THERAPYED'S

National Speech-Language Pathology Examination Review & Study Guide

2nd EDITION

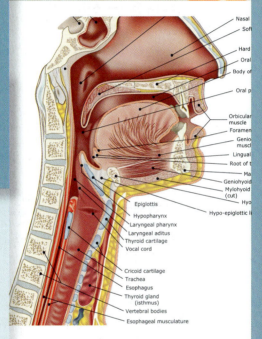

GREGORY L. LOF, PhD, CCC-SLP
ASHA Fellow
Professor Emerita
Department of Communication Sciences and Disorders
MGH Institute of Health Professions
Boston, Massachusetts

ALEX F. JOHNSON, PhD, CCC-SLP
ASHA Fellow; ASHA Honors
Provost and Vice President for Academic Affairs
Professor
Department of Communication Sciences and Disorders
MGH Institute of Health Professions
Boston, Massachusetts

TherapyEd
Evanston, Illinois
United States of America

Copies of this book and software may be obtained from:
TherapyEd
Telephone (847) 328-5361
Fax (847) 328-5049
www.TherapyEd.com

▶ Preface

TherapyEd's *National Speech-Language Pathology Examination Review & Study Guide* is designed to assist U.S. and internationally educated candidates in their preparation for the Praxis II: Speech-Language Pathology Examination. This *Review and Study Guide* provides a comprehensive overview of the depth and breadth of current speech-language pathology practice according to the field's seminal textbooks, the American Speech-Language-Hearing Association's (ASHA's) *Scope of Practice of Speech-Language Pathology*, ASHA's *Code of Ethics*, and ASHA's *Practice Policy Documents*. In addition to students studying in the field of speech-language pathology, this review text also can be helpful to practitioners who are new to the field, those who are changing practice areas, and those initiating a new role (e.g., clinical supervisor).

The text chapters cover all of the practice domains established by the most current ASHA-commissioned survey of speech-language pathology practice. While the text authors or contributors did not have access to an actual examination or to specific examination items, all chapter content and the online examinations are based on the authors' critical review of recent publications and the textbooks and research articles that are likely to be foundational for the examination. Because the Speech-Language Pathology Examination items cover the entirety of the speech-language pathology profession, information that is foundational to entry-level, speech-language pathology practice is provided. This solid foundation is required to clinically reason through examination items and ensure that the exam candidate acquires what ASHA refers to as the "understanding of essential content and current practices" in speech-language pathology.

Specific methods of evaluation and intervention are provided in chapters organized according to communicative disorder diagnoses across the lifespan.

Appropriate references are made in chapters when applicable, in order to provide a well-rounded approach to the field of speech-language pathology. This holistic, integrative approach allows for in-depth coverage while eliminating redundancy and reductionism. References for sources that served as the foundation for text content are provided at the end of each chapter.

Each chapter in this *Review & Study Guide* is presented in an outline format that is easy to read and provides a helpful guide for organizing a study plan. Upon reviewing each chapter's outline, the exam candidate will be able to assess his/her level of comfort with, and mastery of, each content area. Identifying areas of strength and weakness can bolster confidence and help focus studying in an efficient and effective manner. This text is not a substitute for primary resources such as classroom lectures and course textbooks. By first using this text, however, the exam candidate will not spend time extensively studying information already known. Rather, specific areas in which further knowledge is required will be identified, and appropriate study time can be planned. End of chapter review questions and three online examinations are provided to help students develop strategies for effective examination preparation and successful test-taking.

Completion of this text's simulated examinations will help exam candidates evaluate their preparedness for the Speech-Language Pathology Examination. Consistent with the Speech-Language Pathology Examination format, this text's examination items are designed to test mastery of professional knowledge by asking the candidate to apply this knowledge to practice situations. Detailed explanations are provided to help exam candidates understand why one answer is considered the best response and the others are incorrect.

It is the authors' wish that this comprehensive review manual be of the utmost help to the reader, whether preparing for the Speech-Language Pathology Examination, Comprehensive exams, or transitioning into a new area of clinical practice. As speech-language pathology is always evolving, due in part to continuous efforts by many wonderful clinicians and researchers, this book shall continue to be updated to reflect new trends and information within the field as they are revealed. By utilizing this approach, the authors hope this review book remains a constant source of information for all readers, present and future.

▶ Table of Contents

Table of Contents

Section III: Acquired Communication Disorders

Section IV: Structural Communication and Swallowing Disorders

Section V: Special Considerations in Speech-Language Pathology Practice

Section VI: Examinations

Contributors

Jean Andruski, PhD
Associate Professor (Retired)
Department of Communication Sciences
 and Disorders
Wayne State University
Detroit, Michigan

Cara Bryan, MA, CCC-SLP
Founder
South Tampa Voice Therapy
Tampa, Florida

Derek E. Daniels, PhD, CCC-SLP
Associate Professor
Department of Communication Sciences
 and Disorders
Wayne State University
Detroit, Michigan

Mark DeRuiter, MBA, PhD, CCC-A/SLP
ASHA Fellow; National Academies of
 Practice Fellow
Director of Doctor of Clinical Science in SLP
Department of Communication Science
 and Disorders
University of Pittsburgh
Pittsburgh, Pennsylvania

Sandra Laing Gillam, PhD, CCC-SLP
ASHA Fellow
Professor
Department of Communicative Disorders and
 Deaf Education
Utah State University
Logan, Utah

Donald M. Goldberg, PhD, CCC-A/SLP
ASHA Fellow; American Academy of Audiology Fellow
Professor
Department of Communication Sciences and Disorders
College of Wooster
Wooster, Ohio
Professional Staff, Section of Allied Hearing, Speech
 and Balance Services
Cleveland Clinic Lerner College of Medicine of Case
 Western Reserve University
Cleveland, Ohio

Margaret Greenwald, PhD, CCC-SLP
Associate Professor
Department of Communication Sciences and Disorders
Wayne State University
Detroit, Michigan

Michelle Gutman, PhD, CCC-SLP
Clinical Professor
Department of Speech, Language and Hearing Sciences
Purdue University
West Lafayette, Indiana

Charles Haynes, EdD, CCC-SLP
Professor
Department of Communication Sciences and Disorders
MGH Institute of Health Professions
Boston, Massachusetts

R. Jordan Hazelwood, PhD, CCC-SLP,
 BCS-S, CCRE
Assistant Professor
Department of Communication Sciences and Disorders
Appalachian State University
Boone, North Carolina

James T. Heaton, PhD
Adjunct Professor
Department of Communication Sciences and Disorders
MGH Institute of Health Professions
Boston, Massachusetts
Associate Professor
Harvard Medical School, Department of Surgery
Massachusetts General Hospital
Boston, Massachusetts

Pamela Hook, PhD
Professor Emerita
Department of Communication Sciences and Disorders
MGH Institute of Health Professions
Boston, Massachusetts

Melanie W. Hudson, MA, CCC-SLP
ASHA Fellow; National Academies of Practice Fellow
National Director
EBS Healthcare
West Chester, Pennsylvania

Alex F. Johnson, PhD, CCC-SLP
ASHA Fellow; ASHA Honors
Provost and Vice President for Academic Affairs
Professor
Department of Communication Sciences and Disorders
MGH Institute of Health Professions
Boston, Massachusetts

Samantha E. Jordan, MS, CCC-SLP
Speech-Language Pathologist
Kevin G. Langan School
Albany, New York

Ann W. Kummer, PhD, CCC-SLP
ASHA Fellow; ASHA Honors
Senior Director (Retired)
Division of Speech-Language Pathology
Cincinnati Children's Hospital Medical Center
Professor of Otolaryngology and Clinical Pediatrics
University of Cincinnati College of Medicine
Cincinnati, Ohio

Gregory L. Lof, PhD, CCC-SLP
ASHA Fellow
Professor Emerita
Department of Communication Sciences and Disorders
MGH Institute of Health Professions
Boston, Massachusetts

Kimberly A. Murphy, PhD, CCC-SLP
Assistant Professor
Communication Disorders and Special Education
Old Dominion University
Norfolk, Virginia

Nancy Naperala, PhD, CCC-SLP
Instructor
Department of Communication Sciences and Disorders
Wayne State University
Detroit, Michigan

Craig W. Newman, PhD, CCC-A
ASHA Fellow
Section Head, Allied Hearing, Speech, and Balance
    Services
Vice Chair of Head and Neck Institute (Retired)
Cleveland Clinic Lerner College of Medicine of Case
    Western Reserve University
Cleveland, Ohio

Marjorie Nicholas, PhD, CCC-SLP
ASHA Fellow
Professor
Department of Communication Sciences and Disorders
MGH Institute of Health Professions
Boston, Massachusetts

Gail Richard, PhD, CCC-SLP
ASHA Fellow
Professor Emerita
Department of Communication Sciences and Disorders
Eastern Illinois University
Charleston, Illinois

Sharon A. Sandridge, PhD, CCC-A
ASHA Fellow
Section Head, Allied Hearing, Speech and Balance
    Services
Co-Director, Tinnitus Management Clinic and
    Audiology Research Laboratory
Cleveland Clinic Lerner College of Medicine of Case
    Western Reserve University
Cleveland, Ohio

Reed Senter, MS, CCC-SLP
Doctoral Student
Special Education and Disability Policy
Virginia Commonwealth University
Richmond, Virginia

Brian B. Shulman, PhD, CCC-SLP
ASHA Fellow; National Academies of Practice Fellow; Association of Schools Advancing Health Professions Fellow
Dean
School of Health and Medical Sciences
Professor
Department of Speech-Language Pathology
Seton Hall University
Nutley, New Jersey

Nina Capone Singleton, PhD, CCC-SLP
Associate Professor
Department of Speech-Language Pathology
Seton Hall University
Associate Professor of Pediatrics
Hackensack Meridian School of Medicine
Nutley, New Jersey

Zachary M. Smith, MS, CCC-SLP
Speech-Language Pathologist
Speech and Swallow Department
Brigham and Women's Hospital
Boston, Massachusetts

Barbara C Sonies, PhD, CCC-SLP, BCS-S
ASHA Fellow; ASHA Honors
Professor Emeritus
Department of Hearing and Speech Disorders
University of Maryland
College Park, Maryland
Chief (Retired)
Speech Language Pathology and Oral Motor Function Laboratory (Retired)
Department of Rehabilitation Medicine
National Institutes of Health
Bethesda, Maryland

Greg Turner, PhD, CCC-SLP
Professor
Communication Disorders Program
School of Human Services
Harmon College of Business and Professional Studies
University of Central Missouri
Warrensburg, Missouri

Sofia Vallila-Rohter, PhD, CCC-SLP
Associate Professor
Department of Communication Sciences and Disorders
MGH Institute of Health Professions
Boston, Massachusetts
SLP Concentration Chair
Speech and Hearing Bioscience and Technology Program
Harvard University
Cambridge, Massachusetts

Maggie Watson, PhD, CCC-SLP
Professor (Retired)
Department of Communicative Disorders
University of Wisconsin, Stevens Point
Stevens Point, Wisconsin

Margaret Wilson, MA, CCC-SLP
Speech-Language Pathologist III
Cincinnati Children's Hospital Medical Center
Cincinnati, Ohio

Aaron Ziegler, PhD, CCC-SLP
Co-Director
The Wellness Group for Voice, Speech and Swallowing
Portland, Oregon

▶ Acknowledgments

In organizing and producing a comprehensive review text for speech-language pathology subject matter, it was essential to involve many valued partners. First, our team at TherapyEd has been invaluable at each step of the way. Tom Pendry and Betsi Pendry have lent their knowledge and experience from their physical therapy and occupational therapy texts to the development of this review guide, which parallels many of their great innovations in test preparation and comprehensive review books. They have also spent time speaking with many colleagues from speech-language pathology to gather input for this second edition.

Our predecessors in this journey, authors Dr. Susan O'Sullivan, Dr. Ray Siegelman, and Dr. Rita-Fleming-Castaldy, have served as excellent role models for us. Also, most valued partners in this work have been our speech-language pathology colleagues (and former students), Zachary Smith and Samantha Jordan. In this edition they have continued as editors and question developers. Their combined and sustained effort has been crucial in producing this book.

This book has many important contributors covering the spectrum of the discipline. How fortunate we are to have these great outstanding colleagues as collaborators. Be assured that as you read their work, you will be prepared for your next milestone in our field!

Finally, special thanks go to those speech-language pathologists who are entering the field, preparing for the examination, or using this guide to prepare for a new area of practice. You were the inspiration for this work.

GL and AJ

SECTION I

Foundational Knowledge for Speech-Language Pathology Practice

1

Preparing for the Speech-Language Pathology Examination

ZACHARY M. SMITH, MS

Speech-Language Pathology Exam Content and Format

Background

1. Speech-language pathology practice analysis.
   a. The American Speech-Language-Hearing Association (ASHA) conducts an SLP practice analysis every 5–7 years, in order to determine "on the job" tasks for speech-language pathologists (SLPs) and to identify any emerging trends or other changes in the practice landscape.
   b. The analysis includes large-scale surveys of practitioners, educators, clinical supervisors, and clinic directors.
   c. The results of the surveys provide information on the knowledge, skills, and abilities needed to be an independent practicing SLP.
2. Council for Clinical Certification in Audiology and Speech-Language Pathology (CFCC) and practice analysis results.
   a. Based on the results of the SLP practice analysis, along with other information from within the field of speech-language pathology, the CFCC receives recommendations of change for the current standards of certification.
   b. The newly published standards of certification include information about requirements for the Speech-Language Pathology Exam.
   c. The most recent standards of certification went into effect on January 1, 2020.
      (1) There were no changes to Standard VI (Assessment), which is the standard governing passing of the Praxis exam.
3. Item development.
   a. The blueprint for the Speech-Language Pathology Exam is derived from the newly released standards for certification, which directly reflect the SLP practice analysis.
   b. Studies are periodically conducted to determine the validity of specific questions and their relevance to new clinicians.
      (1) These studies also determine the number of questions that a candidate must answer correctly in order to achieve a passing score.
      (2) The CFCC uses the results of these studies to determine the final passing score criterion.
   c. From the results of all previously mentioned studies, ASHA proposes content areas for the Speech-Language Pathology Exam, and examination committees work with Educational Testing Services (ETS) to develop the exams.

(1) The examination committees are made up from ASHA-certified speech-language pathology members who work to develop questions.

Speech-Language Pathology Exam Content

1. Practice domains.
   a. The Speech-Language Pathology Exam contains three domains of speech-language pathology practice, with each comprising a preset percentage of the exam. As of September 2014, these domains are (ASHA, 2014b):
      (1) Foundations and Professional Practice (44 questions).
         (a) Foundations.
            • Typical development and performance across the lifespan.
            • Factors that influence communication, feeding, and swallowing.
         (b) Professional practice.
            • Wellness and prevention.
            • Culturally and linguistically appropriate service delivery.
            • Counseling, collaboration, and teaming.
            • Documentation.
            • Ethics.
            • Legislation and client advocacy.
            • Research methodology and evidence-based practice (EBP).
      (2) Screening, Assessment, Evaluation, and Diagnosis (44 questions).
         (a) Screening.
            • Communication disorders.
            • Feeding and swallowing disorders.
         (b) Approaches to assessment and evaluation.
            • Developing case histories.
            • Selecting appropriate assessment instruments, procedures, and materials.
            • Assessing factors that influence communication and swallowing disorders.
            • Assessment of anatomy and physiology.
            • Referrals.
         (c) Assessment procedures and assessment.
            • Speech sound production.
            • Fluency.
            • Voice, resonance, and motor speech.
            • Receptive and expressive language.

- Social aspects of communication, including pragmatics.
- Cognitive aspects of communication.
- Augmentative and alternative communication.
- Hearing.
- Feeding and swallowing.

(d) Etiology.
- Genetic.
- Developmental.
- Disease processes.
- Auditory problems.
- Neurological.
- Structural and functional.
- Psychogenic.

(3) Planning, Implementation, and Evaluation of Treatment (44 questions).

(a) Treatment planning.
- Evaluating factors that can affect treatment.
- Initiating and prioritizing treatment and developing goals.
- Determining appropriate treatment details.
- Generating a prognosis.
- Communicating recommendations.
- General treatment principles and procedures.

(b) Treatment evaluation.
- Establishing methods for monitoring treatment progress and outcomes to evaluate assessment and treatment plans.
- Follow-up on post-treatment referrals and recommendations.

(c) Treatment.
- Speech sound production.
- Fluency.
- Voice, resonance, and motor speech.
- Receptive and expressive language.
- Social aspects of communication, including pragmatics.
- Communication impairments related to cognition.
- Treatment involving augmentative and alternative communication.
- Hearing and aural rehabilitation.
- Swallowing and feeding.

Speech-Language Pathology Exam Format

1. The exam consists of 132 selected response questions.
2. All 132 questions are Multiple-Choice, requiring the test-taker to choose the best answer from four possible choices. To choose the correct answer the test-taker must click the checkbox of their choice on the exam.
   a. The questions will often contain the phrase "which of the following" embedded somewhere in the question.
   b. Also look for the words *not*, *least*, and *except*.
      (1) When the item contains one of these words, the examinee must select the answer that does not belong.
      (2) Reading these questions carefully is important to answering correctly.
   c. If an item includes graphs or images (e.g., audiograms, spectrograms), it is important to provide information pertinent only to the question being asked.

Examination Scoring and Reporting

1. Equating Speech-Language Pathology Exam scores.
   a. The passing score for the exam is established by ASHA and ETS, after statistical analysis of past test performance.
   b. Using performance of past exam candidates, ASHA and ETS are able to establish a criterion score that is fair and is reflective of passing performance.
2. Scoring procedures.
   a. Only questions answered correctly contribute to the final score, so it is better to answer questions that promote certainty, while moving on from difficult questions.
      (1) Remember, the more questions answered means more likely increases in the raw score.
      (2) Difficult questions can always be revisited after going through the remainder of the test.
   b. Each selected response question (e.g., multiple choice, multiple select) is worth 1 point toward the raw score.
      (1) These questions are automatically scored by computer.
   c. The raw score (number of questions answered correctly) is converted into a scaled score that adjusts for the difficulty of the test.
      (1) There are multiple versions of the Speech-Language Pathology Exam that are administered, and each contains different combinations of questions.
      (2) Using a scaled score ensures that all exam candidates have as fair a chance as possible to pass the exam.
3. Scoring schedule and score reporting.
   a. Because the Speech-Language Pathology Exam is offered in specific testing windows, scores are available 10–16 days after each testing window is over.
      (1) Each testing window is approximately 12 days in length.

b. Exam candidates are encouraged to make an online ETS account, as score reports are available through the account.

(1) Scores are available for exactly 1 year after their initial release, so exam candidates are also encouraged to save a copy of the score report to refer to later if needed. Scores may be requested for up to 10 years for a fee.

c. In addition to exam candidates receiving their score, the score report is also sent to the candidate's graduate institute and to ASHA, for certification purposes.

(1) The code to enter to ensure that ASHA receives Speech-Language Pathology Exam scores is R5031.

(2) Codes for different graduate programs can be found at www.ets.org/s/praxis/pdf/aud_slp_attending_institution_recipient_codes.pdf.

(3) **As of 2020, passing Speech-Language Pathology Exam for ASHA certification is a scaled score of 162, on a 100- to 200-point scale.**

d. Aggregate score reports are provided to the program directors for graduate programs in speech-language pathology for candidates who are graduates of the program.

▶ Effective Exam Preparation

Overview and General Guidelines

1. Types of questions on the Speech-Language Pathology Exam.
   a. There are four levels of objective examination questions, summarized in Table 1-1.
2. Critical and clinical reasoning.
   a. The ability to critically and clinically reason and evaluate questions is a skill necessary for success on the Speech-Language Pathology Exam.
      (1) Table 1-2 summarizes types of critical reasoning to use during the exam.

(2) Keeping one's "eyes on the prize" of becoming a licensed and certified SLP can help keep work and study at the forefront and can help manage fear and anxiety.

c. If a previous attempt at taking the exam was not successful, critique previous performance, including study habits and methods, to evaluate the source of difficulty.

(1) Knowing specific deficiencies in content or clinical reasoning/problem-solving can be critical to improvement on the next test.

d. Table 1-3 summarizes psychological outlook and its relationship to success with the Speech-Language Pathology Exam.

Psychological Outlook

1. Psychological outlook as a factor for success.
   a. Positive outlook is a necessary foundation for effective studying and test taking, as it puts exam candidates in a mind-set for success.
      (1) Use previous successful academic and clinical experiences to bolster confidence in being prepared for the exam.
      (2) Discuss areas of strength and areas that might benefit from additional study time with professors, clinical supervisors, and classmates. This feedback can provide a realistic picture that can build confidence.
   b. Doubt and negative outlook can be detrimental to performance on the Speech-Language Pathology Exam.
      (1) If developing a positive outlook is difficult, be sure to access others who can be supportive and encouraging.

Reviewing Professional Education

1. Establish current knowledge and skill level.
   a. The chapters of this review guide will help establish a plan of action for studying all pertinent aspects within the scope of SLP practice.
      (1) While proceeding through the chapters, make a "knowledge scale" consisting of (1) know very well, (2) know adequately, (3) know little, and (4) know nothing.
         (a) Focus studying efforts on the content that falls toward the "know nothing" end of the scale to solidify knowledge in all content areas.
   b. Using clinical reasoning skills gained during clinical placements will help navigate the questions posed on the Speech-Language Pathology Exam.
      (1) The exam features questions that are structured to test clinical reasoning and a factual knowledge base.

Table 1-1

Levels of Examination Questions

QUESTION LEVEL AND DESCRIPTION	RELEVANCE TO SPEECH-LANGUAGE PATHOLOGY EXAM	SPEECH-LANGUAGE PATHOLOGY EXAM PREPARATION STRATEGY
1. **Knowledge** Recall of basic information.	A solid knowledge foundation of all information related to entry-level SLP practice is required to answer practice scenario items. It is highly likely that little to no items on the Speech-Language Pathology Exam are solely at this level.	A strong commitment to studying is needed to remember all the information acquired during your SLP education. Fortunately, this text provides extensive information in an outline format to ease your review. Memorization of this information is required to be able to readily recall it when taking the 132-question exam.
2. **Comprehension** Understanding information to determine significance, consequences, or implications.	The Speech-Language Pathology Exam is not a matching-column type of test; therefore, you cannot just recall information to be able to succeed on this exam. You must fully understand the content to be able to understand the nuances of an exam item. A few items on the exam may be at this level.	When studying the text to review basic content and acquire your foundational knowledge, ask yourself how and why this fundamental information is important. Studying with a peer or a study group can provide you with additional insights about the relevance, significance, consequences, and implications of the information. Do not enter the exam without strong comprehension of all major areas of SLP practice.
3. **Application** Use of information and application of rules, procedures, or theories to new situations.	The Speech-Language Pathology Exam requires you to use your knowledge and comprehension as described above, along with the competencies you developed during your clinical placements, in a manner that best fits the specific practice scenario in an exam item. Many items from the exam are at this level, for a main goal of the exam is to assess your ability to respond competently to different situations.	Once you have acquired a solid knowledge base and good comprehension skills in all domains of SLP as put forth in this text, you should take practice exams. This type of exam requires you to apply your knowledge in a manner similar to the Speech-Language Pathology Exam. Upon completion of these exams, you should analyze your performance to determine how well you are applying your knowledge.
4. **Analysis** Recognition of interrelationships between principles and interpretation or evaluation of data presented.	The Speech-Language Pathology Exam assumes that you have mastered entry-level knowledge and that you can competently apply this information to diverse situations; therefore, it will ask you to analyze and respond to ambiguous, not "straight from the book," situations. Many items from the exam are also at this level, to determine your ability to be competent in complex practice situations.	Use the analyses of practice exams described above to reflect on your reasoning mistakes. Critically review the extensive rationales provided in this text for the correct exam answers. Reflecting with a peer or study group can be helpful in determining your gaps in analysis of exam items. Review the text's section on critical thinking skills and reflect on the questions provided in Table 1-5 to ascertain the actions you need to take to adequately prepare for the complexities of the Speech-Language Pathology Exam.

Source: Fleming-Castaldy & Inda, 2019.

c. Review coursework history in order to establish strengths and weaknesses.
   (1) Knowing which aspects of SLP practice that have been most challenging will determine a place to begin studying.
2. Establish a study plan of action.
   a. Items rated as "know little" or "know nothing" from the previously mentioned knowledge scale will become the most pertinent items for critical studying.
   b. Items rated as "know very well" or "know adequately" from the knowledge scale will become the items that require more review than critical study.
      (1) For example, if one has a strong knowledge base of assessment of the different disorders treated under the SLP's scope of practice but has difficulty making goals or providing appropriate intervention approaches, one's studying may focus on intervention methods across disorders (i.e., treatment of speech-sound disorders or adult-acquired language disorders).

   (2) Finding trends throughout the chapters will help draw conclusions and provide an integrative learning experience that will prove to be invaluable in preparation for the exam.
c. Remember that the Speech-Language Pathology Exam encompasses three distinct areas of practice equally, so be prepared to spend equal amounts of time studying each area.
   (1) Foundations and Professional Practice.
   (2) Screening, Assessment, Evaluation, and Diagnosis.
   (3) Planning, Implementation, and Evaluation of Treatment.
d. Allow adequate time to prepare for the test, taking into account strengths and weaknesses as an exam-taker.
   (1) Determine the appropriate time during graduate education to begin studying in order to achieve mastery of all material, including those that fall under the "know nothing" category.

Chapter 1 PSL

Table 1-2

Critical Reasoning Applied to Speech-Language Pathology Exam Items

TYPE OF REASONING	QUESTIONS TO CONSIDER	RELATIONSHIP TO EXAM SUCCESS
Procedural Reasoning Requires the systematic gathering and interpreting of data to identify problems, set goals, plan intervention, and implement treatment strategies. It is the "doing" of practice.	What does the exam item tell/ask you about: Diagnosis? Symptoms? Prognosis? Assessment methods? Treatment protocols? Theories/practice frameworks to support procedures?	Correct answers on the Speech-Language Pathology Exam will be consistent with the published evaluation standards and intervention protocols for a given clinical condition and will be congruent with established theories and relevant practice framework.
Interactive Reasoning Focuses on the client as a person and involves the therapeutic relationships among the practitioner, the individual, caregivers, and significant others.	What does the exam item tell/ask you about: Rapport building? Family/caregiver involvement? Therapeutic use of self? Teaching/learning styles? Successful collaboration?	Correct answers on the exam will have the therapist engaging with the person, family, caregivers, and others in an empathic, caring, respectful, collaborative, and empowering manner.
Pragmatic Reasoning Considers the context of service delivery, including the person's situation and the practice environment to identify the real possibilities for a person in a given setting.	What does the exam item tell/ask you about: Person's client factors? Practice setting characteristics? Reimbursement issues? Legal parameters? Referral options?	Correct answers on the Speech-Language Pathology Exam will be realistic given the person's assets and limitations, his/her environmental supports and barriers, and the practice setting's inherent opportunities or constraints.
Conditional Reasoning Represents an integration of procedural, interactive, and pragmatic reasoning in the context of the client's narrative.[a] Focuses on past, current, and possible future social contexts.	What does the exam item tell/ask you about: The individual's unique roles, values, goals? Impact of illness on this person's function? How the condition's course will influence the person's future? Where the person will be able to live after discharge?	Correct answers on the exam will consider all case information that is provided in the item scenario. The exam items do not include extraneous details, so carefully reflect on the relevance of the information provided in each item scenario to determine the best answer.

Source: Fleming-Castaldy & Inda, 2019.

[a]The application of narrative reasoning is not likely required during the exam, since this type of reasoning deals with the individual's speech-language story and uses critical imagination to help the person reach an imagined future. This important process is not readily measured by objective exam questions.

(2) Be aware of any constraints as a test-taker (e.g., difficulty memorizing information, difficulty parsing out the important information to study) and make schedule adjustments accordingly.

e. Assess study habits formed during professional program schooling and choose a route that is most effective.

f. Create a strict study plan and follow through. Some study tips are as follows:

(1) Study one major content area per session. This can include studying one of the comprehensive chapters in this book.

(2) Limit any possible interruptions.

(a) Turn off any electronics that are not essential to studying.

(b) Parents/caregivers should make sure to arrange for help to allow ample opportunity to study without distraction.

(c) Do not study by a computer or other devices, unless Internet restrictions for distracting websites can be enabled.

(3) If something occurs that forces deviation from study schedules, immediately make an attempt to reschedule study time to make up for lost time.

3. Appropriate timing for taking practice assessments and exams.

a. Completing a practice exam before having adequately studied all areas of exam content will reinforce feelings of fear and anxiety by demonstrating that continued gaps in knowledge exist.

b. Completing a practice exam after having adequately studied the content areas will allow demonstration of the amount of knowledge gained while studying.

(1) Taking practice exams at this point in studying will enforce feelings of confidence and self-esteem in knowledge of the material that a practicing SLP would encounter.

(2) This will also give an opportunity to discover which areas of exam content may continue to be difficult and allow more time to focus on this material.

4. Using the practice exams that accompany this book can assist in determining a test-taking personality.

a. Knowledge of test-taking personalities helps identify particular characteristics and strategies to aid in studying and test-taking (Table 1-4).

5. It is important to take practice exams within the allotted time that would be given during the actual Speech-Language Pathology Exam.

a. This will allow practice with the visual, psychological, and cognitive demands that come with taking

Table 1-3

Psychological Outlook and the Speech-Language Pathology Exam

CONCEPT	PRINCIPLE	ACTIONS
Control	Only you can determine your future.	• Take charge; determine exactly what is needed to succeed. • Set goals to meet these needs. • Develop and implement concrete plans to succeed.
Self-awareness	Knowing your innate capabilities enables you to build on strengths and effectively deal with limitations.	• Critically analyze test-taking errors and content knowledge gaps. • Be honest about your test-taking and content knowledge, strengths, and limitations. • Avoid self-defeatist behavior.
Self-confidence	Your past accomplishments provide a solid foundation for future success.	• Review exam content prior to completing practice exams. • Use a diversity of learning methods to achieve mastery. • Recognize and celebrate your successes and achievements.
Self-fulfilling prophecy	Your self-expectancy will influence the outcomes of your efforts.	• Expect success. • Use positive self-talk throughout exam preparation. • Continue to think positively during the exam administration.
Self-esteem	You are a person capable of excellence.	• Remember your personal and academic achievements. • SLP academic coursework and fieldwork are demanding; give yourself well-earned credit for your success.
Motivation	Your desire to succeed and a fear of failure can be channeled for success.	• Understand that the early stages of studying will have uncertain results. • Remind yourself of what initially motivated you to pursue a career as an SLP. • Harness fear and establish a doable study plan.
Courage	Taking responsibility for one's failures is key to success.	• Honestly critique precipitators/reasons for an exam failure. • Do not make excuses. • Do not strive for perfection.
Perseverance	You can only succeed if you persevere.	• Reestablish goals. • Seek support for goal attainment. • Utilize multiple resources to stay on track.
Freedom	You can freely choose your attitude.	• View test-taking as an opportunity. • Keep your "eyes on the prize." • Exam success equates the achievement of your goal to become an SLP practitioner.

Source: Fleming-Castaldy & Inda, 2019.

an extended standardized test and becoming comfortable with them.

    b. Practicing the test-taking strategies presented in this chapter during practice exams will help with generalization of skills to the real exam.

6. Do not try to memorize any specific question that appears on any practice item used. Use questions to help assess knowledge.

    a. It is most important to review information and become comfortable with the structure of exam questions.

Key Preparation Resources

1. Effective preparation for the Speech-Language Pathology Exam requires understanding two components to exam success: adequate content knowledge and effective test-taking skills.

2. This *Review and Study Guide* has been designed as a knowledge resource for individuals studying for the exam and is a comprehensive compilation of information to help test-takers succeed on the exam and as a practicing SLP.

    a. The chapter authors are leading professionals in their respective areas of the field and draw from foundational textbooks and important research findings to form their chapters.

    b. Referring to the reference lists associated with each chapter may provide advanced knowledge of areas of SLP practice with which there may be weakness.

3. Reaching out to fellow students can prove to be a valuable resource.

    a. Forming study groups can help fill in knowledge gaps for all members.

    b. Fellow students and friends can also serve as a psychological support, in the event that fear and anxiety surrounding the exam escalate.

4. Consulting academic and clinical resources, including professors and clinical supervisors, can help fill in gaps in knowledge from individuals who are experts in the field.

    a. Both professors and supervisors care about student clinicians' well-being and success within the field and have advanced knowledge of the content required for a successful career as an SLP.

Table 1-4

Personalities of Test-Takers

PERSONALITY TYPE	CHARACTERISTICS	ACTIONS
The rusher	• Impatient. • Jumps to conclusions. • Skips key words. • Inadequate consideration of exam items.	• Take practice exams in a timed manner to establish a nondesperate pace and help realize that the time allotted for the exam is sufficient. • Use positive self-talk and relaxation techniques during the exam. • Employ the strategies provided in Tables 1-5 and 1-6 to slow your pace and avoid the errors that are endemic to rushing.
The turtle	• Overly slow and methodical. • Overattention to extraneous detail. • Reads and rereads exam items' details. • Misses the theme of exam items.	• Take practice exams in a timed manner to establish the pace of completing practice exams in 150 minutes, which is the amount of time given during the real examination. • Study in bullet format. • Use the strategies in Tables 1-5 and 1-6 to identify each item's focus and select the best answer, and then move on to the next item.
Squisher/ procrastinator	• Puts things off. • Does not reschedule missed study time. • Mastery of exam content is not attained and major knowledge gaps remain.	• Focus on developing a step-by-step plan. • Dig in and get started. • Adopt a "no excuses" attitude. • Join a study group or work with a study partner to stay on track.
Philosopher	• Is a thoughtful, talented, intelligent, and disciplined student. • Excels in essay questions. • Overanalyzes and reads into exam items. • Wants to know everything and answer everything about the topic. • Overapplies clinical knowledge.	• Study in bullet, not paragraph, form. • Focus only on the exam item. • Look for simple, straightforward answers. • Remind yourself that your "job" on the exam is to select the best answer for the question posed, not to address all possible aspects of an item's scenario. • Apply the strategies provided in Tables 1-5 and 1-6 to stay focused on answering each item as it is presented.
Lawyer	• Is a thoughtful, talented, intelligent, and disciplined student. • Picks out some bit of information and builds a case on that. • Reads into exam items to make a case for a preferred answer instead of determining what the question is asking.	• Focus on what the exam item is asking, and only what the exam item is asking. • Remind yourself that your "job" is to pass the exam, not to prove a point. • Remember that you can train to be a Speech-Language Pathology Exam item writer and write "better" exam items after you pass the exam.

Second-guesser	• Often a philosopher who reads into an item.
	• Frequently looks at the exam item from every angle.
	• Keeps changing answers, increasing anxiety, thinking less clearly, and then changing answers more rapidly.
		• Apply a "lightbulb" strategy.
		  ○ Identify a good reason to reject your first answer (i.e., missing a key word).
		  ○ Identify a good reason to select a new answer (i.e., obtaining a solid hint from a subsequent exam item).
		  ○ If you do not experience a lightbulb moment, do not change your answer.

Source: Fleming-Castaldy & Inda, 2019.

Critical Thinking and Speech-Language Pathology Exam Performance

Critical Thinking and the Speech-Language Pathology Exam

1. *Critical thinking* can be thought of as a process of evaluating and analyzing situations by drawing strengths from a person's knowledge, skills, experiences, and objective logic in order to form reasonable conclusions.

a. Critical thinking encompasses a variety of subskills, including:
   (1) Analysis.
   (2) Inference.
   (3) Evaluation.
   (4) Explanation.
   (5) Self-examination.
   (6) Self-correction.
   (7) Inductive and deductive reasoning.

2. Being able to think critically is a skill that is absolutely necessary for success on the Speech-Language Pathology Exam.

   a. The exam does not simply test one's ability to reproduce information printed in a textbook or taught in lecture.

   b. Questions on the exam require a strong knowledge foundation, but the ability to think critically, from the perspective of a future speech and language clinician, can help examination candidates arrive at appropriate answers in an organized fashion.

   c. The exam integrates the knowledge, skills, and critical-thinking behaviors necessary for success as an entry-level SLP.

3. Because critical-thinking skills are employed on a daily basis as an SLP, it is important that these skills begin to be used long before taking the exam.

   a. Most of the exam questions are designed to be contextualized to the work an SLP would perform while in the field, which necessitates critical thinking in order to answer appropriately.

   b. Graduate academic and clinical work in speech-language pathology have started the foundation of critical-thinking skills, and it is important to draw from these experiences while studying for and during the Speech-Language Pathology Exam.

Analysis

1. *Analysis* is the ability to identify both the intended and actual relationships between concepts, facts, questions and descriptions of statements, beliefs, and so on.

   a. This skill helps one examine concepts and the relationships between them.

2. Analysis is used in SLP practice through interpreting assessment results, reviewing case history information to retrieve important information (e.g., number of words spoken by a child, presenting medical illness for an adult), and formulating a diagnosis for clients (e.g., Broca's aphasia, language disorder).

3. Analysis is required while answering many questions presented on the Speech-Language Pathology Exam.

   a. Information presented in graphs, charts, or tables will mandate some form of analysis in order to correctly interpret information and determine its meaning.

4. Questions that tap an examination candidate's analysis skills can seem frustrating, due to potential lack of information. However, this closely simulates what a practicing SLP may encounter, as that SLP is rarely given a complete picture of the person with whom he/she works.

Inference

1. *Inference* is the ability to identify and secure elements needed to draw reasonable conclusions, to develop hypotheses, to consider relevant information, and to form conclusions from data, statements, and so on.

   a. This skill utilizes a specific knowledge base to make reasonable assumptions about new information.

2. Inference is used in SLP practice during assessment selection and when therapists infer potential client/patient symptoms based on limited information.

   a. For example, a note dictates that a new client does not make all of her sounds correctly, possibly necessitating the selection of an articulation/phonology assessment battery.

   b. As another example, while reviewing a patient's medical chart, the therapist notices "left MCA stroke," which leads him to infer the presence of aphasia.

3. Inference is also used in SLP practice to determine the best possible route of intervention for particular clients.

   a. Although all inferences should be based in some form of knowledge, they are not guaranteed to be 100% accurate. For example, when treating a child with a phonological disorder, the therapist cannot be certain that cycles approach would lead to the greatest gains for that child. For this reason, inference must utilize a clinician's knowledge and experience.

4. Because inference is regularly used in SLP practice and decision-making, it makes sense that this skill is important for success on the Speech-Language Pathology Exam.

   a. There are questions that prompt the examination candidate to determine likely presentations of disorders or appropriate approaches to treatment/intervention that require inferential reasoning.

   b. Inference should be used cautiously when answering exam questions because, if the information presented has not been considered appropriately or logically, an incorrect answer could be selected.

5. As inference is used frequently in daily SLP practice, it is not surprising that many of the exam questions require some level of inference.

Evaluation

1. *Evaluation* is the ability to assess the credibility of statements that represent a person's perceptions, experience, and judgment, as well as the ability to assess the logical strength of the relationship between statements, descriptions, and questions.

   a. Evaluation aids in deciding whether or not a conclusion is valid, based on the facts presented.

2. Evaluation is used in SLP practice when difficult decisions need to be made and there is no obvious answer or approach to use.
   a. In SLP practice, evaluation should be a conscious process to determine the trustworthiness of information used in generating a course of action.
      (1) Evaluation should be approached cautiously, as assigning too much value to information that has little relevance to a present case can lead to unintended consequences.
   b. Being able to assess the validity of research, in order to provide the best EBP, is something that requires keen evaluative skills.
   c. Situations that arise while in the field can be ambiguous and require an SLP to weigh sources of information for reliability, validity, and applicability to the current situation in order to achieve the best result.
      (1) For example, while working to improve swallowing endurance in a patient who has a pulmonary disorder, the patient begins to experience shortness of breath. The clinician must evaluate whether or not to alert the patient's nurse.
3. Evaluation is required when answering questions on the Speech-Language Pathology Exam that deal with ethical dilemmas or when evaluating statements posed by research.
   a. In studying for the exam, it helps to familiarize oneself with the evaluative process and practice evaluating statements made in research articles and case studies.

Explanation

1. An *explanation* states the results of the process of critical thinking in a way that justifies the reasoning used in reaching a conclusion.
   a. An explanation interprets results based on the information that was gathered to reach a conclusion.
2. Explanation is used in SLP practice when reaching a decision about a client's diagnosis using given information, when definitively explaining why a particular treatment approach may prove to be beneficial, and while advocating for the populations that SLPs serve.
   a. Explanation relies on solid foundational knowledge and skills, including knowledge of effects of diseases/deficits/disorders, the implications of treatment processes, and the effect of communication and swallowing disorders on the quality of life affecting clients and patients.
3. Explanation on the Speech-Language Pathology Exam comes in the form of selecting the appropriate answer(s) for questions.
   a. Although there is no "checkbox" in real situations, the checkbox scenario found in the exam directly assesses an examination candidate's explanation

ability. By selecting the correct answers, a capacity for explanation has been shown.

Self-Examination

1. *Self-examination* is the ability to consciously reflect on previous occurrences in order to determine areas or acts of strengths in performance while also being able to interpret areas in which one could use improvement and why these could be improved.
2. Self-examination is typically used in SLP practice after assessment or treatment has been completed, in order to properly assess what behaviors have or have not been successful in that SLP's interactions with his/her clients.
   a. Engaging in self-examination after missteps in client interactions is important, because it allows the SLP to identify what behaviors caused the problem and how to effectively remedy these problems moving forward.
   b. Engaging in self-examination after successes is just as important for the therapist–client relationship, as it allows the SLP to determine what works well for particular clients in order to maximize the gains seen in treatment.
3. While the Speech-Language Pathology Exam may pose questions asking about changes to interaction style or therapy approach, it is likely that this skill is not going to feature prominently on the exam itself.
   a. The skill of self-examination is important during the study period for the exam. If the amount of gains made during studying is not ideal, it is important to reflect on what is causing this, in order to make appropriate changes.
      (1) This is a continuing process throughout the time spent preparing for the exam, as new problems may spring up farther down the road of studying.

Self-Correction

1. Using all of the other areas of critical thinking, *self-correction* allows a person to change his/her behavior for future occurrences that are similar to a preceding event (e.g., future therapy session, future evaluations).
2. Self-correction is used in SLP practice after having engaged in self-examination so that one may move forward with appropriate changes.
   a. For example, perhaps an SLP's cueing or instructions were not effective during a particular session. After engaging in self-examination, that SLP can determine an appropriate correction in behavior in order to maximize the client's potential.
      (1) Invoking this change in behavior engages the SLP's self-correction abilities.

3. While self-correction can often be employed as a working SLP, this is a subskill of critical thinking that may not be employed as readily during the Speech-Language Pathology Exam.
   a. Because of the time limits during the administration of the exam, it is important to work efficiently and to utilize self-correction only on an as-needed basis.

Inductive and Deductive Reasoning

1. Inductive reasoning is the process in which the assumptions of an argument are believed to endorse the conclusion but do not guarantee it.
   a. This type of reasoning begins in specific situations and evolves over time to encompass more generalized situations.
   b. Inductive reasoning is used as a part of the diagnostic process, to help form assumptions about what to expect from a diagnosis and its evolution over time.
   c. This process may start with observations in a specific instance or situation and then lead to drawing conclusions about other circumstances. As such, it can lead to flawed reasoning.
      (1) For example, after observing a patient admitted to a hospital with a left middle cerebral artery (MCA) stroke who presents with nonfluent aphasia, an SLP assumes that all persons with a left MCA stroke will have nonfluent aphasia, which is untrue.
   d. Inductive reasoning should be used cautiously when answering questions on the Speech-Language Pathology Exam, because situation-specific knowledge is not an adequate foundation for making universal assumptions.
2. Deductive reasoning is the process of reasoning in which conclusions are based on facts, laws, rules, or accepted principles, and is the opposite process of inductive reasoning.
   a. This process begins with information about larger circumstances and broader principles, and applies this knowledge to specific circumstances that may be encountered clinically.
   b. Deductive reasoning should be used cautiously when answering questions on the exam, because erroneous assumptions about the premises of a theory can be made and then mistakenly applied to a specific circumstance.

Developing Critical-Thinking Skills

1. Critical thinking entails a particular set of skills that are developed over an extended period of time and that continue to be refined over the course of one's career as an SLP.
   a. Time spent as a graduate student SLP clinician gives ample opportunity to begin forming these skills, but it is essential to continue to practice.
2. When studying for the Speech-Language Pathology Exam, capitalize on opportunities that arise for practice of any of the subskills of critical thinking.
3. Identifying any areas of potential weaknesses in critical thinking is a great way to practice critical-thinking skills.
   a. This identification establishes a foundation to analyze performance, make evaluations, engage in self-examination, and make corrections in order to continue on the right path toward success.
   b. Ask yourself the questions found in Table 1-5 and determine if they are reflective of your examination performance.
      (1) Questions that are answered affirmatively can help you identify critical reasoning skills that can be improved.

▶ The Examination Day and Beyond

Preparation and Planning

1. Be prepared physically and mentally.
   a. Get a good night's sleep prior to the exam.
   b. Eat a well-balanced breakfast the morning of the exam.
   c. Although coffee and tea may aid long nights of studying during professional programs, avoid too much caffeine prior to the test.
   d. Wear appropriate clothing for warm or cold testing centers, and make sure to wear layered clothing that can be changed easily (e.g., long sleeves that can easily be rolled up in the event that the temperature rises in the testing center).
      (1) Keep in mind that the time allotted for the test remains the same and is not paused for clothing adjustments.
   e. Make sure to use the restroom before entering the test room.

Table 1-5

Critical Reasoning Self-Assessment Questions

OBSERVED EXAM DIFFICULTY	REASONING CHALLENGE	SPEECH-LANGUAGE PATHOLOGY EXAM PREPARATION STRATEGY
Do you: • Have difficulty with taking specific information and applying it to large populations? • Select incorrect answers because you cannot generalize your knowledge?	Inductive reasoning	When studying a specific content area, think about how the discrete information that you are reviewing can be applied to a diversity of situations. Use a reflective "what if" stance to think how this information may be generalized to a broader context. This can be a fun and effective study group activity.
Do you: • Prefer to follow your instincts rather than the guidelines that a protocol may provide? • Select incorrect answers because you are unfamiliar with established practice standards or major theoretical approaches?	Deductive reasoning	When you study, be sure that you master all major facts, laws, rules, and accepted principles that guide SLP practice. Carefully review all of the frames of reference, practice models, and intervention protocols and procedures provided in the chapters of the *Review & Study Guide* and the ASHA Code of Ethics and legislation information provided in Chapter 6.
Do you: • Tend to misinterpret information provided, make poor judgments, and apply inadequately conceived assumptions about it? • Select incorrect answers because you misjudged the effects of a clinical condition on communication, swallowing, or cognitive-linguistic performance?	Analysis	Be sure to develop a solid knowledge of all major clinical conditions and their symptoms, diagnostic testing and criteria, anticipated sequelae, and expected outcomes. This information is extensively reviewed in the following chapters of this *Review & Study Guide* to help you make accurate judgments and correct assumptions about the potential impact of a clinical condition on communication, swallowing, or cognitive-linguistic performance.
Do you: • Have difficulty with thinking about how clinical conditions and practice situations may evolve over time? • Assume information is valid when in fact it is not true? • Select incorrect answers because you have difficulty deciding the best course of action in a practice scenario?	Inference	When studying the clinical conditions in the chapters of this *Review & Study Guide*, be sure to think about how the presentation of these conditions may sometimes vary from textbook descriptions. Use the knowledge and experience you acquired during your clinical practicums/externships to assess the trustworthiness of your assumptions.
Do you: • Feel anxious when you have exam items that are ambiguous and you cannot find answers to them in a textbook? • Rely on protocols and guidelines more than gut instinct? • Select incorrect answers because you become overwhelmed by questions that present ethical dilemmas?	Evaluation	When reviewing specific content, think about the practice ambiguities and ethical dilemmas you observed during your clinical practicums/externships related to those areas.

Source: Fleming-Castaldy & Inda, 2019.

2. Be prepared emotionally.
   a. Before taking the exam, make sure to recall successes made throughout studying for the exam.
      (1) This will enforce a positive mind-set before entering the testing center.
   b. Make sure to arrive early, to minimize any anxiety that could occur from potentially being late.
   c. Think about going to the testing center before the actual exam day so routes can be mapped, including potential conflicts with public transportation, traffic, and so on.
3. If something arises before the exam that requires cancellation of a test date, make sure to follow the procedures for cancellation outlined on the ETS website.

Test Center Procedures

1. Make sure to arrive at the test center at least 30 minutes prior to the start of the exam to allow ample time for check-in.
   a. Examination candidates who are late to the testing center may *not* be allowed into the exam and will have to forfeit any and all registration fees paid.
   b. Be aware that sometimes inclement weather or other conditions may cause a delay or cancellation of an exam time.

2. Before entering the testing center, the confidentiality agreement supplied by ETS must be signed.
   a. If the confidentiality agreement is not signed, entrance into the testing center will be denied and registration fees will not be refunded.
3. In order to sign in, a valid form of government-issued identification must be shown (see below for examples).
   a. The ID supplied must contain the examination candidate's name, picture, and signature.
      (1) The name and signature used needs to match the name used when registering for the Speech-Language Pathology Exam.
         (a) Individuals who have a two-part last name or whose name has changed from the time they registered for the exam will still need to provide a form of ID that matches the registration name.
         (b) If the form of ID does not contain a signature, it must be signed, or a supplemental form of ID must be produced as well.
   b. All documents and forms of identification used must be original and not expired.
      (1) No copies of any form of identification will be accepted by the testing center.
   c. If an acceptable form of ID is not brought, entrance to the testing center will be denied.
      (1) Acceptable forms of ID include:
         (a) Passport.
         (b) Valid, government-issued driver's license.
         (c) State or province ID provided by a motor vehicle registry.
         (d) National ID.
         (e) Military ID.
4. It is important to recognize that certain items are not allowed inside the testing center under any circumstance.
   a. Cell phones, smartphones, electronic watches, recording devices, scanning devices, and photography equipment are not allowed, and if brought into the testing center, the examination candidate risks being released from the testing center with no refund of registration fee.
   b. Do not bring pencils, erasers, or scrap paper, as these will be supplied at the testing center.
   c. The items that should be brought include:
      (1) An admissions ticket.
      (2) A valid form of ID.
      (3) Any health-related equipment needed.
         (a) Permission from respective testing centers needs to be received in order to bring such equipment.
   d. A locker will be supplied by the testing center to store personal items. Before entering the testing room, a search for banned personal items may be conducted.
      (1) Personal items may not be accessed at any point during the test or on any breaks.
5. Before starting the exam, a 30-minute practice time period will be given to allow examination candidates time to become familiar with the computer system.
   a. This practice period is designed to make sure that the exam moves smoothly.
   b. Scratch paper is not allowed during the practice time period.
6. During the exam, if any computer-related difficulties are experienced, testing center policy dictates that examination candidates raise their hand for a testing center employee's assistance.

Examination Time and Timekeeping

1. There are 150 minutes allotted to complete the Speech-Language Pathology Exam.
   a. There is an on-screen clock that will keep track of time as examination candidates continue through the exam.
   b. Although there is an on-screen clock, it is up to the examination candidates to keep their own pace.
      (1) The test is taken as a whole and is not broken into sections. As such, it is important to keep a steady pace throughout the exam.
      (2) If questions that are particularly difficult are encountered, it may be beneficial to move on to other questions in an attempt to answer as many questions as possible.
         (a) Remember, only questions that are answered correctly are counted toward the raw score, so the more questions that are answered, the higher the raw score will be.
   c. Allow a per question time limit and stick to it in order to move through the exam at an appropriate pace.

Question-Answering Strategies

1. Table 1-6 suggests general strategies for answering the questions that may be encountered while taking the Speech-Language Pathology Exam.
2. Table 1-7 suggests specific strategies for answering selected response questions on the exam.
   a. These types of questions make up the bulk of the exam, so it is important to internalize these strategies!

Table 1-6

General Strategies for Answering Speech-Language Pathology Exam Questions
Read the exam item carefully before selecting a response to the question.
Employ relevant clinical experience. • Remember trends and consistent cases in your experience. • Do not call on unusual cases or atypical presentations.
Read the exam item for key words that set a priority (e.g., *pain, acute care*).
Apply clinical reasoning skills to determine the relevance of item info (e.g., diagnosis, setting, intervention, and theoretical principles).
Use your knowledge of medical terminology to decipher unknown terms by applying the meaning of known prefixes, suffixes, and root words.
Select responses that most closely reflect the fundamental tenets of SLP (e.g., ethical actions, the use of functional communication).
Choose client-centered, person-directed actions.
Identify choices that focus on the emotional well-being of the person.
Use your clinical judgment to support the best answer.
Check your answer to see if it is: • Theoretically consistent with the exam scenario. • Diagnostically consistent with the exam scenario. • Developmentally consistent with the exam scenario.
Eliminate choices that contain contraindications, as these must be incorrect.
Consider eliminating options that state "always," "never," "all," or "only," as there are few absolutes in SLP practice.
Eliminate unsafe options.
Choose answers that reflect entry-level SLP practice.
Remember the Speech-Language Pathology Exam is not a specialty certification exam.

Table 1-7

Specific Strategies for Answering Selected Response Questions
Identify the theme of the selected response questions. Ask yourself, "What is the question posed REALLY asking?"
Avoid "reading into" the selected response item. Read the question asked and nothing but the question.
Identify choices that seem similar or equally plausible. • If two choices basically say the same thing, or use synonyms in their answers, both cannot be right; therefore, both can be eliminated.
Carefully consider choices that are opposites of one another. If you cannot eliminate both opposites right away, one may be the correct answer.
Determine the best answer using strategies identified in Table 1-5. • More than one answer may be "correct." Choose the one that is MOST correct.
Select positive, active choices rather than passive, negative ones.
Before changing an answer, make sure that you have a good reason to eliminate your original choice and a good reason to make your new choice. • Good reasons include realizing that you missed the theme or a key word (e.g., screening) of the exam item or you gained a clue from subsequent exam items (e.g., areas of the brain).
Do not let second-guessing talk you out of the correct answer.

Waiting for and Receiving Examination Results

1. The first step after completion of the exam is to accept that the exam is over and that there is a waiting period for receiving scores.
2. Focus on success and know that all questions were answered with the best reasoning possible.
3. Avoid focusing on any difficulties encountered during the exam, as this will increase feelings of fear and anxiety while waiting for scores.
4. Examination candidates should surround themselves with positivity, including friends, family members, and other students.
5. Avoid discussions about the fairness of the exam and about the ability to pass the exam.
6. After receiving score reports, if a passing score is achieved, look forward to beginning a clinical fellowship (CF) and to the start of a rewarding career as an SLP.
   a. If a passing score was not achieved, know that there is always another attempt and that passing the Speech-Language Pathology Exam and becoming an SLP is still an attainable goal.

Retaking the Exam

1. Each Speech-Language Pathology Exam that is taken requires separate registration; however, the same online ETS account from the first attempt may be used repeatedly.
2. Eligibility to retake the exam begins during the next available testing window.
   a. Testing windows for the exam occur in March, June, July, August, September, and December.
   b. In the time spent waiting for the next selected testing window, there are several things to do:
      (1) Surrounding oneself with a supportive network of people may prove necessary in overcoming negative feelings of disappointment.
      (2) Review exam results and identify areas of strengths and weaknesses, in order to establish areas that should be reviewed while waiting.
      (3) Identify anything that may have caused the lack of success on the first attempt at passing the exam. Reduce the chance of reoccurrence by minimizing these hindrances during a second attempt. These include behaviors such as:
         (a) Taking too long to answer certain questions.
         (b) Experiencing anxiety over questions that proved difficult or those that provoked feelings of ambiguity.
         (c) Becoming distracted by how quickly other test-takers are advancing through their tests.
         (d) Not arriving to the testing center with enough time to ease into the situation.
         (e) Either forgetting or forgoing assistance for the Speech-Language Pathology Exam if qualifications for disability assistance are met.
3. Be realistic about obstacles to success that can and cannot be changed. Evaluate those that can be changed, and come up with a solution that works.
4. Continue taking practice exams, in order to increase comfort with lengthy, computer-based standardized tests.
5. Know that having to retake the Speech-Language Pathology Exam will not prevent examination candidates from becoming well-rounded SLPs!

References

American Speech-Language-Hearing Association. (1997). Council for clinical certification in audiology and speech-language pathology. Available at www.asha.org/About/governance/committees/CommitteeSmartForms/Council-for-Clinical-Certification-in-Audiology-and-Speech-Language-Pathology/.

American Speech-Language-Hearing Association. (2014a). About the speech-language pathology Praxis exam. Available at www.asha.org/Certification/praxis/About-the-Speech-Language-Pathology-Praxis-Exam/.

American Speech-Language-Hearing Association. (2014b). Speech-language pathology exam (5331) content. Available at www.asha.org/Certification/praxis/Speech-Language-Pathology-Exam-5331-Content/.

American Speech-Language-Hearing Association. (2014c). Speech-language pathology practice analysis and curriculum study. Available at https://www.asha.org/Certification/SLP-Practice-Analysis-and-Curriculum-Study/.

Educational Testing Services. (2015a). On test day overview. Available at www.ets.org/praxis/test_day/.

Educational Testing Services. (2015b). Praxis scores overview. Available at www.ets.org/praxis/scores/.

Educational Testing Services. (2015c). Praxis subject assessments overview. Available at www.ets.org/praxis/about/praxisii/.

Educational Testing Services. (2015d). The Praxis Study Companion: Speech-Language Pathology. Ewing, NJ: Educational Testing Services. Available at www.ets.org/s/praxis/pdf/5331.pdf.

Educational Testing Services. (2015e). Praxis subject assessments test content and structure. Available at www.ets.org/praxis/about/praxisii/content/.

Educational Testing Services. (2015f). Registration, test dates and centers. Available at www.ets.org/praxis/register/.

Facione, P. (1990). Critical Thinking: A Statement of Expert Consensus for Purposes of Educational Assessment and Instruction. Research Findings and Recommendations. Newark, DE: American Psychological Association.

Facione, P. (2006). Critical Thinking: What It Is and Why It Counts. Millbrae, CA: California Academic Press.

Facione, N. C., & Facione, P. A. (2006). The Health Sciences Reasoning Test HSRT: Test Manual 2006 Edition. Millbrae, CA: California Academic Press.

Fleming-Castaldy, R. P. (2014). National Occupational Therapy Certification Exam: Review and Study Guide, 7th ed. Evanston, IL: TherapyEd.

Fleming-Castaldy, R. P., & Inda, K. (2019). "Principles of Effective Examination Preparation." In R. Fleming-Castaldy (Ed.), National Occupational Therapy Certification Exam: Review & Study Guide, 9th ed. Evanston, IL: TherapyEd.

Much of the material in this chapter was used, with permission, from Rita Fleming-Castaldy's National Occupational Therapy Certification Exam Review and Study Guide, 7th edition (2014). Adaptations to fit the profession of speech-language pathology were made and new material was added.

2

Anatomy and Physiology of Communication and Swallowing

JAMES T. HEATON, PhD
SOFIA VALLILA-ROHTER, PhD

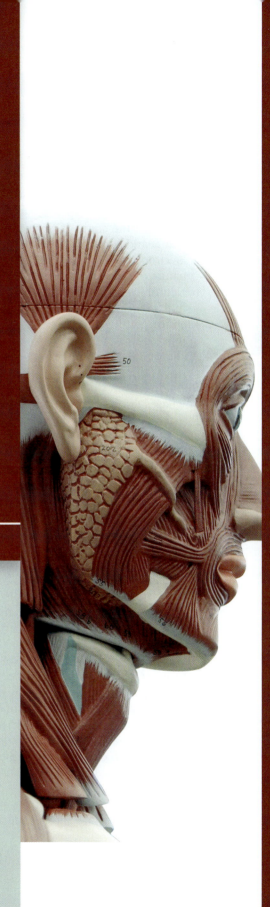

▶ The Study of Speech, Language, and Swallowing

Areas of Study

1. Anatomy: the bodily structure of an organism and its parts.
2. Physiology: the study of normal function of bodily structure and parts.
   a. Electrophysiology: the study of the bioelectrical nature of cells.
   b. Neurophysiology: the study of the nervous system's function.
3. Kinesiology: the study of physiological, mechanical, and psychological mechanisms of movement.
4. Audiology: the study of hearing disorders, evaluation, and rehabilitation.
5. Phonology: the study of how sound is used across languages to convey meaning.
6. Psychology: the study of mental processes and behavior.

Basic Elements of Anatomy

1. There is a hierarchical organization to the body's form and function.
   a. Atoms: the basic units of matter that, it is believed, cannot be divided into smaller stable forms of matter.
   b. Molecules: two or more atoms bound together by the sharing of electrons.
   c. Tissues: integrated cells from the same developmental origin that together carry out a common function.
   d. Organs: structures made of two or more tissues that together perform a common function.
   e. Organ systems: formed by multiple organs that together perform a particular body function (e.g., muscular system, skeletal system).
      (1) Each anatomical element described is composed of contributions from earlier components of the hierarchy (e.g., tissues are made up of multiple cell types).
2. The main tissue types for animals are epithelial, connective, muscular, and nervous (detailed below).

Parts of the Body

1. Planes of section and directional nomenclature.
   a. Anatomy is typically described from a particular perspective or plane of a section. When examining the body as a whole, the frame of reference for planes and directional terms is the *standard anatomical position*.

(1) For humans (bipeds), standard anatomical position is the body standing upright with the arms at the sides and palms facing forward.
(2) For four-legged animals (quadrupeds), standard anatomical position is where all four feet are on the ground while standing.
(3) Planes and directional terms are in relation to the long axis of a structure or the relative position or movement of two or more structures (Fig. 2-1).
   b. Planes of section.
   (1) Frontal (coronal) plane: divides the body vertically into anterior (front) and posterior (back) parts.
   (2) Sagittal (median) plane: divides the body vertically into right and left sides.
      (a) When the right/left dividing line is in the center, the plane can be called *midsagittal*.
      (b) When the right/left dividing line is off from the midline, the plane can be called *parasagittal* or *lateral*.
   (3) Horizontal (axial) plane: divides the body along the horizon into upper and lower parts.
      (a) This is the same as the transverse plane, which divides a structure perpendicular to its long axis (e.g., cutting a loaf of bread into slices).
   c. Directional nomenclature.
   (1) Superior or cranial is toward the head, whereas inferior or caudal is toward the feet.
   (2) Anterior or ventral is toward the front, whereas posterior or dorsal is toward the back.
      (a) Rostral, from the Latin term *beak* or *nose*, means "toward the nose."

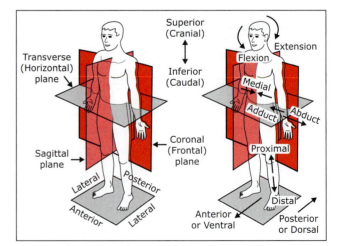

Figure 2-1 **Planes of Section and Directional Nomenclature**

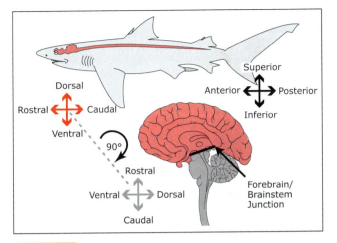

Figure 2-2   **Directional Terminology for the Human Brain**

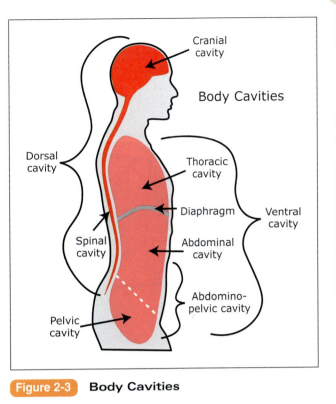

Figure 2-3   **Body Cavities**

(3) Medial is toward the body midline, whereas lateral is away from the midline (e.g., the big toe is on the medial edge of the foot, and the ear is on the lateral surface of the head).

(4) Proximal is toward the trunk or origin of a part, whereas distal is away from the trunk or the origin of a part (e.g., the proximal end of the humerus bone attaches to the scapula at the shoulder, and the distal end articulates with the ulna and radius bones at the elbow).

(5) Flexing decreases a joint angle, whereas extending increases a joint angle.

  (a) For the head and neck, tucking the chin toward the sternum is flexion, and moving the back of the head toward the shoulder blades is extension.

  d. Directional terminology for the human brain.

  (1) Because the forebrain is turned 90° "forward" in the skull relative to the rest of the nervous system and body, the orienting names for the brain need to be adjusted relative to the body (e.g., the dorsal surface of the brain resides at the superior aspect of the body) (Fig. 2-2).

2. Body cavities.

  a. Major body cavities include the dorsal cavity and ventral cavity (Fig. 2-3).

  b. Dorsal cavity is formed by the skull and vertebral column, containing the brain and spinal cord, respectively.

  c. Ventral cavity is subdivided into the thoracic and abdominal cavities, which are divided from each other by the diaphragm muscle located inferior to the lungs.

  (1) Thoracic cavity contains the heart, lungs, trachea, esophagus, large blood vessels, and nerves.

  (2) Abdominal cavity contains the digestive system from the stomach to the colon, as well as the kidneys and adrenal glands.

  (a) The inferior-most portion of the abdomen located within the pelvic skeleton is called the pelvic cavity and contains most of the urogenital system and rectum.

Tissue Types

1. Epithelial layers.

  a. Epithelial layers are tightly joined cells that form coverings for the exterior body surface, as well as the interior surfaces on organs, cavities, and aerodigestive tract.

  b. These layers are categorized according to how many cell layers they have (single vs. multiple) and cell shape.

  c. Simple epithelial layers of a single cell thickness are listed below (Fig. 2-4).

  (1) Ciliated epithelium: lines the airway from the bronchi through the nasal cavities, paranasal sinuses, and false vocal folds (but not the true vocal folds).

  (2) Ciliated pseudostratified columnar epithelium: lines the trachea and the upper respiratory tract.

  (a) Respiratory epithelium is technically a single cell layer attached to a basement membrane (which underlies all epithelial and endothelial layers). It includes multiple cell types such as basal cells (for repairing damage) and goblet cells (which secrete mucus).

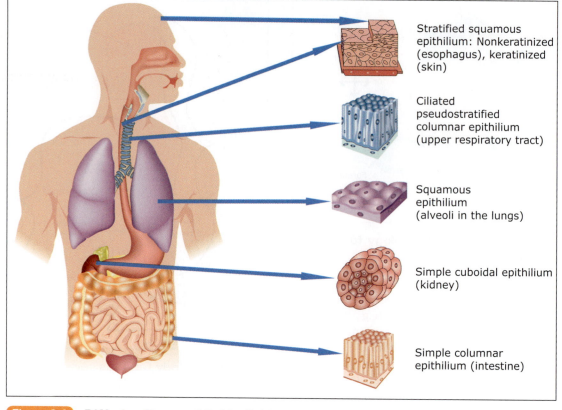

Stratified squamous epithilium: Nonkeratinized (esophagus), keratinized (skin)

Ciliated pseudostratified columnar epithilium (upper respiratory tract)

Squamous epithilium (alveoli in the lungs)

Simple cuboidal epithilium (kidney)

Simple columnar epithilium (intestine)

Figure 2-4   Differing Types of Epithelial Layers

(b) The upwardly (cranially) beating cilia of respiratory epithelium in the trachea transport particles caught on the epithelial surface toward the pharynx. One can then swallow or spit them out and maintain a clean airway.

(3) Squamous epithelium: lines alveoli in the lungs and interior surface (or endothelium) of lymph and blood vessels.

(4) Cuboidal epithelium: lines the kidney tubules and glands.

d. Compound epithelial layers of multiple cell thickness offer more protection against friction/abrasion, microbial invasions, and desiccation (drying out) than do simple epithelium.

e. Compound epithelial layers of multiple cell thickness are listed below.

(1) Nonkeratinized stratified squamous epithelium ("mucosa"): lines the mouth, pharynx, esophagus, true vocal folds, rectum, and some of the female reproductive tract.

(2) Keratinized stratified squamous epithelium: forms the skin and has an outer layer of dead cells (rich in the protein keratin) that provides a tough, waterproof barrier.

(3) Stratified cuboidal and columnar epithelia: relatively rare and often line ducts within glands but are found in some other locations as well.

2. Connective tissue.

a. Connective tissue connects and supports other tissues.

b. Loose connective tissue: contains loosely woven collagen and elastin fibers that hold organs in place while still allowing a generous range of movement.

c. Fibrous connective tissue: contains densely packed collagen fibers that bind muscle to bone or other regions of muscle (i.e., tendons) or bind skeletal components together (i.e., ligaments) to limit range of movement.

d. Adipose tissue (fat): stores metabolic fuel in the form of free fatty acids.

e. Cartilage.

(1) A pliable tissue that comes in a wide range of density and pliability to serve different purposes.

(2) Fibrocartilage is white in color and contains a mixture of cartilage and collagen (type I).

(a) It is found in the pubic symphysis, intervertebral discs, and in some joints, including the knee and temporomandibular joint (TMJ).

(3) Hyaline cartilage is bluish white in color, firm, and very elastic.

(a) It helps maintain a patent (open) airway by forming rings in the bronchi, partial rings in the trachea, and most cartilages of the larynx.

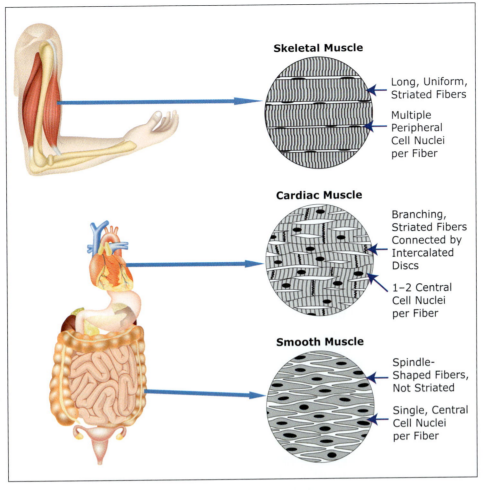

Skeletal Muscle

Long, Uniform, Striated Fibers

Multiple Peripheral Cell Nuclei per Fiber

Cardiac Muscle

Branching, Striated Fibers Connected by Intercalated Discs

1–2 Central Cell Nuclei per Fiber

Smooth Muscle

Spindle-Shaped Fibers, Not Striated

Single, Central Cell Nuclei per Fiber

Figure 2-5   **Differing Types of Muscular Tissues**

(b) It covers the articular surfaces of bones and forms the cartilaginous portions of ribs (portion attached to the sternum).

(4) Elastic cartilage contains many yellow elastic fibers in addition to collagen (type II) and elastin, giving it great flexibility.

    (a) It is found in the epiglottis of the larynx and pinnae of the ears.

f. Bone.

(1) Bone is a dense tissue that is strong and hard due to crystalline minerals in compact regions.

(2) Bone has a spongy core that contains marrow for blood cell production.

g. Blood.

(1) Blood is a suspension of cells in a liquid matrix.

(2) Transports gasses, nutrients, chemicals, and waste products to/from cells throughout the body.

3. Muscular tissue.

a. Muscular tissue is tissue composed of cells (fibers) that serve the function of movement and generation of force.

b. Muscle cells are classified as skeletal, cardiac, or smooth (Fig. 2-5).

(1) In all three classes, the cells are relatively long, with alternating layers of partially overlapping contractile filaments organized lengthwise.

c. When stimulated, muscle cells increase the amount of filament overlap along their length, causing them to shorten.

d. Skeletal muscle.

(1) Is striated and under voluntary control.

(2) Has a repeating pattern of partially overlapping filaments, giving it a striped or striated appearance when viewed under a microscope.

(3) Is the longest muscle cell type, with uniform diameter and multiple nuclei per cell (due to the fusion of multiple cells in early development).

(4) Is attached to the skeletal frame by tendons.

(5) Generates voluntary body movements.

(6) Multiple fiber types have different forms of contractile filaments, determining how quickly they contract and their relative resistance to fatigue.

    (a) Slow-twitch fibers contract relatively slowly and are fatigue resistant.

(b) Fast-twitch fibers contract relatively rapidly and vary in fatigability, depending on subtype.

e. Cardiac muscle.

(1) Is striated and contracts involuntarily.

(2) Found in the heart wall and contracts to propel blood through the heart chambers (two atria and two ventricles).

(3) Fibers are striated like skeletal muscle but have only one or two nuclei and have branching patterns that fuse with one another at their ends.

(4) Fibers are interconnected along their length by intercalated discs that pass electrical impulses from cell to cell (causing contraction).

(a) This mechanically binds cells together, thus synchronizing the contraction of adjacent heart walls.

(5) Specialized cardiac cells form nodes that act as internal pacemakers for the other cells, initiating about 60–100 contractions (beats) per minute without neuronal innervation.

(a) Nervous system input can reduce (parasympathetic) or increase (sympathetic) heart rate but is not required to generate resting heart rhythm.

f. Smooth muscle.

(1) Is not striated and contracts involuntarily.

(2) Fibers have a single nucleus and are spindle-shaped (widest in the middle) with staggered patterns of overlapping filaments, making them homogenous in appearance (not striated).

(3) Specialized for relatively slow, sustained contraction in the internal organs, blood vessels, lens and iris of the eye, and hair follicles.

(4) Fibers contract in response to many different stimuli, depending on location/function.

(a) Hormones, endogenous chemicals, and ingested chemicals/drugs.

(b) Stretch and gasses in the airway and blood vessels.

(c) Motoneuron input from peripheral nerves.

(d) Via local circuit neurons acting as intrinsic pacemakers for rhythmic contraction.

4. Nervous tissue.

a. Nervous tissue comprises multiple cell types that together receive, integrate, interpret, and direct the response to internal and environmental stimuli.

(1) Neurons are cells specialized for receiving and transmitting information over long distances in the form of electrochemical impulses (action potentials [APs]).

(a) Neurons respond to a wide range of stimuli (e.g., mechanical, noxious, chemical, thermal, light) either directly or in conjunction with transducer cells (e.g., rods/cones in retina, acoustic and vestibular hair cells, touch receptors).

(b) Within the brain and spinal cord, neurons have multiple processes extending from their cell body, with dendrites that are highly receptive to chemical signals (input) and an axon that can extend long distances to send signals (output) to other neurons or drive the activity of glands and muscles to control behavior.

(2) Support cells (glial cells) include multiple cell types that provide structural support, form protective barriers, clear waste materials, and electrically insulate axons to facilitate AP transmission.

▶ Neuroanatomy and Neurophysiology for Speech, Language, and Swallowing

Nervous System (NS)

1. A complex information-processing system that enables interaction with the environment for survival and reproduction.

NS Cell Types

1. Neurons.

a. Neurons are cells specialized for information reception and transmission.

(1) Information processing, learning, and memory are accomplished by changes in the strength and number of connections among neurons.

b. Neurons have a cell body (soma) containing a single nucleus, along with one or more extensions called *processes* or *poles* from the soma.

(1) Dendrites: processes specialized for receiving signals from other neurons or environmental stimuli.

(2) Axons: processes specialized for transmitting or propagating APs in order to communicate with other neurons, contract muscle, or cause glands to secrete.

(a) APs originate at the axon's trigger zone, the axon hillock, located at the initial segment of the axon.

c. Neurons can be classified as multipolar, bipolar, or unipolar based on how many "poles" or processes extend from their cell body (Fig. 2-6).

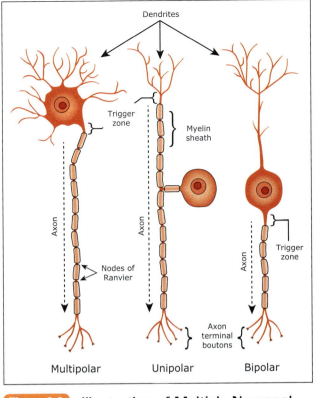

Figure 2-6 **Illustration of Multiple Neuronal Types**

(1) Multipolar neurons: have multiple dendrites and a single axon extending a relatively far distance from their soma.
  (a) Are found throughout the central nervous system (CNS; brain and spinal cord).
  (b) Include lower motor neurons, which have axons extending sometimes several feet from the brainstem and spinal cord of the CNS to muscles via nerves in the peripheral nervous system (PNS).
(2) Bipolar neurons: have two processes (poles) extending from the soma, with one serving as an axon and the other usually serving as a dendrite (an exception is bipolar cells of the cochlea's spiral ganglia, which have two axon extensions from their soma).
  (a) Are found in PNS sensory pathways for special senses of the head (i.e., taste, olfaction, vision, hearing, and vestibular sensation).
(3) Unipolar neurons: have a single, fused process, the distal-most portion of which serves as a dendrite, while the remainder serves as an axon.
  (a) Are found in PNS sensory pathways for senses represented throughout the body, including fine touch, vibration, proprioception, pressure, pain, and temperature.
  (b) These are also called *pseudounipolar neurons*.

d. Most axons are electrically insulated from surrounding tissues/fluid by a coating of glial cells forming a myelin sheath.
  (1) Myelinating cells have a high lipid (fat) content, which gives a white appearance to fiber pathways (like white fat in milk).
e. Axons terminate in a branching pattern onto their target(s), with small enlargements or swelled locations at their very ends, called *terminal boutons*.
  (1) Boutons contain neurotransmitters for chemical signaling.
2. Glia.
  a. *Glia* is a label for multiple cell types that play supportive, critical roles in neuronal function.
  b. Glia physically support neurons, remove metabolic waste products, and prevent toxic buildup of chemicals used in neural signaling.
  c. Glia help form the barrier between neurons and circulating blood in the CNS (blood-brain barrier) by covering the capillaries and acting as a filter.
  d. Glia also respond to neuronal injury by removing dead cells and forming neural scar tissue.
  e. One of the most important glial cell functions is the formation of myelin sheaths on axons, which provide electrical insulation and thereby increase the speed of APs (see the next section).
    (1) Oligodendrocytes myelinate axons in the CNS. A single oligodendrocyte can provide a small length of myelin to multiple axons.
    (2) Schwann cells myelinate axons in the PNS. Each Schwann cell provides myelin to a small length of just one axon of the PNS.

Neural Signaling

1. Resting membrane potential, concentration, and electrical gradients.
  a. Neurons have a cell membrane that restricts the flow of particles into and out of the cell.
    (1) The membrane is a phospholipid bilayer with channels spanning across the membrane that open/close to determine the flow of particles.
  b. By controlling the flow of charged particles (ions) across the membrane, neurons are able to generate electrical potentials used in neural signaling.
  c. Neurons have relatively high intracellular concentrations of potassium ions (K^+) and negatively charged organic molecules (A^-). Sodium ions (Na^+) and chloride ions (Cl^-) are also present inside neurons.
  d. A neuron's extracellular environment has relatively high concentrations of Na^+ and chloride (Cl^-). K^+ ions are also present extracellularly.
  e. At rest, neurons maintain a resting potential of about -65 mV on the inside of the cell compared to the outside of the cell. Because it has a charge, the cell membrane is described as being *polarized*.

(1) This negative potential keeps the neuron prepared to "fire," or send a signal down the length of its axon.

f. Differences in ion concentrations inside and outside of the cell lead to concentration gradients.

(1) The high concentration of Na^+ ions outside the cell relative to inside the cell creates an inward directed concentration gradient (Na^+ ions want to move into the cell to a region of lower Na^+ concentration).

(2) The high concentration of K^+ ions inside the cell relative to outside the cell creates an outward directed concentration gradient.

g. Differences in intra- and extracellular charge lead to electrical gradients.

(1) The resting potential of –65mV inside attracts Na^+ ions toward the inside of the cell (opposite charges attract!). This is referred to as an *inward directed electrical gradient.*

(2) The electrical gradient for K^+ is also inward directed.

h. Notice that the concentration and electrical gradients for Na^+ are both directed inward. Interestingly for K^+, the concentration gradient is outward directed, while the electrical gradient is inward directed (at rest).

(1) If Na^+ was able to flow freely, it would enter the neuron due to both concentration and electrical gradients. By default, Na^+ channels are closed, preventing such free flow.

(2) If K^+ is able to flow freely, opposing concentration and electrical gradients lead K^+ ions to operate on more of a "one in, one out" type of movement. Some K^+ channels are open at rest, allowing K^+ to "leak" in and out of the cell slowly.

2. Synaptic potentials.

a. Dendrites contain chemically gated channels.

b. These channels act as receptors that open in response to chemical signals (neurotransmitters) released by other neurons.

c. When neurotransmitter molecules bind to chemically gated channels, this causes the channels to open, allowing positively or negatively charged ions to enter the cell, leading to synaptic potential.

d. The type of receptor, where the input is received, and what other inputs are received will determine the impact of a synaptic potential.

(1) Synaptic potentials that make neurons more likely to fire an action potential are called *excitatory postsynaptic potentials* (EPSPs). These are depolarizing potentials (they make the membrane less polarized, or less negative).

(2) Synaptic potentials that make neurons less likely to fire an action potential are called inhibitory postsynaptic potentials (IPSPs).

These are hyperpolarizing (they make the membrane more polarized, or more negative).

e. Synaptic potentials are generally small, meaning that many occurring simultaneously may be needed to cause an action potential (AP) to fire. In addition, synaptic potentials are graded potentials. This means that they become smaller as they move away from the synapse.

f. If synaptic potentials depolarize a neuron sufficiently, they will trigger an AP.

3. Action potentials (APs).

a. When summed synaptic potentials depolarize a neuron at its trigger zone by about 15 mV (thus bringing the resting potential to around –50mV), voltage-gated Na^+ channels open.

b. Once voltage-gated channels open, they allow an influx of Na^+ due to strong inward-directed concentration and electrical gradients.

c. This rapid influx of Na^+ causes a rapid depolarizing current (a "spike" or "impulse") that is called an *action potential* (AP).

d. The voltage-gated channels that allow Na^+ to enter the neuron during an AP are open for only a very brief amount of time (about 0.5 ms) before rapidly becoming inactivated, stopping the flow of Na^+.

(1) Na^+ inactivation limits the duration of the AP's positive spike and makes the AP brief in duration.

(2) During Na^+ inactivation, it is impossible to open these voltage-gated channels, causing an absolute refractory period. During the absolute refractory period (about 1 to 2 ms), another AP cannot fire.

e. During Na^+ inactivation, voltage-gated K^+ channels open.

f. K^+ rushes out of the cell, as the concentration gradient and electrical gradients are now both outward directed (remember that Na^+ has rushed in, so now the membrane potential is positive rather than negative) (Fig. 2-7).

g. This efflux of K^+ causes a brief period of hyperpolarization (K^+ ions rushing out make the cell negative again) immediately after the AP spike.

(1) During this period, it is relatively more difficult to bring the neuron to threshold because of the hyperpolarized state (compared to the resting potential). This period is called the *relative refractory period.*

(2) Only very strong stimuli can overcome hyperpolarization during this relative refractory period and cause action potentials.

h. After an AP, the resting potential is restored by the active transport of Na^+ to the outside and K^+ to the inside of the cell membrane by sodium-potassium pumps embedded like channels in the cell membrane.

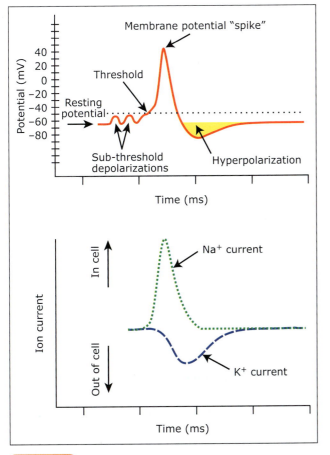

Figure 2-7   **Summary of Action Potentials**

i. Action potentials are all-or-none events because the threshold for opening voltage-gated channels is either reached or it is not.

j. The process of an AP is re-created down the entire length of an axon.
   (1) Brief (1 ms) electrical "spikes" propagate down the axon at a uniform speed and magnitude, regardless of the input strength.
   (2) The amount of stimulation a neuron receives is represented by its AP firing rate (how rapidly the APs occur back-to-back), rather than the strength of individual APs (which are all the same "size").

4. Saltatory conduction.
   a. As noted earlier, most axons are electrically insulated along a vast majority of their length by a sheath of myelin.
   b. There are short noninsulated gaps between myelinating cells called *nodes of Ranvier*, where voltage-gated channels are concentrated.
   c. This enables APs to jump along the axon from gap to gap (called *saltatory conduction*).
   d. Saltatory conduction carries signals at speeds much faster than nonmyelinated axons, where voltage-gated channels must sequentially open along the entire axon surface/length.
   e. Myelinated axons propagate APs at a rate of about six times the axon diameter.
      (1) The fastest myelinated axons are about 20 μm in diameter and transmit at 120 m/sec.
      (2) Axons that are not myelinated tend to be small in diameter and transmit at only 2–8 m/sec.

5. Neurotransmitter release and end-plate potentials.
   a. When an AP reaches a bouton, it opens voltage-gated calcium ion (Ca$^+$) channels, causing an influx of Ca$^+$.
   b. In the presence of Ca$^+$, synaptic vesicles within the terminal bouton that contain neurotransmitter fuse with the cell membrane and squirt their neurotransmitter into the synaptic gap through a process called *exocytosis*.
   c. Exocytosis is how neurons communicate with other neurons, muscles, and glands via the release of chemical signals (neurotransmitters) onto the surface of their targets.
   d. Chemical signals released from terminal boutons into the synaptic clefts (gaps) between axon terminals and their targets contribute to synaptic potentials (see #2) when the signals are received by dendritic receptors of nearby neurons.
      (1) Recall that synaptic potentials can be excitatory (bringing a neuron closer to AP firing threshold) or inhibitory (bringing a neuron farther away from AP firing threshold).
      (2) Importantly, released neurotransmitters can also be described as receptor agonists that open channels, or receptor antagonists that block channel openings.
         (a) When receptor agonists open channels and allow ions to enter the cell, the cell can come closer to firing (depolarizing potential) or farther from firing an action potential (hyperpolarizing potential), depending on whether the flowing ions are positively or negatively charged, respectively.
         (b) When receptor antagonists block channel openings, this can block signals normally causing hyperpolarizing or depolarizing synaptic potentials.
   e. Neurotransmitter rapidly clears the synaptic cleft by passive diffusion, active reuptake (by the boutons), and/or enzymatic destruction in order to prevent a prolonged effect of released transmitter (e.g., to prepare the synapse for new signal transmission).

6. An example of the neural signaling process.
   a. Acetylcholine (ACh) is a commonly occurring neurotransmitter found in the vesicles of motor neurons, visceral efferent neurons, and numerous brain pathways.

b. When a motor neuron fires an action potential, ACh is released from the neuron's terminal bouton.

c. Motor neurons (motoneurons) contact muscle cells (fibers) at specialized end-plate regions where the fibers have numerous ACh receptors called *nicotinic receptors*.

d. ACh is an agonist to nicotinic receptors, meaning that ACh binds with the receptors and opens them.

e. Opening the receptors allows Na^+ to enter the muscle fiber, depolarizing the muscle cells and causing them to contract (shorten).

f. ACh receptor antagonists, which block receptors from opening, can be used in anesthesia, for example, to block the action of ACh and relax muscles.

g. ACh binding does not always lead to an excitatory postsynaptic potential. ACh is also an agonist to muscarinic receptors of the heart. Interestingly, when ACh binds with *these* receptors, it triggers a chain of events that are inhibitory and slow the heart.

h. Thus, ACh can act as a receptor agonist that either brings a cell closer to firing (e.g., when taken up by nicotinic receptors of muscles) or brings a cell farther away from firing (e.g., when taken up by muscarinic receptors of the heart).

i. ACh receptor antagonists would block either of these actions.

j. Exocytosis can also be blocked in other ways. Botulinum toxin can be used as a medication to intentionally prevent exocytosis of ACh. When botulinum (Botox) is injected into a muscle, it enters the terminal boutons of the innervating motor nerve, permanently inactivates proteins critical to the process of vesicle fusion with the cell membrane, and thereby stops the release of ACh. The injected muscle is weakened or even paralyzed for several months until new boutons have time to sprout from the axon terminals and restore ACh release.

Central and Peripheral NS

1. In the developing embryo, a neural tube forms that eventually becomes the brain and spinal cord, referred to as the *central nervous system*.
   a. The PNS comprises peripheral nerves, in communication with the CNS, that stem from neural crest cells in the developing embryo. Therefore, the distinction between CNS and PNS is not arbitrary, but rather relates to their different embryological origins.
2. Two important differences between CNS and PNS include regenerative capability and exposure to blood circulation.

a. CNS neurons have little regenerative capabilities due to their inherent tendency to retract their processes and/or die after injury rather than survive and sprout new growth. Their regeneration is actively inhibited by chemicals released from surrounding glia and glial scars.

b. In contrast, when axons are injured in PNS motor or sensory nerves, they send numerous sprouts from the site of injury in a robust attempt to regenerate. This is actively facilitated by Schwann cells and the nerves' connective tissues.

c. Neurons and glia within the CNS are limited in what they can receive from circulating blood due to the blood-brain barrier (BBB). The BBB is formed primarily by tight junctions between capillary endothelial cells in the CNS, which limit what molecules can diffuse from circulating blood.

d. In contrast, neurons and glia in the PNS receive a diffusion of blood-borne molecules that is less filtered than what reaches the brain and is therefore more on the "body side" of the BBB.

Major Divisions of the PNS

1. Somatic and autonomic NS.
   a. The PNS can be subdivided into somatic NS and autonomic NS components (Fig. 2-8).
   b. The somatic NS supports sensations and motor functions of the body (soma) that are consciously perceived and volitionally controlled, respectively.
      (1) It allows one to be aware of the external environment and to act on that information.
   c. The autonomic NS (also called the *visceral NS*) functions mostly below conscious awareness or control, regulating visceral functions such as digestion, heart rate, blood pressure, respiration, and gland secretion. It detects and acts on the body's internal environment.
      (1) The parasympathetic division of the autonomic NS helps maintain homeostasis ("rest-and-digest") through balancing functions such as respiration, blood perfusion, and food digestion in relation to metabolic needs.
         (a) The efferent (outward-flowing) signals of the parasympathetic division originate from the cranial nerves and sacral region of the spinal cord, so it is also called the craniosacral division of the autonomic NS.
      (2) The sympathetic division of the autonomic NS is activated in times of perceived threat, preparing one for fight or flight by inhibiting nonessential bodily functions (like digestion); increasing heart rate, blood pressure, sweat production, respiratory rate; and diverting blood to

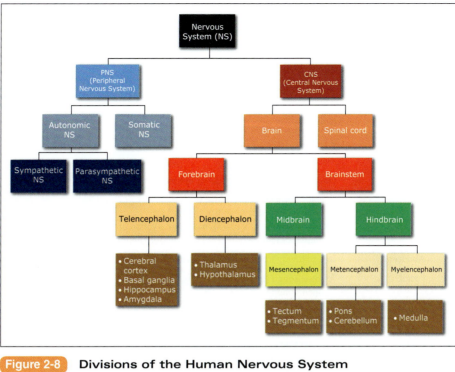

Figure 2-8   **Divisions of the Human Nervous System**

the skeletal muscles in preparation for physical exertion.

(a) The efferent signals of the sympathetic division originate from the thoracic and lumbar regions of the spinal cord, so it is also called the thoracolumbar division of the autonomic NS.

2. Cranial and spinal nerves.

a. The CNS communicates with the body (and thereby the environment) via peripheral nerves in the PNS.

b. Twelve pairs of nerves leave the skull to communicate between the CNS and the head, neck and viscera of the thorax and abdomen. These are called cranial nerves because they enter/exit the cranium (skull) (Fig. 2-9).

c. Thirty-one pairs of nerves exit the spinal column and carry information to and from the PNS (peripheral nerves) and CNS (spinal cord and brain). These are called *spinal nerves* because they enter/exit the spine (Fig. 2-10).

d. The cranial nerves are numbered more or less according to their order of appearance on the ventral brain surface from rostral to caudal (see Fig. 2-9).

e. There are 12 pairs of cranial nerves, often referred to by Roman numerals I through XII.

f. Cranial nerves can be composed entirely of motor axons, entirely of sensory axons, or a mixture of motor and sensory axons.

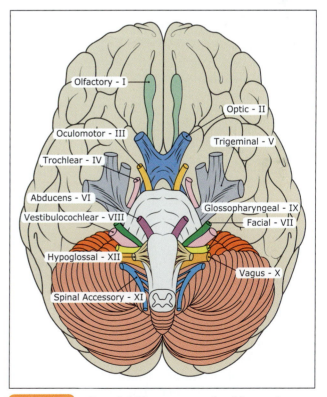

Figure 2-9   **Cranial Nerves on the Ventral Surface of the Brain**

Chapter 2 APC

Table 2-1

NERVE	S: SENSORY M: MOTOR B: BOTH	NAME	FUNCTION	SPEECH/SWALLOW CONTRIBUTION
			Cranial Nerves	
CN I	S	Olfactory	Smell	
CN II	S	Optic	Vision	
CN III	M	Oculomotor	Eye movement, upper eyelid elevation, pupil constriction	
CN IV	M	Trochlear	Downward and lateral (midline) eye movement	
CN V	B	Trigeminal	3 major branches: ophthalmic (V1), maxillary (V2), mandibular (V3) Face sensation (V1, V2, V3), motor innervation of muscles of mastication (V3), and tensor tympani	Oral stage of swallowing: chewing, bolus sensation, dampening of internal chewing sounds by contracting tensor tympani
CN VI	M	Abducens	Lateral (away from midline) eye movement	
CN VII	B	Facial	Taste sensation (anterior ⅔ of tongue), motor innervation to muscles of facial expression, lacrimation, salivation	Oral stage of swallowing: taste, bolus formation Speech: articulation
CN VIII	S	Vestibulocochlear	Hearing and vestibular sensation	Hearing, sound localization
CN IX	B	Glossopharyngeal	Taste sensation (posterior ⅓ of tongue), sensation from middle ear, upper pharynx, and carotid body (blood gases and pressures), salivation (parotid), motor innervation of stylopharyngeus	Oral and pharyngeal stages of swallowing: taste, salivation, pharynx elevation, gag reflex
CN X	B	Vagus	Sensation from lower pharynx, motor innervation of pharyngeal and laryngeal muscles of the soft palate, heart, lungs, and digestive tract	Velum elevation, gag reflex, vocal fold tension, adduction, and abduction (SLN & RLN)
CN XI	M	Spinal accessory	Motor innervation of sternocleidomastoid and trapezius muscles	Head turning, shoulder elevation
CN XII	M	Hypoglossal	Motor innervation of intrinsic tongue muscles	Oral stage of swallowing: bolus manipulation and propulsion, speech articulation

(1) Sensory axons in cranial nerves are from bipolar or unipolar neurons with their somas clustered in peripheral ganglia at some point along the nerve, similar to the spinal nerve dorsal root ganglia.

(2) Motor axons in cranial nerves are from multipolar neurons clustered in the brainstem (nerves III–VII, IX, X, and XII) or in the upper cervical spinal cord (nerve XI).

g. Individual cranial nerve functions are often described in terms of being afferent (sensory) versus efferent (motor), general (body-wide) versus special (peculiar to the head), and somatic versus visceral (autonomic).

(1) Each cranial nerve can have several functions, including combinations of all the above (Table 2-1).

h. The spinal nerves are named in relation to the region of the vertebral column from which they exit the vertebral canal (see Fig. 2-10).

i. Spinal nerves all contain a mixture of motor (outward-flowing or efferent) and sensory (inward flowing or afferent) fibers at the point where they exit the vertebral column.

(1) Axons entering the spinal cord through the dorsal roots are from unipolar sensory neurons. First order sensory neuron cell bodies are clustered in dorsal root ganglia.

(2) Axons leaving the spinal cord through the ventral roots are from multipolar lower motor neurons. Lower motor neuron cell bodies are clustered in the ventral horns of the spinal cord.

(3) The dorsal and ventral roots converge as they travel between the vertebrae to form the 31 pairs (right and left) of mixed sensory/motor spinal nerves (see Fig. 2-11).

Central Nervous System

1. Meninges.

a. The CNS is covered by three layers of protective membranes called the *meninges* (Fig. 2-12).

b. To remember these layers, think of them as a protective PAD (pia, arachnoid, and dura mater, listed from deep to superficial) of the brain and spinal cord.

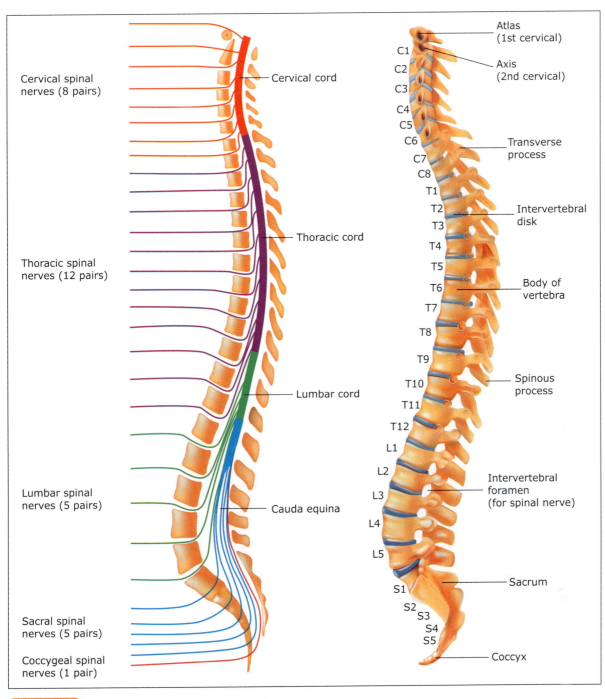

Figure 2-10   Spinal Nerves and Spinal Column

c. Pia mater (Latin: "tender mother"): a thin, delicate fibrous sheet that is tightly adhered to the surface of the brain and spinal cord. This layer adheres tightly to all of the contours of the brain.

d. Arachnoid mater: composed of a spiderweb-like mesh of fibers (thus the name) providing a region through which cerebral spinal fluid (CSF) can flow.
   (1) The brain essentially floats in this layer of CSF, which provides an important cushion to protect the brain from mechanical injury.

e. Dura mater (Latin: "tough mother"): a tough or durable sac made of dense fibrous tissue that surrounds the entire brain and spinal cord.
   (1) It has two layers that are tightly attached to one another in most locations. The outermost layer is attached to the inner surface of the skull and spinal column. The innermost surface contacts the arachnoid mater.
   (2) There are specialized regions where the two layers of the dura are not attached to one another, which creates cavities or dural sinuses where

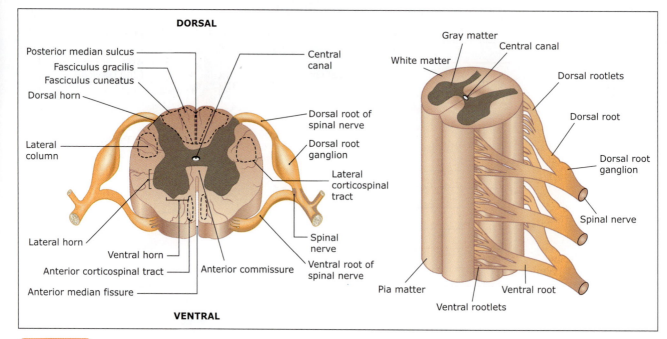

Figure 2-11   Anatomy of the Spinal Cord

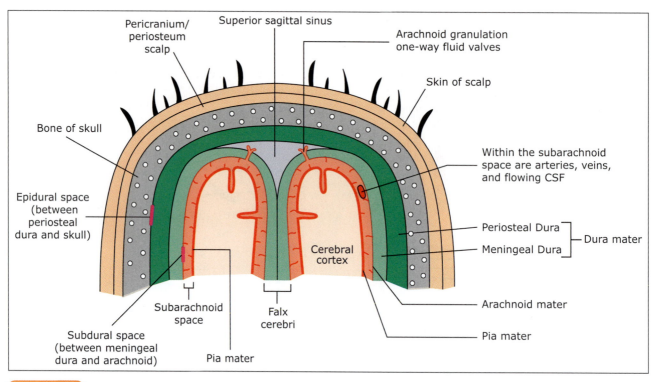

Figure 2-12   Illustration of the Meninges

deoxygenated blood from the brain's blood vessels can flow.

  (a) These sinuses converge on the right and left sides on the ventral (under) surface of the brain and exit the skull as the jugular veins, sending the depleted blood back to the heart.

(3) The dura not only covers the brain, but also physically separates major regions of the brain.

  (a) Dura extends between the right and left cerebral hemispheres (falx cerebri), between the cerebral hemispheres and the cerebellum (tentorium cerebelli), and between the cerebellar hemispheres (falx cerebelli).

(b) These extensions act as barriers, which help protect the brain by limiting its movement within the skull.

2. Ventricular system.
   a. During early fetal development, the CNS is a fluid-filled tube. As the brain and spinal cord develop, they maintain this fluid-filled core, which ultimately forms the ventricular system of the brain and the central canal of the spinal cord.
   b. CSF is a clear fluid created in the ventricular system by highly vascular, sponge-like tissue called *choroid plexus*.
      (1) CSF slowly flows through the ventricular system and fills the subarachnoid space, ultimately reentering the blood stream by flowing into the dural sinus through one-way valves called *arachnoid granulations* (or arachnoid villi).
      (2) Standing volume of CSF in the NS is about 150 ml, which turns over about three to four times per day (daily production of about 500 ml).
      (3) If the flow of CSF through the ventricular system is blocked, it causes elevated CSF pressure in a condition known as *hydrocephalus* (water on the brain).
         (a) This can be treated surgically by removing the obstruction or providing an alternative route of CSF flow (shunting).
   c. There are four ventricles within the brain (Fig. 2-13).
      (1) The right and left lateral ventricles at the core of the cerebral hemispheres.
      (2) The third ventricle on the midline of the brain below the corpus callosum.
      (3) The fourth ventricle at the base of the cerebellum.
         (a) CSF flows between the third and fourth ventricle through the cerebral aqueduct.

3. Major "encephalon" divisions.
   a. By the fifth week of embryological development, five major divisions of the brain are identifiable.
   b. These include the telencephalon and diencephalon (forebrain), mesencephalon (midbrain), metencephalon, and myelencephalon (rhombencephalon) (see Fig. 2-8).
      (1) The telencephalon further develops into the cerebral hemispheres.
      (2) The diencephalon further develops into the thalamus and hypothalamus.
      (3) The mesencephalon develops into the midbrain.
      (4) The metencephalon further develops into the pons and cerebellum.
      (5) The myelencephalon further develops into the medulla.
   c. Each of these divisions will be discussed in further detail below.

Forebrain: Telencephalon

1. Consists of right and left cerebral hemispheres, basal ganglia, hippocampus, and amygdala.
2. Cerebral hemispheres are divided along the midline by a longitudinal fissure and connected horizontally via fibers of the corpus callosum.
3. The outer surface of each cerebral hemisphere is a convoluted (folded), cell-rich, six-layered structure called the *cerebral cortex*.
4. The cortex varies in thickness from about 2 to 4 mm across the brain.
5. In fresh tissue, the cortex appears relatively gray due to a high cell content, whereas the deeper fiber pathways into and out of the cortex appear relatively white because of the high myelin content of the myelinated (insulated) axons.
6. The six horizontal layers of the cortex have different connections (Fig. 2-14), with the outer layers being primarily receptive (where incoming axons synapse) and the inner layers containing cell bodies of neurons that project to other brain areas.
7. Layer IV, the fourth deepest cell layer, receives sensory information from the thalamus and is relatively thick in regions of primary sensory cortex.

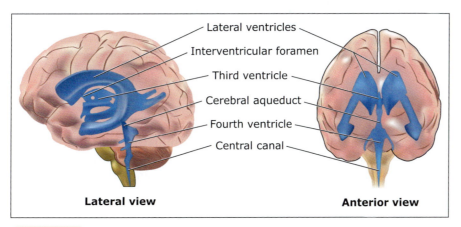

Lateral ventricles

Interventricular foramen

Third ventricle

Cerebral aqueduct

Fourth ventricle

Central canal

Lateral view   **Anterior view**

Figure 2-13   **Ventricular System of the Human Brain**

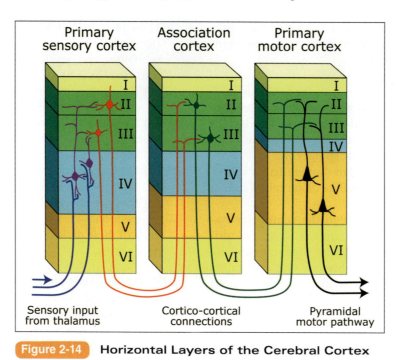

Figure 2-14   Horizontal Layers of the Cerebral Cortex

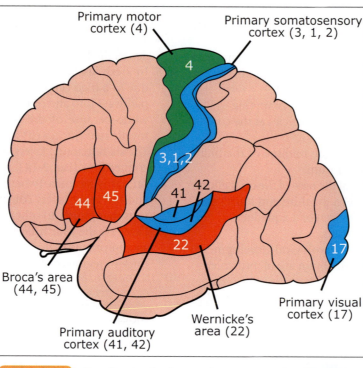

Figure 2-15   Brodmann's Areas Important for Speech
Production and Perception

8. Layer V contains large projection neurons (Betz cells) that send motor commands to the brainstem and spinal cord and is relatively thick in regions of primary motor cortex.

9. Layer III contains neuronal cell bodies projecting to other cortical areas and is relatively thick in regions of association cortex.

10. Korbinian Brodmann, a German neurologist, identified 52 distinct cortical regions based on unique anatomical features (e.g., layers) in the early 1900s. His anatomically numbered regions, called Brodmann's areas, are well known today because they relate to particular brain functions (Fig. 2-15).

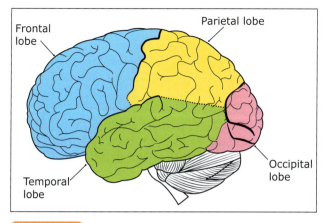

Figure 2-16   **Lobes of the Cerebral Hemispheres**

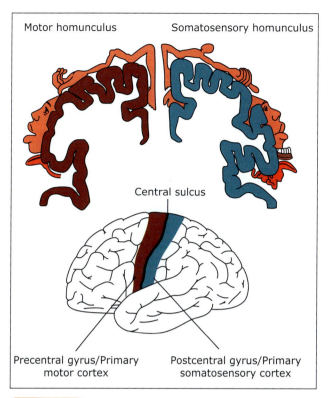

Figure 2-17   **Cortical Representations of the Motor and Sensory Homunculi**

11. In each hemisphere, the central sulcus marks the anatomical and functional demarcation between the frontal and parietal lobes (see lobe anatomy in the following section).
12. Each cerebral hemisphere is divided into four major lobes: frontal, parietal, temporal, and occipital lobes (Fig. 2-16).

Lobes of the Brain (Telencephalon)

1. Frontal lobe.
   a. The frontal lobe is anterior to the central sulcus and superior to the lateral fissure.
   b. The anterior-most portion of the frontal lobe, the prefrontal cortex, contributes to executive control, important for attention, monitoring, planning, and decision-making.
   c. Within the prefrontal cortex is the inferior frontal gyrus, the site of Broca's area in the left hemisphere, important for language production.
   d. Posterior to the prefrontal cortex is a region called the *premotor cortex*, involved in the performance of skilled movements (such as those necessary for speech) and regulation of the primary motor cortex.
   e. Posterior to the premotor cortex is an important outward fold of cortex just anterior to the central sulcus: the precentral gyrus, site of the primary motor cortex.
      (1) This motor strip is the source of half or more of all body motor control signals (Brodmann's area four).
      (2) There is a body mapping or topography across this strip called the *homunculus* (little human). The distortions of the mapping relative to true body proportions reveal that functions requiring relatively more neural processing take up relatively more cortex (see Fig. 2-17). For example, precisely controlled regions of the body (like the face) have relatively large cortical representations.

2. Parietal lobe.
   a. The parietal lobe is posterior to the central sulcus and superior to the lateral fissure.
   b. The anterior-most portion of the parietal lobe, the postcentral gyrus, is the site of the primary somatosensory cortex.
      (1) This somatosensory strip receives body sensations (excluding the special senses such as hearing and vision).
      (2) Like the motor strip, body mapping is topographically organized across the strip with highly sensitive regions taking up relatively more cortex.
3. Temporal lobe.
   a. The temporal lobe is inferior to the lateral sulcus and anterior to the occipital lobe; contains three important surface gyri: the superior, middle, and inferior gyri.
   b. The primary auditory cortex is located within the superior surface of the temporal lobe on a gyrus medial to the superior temporal gyrus called *Heschl's gyrus*.
   c. The posterior portion of the left superior temporal gyrus, adjacent to the primary auditory cortex, is the site of Wernicke's area, important for language comprehension.
4. Occipital lobe.
   a. The occipital lobe is the most posterior lobe of the brain with no natural lateral boundary separating it from the parietal and temporal lobes.

b. The occipital lobe contributes to higher-order processing of visual information and is the site of the primary visual cortex and of secondary visual integration areas.

5. Limbic cortex.

a. The limbic cortex, sometimes referred to as the *limbic lobe*, extends across portions of the temporal, parietal, and occipital lobes.

b. This "lobe" is primarily composed of the cingulate and parahippocampal gyri, and with its interconnected structures (the hippocampus, amygdala, fornix, mammillary body, and septal nuclei), it makes up the limbic system, which is important for memory, emotion, and drive-related behavior.

c. Limbic cortex is important for primitive behaviors and has fewer layers than a majority of our more highly evolved cortex (called *neocortex*).

Basal Ganglia (Telencephalon)

1. Deep in the gray and white matter of the cerebral cortex lies a collection of interconnected nuclei called the *basal ganglia*, or *basal nuclei*.

2. These nuclei act together to guide behavior, mostly through inhibition.

3. Subdivisions of the basal ganglia include the striatum, globus pallidus, substantia nigra, and subthalamic nucleus.

4. Striatum: composed of the caudate and putamen; functionally one structure divided by the main fiber highway into/out of the cortex called the *internal capsule*.

5. Globus pallidus (GP): comprises external and internal subdivisions.

6. Substantia nigra (SN): comprises two regions: the pars compacta and the pars reticulata.

a. Substantia nigra pars compacta (SNc): located in the midbrain and contains dopamine-producing cells that send strong projections to the striatum.

b. Substantia nigra pars reticulata (SNr): contains cells that produce the inhibitory neurotransmitter gamma-aminobutyric acid (GABA) that projects onto motor regions of the thalamus, which in turn projects to the motor cortex.

7. Subthalamic nucleus (STN): nucleus that receives a projection from the external segment of the GP and projects back to the internal segment.

Diencephalon

1. Diencephalon is the region of brain spanning between the cerebral hemispheres and the midbrain (uppermost part of the brainstem).

2. It is divisible into four major regions: the epithalamus, the thalamus, the subthalamus, and the hypothalamus.

3. The epithalamus contains the pineal gland (or body), as well as cellular regions and fiber pathways associated with the limbic system.

a. These structures play a role in the regulation of sleep/wake cycles, stress responses, and emotions.

b. Atrophy of the epithalamus has been found in cases of severe depression.

4. The thalamus surrounds the third ventricle (see above) on the brain midline below the corpus callosum. It contains many subdivisions that process sensory and motor information.

a. Almost all sensory information reaching the cerebral hemispheres that we consciously perceive is relayed through (and is processed by) the thalamus.

b. Motor pathways of the basal ganglia and cerebellum travel through motor subdivisions of the thalamus en route to the motor cortex.

c. Some movement disorders are treated by placing deep brain stimulator electrodes into motor regions of the thalamus.

5. The subthalamus contains the subthalamic nucleus, which is an important component of the basal ganglia motor control circuit (see section on subthalamic nucleus [STN]).

6. The hypothalamus is located on the floor of the diencephalon, between the optic chiasm to the mammillary bodies (about the size of an almond).

a. The hypothalamus communicates with the pituitary gland through a stalk of neural and vascular tissue.

b. It interacts with the pituitary to maintain body homeostasis of metabolic and endocrine (hormonal) functions such as body temperature, thirst, hunger, fatigue, circadian rhythms, and sleep/wake cycles.

Brainstem (Mesencephalon, Metencephalon, and Myelencephalon)

1. This is a relatively conserved ("older" or less evolved) region of the brain spanning between the forebrain and the spinal cord. It serves several life-sustaining functions and is the route through which nearly all neural information travels between the body and the brain (aside from vision and olfaction).

3. The brainstem comprises three major segments: the midbrain, the pons, and the medulla oblongata.

3. Midbrain: the most rostral (highest) portion of the brainstem, located just below the cerebral hemispheres and above the pons.

a. It has four prominent bulges on the posterior surface (two on each side), including two superior colliculi and two inferior colliculi, which process visual and acoustic information, respectively.

b. Just inferior to the colliculi is a cell-rich region of gray matter surrounding the cerebral aqueduct called the *periaqueductal gray* (PAG).

(1) The PAG receives and processes pain information and plays a critical role in coordinating phonatory, articulatory, and respiratory movements for sound production in all vocalizing animals studied to date.

(2) In humans, it appears that PAG lesions can cause mutism.

4. Pons: the region of brainstem with a prominent ventral bulge located immediately anterior to the cerebellum between the midbrain and the medulla.
   a. The posterior surface contains thick bundles of axons going to/from the cerebellum called *cerebellar peduncles.*
   b. Several cranial nerves have their associated nuclei (clusters of neuron cell bodies) located within the pons, including the motor nuclei for mastication (chewing) via nerve V, facial expressions via nerve VII, some eye movements via nerve VI, sensory nuclei for the head via nerve V, and vestibular and cochlear sensory functions via nerve VIII.
5. Medulla oblongata: the lowest segment of the brainstem spanning from the pons to the spinal cord.
   a. It contains neuronal circuitry guiding several autonomic functions, including respiration, cardiac rate, vascular contraction/dilation, and integration of sensory information for reflex motor responses such as coughing, vomiting, and swallowing.
   b. Nucleus ambiguus in the medulla contains motoneurons that innervate muscles of the larynx, pharynx, and the upper esophagus via branches of nerve X (vagus nerve).
   c. The hypoglossal motor nucleus in the medulla controls the tongue via nerve XII (hypoglossal nerve).
6. The reticular formation is a column of interconnected nuclei that course throughout the brainstem and caudal forebrain.
   a. Cells of the reticular formation help coordinate motor functions of the body (such as posture) and of the head (such as mastication and articulation).
   b. The reticular formation is important for regulating sleep/wake cycles and actively generating both wakeful and sleeping states.
   c. It also directs attention to help us ignore repetitive stimuli but respond to novel or salient events.
   d. Connections of the reticular formation with the cerebral cortex that guide attention/arousal are part of the reticular activating system.

Cerebellum (Metencephalon)

1. Meaning "little brain" in Latin, the cerebellum has right and left hemispheres with multiple lobes and folds of cortex similar to the cerebral hemispheres.
2. The cerebellar cortex is thinner and much more tightly folded than the cerebrum.
3. The cerebellum plays an important role in motor control by comparing motor intent with motor outcome, enabling it to guide ongoing movements (and improve future movements) by sending error correction information to the motor cortex of the cerebrum.
4. Lesions of the cerebellum do not cause paralysis but disrupt the coordination and precision of motor behavior in a condition known as *ataxia.*

Spinal Cord

1. The division between the medulla oblongata and spinal cord occurs at the foramen magnum, which is the prominent opening in the skull at the beginning of the vertebral canal.
2. There is continuity in much of the neuroanatomy between the brainstem and the spinal cord (i.e., it is not an abrupt distinction), but one identifying feature is that most of the corticospinal fibers in the pyramidal tracts cross the midline (decussate) in the medulla and then travel in the lateral corticospinal tracts within the spinal cord.
3. Features of the spinal cord.
   a. Extends the full length of the vertebral canal in newborns, but with growth it does not keep pace and only reaches the beginning of the lumbar vertebrae in adulthood.
   b. It is about 18 inches long (45 cm) and varies in width from approximately ¼ inch in the thoracic region to ½ inch in the cervical and lumbar regions (which are enlarged due to the additional motor and sensory functions associated with the arms and legs, respectively).
   c. Has a butterfly-shaped, cell-rich (gray matter) central region surrounded by dense bundles of axons (white matter) carrying motor commands from the brain to motor neurons in the cord gray matter, or carrying sensory signals from the body to the brain (see Fig. 2-13).
   d. Axons entering the dorsal or posterior side of the cord carry sensory signals, while axons exiting the ventral or anterior side carry motor signals.
   e. The spinal cord has local neuronal connections (circuits) that enable it to receive incoming sensory information and respond rapidly with a motor response (e.g., withdrawal reflexes to painful stimuli, stretch reflexes).
      (1) Descending signals from the brain can modulate or even override some spinal reflexes.
      (2) A change in reflexes can indicate brain damage (e.g., when the toes flare outward instead of curling inward in response to stroking the sole of the foot: known as a positive Babinski sign).

Fiber Connections

1. The CNS is an interconnected system, structurally and functionally linked through various fiber bundles, characterized as projection, association, and commissural fibers.
2. Association fibers are fibers within a cerebral hemisphere and either form short connections between adjacent gyri or longer connections between lobes.
3. Commissural fibers are transverse fibers that connect the two hemispheres of the brain.
4. Efferent and afferent projection fibers link the cortex with the brainstem and spinal cord.

Neural Pathways

Neural Pathways Overview

1. Neural pathways connect portions of the nervous system.
2. As previously described, nerve impulses, or APs, are generated at cell bodies or sensory nerve endings, and information is then rapidly conveyed to parts of the brain or body through axons.
3. APs are all-or-none electrochemical impulses that code information via their frequency, connections, and receptor types.
4. Our nervous system contains important descending and ascending neural pathways that contribute to our movement and sensation, respectively.
   a. Damage to these pathways can occur from trauma, disease, toxins, or restricted blood supply.
   b. Damage can affect nerve activity and impacts the way we regulate and respond to our internal and external environment.

Direct Motor Pathways

1. The direct motor pathway, often referred to as the *pyramidal system*, comprises axons that descend from upper motor neurons in the cerebrum to lower motor neurons in the spinal cord and brainstem.
   a. Axons that go from cortex to lower motor neurons of the spinal cord form the corticospinal tract.
   b. Axons that go from cortex to cranial nerve neurons in the brainstem form the corticobulbar tract.
2. Nerve impulses carried away from the brain are described as *efferent signals* or simply *efferents* (Hint: *eff*erents *ex*it the brain).
3. The function of the direct motor pathway is to control skilled, voluntary movements.
4. The corticospinal tract is one of two major tracts (pathways) of the pyramidal system. It is further subdivided into two pathways: the lateral corticospinal tract and the anterior corticospinal tract (described later in detail).

Corticospinal Tract

1. Upper motor neurons of the corticospinal tract originate from the primary and premotor cortex, as well as from supplementary motor areas and the parietal lobe.
2. Approximately 3% of these cortical motor neurons are exceptionally large cells (called *Betz cells*) that look like inverted pyramids, giving rise to the name *pyramidal tract*.

3. Corticospinal tract fibers descend through the internal capsule.
   a. The internal capsule is a thick layer of white matter located above the midbrain.
   b. It carries ascending and descending axons that connect the cortex with the brainstem and spinal cord.
4. Fibers then descend into the midbrain with many other axons in a white matter bundle called the *cerebral peduncles*.
5. In the brainstem, fibers descend through the ventral portion of the pons to the ventral surface of the medulla in pyramid-shaped fiber bundles called the *medullary pyramids* (thus reinforcing the name *pyramidal tract*).
6. When the descending pyramidal tract fibers reach the transition point from the brainstem to the spinal cord (cervicomedullary junction), 85% of all corticospinal tract fibers cross over in the pyramidal decussation and control muscles on the opposite (contralateral) side of the body.
7. Fibers that decussate form the main subdivision of the corticospinal tract called the *lateral corticospinal tract* (Fig. 2-18).
   a. The primary function of the lateral corticospinal tract is contralateral, fine, rapid limb control.
   b. Axons of the lateral corticospinal tract synapse with lower motor neurons (or nearby interneurons that then synapse with lower motor neurons) in the gray matter of the anterior horn of the spinal cord (also called the *ventral horn*).
   c. Axons that project from lower motor neurons contact striated muscle and are often referred to as the final common pathway.
   d. Damage to the final common pathway results in paresis (partial paralysis) or paralysis, muscle atrophy, fibrillations (random, spontaneous contractions) from denervated muscle cells, fasciculations (whole motor unit twitches) from spontaneous axon discharges, and decreased reflexes (hyporeflexia).
8. Fifteen percent of corticospinal fibers that *do not* decussate in the pyramidal decussation form the anterior corticospinal tract.
   a. These axons synapse contralaterally or bilaterally in the spinal cord anterior horns at the level of an action.
   b. They are involved in the control of midline (trunk) musculature.

Corticobulbar Tract

1. The corticobulbar tract, whose axons course from upper motor neurons in the cerebrum to lower motor neurons in the brainstem, is the other major tract of the direct motor pathway.

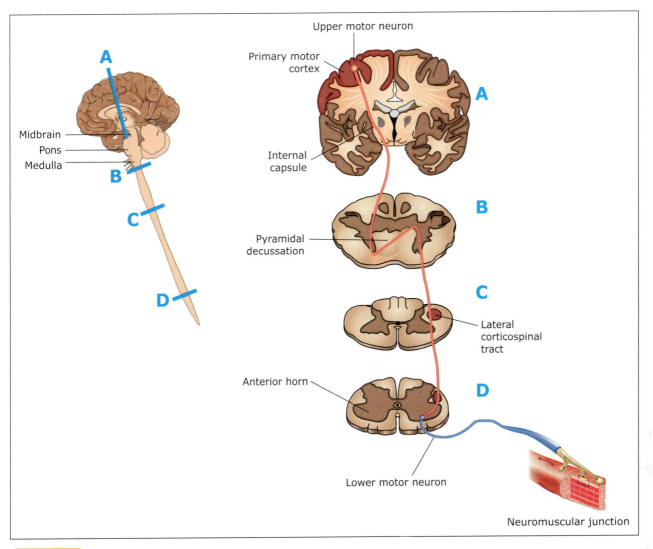

Figure 2-18   **Corticospinal Motor Pathways**

2. The function of the corticobulbar tract is to control muscles of the face, head, and neck.
3. Upper motor neurons of the corticobulbar tract originate from a lateral portion of the motor cortex close to the Sylvian fissure.
4. Similar to the corticospinal tract, fibers of the corticobulbar tract descend ipsilaterally through the internal capsule and then through the ventral portion of the midbrain cerebral peduncles.
5. Within the pons and medulla, axons of the corticobulbar tracts project contralaterally or bilaterally onto cranial nerve motor nuclei.
6. Axons from the motor nuclei then exit the brainstem ipsilaterally at various levels, forming the motor components of the cranial nerves.

Indirect Motor Pathways

1. The motor system also contains descending pathways that are indirect, forming part of the extrapyramidal system (Table 2-2).

2. The cortex projects onto multiple brainstem motor centers, which then project onto lower motor neurons to exert their control (hence the indirect motor pathway).
3. These targets include the tectum (corticotectal), red nucleus (corticorubral), and reticular formation (corticoreticular).
4. The indirect activation pathway is involved in reflexes and coordination of multiple muscle groups, as well as in the modulation and regulation of posture, balance, tone, and some voluntary movements.
5. Rubrospinal tract.
   a. Rubrospinal tract fibers originate in the red nucleus of the midbrain and descend into the lateral column of the spinal cord.
   b. This tract is relatively rudimentary in humans and contributes to postural control through its regulation of muscle tone and inhibition of extensor movement.
6. Reticulospinal tract.
   a. Medial and lateral reticulospinal tracts receive inputs from the cortex through the corticoreticular

Table 2-2

Summary of the Indirect Motor Pathway

EXTRAPYRAMIDAL MOTOR SYSTEM		CONTROL CIRCUITS: MODULATE DESCENDING MOTOR OUTPUT		
CORTICORETICULAR	**RUBROSPINAL**	**BASAL GANGLIA**		**CEREBELLUM**
Inputs: from the pre-motor, motor, and sensory cortices	Inputs to red nucleus (midbrain): from cerebellum and motor cortex	Inputs to striatum: from motor cortex and substantia nigra pars compacta		Inputs to cerebellum: cerebral cortex sensory systems, brainstem, spinal cord
Outputs: to reticular formation of the brainstem	Outputs: to spinal cord	Outputs: to motor systems of cortex and brainstem		Outputs: to motor systems of cortex and brainstem
		Direct Pathway of BG	**Indirect Pathway of BG**	
Function: contributes to regulation of somatic motor control, automatic gait movements, and automatic posturing; controls proximal and axial extensors of the upper extremities	Function: contributes to movement of extremities, automatic gait movements (arm swinging), and automatic posturing; controls flexors of the upper extremities	Function: tends to facilitate movement	Function: tends to inhibit movement	Function: coordination (limbs, trunk), balance, motor planning
		Associated Disorders		
Damage can lead to decorticate posturing: hyperflexion of upper extremities.	Damage can lead to decerebrate posturing: hyperextension of upper extremities.	Parkinson's disease: loss of dopamine net inhibition of movement Huntington's disease: caudate and putamen neuron degeneration, less inhibition of thalamus, early stage hyperkinetic movement		Ataxia: uncoordinated movement

tract and also have origins in the reticular formation of the pons and medulla.

b. These tracts play a role in the control of autonomic function and in the regulation of somatic motor control.

7. Vestibulospinal tract.

a. The vestibulospinal tract originates in the vestibular nuclei of the lower pons and medulla.

b. This tract contributes to body and limb adjustments related to balance.

Extrapyramidal System Control Circuits

1. Cerebellar control circuits.

a. As previously noted, the cerebellum contributes to planning, coordination, timing, precision of movements, and motor learning.

b. The cerebellum integrates afferent and efferent inputs from the brain and spinal cord.

c. Through this process of integration, the cerebellum compares motor intent with actual motor execution such that motor programs can be altered to most accurately match output goals.

d. Damage to cerebellar control circuits can lead to incoordination, intention tremor, limb ataxia,

hypotonia, disequilibrium, dysarthria, and dysmetria.

2. Basal ganglia control circuits.

a. The basal ganglia contain multiple interconnected loops, sending projections between basal ganglia nuclei and the cortex (via the thalamus), as well as to the brainstem; this is critical to the regulation of motor activity (these loops serve additional functions related to cognition, emotion, and motivation).

b. The basal ganglia do not exert direct motor control; instead, circuits contribute inhibitory or facilitatory input to the cortex, modulating cortical output on a time scale of hundreds of milliseconds.

c. When functioning correctly, the basal ganglia refine movements, increasing precision and form while reducing extraneous activity.

d. There are two predominant pathways within the basal ganglia: the direct pathway and the indirect pathway (Fig. 2-19).

(1) The direct and indirect pathways of the basal ganglia receive input from the cortex (in the form of glutamate).

(2) Direct and indirect pathways of the basal ganglia also receive input from the substantia nigra pars compacta (SNc) (in the form of dopamine).

e. Glutamatergic input from the cortex is excitatory to the striatum.

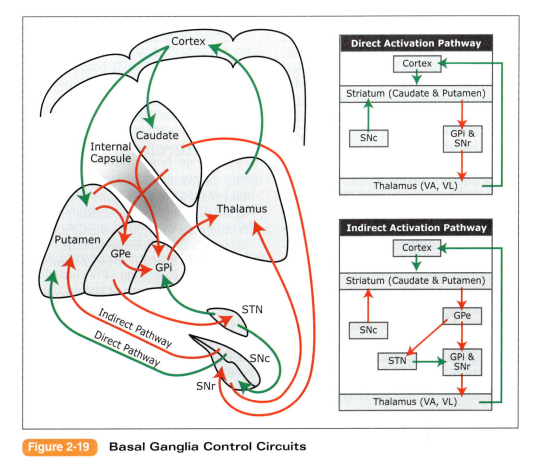

Figure 2-19   **Basal Ganglia Control Circuits**

f. Dopaminergic input from the SNc (which is lost in Parkinson's disease) to the striatum is both excitatory and inhibitory to the striatum, depending on which particular cells receive the transmitter.

g. Dopamine uptake in the direct pathway leads to an EPSP (excitation).

h. Dopamine uptake in the indirect pathway leads to an IPSP (inhibition).

i. The net result of cortical input to the direct pathway is to facilitate movement.

j. As noted above, dopaminergic input from the SNc to the direct pathway is excitatory and also leads to a facilitation of movement.

k. In contrast, the net result of cortical input to the indirect pathway, which contains additional loops through the external segment of the globus pallidus (see Fig 2-19), is to reduce movement. In this manner, the direct and indirect pathways of the basal ganglia work together to increase or reduce movement.

l. Dopaminergic input from the SNc to the indirect pathway is inhibitory.

m. Dopamine inhibits the overall reduction of movement brought about by the indirect pathway, therefore facilitating movement (i.e., inhibiting inhibition = facilitation).

n. Interruption of either of these pathways leads to movement disorders of initiation or muscle tone,

each with different manifestations based on the location of damage. These include, but are not limited to:

(1) Tremors: rhythmic alternating contraction of opposing muscles.

(2) Athetosis: slow, repetitive writhing movements.

(3) Ballism: sudden, jerky flinging movements.

(4) Chorea: rhythmic, repetitive jerking movements.

Ascending Pathways: Overview of Sensory Systems

1. Sensory pathways convert environmental stimuli into neural signals that the brain interprets as particular sensations based on where they go in the brain.

2. They are called *ascending pathways* because sensory signals typically ascend as they enter the CNS and get processed by progressively higher and higher brain regions.

3. Sensory signals are called *afferent signals* (Hint: *afferents arrive*) because information propagates from the body's periphery *to* the brain.

4. Afferent signals originate from nerve endings found throughout the body (except in the brain itself) that are either "bare" or that contact specialized transducer cells (sensory receptors).

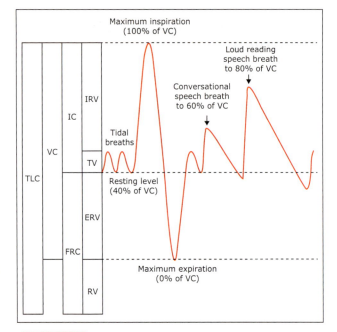

Figure 2-25 **Respiratory Volumes and Capacities**

(1) Approximately 4 L in women, 5 L in men.
(2) Vital capacity = IRV + TV + ERV.
b. Functional residual capacity (FRC)/resting/relaxation volume: volume of air in the lungs at the end of the expiratory phase of tidal breathing.
(1) Functional residual capacity = ERV + RV.
c. Inspiratory capacity (IC): maximum volume of air that can be inspired when starting at resting level.
(1) Inspiratory capacity = TV + IRV.
d. Total lung capacity (TLC): = IRV + TV + ERV + RV.

Anatomy of Phonation and Swallowing

The Larynx

1. An organ critical to airway protection and phonation (Fig. 2-26).
   a. Located in the neck, at the level of C3–C6.
   b. Connects the oropharynx and laryngopharynx to the trachea.
2. Comprises cartilages, connective tissues, epithelia, nerves, and muscles.
   a. The larynx has prominent folds of tissue (vocal folds or cords) that can be positioned to interact with the flow of air from the trachea and generate sound, or squeezed together to act as a sphincter that closes off the airway for protection or when generating high thoracic/abdominal pressures for heavy lifting, defecation, childbirth, and so on.
   b. Multiple pairs of muscles attach to the cartilages of the larynx, which enable one to control vocal fold position, length, and tension to manipulate vocal frequency and amplitude (in conjunction with the respiratory system).
3. The larynx also plays a critical role in airway protection during swallowing.

Laryngeal Cartilages

1. The larynx has a framework of single midline cartilages (thyroid, cricoid, and epiglottis) and smaller right/left cartilage pairs (arytenoid, corniculate, cuneiform).
   a. These cartilages, and the muscles that move them, maintain an open airway for respiration and enable one to control the flow of air and prevent aspiration.
2. Thyroid cartilage.
   a. The largest cartilage of the larynx, the thyroid is formed by two hyaline plates that join at the front of the neck in a shape like a shield and are open in the back.
   b. Laryngeal prominence: an anterior projection where left and right thyroid plates fuse.
      (1) Often called the Adam's apple because it is larger and more visible in males.
      (2) The angle of fusion is more acute in males (90°) than in females (120°), causing greater anterior projection in males.
   c. Superior horns: superior extensions or cornu (Latin for "horn") from the thyroid plates that attach to the hyoid bone via the hyothyroid ligaments.

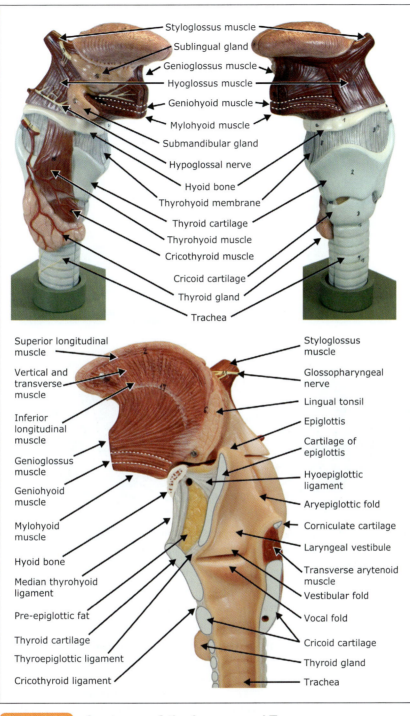

Figure 2-26   **Anatomy of the Larynx and Tongue**

d. Inferior horns: smaller, inferior extensions from the thyroid plates that form joints with the cricoid cartilage.
3. Cricoid cartilage.
   a. A complete ring of cartilage attached to the superior end of the trachea that forms the base of the larynx.
   b. Connects to the first tracheal semicircular ring.
   c. Has a signet shape whereby the anterior height (arch in front) is about 7 mm tall but the posterior

portion is three times as tall. The relatively narrow anterior height can be felt with your fingertip by pressing into the cricothyroid ligament (connecting the cricoid and thyroid cartilages) at the front of your neck.
   d. Posterior lamina: large, flattened posterior portion of the cricoid. The superior edge has right and left facets on which the arytenoid cartilages sit and articulate (rock back/forth and slide front/back).

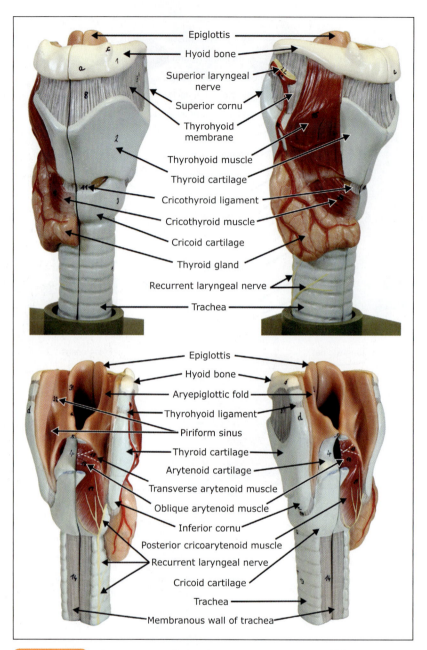

Figure 2-26   Anatomy of the Larynx and Tongue (*Continued*)

4. Arytenoid cartilages.
   a. Two small cartilages that articulate on saddle-shaped joints located on the right and left superior, posterior surface of the cricoid.
   b. Pyramid- or cone-shaped.
   c. Muscular process: projection at the lateral base of each arytenoid.
      (1) The muscular process is the connection point for:
         (a) Posterior cricoarytenoid muscle.
         (b) Lateral cricoarytenoid muscle.
         (c) Thyroarytenoid muscle.
   d. Vocal process: projection at the anterior base of each arytenoid.

   (1) Vocal process is the posterior connection point for the vocal folds and is a part of the posterior ⅓ ("cartilaginous") portion of the vocal folds.

5. Epiglottis.
   a. Mucous-membrane-covered elastic cartilage that originates just below the thyroid notch and extends upward toward the hyoid bone.
   b. Teardrop shaped (inverted).
   c. Made of highly flexible, perforated elastic cartilage.
   d. Aryepiglottic folds: folds made up of connective tissue and muscle that extend posteriorly between the lateral sides of the epiglottis and the arytenoid cartilages.

(1) The aryepiglottic folds form a division between the laryngeal opening and the pyriform sinuses.

(2) Contraction of the muscle of the aryepiglottic folds inverts the epiglottis.

e. The coordinated anterior and superior motion of the hyoid and larynx during swallowing leads to epiglottic inversion, protecting the airway.

Hyoid Bone

1. A free-floating bone anchored by muscle and ligament connections to the tongue, jaw, skull, pharynx, laryngeal cartilages, sternum, and scapula.
2. Horseshoe-shaped.
3. Not technically part of the larynx, but an important contributor to laryngeal and tongue positioning.

Intrinsic Muscles of the Larynx

1. Muscles that span between two or more laryngeal cartilages (Table 2-3.)
2. The primary function of two of the intrinsic laryngeal muscles is to control vocal fold length and tension.
3. Thyroarytenoid muscles (TA).
   a. Make up the body of the vocal folds (along with the vocal ligament).
   b. Span from the interior surface of the thyroid cartilage to the vocal and muscular processes of the arytenoids.
   c. Sometimes described in terms of two muscular divisions:
      (1) Thyromuscularis: lateral division.
      (2) Thyrovocalis/vocalis: medial division.
   d. Contraction typically draws the arytenoid cartilages forward.

e. Contraction shortens and tenses the body of the vocal folds.

4. Cricothyroid muscles (CT).
   a. Span from the anterior/superior surface of the cricoid cartilage to the inferior edge and inferior horns of the thyroid cartilage.
   b. Two subdivisions:
      (1) Pars rectus: medial division.
      (2) Pars oblique: lateral division.
   c. Contraction typically draws the cricoid and thyroid cartilages together anteriorly.
   d. Contraction rocks the cricoid cartilage backward at the location of the arytenoid cartilages, which stretches the vocal folds and contributes to raising pitch.

Vocal Fold Adductors

1. Lateral cricoarytenoid muscles (LCA).
   a. Span from the lateral/superior surface of the cricoid cartilage to the muscular process of the arytenoids (anterior surface).
   b. Contraction draws the muscular processes of the arytenoids forward and medially (together), adducting the vocal folds.
2. Transverse and oblique interarytenoid muscles (IA).
   a. Span from the posterior surfaces of the arytenoid cartilages to the opposite posterior arytenoid cartilage surface.
   b. Fibers of the single midline transverse muscle run horizontally.
   c. Right and left oblique muscles have fibers that cross diagonally and either attach to the apex of the contralateral arytenoid cartilage or continue beyond the arytenoid and reach the epiglottis within the aryepiglottic fold (forming the aryepiglottic muscle).

Table 2-3

Intrinsic Muscles of the Larynx	
VOCALIS MUSCLES[a]	**THYROARYTENOIDS (TA)**
Action: Form vibrational mass of vocal folds Function: Change thickness/tense vocal folds, change vocal tone Motor Innervation: CN X–RLN	Action: Draw arytenoids cartilages forward Function: Tense, shorten vocal folds Motor Innervation: CN X–RLN
CRICOTHYROIDS (CT)	**LATERAL CRICOARYTENOIDS (LCA)**
Action: Tilt anterior cricoid cartilage superiorly (toward thyroid cartilage), stretching vocal folds Function: Work with the TA muscles to raise pitch Motor Innervation: CN X–SLN	Action: Medially rotate arytenoid cartilages Function: Adduct vocal folds Motor Innervation: CN X–RLN
TRANSVERSE AND OBLIQUE INTERARYTENOIDS (IA)	**POSTERIOR CRICOARYTENOIDS (PCA)**
Action: Draw arytenoids together Function: Adduct vocal folds Motor Innervation: CN X–RLN	Action: Externally rotate arytenoid cartilages Function: Abduct vocal folds Motor Innervation: CN X–RLN

[a] Often considered a subdivision of the TA muscles.
RLN = recurrent laryngeal nerve; SLN = superior laryngeal nerve

d. Contraction draws the arytenoids together, adducting the vocal folds and closing the posterior glottis. Contraction of the oblique interarytenoid and aryepiglottic fibers narrows the laryngeal inlet and draws the epiglottis posteriorly to protect the airway during swallowing.

Vocal Fold Abductors

1. Posterior cricoarytenoid muscles (PCA).
   a. Span from the cricoid laminae (posterior surface) to the muscular processes of the arytenoids (posterior surface).
   b. Contraction pulls the muscular processes of the arytenoids posteriorly. From a superior view,

contraction of the PCA can be seen to rotate the left arytenoid cartilage counterclockwise and the right arytenoid clockwise, abducting the vocal folds.

Motor Innervation of Intrinsic Laryngeal Muscles

1. All laryngeal muscles are innervated by branches of the vagus nerve (cranial nerve X).
2. The CT muscles receive motor innervations through the external branch of the superior laryngeal nerve (eSLN).
3. All remaining intrinsic laryngeal muscles receive motor innervations via the recurrent laryngeal nerve (RLN) (Fig. 2-27).

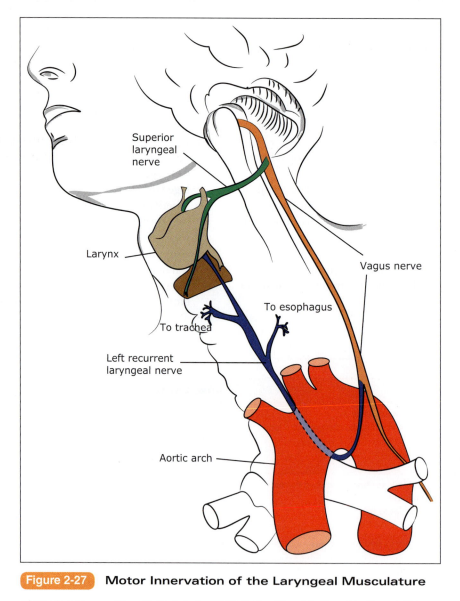

Superior laryngeal nerve

Larynx

To trachea

To esophagus

Vagus nerve

Left recurrent laryngeal nerve

Aortic arch

Figure 2-27   Motor Innervation of the Laryngeal Musculature

Adapted from "Laryngeal Nerve" by Truth-Seeker (2004). Retrieved from http://en.wikipedia.org/wiki/Recurrent_laryngeal_nerve.

Extrinsic Muscles of the Larynx

1. Muscles connected to the hyoid bone or laryngeal thyroid cartilage vertically position and support the hyolaryngeal complex.
   a. The hyoid bone and thyroid cartilage of the larynx are attached via the thyrohyoid ligament and thyrohyoid membrane, so they tend to move as a unit, or complex (Table 2-4).
2. Suprahyoid muscles.
   a. Contribute to hyoid elevation, and their action may raise the larynx, tensing the vocal folds and contributing to increased pitch.
   b. Help widen the pharynx and esophageal opening during swallowing.
   c. Mylohyoid.
      (1) Spans from the mandible to the hyoid.
      (2) Flat muscle that forms a majority of the floor of mouth.
      (3) Contraction elevates the hyoid bone and draws it forward or lowers the jaw if the hyoid bone is fixed (held stable by other muscles).
      (4) Motorically innervated by the mandibular nerve, a division of the trigeminal (CN V).
   d. Geniohyoid.
      (1) Spans from the mandible to the hyoid.
      (2) Cylindrical muscle that lies superior to the mylohyoid.
      (3) Contraction elevates the hyoid bone and draws it forward.
      (4) Motorically innervated by cervical spinal nerve (C1) axons traveling with the hypoglossal nerve (CN XII).

   e. Stylohyoid.
      (1) Spans from the styloid process of the temporal bone to the hyoid.
      (2) Cylindrical muscle that is identifiable near its attachment to the hyoid bone because the posterior digastric pierces through the middle of the muscle.
      (3) Contraction elevates the hyoid bone and draws it backward.
      (4) Motorically innervated by the facial nerve (CN VII).
   f. Digastric muscle.
      (1) Comprises two parts: anterior belly and posterior belly, with a common tendon attached to the hyoid bone.
         (a) Anterior belly of the digastric.
            • Originates from the mandible.
            • Motorically innervated by the mandibular nerve, a division of the trigeminal (CN V).
         (b) Posterior belly of the digastric.
            • Longer than the anterior belly.
            • Originates from the mastoid process of the temporal bone.
            • Motorically innervated by the digastric nerve, a branch of the facial nerve (CN VII).
      (2) Anterior and posterior bellies join at an intermediate tendon.
      (3) The intermediate tendon passes through a fibrous sling connected to the hyoid bone.
      (4) The fibrous sling allows the tendon to slide forward and backward.
      (5) Contraction elevates and steadies the hyoid bone.

Table 2-4

Extrinsic Muscles of the Larynx

SUPRAHYOID MUSCLES: CONTRIBUTES TO HYOID ELEVATION	
Mylohyoid Action: Elevates hyoid, tenses floor of mouth Innervation: CN V	**Stylohyoid** Action: Elevates and retracts hyoid bone, lengthens floor of mouth Innervation: CN VII
Geniohyoid Action: Elevates and advances hyoid widening pharynx during swallow, shortens floor of mouth Innervation: C1 (via CN XII)	**Digastric** Action: Elevates hyoid, supports hyoid during swallow, depresses mandible Anterior belly innervation: CN V Posterior belly innervation: CN VII
INFRAHYOID (STRAP) MUSCLES: CONTRIBUTE TO HYOID/THYROID DEPRESSION	
Sternohyoid Action: Depresses hyoid bone, helps steady hyoid Innervation: C1–C3 (ansa cervicalis)	**Sternothyroid** Action: Depresses hyoid bone and larynx Innervation: C1–C3 (ansa cervicalis)
Thyrohyoid Action: Depresses hyoid or elevates larynx toward hyoid bone for airway protection during swallow Innervation: C1 (via CN XII)	**Omohyoid** Action: Depresses, retracts, and steadies hyoid bone during speaking and swallowing Innervation: C2, C3 (ansa cervicalis)

(6) Contraction may also draw the hyoid bone forward (anterior belly) or backward (posterior belly).

3. Infrahyoids (strap muscles).
   a. The infrahyoid muscles (strap muscles) contribute to hyolaryngeal depression.
   b. Sternohyoid.
      (1) Spans from the sternum and inner clavicle to the lower edge of the hyoid bone.
      (2) Long, flat, vertically coursing muscle.
      (3) Contraction lowers the hyoid bone or steadies the hyoid bone in the context of opposing contractions.
      (4) Motorically innervated by the ansa cervicalis, which is a nerve arising from motor axons of spinal nerves C1, C2, and C3.
   c. Omohyoid.
      (1) From the scapula (shoulder blade) to the lower edge of the hyoid bone.
      (2) Comprises two parts: anterior and posterior.
      (3) Anterior and posterior portions connect at an intermediate tendon, passing through a fascial sling.
      (4) The fascial sling is attached to the clavicle, maintaining the tendon's positioning.
      (5) Contraction lowers the hyoid bone and draws it backward and steadies the hyoid bone in the context of opposing contractions.
      (6) Motorically innervated by the ansa cervicalis.
   d. Thyrohyoid.
      (1) Spans from the thyroid cartilage to the lower edge of the hyoid bone.
      (2) Contraction lowers the hyoid bone and elevates the larynx.
      (3) Motorically innervated by C1 axons traveling with the hypoglossal nerve (CN XII).
   e. Sternothyroid.
      (1) Spans from the manubrium of the sternum to an oblique line across the anterior surface of the thyroid cartilage.
      (2) Runs over portions of the thyroid gland and may limit thyroid gland expansion.
      (3) Contraction lowers the larynx or steadies the larynx in the context of opposing contractions.
      (4) Motorically innervated by ansa cervicalis.

The Vocal Folds

1. Two pliable mucous membranes within the larynx that extend from the anterior thyroid cartilage to the vocal process of the arytenoids (Fig. 2-28).
2. The vocal folds are a layered structure, covered in a nonkeratinized stratified squamous epithelium (see "Tissue Types" section above).
3. Vocal fold layers (from internal to external structures).
   a. Vocalis muscle/thyrovocalis (internal/medial division of the TA muscle).
   b. Lamina propria (LP): thin layer of connective tissue that, together with the epithelium, forms a mucous membrane.
      (1) Deep lamina propria (DLP): primarily collagen fibers.
      (2) Intermediate lamina propria (ILP): primarily elastic fibers.
      (3) Superficial lamina propria (SLP): few elastic and collagenous fibers.

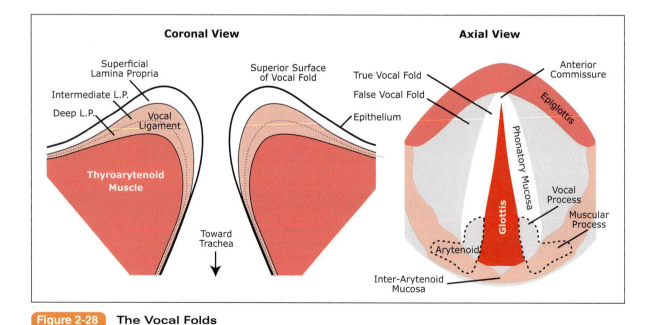

Figure 2-28   The Vocal Folds

c. Epithelium: external tissue that covers the entire body of the vocal folds.

4. The glottis: term used to describe the space between the right and left vocal folds.

5. The vocal folds are often described in terms of the *body* and *cover*.
   a. The body comprises the thyroarytenoid muscle, the deep LP and the intermediate LP.
   b. The cover is highly gelatinous and pliable; comprises the superficial LP and epithelium.
   c. The body is stiffer than the cover.

6. Factors such as radiation therapy or vocal fold pathologies such as nodules and polyps may affect stiffness and pliability.

Myoelastic Aerodynamic Theory

1. A theory that describes the driving force and process of vocal fold vibration in terms of three major components.

2. *Myo-* means "muscle."
   a. Muscle contractions of intrinsic and extrinsic laryngeal muscles affect the tension and positioning of the vocal folds.
   b. Vocal folds are drawn together (adducted) during voicing.
   c. Vocal folds are drawn apart (abducted) during breathing and for the production of voiceless phonemes.

3. Elastic.
   a. Refers to the elastic, pliable property of the LP.
   b. The elastic nature of superficial vocal fold layers leads to vibration that is wavelike, rather than rigid.
   c. Vocal fold vibration produces a mucosal wave.
   d. Contraction of the intrinsic and extrinsic laryngeal muscles will impact the stiffness of the body and cover.

4. Aerodynamic.
   a. Vocal fold vibration depends on vocal fold tension, positioning, and airflow.

b. Air pressure and airflow provide the forces that drive phonation.

5. Typical cycle of voicing.
   a. The vocal folds are adducted, closing the glottis.
   b. Subglottal air pressure (pressure below the vocal folds) builds up.
   c. Air pressure eventually blows apart the vocal folds, partially opening the glottis.
      (1) Inferior portions open before superior portions, producing a wavelike motion from bottom to top.
      (2) Described as a mucosal wave.
   d. As explained by Bernoulli's principle, as air rushes through the narrow glottis opening, pressure decreases between the vocal folds.
   e. The decrease in pressure, paired with the pliable nature of the vocal folds, draws the vocal folds together and closes the glottis.
   f. With the glottis closed, pressure once again builds up, leading to another cycle of vibration.

6. Glottal pulse: each puff of air that is emitted as vocal folds blow apart.
   a. Glottal pulse rate determines a person's fundamental frequency (F0).
   b. Glottal pulse rate/F0 varies across individuals.
      (1) A typical male F0 is around 125 Hz while a typical female F0 is around 210 Hz.
      (2) Male F0 is typically lower due to greater mass per unit length of the vocal folds.

Muscles of Mastication

1. There are four primary muscles of mastication responsible for vertical and lateral motion of the jaw. Movement of the mandible is critical to the oral preparatory stage of swallowing and for speaking (Fig. 2-29).
   a. Masseter muscles.
      (1) Contribute to mandible elevation.

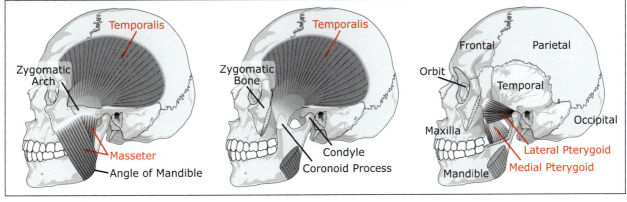

Figure 2-29   **Muscles of Mastication**

b. Temporal muscles.
   (1) Contribute to mandible elevation.
   (2) Contraction of posterior fibers of the temporal muscles retracts the mandible.
c. The medial (or internal) pterygoid muscles.
   (1) Contribute to mandible elevation.
d. The lateral (or external) pterygoid muscles.
   (1) Responsible for depressing and protruding the mandible.
   (2) The suprahyoid muscles assist in mandible depression.
e. Alternating contraction of the medial and lateral pterygoid muscles produces side-to-side motion of the jaw.
2. All muscles of mastication are paired, meaning that there is a left and right muscle.
3. The muscles of mastication are innervated by the mandibular division of the trigeminal nerve (CN V).
4. The temporomandibular joint (TMJ).
   a. The TMJ, a small hinge joint located at the boundary of the temporal bone and the mandible, makes jaw motion in three planes of direction possible (lateral, vertical, and anterior-posterior).
   b. The TMJ is divided into two parts by the articular disc, a small piece of fibrocartilaginous tissue.
      (1) There is a superior joint that connects the temporal bone with the articular disc, and an inferior joint that connects the articular disc with the mandible.
   c. The TMJ is involved in speaking, chewing, and swallowing and is susceptible to dysfunction or dislocation.

The Tongue

1. The tongue is a large mass of muscles extending from the oropharynx to the oral cavity and covered by a mucous membrane.
   a. This muscular hydrostat, so called because of its primarily muscular composition without skeletal support, is capable of making highly complex, controlled movements important for speaking, chewing, swallowing, and, to some degree, maintaining dental hygiene.
2. The tongue is also important for taste, containing small prominences on its surface (buds) that contain taste receptors.
3. The tongue comprises multiple parts: a root, body, apex, dorsum, and inferior surface.
   a. The anterior and posterior portions of the tongue are separated by a V-shaped groove called the *terminal groove*.
4. On the inferior surface of the tongue there is a small fold of mucous membrane called the *lingual frenulum* that attaches the undersurface of the tongue to the floor of the mouth.

5. Blood is supplied to the tongue through the lingual artery, a branch of the external carotid artery.
6. The tongue is composed of eight major muscles, divided into two groups: the intrinsic and the extrinsic muscles.
7. All of the muscles of the tongue receive innervation from CN XII, the hypoglossal nerve, with the exception of the palatoglossus (see below).

Tongue Muscles

1. Intrinsic muscles (Table 2-5).
   a. There are four intrinsic muscles of the tongue, grouped together because they are not attached to any bone and therefore exist only within the tongue.
   b. These muscles, whose contraction leads to shape changes of the tongue, are the superior longitudinal, inferior longitudinal, transverse, and vertical muscles (Fig. 2-26).
      (1) Superior longitudinal muscles: contain fibers that run anteriorly to posteriorly underneath the mucous membrane of the tongue dorsum.
         (a) Contraction of the superior longitudinal muscles shortens the tongue or elevates the tongue tip and sides of the tongue.
      (2) Inferior longitudinal muscles: a narrow band of fibers that course along the inferior surface of the tongue whose contraction shortens the tongue or causes the apex of the tongue to curl down.
      (3) Transverse muscles: course deeper than the superior longitudinal muscles and contain fibers that originate in the median plane of the tongue and extend laterally.
         (a) Contraction of these muscles narrows and elongates the tongue.
      (4) Vertical muscles: run top to bottom in the tongue and flatten the tongue when contracted.
2. Extrinsic muscles (Table 2-5).
   a. The four extrinsic muscles of the tongue originate from bone and extend into the tongue. Contraction of these muscles primarily contributes to tongue motion and positioning.
      (1) Genioglossus: a large, fan-shaped muscle that constitutes the majority of the tongue body.
         (a) Originates in the mental spine (posterior midline) of the mandible and inserts into the hyoid bone and tongue dorsum.
         (b) Contraction of the genioglossus protrudes the tongue and can also produce side-to-side movement of the tongue when contracted unilaterally.
      (2) Hyoglossus: a thin, square-shaped muscle (when viewed laterally) that courses from the body and greater horn of the hyoid to each side of the tongue.

Table 2-5

Intrinsic and Extrinsic Muscles of the Tongue

MUSCLES	ORIENTATIONS/CONNECTIONS	ACTION	CONTRIBUTIONS TO SPEECH AND SWALLOWING
Intrinsic Muscles: Within the Tongue (all innervated by CN XII)			
Superior longitudinal	Superficial anteroposterior fibers	Tongue shortening, tongue tip elevation, lateral edge elevation	Intrinsic tongue muscles produce fine lingual shape changes important to speech articulation, mastication, and swallowing
Inferior longitudinal	Deep anteroposterior fibers	Tongue shortening, tongue tip depression	
Transverse	Side-to-side fibers, interwoven with vertical muscles	Tongue narrowing and elongation	
Vertical	Top-to-bottom fibers, interwoven with transverse muscles	Tongue flattening	
Extrinsic Muscles: From Tongue to Other Structures (almost all innervated by CN XII)			
Genioglossus	Body of mandible to root, dorsum, blade, and tip of tongue. Bulk of tongue	Tongue protrusion/anterior movement, side-to-side movement	Extrinsic muscles contribute to gross positioning and movements of the tongue important for mastication, swallow initiation, and swallowing
Hyoglossus	Greater horn of hyoid to inferior sides of tongue	Tongue body lowering, backward movement	
Styloglossus	Styloid process to sides of tongue	Tongue retraction, shortening, lateral edge elevation	
Palatoglossus[a]	Soft palate to sides of tongue, forms anterior faucial pillars	Posterior tongue elevation, soft palate depression	

[a] Palatoglossus innervated by CN IX and X via the pharyngeal plexus

(a) Contraction of the hyoglossus pulls the tongue edges down and helps shorten the tongue.

(3) Styloglossus: runs from the lower end of the styloid process to the sides and inferior aspects of the tongue.

  (a) Contraction of the styloglossus shortens the tongue and curls the edges up, helping create a narrow trough in the tongue center through which a bolus can cohesively move during deglutition.

(4) Palatoglossus: a narrow muscle joining the posterior border of the hard palate (the palatine aponeurosis) with the posterolateral tongue.

  (a) Some fibers of the palatoglossus pass deeply into the tongue and intermingle with the intrinsic transverse muscles.

  (b) Contraction of the palatoglossus lowers the soft palate or elevates the posterior tongue. Contraction of the palatoglossus is essential for swallowing in order to constrict the isthmus of fauces, a constricted space that connects the mouth and the pharynx.

  (c) The palatoglossus is the only tongue muscle not innervated by CN XII (it is innervated by CN IX and X via the pharyngeal plexus).

Muscles of the Face

1. Several facial muscles are critical to speech production and swallowing, in addition to producing facial expressions used in nonverbal communication.
2. Orbicularis oris: comprises intertwined fibers, forms a ring around the lips, and when contracted, contributes to opening and closing of the lips, puckering, and vertical or lateral movements of the lips.
3. Buccinator: a broad muscle with horizontally coursing fibers that originate from several locations, including the outer alveolar processes of the maxilla and mandible (above and below the cheek wall, respectively), as well as the pterygomandibular ligament that separates it from the superior pharyngeal constrictor posteriorly.
  a. Inserts into the upper and lower lip.
  b. Forms part of the cheek wall; contraction produces tension that pulls the cheek against the teeth.
4. Risorius: sometimes referred to as the "laughter muscle"; narrow bundle of horizontally coursing fibers that originates from the masseter muscle and inserts at the angle of the mouth.
  a. Contraction retracts the angle of the mouth.
5. Five paired muscles contribute to the raising or lowering of the lips.

a. The levator labii superioris, levator labii superioris alaeque nasi, and the zygomatic minor insert into the upper lip and contribute to elevating or everting (turning it outward) the upper lip. Contraction of the zygomatic minor also pulls the corners of the mouth upward.

b. The zygomatic major originates from the zygomatic bone and inserts into the corner of the mouth. Contraction draws the corners of the mouth backward, simultaneously lifting and pulling the corners of the mouth sideways.

c. The depressor labii inferioris is a flat muscle that originates from the anterior surface of the mandible, coursing upward to insert into the lower lip. Contraction depresses and turns the lower lip outward.

6. Mentalis: originates from the mandible inferior to the incisor teeth and courses downward into the chin.

a. This muscle is often referred to as the "pouting muscle" due to its contraction, which forces a curling of the lower lip.

7. Paired levator anguli oris and depressor anguli oris muscles draw the corners of the mouth up and down, respectively. Contraction of each of these muscles can also draw the lips together.

8. Beneath the levator anguli oris and depressor oris are the incisivus labii superioris and incisivus labii inferioris. Contraction of these muscles pulls the corners of the mouth upward toward the midline or downward toward the midline.

9. Platysma: a broad, superficial muscle with infra- and supraclavicular origins that courses medially and obliquely up the neck, inserting into the lower edge of the mandible and into muscles of the lower face.

a. Contraction of the platysma can depress the lower lip and corners of the mouth or produce a vertical wrinkling of the skin of the neck as the skin of the neck is drawn toward the mandible.

Systems Involved in Speech Production

1. Three major systems contribute to speech production: the respiratory system, the laryngeal system, and the supralaryngeal system.

2. The respiratory system provides the driving force behind voice production and other articulated sounds of speech.

3. The laryngeal system, located on top of the trachea, acts as a valve for airway protection, closing like a sphincter during swallowing to prevent aspiration and generating voice with specialized vocal folds or cords when powered by the respiratory system.

a. Periodic vocal fold vibration is the principle sound source of speech.

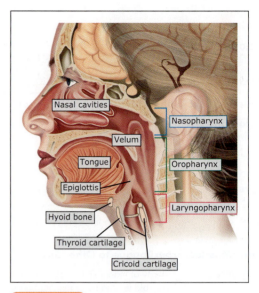

Figure 2-30   **Major Cavities of the Supralaryngeal System**

4. The supralaryngeal system comprises articulators and cavities that filter and shape phonation and glottal aspiration sounds.

5. The three major cavities of the supralaryngeal system are the pharyngeal cavity, the oral cavity, and the nasal cavity (Fig. 2-30).

a. The pharynx, a cavity that can be divided into the nasopharynx, the oropharynx, and the laryngopharynx, is a tube of tendon and muscle that extends from the base of the skull to behind the larynx where it is continuous with the esophagus.

b. The oral cavity, or mouth cavity, is bounded by the palate, the oropharynx, and the cheeks and lips.

(1) The anterior portion of the palate, the hard palate, is bony, while the posterior portion, the soft palate, consists of fleshy mucous membrane, muscular fibers, and mucous glands. Together, these form the roof of the mouth.

(2) The velum consists of the soft palate and uvula (a fleshy tissue and muscle extension of the soft palate in the back of the throat).

(3) Paired contraction of the tensor veli palatini and the levator veli palatini elevates the velum and draws it backward, making contact with the posterior pharyngeal wall.

c. Contact between the velum and the posterior pharyngeal wall stops the passage of air through the nasal cavity, the large air-filled space behind the nose.

6. These cavities act as resonating tubes that amplify and dampen frequencies that radiate through them.

a. These amplified resonant frequencies produce the formants that are used to describe and recognize vowels.

7. In order to articulate consonants and vowels, fine motor movements are made with the lips, tongue, mandible, and glottis to further shape sound as it resonates through the supralaryngeal cavities.

   a. The lower lip, tongue, and glottis move during the production of speech and are considered active speech articulators.

   b. Active articulators approach or make contact with structures such as the upper lip, teeth, alveolar ridge, hard palate, soft palate, uvula, and pharynx, which remain fixed during speech and are considered passive articulators.

8. The interaction of respiratory, laryngeal, and supralaryngeal systems in speech is often described as a source (respiratory drive of voice) interacting with a filter (supralaryngeal tubes and constrictions) in the source filter theory. This acoustic theory describes speech production based on two fundamental processes: sound production and sound filtering.

References

Barnett, M. W., & Larkman, P. M. (2007). The action potential. *Practical Neurology, 7*(3), 192–197.

Bhatnagar, S. C. (2013). *Neuroscience for the Study of Communicative Disorders*, 4th ed. Philadelphia: Wolters Kluwer Health/Lippincott Williams & Wilkins.

Blumenfeld, H. (2010). *Neuroanatomy through Clinical Cases*, 2nd ed. Sunderland, MA: Sinauer Associates.

Burdett, E., & Mitchell, V. (2011). Anatomy of the larynx, trachea and bronchi. *Anaesthesia and Intensive Care Medicine, 12*(8), 335–339.

Colton, R. H., Casper, J. K., & Leonard, R. (2011). *Understanding Voice Problems: A Physiological Perspective for Diagnosis and Treatment*, 4th ed. Philadelphia: Wolters Kluwer Health/Lippincott Williams & Wilkins.

Davis, M. C., Griessenauer, C. J., Bosmia, A. N., Tubbs, R. S., & Shoja, M. M. (2014). The naming of the cranial nerves: A historical review. *Clinical Anatomy, 27*(1), 14–19.

Fuller, D. R., Pimentel, J. T., & Peregoy, B. M. (2012). *Applied Anatomy & Physiology for Speech-Language Pathology & Audiology*. Philadelphia: Wolters Kluwer Health/Lippincott Williams & Wilkins.

Gray, H., Standring, S., Ellis, H., & Berkovitz, B. K. B. (2005). *Gray's Anatomy: The Anatomical Basis of Clinical Practice*, 39th ed. Edinburgh, UK: Elsevier Churchill Livingstone.

Hixon, T. J., Weismer, G., & Hoit, J. D. (2014). *Preclinical Speech Science: Anatomy, Physiology, Acoustics, Perception*, 2nd ed. San Diego, CA: Plural Publishing.

Hodgkin, A. L., & Huxley, A. F. (1952). Propagation of electrical signals along giant nerve fibers. *Proceedings of the Royal Society of London. Series B: Biological Sciences, 140*(899), 177–183.

Kandel, E. R. (2013). *Principles of Neural Science*, 5th ed. New York: McGraw-Hill Medical.

Mildner, V. (2006). *The Cognitive Neuroscience of Human Communication*. Mahwah, NJ: Lawrence Erlbaum Associates.

Moon, J., & Alipour, F. (2013). Muscular anatomy of the human ventricular folds. *Annals of Otology, Rhinology and Laryngology, 122*(9), 561–567.

Myers, P. S. (1999). *Right Hemisphere Damage: Disorders of Communication and Cognition*. San Diego, CA: Singular Publishing.

Osborn, A. G., Jacobs, J. M., & Osborn, A. G. (1999). *Diagnostic Cerebral Angiography*, 2nd ed. Philadelphia: Lippincott-Raven.

Seikel, J. A., King, D. W., & Drumright, D. G. (2010). *Anatomy & Physiology for Speech, Language, and Hearing*, 4th ed. Clifton Park, NY: Delmar Cengage Learning.

Titze, I. R. (2006). *The Myoelastic Aerodynamic Theory of Phonation*. Iowa City, IA: National Center for Voice and Speech.

Van Den Berg, J. (1958). Myoelastic-aerodynamic theory of voice production. *Journal of Speech and Hearing Research, 1*(3), 227–244.

Zeitels, S. M., & Healy, G. B. (2003). Laryngology and phonosurgery. *New England Journal of Medicine, 349*(9), 882–892.

Review Questions

1. Which plane of section divides the body vertically into anterior and posterior parts?

   a. Frontal.
   b. Sagittal.
   c. Horizontal.
   d. Distal.

2. Which part of the neuron is specialized for receiving signals from other neurons or environmental stimuli?

   a. Axon.
   b. Neurotransmitter.
   c. Dendrite.
   d. Soma.

3. What is cranial nerve VII?

   a. Trochlear.
   b. Trigeminal.
   c. Facial.
   d. Vagus.

4. What is cranial nerve X?

   a. Abducens.
   b. Glossopharyngeal.
   c. Vagus.
   d. Hypoglossal.

5. What are the names of the meninges?

   a. Pia mater, arachnid mater, durable mater.
   b. Pia mater, arachnoid mater, dura mater.
   c. Pterygoid mater, anastomosis mater, durable mater.
   d. Falx mater, subarachnoid mater, epidural mater.

6. How many ventricles are in the brain?

   a. 2.
   b. 3.
   c. 4.
   d. 5.

7. Which portion of the brainstem houses neuronal circuits guiding respiration?

    a. Medulla oblongata.
    b. Midbrain.
    c. Pons.
    d. Cerebellum.

8. In which lobe of the brain will you find the primary motor cortex?

    a. Parietal lobe.
    b. Occipital lobe.
    c. Temporal lobe.
    d. Frontal lobe.

9. Almost all sensory information that reaches the cerebral hemispheres is relayed through which structure of the brain?

    a. Limbic cortex.
    b. Cerebellum.
    c. Thalamus.
    d. Basal ganglia.

10. When a person moves their right leg, which of the following describes the appropriate pathway?

    a. Right upper motor neuron signals carried along the corticospinal pathway.
    b. Right upper motor neuron signals carried along the corticobulbar pathway.
    c. Left upper motor neuron signals carried along the corticospinal pathway.
    d. Left upper motor neuron signals carried along the corticobulbar pathway.

11. From where does the anterior blood supply to the brain originate?

    a. Anterior cerebral artery.
    b. Carotid artery.
    c. Middle cerebral artery.
    d. Posterior communicating artery.

12. What term refers to the volume of air exchanged between a maximum inspiration and a maximum expiration?

    a. Tidal volume.
    b. Vital capacity.
    c. Functional residual capacity.
    d. Total lung capacity.

13. What is the name for the paired cartilages located on the superior, posterior surface of the cricoid cartilage?

    a. Thyroid cartilage.
    b. Epiglottis.
    c. Aryepiglottic cartilage.
    d. Arytenoid cartilage.

14. What is the free-floating bone that serves as an important contributor to laryngeal positioning?

    a. Hyoid bone.
    b. Zygomatic bone.
    c. Maxillary bone.
    d. Styloid bone.

15. Which laryngeal muscle acts as a vocal fold abductor?

    a. Lateral cricoarytenoid muscle.
    b. Transverse interarytenoid muscle.
    c. Oblique interarytenoid muscle.
    d. Posterior cricoarytenoid muscle.

16. Which cranial nerve innervates all laryngeal muscles?

    a. Facial nerve (CN VII).
    b. Glossopharyngeal nerve (CN IX).
    c. Vagus nerve (CN X).
    d. Hypoglossal nerve (CN XI).

17. Which muscle is responsible for mandibular depression?

    a. Masseter muscle.
    b. Temporal muscle.
    c. Lateral pterygoid muscle.
    d. Medial pterygoid muscle.

18. Which muscle forms a majority of the cheek wall?

    a. Mentalis.
    b. Platysma.
    c. Risorius.
    d. Buccinator.

19. Which extrinsic tongue muscle contributes to lingual protrusion?

    a. Hyoglossus.
    b. Genioglossus.
    c. Styloglossus.
    d. Palatoglossus.

20. Which intrinsic tongue muscle contributes to tongue narrowing and elongation?

    a. Superior longitudinal.
    b. Inferior longitudinal.
    c. Transverse.
    d. Vertical.

Acoustics

JEAN ANDRUSKI, PhD

▶ Graphical Representations of Sounds

Waveforms

1. Waveforms: show variations in amplitude, pressure, or intensity of a sound over time (Table 3-3).
   a. X-axis is time.
   b. Y-axis may be amplitude, pressure, or intensity.
2. Waveform use.
   a. Finding the exact fundamental frequency (F_0).
   b. Measuring time-related cues such as voice onset time (VOT).
   c. Determining whether a signal is periodic or aperiodic.

Table 3-3

Summary of Most Common Graphical Representations of Speech and Their Characteristics			
TYPE OF ANALYSIS	**X -AXIS**	**Y -AXIS**	**NOTES**
Waveform	Time	Amplitude or a related measure	Frequency can be measured indirectly, by finding the period (*T*) and taking the inverse ($f = 1/t$) (e.g., if $T = 0.005$ sec, $f = 1/0.005$, or 200 Hz). Provide information on manner of articulation—for example, whether a sound is resonant (periodic) or obstruent (aperiodic). Also helpful for time-related measurements such as VOT.
Spectrum	Frequency	Amplitude or a related measure	No time axis. Always averaged over some period of time. Used to measure harmonic amplitude, verify formant locations, measure noise characteristics such as center of gravity. To clearly see harmonics, F_0 and vowel quality must be held steady.
Spectrogram	Time	Frequency	Amplitude shown by level of darkness; darker regions have higher amplitude. Most useful analysis for examining speech sounds. Narrowband: precise frequency detail. Broadband: precise time detail.

d. Other analyses based on waveforms.
e. Pitch contours.
f. Voice quality analyses that relate to periodicity.

Spectrograms

1. Spectrograms: show regions of high-amplitude energy and changes over time.
   a. X-axis is time.
   b. Y-axis is frequency.
      (1) Level of detail on the Y-axis (frequency) can be adjusted by changing analysis bandwidth.
         (a) Broadband: averages amplitude across a wide band of frequencies (e.g., 300 Hz). Details can be seen along time axis (X-axis) but not the frequency axis.
         (b) Narrowband: averages amplitude across a narrow band of frequencies (e.g., 60 Hz). Details can be seen along the frequency axis but not the time axis.
   c. Darkness dimension on a spectrogram shows amplitude or intensity at different frequencies.
      (1) No scale is provided to interpret this dimension.
   d. Most frequently used tool in speech analysis.
2. Spectrogram use.
   a. Broadband.
      (1) Finding different sounds by manner of articulation and voicing.
      (2) Measuring time-related cues such as VOT.
      (3) Measuring frequency-related cues such as formant frequencies.
   b. Narrowband.
      (1) Checking pitch contour accuracy by comparing it with harmonic contours.
      (2) Estimating periodicity by examining number of harmonics that are clearly visible.

Amplitude Spectra

1. Amplitude spectra: show amplitude of individual sinusoids present in a sound.
   a. X-axis is frequency.
   b. Y-axis is amplitude, pressure, or intensity.
2. Amplitude spectra use.
   a. Measure amplitude of individual harmonics.
   b. Measure the highest-amplitude harmonic within a formant.
   c. Examine how energy is distributed across the frequency spectrum in aperiodic sounds such as fricatives and stop bursts.

Types of Sounds and Their Graphical Representations

Sinusoids

1. Sinusoids consist of a single frequency.
   a. Called *simple sounds* or *pure tones*.
   b. Exhibit simple harmonic motion (SHM).
      (1) Examples of SHM.
         (a) Motion of a pendulum.
         (b) Motion of a weight attached to a spring.
   c. Adding sinusoids of the same frequency gives another sinusoid with the same frequency.
   d. Adding sinusoids of different frequencies gives a complex sound.

Waveforms of Sinusoids

1. Waveforms of sinusoids show simple repetitive patterns.
   a. Cycle of a sinusoid is the simple, symmetrical, up-and-down motion around the 0 axis.
   b. Number of oscillations (cycles) per second is the frequency of the sinusoid.
   c. Greatest distance of sinusoid from 0 axis is its peak amplitude.
   d. Peak amplitude always occurs at 90° and 270° of a sinusoid's cycle.
2. Amplitude spectrum of a sinusoid consists of a single vertical line.
   a. X-axis: top of the line gives peak amplitude.
   b. Y-axis: line location gives sinusoid's frequency.

c. Sinusoids can be completely described by A and f or by A and T.
   (1) Since T can be calculated from f and vice versa, only one of these two numbers is needed.
3. Spectrograms are not needed to examine sinusoids.
   a. Contain only one f that does not change over time.
4. Complex sounds: produced by adding sinusoids of *different* frequencies.
   a. May be periodic or aperiodic.
   b. Vocal fold vibration is a complex sound.
      (1) Often referred to as *periodic* but is never perfectly periodic.
      (2) More accurately referred to as *quasi-periodic* (somewhat periodic).
5. Periodic complex sounds: each sinusoidal frequency is an integer multiple of a greatest common denominator (GCD).
   a. GCD: largest whole number (integer) that can be multiplied to give the frequencies of all sinusoids present in the sound.
      (1) Called the *fundamental* frequency (F_0) of the sound.
      (2) As with f, F_0 of a complex periodic sound is the inverse of T.
   b. Sinusoids in a periodic complex sound are said to be in a harmonic relationship with F_0.
      (1) Each is an integer multiple of F_0.
      (2) Referred to as harmonics (Table 3-4 and Table 3-5).

Table 3-4

Frequency of Harmonics and the Related Greatest Common Denominator					
FREQUENCY (HZ) OF THE FIRST FOUR HARMONICS IN A SOUND				THE GREATEST COMMON DENOMINATOR (GCD)	NOTES
H1	H2	H3	H4	(INTEGER MULTIPLES THAT ARE PRESENT)	
100	200	300	400	**100** (1 × 100, 2 × 100, 3 × 100, 4 × 100)	In these sounds, the GCD and H1 have the same f. Another way of saying this is that H1 = F_0 = GCD. Every integer multiple of the GCD is present.
200	400	600	800	**200** (1 × 200, 2 × 200, 3 × 200, 4 × 200)	This kind of harmonic sequence is produced by the human voice: H1 is the GCD and every multiple of the GCD is present.
500	750	1,000	1,250	**250** (2 × 250, 3 × 250, 4 × 250, 5 × 250)	In these sounds, H1 is *not* the GCD. The "real" H1 is missing. This is deliberately done for telephone signals (frequencies below ~300 Hz and above ~3.5 kHz are filtered out). As a result, H1 is usually not present in a telephone signal.
300	450	600	750	**150** (2 × 150, 3 × 150, 4 × 150, 5 × 150)	Although H1 is absent, F_0 is still equal to the GCD. In addition, we still *perceive* F_0 to be the GCD.
100	300	500	700	**100** (1 × 100, 3 × 100, 5 × 100, 7 × 100)	In these sounds, only the *odd multiples* of the GCD are present. When only the odd multiples are present, result is a square wave. The human voice does not produce this type of signal.
150	450	750	1,050	**150** (1 × 150, 3 × 150, 5 × 150, 7 × 150)	Signals of this type are often used in digital circuits.

Table 3-5

Summary Information on Sound Type and Associated Characteristics

SOUND TYPE	NUMBER OF FREQUENCIES PRESENT	RELATIONSHIP BETWEEN COMPONENT FREQUENCIES	NOTES ON FINDING FREQUENCY
Sinusoid *Speech example:* individual harmonics of the human voice.	1	N/A	Count number of cycles in 1 second on a waveform. Find T and take the inverse (e.g., if $T = 0.01$ sec, $f = \frac{1}{0.01}$, or 100 Hz). T = Period (time to complete one cycle). Measure f of the single line that is present in an amplitude spectrum.
Complex periodic *Speech examples:* vowels, resonant consonants.	Greater than 1 to an infinite number. Complex periodic speech sounds contain an infinite number of sinusoids.	Harmonic (i.e., all component sinusoids are integer multiples of a fundamental frequency). In speech, all integer multiples (odd and even) are present unless the signal has been filtered (e.g., during a telephone call).	Count number of cycles in 1 second on a waveform. Find T and take the inverse. Measure f of any two harmonics in an amplitude spectrum or narrowband spectrogram and find the interval between them (e.g., if H5 = 1,000 Hz and H6 = 1,200 Hz, F_0 = 1,200 − 1,000 = 200 Hz). Measure f of any harmonic and divide by its harmonic number (e.g., if H10 = 1,000 Hz, $F_0 = \frac{1,000}{10} = 100$ Hz).
Complex aperiodic *Speech examples:* fricatives, stops.	Greater than 1 to an infinite number. Complex aperiodic speech sounds contain an infinite number of sinusoids.	Random	N/A: Aperiodic sounds do not have a frequency. To have a period and a frequency, sounds must have a cycle. Aperiodic sounds do not have a cycle.

(3) Look at the first four harmonics listed for each sound and find the GCD. Most, but not all, of these harmonic sequences could be found in recordings of the human voice.

6. Waveforms of complex periodic sounds show a repetitive pattern (the cycle) that is more complex than a sinusoid.

7. Amplitude spectrum of a periodic complex sound: always has more than one line since more than one sinusoidal frequency is present.
   a. Each line represents a harmonic.
   b. Harmonics are regularly spaced since they occur at integer multiples of F_0.
   c. In the human voice, harmonics are infinite in number.

8. Narrowband spectrograms of complex periodic sounds show individual harmonics and how their frequencies change over time.

9. Aperiodic complex sounds: the sinusoidal frequencies are *not* integer multiples of any common denominator other than 1.
   a. Relationship between sinusoidal frequencies is random.
   b. Individual sinusoids are *not* harmonics.
   c. Aperiodic sounds are often referred to as *noises*.

10. Waveforms of aperiodic complex sounds do not show a repetitive pattern (i.e., do not have a cycle).
    a. Since there is no cycle, aperiodic sounds do not have F_0.

11. Amplitude spectra of aperiodic sounds: show average amplitude of sinusoids across the frequency spectrum.
    a. Individual sinusoids not usually visible.

▶ Periodic Complex Sounds in Speech

Glottal Source

1. Glottal source: complex periodic sound produced by vocal fold vibration.
   a. Also referred to as *phonation* or *voicing*.
   b. Source of sound energy for voiced sounds (e.g., vowels and resonant consonants).

(1) Although all voiced sounds have some vocal fold vibration, vocal folds often do not vibrate continuously during voiced obstruents.
   c. A quasi-periodic sound, often called *periodic*.
      (1) Vocal folds do not vibrate in a perfectly periodic pattern.
   d. Contains an infinite number of harmonics.

2. So
so
a.
b.
3. So
qu
a. T

Am

1. Sinu
cies]
a. Si
to
b. At
su
th
c. Th
de
to
(1)
(2)

d. Re
pea
tiv
(1)

Lette

1. Includ
uids, a
2. SLVT s
a. Vow
3. No ape
resona
a. Defa
b. Char
(1) F
a
(2) F
w

e. Harmonic amplitude decreases as harmonic frequency increases.
   (1) For each octave increase in frequency, harmonic amplitude decreases by ~12 dB.
   (2) Sometimes referred to as *spectral roll-off*.
2. Determines vocal pitch and voice quality.
  a. Vocal pitch: determined by rate of vocal fold vibration.
   (1) Changes in F_0 perceived as intonation.
    (a) Intonation is an important element of prosody.
  b. Languages use vocal pitch in different ways.
   (1) Intonation contributes to perception of emotions and attitudes in all languages.
   (2) In English, F_0 contributes to perception of word and sentential stress.
    (a) F_0 typically rises on stressed syllables and words.
   (3) In many East Asian and African languages, pitch is phonemic (i.e., it can change word meaning).
    (a) Referred to as tone languages (e.g., Mandarin Chinese and all other Chinese languages).
    (b) Tones are classified by pitch height and contour (e.g., Mandarin Chinese has four tones—a high level, a mid-rising, a low dipping, and a high-falling).
   (4) Some languages have a restricted tonal system called *pitch accent* (e.g., some Scandinavian languages and Japanese).
    (a) Pitch accent systems usually have only two tones, high and low.
    (b) Mode of vocal fold vibration and degree of regularity or irregularity in the glottal cycle are perceived as voice quality.
  c. Languages use voice quality in different ways.
   (1) In some tone languages, both pitch and voice quality are phonemic.
    (a) For example, in Hmong languages of Southeast Asia, using modal versus breathy or creaky voice may change word meaning.
   (2) Amplitude of the glottal source determines overall loudness of the voice.

▶ Aperiodic Complex Sounds in Speech

Production and Types

1. Produced by impeding or obstructing airflow.
2. Impulse noises: very brief aperiodic sounds.
  a. Can be produced by suddenly releasing air pressure that has built up behind a blockage.
   (1) For example, stop consonant bursts.
  b. Can be produced by sucking the tongue against the roof of the oral cavity, then pulling it away to produce a click.
   (1) In English, clicks are not speech sounds but can still have a meaning.
   (2) For example, lateral click is used to mean "giddy-up" to a horse.
   (3) Clicks are used as phonemes of speech in some African languages.
3. Turbulent noises—have longer duration than impulse noises.
  a. Molecules set into turbulent motion by forcing air through a narrow channel or against an obstruction such as the teeth.
   (1) For example, continuant obstruents (fricatives).
4. Obstruent sounds always include aperiodic noise as a sound source.
  a. Voiceless obstruents: aperiodic noise is the only sound source.
  b. Voiced obstruents: aperiodic noise combined with vocal fold vibration.
5. Adding turbulent noise to a periodic sound results in amplitude modulated noise.

▶ The Source-Filter Theory of Speech Production

Acoustic Theory of Speech Production

1. Also called the *acoustic theory of speech production*.
2. States that speech is produced by passing a sound source through a sound filter.
3. Mathematically, source-filter theory can be expressed as $U(f) \times T(f) \times R(f) = P(f)$.
  a. $U(f)$ = the source function.
   (1) Most common sound source is vocal fold vibration.
   (2) Turbulent and impulse noises also act as sound sources for speech.

(1) This is described as a "diffuse flat" or "diffuse falling" spectrum.

b. In alveolar stops, the burst spectrum tends to rise gradually, especially in the region up to about 5,000 Hz (higher for women and children).

(1) This is described as a "diffuse rising" spectrum.

c. In velar stops, the burst spectrum tends to have peaks in the region of F1 and F2 for the adjacent vowel.

(1) This is described as a "compact" spectrum.

Acoustic Measurement of Vocal Fold Vibration

Frequency

1. Frequency, stability, and manner of vocal fold vibration are perceived as pitch and voice quality.
2. Frequency of vocal fold vibration (F_0) is most often measured from a waveform or pitch contour.
   a. From a waveform, select exactly one cycle and find its period (T).
      (1) Calculate F_0 as $1/T$.
      (2) F_0 measurements are very accurate, providing a cycle can be detected.
      (3) Although changes in F_0 are visible in waveforms, waveforms are not convenient for analyzing pitch over time.
   b. Pitch contours are the best display for examining F_0 over time.
      (1) To create an accurate pitch contour, acoustic analysis software must detect the cycle.
      (2) This can be difficult or impossible in disordered voices.
         (a) Pitch contour accuracy should be checked even in healthy voices.
         (b) Accuracy is most easily checked by showing a narrowband spectrogram behind the pitch contour.
         (c) If accurate, pitch contour shape will closely resemble the curves of the harmonics.
      (3) Pitch contour measurements are an average of cycles around the measurement point.
         (a) Measurements may not perfectly match waveform measurements at the same location.
   c. It may not be possible to create an accurate pitch contour for some disordered voices.
      (1) Estimates of F_0 may be obtainable from the waveform or narrowband spectrogram.

Summary Statistics

1. Summary statistics on F_0 across time can assist in objectively evaluating vocal health (Table 3-10).
   a. Results can be compared with published values for the speaker's sex and age group.
      (1) F_0 units must be the same as published values (e.g., semitones RE: 100 Hz) and should optimally be made from the same type of vocal sample.

Table 3-10

F_0 Statistics and the Vocal Samples Used to Obtain Them

F_0 STATISTIC	TYPICAL VOCAL SAMPLE
Average speaking fundamental frequency (SFF)	Mean F_0 from a read passage or conversational speech
F_0 SD	SD of F_0 from a read passage or conversational speech
Speaking F_0 range	Distance between the minimum and maximum F_0 values in a read passage or conversation
Maximum phonational frequency range (MPFR)	Distance between the minimum and maximum F_0 values from an /a/ that glides from a comfortable pitch to the highest pitch a speaker can reach and an /a/ that glides from a comfortable pitch to the lowest pitch a speaker can reach
Cycle-to-cycle frequency variability (jitter)	A sustained /a/
Cycle-to-cycle amplitude variability (shimmer)	A sustained /a/

Table 3-11

A Comparison of Different Voice Qualities

VOICE QUALITY	SPECTRUM	NOTES
Modal voice		H1 and H2 are approximately equal in amplitude.
Creaky voice		H1 is lower in amplitude than H2.
Breathy voice		H1 is higher in amplitude than H2.

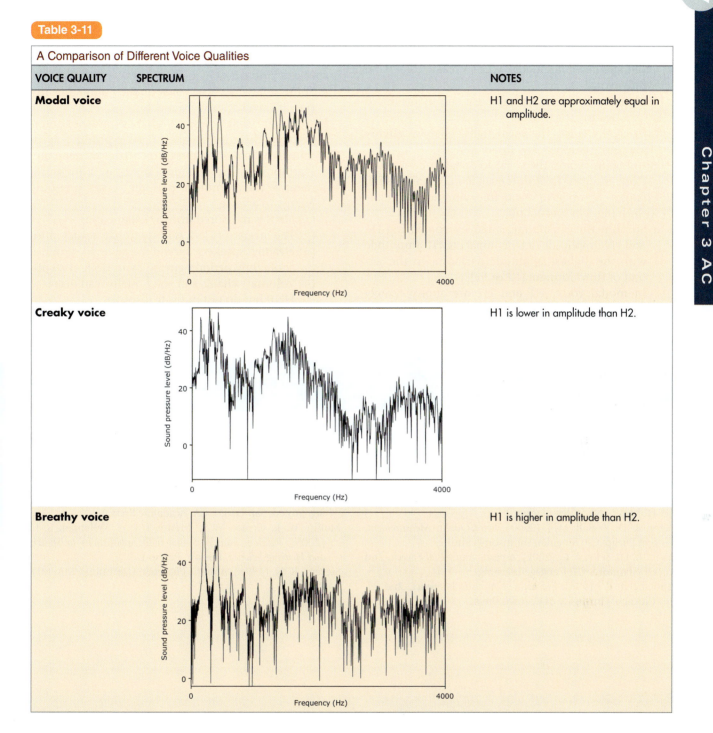

Stability

1. Stability of vocal fold vibration.
   a. Jitter is cycle-to-cycle variability in frequency.
   b. Shimmer is cycle-to-cycle variability in amplitude.
   c. Jitter and shimmer should be measured from a sustained /ɑ/.
      (1) Healthy speakers can voluntarily produce voice qualities that appear disordered.
      (2) It is important to have the speaker produce /ɑ/ in the "clearest" voice he/she can generate.
   d. Calculations of jitter, frequency, or amplitude of each cycle in the recorded sample is compared with one, two, or three cycles on either side.
      (1) To accurately determine the amount of jitter and shimmer, acoustic analysis software must accurately find the cycles.
      (2) Only the user can determine whether or not the software has accurately found the individual cycles in the speech sample.
   e. Jitter and shimmer measurements can be compared with published thresholds for disorder.

Voice Quality

1. Often divided into modal voice, creaky voice, and breathy voice.
   a. Modal voice is the typical voice quality produced by a healthy speaker.
   b. In creaky voice, the vocal folds pulse irregularly and often at a very low frequency.
   c. In breathy voice, the vocal folds never completely close, resulting in airflow even at maximal closure.
2. Changes in mode of vocal fold vibration correlate with changes in spectral tilt.
   a. Spectral tilt can be measured by comparing H1 and H2 amplitude or by comparing H1 amplitude with the highest-amplitude harmonic in the second or third formant (F2 or F3).
   b. In modal voice, H1 and H2 are approximately equal in amplitude.
   c. In creaky voice, H1 is lower in amplitude than H2.
   d. In breathy voice, H1 is higher in amplitude than H2.
3. Voice quality can be voluntarily changed by healthy speakers (Table 3-11).
   a. Some languages use voice quality phonemically (i.e., it can change word meaning).
   b. To ensure that voluntary changes are not interpreted as disorder, speakers need to produce a sustained /ɑ/ in the "clearest" voice they can generate.
   c. Harmonics-to-noise ratio (HNR) is a measurement of the amount of periodic versus aperiodic energy in a voice.
      (1) HNR is measured from a sustained /ɑ/.
      (2) The inverse of HNR is noise-to-harmonics ratio.
      (3) Healthy speakers should be able to produce about 99% periodic energy, or an HNR of 20 dB.
      (4) Voluntary changes in voice quality can decrease HNR but do not indicate disorder.

References

Behrman, A. (2012). *Speech and Voice Science*, 2nd ed. San Diego, CA: Plural Publishing.

Durrant, J. D., & Lovrinic, J. H. (1995). *Bases of Hearing Science*, 3rd ed. Baltimore: Williams & Wilkins.

Johnson, K. (2011). *Acoustic & Auditory Phonetics*, 3rd ed. Hoboken, NJ: Wiley-Blackwell.

Kent, R. D., & Ball, M. J. (2000). *Voice Quality Measurement*. San Diego, CA: Singular/Thomson Learning.

Kent, R. D., & Read, C. (2001). *Acoustic Analysis of Speech*, 2nd ed. Stamford, CT: Cengage Learning.

Ladefoged, P. (1996). *Elements of Acoustic Phonetics*, 2nd ed. Chicago: University of Chicago Press.

Ladefoged, P., & Disner, S. F. (2012). *Vowels and Consonants*, 3rd ed. Hoboken, NJ: Wiley-Blackwell.

Laver, J. (1994). *Principles of Phonetics*. New York: Cambridge University Press.

Moore, B. C. J. (2003). *An Introduction to the Psychology of Hearing*, 5th ed. San Diego, CA: Academic Press.

Mullin, W. J., Gerace, W. J., Mestre, J. P., & Velleman, S. L. (2003). *Fundamentals of Sound with Applications to Speech and Hearing Science*. Boston: Pearson.

Stevens, K. N. (1998). *Acoustic Phonetics*. Cambridge, MA: MIT Press.

Review Questions

1. In sound vibration, what term refers to an area of higher density and pressure?

   a. Rarefaction.
   b. Condensation.
   c. Evaporation.
   d. Sublimation.

2. What is frequency?

   a. Physical measurement of the extent of vibrational change from resting position.
   b. The number of repetitions of a cyclic pattern in 1 second.
   c. Intervals between sounds.
   d. The maximum pressure reached by a sound pressure wave.

3. What term refers to the distance traveled by a sound during a single cycle?

   a. Intensity.
   b. Duration.
   c. Wavelength.
   d. Frequency.

4. For what purpose would a narrowband spectrogram be used?

   a. Finding the exact fundamental frequency.
   b. Finding different sounds by manner of articulation.
   c. Checking pitch contour accuracy.
   d. Measuring frequency-related cues.

5. What is a sinusoid?

   a. A sound consisting of multiple frequencies.
   b. A sound consisting of a single frequency.
   c. The peak amplitude observed in a spectrum.
   d. A complex sound produced by vocal fold vibration.

6. In the source-filter theory of speech production, what acts as the filter?

   a. Vocal fold vibration.
   b. Supralaryngeal vocal tract.
   c. Sound radiation from the lips.
   d. Speech.

7. In the source-filter theory of speech production, what acts as the source?

   a. Vocal fold vibration.
   b. Supralaryngeal vocal tract.
   c. Sound radiation from the lips.
   d. Speech.

8. Formant 1 (F1) is most closely associated with which factor?

   a. Pharynx size.
   b. Oral cavity size.
   c. Distinguishing retroflexed vowels.
   d. Listener perception.

9. Formant 3 (F3) is most closely associated with which factor?

   a. Oral cavity size.
   b. Listener perception.
   c. Pharynx size.
   d. Distinguishing retroflexed vowels.

10. Nasal consonants have a complete closure in which location?

   a. Oral cavity.
   b. Nasal cavity.
   c. Glottis.
   d. Subglottis.

11. What is a distinguishing feature of /r/ on spectrographic analysis?

   a. High F1.
   b. High F2.
   c. Low F2.
   d. Low F3.

12. What is characteristic of stop consonants on a spectrogram?

   a. A period of silence followed by a burst.
   b. Continuous high-frequency noise.
   c. A low-frequency formant.
   d. Close resemblance to vowels.

13. What is a distinguishing feature between voiced and voiceless obstruent cognate pairs?

   a. Only voiceless sounds can be obstruents.
   b. Voiced obstruents have a shorter duration.
   c. Voice obstruents have a longer duration.
   d. Voiceless sounds cannot be obstruents.

14. What is a distinguishing feature between sibilant and nonsibilant fricatives?

   a. Sibilant fricatives appear as noise on a spectrogram.
   b. Nonsibilant fricatives appear as noise on a spectrogram.
   c. Sibilant fricatives have higher amplitude noise than nonsibilant fricatives.
   d. Nonsibilant fricatives have higher amplitude noise than sibilant fricatives.

15. What do changes in mode of vocal fold vibration correlate with?

    a. Spectral harmony.
    b. Spectral tilt.
    c. Spectral frication.
    d. Spectral energy.

16. What is cycle-to-cycle variability in frequency?

    a. Fundamental frequency.
    b. Jitter.
    c. Aperiodicity.
    d. Shimmer.

17. What is cycle-to-cycle variability in amplitude?

    a. Jitter.
    b. Shimmer.
    c. Aperiodicity.
    d. Fundamental frequency.

18. Which of the following is true regarding voice onset time (VOT) for stop consonants?

    a. Alveolar stop consonants have a longer VOT than velar consonants.
    b. Bilabial stop consonants have a shorter VOT than alveolar consonants.
    c. Bilabial stop consonants have a longer VOT than velar consonants.
    d. Velar stop consonants have a longer VOT than alveolar consonants, but only for voice sounds.

19. What is an appropriate description for the effect a stop burst of a bilabial consonant has on a spectrogram?

    a. It leads to a diffuse flat spectrogram.
    b. It leads to a diffuse rising spectrogram.
    c. It leads to a diffuse compact spectrogram.
    d. Bilabial consonants do not have a stop burst.

20. What is a nasal formant?

    a. A high-frequency formant caused by a large, vibrating pocket of air in the nasal cavity.
    b. A low-frequency formant caused by a large, vibrating pocket of air in the nasal cavity.
    c. A high-frequency formant caused by a large, vibrating pocket of air at the site of constriction.
    d. A low-frequency formant caused by a large, vibrating pocket of air at the site of constriction.

4

Language Acquisition: Preverbal and Early Language

NINA CAPONE SINGLETON, PhD
BRIAN B. SHULMAN, PhD

Chapter Outline

Language

Symbols and Parameters

1. A complex and dynamic system of conventional symbols that is used in various modes for thought and communication.
   a. Language evolves within specific historical, social, and cultural contexts.
   b. Language is a rule-governed behavior.
   c. Language is independent of the modality of expression used to convey messages.
2. Language parameters (domains).
   a. Language domains characterize the form (phonologic, morphologic, syntactic), content (semantic), and use (pragmatic) of language.

Learning and Use

1. Language learning and use are determined by the interaction of biological, cognitive, psychosocial, and environmental factors.
2. Effective use of language to communicate requires a broad understanding of human interaction, including nonverbal cues, motivation, and sociocultural roles.
3. The spoken modality can be understood and produced.
   a. Receptive language or comprehension is the understanding of language.
   b. Expressive language is the production of language or what is written or signed.
4. Each aspect of language has a course of development.

Pragmatics

Function, Competence, and Social Interaction

1. The domain of language that governs communication to be functional and socially appropriate within a given context.
2. *Pragmatics* refers to communicative competence.
3. Pragmatic rules guide the use of language in social interactions in a variety of contexts.
4. Pragmatics includes the use of gestures and proxemics.
   a. Gestures are not the same as a signed language.
   b. Gestures are body, facial, or hand movements that can reflect the referent's form (holding up two fingers in V to represent a bunny) or function (stirring to represent a bowl), the relationship between two entities or the path of movement (moving one hand from above to under the other hand). Gestures can also indicate movements such as pointing to what is being referred to in the environment (indicating "up" in a story retelling about finding cookies in a high cabinet yesterday).
   c. Proxemics is nonverbal communication through the use of space between individuals.
      (1) For example, the knowledge of how much space is appropriate between individuals when speaking and how that differs when speaking to a friend, to a teacher, and to a police officer falls under the domain of pragmatics by the rules of proxemics.

Stages of Pragmatic Development

1. Perlocutionary stage.
   a. Birth–8 months.
   b. Adults infer communicative intent from unintentional, vegetative behaviors such as the infant's cough or burp.
2. Illocutionary stage.
   a. 8–12 months.
   b. The use of gestures and vocalizations but no words to express intentions to communicate.
   c. Infants SHOW objects and shortly after GIVE objects over to adults to initiate interaction.
   d. Infants also use ritual request gestures to request action or attention.
      (1) For example, touching the adult's arm and making eye contact.
   e. Pointing to objects emerges as the infant approaches the first birthday.
   f. Pointing precedes and predicts first words in hearing children and first signs in hearing-impaired children exposed to sign language.
3. Locutionary stage.
   a. 12 months–lifespan.
   b. The use of words to express intentions to communicate.
   c. Gesture and other nonverbal behaviors become integrated with spoken language.

Communicative Behaviors

1. Nonverbal behaviors (e.g., eye contact, gestures, proxemics).
2. Intention expressed in spoken and nonverbal communication.
3. Discourse-related skills.
4. Theory of mind.
   a. Falls within the subdomain of social cognition.
   b. The ability to connect emotional states to self and others.
   c. Understanding that others have knowledge, desires, and emotions that may differ from one's own.
   d. The ability to take the perspective of another and modify language use accordingly.

Pragmatic Skills in Infancy

1. Pragmatic skills present in infancy that are the foundation for the social use of language.
   a. Eye contact.
   b. Turn-taking.
   c. Joint attention.
      (1) Requires mutual engagement for a social purpose.

Children's Communicative Intentions

1. Children express their intentions using gestures, vocalizations, or words.
   a. Intention refers to how language and other behaviors accomplish things in the world.
   b. Communicative intentions (also referred to as *speech acts*) expressed by infants and toddlers.
      (1) Requesting action.
      (2) Naming or labeling.
      (3) Protesting.
      (4) Greeting.
      (5) Repeating.
      (6) Calling.
      (7) Practicing.
      (8) Answering.
   c. Communicative intentions expressed by preschoolers.
      (1) Requesting permission.
      (2) Acknowledging.
      (3) Asking questions.
      (4) Making jokes.
      (5) Relating a story.
      (6) Suggesting.
      (7) Indirect requesting.
   d. Analyses of early pragmatic development.
      (1) Dore's Primitive Speech Acts.
      (2) Dore's Conversational Acts.
      (3) Martlew's Conversational Moves.

Children's Use of Gestures

1. Children use gestures to communicate.
   a. Children express intentions via gesture and vocalizations before words (e.g., pointing to guide adult attention).
      (1) By 12 months
   b. Iconic gestures (sticking tongue out to represent frog) and conventional gestures (nodding head, waving) emerge at the time of first words.
      (1) 12 months and older
   c. Gestures are initially produced in isolation but gradually become integrated with spoken language by 2 years of age.
      (1) Pointing and saying a word (point + "car") emerges by 16 months of age.

Longer Linguistic Units

1. Discourse includes conversation, narrative, expository, and procedural.
2. Engaging in longer linguistic units of discourse is a pragmatic skill that requires the integration of all five domains of language.
   a. A narrative is a decontextualized monologue that conveys a story, personal recount, or retelling of a book or movie told to a listener with little support for the speaker.
      (1) Narratives are rule-governed in their organization.
         (a) Establish the central event.
         (b) Sequence events that are related to each other.
         (c) Specify the outcome.
      (2) Narratives reflect the culture of the speaker and the listener.
      (3) Two-year-old children tell proto-narratives characterized by related utterances that do not require sequencing.
      (4) Children gradually chain-link events to one another in an additive manner.
      (5) Children accurately describe a sequence of events in late preschool.
      (6) Narratives have a grammar:
         (a) Setting + episode(s).
         (b) Setting: introduces main characters, protagonist, place.
         (c) Episode: initiate the event, plan and attempt to solve the problem, internal response of the character, consequence of attempts, and character reaction.
         (d) Developmental course begins at 2 years of age, with all grammar units present by 9 years of age.
   b. A conversation is a dialogue between two communicative partners that emerges in toddlerhood and is refined through the preschool years.

(1) Initiating a topic of conversation, maintaining a topic, transitioning to related topics, taking turns, and clarifying misunderstandings given verbal and/or nonverbal cues by the listener are skills that characterize a competent conversationalist.

(2) Two-year-olds engage in short dialogues with few interruptions; however, these changes are highly scaffolded by the caregiver, who explicitly requests clarifications.

(3) Preschoolers engage in conversations that refer to the immediate context or specific past events.

c. A monologue other than a narrative is characterized by self-conversation during focused, goal-directed activities, with no desire to involve others.

(1) Emerges in preschool years.

d. Expository discourse is an academic discourse device that develops in school-age children.

e. Cohesion devices make communication efficient early in preschool.

(1) Pronouns (*me, mine, you, he, she, they*).

(2) Conjunctions (*and, because*).

f. Ellipses and deixis refer to the omission of redundant information in discourse.

(1) Ellipses refer to deleting already said information even if it results in an ungrammatical sentence (e.g., Did Mary eat the cookie? Yes, she did. . . .).

(2) Deixis devices are words or gestures that rely on context to glean meaning, such as pointing and using personal or other pronouns (*this, that, here, there*).

(3) At least one deixis term is present in the first 50-word vocabulary, but mastery continues through school-age years.

g. The style of speech varies by speaker and context.

(1) Dialect differences and register changes related to ethnicity, gender, region, and generation.

(2) Preschool children use *caregiverese* when talking with younger children and take on various roles in play.

(a) Caregiverese is traditionally referred to as *motherese*.

(3) Appropriate volume and tone of voice when communicating.

(4) Politeness (e.g., *please, thank you*).

h. Grice's maxims are the rules for effective communication.

(1) Quantity: be informative without giving too much information or too little information.

(2) Quality: be truthful in the information that is given.

(3) Relevance: say things that relate to the discussion at hand without being irrelevant.

(4) Manner: be clear, brief, and unambiguous.

Social Communication

1. Components of social communication include:
   a. Social interaction.
   b. Social cognition.
   c. Language processing: expressive and receptive language.
      (1) All domains that include pragmatics (verbal and nonverbal communication).

Theory of Mind

1. Ability to take the listener's point of view, including what they may believe, know, or feel.
2. Must be taken into account to convey sufficient and accurate information to a listener.
   a. For example, providing the referent for subsequent pronoun use or providing all background or introduction information to establish a topic of discourse.

Phonology

System of Sound

1. Sound system of a language and the rules that govern the sound combinations.
2. The smallest linguistic unit that signals a difference in word meaning is the phoneme.
   a. C = consonant.
   b. V = vowel.
3. Phonemes are transcribed using the International Phonetic Alphabet (IPA).

Phonological Rules

1. Phonological rules govern the form of phonemes.
   a. *Place of articulation* refers to where the articulators approximate each other to create a sound source for consonants.
   b. *Manner of articulation* refers to how the sound is modified along the vocal tract for consonants.
   c. *Voicing* refers to whether or not there is vocal fold vibration during sound production for consonants.

(1) For example, /b/.
   (a) Place of articulation is bilabial.
   (b) Manner of articulation is stop.
   (c) The phoneme is voiced.
(2) For example, /h/.
   (a) Place of articulation is glottal (vocal fold level).
   (b) Manner of articulation is fricative.
   (c) The phoneme is voiceless (no vocal fold vibration).

d. Vowels are characterized by lingual (tongue) height and anterior-posterior lingual posture in the oral cavity.
(1) Vowels are high, mid, or low in lingual height.
(2) Vowels are front, central, or back in lingual posture.
   (a) Vowel /i/ is a high, front vowel.
   (b) Vowel /a/ is a low, back vowel.
(3) Vowels are also characterized by tension (/i, u, e, o/) and rounding (/u, ʊ, o, ɑ/).

e. Vowels are always voiced.

2. Phonological rules govern how phonemes are sequenced in syllables.
a. Phonotactic probability is the frequency with which certain sound sequences occur in a language.
(1) Established through experience with the ambient language.
(2) Sound sequences comprised of common phonotactic probability sequences occur often.
(3) Sound sequences comprised of rare phonotactic probability sequences occur infrequently.
(4) Common sequences are perceived and produced more quickly than rare sequences.
(5) Awareness of phonotactic probabilities emerges at approximately 9 months of age.

3. Phonological rules govern how syllables are structured.
a. Syllables require a V and can have a variety of C and V configurations.
(1) Examples of syllable structures are V (*a*), VC (*in*), CV (*to*), CVC (*cat*), CVCV (*baby*), CVCC (*walk*), and CCVC (*stop*).

Phonological Development

1. Early phonological development is fairly consistent across children.
a. First words consist of a single CV syllable, single V, and CVCV syllables.
b. Early sound repertoire includes phonemes /p, b, t, d, g, k, h, m, w, n/.
c. Production of phonemes is variable.
d. Children are more likely to attempt to say new words that contain phonemes already in their phonological repertoire.
e. Phonological development is initially holistic but the child is eventually able to segment phonemes within a word.

2. When children reach a threshold of vocabulary, they begin to evince phonological processes.
a. Usually emerges between 18 and 24 months of age.
b. A phonological process is a pattern of speech production in which a child simplifies the adult form of a production.
c. Phonological processes have a typical course of use and resolution.
(1) For example, reduplication, such as saying "baba" for *bottle*.
(2) For example, final consonant deletion, such as saying "ca" for *cat*.
d. An analysis of the phonological processes used by the child is used to evaluate the timeliness of resolution.

3. When evaluating a child for phonological aspects of speech intelligibility, ASHA (1983) has stated that "no dialectal variety of English is a disorder or a pathological form of speech or language."
a. Children can be bilingual or multilingual (e.g., English, Portuguese, and Chinese).
b. Children may speak English as a second language (English learning after proficiency in another language).
c. Children may speak a dialect variation of English (there is no standard English).
d. Children may speak the English of a specific country (American English, British English, Australian English).
e. The phonological characteristics vary between languages.
f. A child's first language affects the child's production of the second language.

4. In the preschool years, children emerge with awareness that words can be deconstructed into phonological parts (sounds, syllables); this is referred to as *phonological awareness* (see Table 4-1).
a. Development of phonological awareness begins by early preschool and continues into the school-age years.
b. Phonological awareness skills begin as rhyming and evolve to identifying the first sound of words, sound comparison between words, and segmentation of words into smaller units.
c. Phonological awareness is strongly correlated with reading and writing skills development.

Table 4-1

Levels of Phonological Awareness

SYLLABLE AWARENESS	ONSET-RIME AWARENESS	PHONEMIC AWARENESS
Syllable segmentation: tell how many syllables are in a word	Judgment: identify whether two words rhyme	Alliteration: phoneme detection at the beginning of words
Syllable completion: finish the word	Oddity: identify which word in a group does not rhyme	Phoneme matching: indicate which words have the same initial sound
Syllable matching: identify the syllables that are the same in two words	Rhyme generation: provide rhyming words for a stimulus	Phoneme isolation: identify a sound in word position
Syllable/word manipulation: manipulate words by deleting, transposing, or substituting syllables		Phoneme completion: provide the sound missing from a word
Syllable/word blending: create new words by combining syllables		Phoneme deletion: say a word without a specific sound
		Phoneme blending: put separately heard sounds together into a word
		Phoneme segmentation: identify how many sounds are in a word
		Spoonerisms: exchange the first sounds in the two words of a phrase
		Phoneme reversal: exchange the sounds in a single word
		Phoneme substitution: change a sound in a word completely

d. The relationship between phonological awareness and literacy appears to be universal across literate languages.

5. Reading is a language-based skill that requires the same linguistic knowledge of language form, content, and use to understand and use oral language.

6. Reading involves the decoding of text, but the remainder of language processing parallels oral language.
   a. Some languages use an alphabetic system (e.g., English).
   b. Some languages use pictographs, where a symbol stands for a whole word (e.g., Chinese uses pictographs).

7. Learning to read and write (literacy) requires direct instruction, but ideas about literacy develop before school, starting in infancy through kindergarten.
   a. Some examples include recognizing signs for familiar products, drawing pictures for words, telling and listening to stories about personal happenings.
   b. Phonological awareness.
   c. Print concepts.

d. Alphabet knowledge.
e. Learning literate language.

8. Joint book reading provides a vehicle for children to learn:
   a. Book orientation.
   b. That ideas are expressed via print.
   c. Page turning.
   d. Left to right reading.
   e. Top to bottom reading.
   f. Literacy socialization.
      (1) Children discuss books with the reader.
      (2) They are involved with explicit attention to features of print.
      (3) Preschoolers who are read to then learn to read earlier and more skillfully than children who are not read to as preschoolers.

9. Dialogic reading.
   a. The caregiver scaffolds the child to be an active participant in reading.
   b. Reading is considered a dialogue between the child and the caregiver.
   c. Use strategies such as prompting and expanding the child's responses.

(Left column - partially cut off)

(3) During th
  accelerate
  new but w
  (a) Weak
    repres
  (b) Richer
    repres
(4) Children
  as they a
  word's me
h. Overgeneraliz
  are semantic
  early vocabul:
  (1) Overgener
    moon, ind:
    is more bi
    (a) Occurs
      details
      separa
    (b) Occurs
      tional
      the ref
  (2) Undergen
    child's "d
    indicates a
    restricted
i. Children inve
  their lexicon,
  ring, and bilir
  one language
  lexical gap.
j. Bilingual chil
  their language
  as *few word eq*
  (1) A word eq
    that refers

Nouns

1. A universal ser
  nouns make up
  vocabulary.
  a. Children wh
    preponderanc
    referred to as
  b. Those who do
    as *expressive ch*
  c. Referential ch
    (1) Have large
    (2) Reach mo
      sooner.
    (3) Have grea
      20 month:

Semantics

System of Meanings

1. System that governs the meanings of words and sentences.
   a. Semantics encompasses the rules for learning and using words, word combinations, and higher-level meaning units (e.g., idioms, metaphors, and other types of figurative language in the school-age years).
   b. Children store words in long-term semantic memory, also referred to as the *lexicon*.

Word Learning

1. Word learning encompasses mapping the word form or label (lexical representation), word meaning (semantic representation), and grammatical specifications (word class information), in addition to making connections between the various phonological representations and articulatory representations.
2. Word learning is a gradual and long-term process that begins with fast-mapping a sketch of the word and subsequently slow-mapping the details of the word.
   a. Fast mapping happens when the initial association or link between the word label and meaning is made and stored in memory.
      (1) Quick Incidental Learning (QUIL) also refers to the fast-mapping process but reflects the more naturally occurring word-learning situations that offer minimal support in ongoing scenes.
   b. *Slow mapping* refers to learning that occurs during the protracted period of word learning after fast mapping has occurred.
      (1) Enrichment of semantic and lexical representations occurs during slow mapping.
         (a) Richer representations result from more frequent experience and high-quality experience.
      (2) Also referred to as *configuration* of the representation.
   c. Words that are more frequently heard in the ambient language are learned more quickly.
   d. Nouns are more easily learned than other word classes.
      (1) Verbs take more exposure to learn than nouns, most likely because a more subtle inference needs to be made about verbs from ongoing events.
      (2) In Korean and German, where cultural practice or structure of the language promotes verb over noun learning, nouns predominate in early lexicons.
   e. Phonological, lexical, and semantic representations of the word itself influence word learning.
      (1) Phonological representations refer to sound representations.
         (a) Infants produce more words comprised of rare phonotactics than common phonotactics.
         (b) Preschoolers learn words comprised of high-phonotactic sequences faster than low-phonotactic probability sequences.
         (c) As phonotactic probability increases in a word, that word is recognized more easily as acceptable in the language
         (d) Rare phonotactic probability sequences trigger new word representations
            • *Triggering* refers to the recognition that a sound sequence is novel and likely a new word to be learned.
      (2) Lexical representations refer to word label representations.
         (a) Neighborhood density of a word refers to the number of possible words (i.e., neighbors) that differ by one phoneme from it.
            • For example, the word *cat* resides in a high-density neighborhood because it has several neighbors, including *sat, pat, cab, rat, coat, cute,* and *can.*
         (b) Children learn more words that are short and from dense neighborhoods (with many neighbors) than long words from sparse neighborhoods.
      (3) Semantic representations refer to meaning or conceptual representations.
         (a) Richness of knowledge and connections.
         (b) Children are more likely to retrieve words with many details stored about them and strong connections between related words.
   f. Neighborhood density is a lexical representation variable that influences word learning.
      (1) A word that resides in a dense neighborhood may be easier to learn because it has many connections between phonologically similar words, but it may be more difficult to perceive or retrieve that word for production because of interference activation from those same phonological neighbors.
   g. Enriching the quality of word exposure hastens fast and slow mapping.
      (1) Richer semantic representations support word retrieval to name words.

Chapter 4 LPE

(2) Weak
recog
ciate
name

The Pho

1. The capaci
nent of wo
with word
a. The pho
manipul
informa
b. The gol
loop is i
c. Childrei
tend to l

Semant

1. The seman
superordir
nate (*poodl*
a. Semanti
in the le
b. Childrer

Retriev

1. Words tha
tered are v
fore vulnei
a. Word-re
the targe
(1) Phor
"chi
milli
(2) Sem
door,
(3) Phor
as "e
b. Indeterr
know,"
related t
c. Persevei
says the
a set tir
correctl
d. Visual
"lollipo

Chapter 5 REP

Table 5-1

Choosing the Appropriate Statistical Analysis

VARIABLES/FACTORS	STATISTICAL ANALYSIS
1+ categorical variables	Chi-square
2+ continuous variables	Correlation
2+ continuous variables with one predictor variable	Regression
1 categorical IV with two unrelated groups or levels (between-subject); 1 continuous DV	Independent t-test
1 categorical IV with two related groups or levels (within-subject); 1 continuous DV	Dependent t-test
1+ categorical IV with two levels each (between-subject); 1 continuous DV	One-way ANOVA (analysis of variance)
2+ categorical IV with 2+ levels each (between subject); 1 continuous DV	Factorial ANOVA
1 categorical IV with 2+ levels (within-subject); 1 continuous DV	Repeated Measures ANOVA
1 categorical IV with 2+ levels (between-subject); 1 categorical IV with 2+ levels (within-subject); 1 continuous DV	Mixed-model repeated measures ANOVA
1+ categorical IV with 2+ levels each (between-subject); 2+ continuous DV	MANOVA (multivariate analysis of variance)

4. *Levels of measurement* describe how variables are measured and determine the appropriate statistical analysis. Values assigned to variables can be categorical (qualitative) or continuous (quantitative). Data are classified into one of four measurement scales: nominal, ordinal, interval, and ratio (NOIR) (Figure 5-6).
5. Statistical analysis.
   a. Choosing the appropriate statistical analysis requires the researcher to correctly classify the level of measurement and elements of the study design:
      (1) Whether variables are categorical (nominal groups) or continuous (interval/ratio scales).
      (2) The nature of independent variable(s).
         (a) Number of IVs.
         (b) Number of groups or levels of IV(s).
         (c) Between-subject or within-subject factors. Refer to Table 5-1.

Evaluating the Evidence

1. Arriving at a clinical decision in evidence-based practice includes reviewing the related literature and clinical practice guidelines (CPGs). CPGs are formed by a group of experts to identify best practices for clinical care and are communicated in terms of strength of recommendation. As for research articles, experimental studies, meta-analyses, and systematic reviews are prevalent types in EBP. The credibility of the level of evidence in a research article is ranked based on convergence of evidence, adequacy of experimental control, reduction of researcher bias, size of treatment effect, and relevance.
2. Experimental treatment studies vary in quality and the strength of evidence. The benefit or treatment effect should be demonstrated by comparison to ade-

quate reporting of baseline performance. Time-series studies include repeated baseline measures prior to treatment and can be strengthened by including control subjects, a second baseline segment after treatment, or multiple alternating treatment and baseline segments.
3. The strongest evidence of credibility comes from:
   a. *Meta-analyses*, which statistically analyze accumulated evidence from multiple studies to evaluate the consistency of results and effect sizes across studies. These are particularly strong when well designed and when based on multiple randomized controlled clinical studies.
   b. *Systematic reviews*, which provide objective and comprehensive overviews of research focused on a particular clinical issue. To promote objectivity, strict criteria are used in selecting and reviewing relevant studies.

Interpreting Research Articles

1. Subjects: the number of subjects sampled from the population of interest and subject selection criteria should be clearly defined.
   a. Adequate sample size affected by study design and the variability of data in that particular study.
   b. Sample of subjects should have similar characteristics to population of interest to be reasonably accurate estimates of population parameters.
   c. Random sampling allows each individual in population of interest an equal chance of being selected for the study.
   d. Generalizability of study results is enhanced when the sample is large and randomly selected from the population of interest (note: many studies in CSD do not use large random samples, as they are difficult to obtain).

e. Studies including a control group generally have stronger designs than studies involving only one group, particularly when the control group is well matched to the experimental group.

f. Randomization of treatment across matched control groups is a stronger design than nonrandomized application of treatment.

2. Methodology: research article should contain sufficient detail to replicate the study, materials should adequately generate or measure the variables under investigation, and the study should demonstrate good validity and reliability.

a. Internal validity: how well the study tests or describes what it is intending to test or describe; depends on methods and procedures used to address the research question(s).

(1) Threats to internal validity.

(a) Subject selection procedures may be biased.

(b) History: extraneous events occurring between the initial measurement and subsequent measurements may contaminate the results.

(c) Reactive pretest: scores on a post-test may be influenced by administration of a pretest.

(d) Statistical regression: if subjects are selected based on extreme scores, their scores on subsequent administrations of the same measure may be closer to the average score even with no treatment.

(e) Researcher bias: the researcher's preconceived notions may influence the way data are interpreted.

(f) The test environment (e.g., noise level) may affect results.

(g) Subject performance may be influenced by the subject's awareness that they are in a research study (i.e., the Hawthorne effect) and how they perceive the consequences of their behavior in the study.

b. External validity: generalizability of results beyond confines of one singular study; can be extended by replication across populations, settings, measurements, or treatments.

(1) Threats to external validity.

(a) The subjects selected may not represent the population to which the researcher is generalizing.

(b) The experimental arrangement (e.g., setting) may influence the study results, thus limiting generalizability of study results to other people who have not experienced the same arrangement.

(c) If multiple sequences or numbers of treatments are studied, the study results may only generalize to other people who have received the same sequences and numbers of treatments.

c. Reliability of measurement: how much we can depend on a measure; the reliability of a measurement can be evaluated in a variety of ways:

(1) Stability: using the test-retest method.

(2) Equivalence: comparing performance on alternate forms of a test.

(3) Internal consistency: the split-half method, in which performance on one half of a test is compared to performance on the other half of items from the same test.

(4) Precise measurements remain relatively stable if repeated with the same research subject under similar conditions; a measurement that is precise may not always be accurate. *Accurate* measurements reflect the level of error that is present.

(5) Sources of potential measurement errors.

(a) Systematic errors such as those resulting from poor equipment calibration.

(b) Unsystematic errors that occur unpredictably, such as from intermittent equipment malfunction

(c) Day-to-day changes in the characteristics of the person being measured.

(d) The behavior of the researcher:

• Interobserver agreement: how consistent two or more researchers are in making a particular measurement.

• Intraobserver agreement: how consistent one researcher is when making the same measurement more than once.

• Agreement coefficients can be calculated to determine the level of interobserver or intraobserver agreement; these coefficients do not tell whether the measure itself is accurate or precise.

3. Results of data analyses: statistical tests and outcomes of analyses that define the data depend on the research design; all studies report descriptive statistics.

a. Measures of central tendency: typical value for a set of data.

(1) Mean: the arithmetic average of scores.

(2) Median: the middle score of the distribution.

(3) Mode: the most commonly occurring score.

b. Measures of variability: how much scores differ from the mean.

(1) Range: the lowest score to the highest score.

(2) Variance: how far each score in the distribution varies from the mean.

(3) Standard deviation (SD): the average amount that all scores in the distribution vary from the mean; small SD indicates more homogeneity.

(4) Standard error of measurement (SEM): the expected variability of a subject's score if the measurement was repeated; small SEM suggests higher reliability.

c. *Parametric tests*: analyze interval or ratio level sample means that estimate population parameters and meet assumptions about the distribution of the data; more powerful statistical test.

d. *Nonparametric tests*: parametric analogues rank scores for analysis of categorical data *or* interval/ratio data that violate assumptions about the distribution; less powerful statistical test. See Table 5-2.

e. *Statistical significance*: likelihood that the relationship between the DV and IV is not due to chance.
   (1) The threshold for significance (alpha level) is set a priori and is often .05; thus $p < .05$ would indicate only a 1 in 20 possibility of the null hypothesis being rejected in error; this finding would be called statistically significant.
   (2) If multiple comparisons are being tested, an adjustment such as the Bonferroni correction may be needed.

f. *Inferential statistics* evaluate differences among data (e.g., ANOVA computes F ratio; statistically significant F indicates difference between groups; greater F value indicates more variance explained).

g. *Correlational statistics* evaluate relationships between data; how variables that are correlated can be described as varying together (e.g., correlation coefficient r indicates how strong the relationship is; the square of the correlation coefficient [r^2] is used to assess its practical meaning; value of r^2 indicates variance explained). See Table 5-3 and Figure 5-7.

Interpreting Tests and Measurements

1. The process of EBP in CSD assists the clinician with interpreting tests. Well-designed and controlled research studies can provide evidence about test sensitivity and specificity and validity of measurements.
   a. *Sensitivity* refers to how well the test detects that a condition (e.g., dysphagia) is present when the

Table 5-2

Parametric and Nonparametric Statistical Tests	
PARAMETRIC TESTS	**NONPARAMETRIC ANALOGUES**
Independent t-test	Mann-Whitney U Test (Ordinal Data)
Dependent t-test	Wilcoxon Signed Rank Test (Ordinal Data)
Pearson Product-Moment Correlation	Spearman Rank-Order Correlation
One-way ANOVA	Kruskal-Wallis one-way ANOVA by ranks
Factorial ANOVA	Friedman's ANOVA by ranks
Repeated-Measures ANOVA	Friedman's ANOVA by ranks

Table 5-3

Strength of a Correlation	
VALUE OF CORRELATION COEFFICIENT	**STRENGTH OF CORRELATION**
$+/- 0.1 < r < +/- 0.29$	Weak
$+/- 0.3 < r < +/- 0.49$	Moderate
$r \geq 0.5$	Strong
$r = +/-1$	Perfect

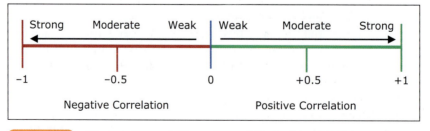

Figure 5-7   **Strength and Direction of Relationship between Variables**

condition actually is present (i.e., the proportion of true positives correctly identified by the test).

b. *Specificity* refers to how well the test detects that a condition (e.g., dysphagia) is not present when the condition actually is not present (i.e., the proportion of true negatives correctly identified by the test).

c. *Content validity* refers to how well the test items measure the characteristics or behaviors of interest.

d. *Criterion validity* refers to how well the measure correlates with a standard that is known to be a good indicator of the characteristic or behavior of interest.

e. *Construct validity* refers to how well the measure reflects a theoretical construct of the characteristic or behavior of interest.

(1) The relationship among clinical signs elicited by different clinical tests and measurements can be quantified in a variety of ways:

(a) Positive predictive value: the number of true positives divided by the combined true and false positives.

(b) Negative predictive value: the number of true negatives divided by the combined true and false negatives.

(c) Positive and negative predictive values should only be calculated from studies reflecting the actual prevalence of the condition or disease in the population of interest at that time because these values are dependent on prevalence.

References

American Speech-Language-Hearing Association. (2003). *National Outcomes Measurement System (NOMS): Adult Speech-Language Pathology User's Guide.* Rockville, MD. Available at www.asha.org.

American Speech-Language-Hearing Association. (2010). *Code of Ethics.* [Ethics]. Available at www.asha.org/policy.

Deviant, S. (2010). *The Practically Cheating Statistics Handbook: The Sequel,* 2nd ed. Jacksonville, FL: Kenrose Media.

Dollaghan, C. A. (2007). *The Handbook for Evidence-Based Practice in Communication Disorders.* Baltimore: Paul H. Brookes Publishing Co.

Douglas, N. F., & Burshnic, V. L. (2019). Implementation science: Tackling the research to practice gap in communication sciences and disorders. *Perspectives of the ASHA Special Interest Groups, 4,* 3–7.

Graziano, A. M., & Raulin, M. L. (2010). *Research Methods: A Process of Inquiry,* 7th ed. Boston: Pearson/Allyn & Bacon.

Horner, J., & Minifie, F. D. (2011). Research Ethics I: Responsible Conduct of Research (RCR)—Historical and contemporary issues pertaining to human and animal experimentation. *Journal of Speech, Language and Hearing Research, 54,* S303–S329.

Hulme, P. (2010). Cultural considerations in evidence-based practice. *Journal of Transcultural Nursing, 21*(3), 271–280.

Kaderavek, J. N., & Justice. L. M. (2010). Fidelity: An essential component of evidence-based practice in speech-language pathology. *American Journal of Speech-Language Pathology, 19,* 369–379.

Nail-Chiwetalu, B. J., & Bernstein Ratner, N. (2006). Information literacy for speech-language pathologists: A key to evidence-based practice. *Language, Speech, and Hearing Services in Schools, 37,* 157–167.

Richardson, W., Wilson, M., Nishikawa, J., & Hayward, R. (1995). The well-built clinical question: A key to evidence-based decisions. *American College of Physicians Journal Club, 123,* A12–13.

Robey, R. R. (2004). Levels of evidence. *ASHA Leader, 9*(7), 5.

Sackett, D. L., Straus, S. E., Richardson, W. S., Rosenberg, W., & Haynes, R. B. (2000). *Evidence-Based Medicine: How to Practice and Teach EBM.* Edinburgh: Churchill Livingstone.

Schiavetti, N., Metz, D. E., & Orlikoff, R. F. (2011). *Evaluating Research in Communicative Disorders,* 6th ed. Boston: Pearson Education.

Stevens, S. S. (1946). On the theory of scales of measurement. *Science, 103,* 677–680.

Tompkins, C. A., Scott, A. G., & Scharp, V. (2008). "Research Principles for the Clinician." In R. Chapey (Ed.), *Language Intervention Strategies in Aphasia and Related Neurogenic Communication Disorders,* 5th ed. Philadelphia: Lippincott, Williams & Wilkins, pp. 163–185.

Review Questions

1. What are the three tenants of evidence-based practice?
   a. Best clinical research, clinical expertise, and needs of the client.
   b. Most recent clinical research, clinical preference, and needs of the client.
   c. Most available clinical research, clinical excellence, and wants of the client.
   d. Best clinical research, clinical excellence, and needs of the client.

2. What is internal validity?
   a. How well a study is utilizing research methods it claims to be using.
   b. How well a study is testing what it claims to be testing.
   c. How well a study is controlling participant variables.
   d. How well a study's results line up with the research procedures used.

3. What is external validity?
   a. How well the results of a study are generalizable.
   b. How applicable the results of a study are to the field at large.
   c. How well a study's results reflect the research process used in a study.
   d. How well the results of a study reflect the hypothesis.

4. What are the four characteristics used in level of measurement?
   a. Identity, maximization, equity of interval, true zero.
   b. Identification, magnitude, equality of interval, rational zero.
   c. Identification, magnitude, equity of interval, rational zero.
   d. Identity, magnitude, equality of interval, true zero.

5. What term indicates how much we can depend on a measure?
   a. Reliability.
   b. Levels of measurement.
   c. Validity.
   d. Standard of error.

6. Research studies can be categorized broadly into what three areas?
   a. Quantitative, time-series, or a combination of the two (mixed methods).
   b. Qualitative, replication, or a combination of the two (mixed methods).
   c. Quantitative, qualitative, or a combination of the two (mixed methods).
   d. Quantitative, clinical practice guidelines, or a combination of the two (mixed methods).

7. Which form of research emphasizes functional service delivery of laboratory-based interventions in clinical settings?

    a. Implementation research.
    b. Clinical research.
    c. Quantitative research.
    d. Translational research.

8. What are typical main sections in research articles?

    a. Review of literature, materials, results, discussion.
    b. Abstract, review of literature, hypothesis, results.
    c. Review of literature, methods, results, discussion.
    d. Abstract, methods, results, discussion.

9. Which of the following terms refers to how well a test detects that a condition is present when the condition actually is present?

    a. Significance.
    b. Specificity.
    c. Sensitivity.
    d. Stability.

10. Which section of a research article provides information regarding the subjects used in the study?

    a. Introduction.
    b. Methods.
    c. Results.
    d. Discussion.

11. Which section of a research article may discuss data distributions from the study?

    a. Introduction.
    b. Methods.
    c. Results.
    d. Discussion.

12. The strongest evidence of credibility in CSD treatment studies comes from:

    a. Meta-analyses and time series.
    b. Systematic reviews and time series.
    c. Meta-analyses and clinical practice guidelines.
    d. Meta-analyses and systematic reviews.

13. How far each score in a data distribution varies from the mean is:

    a. Stability.
    b. Equivalence.
    c. Variance.
    d. Range.

14. Researcher bias is a threat to:

    a. Criterion validity.
    b. Internal validity.
    c. External validity.
    d. Construct validity.

15. What *p* value is typically accepted as indicating significance?

    a. <0.5.
    b. <0.05.
    c. <0.005.
    d. <0.0005.

16. Subjective aspects of behavioral performance can be explored using what kind of research design?

    a. Randomized.
    b. Qualitative.
    c. Quantitative.
    d. Continuous.

17. An active independent variable is:

    a. Characterized as an outcome.
    b. Manipulated by the researcher.
    c. Constrained as extraneous.
    d. A response of interest.

18. To what does treatment efficacy refer?

    a. The degree to which actual implementation of the treatment in the real-world is consistent with the prototype treatment.
    b. When there is clinical improvement from the treatment when applied in a real-world context.
    c. When research is aimed at demonstrating the benefits of treatment through well-controlled studies.
    d. When research provides best practice guidelines for implementation of treatment methods.

19. What is a positive predictive value?

    a. The number of true positives divided by the combined true and false positives.
    b. The number of true positives divided by the combined true and false negatives.
    c. The number of true negatives divided by the combined true and false positives.
    d. The number of true negatives divided by the combined true and false negatives.

20. Which statistical analysis procedure is most appropriate to use when there are two or more continuous variables?

    a. Correlation.
    b. One-way ANOVA.
    c. MANOVA.
    d. Repeated Measures ANOVA.

6

The Practice of Speech-Language Pathology

MARK DERUITER, MBA, PHD
MELANIE W. HUDSON, MA

Chapter Outline

History of Speech-Language Pathology

First Organizational Meeting

1. First meeting of the National Association of Teachers of Speech (NATS) in 1925.
   a. Organized by Carl Seashore and Lee Edward Travis of the University of Iowa.
   b. There were 25 charter members.
2. Ultimately evolved into today's American Speech-Language-Hearing Association (ASHA).

Disorders Addressed in the Early History

1. 1920s and 1930s: stuttering (Lee Edward Travis, Wendell Johnson, and others).
   a. Members of the early group were interested in fluency disorders.
   b. Wanted to protect the public from spurious treatments.

2. Late 1930s and 1940s: adult neurological disorders and motor speech (Karl Goldstein, Norman Geschwind).
3. 1943: childhood aphasia (Mildred Berry, Jon Eisenson).
4. Early and mid-1940s: aphasia and hearing loss from war injuries (Jon Eisenson and Joseph Wepman).

Professional Development

1. Original group became the American Speech Correction Association (ASCA) in 1934.
2. A Code of Ethics was written for the ASCA in 1935.
3. The *Journal of Speech Disorders* was first published in 1936.
4. The ASCA became the American Speech and Hearing Association (ASHA) in 1947.
5. The first standards for clinical certification were established in 1952.
6. Throughout the rest of the century, the scope of practice, name, and activities of the organization and research publications continued to expand exponentially.

Scope of Practice

Focus

1. The *ASHA Scope of Practice in Speech-Language Pathology* document is a "living document" of the organization.
   a. It is considered a living document because it is updated approximately every 5 years.
   b. The *Scope of Practice* reflects the dynamics of service delivery at the time it is written.
   c. The document is written broadly to consider all practice settings and a wide variety of practice scenarios.
   d. The *Scope of Practice* does not supersede state law.

Introduction, Purpose, Definitions, and Service Delivery Areas

1. Introduction.
   a. Defines the SLP as the professional who engages in professional practice in the areas of communication and swallowing across the lifespan.
   b. Delineates practice areas in the context of eight domains of speech-language pathology service delivery: collaboration; counseling; prevention and wellness; screening; assessment; treatment; modalities, technology, and instrumentation; and population and systems.
   c. Delineates five domains of professional practice for the SLP: advocacy and outreach, supervision, education, research, and administration/leadership.
2. Purpose.
   a. Delineate areas of professional practice.
   b. Inform others about professional roles and responsibilities of qualified SLPs.
   c. Support SLPs in the provision of high-quality, evidence-based services to individuals with communication, feeding, and/or swallowing concerns.
   d. Support SLPs in the conduct and dissemination of research.
   e. Guide the educational preparation and professional development of SLPs to provide safe and effective services.
      (1) SLPs are not expected to provide services in all areas. Instead, they are expected to consider the ASHA Code of Ethics regarding competency as they engage with different areas of practice.

3. Definitions of Speech-Language Pathologist and Speech-Language Pathology.
   a. Speech-language pathologists, as defined by ASHA, are:
      (1) professionals who hold the appropriate graduate degree and ASHA Certificate of Clinical Competence in Speech-Language Pathology (CCC-SLP).
         (a) Certification is granted after completion of educational requirements and a mentored postgraduate professional experience as well as passing a national examination.
      (2) SLPs demonstrate continued professional development for the maintenance of the CCC-SLP and other required credentials (e.g., state licensure, teaching certification, specialty certification).
   b. Speech-language pathology contains a broad area of practice that includes both speech-language pathology service delivery and professional practice domains.
   c. SLPs are autonomous professionals who are the primary care providers of speech-language pathology services.
4. Speech-language pathology service delivery areas are considered across eight main areas, with the inclusion of elective services (e.g., accent modification, business communication, transgender communication).
   a. Fluency
   b. Speech production
   c. Language
   d. Cognition
   e. Voice
   f. Resonance
   g. Feeding and swallowing
   h. Auditory habilitation/rehabilitation

Themes within the Scope of Practice

1. The *Scope of Practice* considers practice areas, domains of professional practice, and service delivery areas within the context of the World Health Organization's International Classification of Function (2001).
2. Supported by other related documents, including the Code of Ethics and other practice guidelines.
3. The *Scope of Practice* does not exclude emerging areas of practice within the dynamic and evolving profession of speech-language pathology.
4. See the complete document, Appendix 6A of the ASHA *Scope of Practice in Speech-Language Pathology*, from which the above information is excerpted at the end of this chapter (page 136).

 Credentialing

Certificate of Clinical Competence (CCC)

1. National credential administered by the Council for Clinical Certification (CFCC) of ASHA.
2. Considered the "gold standard" credential for speech-language pathologists and required of employees in many clinical, medical, and educational settings.
3. Reciprocal credential for state licensure since most state licensure laws parallel CCC requirements.
4. Universally required for supervising students in training and mentors of clinical fellows who are candidates for ASHA certification.
5. Students from a graduate program accredited by the Council on Academic Accreditation (CAA) applying less than 3 years postgraduation complete only the demographic and attestation portions of the CCC application.
6. New standards are in effect as of 2020.

7. Requirements:
   a. Master's, doctoral, or other graduate degree.
   b. 75 semester credit hours (SCH) of study focused on the knowledge and skills pertinent to the field of speech-language pathology, at least 36 SCH at the graduate level.
   c. Graduate coursework and clinical practicum initiated and completed in a CAA-accredited program.
   d. Prerequisite knowledge (one course each) in biological science, statistics, social science, and either physics or chemistry.
   e. Knowledge of the bases of human communication and swallowing processes, including:
      (1) Biological.
      (2) Neurological.
      (3) Acoustic.
      (4) Psycholinguistic.
      (5) Linguistic.
      (6) Cultural.

f. Knowledge of the nature of communication disorders, differences, and swallowing disorders in the ("Big 9") areas of:
(1) Articulation.
(2) Fluency.
(3) Voice and resonance, including respiration and phonation.
(4) Receptive and expressive language (phonology, morphology, syntax, semantics, and pragmatics) in speaking, listening, reading, writing, and manual modalities.
(5) Hearing, including the impact on speech and language.
(6) Swallowing (oral, pharyngeal, esophageal, and related functions, including oral function for feeding; orofacial myofunction).
(7) Cognitive aspects of communication (attention, memory, sequencing, problem-solving, and executive functioning).
(8) Social/pragmatic aspects of communication (including challenging behavior, ineffective social skills, and lack of communication opportunities).
(9) Communication modalities (including oral, manual, augmentative, and alternative communication techniques and assistive technologies).
g. Knowledge of prevention, assessment, and intervention for the disorders listed in (f) above.
h. Knowledge of ethical standards.
i. Knowledge of research principles and integrating those principles into evidence-based practice.
j. Knowledge of contemporary professional issues.
k. Knowledge about national, state, and specialty credentialing.
l. Skills in assessment, intervention, and interaction across disorders and the lifespan and with clients from all backgrounds.
m. Skills in oral and written communication sufficient for professional practice.
n. Clinical experience during the educational program of at least 400 clock hours (25 in observation and 375 in direct contact); 325 clock hours must be obtained at the graduate level, and experience must be obtained with clients:
(1) Across the lifespan.
(2) With a variety of disorders.
(3) From diverse backgrounds.
(4) While being supervised by an individual who meets ASHA supervision requirements.
o. Ongoing assessment of student skills and knowledge must be conducted throughout the graduate program.
p. Must pass a national examination.
(1) PRAXIS II in speech-language pathology, administered by the Educational Testing Service (ETS).

q. After graduation, complete a minimum of 36 weeks of full-time employment with periodic assessment and recommendation for certification by a mentor meeting ASHA supervision requirements.
(1) The 2020 CFSI (skills inventory) document can be found on the ASHA website: https://www .asha.org/siteassets/uploadedfiles/2020-clinical -fellowship-skills-inventory.pdf

State Licensure

1. Legal requirement to practice as an SLP in all 50 states and the District of Columbia.
2. Defines the minimum qualifications for practicing in the state (often the same as ASHA CCC requirements, but not always).
3. States grant an individual the right to practice in a defined scope of practice (may be narrower than in the ASHA *Scope of Practice*).
4. Licensure laws are typically designed to protect the public health and welfare, not to protect/preserve/ uplift the profession.
5. Most laws prohibit unlicensed persons from using the title of speech-language pathologist, and doing so is a violation of the law.
6. May exempt certain individuals from the licensure requirement, including:
   a. Individuals practicing in the schools with a teaching credential.
   b. Federal employees.
7. Most boards require evidence of continuing education to maintain the license.
8. Clinical fellowship may be administered through registration or temporary/provisional license prior to full licensure, depending on state statute.
9. Typically allow some level of reciprocity from state to state.
10. Holding the CCC makes the holder eligible for state licensure.
11. Typically administered by a board of examiners through a state board of examiners for speech-language pathology.
    a. Members of the board are often appointed by the governor or other elected official.
    b. May be recommended by the state speech-language-hearing association to the person making appointments, but official may not be bound to act on the recommendations.

Teacher Certification

1. All states regulate practice in educational settings through teacher credentialing requirements.
2. Typically administered by state departments of education.

3. Practicing in schools may require state license from board of examiners in speech-language pathology in addition to teacher credential or only teacher credential; varies from state to state.
4. Requires bachelor's or master's degree, depending on state regulations.
5. Usually valid for serving children kindergarten through 12th grade.

Specialty Recognition

1. Voluntary program recognizing advanced knowledge in a given specialty area.

2. Awarded in addition to basic credential, such as the CCC.
3. ASHA has four specialty recognition credentials:
   a. Child language.
   b. Fluency disorders.
   c. Swallowing and swallowing disorders.
   d. Intraoperative monitoring.
4. Academy of Neurologic Communication Disorders and Sciences (ANCDS) grants board certification for expertise in neurological communication disorders (BC-NCD) of children, adults, or children and adults (dual).

Professional Organizations

American Speech-Language-Hearing Association (ASHA)

1. ASHA is the largest and oldest scientific and professional association representing both speech-language pathology and audiology.
2. National office is in Rockville, Maryland.
3. Vision: "Making effective communication a human right, accessible and achievable for all" (ASHA 2011).
4. Mission: "Empowering and supporting speech-language pathologists, audiologists and speech, language and hearing scientists" (ASHA 2011).
   a. Advocating on behalf of persons with communication and related disorders.
   b. Advancing communication science.
   c. Promoting effective human communication.
5. Membership.
   a. As of 2019, there were approximately 211,000 certified members, noncertified members, international affiliates, and nonmember certificate holders who are speech-language pathologists, audiologists, and speech, language and hearing scientists. Almost 13,000 others are student members or affiliated support personnel.
   b. Approximately 86.2% of members/certificate holders are female.
   c. Slightly more than 3% of members/certificate holders are members of ethnic minorities, and 8.6 % are members of racial minorities.
6. Standards.
   a. The Council for Clinical Certification (CFCC) reviews and establishes standards for practice and competence for individual members.

b. The Council on Academic Accreditation (CAA) determines standards for academic training programs.
7. Examples of member services supported by work clusters within the ASHA national office.
   a. Membership.
   b. Public relations, communication, and marketing.
   c. Professional education and materials.
   d. Governmental relations and public policy.
   e. State-national relations.
   f. Science, research, and evidence-based practice.
   g. Scholarly and professional publications.
   h. Academic affairs and accreditation.
   i. Practices.
   j. Certification and specialty recognition.
   k. Ethics.
   l. Special interest groups.
   m. International relationships/affiliations.
   n. Multicultural affairs.
   o. General and financial operations.
8. Special interest groups (SIGs).
   a. Established within ASHA to promote knowledge and skills in targeted areas.
   b. Currently 19 SIGs.
   c. Groups are comprised of members with similar interests/expertise with access to educational programs, research, publications, and dialogue.
   d. Examples of SIGs include fluency disorders, voice disorders, administration and supervision, school-based issues, augmentative and alternative communication, and so on.
9. Authority for conducting the business of the association is vested in an elected board of directors.

State Organizations

1. State organizations are often affiliated with a larger national organization with similar purposes and structure.
2. Many state associations for speech-language pathologists and audiologists are recognized affiliates of ASHA.
3. ASHA provides information, advocacy, and sometimes monetary support to affiliated state organizations for legislation, licensure, and other state-focused issues.
4. State organizations are influential in practice issues, regulations, funding decisions, and other aspects of practice for a specific locale.

National Student Speech Language Hearing Association (NSSLHA)

1. Student organization for speech-language pathology students and audiology students.
2. As of 2011, NSSLHA was integrated into ASHA. NSSLHA remains a student-led organization within the larger association, and its national advisor holds a position on the ASHA board of directors.
3. Membership is targeted to students with an interest in normal and disordered human communication who are enrolled in a training program (graduate or undergraduate) in communication sciences and disorders.

4. Local chapters allow for leadership development, volunteerism, philanthropic work, and professional networking.
5. Members of NSSLHA receive reduced fees for membership and convention attendance at state and national professional meetings.

International Organizations

1. International Association of Logopedics and Phoniatrics (IALP) provides membership and education opportunities for speech-language pathologists worldwide.
2. Many countries have national organizations for the profession of speech-language pathology with similar missions/visions to ASHA.

Related Professional Organizations

1. Organizations for individuals who have specialized research or clinical or educational interests not addressed within the scope of ASHA or state organizations.
2. May be of interest to the student or professional in areas not included in the array of SIGs.

Ethical Issues

Considerations

1. Professionals have special expertise and render services to individuals in the area(s) of expertise.
2. Highly specialized skills create an obligation to serve individuals in a highly competent manner.
3. Professionals abide by legally specified standards and also a code of ethics.
4. Codes of ethics are developed by the profession itself, and the standards of conduct exceed legal standards.
5. As a member of a profession, one agrees to uphold the principles of the code of ethics.
6. Ethical behavior is constant across employment settings and client populations (Table 6-1 and Table 6-2).

Table 6-1

Five Philosophical Concepts Underlying Ethical Standards
1. **Utilitarian approach:** What action will do the most good and the least harm?
2. **The rights approach:** What action best respects the rights of all stakeholders?
3. **Fairness/justice approach:** Which option treats people equally or proportionally?
4. **Common good approach:** What action best serves the whole community and not just some members?
5. **Virtue approach:** Which option causes me to act as the sort of person I want to be?

Table 6-2

Components of Codes of Ethics (from General to Specific)
Preamble or Introduction: the vision statement and audience to whom it applies.
Terminology: basic terms that may be required to interpret the code.
Principles: the goals to be maintained.
Rules: more specific "dos and don'ts" of each principle.

ASHA Code of Ethics

1. Preamble.
   a. To discharge obligations responsibly, the highest standards of integrity and ethical principles must be set forth.
   b. All individuals who are ASHA members, certificate holders, and applicants for certification (including clinical fellows) must abide by the code.
2. The code is both aspirational and inspirational in nature.
3. Principles of ethics and rules govern responsibility to:
   a. Persons served.
      (1) Hold paramount the welfare of the persons served.
      (2) Holds true for clients and research subjects and extends to humane research with animals.
   b. Achieving and maintaining high levels of professional competence and performance.
      (1) Hold the CCC for the area in which services are provided.
      (2) Engage in activities within the scope of practice.
      (3) Maintain competence through lifelong learning.
      (4) Supervise staff and maintain clinical equipment responsibly.
      (5) Use and maintain technology and instrumentation appropriately.
      (6) All research should be conducted within governing regulations.
   c. The public.
      (1) Promoting public understanding of the professions.
      (2) Supporting the development of services to fulfill unmet needs.
      (3) Providing accurate information when communicating about the professions.
   d. Uphold the professions and relationships with colleagues, students, and other professionals.
      (1) Maintain the dignity and autonomy of the profession.
      (2) Practice with honesty and integrity.
      (3) Adhere to guidelines in scholarly work.
      (4) Adhere to principles of nondiscrimination in professional relationships.
      (5) Self-report misdemeanors or felonies where there has been a conviction, guilty plea, or record of no contest.
      (6) Self-report public sanctions or licensure or professional credential denials.
      (7) Comply fully with policies of the board of ethics and report suspected violations of others. Note: The Code of Ethics of the American Speech-Language-Hearing Association (2016) is contained in Appendix 6B at the end of this chapter (page 151).

Issues in Ethics Statements

1. Provide additional guidance concerning specific issues of ethical conduct.
2. Intended to increase sensitivity and awareness.
3. Assist in self-guided ethical decision-making.
4. Currently approximately 20 different topic areas related to practice, professional behaviors, and supervision.

Violations of the Code of Ethics

1. All members are responsible for adhering to the Code of Ethics and reporting when others violate the Code.
2. Reasons for sanctioning.
   a. Penalize the person in violation.
   b. Educate and rehabilitate.
   c. Inform the public.
   d. Inform other members that the Code is enforced and that penalties are enforced.
3. Types of sanctions that can be imposed by the Board of Ethics (BOE).
   a. Reprimand: perform privately to the person who made a minor or inadvertent violation and to the complainant.
   b. Censure: public reprimand, published to the membership.
   c. Suspension: for serious violations; membership and certification are revoked for a shorter period, typically 6 months; reinstatement at the end of the suspension can be addressed directly to ASHA and does not need BOE approval; published to the members.
   d. Revocation: for serious violations; membership and certification can be revoked for a year, multiple years, or life; published to the membership; must seek reinstatement at the end of the revocation period from BOE.
   e. Withholding: for clinical fellows in violation; may withhold ability to apply for the CCCs for a period determined by the BOE; published to the members.
   f. Cease and desist: BOE may specify a particular action that must stop immediately; failure to do so is also a violation of the Code.

Workforce Issues and Employment (Table 6-3)

Table 6-3

Settings
Clinical/medical settings—approximately 40% of employed SLPs. • Acute care hospitals. • Rehabilitation hospitals. • Community clinics. • Private practice. • University-based clinics. • Long-term care facilities.
Educational settings—approximately 54% of employed SLPs. • Public schools. • Private schools. • Colleges and universities—approximately 3% employed in higher education.

Service Delivery Models

1. Multidisciplinary: client is seen by multiple professionals with some communication between disciplines in regard to referral and follow-up, little cooperative service delivery, independent assessment, and treatment by all disciplines.
2. Interdisciplinary: client is seen by multiple professionals, possibly even providing treatment simultaneously, who communicate regarding treatment and share information about overall status; independent assessment by all disciplines.
3. Transdisciplinary: professionals cooperate in service delivery and communicate frequently; assessment and treatment are often delivered by multiple professionals in a more natural environment.

General Laws Governing Nondiscriminatory Employment and Practice

1. Title VII of the Civil Rights Act of 1964: prohibits employment discrimination based on race, color, sex, religion, and national origin and prohibits sexual harassment.
2. The Age Discrimination and Employment Act of 1967: prohibits discrimination against persons from 40 to 70 years of age in any area of employment.
3. The 1973 Rehabilitation Act: prohibits discrimination based on disability in any facility receiving federal support, including Medicare and Medicaid.
4. The Americans with Disability Act (ADA), 1990: prevents discrimination against individuals with disabilities and ensures their integration into mainstream American life; requires reasonable accommodations in the workplace.

Health Care Environment

Regulations

1. Health care is highly regulated, mostly by laws at the state and federal levels.
2. Legal regulations are set by the Centers for Medicare & Medicaid Services (CMS) of the U.S. Department of Health and Human Services.
3. SLPs must conform to the laws and regulations for billing and reimbursement in order to be paid for services.

Health Care Legislation

1. Social Security Act Amendments, 1965–1996.
   a. Title XVIII of the Social Security Act, Medicare.
      (1) Provides health insurance for individuals age 65 and older.
      (2) Provides health insurance for disabled individuals, notably those with kidney failure, under the age of 65.
      (3) Part A covers patients in hospitals, skilled nursing facilities, and hospice care.
      (4) Part B covers physician visits and outpatient services.
      (5) Each patient pays a monthly premium.
      (6) Does not cover all medical expenses.
      (7) Physician must prescribe SLP services covered under Medicare.
   b. Title XIX of the Social Security Act, Medicaid.
      (1) A joint state and federal program.
      (2) Provides health care services to the poor, elderly, and disabled, regardless of age, who do not receive Medicare benefits.
      (3) Benefits vary from state to state.

(4) Preauthorization is needed by a physician before SLP can treat.

c. Social Security Act Amendments of 1982, 1983: eliminated reimbursement to hospitals for direct costs and provided strong incentives for efficient services.

  (1) Impact on SLPs was reduction in inpatient services.

  (2) Shift from language-based inpatient services to dysphagia.

d. Technology-Related Assistance for Individuals with Disabilities Act of 1988 (and reauthorization of 1998).

  (1) Provided assistive technology devices and services, including augmentative and alternative communication (AAC) devices prescribed by SLPs.

  (2) Reauthorization included provisions for low-interest loans for purchasing assistive technology.

e. Health Insurance Portability and Accountability Act (HIPAA) of 1996.

  (1) Protects availability of health insurance coverage for workers when they move from one employer to another.

  (2) Strong emphasis on protection of confidentiality for medical records, especially targeting record storage and transmission.

2. Omnibus Budget Reconciliation Acts: change in payment systems in order to cut costs and reduce waste.

3. Social Security Act Amendments of 1993.

a. Defined speech-language pathology services and speech-language pathologist for the first time.

  (1) Speech-language services: speech, language, and related function assessment and rehabilitation services furnished by a qualified speech-language pathologist.

  (2) Qualified speech-language pathologist: an individual with a master's or doctoral degree in speech-language pathology who is licensed by the state in which services are furnished or who meets equivalent qualifications if providing services in a state that does not license SLPs.

  (3) Health care coding.

    (a) Charges for services in SLP required under HIPAA.

      • Reporting of diseases and disorders is required using the *International Classification of Disease,* 10th edition, *Clinical Modification.*

      • Procedures must be identified using *Current Procedural Terminology* (CPT) codes.

4. Balanced Budget Act of 1997: imposed an annual cap of $1,500 on SLP (combined with physical therapy) services to outpatients; subsequent actions by Congress have placed a continuing moratorium on the therapy caps.

5. Patient Protection and Affordable Care Act of 2010.

a. Provided more health care coverage to more individuals.

b. Of importance to SLPs, the act provides coverage for "habilitative" care (issues associated with developmental delays) and not restricted to "rehabilitative" care (issues that are acquired).

c. The Affordable Care Act's implementation has affected and defined health care and is subject to changes through legislative, judicial, and executive action.

6. Medicare Access and CHIP Reauthorization Act of 2015.

a. Shifts from volume-based payment models to a patient-centered model under Medicare Part B.

b. Established Merit-based Incentive Payment System (MIPS) and Advanced Alternative Payment Models (AAPMs), both based upon quality and value of services for Medicare Part B beneficiaries.

c. Speech-language pathologists may participate under an alternative payment model (APM) if their practice meets specific guidelines.

d. Patient-Driven Payment Model (PDPM) expands the APM beyond Medicare Part B.

e. PDPM has dramatically shifted reimbursement for services offered in skilled nursing facilities (SNFs).

f. Under Patient-Driven Groupings Model (PDGM) payment is value-based on patient characteristics versus the number of therapy services that are provided.

g. PDGM is an APM for home health services.

SLP Roles in the Medical Setting

1. Assessment and treatment of disorders of swallowing and communication as a result of a medical condition.

2. Providing counseling regarding surgery that may impact communication or swallowing.

3. Collaborating with medical and other health care staff in treating patients.

4. Use of all modes of service delivery, including those that are technology based.

5. Participation in the evaluation and selection and use of assistive devices or voice prostheses.

6. Participation in the continuum of health care, including prevention.

7. Counseling patients, families, and caregivers regarding assessment and treatment.

8. Consulting with other professionals and agencies regarding patient management.

▶ Educational Service Delivery

Regulations

1. Education policy has directed SLP service delivery in the schools.
2. Students must be identified and ruled eligible to receive services; all decisions and services must be documented, and dismissal must be warranted based on achievement.
3. Positive effects of federal legislation on SLP services include team approach to management, the use of outcomes measurement, evidence-based practice, and inclusion of literacy in service delivery.

Legislation and Legal Decisions Affecting SLP Services in Schools

1. *Brown vs. the Board of Education*, 1954: eliminates segregated education.
2. Elementary and Secondary Education Act (ESEA) of 1965: the most far-reaching federal legislation ever passed by Congress; provided federal funding for primary and secondary public education.
3. PL 94-142: The Education for All Handicapped Children Act of 1975.
   a. All children have the right to a free and appropriate public education.
   b. Their rights and the rights of their parents are protected by due process.
   c. States and local school districts are to receive federal support for providing the services.
   d. Effectiveness of education programs are to be assessed.
   e. An Individualized Education Program (IEP) is to be the written record of the commitment to meet a student's goals as determined by school personnel and the child's parents.
   f. Defines special education and mandates a process to include handicapped children in regular schools and in the least restricted environment.
   g. Has a pervasive and profound effect on public school speech-language and hearing programs.
   h. Defines the categories of children to be served in special education and related services.
   i. Speech-language therapy is defined as a related service for most children.

4. PL 99-457: Education for the Handicapped Act Amendments of 1986.
   a. Requires states to use qualified personnel to provide special education and related services.
   b. Provide services to children age 3 years and younger with special needs.
5. PL 101-476: Individuals with Disabilities Education Act (IDEA), 1990.
   a. Replaces the word *handicap* in previous legislation with the word *disability.*
   b. Expands the original law to include instruction in all settings.
   c. Adds categories of treatment for children, including autism and traumatic brain injury.
   d. Reauthorizations of this act have changed the scope or requirements for documenting efficacy over time.
   e. Most significant change to IDEA came in 2004, which sought to improve the original act, particularly improving outcomes for special education and to make IDEA consistent with No Child Left Behind (NCLB).
6. PL 107-110: No Child Left Behind Act of 2001.
   a. Sought to improve outcomes through:
      (1) Highly qualified teachers and paraprofessionals.
      (2) Use of accommodations, modifications, and alternative assessments for children with disabilities.
      (3) Assessment of English-language learners.
      (4) Sanctions for schools identified as in need of improvement.
      (5) Requiring accountability and adequate yearly progress.
   b. As an unfunded mandate, NCLB has resulted in dissatisfaction with excessive reliance on achievement test outcomes and conflicts with IDEA.
7. Every Student Succeeds Act (ESSA), 2015: reauthorization of the Elementary and Secondary Education Act of 1965.

Role of the SLP in the School Setting

1. Identification of eligible children: typically by referral from parents, teachers, and outside agencies.
2. Evaluation: if children fail screening, the SLP must have informed consent signed by the parents giving permission to evaluate.

3. Determining eligibility: the evaluation must determine eligibility for special education and related services as well as educational needs.
4. Developing the IEP: developed by the IEP team for all children age 3 or older who qualify for speech-language services and is developed to meet each child's individual needs.
5. IEP implementation: with parental consent, the IEP's goals and objectives are implemented through a program of therapy.
6. Dismissal: the IEP team must agree that goals have been achieved and termination is warranted.
7. Language-learning connection to literacy has received prominent attention in recent years.
   a. SLPs participate in literacy/reading intervention.
   b. Literacy/reading intervention often occurs in the classroom.

c. Children who are not achieving are often seen by SLPs in services referred to as Response to Intervention (RTI) or Multi-Tiered System Supports (MTSS)—essentially trial therapy or classroom support to determine if difficulties can be overcome without resorting to special education services. These services are provided through general education funding sources and are not considered special education programs, and may apply to more than language-learning and literacy.
8. Caseload/workload may be mandated by state regulations or local district guidelines and includes indirect and direct services; *caseload* refers to the number of students mandated to receive the services of the SLP. *Workload* refers to all activities required of and performed by the SLP.

Early Intervention

Regulation

1. Governed by IDEA 1997 (PL 105-17); Part C recognizes an urgent need to:
   a. Enhance the development of infants and toddlers with disabilities.
   b. Reduce educational costs by minimizing later special education needs.
   c. Minimize need for institutionalization and maximize potential for independent living.
   d. Enhance families' capacities to meet the needs of their infants and toddlers with disabilities.
   e. Enhance the capacity of education agencies and service providers to identify, evaluate, and manage young children from underrepresented groups.
   f. Provide services to children age 3 years and younger with special needs.

Role of the SLP

1. Developmental screening: requires states to have policies and procedures to identify infants and toddlers with developmental delays.
2. Evaluation: timely, comprehensive, and multidisciplinary evaluation.

3. Assessment of results: must delineate appropriate services to meet the child's special needs.
4. Individualized Family Service Plan (IFSP): goals and objectives for the child and family, services to be provided, preservice levels, plan for intervention, and evaluation of services/outcomes.
5. Work with the service coordinator and other members of the service delivery team to provide competent and comprehensive services.

Guiding Principles for Early Intervention Services

1. Services are family centered and culturally and linguistically responsive.
2. Services are developmentally supportive and promote children's participation in their natural environments.
3. Services are comprehensive, coordinated, and team based.
4. Services are based on the highest quality evidence that is available.
   a. American Speech-Language-Hearing Association's (2008) *Roles and Responsibilities of Speech-Language Pathologists in Early Intervention: Guidelines*; American Speech-Language-Hearing Association's (2020) "Early intervention" web page.

▶ Professional Liability and Responsibility

Autonomy Entails Responsibilities, Duties, and Liabilities

1. Liabilities arise from promises made to abide by standards of practice and codes of ethics.
2. Lapses in professional judgment, lack of care in evaluation, or treatment methods or failure to use best practices or conform to applicable law create situations in which the SLP may be liable for professional misconduct.
3. Licensure laws protect the health, safety, and welfare of citizens.
4. Citizens or others may enter a complaint to the licensure board regarding professional misconduct, and the licensure board must investigate the allegation.

5. Professionals manage risks by adhering to scope of practice, practice guidelines, and policies and procedures; by participating in continuing education; and by committing to quality improvement.
6. SLPs should carry professional liability insurance coverage provided by their employer or obtained from an insurance company.
7. Professional liability insurance covers errors in judgment but not willful or intentional acts of malfeasance.
8. Errors in judgment should immediately be reported and guidance sought as to how to correct or limit the result of the error.
9. Errors in judgment should never be covered up or ignored.

▶ Policies and Procedures

Typical Policies and Procedures

1. Some policies and procedures are typical from setting to setting, and SLPs will expect to find such requirements in place wherever they work. It is typical for each unit in a facility to have a policies and procedures handbook that contains institutional, departmental, and programmatic policies, including:
   a. Applicable accrediting and regulatory requirements.
   b. Legal considerations.
   c. Infection control: universal precautions that prevent the spread of disease through the use of barriers (gloves), good hygiene (hand washing), and sterilization of materials.
   d. Continuous quality improvement program: parameters for developing and implementing.

Rules and Regulations

1. Dress code.
2. Attendance/leave policies.
3. Procedures to institute in case of emergency.
4. Patient admission and discharge procedures.
5. Confidentiality for protected patient information.
6. Ethics.
7. Taking/reporting disciplinary actions.
8. Roles of professionals in the unit.
9. Evaluation and treatment protocols.
10. Continuing education and student training requirements.
11. Patient safety.
12. Incident reporting protocols.

▶ Serving Multicultural Populations

Providing Services in a Multi-ethnic Society

1. Approximately 7% of SLPs come from culturally and linguistically diverse (CLD) backgrounds, far less than the number of patients to be seen.

2. SLPs are required to provide services competently (by Code of Ethics).
3. This requirement includes cultural competence or humility.
4. CLD populations have traditionally included Native Americans, Hispanics, African Americans, and Asian Americans.

5. Also includes diversity related to age, gender, race, ethnicity, language, religion, politics, sexual orientation, and socioeconomic status, according to ASHA.
6. Caseloads in all settings reflect a growing diversity.
   a. ASHA (2017). Issues in ethics: Cultural and linguistic competence is a resource for clinicians.

Issues Associated with CLD Populations

1. Bilingualism or second-language acquisition: may be addressing a primary language in the home and English as the second language (ESL) in the school environment.
2. Respect for the culture of the home and assisting acculturation in the environment.
3. Interactions of testing and treatment may affect clinical outcomes.
4. Use of interpreters may affect clinical decisions and outcomes.
5. Test instruments may lack sensitivity to cultural diversity and result in invalid data.
   a. Modification of test instruments may be necessary to eliminate bias.
   b. Dynamic assessment in the client's environment may reveal better information than standardized testing.
   c. Cultural differences may include perception of gender roles.
   d. Advice regarding cultural differences and competence in addressing them should be sought in order to provide services competently.
   e. Clinicians should develop therapeutic relationships with clients and their families in order to increase understanding and success.

Supervision

Types of Supervision

1. Students must be supervised by someone who holds the CCC-SLP, has 9 months of full-time clinical experience after earning the CCC-SLP, and has completed 2 hours of professional development in the area of supervision in order for the hours to count toward certification requirements. Allowing clock hours to count when students are supervised by individuals in other professions is part of the current discussion associated with interprofessional practice.
2. SLPs often supervise students in externships but also supervise clinical fellows in a variety of employment settings. The goal is to assist the learner in becoming an independent practitioner.
   a. Goal of supervision is for both supervisor and supervisee to experience professional growth resulting in better client outcomes.
   b. Skills for effective supervision for students and CFs:
      (1) Relinquish control as appropriate relative to the knowledge and skills of the supervisee.
      (2) Promote problem-solving and critical thinking.
      (3) Teach clinical competence in assessment, intervention, and documentation.
      (4) Good interpersonal communication.
      (5) Conduct effective supervisory conferences.
      (6) Evaluate growth of the supervisee.
      (7) Clinical acumen that serves as a role model to the learner.
      (8) Ability to model and teach professional and ethical behavior.
      (9) Assist the student/CF to achieve clinical independence.
3. SLPs supervise speech-language pathology assistants (SLPAs), who work under the direction of the SLP and are not intending to become independent practitioners.
   a. Appropriate use of SLPAs: The SLP should be knowledgeable of current state regulations, required training and supervision, and appropriate policy documents. SLPAs may work in a variety of settings.
   b. Role of the SLPA—to supplement—not supplant—the services of the ASHA-certified SLP. The SLPA may, at the direction of the SLP:
      (1) Assist with screenings without making interpretations.
      (2) Follow treatment plans or protocols developed by the SLP.
      (3) Document client performance through charts or tables and report this information to the supervising SLP.
      (4) Assist with assessment exclusive of administration and/or interpretation.
      (5) Assist the SLP with bilingual translation during screening and assessment activities exclusive of interpretation.
      (6) Provide guidance and treatment via telepractice to students, patients, and clients who are selected by the supervising SLP as appropriate for this service delivery model.
      (7) Program and provide instruction in the use of augmentative and alternative communication devices.

(8) Demonstrate or share information with patients, families, and staff regarding feeding strategies developed and directed by the SLP.

(9) Serve as interpreter for patients/clients/students and families who do not speak English.

(10) Provide services under SLP supervision in another language for individuals who do not speak English and English-language learners.

(11) Assist with preparing materials, scheduling, or clerical duties.

(12) Check and maintain equipment.

(13) Assist with departmental operations.

(14) Provide support for projects or training programs conducted by the SLP, including advocacy and prevention initiatives.

(15) ASHA currently has a certification program for SLPAs (ASHA, 2020b).

Telepractice

Definition

1. An encounter with real-time audio and video connection between client(s) and a clinician, similar to an in-person session.
   a. May also utilize software or other digital media as accompaniment to live interaction.
   b. Live events may be supplemented with other contacts (phone, email, etc.).
   c. May include any service delivery venue where the technology is available.
   d. Must conform to professional standards of ethics and best clinical practices and should be evaluated for efficacy and quality on an ongoing basis.
   e. Assumption is that services provided via telepractice will have same outcome as those delivered face-to-face.
   f. All rules for privacy and confidentiality of patient information must be followed.
   g. Variability of licensure rules exists; however, states typically require the telepractitioner to be licensed in the state where the services are delivered.
   h. States and other professional groups are working on assistance with the licensure issue such as limited license.
   i. Telepractice has the potential to improve access to SLP services.
   j. Research is needed as to the efficacy of telepractice in comparison to direct face-to-face services.
   k. Some possibilities exist for asynchronous (store and forward) services where patients store speech samples for review by the clinician.

Evidence-Based Practice (EBP)

Definition

1. "The conscientious, explicit, and judicious use of current best evidence in making decisions about the care of individual patients . . . [by] integrating individual clinical expertise with the best available external clinical evidence from systematic research" (Sackett et al., 1996).
   a. Evidence must be supplemented with clinical expertise and patient values while identifying and making use of the best evidence available.
   b. Practitioners should gain evidence from their own study but look for efficiencies by going to "high-yield" sources.
   c. Knowledge is continually changing, so reference scholarly journals available online or from evidence compilers such as professional organizations.
   d. ASHA has the National Center for Evidence-Based Practice (NCEP) in addition to journals—sources that provide relevant evidence across a wide range of disorders/areas of practice.
   e. NCEP conducts several comprehensive, systematic reviews each year for the benefit of members and practitioners in SLP.
   f. The ASHA website provides a practice portal, evidence maps, and all published material in ASHA publications, including the scholarly journals, by search topic.

g. Other specialty organizations and special interest groups have focused information as well.

h. Practitioners must assess evidence critically to determine if it is pertinent and of sufficient strength and quality.

i. Questions the practitioner might ask:

(1) Were there significant differences between treated and untreated groups?

(2) Were outcome measures reliable and valid?

(3) Were patients randomly assigned to groups?

(4) Were investigators blind to group assignment?

(5) Were group differences acceptable?

j. EBP offers a means by which practitioners can improve as clinicians.

References

American Speech-Language-Hearing Association. (2010a). *Code of Ethics* [Ethics]. Available at www.asha.org/policy.

American Speech-Language-Hearing Association. (2010b). Professional issues in telepractice for speech-language pathologists [Professional Issues Statements]. Available at www.asha.org/policy.

American Speech-Language-Hearing Association. (2011). *ASHA Strategic Pathway to Excellence*. Available at www.asha.org/uploadedFiles/ASHAPublicPathwayHandout.pdf#search=%22mission%22.

American Speech-Language-Hearing Association. (2018). *2018 ASHA Member Counts:* Available at https://www.asha.org/uploadedFiles/Year-End-2009-2018.pdf.

American Speech-Language-Hearing Association. (2016). Scope of Practice in Speech-Language Pathology [Scope of Practice]. Available at www.asha.org/policy/.

American Speech-Language-Hearing Association. (2017). Issues in cultural and linguistic competence. Available at www.asha.org/Practice/ethics/Cultural-and-Linguistic-Competence/.

American Speech-Language-Hearing Association. (2020a). Early intervention. Available at www.asha.org/practice-portal/professional-issues/early-intervention/.

American Speech-Language-Hearing Association (2020b). Assistants program. Available at: https://www.asha.org/assistants-certification-program/.

Colorado Department of Education, Special Education Services Unit. (2004). Fast Facts: Speech-Language Pathology Assistants (SLPA). Available at www.cde.state.co.us.

Dollaghan, C. (2004). Evidence-based practice: Myths and realities. *The ASHA Leader*, April 13, 2004. Available at https://www.asha.org/uploadedFiles/Year-End-2009-2018.pdf.

Duchan, J. F. (2002). What do you know about your professions' history and why it is important? *The ASHA Leader*, December 24, 2002. Available at https://leader.pubs.asha.org/doi/10.1044/leader.ftr.07232002.4.

Hudson, M., & DeRuiter, M. (2021). *Professional Issues in Speech-Language Pathology and Audiology*, 5th ed. San Diego, CA: Plural Publishing.

Lusis, I. (2010). New health care law brings changes. *The ASHA Leader*, April 27, 2010. Available at https://leader.pubs.asha.org/doi/10.1044/leader.pa.15052010.1.

Markula Center for Applied Ethics. (2009). A framework for thinking ethically. Santa Clara University. Available at https://slideplayer.com/slide/2477335/.

McCready, V. (2007). Supervision of speech-language pathology assistants: A reciprocal relationship. *The ASHA Leader*, May 8, 2007. Available at https://leader.pubs.asha.org/doi/10.1044/leader.ftr2.12062007.10.

Sackett, D. L., Rosenberg, W. M. C., Gray, J. A. M., Haynes, R. B., & Richardson, W. S. (1996). Evidence-based medicine: What it is and what it isn't. Article based on an editorial from the *British Medical Journal*, 312, 71–72.

Research

SLPs conduct and participate in basic and applied/translational research related to cognition, verbal and nonverbal communication, pragmatics, literacy (reading, writing and spelling), and feeding and swallowing. This research may be undertaken as a facility-specific effort or may be coordinated across multiple settings. SLPs engage in activities to ensure compliance with Institutional Review Boards and international laws pertaining to research. SLPs also collaborate with other researchers and may pursue research funding through grants.

Administration and Leadership

SLPs administer programs in education, higher education, schools, health care, private practice, and other settings. In this capacity, they are responsible for making administrative decisions related to fiscal and personnel management; leadership; program design; program growth and innovation; professional development; compliance with laws and regulations; and cooperation with outside agencies in education and healthcare. Their administrative roles are not limited to speech-language pathology, as they may administer programs across departments and at different levels within an institution. In addition, SLPs promote effective and manageable workloads in school settings, provide appropriate services under IDEIA (2004), and engage in program design and development.

References

American Psychiatric Association. (2013). *Diagnostic and statistical manual of mental disorders* (5th ed.). Washington, DC: Author.

American Speech-Language-Hearing Association. (2005). *Evidence-based practice in communication disorders* [Position statement]. Available from www.asha.org/policy.

American Speech-Language-Hearing Association. (2014). *Interprofessional education/interprofessional practice (IPE/IPP).* Available from www.asha.org/Practice/Interprofessional-Education-Practice/

Bridges, D. R., Davidson, R. A., Odegard, P. S., Maki, I. V., & Tomkowiak, J. (2011). Interprofessional collaboration: Three best practice models of interprofessional education. *Medical Education Online, 16.* doi:10.3402/meo.vl6i0.6035. Retrieved from www.ncbi.nlm.nih.gov/pmc/articles/PMC3081249/

Craddock, D., O'Halloran, C, Borthwick, A., & McPherson, K. (2006). Interprofessional education in health and social care: Fashion or informed practice? *Learning in Health and Social Care, 5,* 220-242. Retrieved from http://onlinelibrary.wiley.eom/doi/10.1111/j.1473-6861.2006.00135.x/abstract

Individuals With Disabilities Education Act of 2004, 20 U.S.C. § 1400 et seq. (2004).

Individuals with Disabilities Education Improvement Act of 2004, 20 U.S.C. § 1400 et seq. (2004).

Lipinski, C. A., Lombardo, F., Dominy, B. W., & Feeney, P. J. (1997, March 1). Experimental and computational approaches to estimate solubility and permeability in drug discovery and development settings. *Advanced Drug Delivery Reviews, 46*(1–3), 3–26. Retrieved from http://www.ncbi.nlm.nih.gov/pubmed/11259830

Rehabilitation Act of 1973, 29 U.S.C. § 701 et seq.

U.S. Department of Education. (2004). *Building the legacy: IDEA 2004.* Retrieved from http://idea.ed.gov/

World Health Organization. (2014). *International Classification of Functioning, Disability and Health.* Geneva, Switzerland: Author. Retrieved from www.who.int/classifications/icf/en/

Resources

American Speech-Language-Hearing Association. (n.d.). *Introduction to evidence-based practice.* Retrieved from http://www.asha.org/Research/EBP/

American Speech-Language-Hearing Association. (n.d.). Practice Portal. Available from http://www.asha.org/practice-portal/

American Speech-Language-Hearing Association. (1991). *A model for collaborative service delivery for students with language-learning disorders in the public schools* [Paper]. Available from www.asha.org/policy

American Speech-Language-Hearing Association. (2003). *Evaluating and treating communication and cognitive disorders: Approaches to referral and collaboration for speech-language pathology and clinical neuropsychology* [Technical report]. Available from www.asha.org/policy

Paul, D. (2013, August). A quick guide to DSM-V. *The ASHA Leader, 18,* 52–54. Retrieved from http://leader.pubs.asha.org/article.aspx?articleid=1785031

U.S. Department of Justice. (2009). *A guide to disability rights laws.* Retrieved from www.ada.gov/cguide.htm

References

American Speech-Language-Hearing Association. (2005). *Evidence-based practice in communication disorders* [Position Statements]. Available at www.asha.org/policy.

American Speech-Language-Hearing Association. (2013). *Speech-Language Pathology Assistant Scope of Practice* [Scope of Practice]. Available at www.asha.org/policy/.

American Speech-Language-Hearing Association. (2016). *Scope of Practice in Speech-Language Pathology* [Scope of Practice]. Available at www.asha.org/policy/.

American Speech-Language-Hearing Association. (2017). Issues in ethics: Speech-language pathology assistants. Available at www.asha.org/policy/.

Chapter 6 PSL

American Speech-Language-Hearing Association. (2018). Scope of practice in audiology. Available at www.asha.org/policy/sp2018-00353/.

American Speech-Language-Hearing Association. (2019). Annual demographic and employment data: 2019 member and affiliation profile. Available at www.asha.org/uploadedFiles/2019-Member-Counts.pdf.

World Health Organization. (2001). *International Classification of Functioning, Disability and Health*. Geneva, Switzerland: Author.

Resources

ASHA Cardinal Documents

American Speech-Language-Hearing Association. (2004). Preferred practice patterns for the profession of speech-language pathology. Available at www.asha.org/policy.

American Speech-Language-Hearing Association. (2016). *Code of Ethics* [Ethics]. Available at www.asha.org/policy.

Council on Academic Accreditation Audiology and Speech-Language Pathology. (2016). Standards for accreditation of graduate education programs in audiology and speech-language pathology. Retrieved from https://caa.asha.org/wp-content/uploads/Accreditation-Standards-for-Graduate-Programs.pdf.

Council for Clinical Certification in Audiology and Speech-Language Pathology of the American Speech-Language-Hearing Association. (2018). 2020 Standards for the Certificate of Clinical Competence in Speech-Language Pathology. Available at www.asha.org/certification/2020-SLP-Certification-Standards.

General Service Delivery Issues

Admission/Discharge Criteria

American Speech-Language-Hearing Association. (2004). Admission/discharge criteria in speech-language pathology [Guidelines]. Available at www.asha.org/policy.

Autonomy

American Speech-Language-Hearing Association. (1986). Autonomy of speech-language pathology and audiology [Relevant Papers]. Available at www.asha.org/policy.

Culturally and Linguistically Appropriate Services

American Speech-Language-Hearing Association. (2003). *American English dialects* [Technical report]. Available at www.asha.org/policy.

American Speech-Language-Hearing Association. (2017). Issues in ethics: Cultural and linguistic competence. Available at www.asha.org/Practice/ethics/Cultural-and-Linguistic-Competence/.

Caseload

American Speech-Language-Hearing Association. (2020). Caseload and workload. www.asha.org/practice-portal/professional-issues/caseload-and-workload/.

Definitions and Terminology

American Speech-Language-Hearing Association. (1982). Language [Relevant Papers]. Available at www.asha.org/policy.

American Speech-Language-Hearing Association. (1986). Private practice. Available at www.asha.org/policy.

Evidence-Based Practice

American Speech-Language-Hearing Association. (2004). Evidence-based practice in communication disorders: An introduction [Technical Reports]. Available at www.asha.org/policy.

American Speech-Language-Hearing Association. (2005). Evidence-based practice in communication disorders: An introduction [Position Statements]. Available at www.asha.org/policy.

American Speech-Language-Hearing Association. (2020). Practice Portal. Available at: https://www.asha.org/practice-portal/.

Private Practice

American Speech-Language-Hearing Association. (2011). Frequently asked questions about business practices. Available at www.asha.org/practice/faq_business_practices_both/.

American Speech-Language-Hearing Association. (2013). Obtaining clients for private practice from primary place of employment [Issues in Ethics]. Available at www.asha.org/policy.

American Speech-Language-Hearing Association. (2015). SLP health care survey 2015: Private practice owners and co-owners. Available at https://www.asha.org/uploadedFiles/2015-SLP-Health-Care-Survey-Private-Practice.pdf.

Professional Service Programs

American Speech-Language-Hearing Association. (2005). Quality indicators for professional service programs in audiology and speech-language pathology [Quality indicators]. Available at www.asha.org/policy.

Speech-Language Pathology Assistants

American Speech-Language-Hearing Association. (2002). Knowledge and skills for supervisors of speech-language pathology assistants [Knowledge & Skills]. Available at www.asha.org/policy.

American Speech-Language-Hearing Association. (2004a). Guidelines for the training, use, and supervision of speech-language pathology assistants [Guidelines]. Available at www.asha.org/policy.

American Speech-Language-Hearing Association. (2004b). Training, use, and supervision of support personnel in speech-language pathology [Position Statements]. Available at www.asha.org/policy.

American Speech-Language-Hearing Association. (2017). Issues in ethics: Speech-language pathology assistants. Available at www.asha.org/policy/.

American Speech-Language-Hearing Association. (2019). Speech-language pathology assistant scope of practice. Available at www.asha.org/policy/SP2013-00337/.

American Speech-Language-Hearing Association. (2020b). Assistants program. Available at: https://www.asha.org/assistants-certification-program/.

Supervision

American Speech-Language-Hearing Association. (2008). Clinical supervision in Speech-language pathology and audiology [Position Statements]. Available at www.asha.org/policy.

American Speech-Language-Hearing Association. (2010). Supervision of student clinicians [Issues in Ethics]. Available at www.asha.org/policy.

American Speech-Language-Hearing Association. (2013). Knowledge, skills and training considerations for individuals serving as supervisors [Final report, Ad Hoc Committee on Supervision]. Available at www.asha.org/uploadedFiles/Supervisors-Knowledge-Skills-Report.pdf.

American Speech-Language-Hearing Association. (2017). Issues in ethics: Responsibilities of individuals who mentor clinical fellows in speech-language pathology. Available at www.asha.org/Practice/ethics/Responsibilities-of-Individuals-Who-Mentor-Clinical-Fellows-in-Speech-Language-Pathology/.

Clinical Services and Populations

American Speech-Language-Hearing Association. (n.d.). Practice portal. Available at www.asha.org/Practice-Portal/.

Apraxia of Speech

American Speech-Language-Hearing Association. (2007a). Childhood apraxia of speech [Position Statements]. Available at www.asha.org/policy.

American Speech-Language-Hearing Association. (2007b). Childhood apraxia of speech [Technical Reports]. Available at www.asha.org/policy.

Auditory Processing

American Speech-Language-Hearing Association. (1996). Central auditory processing: Current status of research and implications for clinical practice [Technical Reports]. Available at https://pubs.asha.org/doi/10.1044/1059-0889.0502.41.

American Speech-Language-Hearing Association. (2004). Preferred practice patterns for the profession of speech-language pathology [Preferred Practice Patterns]. Available at www.asha.org/policy.

American Speech-Language-Hearing Association. (2005a). (Central) auditory processing disorders [Technical Reports]. Available at www.asha.org/policy.

American Speech-Language-Hearing Association. (2005b). (Central) auditory processing disorders—the role of the audiologist [Position Statements]. Available at www.asha.org/policy.

American Speech-Language-Hearing Association. (2018). Facilitated communication [Position Statements]. Available at from www.asha.org/policy/.

Aural Rehabilitation

American Speech-Language-Hearing Association. (2001). Knowledge and skills required for the practice of audiologic/aural rehabilitation [Knowledge & Skills]. Available at www.asha.org/policy.

American Speech-Language-Hearing Association. (2004). Preferred practice patterns for the profession of speech-language pathology [Preferred Practice Patterns]. Available at www.asha.org/policy.

Autism Spectrum Disorder

American Speech-Language-Hearing Association. (n.d.). Autism. Available at www.asha.org/Practice-Portal/Clinical-Topics/Autism/.

American Speech-Language-Hearing Association. (2006). Roles and responsibilities of speech-language pathologists in diagnosis, assessment, and treatment of autism spectrum disorders across the life span [Position Statements]. Available at www.asha.org/policy.

American Speech-Language-Hearing Association. (2020). Autism practice portal. Available at: www.asha.org/practice-portal/clinical-topics/autism/.

Ha, S., Sohn, I. J., Kim, N., Sim, H. J., & Cheon, K. A. (2015). Characteristics of brains in autism spectrum disorder: Structure, function and connectivity across the lifespan. Experimental Neurobiology, 24(4), 273–284. Available at https://doi.org/10.5607/en.2015.24.4.273.

Cognitive Aspects of Communication

American Speech-Language-Hearing Association. (1990). Interdisciplinary approaches to brain damage [Position Statements]. Available at www.asha.org/policy.

American Speech-Language-Hearing Association. (2003). Evaluating and treating communication and cognitive disorders: Approaches to referral and collaboration for speech-language pathology and clinical neuropsychology [Technical Reports]. Available at www.asha.org/policy.

American Speech-Language-Hearing Association. (2004). Preferred practice patterns for the profession of speech-language pathology [Preferred Practice Patterns]. Available at www.asha.org/policy.

American Speech-Language-Hearing Association. (2005a). Knowledge and skills needed by speech-language pathologists providing services to individuals with cognitive-communication disorders [Knowledge & Skills]. Available at www.asha.org/ policy.

American Speech-Language-Hearing Association. (2005b). Roles of speech-language pathologists in the identification, diagnosis, and treatment of individuals with cognitive-communication disorders [Position Statements]. Available at www.asha.org/policy.

Deaf and Hard of Hearing

American Speech-Language-Hearing Association. (2004a). Roles of speech-language pathologists and teachers of children who are deaf and hard of hearing in the development of communicative and linguistic competence [Guidelines]. Available at www.asha.org/policy.

American Speech-Language-Hearing Association. (2004b). Roles of speech-language pathologists and teachers of children who are deaf and hard of hearing in the development of communicative and linguistic competence [Position Statements]. Available at www.asha.org/policy.

Dementia

American Speech-Language-Hearing Association. (2005a). The roles of speech-language pathologists working with dementia-based communication disorders [Position Statements]. Available at www.asha.org/policy.

American Speech-Language-Hearing Association. (2005b). The roles of speech-language pathologists working with dementia-based communication disorders [Technical Reports]. Available at www.asha.org/policy.

Early Intervention

American Speech-Language-Hearing Association. (2004). Preferred practice patterns for the profession of speech-language pathology [Preferred Practice Patterns]. Available at www.asha.org/policy.

American Speech-Language-Hearing Association. (2008). Roles and responsibilities of speech-language pathologists in early intervention. [Position Statements, Technical Reports, Guidelines, and Knowledge & Skills].

National Joint Committee on Learning Disabilities. (2006). Learning disabilities and young children: Identification and intervention. Available at www.ldonline.org /article/11511?theme=print.

Fluency

American Speech-Language-Hearing Association. (2004). Preferred practice patterns for the profession of speech-language pathology [Preferred Practice Patterns]. Available at www.asha.org/policy.

Hearing Screening

American Speech-Language-Hearing Association. (n.d.) Adult hearing screening. Available at www.asha.org/Practice -Portal/Professional-Issues/Adult-Hearing-Screening/.

American Speech-Language-Hearing Association. (n.d.) Childhood hearing screening. Available at www.asha.org /PRPSpecificTopic.aspx?folderid=8589935406&section =Key_Issues.

American Speech-Language-Hearing Association. (2004). Preferred practice patterns for the profession of speech-language pathology [Preferred Practice Patterns]. Available at www.asha.org/policy.

American Speech-Language-Hearing Association. (2017). Clinical practice by certificate holders in the profession in which they are not certified [Issues in Ethics]. Available at www.asha .org/Practice/ethics/Clinical-Practice-by-Certificate-Holders -in-the-Profession-in-Which-They-Are-Not-Certified/.

Language and Literacy

American Speech-Language-Hearing Association. (n.d.). Spoken language disorders. Available at www.asha.org /PRPSpecificTopic.aspx?folderid=8589935327&section =Assessment.

American Speech-Language-Hearing Association. (2001). Roles and responsibilities of speech-language pathologists with respect to reading and writing in children and adolescents [Position Statements]. Available at www.asha.org/policy.

American Speech-Language-Hearing Association. (2004). Preferred practice patterns for the profession of speech -language pathology [Preferred Practice Patterns]. Available at www.asha.org/policy.

American Speech-Language-Hearing Association. (2008). Adolescent literacy and older students with learning disabilities [Technical Reports]. Available at www.asha.org/policy/.

Orofacial Myofunctional Disorders

American Speech-Language-Hearing Association. (n.d) Orofacial myofunctiuonal disorders. Available at www.asha .org/PRPSpecificTopic.aspx?folderid=8589943975& section=Treatment.

American Speech-Language-Hearing Association. (2004). Preferred practice patterns for the profession of speech -language pathology [Preferred Practice Patterns]. Available at www.asha.org/policy.

Prevention

American Speech-Language-Hearing Association. (1987). Prevention of communication disorders [Position Statements]. Available at www.asha.org/policy.

American Speech-Language-Hearing Association. (2004). Preferred practice patterns for the profession of speech -language pathology [Preferred Practice Patterns]. Available at www.asha.org/policy.

Severe Disabilities

American Speech-Language-Hearing Association. (2004). Preferred practice patterns for the profession of speech-language pathology [Preferred Practice Patterns]. Available at www.asha.org/policy.

National Joint Committee for the Communication Needs of Persons with Severe Disabilities. (1992). Guidelines for meeting the communication needs of persons with severe disabilities [Guidelines]. Available at https://www.asha .org/policy/GL1992-00201/.

National Joint Committee for the Communication Needs of Persons with Severe Disabilities. (2002). Access to communication services and supports: Concerns regarding the application of restrictive "eligibility" policies [Technical Reports]. Available at www.asha.org/policy.

National Joint Committee for the Communication Needs of Persons with Severe Disabilities. (2003). Access to communication services and supports: Concerns regarding the application of restrictive "eligibility" policies [Position Statements]. Available at www.asha.org/policy.

Social Aspects of Communication

Adams, C., Lockton, E., Freed, J., Gaile, J., Earl, G., McBean, K., Green, J., Vail, A., & Law, J. (2012). The Social Communication Intervention Project: A randomized controlled trial of the effectiveness of speech and language therapy for school-age children who have pragmatic and social communication problems with or without autism spectrum disorder. *International Journal of Language and Communication Disorders, 47*(3), 233–244.

American Psychiatric Association. (2013). *Diagnostic and Statistical Manual of Mental Disorders*, 5th ed.

Swallowing

American Speech-Language-Hearing Association. (n.d.). Adult Dysphagia. Available at www.asha.org/Practice-Portal /Clinical-Topics/Adult-Dysphagia/.

American Speech-Language-Hearing Association. (2001a). Knowledge and skills needed by speech-language pathologists providing services to individuals with swallowing and/or feeding disorders [Knowledge & Skills]. Available at www.asha.org/policy.

American Speech-Language-Hearing Association. (2001b). Knowledge and skills for speech-language pathologists performing endoscopic assessment of swallowing functions [Knowledge & Skills]. Available at www.asha.org/policy.

American Speech-Language-Hearing Association. (2001d). Roles of speech-language pathologists in swallowing and feeding disorders [Technical Reports]. Available at www .asha.org/policy.

American Speech-Language-Hearing Association. (2004a). Guidelines for speech-language pathologists performing videofluoroscopic swallowing studies [Guidelines]. Available at www.asha.org/policy.

American Speech-Language-Hearing Association. (2004b). Knowledge and skills needed by speech-language pathologists performing videofluoroscopic swallowing studies. Available at www.asha.org/policy.

American Speech-Language-Hearing Association. (2004c). Preferred practice patterns for the profession of speech-language pathology [Preferred Practice Patterns]. Available at www.asha.org/policy.

American Speech-Language-Hearing Association. (2004d). Role of the speech-language pathologist in the performance

and interpretation of endoscopic evaluation of swallowing [Guidelines]. Available at www.asha.org/policy.

American Speech-Language-Hearing Association. (2004e). Role of the speech-language pathologist in the performance and interpretation of endoscopic evaluation of swallowing [Position Statements]. Available at www.asha.org/policy.

American Speech-Language-Hearing Association. (2004f). Role of the speech-language pathologist in the performance and interpretation of endoscopic evaluation of swallowing [Technical Reports]. Available at www.asha.org/policy.

American Speech-Language-Hearing Association. (2004g). Speech-language pathologists training and supervising other professionals in the delivery of services to individuals with swallowing and feeding disorders [Technical Reports]. Available at www.asha.org/policy.

Voice and Resonance

American Speech-Language-Hearing Association.(.n.d.) Prosthetic devices for voice, speech, and swallowing. Available at www.asha.org/SLP/clinical/Prosthetic-Devices-Voice-Speech-Swallowing/.

American Speech-Language-Hearing Association. (1998). The roles of otolaryngologists and speech-language pathologists in the performance and interpretation of strobovideolaryngoscopy [Relevant Papers]. Available at www.asha.org/policy.

American Speech-Language-Hearing Association. (2004a). Evaluation and treatment for tracheoesophageal puncture and prosthesis [Technical Reports]. Available at www.asha.org/policy.

American Speech-Language-Hearing Association. (2004b). Knowledge and skills for speech-language pathologists with respect to evaluation and treatment for tracheoesophageal puncture and prosthesis [Knowledge & Skills]. Available at www.asha.org/policy.

American Speech-Language-Hearing Association. (2004c). *Preferred Practice Patterns for the Profession of Speech-Language Pathology* [Preferred Practice Patterns]. Available at www.asha.org/policy.

American Speech-Language-Hearing Association. (2004d). Roles and responsibilities of speech-language pathologists with respect to evaluation and treatment for tracheoesophageal puncture and prosthesis [Position Statements]. Available at www.asha.org/policy.

American Speech-Language-Hearing Association. (2004e). Vocal tract visualization and imaging [Position Statements]. Available at www.asha.org/policy.

American Speech-Language-Hearing Association. (2004f). Vocal tract visualization and imaging [Technical Reports]. Available at www.asha.org/policy.

American Speech-Language-Hearing Association. (2005a). The role of the speech-language pathologist, the teacher of singing, and the speaking voice trainer in voice habilitation [Technical Reports]. Available at www.asha.org/policy.

American Speech-Language-Hearing Association. (2005b). The use of voice therapy in the treatment of dysphonia [Technical Reports]. Available at www.asha.org/policy.

Health Care Services Delivery

American Speech-Language-Hearing Association. (2002). Knowledge and skills in business practices needed by speech-language pathologists in health care settings [Knowledge & Skills]. Available at www.asha.org/policy.

American Speech-Language-Hearing Association. (2004). Knowledge and skills in business practices for speech-language pathologists who are managers and leaders in health care organizations [Knowledge & Skills]. Available at www.asha.org/policy.

Neonatal Intensive Care Unit

American Speech-Language-Hearing Association. (2004a). Knowledge and skills needed by speech-language pathologists providing services to infants and families in the NICU environment [Knowledge & Skills]. Available at www.asha.org/policy.

American Speech-Language-Hearing Association. (2004b). Roles and responsibilities of speech-language pathologists in the neonatal intensive care unit [Guidelines]. Available at www.asha.org/policy.

American Speech-Language-Hearing Association. (2004c). Roles and responsibilities of speech-language pathologists in the neonatal intensive care unit [Position Statements]. Available at www.asha.org/policy.

Telepractice

American Speech-Language-Hearing Association. (n.d.). Telepractice. Available at www.asha.org/Practice-Portal/Professional-Issues/Telepractice/.

American Speech-Language-Hearing Association. (2004). Preferred practice patterns for the profession of speech-language pathology [Preferred Practice Patterns]. Available at www.asha.org/policy/.

School-Based Service Delivery

American Speech-Language-Hearing Association. (2002). A workload analysis approach for establishing speech-language caseload standards in the school [Position Statements]. Available at www.asha.org/policy.

American Speech-Language-Hearing Association. (2010a). Roles and responsibilities of speech-language pathologists in schools. Available at www.asha.org/policy.

American Speech-Language-Hearing Association. (2010b). Working for change: A guide for speech-language pathologists and audiologists in schools. Available at www.asha.org/uploadedFiles/Working-Change-Schools-SLPs-Audiologists-Guide.pdf.

American Speech-Language-Hearing Association. (2020). School-based service delivery in speech-language pathology. Available at: https://www.asha.org/slp/schools/school-based-service-delivery-in-speech-language-pathology/.

McGinty, A., & Justice, L. (2006). Classroom-based versus pull-out interventions: A review of the experimental evidence. *EBP Briefs*, 1, 3–25.

Moore, B. J., & Montgomery, J. K. (2008). *Making a Difference for America's Children: Speech-Language Pathologists in Public Schools*, 2nd ed. Austin, TX: Pro-Ed.

Medicare, Medicaid, and Reimbursement Issues

American Speech-Language-Hearing Association. (n.d.). Billing and reimbursement. Available at www.asha.org/practice/reimbursement/.

Centers for Medicare and Medicaid Services (n.d.). Cms.gov. Available at www.cms.gov/.

Code of Ethics

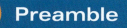

Preamble

The preservation of the highest standards of integrity and ethical principles is vital to the responsible discharge of obligations by speech-language pathologists, audiologists, and speech, language, and hearing scientists. This Code of Ethics sets forth the fundamental principles and rules considered essential to this purpose.

Every individual who is (a) a member of the American Speech-Language-Hearing Association, whether certified or not, (b) a nonmember holding the Certificate of Clinical Competence from the Association, (c) an applicant for membership or certification, or (d) a Clinical Fellow seeking to fulfill standards for certification shall abide by this Code of Ethics.

Any violation of the spirit and purpose of this Code shall be considered unethical. Failure to specify any particular responsibility or practice in this Code of Ethics shall not be construed as denial of the existence of such responsibilities or practices.

The fundamentals of ethical conduct are described by Principles of Ethics and by Rules of Ethics as they relate to the responsibility to persons served, the public, speech-language pathologists, audiologists, and speech, language, and hearing scientists, and to the conduct of research and scholarly activities.

Principles of Ethics, aspirational and inspirational in nature, form the underlying moral basis for the Code of Ethics. Individuals shall observe these principles as affirmative obligations under all conditions of professional activity.

Rules of Ethics are specific statements of minimally acceptable professional conduct or of prohibitions and are applicable to all individuals.

 ## Principle of Ethics I

Individuals shall honor their responsibility to hold paramount the welfare of persons they serve professionally or who are participants in research and scholarly activities, and they shall treat animals involved in research in a humane manner.

Rules of Ethics

A. Individuals shall provide all services competently.

B. Individuals shall use every resource, including referral when appropriate, to ensure that high-quality service is provided.

C. Individuals shall not discriminate in the delivery of professional services or the conduct of research and scholarly activities on the basis of race or ethnicity, gender, gender identity/gender expression, age, religion, national origin, sexual orientation, or disability.

D. Individuals shall not misrepresent the credentials of assistants, technicians, support personnel, students, Clinical Fellows, or any others under their supervision, and they shall inform those they serve professionally of the name and professional credentials of persons providing services.

E. Individuals who hold the Certificate of Clinical Competence shall not delegate tasks that require the unique skills, knowledge, and judgment that are within the scope of their profession to assistants, technicians, support personnel, or any nonprofessionals over whom they have supervisory responsibility.

F. Individuals who hold the Certificate of Clinical Competence may delegate tasks related to provision of clinical services to assistants, technicians, support personnel, or any other persons only if those services are appropriately supervised, realizing that the responsibility for client welfare remains with the certified individual.

G. Individuals who hold the Certificate of Clinical Competence may delegate tasks related to provision of clinical services that require the unique skills, knowledge, and judgment that are within the scope of practice of their profession to students only if those services are appropriately supervised. The responsibility for client welfare remains with the certified individual.

H. Individuals shall fully inform the persons they serve of the nature and possible effects of services rendered and products dispensed, and they shall inform participants in research about the possible effects of their participation in research conducted.

I. Individuals shall evaluate the effectiveness of services rendered and of products dispensed, and they shall provide services or dispense products only when benefit can reasonably be expected.

J. Individuals shall not guarantee the results of any treatment or procedure, directly or by implication; however, they may make a reasonable statement of prognosis.

K. Individuals shall not provide clinical services solely by correspondence.

L. Individuals may practice by telecommunication (e.g., telehealth/e-health), where not prohibited by law.

M. Individuals shall adequately maintain and appropriately secure records of professional services rendered, research and scholarly activities conducted, and products dispensed, and they shall allow access to these records only when authorized or when required by law.

N. Individuals shall not reveal, without authorization, any professional or personal information about identified persons served professionally or identified participants involved in research and scholarly activities unless doing so is necessary to protect the welfare of the person or of the community or is otherwise required by law.

O. Individuals shall not charge for services not rendered, nor shall they misrepresent services rendered, products dispensed, or research and scholarly activities conducted.

P. Individuals shall enroll and include persons as participants in research or teaching demonstrations only if their participation is voluntary, without coercion, and with their informed consent.

Q. Individuals whose professional services are adversely affected by substance abuse or other health-related conditions shall seek professional assistance and, where appropriate, withdraw from the affected areas of practice.

R. Individuals shall not discontinue service to those they are serving without providing reasonable notice.

Principle of Ethics II

Individuals shall honor their responsibility to achieve and maintain the highest level of professional competence and performance.

Rules of Ethics

A. Individuals shall engage in only those aspects of the professions that are within the scope of their professional practice and competence, considering their level of education, training, and experience.

B. Individuals shall engage in lifelong learning to maintain and enhance professional competence and performance.

C. Individuals shall not require or permit their professional staff to provide services or conduct research activities that exceed the staff member's competence, level of education, training, and experience.

D. Individuals shall ensure that all equipment used to provide services or to conduct research and scholarly activities is in proper working order and is properly calibrated.

Principle of Ethics III

Individuals shall honor their responsibility to the public by promoting public understanding of the professions, by supporting the development of services designed to fulfill the unmet needs of the public, and by providing accurate information in all communications involving any aspect of the professions, including the dissemination of research findings and scholarly activities, and the promotion, marketing, and advertising of products and services.

Rules of Ethics

A. Individuals shall not misrepresent their credentials, competence, education, training, experience, or scholarly or research contributions.

B. Individuals shall not participate in professional activities that constitute a conflict of interest.

C. Individuals shall refer those served professionally solely on the basis of the interest of those being referred and not on any personal interest, financial or otherwise.

D. Individuals shall not misrepresent research, diagnostic information, services rendered, results of services rendered, products dispensed, or the effects of products dispensed.

E. Individuals shall not defraud or engage in any scheme to defraud in connection with obtaining payment, reimbursement, or grants for services rendered, research conducted, or products dispensed.

F. Individuals' statements to the public shall provide accurate information about the nature and management of communication disorders, about the professions, about professional services, about products for sale, and about research and scholarly activities.

G. Individuals' statements to the public when advertising, announcing, and marketing their professional services; reporting research results; and promoting products shall adhere to professional standards and shall not contain misrepresentations.

Principle of Ethics IV

Individuals shall honor their responsibilities to the professions and their relationships with colleagues, students, and members of other professions and disciplines.

Rules of Ethics

A. Individuals shall uphold the dignity and autonomy of the professions, maintain harmonious interprofessional and intraprofessional relationships, and accept the professions' self-imposed standards.

B. Individuals shall prohibit anyone under their supervision from engaging in any practice that violates the Code of Ethics.

C. Individuals shall not engage in dishonesty, fraud, deceit, or misrepresentation.

D. Individuals shall not engage in any form of unlawful harassment, including sexual harassment or power abuse.

E. Individuals shall not engage in any other form of conduct that adversely reflects on the professions or on the individual's fitness to serve persons professionally.

F. Individuals shall not engage in sexual activities with clients, students, or research participants over whom they exercise professional authority or power.

G. Individuals shall assign credit only to those who have contributed to a publication, presentation, or product. Credit shall be assigned in proportion to the contribution and only with the contributor's consent.

H. Individuals shall reference the source when using other persons' ideas, research, presentations, or products in written, oral, or any other media presentation or summary.

I. Individuals' statements to colleagues about professional services, research results, and products shall adhere to prevailing professional standards and shall contain no misrepresentations.

J. Individuals shall not provide professional services without exercising independent professional judgment, regardless of referral source or prescription.

K. Individuals shall not discriminate in their relationships with colleagues, students, and members of other professions and disciplines on the basis of race or ethnicity, gender, gender identity/gender expression, age, religion, national origin, sexual orientation, or disability.

L. Individuals shall not file or encourage others to file complaints that disregard or ignore facts that would disprove the allegation, nor should the Code of Ethics be used for personal reprisal, as a means of addressing personal animosity, or as a vehicle for retaliation.

M. Individuals who have reason to believe that the Code of Ethics has been violated shall inform the Board of Ethics.

N. Individuals shall comply fully with the policies of the Board of Ethics in its consideration and adjudication of complaints of violations of the Code of Ethics.

Review Questions

1. What is the professional organization for speech-language pathologists (SLPs) and audiologists that develops standards of practice for both disciplines?

   a. American Speech Correction Association.
   b. American Speech-Language-Hearing Association.
   c. American Speech and Hearing Association.
   d. American Communication and Swallowing Association.

2. Which division of ASHA administers the certificate of clinical competence (CCC)?

   a. Council for Clinical Certification (CFCC).
   b. Council for Academic Accreditation (CAA).
   c. Board of directors (BOD).
   d. Officer-committee board (OCB).

3. How many "big" areas of practice make up the speech-language pathology scope of practice?

   a. 5.
   b. 7.
   c. 9.
   d. 11.

4. In what area of language must SLPs be knowledgeable in?

   a. Respiration.
   b. Morphology.
   c. Orofacial myofunction.
   d. Challenging behaviors.

5. Which of the following is a legal requirement that most SLPs must attain?

   a. The certificate of clinical competence (CCC-SLP).
   b. A passing Praxis score.
   c. State licensure.
   d. Advanced specialty credentialing.

6. What are ASHA special interest groups?

   a. Groups within ASHA that are targeted at raising awareness of SLP practice.
   b. Groups within ASHA that are targeted at raising awareness of benefits of certification.
   c. Groups within ASHA that establish standards for use of evidence-based practice.
   d. Groups within ASHA that engage members in fostering the interchange of information among affiliates who share common professional interests.

7. Which philosophical concept asks what action will do the most good and least harm?

    a. Utilitarian approach.
    b. Rights approach.
    c. Fairness/justice approach.
    d. Virtue approach.

8. Which philosophical concept considers whether people are treated equally or proportionally?

    a. Utilitarian approach.
    b. Rights approach.
    c. Fairness/justice approach.
    d. Virtue approach.

9. Which philosophical concept considers whether an individual acts as the type of person they would like to be?

    a. Utilitarian approach.
    b. Rights approach.
    c. Fairness/justice approach.
    d. Virtue approach.

10. Which philosophical concept considers the action that best respects the rights of all stakeholders?

    a. Utilitarian approach.
    b. Rights approach.
    c. Fairness/justice approach.
    d. Virtue approach.

11. What are the three components of the ASHA Code of Ethics?

    a. Preamble, Rules, Regulations.
    b. Preamble, Principles, Rules.
    c. Rules, Regulations, Principles.
    d. Preamble, Rules, Stipulations.

12. What type of sanction is delivered privately to a person who has made a minor or inadvertent violation?

    a. Censure.
    b. Revocation.
    c. Reprimand.
    d. Suspension.

13. What type of sanction involves repealing membership and certification for some amount of time, in response to a serious violation?

    a. Reprimand.
    b. Revocation.
    c. Warning.
    d. Suspension.

14. What type of sanction involves suspending a clinical fellow's ability to apply for the certificate of clinical competence?

    a. Reprimand.
    b. Suspension.
    c. Withholding.
    d. Cease and desist.

15. What is a multidisciplinary service delivery model?
   a. When a client is seen by multiple professionals who communicate with each other regarding treatment and share information about overall status.
   b. When a client is seen by multiple professionals with some communication between disciplines in regard to referral and follow-up.
   c. When professionals cooperate in the assessment and treatment of a client in a more natural environment.
   d. When a client is seen by a single professional for assessment and treatment of a particular medical condition.

16. What is an interdisciplinary service delivery model?
   a. When a client is seen by multiple professionals who communicate with each other regarding treatment and share information about overall status.
   b. When a client is seen by multiple professionals with some communication between disciplines in regard to referral and follow-up.
   c. When professionals cooperate in the assessment and treatment of a client in a more natural environment.
   d. When a client is seen by a single professional for assessment and treatment of a particular medical condition.

17. What is a transdisciplinary service delivery model?
   a. When a client is seen by multiple professionals who communicate with each other regarding treatment and share information about overall status.
   b. When a client is seen by multiple professionals with some communication between disciplines in regard to referral and follow-up.
   c. When professionals cooperate in the assessment and treatment of a client in a more natural environment.
   d. When a client is seen by a single professional for assessment and treatment of a particular medical condition.

18. What is the role of an SLP in a medical setting?
   a. Assessment and treatment of disorders of swallowing and communication as a result of an underlying medical condition.
   b. Identification, evaluation, and determination of eligible children for receiving speech and language services.
   c. Developmental screening of infants and toddlers.
   d. Billing insurance for services rendered.

19. What is the role of an SLP in a school-based setting?
   a. Assessment and treatment of disorders of swallowing and communication as a result of an underlying medical condition.
   b. Identification, evaluation, and determination of eligible children for receiving speech and language services.
   c. Developmental screening of infants and toddlers.
   d. Billing insurance for services rendered.

20. What is the role of an SLP in an early intervention setting?
   a. Assessment and treatment of disorders of swallowing and communication as a result of an underlying medical condition.
   b. Identification, evaluation, and determination of eligible children for receiving speech and language services.
   c. Developmental screening of infants and toddlers.
   d. Billing insurance for services rendered.

SECTION II

Developmental Communication Disorders

7

Speech Sound Disorders in Children

GREGORY L. LOF, PhD
MAGGIE WATSON, PhD

(f) How would you estimate the child's level of severity?

(g) What is the child's reaction to not being understood?

2. Gather information from other professionals who may have provided services to the client.
   a. Teachers.
   b. Physicians.
   c. Other therapists.

3. Conduct an oral interview with caregivers and other professionals.
   a. Obtain additional information from the caregiver(s).
   b. Clarify written case history information.
   c. Provide information to the caregiver(s) about the assessment procedures.

4. Perform a hearing screening.
   a. To determine if the client may have a hearing loss and is in need of further hearing testing.
   b. Typically screened at frequencies of 500; 1,000; 2,000; and 4,000 Hz at 20 or 25 dB.
   c. Those failing the hearing screening should be referred for a full audiological evaluation.

5. Use standardized measures of speech sound production abilities.
   a. Characteristics of standardized tests.
      (1) Most often elicit sound productions from a single word using picture stimuli.
      (2) Most consonants elicited across word positions (initial, medial, final) at least once, with vowels and consonant clusters minimally evaluated.
      (3) Allow for recording of omissions, substitutions, distortions, and additions, as well as any patterns of error productions.
      (4) Most generate a standard score and percentile ranking.
      (5) Some have standardized stimulability assessment.
   b. Scoring.
      (1) Correct productions and errors are noted. Typically use broad phonetic transcription.
      (2) Types of errors include omissions, substitutions, distortions, and additions.
   c. Concerns.
      (1) Single-word responses are not representational of the child's speech sound system, especially in conversational speech.
      (2) Tests do not provide in-depth information about the child's sound system.
      (3) Speech sounds are assessed in limited phonetic contexts.
      (4) Often vowels and consonant clusters are not adequately sampled.

6. Collect a connected speech sample of at least 80–100 different words.
   a. More representative of natural speaking abilities.
   b. The data can be analyzed using independent and relational analysis (see next section for procedures).

c. Can yield suprasegmental information.
d. Concerns.
   (1) Transcription and analysis is often laborious.
   (2) Difficult to transcribe the targets from highly unintelligible speakers.
   (3) Analysis results do not yield a standard score.
   (4) Low frequency/infrequently used sounds may not be attempted during the sample.

7. Examine the oral-motor system.
   a. Purpose of examination.
      (1) Determine the structural integrity of the speech mechanism.
      (2) Determine the functional integrity of the speech mechanism.
   b. Synonymous terms for this examination.
      (1) Oral mechanism examination.
      (2) Oral peripheral examination.
      (3) Oral facial examination.
      (4) Oral motor examination.
   c. Structural integrity of the various articulators.
      (1) Dentition.
         (a) Occlusion patterns of the teeth (normal, overbite, underbite).
         (b) Overall structure.
      (2) Tongue.
         (a) Ankyloglossia: restricted lingual frenum (tongue tied).
         (b) Size (macroglossia: too large a tongue; microglossia: too small a tongue).
      (3) Hard and soft palate.
      (4) Lips.
      (5) Face, nose, mouth symmetry.
   d. Movement of lips, mandible, tongue, and velum using both speech (e.g., the production of syllables) and nonspeech (e.g., moving tongue back and forth) tasks.
   e. Measure diadochokinesis (DDK), or rate of repetition of syllables.
      (1) Also called *alternating motion rates* (AMRs) or *sequential motion rates* (SMRs).
      (2) Includes repetition of identical syllables (/pʌpʌ/) and different syllables (/pʌtʌkʌ/).
      (3) Limited data are available for comparison of DDK rates for children.
      (4) Movements are examined for rate, accuracy, and ease or smoothness.
   f. Medical issues such as enlarged tonsils, health of teeth and gums, and so on, may also be discerned.

8. Assess stimulability of sounds in error.
   a. Should be conducted once erred sounds are determined through other testing.
   b. Involves the use of a variety of cues to help the client achieve correct production; typical cue is to focus on "listen and watch."
   c. Can be used for prognostic information and determining treatment targets.

(1) Generally, high stimulability is associated with a positive prognosis with and without treatment.

(2) Sounds that are stimulable may be more easily remediated than sounds with little or no stimulability.

(3) Targeting unstimulable sounds in intervention may lead to generalization to erred sounds not receiving treatment.

d. Stimulability methods.

(1) Providing auditory and visual cues related to production in isolation or syllable level.

(2) Usually sitting across from child, emphasizing the cues of "listen and watch" as examiner produces the stimuli.

(3) Describing how to produce the speech sound(s).

(4) Varying phonetic contexts to facilitate correct production.

(5) Providing direct stimulation of the articulators or providing placement cueing.

9. Assess phonological and phonemic awareness skills.

a. Assesses the awareness of the phonological structure of language.

b. Phonemic awareness, a component of phonological awareness, is the ability to understand that words are comprised of individual sounds and is crucial for the development of early word decoding.

c. Children with phonological impairment are at risk for the lack of development of phonemic awareness skills, especially if other language problems exist.

d. Phonemic awareness skills may be assessed with a standardized test or informally.

e. See Chapter 10 on written language disorders for more information.

10. Determine intelligibility level.

a. An overall impression or rating of how well the clinician understands the child.

b. Information from standardized tests are not a good indicator of intelligibility.

c. Intelligibility can be a primary determination of need for therapy.

d. Three ways to determine intelligibility level.

(1) Simple tally.

(a) Count the number of words that were understood and the number of words not understood during a 100-word conversational sample.

(b) This method probably has poor validity in determining actual intelligibility level.

(2) Scaling procedure.

(a) Asks listeners to rate intelligibility along a continuum (e.g., 1–10; unintelligible–somewhat intelligible–intelligible).

(b) Quick and easy to complete.

(c) Can be determined by different listeners who are familiar and unfamiliar with the child's speech.

(d) May be inaccurate and have poor reliability across listeners.

(3) Item identification procedure.

(a) The child speaking a set of known words or phrases is presented to a listener who writes down what he/she thinks the child said.

(b) Scored as a percentage of the number of times there was a match.

(c) Can be time-consuming to gather the child's speech and then have listener write down what is heard.

(d) Can be an accurate estimation of intelligibility.

(e) Can be used over time to determine progress in therapy.

11. Determine severity.

a. Some standardized articulation tests have a severity index.

b. PCC can be used as a severity metric.

(1) Examiner makes correct/incorrect judgments about the accuracy of individual sounds produced.

(2) Data can be obtained from an articulation test or conversational speech sample.

(3) Simple calculation comparing correct consonant productions out of all the consonants (correct and incorrect) produced.

(4) Determines a severity level based on percentage of correctly produced consonants.

(a) <50% is severe.

(b) 50%–65% is moderate/severe.

(c) 65%–85% is mild/moderate.

(d) 85%–95% is mild.

12. Assess language and other communication skills.

a. See other chapters in this book for details.

13. Assess speech discrimination skills.

a. Assess the client's ability to determine correct versus incorrect productions of erred sounds.

b. Locke's procedure (i.e., Locke's SPPT procedure) is often used for this discrimination task.

Using the Assessment Data

1. Analysis of productions.

a. Relational analysis procedures compare the client's productions to the adult standard productions.

(1) Percentage consonants correct (PCC) (see previous section).

(2) Error patterns.

(a) Place-manner-voicing (PVM) displays production abilities within the broad categories of place, manner, and voicing characteristics of phonemes.

(b) Distinctive feature analysis categorizes children's productions and errors according to distinctive features that are present.

(c) Phonological processes analysis (also called Phonological Error Patterns Analysis) typically uses the error pattern categories (see Table 7-16).

(3) Traditional analysis.

(a) Records errors as omissions, substitutions, additions, and distortions.

(b) Most useful for those who have few speech errors that are not phonologically based.

(c) Typically uses a standardized articulation test that provides a standard score and percentile ranking, which may be important for qualifying clients for intervention services across a number of settings.

b. Independent analysis procedures examine the child's speech sound production skills without comparison to the adult model.

(1) Phonetic inventory (PI) determines which consonants and vowels the client produced without considering correct versus incorrect productions.

(a) Sounds produced only once or twice are typically not included in the inventory or are considered "marginal."

(b) Typically organized by manner and place of production, as well as by word and/or syllable position.

(c) Can be used to determine production strengths and weaknesses.

(2) Analysis of use of words and syllable shapes.

(a) Provides a tally of the client's production of syllable types and how syllables are used to form words.

(b) Can be used to determine syllabic strengths and weaknesses and syllable constraints.

2. Determine a diagnosis of speech sound disorder.

a. Interpretation of standardized scores and percentile ranks to determine if the client is eligible for speech intervention services using predetermined eligibility criteria.

b. Compare results to information provided by speech sound developmental charts to determine age-appropriateness of production skills.

c. Determine if phonological error patterns are age appropriate and contributing to unintelligibility.

d. Determine that errors are not related to use of a dialect or influence of other languages.

3. Nature of the disorder.

a. Characteristics of articulation disorders.

(1) Few errors and a pattern of error(s) cannot be discerned.

(2) Sound errors are related to some type of structural or functional problem.

(3) Client does not have problems with the phonological rules of language.

b. Characteristics of phonological disorders.

(1) Many errors and pattern(s) of errors can be discerned.

(2) Highly unintelligible.

(3) Limited production of word and syllable shapes.

(4) Limited phonetic inventory.

(5) Client has difficulty using the phonological rules of language.

4. Analysis and interpretation of prognostic variables.

a. A prognosis speculates clients' ability to benefit from treatment based on a variety of variables.

(1) Severity: poorer prognosis associated with severity.

(2) Chronological age: better prognosis associated with intervention at earlier ages.

(3) Motivation: better prognosis associated with higher motivation.

(4) Inconsistent errors: speech sounds produced correctly some of the time may not need to be treated or may be remediated quickly.

(5) Stimulability: if stimulable for a sound, more likely to master the sound with no or limited therapy.

(6) Attention: lack of focus and inattention associated with poorer performance.

(7) Family support: strong family support associated with better performance.

5. Considerations for assessing clients who are culturally and linguistically diverse.

a. Essential information when assessing a nonnative English speaker or a speaker of multiple languages.

(1) Characteristics of the client's primary (or first) language that are different from other spoken languages.

(2) Determine if and how the first language may be influencing acquisition of the second language.

(3) Determine if the client demonstrates a speech sound disorder in both languages.

b. Types of phonological errors often related to second language learning.

(1) Underdifferentiation of phonemes (i.e., not differentiating phonemes in the second language if they are not differentiated in the first language).

(2) Overdifferentiation of phonemes (i.e., producing allophonic variations of a phoneme in the second language as two separate phonemes if those variations are two separate phonemes in the first language).

(3) Substitution of phonemes (i.e., substituting a phoneme from one language for one in the other language, especially if the phonemes share similar characteristics).

(4) Omission of phonemes (i.e., a phoneme from the second language may be omitted if it is not a part of the first language).

c. Theoretical positions on second language acquisition and phonology.
  (1) Two separate phonological systems (differentiated) or one phonological system (undifferentiated).
    (a) This debate is most applicable to speakers who acquire a second language simultaneously.
    (b) Speakers who acquire a second language after the establishment of a first language probably maintain differentiated phonological systems.
  (2) Critical age for second language acquisition and phonological development.
    (a) Critical age for second language acquisition and development of "native-like" phonological skills not established.
    (b) Generally, research shows that native-like phonological skills for second language acquisition is associated with age.

    (c) Propensity of native-like phonological skills for second language acquisition is influenced by numerous variables, including biological, environmental, instructional, and motivational.
d. Intervention considerations.
  (1) Culturally and linguistically diverse children do not require unique treatment approaches.
  (2) Treatment targets should consider characteristics of first and second language and what will improve intelligibility in the client's primary language the most.

Childhood Apraxia of Speech (CAS)

1. Distinguishing between CAS, dysarthria, and SSD (Table 7-17).
2. See Chapter 14 on motor speech disorders in this book.

Table 7-17

Differentiating between CAS, Dysarthria, and SSD

CAS	DYSARTHRIA	SPEECH SOUND DISORDER
No weakness, incoordination, or paralysis of speech musculature.	Decreased strength and coordination or speech musculature that leads to imprecise speech production, slurring, and distortions.	No weakness, incoordination, or paralysis of speech musculature.
No difficulty with involuntary motor control for chewing, swallowing, and so on, unless there is also oral apraxia.	Difficulty with involuntary motor control for chewing, swallowing, and so on, due to muscle weakness and incoordination.	No difficulty with involuntary control for chewing and swallowing.
Inconsistencies in articulation performance—the same word may be produced several different ways.	Articulation may be noticeably "different" due to imprecision, but errors generally consistent.	Consistent errors that can usually be grouped into categories (fronting, stopping, etc.).
Errors include substitutions, omissions, additions, and repetitions; frequently includes simplification of word forms. Tendency for omissions in initial position. Tendency to centralize vowels to /ə/.	Errors are generally distortions.	Errors may include substitutions, omissions, distortions, and so on. Omissions in final position more likely than initial position. Vowel distortions not as common.
Number of errors increases as length of word/phrase increases.	May be less precise in connected speech than in single words.	Errors are generally consistent as length of words/phrases increases.
Well-rehearsed, "automatic" speech is easiest to produce; "on demand" speech most difficult.	No difference in how easily speech is produced based on situation.	No difference in how easily speech is produced based on situation.
Receptive language skills are usually significantly better than expressive skills.	Typically no significant discrepancy between receptive and expressive language skills.	Sometimes difference between receptive and expressive language skills.
Rate, rhythm, and stress of speech are disrupted; some groping for placement may be noted.	Rate, rhythm, and stress are disrupted in ways specifically related to the type of dysarthria (spastic, flaccid, etc.).	Typically no disruption of rate, rhythm, or stress.
Generally good control of pitch and loudness; may have limited inflectional range for speaking.	Monotone voice, difficulty controlling pitch and loudness.	Good control of pitch and loudness; not limited in inflectional range for speaking.
Age-appropriate voice quality.	Voice quality may be hoarse, harsh, hypernasal, and so on, depending on type of dysarthria.	Age-appropriate voice quality.

Determining Goals and Objectives

1. Long-term goals target broad communication behaviors that may take a relatively long time to achieve such as:
   a. Increased intelligibility to a specific level.
   b. Age-appropriate use of speech sounds.
2. Short-term goals that target specific phonological and articulation abilities, such as:
   a. Increased use of specific speech sounds.
   b. Reduced use of specific error patterns.
3. General factors to consider when choosing treatment objectives.
   a. Targets that will make a significant impact on overall communication abilities.
   b. Targets that will be used and reinforced in the natural environment.
   c. Targets that will allow the client to further develop communication skills.
   d. Targets that are considered culturally and linguistically appropriate.
   e. Targets that facilitate the development of literacy skills.
4. Specific factors to consider for choosing targets in intervention.
   a. Age of child and age appropriateness of error(s).
      (1) Use normative data.
         (a) Choose speech sounds that are considered age appropriate.
            • Belief that speech sounds develop in sequence.
            • Acquisition of speech sounds becomes more complex with age.
            • Earlier developing speech sounds considered easier to produce.
         (b) Choose speech sounds that are considered developmentally complex.
            • Belief that by targeting more complex sounds, less complex sounds will generalize without intervention.
      (2) Problems with using developmental norms for choosing intervention targets.
         (a) Great deal of variability in development across children.
         (b) Conflicting evidence on when speech sounds are considered to be developed.
         (c) Not certain that children with SSD acquire speech sound skills in the same way and in the same time frame as typically developing children.
         (d) Confusing developmental mastery with therapy appropriateness.
   b. Effect on intelligibility: error type.
      (1) Choose sounds that have the greatest impact on intelligibility based on type of error.
         (a) Deleted sounds have the greater impact on intelligibility.
         (b) Substitutions have the next greatest impact.
         (c) Other error types (additions and distortions) affect intelligibility much less.
   c. Effect on intelligibility: deviancy.
      (1) Choose targets that have the greatest impact on intelligibility based on unusual error types.
         (a) Patterns that are deviant, unusual, or idiosyncratic to the child affect intelligibility the most and should be primary targets.
         (b) For example: backing, voicing, deleting initial consonants, sound preferences.
   d. Stimulability.
      (1) Stimulable speech sounds may indicate that the child will acquire the sounds without treatment.
      (2) Not stimulable sounds indicate that the child is not likely to improve without intervention.
         (a) Some research has shown greater generalization than for the remediation of stimulable sounds.
         (b) Stimulable sounds may improve without direct intervention as a result of targeting nonstimulable sounds.
   e. Frequency of sound occurrence in the language.
      (1) Sounds that occur most frequently should be targeted first.
      (2) See Table 7-18 for a listing of the order of the most frequently used sounds.
   f. Homonymy.
      (1) This is the production of one phonetic form for several adult forms.
      (2) Excessive homonymy has negative implications for intelligibility.
      (3) For example: the child produces [bi] for the words beach, beat, beak, bike.
   g. Markedness.
      (1) In phonology, some aspects are more common (or natural) than others, so they are unmarked or "unremarkable."
      (2) The sounds that have more features are considered more marked.
      (3) Targeting marked (versus unmarked) sounds can lead to better generalization.
         (a) Remediating unmarked sounds will aid in improvements to that targeted sound.
         (b) Remediating the marked sound will cause improvements in the marked sound, and the unmarked sound may not need to be worked on in therapy.
      (4) See Table 7-19 for examples of markedness.
   h. Morphological status of speech sound errors.
      (1) Important for children with both SSD and language problems.
      (2) Evaluate and target the tense markers and language structures that mark agreement.

Table 7-18

Most Frequently Used Sounds

ORDER	SOUND
1	n
2	t
3	s
4	r
5	l
6	d
7	ð
8	k
9	m
10	w
11	z
12	b
13	p
14	v
15	f
16	h
17	g
18	j
19	ŋ
20	θ
21	dʒ
22	ʃ
23	tʃ
24	ʒ

Table 7-19

Examples of Markedness Features

MORE MARKED	LESS MARKED
Fricatives	Stops
Affricates	Fricatives
Clusters	Singletons
Voiced	Voiceless

Table 7-20

Examples of Morphological Markers with Complex Endings

MORPHOLOGICAL STATUS	EXAMPLE
Present progressive	barking
Regular plural	dogs
Possessive	baby's
Regular past	jumped
Regular third person	she eats
Contractable copula	he's the baby
Contractable auxiliary	she's going slow

    i. Phonetic inventory.
      (1) Determine the presence and absence of sounds produced.
      (2) If nearly complete inventory, need to make this inventory more usable in the child's phonological system.
      (3) If sounds missing from the inventory, need to provide therapy to add to the sound repertoire.
    j. Relevancy to the child.
      (1) Select sounds/patterns that are important to the child.
      (2) For example, if the child's name is Sue but she pronounces it as "too," then the /s/ is an important and relevant sound to target.

    (3) Targeting these complex final clusters can enhance productions through generalization.
    (4) See Table 7-20 for examples of morphological markers with complex endings.

Treatment of Speech Sound Disorders

Selecting Intervention Targets

1. Target selection follows a complete assessment.
2. Generalization.
    a. Intervention targets should be chosen to achieve "in-class" and "across-class" generalization.
      (1) "In-class" generalization involves skills generalizing to untreated sounds within the same sound class (e.g., working on /s/ generalizes to other fricatives).
      (2) "Across-class" generalization involves skills generalizing to untreated sounds in different sound classes.
    b. Complexity and generalization.
      (1) Choosing targets that are not complex, are inconsistently in error, and are highly stimulable

may produce early success in intervention but not in widespread generalization.

(2) Choosing targets that are complex, are consistently in error, and are not stimulable may result in more widespread generalization.

3. There are two broad methods for choosing targets.
   a. Developmental approach.
      (1) Uses the sequence of normal development of speech sounds for choosing targets that would be developmentally appropriate.
   b. Complexity approach.
      (1) Involves choosing intervention targets that are complex relative to the client's abilities.
      (2) Where the speech sound is on the developmental chart is not important.

4. Clinicians may choose to target individual phonemes or groups of phonemes, or to reduce the client's use of error patterns (i.e., phonological processes).

5. Target phonemes of which the client has the least productive phonological knowledge (PPK).
   a. Children's productions of phonemes are ranked on a six-point continuum from "most knowledgeable" (i.e., always accurately produced) to "least knowledgeable" (i.e., sounds not in the client's inventory).
   b. Some research has shown that targeting sounds with the least PPK results in more widespread generalization.

6. Considerations for choosing targets for bilingual speakers.
   a. Target errors that are demonstrated with similar frequency in both languages.
      (1) Typically, these targets will make an impact on the client's speaking skills in both languages.
   b. After targeting errors that have equal frequency in both languages, target errors that are exhibited with unequal frequency in both languages.
   c. Next, target errors demonstrated in only one language.

7. Number of sounds or patterns to teach.
   a. *Goal attack strategy* is the term used to organize intervention to improve speech skills.
      (1) Horizontal goal attack strategy is where several sounds or sound error patterns are taught in sequence.
      (2) Vertical goal attack strategy is where each sound is targeted until a specific level of correct sound production is achieved.
   b. Some research has examined the efficacy of targeting a single error or multiple errors.
      (1) Targeting two erred sounds using a minimal pair format produced greater improvement than targeting one erred sound.

8. Learnability theory.
   a. Providing children with complex input has been shown to assist learning.

b. Exposure to more complex language pushes children to learn and use more complex structures.

c. Exposure to complexity gives children the opportunity to detect and change their own phonological errors.

d. Following learnability theory, targeting complex phonological targets predicts the greatest amount of change in the children's sound system.

Intervention Approaches

1. Variables to consider when choosing an intervention approach.
   a. Phonetic vs. phonemic errors.
      (1) Phonetic errors tend to be consistent errors and are attributed to faulty motor learning.
         (a) Intervention emphasizes helping the client learn how to produce individual speech sounds that are in error.
         (b) These are typically considered to be "articulation" therapy approaches.
      (2) Phonemic errors tend to involve groups of sounds or sound sequences.
         (a) Intervention emphasizes helping the client learn how speech sounds function in language to signal meaning.
         (b) These are typically considered to be phonological approaches.
         (c) Clients with phonemic errors are often described as having reduced phonological contrasts.
         (d) This lack of contrast often results in the production of homonyms (e.g., saying "tu" for a number of words, such as *shoe*, *sue*, and *two*).
         (e) The errors are usually described by a phonological rule/pattern/process.
   b. Client variables to consider.
      (1) Stimulability skills.
      (2) Ability to self-monitor.
      (3) Attention, effort, and motivation.
      (4) Cognitive skills.
      (5) Linguistic skills.
      (6) Oral motor skills.
      (7) Hearing acuity.
      (8) Age.

2. Intervention approaches for phonetic errors (articulatory based approaches).
   a. These approaches tend to treat speech sounds individually (vertical approach), and a specific therapeutic sequence is often followed, then gradually increased in complexity.
   b. Emphasis of intervention is placement and movement of the articulators.

Van Riper Traditional Approach
Hierarchical progression

Sensory-Motor Approach
Productions in syllables

Multiple Phoneme Approach
Therapy aimed at correcting multiple sound errors at once

Paired Stimuli Approach
Use key words to facilitate productions

Enhanced Stimulability Approach
Moving from nonstimulalbe to stimulable sounds

Figure 7-4   **Five Approaches for Articulation Therapy**

c. Typical phonetic techniques and strategies used in intervention.
 (1) Visual and auditory cues.
 (2) Description of articulator movements.
 (3) Providing a metaphor (i.e., the /s/ sound is called the "silly snake sound").
 (4) Shaping from other sounds.
 (5) Encouraging self-monitoring and evaluation.
 (6) Use of motor learning principles.
  (a) Repetition of the target in syllables, then gradually increasing phonetic complexity.
  (b) Early in treatment, using block practice and then later using random practice.
  (c) As accuracy improves, increasing specific feedback.
  (d) Over time, reducing extrinsic feedback.
d. Specific phonetic approaches (Fig. 7-4).
 (1) Van Riper (traditional) approach.
  (a) General therapy sequence of intervention.
   • Sensory-perceptual training (ear training): the client is trained to distinguish the "target" phoneme from other speech sounds.
   • The client is not asked to produce the target yet, and this step may proceed in the following stages:
    – Identification of the clinician's production of the target versus other sounds (this is done using isolation sound productions that may exaggerate certain aspects of the target).
    – Isolation involves having the client indicate every time the clinician produces the target in a variety of words and contexts.
    – In the stimulation stage, the clinician bombards the client with production of the target sound, and those productions will vary in loudness and rate and can include listening to audio productions by different speakers (the client will also identify when the target is produced).
    – In the discrimination stage, the clinician produces both the correct production of the target and the client's error in a variety of contexts (the client identifies the erred phoneme and may also tell the clinician how to correct the error).
  (b) Elicit and establish the sound in isolation or at syllable level using a variety of sound establishment techniques (Fig 7-5).
   • Imitating verbal models.
   • Following visual cues.
   • Telling the client where to put the articulators.
   • Shaping the new sound from a sound the child can produce (e.g., using /s/ to shape /ʃ/).
   • Using phonetic context of known sounds to stimulate the new sound (e.g., having the client attempt /s/ in the context of /ts/ syllable endings).
  (c) Sound stabilization (Fig. 7-6).
   • A gradual increase of the phonetic complexity in which the client can successfully produce the target (proceeds in the following stages):
    – Isolation.
    – Nonsense syllables.
    – Words that systematically vary where the target is located, including position (initial, intervocalic, final), number of syllables, clusters (initial, intervocalic, final).
    – Phrases, which may begin with carry phrases.

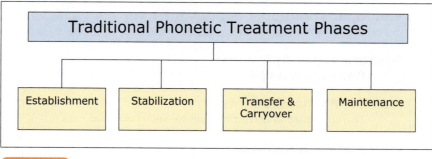

Figure 7-5 **Phases of Traditional Phonetic Treatment Approaches**

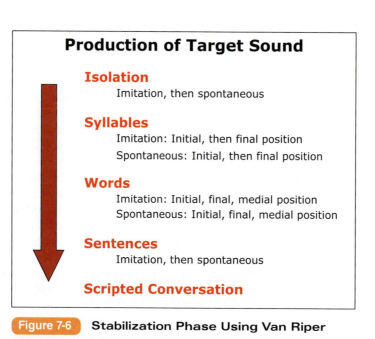

Figure 7-6 **Stabilization Phase Using Van Riper Traditional Hierarchy Approach**

– Sentences that gradually increase in length and complexity.
– Conversation (structured and unstructured).
(d) Transfer and carryover.
  • Also referred to as *generalization*.
  • Emphasis on correct sound production outside the clinical setting with a variety of communication partners.
(e) Maintenance.
  • The clinician may schedule follow-up sessions or interview others to ensure the child is maintaining the target.
(2) Sensory-motor approach.
  (a) Stresses the production of bisyllable units.
  (b) Key concepts.
    • Using facilitative phonetic contexts.
    • Gradual and systematic change of production units.

(c) Begins with the production within a phonetic context in which the target is produced correctly (i.e., a facilitative phonetic context).
(d) Intervention proceeds across various phases.
  • Production of bisyllables consisting of phonemes not in error.
    – Production varies in terms of loudness, rate, and intonation patterns.
    – Production characteristics of different types of sounds are compared and contrasted.
  • Initially, production of the target sound in facilitating phonetic contexts is practiced (i.e., bisyllabic productions).
  • Gradual and systematic expansion of the phonetic contexts in which the client can produce the target successfully.

(3) Multiple phoneme approach.
  (a) Developed for children with multiple phoneme errors.
  (b) Simultaneous instruction on erred phonemes; a client may be at a different phase or step for each erred phoneme.
  (c) A highly structured approach with guidelines for number and type of stimuli to evoke correct productions, strict criteria for advancing to subsequent steps and phases of the program, type of stimuli, and reinforcement schedule.
  (d) Consists of three phases, with substeps within each phase.
    • Establishment phase.
      – Correct production in isolation.
      – Productions are elicited by using graphemes.
      – Maximal cuing (auditory, visual, and tactile) is provided initially.
      – Amount of cuing is gradually reduced.
      – Targets may be placed in a "holding" phase if accuracy at the isolation level is reached, but intervention cannot progress to the syllable level.
    • Transfer phase.
      – Intervention increases complexity, proceeding from syllables, to words, to phrases/sentences, to reading or story-telling, to conversation.
      – Once the child reaches the phrase/sentence level, whole-word accuracy is the goal (instead of individual phonemes in words) and self-monitoring is emphasized.
    • Maintenance phase.
      – The goal is 90% accurate production of whole words within conversations across different settings and with different listeners.
      – Accuracy rate must be achieved without direct intervention.
      – Authors recommend that the client be monitored for 3 months.
(4) Paired-stimuli approach.
  (a) Highly structured, sequenced approach.
  (b) Proceeds from single words, to sentences, to conversations.
  (c) Begins with the target being produced correctly in four "key words" (i.e., two with correct productions in the initial position and two with correct productions in the final position).
  (d) About 10 training words, or words in which the client produces the target in error, are then selected.
  (e) A picture board is created by placing a picture of the key word in the center, surrounded by pictures of the training word, keeping position of the target consistent across stimuli (e.g., all initial position).
  (f) The client alternates production of the key word with each training word until criterion is reached.
  (g) Next, the key word is changed to the final position and intervention continues until criterion is reached.
  (h) Intervention continues with the word pairings, but the client is encouraged to say the word pairs more quickly in succession.
    • The amount of reinforcement is reduced.
  (i) At the sentence level, the client is required to use the key word and each of the training words in sentences.
    • Complexity is increased by including words with the target in the initial and final position in each sentence.
  (j) At the conversation level, the clinician reinforces correct production of the target in any word.
(5) Enhancing stimulability.
  (a) Designed to increase stimulability of unstimulable sounds and increased verbal communication attempts.
  (b) Associates the verbal production of sounds with a movement or gesture and a character (e.g., /f/ is paired with "fussy fish" and a hand motion).
  (c) Multiple sounds are targeted simultaneously, including both stimulable and non-stimulable sounds.
  (d) Games are played involving the characters, and the client can respond with the sound, word, or gesture.
  (e) Intervention techniques also include modeling and requesting imitation.
3. Intervention approaches for phonemic errors (linguistic-based approaches).
  a. These approaches target groups of sounds or how sounds make up syllables (e.g., creating closed syllables, producing consonant clusters).
  b. Often most appropriate for children with multiple errors.
  c. Emphasis of intervention is helping the client develop and use appropriate phonological contrasts in natural communicative contexts.
  d. These approaches deemphasize phonetic training of sound productions.
  e. Intervention usually begins at the word level, and words are often presented in pairs to demonstrate phonemic contrasts (e.g., "tea" versus "key").

f. Typically, more than one sound is targeted in intervention at a time.

g. The goal is for the client to generalize new skills to erred sounds not targeted in therapy.

h. Specific phonemic approaches.

(1) Distinctive features approach.

(a) Focus of intervention is on the distinctive feature(s) the client is missing from the phonological system.

(b) Lack of distinctive features leads to reduced contrast in the client's repertoire.

(c) The missing distinctive feature(s) are taught (e.g., continuant) in a few phonemes, and the client will generalize to other phonemes that share that feature.

(d) Some distinctive features programs include the use of nonsense syllables.

(2) Phonological contrast intervention.

(a) The goal of contrast therapy approaches is to create phonological contrasts in the client's speech.

(b) In contrast intervention, the client's tendency to produce multiple word forms the same way (homonymy) is directly addressed.

(c) Careful consideration is given to choosing treatment targets to maximize generalization.

(d) Intervention is structured to show the client the need to produce different phonemes.

  • The listener will be confused unless the client produces a different word for each stimulus in the word pairs.

(e) The sequence of intervention for contrast intervention is similar across the different types of contrasts used (although multiple oppositions use multiple stimuli at one time).

  • Choose word pairs and familiarize the client with the pictures.

  • The clinician directs the client to point to the various pictures used in an activity.

  • The client produces the word pairs for the clinician in naturalistic activities.

  • Communication breakdowns will occur if the client fails to produce the appropriate contrasts.

  • The clinician provides appropriate feedback and opportunity for the child to produce the correct contrasts.

  • Some clients may need to receive articulatory instruction on correct sound production to succeed with the intervention tasks.

(f) There are several variations of contrast therapy methods.

  • Minimal pairs (minimal contrast method).

    – The goal is to eliminate the client's creation of homonyms (e.g., saying "tea" for both *tea* and *key*).

    – Minimal pairs are sets of words that differ by one phoneme, and that difference creates two different words.

    – The word pairs usually contrast the child's error with the target.

    – Typically, the focus of intervention is to present pairs of different words that the client typically produces as homonyms.

    – Intervention emphasizes the need to say the words in each pair differently (i.e., produce the phonological contrast).

    – Minimal pair intervention follows the theoretical positions of natural phonology (i.e., targeting phonological error patterns) and the principle of informativeness (i.e., speakers using their listeners' feedback to improve speech).

    – Generalization to other phonemes is expected.

  • Maximal oppositions (maximal contrasts).

    – Word pairs in which the target is contrasted with another sound that is maximally distinct (differs across a variety of features) are the focus of intervention (e.g., contrasting "key" with "me").

    – This approach exposes the child to more information about the sound system.

    – The reduction of homonymy is indirectly addressed.

    – Intervention emphasizes the need to say the words in each pair differently.

    – Generalization to other phonemes is expected.

  • Multiple oppositions.

    – This approach is useful for clients who have phoneme collapse or use one sound as a substitute for multiple sounds (e.g., /t/ is substituted for /k/, /s/, /ʃ/, /tʃ/, /f/, /ð/, /l/, and /st/).

    – The target is contrasted with several different sounds based on the client's unique phoneme collapse(s), attempting to disrupt the client's unique deviant rule patterns.

    – Targets used in this approach should also be maximally distinct from each other.

    – The client is presented with a range of new sounds and exposed to different phonological patterns.

    – A variety of erred sounds are treated simultaneously (e.g., the client is presented with pictures of "two/sue," "two/coo," "two/shoe," and "two/chew").

– A great deal of focused input during intervention is recommended, along with production opportunities and specific feedback about the semantic content of the child's productions.

– This approach attempts to reduce the client's tendency to use one phoneme to represent a variety of other sounds.

- Empty set.
  – Word pairs that contrast two erred sounds are used.
  – Maximal contrast is recommended (i.e., "chip" vs. "rip").

(3) Cycles remediation approach.

  (a) A main feature of this approach is the cyclical goal attack strategy.
    - Different targets are addressed in succession without the need to reach criterion.

  (b) Specific phonemes are targeted in an effort to reduce the client's use of error patterns.
    - Generalization is expected.

  (c) Each error pattern is addressed for approximately 2–6 hours, and once all significant error patterns are addressed, the first cycle is completed.

  (d) Only one phoneme is targeted per session, with a different phoneme targeted each session.

  (e) The authors provide suggestions for sequencing targets in intervention, generally following a developmental approach.

  (f) Underlying tenets of this approach.
    - Phonological development is gradual.
    - Listening is a key component of phonological acquisition.
    - Facilitating phonetic contexts are important for helping the client develop the movement and auditory awareness associated with phoneme production.

  (g) Additional aspects of this approach.
    - Auditory bombardment (at the onset and end of each intervention session) of words containing the targeted phoneme of the day.
    - Targets such as s-clusters and liquids are addressed early.
    - Addresses multisyllabic words and phonemic awareness skills in later cycles.

(4) Naturalistic speech.

  (a) A conversation-based approach to treating phonological errors.

  (b) Intervention occurs in natural place activities.
    - Activities can be designed to contain a high frequency of words with the target.

  (c) Frequent models and recasts of errors.
    - Few direct elicitations of language and no direct reinforcement.

(5) Whole-language treatment approach.

  (a) Especially useful for children with phonological impairments and concomitant delays in other language skills.

  (b) Based on the premise that phonological skills are influenced by a multitude of other variables.

  (c) Improvements in one area of language can enhance changes in other areas of language.

  (d) Multiple areas of language are often targeted simultaneously.

  (e) Therapy is conducted in the context of meaningful and functional activities that reflect the client's development level, including:
    - Play.
    - Daily routines.
    - Storytelling and retelling.
    - Conversations.

  (f) The therapist's role is to help the client verbally contribute to the conversation without correcting and evaluating communication performance.

  (g) The therapist reacts to the client's utterances with a response that is more complex, anticipating the client will use the information to produce a more complex utterance.

  (h) Typical techniques include modeling, recasting, and using visual information.

  (i) Clients change their speech productions as they also advance the complexity of their language system.

  (j) Changes in higher-level language processes (i.e., narration) are associated with changes in lower-level processes (i.e., phoneme production).

(6) Morphosyntax approach.

  (a) Designed for preschoolers who demonstrate SSD along with syntactic and morphological (morphosyntactic) errors in their speech.

  (b) Emphasis is on finite grammatical markers that mark tense and number.
    - Also, complex morphemes that create final consonant clusters.

  (c) Efficiency in intervention is accomplished by incorporating both grammar and phonology, thus capitalizing on a "cross-domain effect" for intervention.

  (d) Generalization is expected to nonmorphological clusters (i.e., not just those involving bound morphemes).

  (e) Generalization is also expected to nontargeted speech sounds.

  (f) Therapy activities can be clinician-directed and naturalistic.

  (g) Often targets are addressed in an alternate speech versus morphosyntactic format.

(h) Focused stimulation is a primary intervention technique.
- Opportunities for natural productions are created (e.g., requesting) while elicited productions are also allowed.

(7) Metaphon.
- (a) Metalinguistic approach to phonological disorders.
- (b) Incorporates phonological awareness (PA) to change expressive phonological skills.
- (c) Attributes phonological errors to the child not acquiring the rules of the sound system and not realizing the negative communication impact.
- (d) Intervention is designed to help children change their deviant rules system by helping them realize they need to change their productions and by giving them the skills to make the appropriate changes to assist in the change.
- (e) Phase 1.
  - Concept level: clinician and child "create" a common vocabulary to describe sound quality (e.g., noisy, short, long, etc.).
  - Sound level: vocabulary created in the concept level is then used to describe speech and nonspeech sounds (e.g., balloons hissing, noisemakers, whispers).
  - Phoneme level: common vocabulary is then used to describe speech sounds.
  - Word level: child listens to word pairs and uses vocabulary to describe differences in the sounds between the word pairs.
- (f) Phase 2.
  - Child produces minimal word pairs.
  - Child continues to use vocabulary to describe sounds.
  - Clinician gives feedback regarding communication function.
  - Later, the child can move on to sentences.

(8) Core vocabulary intervention.
- (a) Designed for children who exhibit an inconsistent phonological disorder.
- (b) Inconsistency may be associated with difficulty selecting and correctly arranging phonemes.
  - Also described as difficulty with phonological planning.
- (c) Typically targets whole words that are functional or important.
- (d) Therapy sessions focus on 10–12 words to be produced for each specific target word.
- (e) The goal is for the child to learn how to sequence phonemes for each specific target word.

(f) Ultimate goal is for the child to produce 70 words consistently.
(g) Once consistency for the 70 words is achieved, generalization of consistency is expected.
(h) Consistent errors (e.g., /w/ for /r/) are accepted.
- These errors may be developmental or something to be targeted later.
(i) Cues include syllable segmentation, imitation, use of alphabet letters.

(9) Metaphonological intervention.
- (a) Intervention integrates both phonological and phonemic awareness skill development, along with speech production skill development.
- (b) Many children with SSD also demonstrate difficulty with phonological and phonemic awareness skills, which can affect later literacy skills.
- (c) Research has shown that integrating PA instruction with therapy for SSD can positively affect literacy skills and speech production abilities.
- (d) PA activities in the context of SSD highlights the target(s) by having the client identify and manipulate sounds in words.
- (e) The client's awareness of sounds can be highlighted through such tasks as identifying specific phonemes in words, comparing words based on phonemic structure, and so on.
- (f) Graphemes are often included to reinforce the client's awareness of the sound structure of words.
- (g) The client's awareness of sounds in words is used to help change erred productions.
- (h) This intervention is designed to increase both accurate speech productions and early literacy development.

(10) Nonlinear phonological intervention.
- (a) The emphasis is awareness and production of phonological forms in context.
- (b) This intervention is based on "nonlinear phonology" theories that describe the hierarchical relationship of phonological forms encompassing individual phonetic features through prosodic phrase.
- (c) Intervention should be preceded by nonlinear phonological analysis to determine appropriate targets.
- (d) Intervention typically addresses prosodic structures and/or speech segments and features.
- (e) Typical therapy techniques include the use of auditory, visual, and tactile-kinesthetic cues to develop new word shapes, stress patterns, and speech segments and features.

References

Baker, E., & McLeod, S. (2011). Evidence-based practice for children with speech sound disorders: Part 1 and Part 2. *Language, Speech and Hearing Services in the Schools, 42,* 102–152.

Bernthal, J. E., Bankson, N. W., & Flipsen, P. (2013). *Articulation and Phonological Disorders: Speech Sound Disorders in Children,* 7th ed. Boston: Pearson.

Bowen, C. (2015). *Children's Speech Sound Disorders,* 2nd ed. Edison, NJ: Wiley-Blackwell.

McLeod, S., & Crowe, K. (2018). Children's consonant acquisition in 27 languages: A cross-linguistic review. *American Journal of Speech-Language Pathology, 27,* 1546–1571.

Shriberg, L.D. (1993). Four new speech and prosody-voice measures for genetics research and other studies in developmental phonological disorders. *Journal of Speech, Language, and Hearing Research. 36(1): 105–40. doi:10.1044 /jshr.3601.105. PMID 8450654.*

Shriberg, L., Kent, R., McAllister, T., & Preston, J. (2018). *Clinical Phonetics,* 5th ed. Boston: Allyn & Bacon.

Williams, A. L., McLeod, S., & McCauley, R. J. (2010). *Interventions for Speech Sound Disorders in Children.* Baltimore: Brooks Publishing.

Review Questions

1. What is it called when there is vibration of the vocal folds when producing a consonant sound?

   a. Voicing.
   b. Voiceless.
   c. Frication.
   d. Syllabification.

2. Which of the following sounds is considered alveolar?

   a. /k/.
   b. /t/.
   c. /h/.
   d. /g/.

3. What is an allophone?

   a. Different use patterns in terms of pronunciation, vocabulary, and grammar.
   b. One of a pair of sounds that is different by just one phonetic feature.
   c. A nondistinctive phonetic variant for a phoneme.
   d. Obstruents.

4. Which is NOT a component of the Behavioral Theory of speech sound acquisition?

   a. Speech sounds are shaped from the time of babbling.
   b. Reinforcement is necessary for acquisition to progress.
   c. It is related to a broader version of behavioristic theories.
   d. Children are an active participant in their learning.

5. Which theory is attributed to Roman Jakobson?

   a. Generative phonology.
   b. Structuralist theory.
   c. Natural phonology.
   d. Prosodic theory.

6. This therapy approach is best known for its specific therapeutic sequence from least complex to most complex.

   a. Van Riper traditional approach.
   b. Minimal pair approach.
   c. Stimulability approaches.
   d. Cycles approach.

7. Which is NOT a part of the minimal contrast therapy method?

   a. To eliminate the child's production of homonyms.
   b. To pair a set of words that differ by one phoneme.
   c. Only correct sound production is accepted and reinforced.
   d. Error patterns of production are the treatment targets.

8. Which theory attempts to explain children's phonological error patterns?

   a. Distinctive features theory.
   b. Generative phonology.
   c. Natural phonology.
   d. Prosodic theory.

9. Which is NOT one of the three broad categories of phonological processes?

   a. Syllable structure processes change the complexity of how words are structured.
   b. Substitution processes change the complexity of words by substituting relatively earlier to produce sounds for more difficult ones.
   c. Assimilatory processes simplify the production of words by changing sounds in words to become more similar to each other.
   d. Distortion processes change the production to a nonstandard sound.

10. When compared with adults, an infant has all of the following, EXCEPT:

   a. A shorter, flatter vocal tract.
   b. A tongue mass that is placed more forward in the oral cavity.
   c. Lower laryngeal placement.
   d. Different shape for the vocal tract.

11. What is canonical babbling?

   a. Reduplicated babbling of strings of similar CV syllables.
   b. Cooing.
   c. First words.
   d. Squeals, raspberries, trills, direction noises.

12. What is the replacement of a fricative consonant with an affricate consonant?

   a. Affrication.
   b. Alveolarization.
   c. Cluster simplification.
   d. Consonant deletion.

13. How intelligible should a child be by age 3?

   a. 0%–25% intelligible.
   b. 25%–50% intelligible.
   c. 50%–75% intelligible.
   d. 75%–100% intelligible.

14. What is it called when you compare the number of consonants produced correctly to the total number of consonants that should be produced?

   a. Percentage consonants correct.
   b. Contextual testing.
   c. Informal measure of intelligibility.
   d. Phonological mean length of utterance.

15. What is the goal of phonological contrast intervention?

    a. Create meaningful differences in the client's speech using minimal pairs.
    b. Increase stimulability of sounds.
    c. Emphasize multiple input modes.
    d. Maximal cueing.

16. At what age would you expect to hear vocal play, squeals, and fully resonated vowels?

    a. Birth–1 month.
    b. 2–3 months.
    c. 4–6 months.
    d. 6–9 months.

17. Which of the following is an example of canonical babbling?

    a. Ba ba ba ba ba.
    b. Oooooo.
    c. Mommy.
    d. Squeals.

18. Which of the following is an example of alveolarization?

    a. Rabbit → wabbit.
    b. Shoe → Sue.
    c. Funny → money.
    d. Bus → bu.

19. What is phonemic awareness?

    a. Standardized measures of speech sound production.
    b. The ability to identify and manipulate individual phones of spoken words.
    c. Ability to be understood by family and unfamiliar listeners.
    d. Ability to attend to and discriminate or manipulate sounds at the word or sentence level.

20. An approach to therapy for children who have multiple phoneme collapse (use one sound as a substitute for multiple sounds) would be:

    a. Minimal pair therapy.
    b. Multiple oppositions therapy.
    c. Maximal contrast therapy.
    d. Traditional Van Riper therapy.

 8

Language Disorders in Young Children

KIMBERLY A. MURPHY, PhD
REED SENTER, MS

Overview of Communication and Language Characteristics

This chapter covers language disorder, evaluation, and intervention for children from birth to preschool. This includes services for infants and toddlers (from birth up to age 3) who may receive early intervention (EI) under the Individuals with Disabilities Education Act (IDEA, 2004), Part C, and for preschool children (starting at age 3) who may receive special education and related services under IDEA, Part B.

Communication Competence

1. Acquiring communication competence is the overall goal of language learning.
2. Communication occurs when information is exchanged between two or more participants.
   a. Assumed to be the primary motivation for language development.
   b. Speech-language pathologists (SLPs) may determine if children's communication skills sufficiently meet their needs.
      (1) Children's communication needs are the demands within social, academic, environmental, and functional contexts.
      (2) Mismatch between language skills and demands are a primary consideration for assessment, intervention planning, and dismissal from therapy.
3. The Speech Chain (Denes & Pinson, 1993) is a model of spoken communication that depicts the transmission of a message from speaker to listener. The message is initiated by a thought in the speaker's mind, converted into language, and expressed through speech, and then it travels through the air as sound waves. The listener receives the sound waves in the auditory system, interprets them as speech sounds, and deciphers them into language (Fig. 8-1).
   a. Communication breakdowns may occur at any point in the chain, leading to a miscommunication or distorted message.
   b. While this chapter focuses on spoken language, similar chains occur with other modalities of communication, including sign language and writing.
4. Communication competence includes initiation, expression, understanding, and responding. All four skills are essential.
5. Communication can be unaided (does not require external equipment; spoken, signed) or aided (relies on external devices; computers, writing, augmentative/alternative communication).
6. Communication can be symbolic (relies on symbols; includes words, signs, picture symbols) or

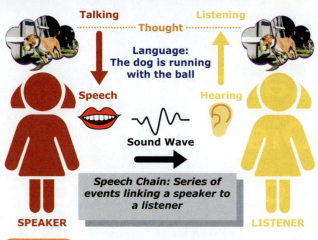

Figure 8-1   The Speech Chain

Storkel, H. (2020). Reprinted with permission.

nonsymbolic (relies on current context; includes facial expressions, gazing, reaching, or touching an object or person).
7. Communication can be verbal or nonverbal (e.g., written, gestural).

Language Characteristics

1. Understanding the characteristics of language is prerequisite to determining the presence of language disorders or typical language-learning patterns. Characteristics shared by all languages include the following:
   a. Languages are symbolic. There is no inherent relationship between a word and its referent.
   b. Socially shared codes are rules governing language form, content, and use and are common to a group of people, thus communicative.
   c. Languages are rule-governed, in that words are not randomly arranged into sentences. Some languages have word-order constraints; others have position constraints.
   d. Language allows for spontaneous, novel, unique, and generative communication, so language users may create a nearly limitless set of individualized utterances.
2. As communication can be verbal or nonverbal, languages can use a spoken (i.e., listening and speaking), written, or other communication symbol system (e.g., American Sign Language, augmentative and alternative communication [AAC] system).

3. Language has been classified as receptive or expressive.

   a. Receptive language describes communication comprehension (e.g., listening and reading); expressive language describes communication production (e.g., speaking and writing).

   b. Language comprehension tends to precede production in development, although there are instances where children attempt to use words or syntactic forms before demonstrating their understanding.

   c. There is evidence that such a dichotomy in language modality may not really exist, however, or at least that current assessment tools are not capable of differentiating receptive and expressive modalities (Tomblin & Zhang, 2006).

4. Language is a synergistic system of five individual domains:

   a. Phonology is the system of sounds in a language, including phonemic inventory and rules that govern sound combinations.

   b. Morphology is the system governing word structure and how word forms are built using morphemes. Bound morphemes include grammatical morphemes (e.g., tense and number) and affixes (prefixes and suffixes). Free morphemes function as words on their own.

   c. Syntax is the system governing rules for sentence construction, including the order and combination of words.

   d. Semantics is the system governing the meaning of words and word combinations/sentences.

   e. Pragmatics is the system governing the use of language in context, including conversation and broader social situations. Pragmatics can be divided into at least three different sets of competencies.

      (1) Communicative intentions represent the functions of language use (e.g., requesting, demanding, negotiating).

      (2) Presupposition involves judging what the listener knows and making appropriate accommodations to facilitate successful communication (e.g., vocabulary choice, sophistication of syntactic structure).

      (3) Discourse management involves the rules for turn-taking, topic initiation and maintenance, etc., that are understood by participants and necessary for successful communication (e.g., do not interrupt when someone is speaking).

5. Bloom and Lahey's (1978) "form, content, and use" framework highlights how language components interface during typical language learning and are asynchronous when a language disorder is diagnosed.

   a. Form includes phonology, morphology, and syntax.

   b. Content includes semantics.

   c. Use includes pragmatics.

   d. Examples of the interface among language components:

      (1) When a child's repertoire of syntactic structures increases (syntax), there is a greater likelihood that he/she also has multiple ways to convey the same request (pragmatics).

      (2) When a child's consistency in the use of grammatical morphemes increases (morphology), there is a greater likelihood that he/she can better specify the setting (i.e., time and place) of a narrative told to a naïve listener (pragmatics).

      (3) When a child's vocabulary grows (semantics), he/she is better able to produce sentences with elaborated noun phrases (NPs) and verb phrases (VPs), an aspect of syntax.

6. Children with language disorders in the spoken modality are at higher risk of developing difficulties with written language (reading, spelling, writing).

Cultural and Linguistic Diversity

1. SLPs must demonstrate cultural and linguistic competence in their practice and are legally and ethically bound to provide services that are culturally and linguistically responsive (American Speech-Language-Hearing Association [ASHA], 2017). Competence includes respect for cultural and linguistic differences, continual efforts to expand knowledge, and making appropriate adaptations in service delivery.

2. To be culturally responsive in interactions with families and children, SLPs must be knowledgeable about cultural expectations of social communication and language style and be careful not to stereotype or make assumptions.

3. Children from culturally and linguistically diverse (CLD) backgrounds may present with variations in language use related to speaking a nonmainstream dialect or learning English as an additional language.

4. A language difference reflects a rule-governed variation in the symbol system used by a group of individuals, based on shared regional, social, or cultural/ethnic factors.

5. It is inappropriate to make assumptions about the culture, language, or dialect of the home based on how a child looks or sounds. This information should be gathered when interviewing caregivers.

▶ Intervention for Language Disorders

Overview

1. The terms *language therapy*, *language treatment*, and *language intervention* all refer to a set of procedures that serve to modify a child's understanding and use of language in everyday interactions.
2. The overall goal of language intervention is to increase a child's functional communication to a level needed to successfully navigate their environments.
3. In language intervention, the SLP makes clear to the child the connection between language symbols (spoken or written or signed) and the contexts where used for communication.
   a. This can be referred to as "mapping language onto context."
   b. The context is the "here and now" for younger children who are less cognitively and linguistically sophisticated, and expands as children develop to include decontextualized language (i.e., talking about events in the past or future).
4. Public policy impacts how intervention services are provided in the United States.
   a. IDEA (2004) mandates that children with disabilities have a right to a free appropriate public education (FAPE) in the least restrictive environment (LRE).
   b. School services may be provided through response to intervention (RtI) or multitiered systems of support (MTSS). These are frameworks that provide multiple levels of academic and behavioral support for students with or, importantly, who are at risk for disabilities. Students therefore do not need to have an identified disability to start receiving preventative services.
5. All aspects of intervention must be culturally responsive and bias-free, including, for example, valuing the language, dialect, and culture of the family, and selecting appropriate goals and materials.
6. For children who are learning English as an additional language, intervention should ideally be provided in the home language or in both languages (Durán et al., 2016).
7. Intervention decisions should be supported by evidence-based practice (EBP), which involves the integration of external scientific evidence (i.e., published research); client and family preferences and perspectives; clinician expertise; and internal practice-based evidence, which is client performance data that has been collected in therapy sessions (Higginbotham & Satchidanand, 2019).

8. Designing appropriate and effective language intervention for a child involves consideration of multiple factors and components, to be described in the next section.

Targets for Language Therapy

1. The general focus of intervention changes across development.
   a. In early intervention with infants and toddlers, the focus is on teaching caregivers to be more responsive to the child's needs and to increase the child's preverbal communication (e.g., eye contact, joint attention, turn-taking), gestures, vocalizations, production and diversity of words and word combinations, social interaction, and meaningful play. For children with complex communication needs, a form of augmentative and alternative communication (AAC) may be implemented.
   b. For preschool children, the intervention focus shifts to directly working with the child to improve specific skills in the domains of language, and should also include emergent literacy given the risk for later literacy difficulties in preschoolers with language disorder.
      (1) Specific language targets may include production of grammatical morphemes, expanding range of communicative functions, vocabulary development, increased length and complexity of sentences, listening comprehension, and narrative skills.
      (2) Emergent literacy targets include skills that support the development of reading and writing, including print concepts, alphabet knowledge, and phonological awareness (National Early Literacy Panel, 2008).
2. Considerations for specific therapy goals include the following goal selection strategies:
   a. Comprehensive assessment data tell us about a child's language abilities and therefore broadly inform our goal-selection strategy. However, specific intervention goals should not be drawn directly from norm-referenced tests. These tests are designed to be diagnostic, not prescriptive (i.e., their purpose is not for intervention planning, and therefore their results should not be used in that manner).
   b. Goals should be functional for the child and should reflect the skills they need for participation in daily activities of home and school. Caregivers

and teachers can provide information about mismatches between the child's language skills and socio-environmental communication demands.

c. Goals should be culturally and linguistically appropriate (e.g., take into account whether the child speaks a different language or dialect or has a different culture).

d. Goals may be chosen based on developmental norms.

e. Goals can be developed using the concept of backward design. Thinking of a task that the child has difficulty with, what are the prerequisite knowledge and skills needed to successfully complete the task?

f. The degree to which a language target is currently in the child's receptive or expressive repertoire may help prioritize targets. Language forms/functions that are used inconsistently (vs. never) may indicate emerging competency; similar to the concept of "stimulability," these language skills may show faster progress during therapy. Forms or functions that are present in the child's repertoire for comprehension, but not expression, may signal foundational knowledge, making it easier and quicker to teach expressively.

3. The SLP should have a clear understanding of task demands—the knowledge and skills required to perform a task and how to break a task down to make it more or less difficult for the child, based on performance. This is important for effective prompting, cuing, and scaffolding.

4. Thoughtful and careful selection and writing of goals is critical for effective intervention. For goal writing resources, see the Goal Functionality Scale III (McWilliam, 2009a) and a tutorial by Diehm (2017). Goals must include the skill, where and how it will be measured, the accuracy level, supports to be provided, and the timeline. SMART goals are specific, measurable, attainable, relevant, and timely.

Stimuli and Materials

1. A stimulus is used to elicit a desired response from the child. Stimuli can be linguistic or nonlinguistic. Examples include:

a. Linguistic: saying the child's name, modeling a target, asking a question, requesting an imitation, or initiating a conversation.

b. Nonlinguistic: making eye contact, touching the child's hand, and using objects, pictures, toys, or books.

2. Linguistic input is often simplified for children in early stages of language development but should still be grammatical.

a. Telegraphic speech, in which the adult omits function words and grammatical markers from an utterance, is not recommended. Instead, use Simplified grammatical input. This can be a phrase or sentence fragment, rather than a complete sentence, but does not violate grammatical rules.

b. Examples of telegraphic and grammatical utterances:

(1) Telegraphic: *more bubble; mommy turn; eat cracker; doggie sleep.*

(2) Grammatical: *more bubbles; mommy's turn; eat the cracker; the doggie is sleeping.*

3. Adding variability to linguistic input can be beneficial (Plante et al., 2014). For example, when working on grammatical morphemes, use several different verbs (e.g., *jumping, sleeping, washing*) to go with the target morpheme (e.g., present progressive *-ing*) instead of just a couple of verbs.

4. Stimuli and materials should engage the child but not distract from the focus and time spent on the language target(s).

5. The SLP should be knowledgeable of and sensitive to the culture of the child and family when choosing stimuli and materials. For example, pictures and texts may relate to specific holidays, depict themes of religion or spirituality or magic and fantasy, or depict foods that may have religious restrictions. Before using such stimuli, use open-ended questions of the family to determine if the themes align with their cultural preferences (e.g., "Tell me about any holidays that your family celebrates)" (Hammond, 2019). If the stimuli are not culturally appropriate, do not use them.

6. For preschool children, use stimuli from the curriculum to facilitate acquisition of the knowledge and skills needed to succeed in school and to help with generalization.

7. Fiction and nonfiction books are excellent stimuli. They are functional and contextual and can be used for a variety of intervention targets, in contrast to worksheets, which often are not functional or contextual. Select books that depict diverse characters, cultures, and themes.

8. Stimuli may be delivered through a computer game or an app.

9. Other materials may be part of the therapy session, such as materials for a specific activity or reinforcer. These should also be chosen thoughtfully.

Therapy Approach

1. Therapy approaches differ along a continuum of naturalness (Fey, 1986) or how close the therapy resembles everyday communication and activities.

a. The dimensions of naturalness include the therapy activity, location, and therapy agent (who is interacting with the child). From most to least natural, examples include:

(1) Activity: daily activities and play, structured games and play, drill.

(2) Location: home, classroom, clinic, or therapy room.

(3) Therapy agent: caregiver, teacher, clinician.

b. Hybrid approaches reflect a midpoint on the continuum (e.g., working 1:1 with a child in the preschool classroom using class materials).

c. The more natural the therapy, the less dramatic the bridge to generalization or carryover to everyday interactions and language use.

d. Natural activities are a good context in which to measure generalization (e.g., can the child use a targeted language form in play or with a caregiver or teacher, with minimal feedback from the clinician).

2. Aligned with the continuum of naturalness, approaches to language therapy also vary along a continuum from child-centered to clinician-directed. The extremes of the continuum are outlined in Table 8-3.

3. In child-centered approaches, the clinician follows the child's lead, using the interests of the child to direct the order and substance of the language intervention session. The focus is often on general communication (e.g., increasing the amount of communication or elaborating the child's output) and not on specific language targets.

4. In clinician-directed approaches, the clinician leads the interaction, chooses the materials and order of activities, and targets specific goals by eliciting a response from the child and providing evaluative feedback.

5. Hybrid approaches borrow characteristics of both clinician-directed and client-centered approaches.

The clinician allows the child to make choices about activities and materials but is deliberate in trying to elicit specific targets during the child's chosen activity.

6. Choice of approach depends on a number of factors, including child characteristics (e.g., age, developmental level, severity of disorder, behavior) and language target (e.g., pragmatic goals may be better suited to more natural contexts). No one approach is inherently better than another, although a particular approach may better align with particular child characteristics and stage of therapy.

7. Therapy mode varies in degree of structure in the therapy session. From most to least structured:

a. Drill is an appropriate therapy mode when the client is motivated, or when a new language target (either rarely observed or absent from the child's repertoire) is a goal.

b. Drill play is an appropriate therapy mode when the client is generally motivated, is being taught a new language target (rarely observed or absent from the child's repertoire), and can tolerate some extraneous activity to promote naturalness or compliance.

c. Structured play is appropriate for children who are becoming acclimated to therapy and cannot tolerate too much structure or who have been working on a language target for a while and are trying to demonstrate independent learning in a more natural setting.

d. Play is an appropriate therapy mode for assessing generalization to a more natural setting because feedback is only intermittently present, if at all.

Table 8-3

Comparison of Child-Centered and Clinician-Directed Therapy Approaches		
	CHILD-CENTERED	**CLINICIAN-DIRECTED**
Naturalness	High (e.g., play-based activities at home)	Low (e.g., drill-based activities in clinic)
Structure	Low	High
Adult control	Low: clinician follows child's lead	High: clinician chooses targets and materials and sets the agenda
Explicitness: degree of direct "teaching"	Low: indirect and implicit	High: direct and explicit
Clinician input	Modeling, contingent responses, interpretation of communicative attempts	Elicit specific form or function from child
Child response	Not required	Required
Measure of dosage	Clinician input: number of models provided or techniques used	Child's productions of the target
Reinforcement	Generally social (e.g., smiling, engagement, high five, "yay!")	Generally tangible (e.g., food, sticker, token, toy)
Feedback	Praise/verbal reinforcement provided if child uses target; usually no explicit error correction	Feedback and error correction usually provided
Theoretical influence	Social interactional	Behavioral/operant

Therapy Techniques

1. The goal of therapy techniques is to provide examples of the targeted forms and functions in meaningful contexts. Techniques will provide the child with support for success during the learning process.
2. Many exaggerated or otherwise highlighted productions create an environment where the targets are more salient than in incidental conversation. Salience of a therapy target can be increased in a number of ways:
   a. Increased prosodic cueing.
   b. Decreased speaking rate.
   c. Multiple exposures.
3. Design of meaningful, if sometimes contrived, contexts will create an environment where the usefulness of the targeted forms and functions is more evident than in incidental conversation.
4. Therapy should be multimodal (supplement auditory with visual and/or tactile).
5. Therapy should provide the child with frequent opportunities for practice, multiple exposures to the language target using multiple exemplars, and feedback.
6. Techniques vary in terms of the explicitness with which a target is taught. Explicit or direct instruction, also called *induction teaching*, uses a systematic set of teaching steps and is more often used in clinician-directed therapy. Indirect techniques, such as language facilitation, use modeling rather than direct teaching of a target.
7. Techniques vary in the degree to which they are child-centered, clinician-directed, or hybrid.
8. Clinician-directed therapy uses discrete trial procedures with drill or drill play. The clinician prompts the child, usually by presenting a stimulus and asking a question, waits for the child's response, and then provides feedback and a reinforcement. In drill play, the clinician adds a play element to make the activity more engaging and motivating for the child.
9. Child-centered therapy uses language facilitation. These are indirect language-stimulation techniques that can be implemented by the caregiver or SLP. In many of the techniques, the language of the caregiver/SLP is contingent upon the child's communication and actions. Table 8-4 provides descriptions and examples of these techniques.
10. Hybrid therapy incorporates techniques from child-centered and clinician-directed therapy.
    a. Focused stimulation: The SLP highlights the language target by providing massed modeling of the target, with multiple exemplars, in a play context. The child simply listens and is not required to produce the target. If the child does respond with an error, the SLP can give feedback in the form of an expansion or continues to model. This technique is often used to prime the child's language system at the beginning of a therapy session before moving to a more explicit approach.
    b. Milieu communication training: The SLP arranges interactive activities that require social communication on the part of the child. The activities take

Table 8-4

Language Facilitation Techniques

TECHNIQUE	DESCRIPTION	EXAMPLE
Self-talk	Adult talks about what she/he is doing, matching language to context; child is not required to say or do anything.	"Mommy's washing the dishes. Here's a cup. Wash the cup."
Parallel talk	Adult talks about what the child is doing, matching language to context; child is not required to say or do anything.	"Look at the truck. You're making the truck go. Drive the truck."
Expansions	Adult adds one or two words to the child's utterance.	Child says, "Bus." Adult says, "Yellow bus."
Recasts	Adult provides a corrected version of a child's word or utterance but stays true to the child's intended meaning and does not introduce additional information to the utterance.	Child says, "Daddy go play," and the adult says, "Daddy is going to play."
Extensions	Adult provides a corrected version of a child's word or utterance and adds semantic information.	Child says, "I like cookies," and the adult says, "I like cookies, too, especially chocolate chip cookies."
Buildup/ breakdown	Adult breaks a sentence down into its constituent parts (phrases and clauses) and then builds it back up.	Child says, "Ball." Adult says, "I'm rolling the big ball to you. The big ball! Rolling the big ball. I'm rolling. I'm rolling the big ball. I'm rolling the big ball to you!"
Sentence recasts	Adult expands the child's utterance into a different type (e.g., question or negative) or more elaborated sentence. Often used for morphosyntax targets.	Child says, "Kitty eating," and the adult says, "Is the kitty eating?"
Asking open-ended questions	Adult asks a question (or prompts for a response) that cannot be answered with a short, one- or two-word answer.	Child says, "I like turtles." Adult says, "Wow! What do you like most about turtles?"

place in everyday settings and have natural consequences for communication. The SLP uses modeling and prompting.

    (1) Prelinguistic milieu teaching is a variation for children who are not yet speaking. It focuses on nonverbal communicative acts, specifically vocalizations, eye gaze, and gesture.

    (2) Enhanced milieu teaching is a variation for children who are using at least 10 words and have an MLU from 1 to 3.5. It is often used as a parent-delivered intervention.

c. Script therapy/joint action routines: The SLP embeds language therapy into routines or scripts familiar to the child, or may develop routines or scripts for a particular purpose.

    (1) The repetitiveness and familiarity of the routine or script alleviates cognitive load, making language learning and focus on the target easier for the child.

    (2) Songs and finger plays are common scripts.

    (3) The SLP can disrupt a familiar routine or script to tempt the child to communicate.

d. Conversational recast therapy: This intervention is used to target grammatical morphemes. The SLP engages the child in play or playlike routines that have been designed such that the target morpheme can be easily and frequently elicited. When the child produces an utterance that requires the target morpheme (whether correct or incorrect), the SLP provides a model of the correct grammatical form by recasting the child's utterance.

e. Dialogic reading (Whitehurst et al., 1988) and other shared book reading methods may be used to target a wide range of skills, including listening comprehension, vocabulary, complex sentences, narrative structure, story retelling, and emergent literacy. These interventions can be implemented by the SLP, or the SLP may train caregivers and teachers to implement them. Strategies include asking questions, performing repeated readings, explicitly teaching meanings of selected words, role playing to reenact the story, and print referencing (Justice & Ezell, 2004; Justice & Pence, 2005).

11. There are many therapy techniques and methods for each of the language domains, as well as therapy programs that often target a combination of language skills. We have not attempted to provide a comprehensive list. SLPs can consult ASHA's practice portal and evidence maps to explore the growing research base for evidence-based practices.

Intervention Stage

1. Children progress in their acquisition of a language target. During these stages, the SLP must vary the stimuli, supports, and procedures.

    a. Establishment. The child is learning the target form or function; SLP uses skilled scaffolding strategies.

    b. Mastery. The child is becoming more independent; the SLP fades the scaffolding/support and builds in procedures to facilitate generalization.

    c. Generalization. The child uses the target form or function independently across contexts (people, places, and activities); SLP facilitates as needed; service focus may become indirect as generalization progresses.

    d. Maintenance. The child sustains use of the target form or function over time; may switch to consultative services only.

2. Generalization is the ability to independently apply a learned skill (i.e., use of the language form or function that was targeted) in a novel situation (i.e., with new activities, people, and places). It can be difficult to achieve, especially if the intervention does not take place in a natural context.

3. SLPs must *plan* for generalization by decreasing the level of support and structure, varying the stimuli, and periodically changing the therapy context—vary the location, communication partners, and service delivery model.

4. There are two kinds of generalization, both of which are desirable for skills acquired through language intervention.

    a. Response generalization refers to a child's production of untrained targets at the same or at a different linguistic level. For example, if the "is + verb + ing" structure was taught with the verbs *catching*, *sleeping*, and *drawing*, and the child produces *is laughing* spontaneously, that would be generalization.

    b. Stimulus generalization refers to a child's production of a trained target in an untrained setting, with new stimuli, or with a new person. For example, the child produces "is + verb + ing" structures with a teacher or uses it while on the playground.

Service Delivery

1. SLPs have a variety of service delivery models (Table 8-5) to choose from, with approaches varying in who delivers the therapy (therapy agent), where

the therapy takes place (therapy setting), and the frequency with which services are provided.

2. No one approach is best for all children or best for an individual child in all circumstances; the SLP should be flexible in making changes as needed.

3. Interprofessional practice and collaboration are essential in each model.

4. Service delivery may vary based on the stage of therapy (e.g., in generalization, we want the child to use new language forms and functions outside of the original therapy context, so we may focus on natural contexts of the home or classroom).

5. In addition to those listed in the table, therapy agents may also be SLP assistants or peers who have been trained to participate in therapy (e.g., in peer-mediated interventions for social communication), and therapy settings may also include other locations such as a playground or lunchroom.

6. Home-based interventions are most commonly provided in early intervention, described next.

Early Intervention

1. Early intervention is a preventative model for the birth-to-age-3 population; its goal is to lessen the effects of a delay or disability.

2. Routines-based interviewing (RBI) is used to learn about the family's most important concerns for the child, to assist with prioritizing intervention goals, and to build on family strengths. Questions are asked regarding the family's day-to-day life and specific routines (times of day and familiar activities). Results guide decisions such as which routines provide the best opportunities for therapy and the highest level of engagement for the child and family, and allow the SLP to write functional goals and objectives driven by the family's choices.

3. Individual Family Service Plans (IFSPs) are developed by the team to monitor presenting performance characteristics, describe the programming to be provided and outcomes to be achieved, periodically document behavior changes, and monitor viability of the service delivery plan. The family's concerns and priorities are of prime importance in the development of the IFSP.

4. Principles of early intervention.
   a. Services are family-centered. As such, they are responsive to each family's unique circumstances and they involve the family in all aspects of service. The whole child within the family unit is the recipient of intervention.
   b. Services are culturally and linguistically responsive. If the child is learning more than one language, caregivers are taught how to implement strategies in their home language.
   c. Services are developmentally supportive and promote children's participation in their natural environments. The therapy setting is most often the home but may also be a child care center, school, or any setting in which young children without disabilities participate. Therapy focuses on daily activities and routines.
   d. Services are comprehensive, coordinated, and team-based. This prevents fragmented service delivery and maximizes outcomes, as there are often multiple service providers working with a child and family. Service providers collaboratively develop interventions that are complementary to one another.
      (1) Transdisciplinary team models are commonly used. This involves role release whereby professionals share expertise, scope of practice, and intervention strategies with each other. The family's primary service provider (PSP) may implement the intervention, incorporating goals and strategies from each of the team members (e.g., physical therapy, speech-language therapy, social work), regardless of the PSP's profession.

Table 8-5

Service Delivery Models

MODEL	SETTING	THERAPY AGENT	DESCRIPTION/DETAILS
Home-based	Home: using daily routines and activities	Caregiver and SLP	The SLP coaches the caregiver, demonstrates techniques, and chooses therapy targets based on the needs of the child and family.
Pull-out	Therapy room (clinic or school)	SLP	The SLP provides therapy 1:1 or in small groups.
Classroom-based direct services	Classroom	SLP and teacher	The SLP and teacher collaborate, providing supports to the child in the classroom, either in whole-group or small-group activities.
Classroom-based indirect services	Classroom	Teacher	The SLP acts as a consultant, guiding the teacher to adjust instructional methods in the classroom to meet the child's needs.

e. Services are based on the highest-quality evidence that is available. This includes external (research) evidence and internal sources, such as family perspectives and clinical expertise and consensus.

5. General treatment approaches include routines-based intervention and caregiver coaching.

   a. In routines-based intervention, everyday activities serve as the context for embedded instruction to increase participation in the natural environment of the child/family. Intervention activities are often implemented by the caregiver while using toys and objects from the home.

   b. Coaching is a model used by the SLP to help caregivers assume the responsibility of and build capacity for facilitating the child's language learning. This is preferable to providing only child-directed services and enhances the caregivers' empowerment and self-esteem. Coaching includes general strategies such as information sharing, observation, and joint interaction, and specific strategies such as direct teaching, demonstration with narration, guided and caregiver practice, feedback, problem-solving, reflection, and review and plan (Family Guided Routines Based Intervention, 2019). The SLP coaches caregivers on how to provide opportunities for practice and feedback and to use responsive communication strategies such as modeling, expansions, imitations, environmental arrangement, and "serve and return" interactions (Center on the Developing Child at Harvard University, 2015).

6. Specific language interventions are also provided by the SLP. This includes strategies that are:

   a. Quantity-based, which vary the amount and complexity of language directed to the child.

   b. Responsive, which are the language facilitation strategies described above.

   c. Directive, which focus on eliciting language production through use of questions (especially open-ended and choice) and prompts to "tell me about . . ."

   d. Multimodal, which combine tactile and visual supports with verbal input.

   e. Engagement-based, which encourage the child to engage in communicative interactions and activities such as play and shared reading.

Factors for Language Intervention Success

1. Child and caregiver motivation.

   a. The SLP should select meaningful and functional targets, stimuli, and activities.

      (1) The child will be more motivated to learn a target that can be immediately useful for better communication.

      (2) The child will have more opportunities for feedback provided indirectly from the environment (was communication successful?) or directly from an adult or peer regarding accuracy or appropriateness of the language used.

   b. The SLP should help the child and caregiver understand the purpose and benefit of the language target.

2. Child's active engagement in the therapy sessions.

   a. SLP should manage the session to ensure active participation of the child.

   b. Level of engagement or on-task behavior may increase the number of exposures and opportunities to practice the language target.

3. Child's level of awareness of their language deficit.

   a. Frustration because of failure to communicate initially may lead to "acting out" behaviors or avoidance of communication attempts.

   b. When usefulness of language targets is demonstrated, child may become more invested in therapy.

4. Dosage and intensity of therapy.

   a. *Dosage* refers to the time spent on the language target within a session. Sessions should be highly productive, with as much time spent on the language target as possible for that child in that situation. As shown in Table 8-3, dosage can be measured as the number of times the SLP models the target or uses the language technique (i.e., the amount of exposure the child receives to the target) or the number of times the child produces or uses the language target.

   b. Frequency is the number of therapy sessions per period of time (e.g., two sessions per week). Duration is the length of the intervention (e.g., therapy lasted 12 weeks).

   c. Cumulative intervention intensity is the product of dose × frequency × duration (Warren, Fey, & Yoder, 2007).

   d. Determining "optimal" intensity is complex, and more research is needed, but emerging evidence supports high dosage with sessions spaced out over time (Justice et al., 2017).

5. Explicitness of therapy provided/needed for learning.

   a. Children differ in terms of the number of examples they need to learn a new language form or function.

   b. Some children will need exposure to a specific rule, led through overgeneralization, and specifically taught exceptions to the rule.

   c. Some children will need more explicit feedback to help them focus on what is most essential in the language-learning task. Children with language disorders generally have difficulty inferring language rules without explicit feedback.

6. Support for new language forms and functions outside the therapy setting (e.g., classroom, home).

a. Are caregivers able and willing to provide the child with opportunities for practice and models of the form or function taught, even when therapy is provided outside the home?

b. Does the child receive support and feedback in the classroom?

c. Does the therapy plan include a systematic plan for incorporating caregiver involvement, to assist with generalization? This can include the use of home programs, where caregivers are asked to monitor the child's use of therapy targets in the home, or training/coaching the caregiver to become the primary therapy agent. Response to coaching methods may be more or less successful with some caregivers, and the SLP must be aware of caregivers' capacity and resources to be directly involved with the child's therapy.

7. The therapy plan accounts for the child's behavior and level of attention. Considerations include salience of the target, schedule of feedback and reinforcement, and the length of therapy sessions.

8. The child's level of competence aligns with the cognitive and linguistic prerequisites for the selected therapy targets and activities. For example, the child should understand the concept of causality and be able to use *do* as an auxiliary form in question structures before the SLP targets comprehension of "why" questions.

Measuring Progress in Therapy

1. Periodic measurement of client performance is critical in ensuring that the intervention is both effective and still required. Progress monitoring is a requirement under IDEA.
   a. Must determine if client is making progress and that progress is due to therapy and not simply maturation.
   b. Compare progress to longer-term goals and shorter-term objectives, and expected rate of change.

2. Purposes for data collection include measuring progress from one session to another (which provides practice-based evidence for making EBP decisions) and documenting and maximizing the overall effectiveness of intervention.

3. Data collection can be quantitative (numbers) or qualitative (descriptive). Rubrics are often used in qualitative data collection. Graphs can be used to visualize quantitative data.

4. Measures of progress should be objective and consider functional outcomes.

5. Results inform decisions regarding therapy continuation, modification, and dismissal.

6. Utilize untrained exemplars to evaluate progress when eliciting language. For example, if the target is third-person singular verb forms and the SLP trained *comes* and *walks*, try to elicit *plays* and *jumps*.

7. Look for use of untrained exemplars in the child's spontaneous language. The SLP may set up a situation or activity in which the particular language form is obligated.

8. If the therapy is not working, the SLP should determine what can be changed to facilitate improvement in the child's performance. This can vary greatly from one child to another and may include:
   a. Changing the examples provided so they are more similar to one another. When examples are too different from one another, they require some generalization to detect similarities. Use of highly similar examples allows the client to focus on essential features of the stimuli.
   b. Using fewer examples. Use of too many examples may be distracting and may make the essential features of the stimuli less obvious.
   c. Providing feedback in a manner conducive to the child's understanding. This may involve increasing the rate of teaching overall (including response latency), particularly provision of feedback. Recheck accuracy and consistency of feedback.
   d. Altering the type or rate of reinforcement.
   e. Looking for an intermediate step in the teaching process. Analyze the task to determine how to revise the objective to a challenging but not frustrating level (zone of proximal development).
   f. Consider the degree to which the therapy is contextualized and relevant to the child's functioning and everyday interactions. Changes in family involvement and location of the therapy may be warranted.
   g. Consider whether therapy should be more or less child-centered or clinician-directed.
   h. An adjustment in therapy intensity (i.e., number of sessions per week, number of minutes per session) may also be warranted.

Dismissal from Therapy

1. ASHA has provided guidelines for appropriate dismissal from therapy (Table 8-6).

2. The discontinuation of direct services does not always mean the end of all services or a permanent end to services. The SLP may choose to provide:
   a. Indirect/consultative support in the classroom.
   b. Follow-up at a later time.
   c. Reevaluation at a later time.
   d. Referral to another SLP, program, or professional.

3. Rather than full dismissal, sometimes a break from therapy is the best choice.

9

Spoken Language Disorders in School-Age Populations

SANDRA LAING GILLAM, PhD

Chapter Outline

14. A randomized controlled trial is a(n):
    a. Analysis of a number of studies related to a specific approach.
    b. Experiment in which participants are not assigned randomly to treatment or control groups.
    c. Experiment in which participants are randomly assigned to treatment and control groups.
    d. Opinion of a respected professional.

15. Which of the following is NOT an example of evaluation criteria for external evidence?
    a. Comparison.
    b. Cultural values.
    c. Random assignment.
    d. Participants.

16. Which of the following best describes genetic syndromes?
    a. They may run in families.
    b. They are likely to be associated with language disorders.
    c. They are presumed to be transmitted in genetic makeup.
    d. All of the above.

17. Which is the most prevalent mental health diagnosis made in childhood?
    a. Attention deficit hyperactivity disorder.
    b. Bipolar disorder.
    c. Specific reading disability.
    d. Intellectual deficit.

18. Which of the following is TRUE about autism spectrum disorders (ASD)?
    a. Separated into ASD, Asperger's, and PDD-NOS diagnostic criteria.
    b. Can be comorbid with intellectual difficulties.
    c. Must involve language disorder before age 3.
    d. Is exclusively a genetic disorder.

19. In Down syndrome, which of the following statements are FALSE?
    a. Language production is more affected than language comprehension.
    b. Syntax is more affected than semantics.
    c. Vocabulary and syntax growth are asynchronous.
    d. Hearing deficits are unlikely to cause language comprehension issues.

20. A student is observed to say the following: "Josh can help with the chores; Bryan can (help with the chores) too," where the information in the parentheses is not stated out loud. This is an example of which of the following?
    a. Register variation.
    b. Presupposition.
    c. Ellipses.
    d. Indirect request.

10

Written Language Disorders in School-Age Populations

CHARLES W. HAYNES, EdD
PAMELA E. HOOK, PhD

Introduction

What Is "Literacy"?

1. According to the United Nations Educational, Scientific and Cultural Organization (UNESCO), *literacy* refers to the "ability to identify, understand, interpret, create, communicate and compute, using printed and written materials."
2. Focus of this chapter.
   a. This chapter outlines key knowledge for understanding, preventing, assessing, and intervening for literacy disorders related to reading and writing.

Roles, Responsibilities, Knowledge, and Skills Required by the Speech-Language Pathologist Involved in Literacy

General Role of SLP in Relationship to Literacy

1. According to the American Speech-Language-Hearing Association policy (ASHA, 2001), SLPs can play direct or collaborative roles in supporting literacy skills in children, adolescents, and adults with developmental and/or acquired literacy communication disorders, including persons with severe or multiple disabilities.

ASHA and Literacy

1. Specific roles and responsibilities of the SLP for reading and writing in children and adolescents (ASHA, 2001):
   a. Preventing written language problems.
   b. Identifying children at risk.
   c. Assessing reading and writing.
   d. Providing intervention and documenting outcomes.
   e. Other roles, such as:
      (1) Assisting general education teachers, parents, and students.
      (2) Adding to the knowledge base.
2. ASHA'S Code of Ethics requires SLPs who serve in these roles to be specifically educated and appropriately trained (ASHA, 2016).
3. Specific knowledge and skills expected of the SLP working with literacy (ASHA, 2002).
   a. Knowledge areas:
      (1) Nature of literacy.
      (2) Typical development of reading and writing.
      (3) Disorders of language and literacy.
      (4) Clinical tools and methods.
      (5) Collaboration, leadership, and research principles.
   b. Skill areas:
      (1) Prevention.
      (2) Identification.
      (3) Assessment.
      (4) Intervention.
      (5) Other roles.

Nature of Literacy: Spoken-Written Language Relationships, Reading and Writing

Characteristics of Written Language

1. Orthography is a secondary symbol system superimposed on the primary oral language system.
2. Reading and writing (written language) consist of receptive processes (reading) and expressive processes (writing).
3. Written language performance is supported by cognitive factors such as attention, executive functions, and memory.
4. Written language is critically influenced by cultural and linguistic differences (e.g., bilingualism, richness of home language and literacy, socioeconomic status, quality and characteristics of school curriculum).

Component Processes That Influence Reading and Writing

1. There is a strong link between spoken and written language. A robust model for the relationship between these elements is Gough and Tunmer's Simple View of Reading (1986):

   Decoding (word identification) × Linguistic Comprehension = Reading Comprehension.

   - Difficulties in either word identification or linguistic comprehension (or both) will affect reading comprehension.

2. A Simple View of Writing mirrors the processes in the Simple View of Reading and underscores the role of working memory in formulation processes (Berninger et al., 2002).

   Transcription (spelling + handwriting) × Linguistic Expression = Written Expression

3. Each element of these models rely heavily on components of working memory (lexical access, manipulation of speech information in a temporary buffer, and monitoring for accuracy).

4. Reading and writing consist of two major elements: word identification/spelling and comprehension/written formulation. Components of word identification/spelling include decoding (phonic word attack) and encoding (spelling) based on phonological structure; structural analysis based on morphological structure; and sight word recognition, which rely heavily on orthographic memory and is necessary for automaticity and fluency.

   a. *Phonic word attack and encoding* involve phonological awareness, grapheme-phoneme correspondence, and syllable recognition skills.

   (1) *Phonological awareness* refers to the capacity to reflect on, analyze, and manipulate speech information; phonological awareness skills, particularly phonemic awareness, predict later word recognition skills. There is a developmental progression for phonological awareness in English:

   (a) *Rhyme awareness* refers to the ability to recognize or produce words that rhyme: "I saw a frog. It sat on a (log)."

   (b) *Word awareness* pertains to the ability to recognize words as units in phrases or sentences: "Clap the words in, *I feel happy today.*"

   (c) *Syllable awareness* involves the ability to recognize syllables as units within words: "Clap the syllables in *happy.*"

   (d) *Onset-rime awareness* refers to the ability to detect and identify initial sounds in onset-rime words (i.e., How are *van* and *pan* different?). Onset-rime awareness is a prerequisite for phonemic awareness.

   (e) *Phonemic awareness* is the capacity to reflect on, analyze, and manipulate speech at the phoneme level.
   - Classic phonemic awareness tasks include blending: /h/ + /ae/ + /p/ + /i/ = happy; segmentation: trip = /t/ + /r/ + /ɪ/ + /p/; and elision or manipulation: trim without /t/ = rim.
   - Phonemic awareness skill correlates significantly with word recognition and spelling performance for regular words.
   - Development of phonemic awareness occurs synergistically with the development of phonic reading and spelling skills.

   (2) *Grapheme-phoneme correspondence*, (commonly referred to as sound-symbol correspondence): the ability to connect letters with corresponding phonemes. English has a complex orthographic system with 26 letters and approximately 44 sounds. Many letters have more than one sound, and many sounds can be spelled in more than one way. For example, in English the digraph *ch* has three sounds: /ch/ as in *chair*, /sh/ as in *champagne*, and /k/ as in *character*. There are at least seven ways to spell the long sound of *a*: a (*baby*), a-e (*gate*), ai (*rain*), ay (*play*), ei (*vein*), eigh (*neighbor*), ey (*they*).

   (a) The complexity of English makes it harder to learn to read and spell than transparent alphabetic languages that have more consistent grapheme/phoneme correspondence, such as Spanish or Finnish.

   (b) Grapheme-phoneme correspondence knowledge and skills are predicted by letter naming performance; together these skills predict and correlate with acquisition of word identification.

   (3) *Syllable types.* Knowledge of syllable types is needed for decoding words once grapheme-phoneme correspondence has been acquired. The six syllable types shown in Table 10-1 provide orthographic cues to vowel pronunciation; knowledge of how to recognize them is critical for struggling readers learning to identify words.

   (4) *Syllabification rules*: In addition to syllable types, knowledge of rules for syllable division is helpful for decoding longer words (Table 10-2).

   b. *Structural analysis*: based on morphological structure. Involves breaking words down according to meaningful morphemes (e.g., prefixes, roots, and suffixes).

   (1) Examples of application of structural analysis would be:

   psych (mind) + *ology* (study of) = *psychology* (study of the mind)

   re- (back) + *tract* (pull) + *-able* (capable of) = *retractable* (able to be pulled back)

Chapter 10 WLD

Table 10-1

Syllable Types

Closed	Has one vowel; ends in one or more consonants—the vowel is short: (C)VC, (C)VCC, (CC)VCC	*at, fit, end, rust, blimp*
Open	Ends in one vowel—the vowel is long: (C)V (usually in a word with two or more syllables)	*she; o-* in *open; mu-* in *music; se-* in *sequin*
Silent e	Ends in a silent e—the vowel is long: (C)VCe, CCVCe	*ate, lime, slope*
Vowel team or vowel combination	Contains a vowel combined with another vowel—the sound is often long or a diphthong: (C)VV(C)	*main, seam, coin, round*
R-controlled	Contains a vowel followed by r in a stressed syllable—the vowel has an unusual sound: Vr	*-ar* in *car; -or* in *fort; -er* in *fern; -ir* in *bird; -ur* in *burn*
Consonant + le	Contains a consonant plus le (in a word with two or more syllables): Cle	*-tle* in *title; -gle* in *bugle; -dle* in *riddle*

Table 10-2

Rules for Syllable Division

VC/CV	Two medial consonants—divide between them	*rab/bit, el/bow, pic/nic*
V/CV or VC/V	Single medial consonant: • Usually divide before the consonant (open first syllable—long vowel)	*pa/per, fi/nal*
	• Sometimes divide after the consonant (closed first syllable—short vowel) (the "flex rule")	*lem/on, cab/in*
VC/CCV or VCC/CV	Three medial consonants—keep blends and digraphs together	*com/press, pil/grim pump/kin, back/hand*

(2) Highest frequency morpheme groups targeted for instruction in English are Anglo-Saxon, Latin, and Greek.

c. *Sight word* reading involves gestalt, or *whole word*, recognition of regular (*dog, sprint, magnet*) or irregular words (*one, friend, yacht*).

(1) The ultimate goal of sight word reading is to achieve the automatic word identification necessary for fluent reading.

(2) Sight word reading places heavy demands on orthographic memory for visual word forms, referred to as *mental graphemic representations* (MGRs).

d. *Automaticity* and *fluency* pertain to reading efficiency (speed and accuracy).

(1) *Automaticity* refers primarily to word recognition skills. When word recognition skills are "automatic," they require minimal cognitive resources. Automaticity contributes to development of fluent reading.

(2) *Fluency* refers to reading at the phrase, sentence, and discourse levels. Fluent oral reading is prosodic, reflecting appropriate rhythm, intonation, and syntactic chunking in combination with automatic word recognition skills.

• Fluent readers leverage syntactic and discourse contexts to anticipate upcoming words and phrases.

(3) Automaticity and fluency contribute to and interact with reading comprehension.

Reading Comprehension

1. *Reading comprehension* refers to the complex cognitive process involving the intentional interaction between reader and text to extract meaning.

a. Spoken and written linguistic factors that influence reading comprehension include, but are not limited to, the reader's knowledge and skills in word identification; reading automaticity and fluency; academic language, including morphology, syntax, and vocabulary; discourse processing; and higher-order thinking.

(1) As previously noted, automaticity of word identification and text-level fluency are important for efficient extraction of meaning from text.

(2) In persons with adequate word recognition skills, *vocabulary* is the individual component language ability that best predicts reading comprehension.

(3) After vocabulary knowledge and skills, sentence processing and production—the capacity to hold in memory, make sense of, and produce word order patterns in sentences of varying length and complexity (syntax)—is the second-most powerful linguistic predictor of reading comprehension performance.

(4) Processing and production of discourse (multi-sentence language) comprises the aggregate operations of semantic, syntactic, and text structure knowledge and skills.

b. Discourse structures fall into two general categories: narrative and expository.

(1) *Narrative,* or *story structure,* is typically more familiar and easier for early-grade-school children to understand and produce than is expository text.

(a) Mainstream middle-class narrative structure typically requires the reader to understand the following sequence of story elements: characters and setting, initiating event, emotional response, internal plan, attempt, consequence, and ending.

(b) African American English, as well as working-class narrative structure, may contain the above elements elaborated with anecdotal, topical associations.

(2) *Expository structure* is informational in nature and is typically found in newspaper reports; content area texts such as geography, science, and biology; and essays. Standard expository structures include, but are not limited to, descriptive, sequential/enumerative, comparison/contrast, and persuasive.

c. Higher-order thinking skills support and direct the reader's interaction with and derivation of meaning from the text. Examples of key higher-order thinking skills include, but are not limited to, getting facts, identifying the main idea, drawing inferences, and drawing conclusions.

(1) Fact-oriented comprehension tasks require the reader to identify or produce key information that is directly represented in the text.

(2) In order to identify the main idea, the reader must differentiate between relevant versus irrelevant details.

(3) Drawing inferences requires the reader to extrapolate information that is implied but not explicitly stated in the text.

(4) In order to identify a main idea or draw an inference, the individual must create a mental model that combines information from the text with prior knowledge. The reader then tests this model to determine viable main ideas and/or draw inferences.

Stages of Reading and Spelling Development

1. Chall's stage theory (Table 10-3) is perhaps the most widely referenced theory for reading acquisition and is representative of most approaches to describing children's development of reading skills. According to this theory, each stage is qualitatively different from the next, with distinctive goals addressed during each of six stages. Each stage relies heavily on children's acquisition of knowledge and skills gained in previous stages. All age and grade ranges are approximate and language skills can be applied in all stages.

Table 10-3

Chall's Stages of Reading Development

	MAIN GOALS	SIGNIFICANCE
Stage 0 (two phases): **Phase 1: Preliteracy** **(Ages 0–3 years)**	Development of basic receptive and expressive language (phonology, morphology/syntax, semantics, pragmatics/discourse)	Unusual significance for early diagnosis and intervention • Preschool language development highly predictive of word recognition, reading fluency, and reading comprehension in grade school • Early intervention for Stage 0 skills shown to be highly effective for later language and literacy learning
Phase 2: Emergent Literacy **(Ages 3–5 years)**	Development of rudimentary phonological awareness, gross concepts of print, early letter knowledge, and book awareness	Emergent literacy skill development and literacy socialization through joint book reading with primary caregivers are significant predictors of literacy attainment in grade school
Stage 1: Decoding/ Encoding (Cracking the Code) (Grades K–1)	Development of numerous word identification skills: • Alphabetic, sound-symbol correspondence • Phonic word attack strategies (decoding) • Phonic spelling strategies (encoding) • Recognition of high-frequency sight words	Lays the foundation for fluency and strong reading comprehension
Stage 2: Automaticity/ Fluency (Ungluing from Print) (Grade 2–early grade 3)	Development of automaticity (speed and accuracy of word recognition) and fluency of text-level decoding (speed, accuracy, and intonational proficiency)	Essential for the development of efficient reading comprehension skills and difficult to attain after third grade
Stage 3: Reading to Learn (Late grade 3–grade 8)	Focus is on learning new information from the text • Expository text predominates • Focus on higher-order thinking skills, involving getting the main idea, summarizing, inferencing, and predicting	• Deficits in decoding, spelling, and/or fluency use up cognitive resources and detract from reading comprehension • Background knowledge and academic language (vocabulary and syntax) become increasingly important
Stage 4: Multiple Viewpoints (Grades 8–12)	Focus on analyzing and synthesizing information from multiple perspectives	Higher-order thinking skills, underlying language base, and background knowledge increasingly important
Stage 5: Construction and Reconstruction (College and beyond)	Involves creation of new theories based on analysis, synthesis, and evaluation of existing sources of information	Higher-order thinking skills, underlying language base, and background knowledge are increasingly important

2. Chall's theory has both strengths and weaknesses.
   a. Strengths of Chall's stage theory are its recognition of the following:
      (1) The importance of early speech and language development prior to the child's exposure to formal literacy instruction in school.
      (2) The reader's mastery of word identification skills is critical for efficiently gaining meaning from print.
   b. Weaknesses of Chall's stage theory are that it does not adequately recognize:
      (1) The importance of ongoing exposure to and development of rich oral language and higher-order thinking skills during the early grades.
      (2) The developmental trajectory for spelling and written language formulation skills.
3. Frith outlined a developmental sequence that accounts for the interaction between reading and spelling processes (Table 10-4).

Components of Writing

1. Components of writing (Table 10-5) largely parallel those involved in word recognition and reading comprehension; they include spelling, language formulation, and cognitive processes of attention, executive function, and memory. Writing places heavy demands on three broad functions: planning, translating, and reviewing.
   a. Writing skill development has been most extensively researched in the areas of spelling and composition, also referred to as *written language formulation*.
      (1) Moats posits that spelling develops in a sequence of five general stages: preliterate, sem-

Table 10-4

Summary of Frith's Developmental Phases of Reading

PHASE	WHAT IS ACQUIRED
Logographic	"Reading" or "spelling" words as pictures, with limited awareness of letter order or letter-sound correspondence. For example, relying on common environmental symbols: a red hexagonal sign at a street corner represents "stop" or yellow arches mean "McDonald's."
Alphabetic	Knowledge of sound-letter correspondence. Spelling with letters or graphemes emerges first and fosters early awareness that sounds are represented by letters. Children then begin to read phonetically, with letter-sound correspondence. Therefore, alphabetic spelling tends to precede alphabetic reading.
Orthographic	Automaticity of sound-symbol skills supports the transition to reading words as orthographic wholes, or gestalts, with fewer cognitive resources spent on alphabetic coding. Orthographic reading tends to precede orthographic spelling.

Table 10-5

Components of Writing

	ELEMENTS

Planning	1. Evaluate the writing assignment, including the topic, audience, and any motivating cues.
	2. Retrieve from long-term memory (LTM) stored knowledge of topic (schema, vocabulary, concepts) and audience (preferences), as well as previously learned strategies and plans for writing.
	3. Set goals for the writing product:
	  • Organize the plan.
	  • Monitor plans being formulated, drawing heavily on attention, executive functioning, and verbal working memory.

Translating	1. Translating comprises formulating underlying language based on plans and converting this language into print. As such, translating requires:
	  • Generation of internal oral language, including word choice, sentence formulation, and text formulation of discourse structures such as narrative or expository forms.
	  • Transcription to print, which involves application of spelling knowledge and skills for:
	    ○ Regular word spelling (/b/ + /ae/ + /t/ = bat; /tS/ + /I/ + /n/ = chin), which draws heavily on mastery of phoneme-grapheme associations.
	    ○ Rule-based spelling ("doubling rule": chip + -ing = chipping; "drop y change rule": party + s = parties), which relies on systematic instruction of such rules.
	    ○ Irregular word (yacht, buoy, any) and homophones (/meIn/ = mane, main, Maine; /saIn/ = sine, sign) spelling, which draws heavily on learning semantic-orthographic associations.
	2. In addition to the above spelling skills, transcription of language to print draws heavily on automaticity of:
	  • Fine motor skills of handwriting and/or digital keyboarding.
	  • Punctuation (commas, colons, end punctuation) and capitalization, both of which rely in part on awareness of sentence prosody and intonation.
	  • Transcription processes, which require ongoing monitoring of execution and draw heavily on cognitive functions of attention, executive functioning, and verbal working memory.

Reviewing	1. Reviewing pertains to reading and editing what has been translated.
	  • Reading relies heavily on decoding skills, as well as monitoring for match versus mismatch between the product, the plan, and the assignment.
	  • Editing involves changing the text to make it approximate the plans and goals.
	  • The process of editing and revising reinvokes transcription processes.
	2. Reviewing, like planning and editing, draws heavily on attention, executive functioning, and verbal working memory.

Table 10-6

Developmental Stages for Spelling (Moats, 2020)	
STAGE	**CHARACTERISTICS CHILDREN DISPLAY**
Preliterate/ Emergent	Awareness that spelling involves making markings on a page intended to communicate language. Example: nonalphabetic squiggles or other marks to record what they have to say.
Semiphonetic/ Letter Name	Letter names used to convey spellings of words. Examples: R U DF = "Are you deaf?"; I M SLE = "I am silly"; KNOPNR = "can opener."
Later Phonetic	Most sounds are represented accurately, with the exception of simplifications of some blends. Examples: JUP = "jump"; LITL = "little"; POWLEOW = "polio."
Syllable Juncture	Spellings reflect emergent knowledge about orthographic patterns within words. Examples: YOUNITED = "united"; EIGHTEY = "eighty"; TAOD = "toad."
Derivational	Spellings are orthographically more accurate, with evidence of developing knowledge of morphological roots and affixes. Examples: BIGG<u>E</u>R, <u>RE</u>HEAT, <u>BIOLOGY</u>

iphonetic, later phonetic, syllable juncture, and derivational (Table 10-6).

(2) Development of composition/formulation skills can be broken down into two broad phases: The emergent and the school age (conventional).

  (a) Phase 1: The emergent writing phase typically occurs between ages 4 and 6. This period is characterized first by drawing of pictures, then by drawing mixed with some alphabetic spelling. Writing serves a social and communicative function; children are telling others their thoughts or are seeking understanding of what others have written.

  (b) Phase 2: The school age, or conventional, writing phase typically occurs from the end of first grade on. This phase has numerous distinguishing characteristics.

- Sentence or multi-sentence writing that follows at least rudimentary writing conventions (i.e., alphabetic, with beginnings and endings of sentences, often with narrative elements).
- Drawing may serve an illustrative function but is distinct from text formulation.
- Early conventional writing is characterized by knowledge telling, with limited planning and monitoring.
- In grades 1 and 2, children primarily learn and develop narrative genre and some object description skills.

    – Students first learn to relate egocentric personal sequence narratives (e.g., *Yesterday, I went skiing with my mom. We rented skis. I went down the easy slope. It was fun.*).

    – Personal sequence narratives are often followed developmentally by third-person story retell structures (e.g., *Mr. Toad had a party. All his friends came. They ate tons of cake and ice cream. Then they all went home. They were stuffed!*).

    – Proto-expository object descriptions may be taught. These structures are rudimentary, typically involving listing of basic adjectival attributes and functions (e.g., *An apple is red. It is sweet. You cook apples in a pie.*).

- In the school-age writing phase, from grades 2 or 3 on, children begin to learn and develop classic expository text structures, first at the paragraph level and then in multiparagraph texts.
- Examples of expository text forms learned include but are not limited to: process, descriptive, persuasive, comparison. Multiparagraph essays often contain combinations of these expository paragraph forms.

(3) Development of writing skills parallels and interacts with development of executive functioning and higher-order thinking skills.

  (a) From grade school through high school, students exhibit increased use of key strategies for enhancing the coherence and quality of their writing, employing intra- and intersentence *cohesive ties* and discourse structure *cohesive devices* to promote textual coherence and integrity.

- Examples of *sentence* and *intersentence cohesive ties* are pronominal referencing, use of conjunctions, and use of synonyms.
- Examples of *discourse-level cohesive devices* are using introductory and concluding sentences within paragraphs; employing introductory and concluding paragraphs within essays.

  (b) Learners' use of cohesive ties parallels and complements skills *for elaboration of content* (e.g., expanding on a statement by adding detail sentences tell *How?* or *Why?* or list examples).

  (c) Students also learn planning and revising strategies for composing and elaborating on different types of narrative and expository structures. They employ and monitor rationales for supporting points of view and analyzing and discussing competing points of view.

Cognitive Factors

1. The cognitive factors of *attention, processing speed, executive functions,* and *memory* are integrally involved in supporting reading and writing.
   a. *Attention* refers to the capacity to attend selectively to stimuli and adaptively shift focus when necessary. Approximately one-third of students with attention deficit disorders exhibit concomitant reading disabilities.
   b. *Processing speed* refers to the individual's general rate of processing cognitive information in different modalities. Slow retrieval speed has a negative effect on automaticity and fluency of reading, which in turn detracts from performance on timed reading comprehension tasks.
   c. *Executive functioning* refers to the mental capacities for planning (strategizing), self-monitoring, and adaptively changing plans when the situation demands it.
      (1) With respect to executive functioning, reading requires the individual to:
         (a) *Form and enact plans* for reading text and for understanding meaning in the text.
         (b) *Self-monitor* for accuracy of reading and accuracy of understanding.
         (c) *Change* strategies when self-monitoring; indicates that the current approach or understanding is inaccurate.
   d. *Memory functions* are vast in scope. A simple model would include long-term memory, short-term memory, and verbal working memory.
      (1) With respect to memory functions, *long-term memory* (LTM) refers to the mind's permanent store of knowledge and associations.
         (a) LTM knowledge and associations for sound-symbol rules, procedures for word-recognition, vocabulary and concept maps, and strategies to support reading comprehension are a few examples of LTM's support for literacy learning.
      (2) *Short-term memory* (STM) is the temporary store for phonological or orthographic information and has practical implications for literacy learning. For example, a child learning to decode words must hold in short-term phonological memory sounds to be blended, or a student reading text must briefly hold in phonological STM an embedded sentence clause in order to extract its meaning.
      (3) Associated with STM, *working memory* (WM) is the mind's capacity to manipulate information held in temporary store. Examples of language and literacy-related tasks relying on phonological WM:
         (a) In the area of phonological awareness: "Say 'split' without the /p/ sound."
         (b) In the area of syntax: "Form a sentence beginning with the word *While*."
      (4) WM can be conceptualized as a *central executive system* supported by two support systems: a *phonological loop* and a *visual-spatial sketch pad* that support literacy learning.
         (a) The *central executive system* employs executive functioning to coordinate the operations of working memory.
         (b) The *phonological loop*, also termed the *phonological* or *verbal rehearsal*, refreshes phonological information in STM.
         (c) The *visual-spatial sketch pad* refreshes visual and orthographic in STM.
         (d) Effective practices for literacy instruction and intervention involve uses of strategies for scaffolding working memory.

Assessment of Literacy Skills

Screening, Diagnostic, Progress Monitoring, and Outcomes

1. Four general types of assessment that serve different purposes: screening, diagnostic, progress monitoring, and outcomes. Although many tests can serve more than one purpose, the goal is to find the most effective and efficient battery.
   a. Screening assessments: typically administered to all children to identify those who are at risk for failure and need additional assessment. Screenings allow for the implementation of extra instructional supports.
   b. Diagnostic assessments: used to determine at-risk students' specific patterns of strengths and weaknesses and their instructional needs. These tests are often individually administered and require lengthy testing sessions.
   c. Progress monitoring assessment (or formative or dynamic assessment): used to determine whether intervention techniques are effective or need to be modified.
      (1) Progress monitoring typically occurs throughout the year to ensure that adequate progress in reading growth is being achieved.

(2) These formative measures of progress are typically criterion-referenced—related to the actual material being taught. These tests may also be based on a specified benchmark or expected level of performance.

(3) Data from progress monitoring is critical for determining a student's "response to intervention" (see below).

d. Outcomes assessment: typically summative in nature and designed to evaluate overall reading/writing achievement.

(1) Students are often compared to other students in the same grade against a standard to determine overall progress.

(2) Outcomes assessment typically involves use of group-administered, norm-referenced achievement tests or "high-stakes tests" designed at the state level.

Preschool and School-Age Identification of Children at Risk

1. Numerous studies have helped to identify factors that can successfully predict young children's school-age literacy performance early, prior to formal instruction in school.

a. Parental histories of dyslexia predict with 40%–50% accuracy the likelihood that a child will have a reading disability.

b. Postnatal assessment of speech perception using elicited response potential (ERP) paradigms can predict with 80%–90% accuracy which children will fail at word recognition in grade school.

c. With respect to early preschool predictors, National Early Literacy Panel (2008) meta-analyses have indicated six additional variables that have medium to large predictive relationships with later literacy performance, independent of IQ or socioeconomic status (SES):

(1) Alphabetic knowledge of letter names and grapheme-phoneme associations.

(2) Phonological awareness of syllables and phonemes.

(3) Rapid automatic naming (RAN) for letters or digits, which involves the ability to rapidly name a sequence of systematically randomized rows of letters or digits.

(4) RAN for objects or colors.

(5) The ability to write letters in isolation on request or to write one's own name.

(6) Phonological memory.

(a) Additional early literacy skills that correlate moderately with at least one of several literacy achievement variables include:

• Concepts of print, referring to the child's knowledge of print conventions (e.g.,

left–right, front–back directionality) and concepts (book cover, author, text).

• Oral language, including vocabulary and grammar.

• Visual processing: the ability to match or discriminate visually presented symbols.

2. For children in kindergarten, predictors of early grade school word recognition skills include:

a. Family history of reading/writing disabilities.

b. Family reading practices.

c. Letter identification.

d. Phonological awareness.

e. Rapid naming.

f. Phonological memory (digit span, nonword repetition).

3. Kindergarten and first-grade predictors of mid- and later grade school text reading fluency include rapid naming (objects, letters, digits) and speed and accuracy of scanning for letter and nonletter shapes.

4. Kindergarten and first-grade predictors of grade school reading comprehension include:

a. Prior informational knowledge.

b. Higher-order thinking skills (concept knowledge, inferential skills, figurative language).

c. Receptive and expressive (oral) vocabulary.

d. Receptive and expressive (oral) sentence processing.

e. Narrative retell skills.

f. Deficits in earlier mentioned predictors of word recognition and reading fluency. This is because deficient decoding and decoding fluency reduces children's abilities to access meaning in text, even in children with strong underlying language skills.

(1) This diagnostic pattern has been referred to as a "decoding bottleneck."

5. Key areas to address when conducting a literacy assessment are underlying spoken language skills, reading and writing skills, underlying processing skills, and cultural context.

a. Underlying language testing should examine skills and metalinguistic awareness in the following areas: morphology, syntax, semantics, and discourse.

b. Assessment of reading and writing should examine both accuracy and automaticity of skills.

(1) Testing should determine the individual's accurate use of knowledge and skills in the areas of letter-sound correspondence, word identification, word attack, sight word reading, and passage comprehension.

(2) Automaticity and fluency assessment should address reading of real words and nonwords, oral reading of paragraphs, and silent reading speed.

(3) Assessment of spelling should address competency with spelling regular and irregular words, application of phonic rules, and knowledge of spelling rules and generalizations.

(4) Testing of written expression should determine the child's sentence and discourse-level formulation skills.

(a) Application of strategies for sentence elaboration and sentence combining should be examined.

(b) In addition, a basic assessment of writing should gather both unedited and self-edited samples of narrative and expository texts.

(c) For informal assessment of writing, writing rubrics allow holistic, criterion-related scoring to determine general level of mastery (e.g., Emerging, Adequate, Proficient, Expert).

(d) Rubrics vary according to general type of writing, narrative or expository; criteria for grade school writing vary according to students' developmental levels; general examples:

- Narrative: student employs basic story elements (setting with place and characters, initiating event or problem, character's internal response, character's attempt/solution, consequence, and emotional reaction); uses specific vocabulary and well-formed sentences; and employs correct mechanics (spelling, capitalization, punctuation, handwriting).

- Expository: student addresses the prompt, communicates goals, organizes ideas, uses specific vocabulary and well-formed sentences, provides and elaborates on rationales, and employs correct mechanics (spelling, capitalization, punctuation, handwriting).

c. Assessment of underlying cognitive processing abilities:

(1) Phonological processing assessment should address phonological awareness, phonological short-term and working memory, and rapid naming.

(2) Visual and orthographic processing can be assessed through standardized tests or can be studied informally through comparison of the student's spelling of regular versus irregular words.

(3) Additional cognitive processing factors such as attention, working memory, and executive functioning can be measured directly or inferred through informal analysis of test behaviors.

(a) In the case of noteworthy concerns regarding any of these factors, referral for neuropsychological assessment should be considered.

d. Cultural context assessment is central and should target extrinsic factors associated with literacy learning.

(1) Determining the language of the home will provide useful information about bilingual or multilingual factors.

(a) For bilingual language learners, it is critical to assess status of first language (L1) mastery level. L1 mastery is a key predictor of degree of success at L2 language learning in both oral and written domains.

(b) An important aspect of assessment is determining a language difference versus a language disorder. Assessment of L1 proficiency should be done by a professional with native or near-native proficiency in all aspects of the first language.

(2) Degree of access to reading materials and literacy practices in the home should be determined because they are crucial factors that influence literacy learning.

(3) The child's history of formal schooling can provide valuable information about quantity and quality of previous literacy instruction.

(4) Economic well-being is a general factor associated with lags in language and literacy learning, because basic resources such as food, clothing, and shelter provide foundational security for learning to take place.

(a) Direct or indirect determination of the child's economic context can help the tester understand the extent to which the child's basic needs are being met.

(6) Societal marginalization is a major factor. Race, ethnicity, gender, gender orientation, and religious beliefs are examples of factors that may result in marginalization of the individual and their family and may result in reduced access to quality literacy learning.

e. For students who are not from mainstream culture, use of standardized tests in their L2 may yield results that are not valid or reliable. Non-biased assessment is critical for accurate differentiation of a language difference versus disorder. Examples of nonbiased assessment strategies are:

(1) Assessment of the child's first language (L1) by a native or near-native speaker of L1.

(2) Repeated observation of the child's communication in multiple settings and with familiar communication partners.

(3) Language sampling of the child's L1 and L2 conducted by a clinician with native or near-native proficiency.

(4) Use of diagnostic teaching using a test-cycle.

(5) Use of a reliable cultural informant who reports on the child's language and literacy skills.

(6) Facilitating assessment through partnering with a trained interpreter.

6. In addition to the above speech-language and literacy factors, classic "exclusionary factors" to rule out in a

differential diagnosis of a specific reading/writing disability include:

a. Peripheral sensory deficits in hearing and/or vision.
b. Global cognitive delay.
c. Primary emotional disturbance.
e. Neurological insult, such as stroke or traumatic brain injury.
f. Limited environmental exposure to language and literacy learning (see cultural factors above).
(1) Confirmatory identification of these exclusionary factors may require participation of professionals from multiple disciplines, including, but not limited to, psychiatry, neurology, ophthalmology, and neuropsychology.

▶ Reading- and Writing-Related Disorders

Reading- and Writing-Related Disorders: Language Learning Disability, Dyslexia, Hyperlexia, and Attention Deficit Disorder

1. Language learning disability (LLD) is often characterized by difficulties in underlying language skills (deficits in vocabulary, morphology, syntax, discourse). In more recent years, this term is used synonymously with school-age developmental language disorder (DLD).
   a. In some cases, coexisting difficulties with word recognition and spelling (orthographic and phonological deficits) are present.
   b. In younger children who have not yet received formal reading or writing instruction, the LLD categorization is often replaced by a diagnosis of specific language impairment (SLI) (now often called a DLD).
2. Dyslexia: definition by the International Dyslexia Association (IDA, 2017): "Dyslexia is a specific learning disability that is neurobiological in origin. It is characterized by difficulties with accurate and/or fluent word recognition and by poor spelling and decoding abilities. These difficulties typically result from a deficit in the phonological component of language that is often unexpected in relation to other cognitive abilities and the provision of effective classroom instruction. Secondary consequences may include problems in reading comprehension and reduced reading experience that can impede growth of vocabulary and background knowledge."
   a. Weaknesses in word recognition and spelling, with deficits in phonological and orthographic processing.
   b. Relative strengths in underlying language skills, with typically average or above average abilities in the areas of vocabulary, morphology, syntax, and discourse.
3. Hyperlexia is typically characterized by:
   a. Deficits in underlying language skills (deficits in vocabulary, morphology, syntax, discourse).
   b. Relative strengths with word recognition and spelling.
4. Attention deficit hyperactivity disorder (ADHD) is characterized by behaviors associated with inattention and/or hyperactivity/impulsivity.
   a. ADHD is comorbid in roughly 30%–40% of cases of reading disabilities.
   b. The degree of overlap between ADHD and reading disability varies, depending on diagnostic criteria and cut-off scores employed for defining reading impairment (LLD or dyslexia) and ADHD.

▶ General Considerations for Reading and Writing Instruction

Top-Down vs. Bottom-Up

1. Debate exists regarding "top-down" versus "bottom-up" or "phonics" approaches to reading and writing instruction.
   a. Top-down, or whole language, approaches to reading and writing emphasize exposure to authentic literature and leveraging of discourse contexts.
   (1) A top-down approach to word-level reading emphasizes reading unfamiliar words through contextual guessing.
   (2) A top-down approach to spelling instruction might stress remembering the global shape of words.
   (3) With respect to written formulation, a top-down or whole language approach might emphasize

exposing students to rich, authentic texts, with the expectation that they will infer sentence and discourse-level writing skills through incidental exposure to texts.

b. Bottom-up approaches to reading, spelling, and written language formulation emphasize graduated, systematic instruction that is multimodal, involving listening, speaking, reading, and writing practice.

(1) A frequently employed bottom-up progression for teaching reading involves phonological awareness, grapheme-phoneme relationships, syllable structure recognition, morphological analysis, and text-level decoding fluency.

(2) A frequently employed bottom-up approach to spelling instruction follows a progression of types of words: regular for reading and for spelling, regular for reading but not for spelling, rule-based, irregular for reading and for spelling (for examples, see "Roles, Responsibilities, Knowledge, and Skills Required by the Speech-Language Pathologist Involved in Literacy," section 2d[2]).

(3) A bottom-up approach to writing formulation might involve multimodal instruction that systematically follows a progression, such as word, phrase, simple sentence, complex sentence, paragraph, essay.

c. Many professionals advocate for a "balanced approach" to reading that incorporates both bottom-up and top-down methods.

(1) At issue with a balanced approach is a lack of nuanced developmental perspective on when and how much bottom-up versus top-down methodology should be employed and how that balance should vary depending on the child's needs.

(2) Many balanced approaches do not employ decodable texts with beginning readers. Therefore, application of phonic word attack strategies when reading uncontrolled texts is quite difficult for readers at this level.

Sociocultural Diversity Factors

1. Social justice, inclusion, equity, and diversity factors have a major influence on children's language and literacy development.

a. As a whole, children in historically marginalized racial and ethnic cultural communities often experience an opportunity gap that results in their lagging behind mainstream peers in high-stakes measures of literacy attainment.

b. "Additive" classroom environments—school contexts that recognize and affirm the child's first language, dialect, and culture—result in higher engagement and higher English reading and writing attainment for minority language and dialect users.

c. Antiracist teaching helps to develop an additive language and literacy learning environment in which racial minority students are supported and are better able to access the curriculum.

d. Instruction of reading and writing skills that is structured and systematic results in higher literacy attainment in language minority learners than does unstructured teaching.

c. Multimodal, thematic instruction that systematically targets emergent bilinguals' (English language learners') vocabulary and sentence skills improves their listening and reading comprehension skills.

Effective Literacy Practices

Multitiered System of Supports

1. Multitiered system of supports (MTSS) blends the response to intervention (RTI) and the positive behavioral interventions and supports (PBIS) tiered frameworks to provide support for struggling students. It includes not only academic growth and achievement (RTI), but also behavioral, social, and emotional needs and absenteeism (PBIS). The goal is to identify struggling students early and intervene quickly. Key elements include:
a. Universal screening.
b. Increasing levels of targeted support.
c. Integrated plans that address academic, behavioral, social, and emotional needs.
d. Use of evidence-based strategies.
e. School-wide approach (teachers, counselors, psychologists, and other specialists).
f. Professional development.
g. Family involvement.
h. Frequent progress monitoring to guide instruction.
(1) RTI tier model.
(a) Tier 1—whole class instruction: designed to provide for the majority of students' instructional needs.
(b) Tier 2—small group intervention: for those students for whom Tier 1 instruction is insufficient.
(c) Tier 3—intensive, individualized support: designed to provide intervention that is intensive, strategic, and supplemental.

(d) While the RTI model has been adapted to varying degrees across the United States, there are challenges to its efficacy.

- There is no uniform agreement as to what comprises "research-based" instructional methods for reading intervention.
- Lack of regular educators' teacher preparation in research-based literacy methods may result in children receiving inadequate instruction in Tiers 1 and 2.
- Delayed detection of children for whom Tier 1 or Tier 2 instruction is insufficient may result in months of time passing before individualized Tier 3 instruction is provided. This has resulted in some calling RTI a "wait until they fail" approach.

i. Positive behavioral interventions and supports (PBIS) model.

(1) Tier 1—school-wide: provides practices and systems to establish a foundation of proactive support and prevent unwanted behaviors for all students.

(2) Tier 2—students at risk for developing more serious problem behaviors: practices and systems to support these students before those behaviors start.

(3) Tier 3—more intensive, individualized support to improve student behavioral outcomes: assessments used to determine needs.

Structured Literacy Approaches

1. Structured literacy approaches have been found to be effective for all learners, and at-risk learners in particular. Structured literacy practices are characterized by a hierarchically structured, systematic approach to reading and writing that is developmentally attuned to a learners' specific literacy needs. These approaches are informed by the science of reading, which provides evidence for effective instruction.

a. According to the International Dyslexia Association, specific features of a structured literacy approach include:

(1) Instruction should be explicit, systematic, cumulative, diagnostic, and responsive. Teach to success; teach within the student's zone of proximal development, ensuring automaticity (promptness and accuracy) of targeted skills before introducing new skills.

(2) Spiral back: revisit and ensure mastery of skills at different levels of language complexity.

(a) Spiraling back involves the review of previously presented concepts such as vowel sounds until students are automatic at retrieval with increasingly more complex words (e.g., CVC, CCVC, CCVCC, two-syllable words).

(b) It also involves practice and mastery of concepts such as the hard versus soft *c* rule (*co-, ca-, cu-* = /k + vowel phoneme/; *ce, cy, ci* = /s + [vowel phoneme]) at the following levels: grapheme-phoneme, syllable, word, phrase, sentence, and discourse.

b. Students with dyslexia benefit from structured approaches to word recognition, decoding, fluency, spelling, and written expression.

c. In addition to receiving systematic instruction in phonics, students with DLD who display concomitant deficits in both word recognition and underlying language should receive oral language enrichment and instruction that increases their prior knowledge and improves their vocabulary and sentence- and discourse-level language skills.

Gradual Release of Responsibility Model

1. Gradual release of responsibility model (GRRM) is considered an effective instructional model for all students struggling with literacy learning.

a. Stage 1: Initial instruction involves extensive teacher monitoring and modeling, with heavily scaffolded practice. Sometimes referred to as "I DO," meaning that the teacher is primarily responsible.

b. Stage 2: Teacher and student work together. Responsibility for practice, learning, and application involve both the teacher and student: "WE DO."

c. Stage 3: Student works independently to apply reading and writing skills: "YOU DO."

Blended Learning

1. Blended learning is a teaching method that combines technology with teacher-led instruction. The use of technology can provide a more personalized approach by providing systematic and structured instruction with scaffolding and immediate feedback at a student's skill level. Students often complete self-paced online activities with offline instruction delivered by a teacher or paraprofessional as necessary.

Systematic Writing Instruction

1. Systematic writing instruction:

a. In the area of spelling, systematic teaching of phonic spelling (encoding) and spelling rules improves accuracy and writing fluency.

b. In the area of written composition:

(1) Sentence-combining practice enhances the quantity and quality of text produced.

(2) Strategy instruction improves the form and content of both expository and narrative texts.

(3) Extensive research supports that self-regulated strategy development develops students' meta-cognitive awareness and application of techniques for supporting elements of their writing, particularly text planning, formulation, and review.

(a) The term *self-regulated* emphasizes the critical role of developing students' executive control of their writing.

▶ Efficacy of Approaches to Reading Depend on Student's Developmental Level

National Early Literacy Panel Analyses

1. National Early Literacy Panel (2008) meta-analyses of preschool literacy research indicate the following effects of different approaches on children's preliteracy skills.

   a. Moderate to large positive effects on children's conventional literacy skills for code-focused interventions (alphabetic knowledge, word-level decoding and encoding).

   b. Large effects on oral language skills for language-enhancement interventions.

   c. Moderate effects on children's print knowledge and oral language skills for book-sharing interventions.

   d. Moderate to large effects on children's oral language skills and general cognitive abilities for parent training in use of home language and cognitive stimulation.

2. The National Reading Panel meta-analyses indicate the following intervention effects for methods for improving grade-school children's reading skills (2000):

   a. Moderate effects for phonological awareness intervention, particularly when linked to letter awareness.

   b. Moderate to large effects for systematic, structured word attack and word identification instruction.

   c. Small to moderate effects for repeated readings to enhance text-level reading fluency.

   d. Positive effects for systematic vocabulary and summary writing to enhance reading comprehension skills.

▶ Legal Supports for Student Literacy

Every Student Succeeds Act

1. The Every Student Succeeds Act (ESSA; Zinskie & Rea, 2016) and the Individuals with Disabilities Education Act (IDEA, 2004).

   a. Two significant amendments to IDEA 2004 through ESSA 2015:

   (1) Changed highly qualified teacher requirements: reduces requirements for all special education personnel to a single requirement—full state certification as a special education teacher, or passed the state special education teacher licensing examination, and holds a license to teach the state as a special education teacher (with a few exceptions).

   (2) Eliminated the reference to the essential components of reading instruction from the "special rule for eligibility determination" but maintained the reference otherwise.

   (3) Essential components of reading instruction is defined as including explicit and systematic instruction in:

   (a) Phonemic awareness.

   (b) Phonics.

   (c) Vocabulary development.

   (d) Reading fluency, including oral reading skills.

   (e) Reading comprehension strategies.

   (4) Maintaining reference to the essential components of reading instruction is important for a learning disability such as dyslexia because often students are found eligible because of poor reading instruction rather than the presence of a learning disability.

Important Elements of IDEA

1. Important remaining elements of IDEA 2004:

   a. IDEA addresses issues around evaluation or assessment and identification of learning disabilities related to "written expression, basic reading skill (and) reading comprehension."

b. In addition, the law addresses RTI in noting the local educational agency's role in using "a process that determines if the child responds to scientific, research-based intervention as a part of the evaluation procedures."

c. Under IDEA, children with a qualifying learning disability are entitled to an Individualized Education Program (IEP) that meets their needs. The IEP process must include:

(1) An initial meeting in which a determination of the child's eligibility for special education is made.

(2) Provision for an independent evaluation if requested by the parents.

(a) "Measurable annual goals" that address the child's specific educational needs.

(b) A description of the setting and services required to provide the child with a free and appropriate public education (FAPE) in the least restrictive environment (LRE).

(c) Considerations for vocational and work placements for a children who are 16 or older.

(d) The parents' right to dispute their child's placement in the school district and take that dispute to an independent party for resolution.

References

The foundational references below reflect a selection of references from key sources, including the American Speech-Language-Hearing Association's (2002), *Knowledge and Skills Needed by Speech-Language Pathologists with Respect to Reading and Writing in Children and Adolescents*, as well as from the International Dyslexia Association's (2011) policy document, *Knowledge and Practice Standards for Teachers of Reading*, and additional salient research.

Aaron, P. G., Joshi, R. M., Gooden, R., & Bentum, K. (2008). Diagnosis and treatment of reading disabilities based on the component model of reading: An alternative to the discrepancy model of LD. *Journal of Learning Disabilities, 41*, 67–84.

Adams, M. J. (1990). *Beginning to Read: Thinking and Learning about Print*. Cambridge, MA: MIT Press.

American Speech-Language-Hearing Association. (1997). *Preferred Practice Patterns for the Profession of Speech-Language Pathology*. Rockville, MD: Author.

American Speech-Language-Hearing Association. (1999). *Guidelines for the Roles and Responsibilities of the School-Based Speech-Language Pathologist*. Rockville, MD: Author.

American Speech-Language-Hearing Association. (2001). *Scope of Practice for Speech-Language Pathology*. Rockville, MD: Author.

American Speech-Language-Hearing Association. (2002). *Knowledge and Skills Needed by Speech-Language Pathologists with Respect to Reading and Writing in Children and Adolescents* [Knowledge and Skills]. Available from www.asha.org/policy.

American Speech-Language-Hearing Association. (2016). Code of ethics [Ethics]. Available from www.asha.org/policy/.

Apel, K. (2009). The acquisition of mental orthographic representations for reading and spelling development. *Communication Disorders Quarterly, 31*(1), 42–52.

Ball, E. W., & Blachman, B. A. (1988). Phoneme segmentation training: Effect on reading readiness. *Annals of Dyslexia, 38*, 208–224.

Bashir, A., & Hook, P. (2009). Fluency: A key link between word identification and comprehension, *Language, Speech and Hearing Services in the Schools, 40*(2), 196–200.

Bear, D., Invernizzi, M., Templeton, S., & Johnston, P. (2000). *Words Their Way*, 2nd ed. Columbus, OH: Merrill.

Beck, I. L., & McKeown, M. G. (2006). *Improving Comprehension with Questioning the Author: A Fresh and Expanded View of a Powerful Approach*. New York: Scholastic.

Beck, I. L., McKeown, M. G., & Kucan, L. (2013). *Bringing Words to Life: Robust Vocabulary Instruction*, 2nd ed. New York: Guilford Press.

Bereiter, C., & Scardamalia, M. (1987). *The Psychology of Written Composition*. Hillsdale, NJ: Erlbaum.

Berninger, V. W., Abbott, R. D., Abbott, S. P., Graham, S., & Richards, T. (2002). Writing and reading: Connections between language by hand and language by eye. *Journal of Learning Disabilities, 35*, 39–56.

Berninger, V. W., & Amtmann, D. (2003). "Preventing Written Expression Disabilities through Early and Continuing Assessment and Intervention for Handwriting and/or Spelling Problems: Research into Practice." In H. L. Swanson, K. R. Harris, & S. Graham (Eds.), *Handbook of Learning Disabilities*. New York: Guilford Press, pp. 345–363.

Berninger, V., Vaughan, K., Abbott, R., Brooks, A., Begay, K., Curtin, G., Byrd, K., & Graham, S. (2000). Language-based spelling instruction: Teaching children to make multiple connections between spoken and written words. *Learning Disability Quarterly, 23*, 117–135.

Berninger, V., & Wolf, B. (2016). *Teaching Students with Dyslexia, Dysgraphia OWL LD, and Dyscalculia*, 2nd ed. Baltimore: Brookes.

Bickart, T. (1998). *Summary Report of Preventing Reading Difficulties in Young Children* (National Academy of Sciences). Washington, DC: U.S. Department of Education.

Biemiller, A. (2005). "Size and Sequence in Vocabulary Development: Implications for Choosing Words for Primary Grade Instruction." In E. H. Hiebert & M. L. Kamil (Eds.), *Teaching and Learning Vocabulary: Bringing Research to Practice*. Mahwah, NJ: Erlbaum.

Birsh, J., & Carreker, S. (Eds.). (2018). *Multisensory Teaching of Basic Language Skills*, 4th ed. Baltimore: Brookes.

Blachman, B. A., Schatschneider, C., Fletcher, J. M., Francis, D. J., Clonan, S., Shaywitz, B., et al. (2004). Effects of intensive reading remediation for second and third graders. *Journal of Educational Psychology*, 96, 444–461.

Brady, S., & Shankweiler, D. (Eds.). (1991). *Phonological Processes in Literacy: A Tribute to Isabelle Y. Liberman*. Hillsdale, NJ: Lawrence Erlbaum Associates.

Carlisle, J., & Rice, M. S. (2003). *Reading Comprehension: Research-Based Principles and Practices*. Baltimore: York Press.

Castles, A., Rastle, K., & Nation, K. (2018). Ending the reading wars: Reading acquisition from novice to expert. *Psychological Science in the Public Interest*, 19(1), 5–51. https://doi.org/10.1177/1529100618772271

Catts, H. W. (1993). The relationship between speech-language impairments and reading disabilities. *Journal of Speech and Hearing Research*, 36, 948–958.

Catts, H. W., Fey, M. E., Zhang, X., & Tomblin, J. A. (1999). Language basis of reading and language disabilities: Evidence from a longitudinal investigation. *Scientific Studies of Reading*, 3, 331–361.

Catts, H., Fey, M., Zhang, X., & Tomblin, J. B. (2001). Estimating the risk of future reading difficulties in kindergarten children: A research-based model and its clinical implementation. *Language, Speech, Hearing Services in Schools*, 32, 38–50.

Catts, H. W., Hogan, T. P., & Adlof, S. M. (2005). "Developmental Changes in Reading and Reading Disabilities." In H. W. Catts & A. Kamhi (Eds.), *The Connections between Language and Reading Disabilities*. Mahwah, NJ: Erlbaum, pp. 25–40.

Catts, H. W., & Kamhi, A. G. (1999). *Language and Reading Disabilities*. Boston: Allyn & Bacon.

Coyne, M., Kameenui, E. J., & Carnine, D. (Eds.). (2010). *Effective Teaching Strategies that Accommodate Diverse Learners*, 4th ed. Upper Saddle River, NJ: Prentice Hall.

Crawford, E. C., & Torgesen, J. K. (2006, July). *Teaching all children to read: Practices from Reading First schools with strong intervention outcomes*. Presented at the Florida Principal's Leadership Conference, Orlando. Retrievable from https://eric.ed.gov/?id=ED498784.

Cunningham, A. E., & Stanovich, K. E. (1997). Early reading acquisition and its relation to reading experience and ability ten years later. *Developmental Psychology*, 33, 934–945.

Cutting, L. E., & Scarborough, H. S. (2006). Prediction of reading comprehension: Relative contributions of word recognition, language proficiency, and other cognitive skills can depend on how comprehension is measured. *Scientific Studies of Reading*, 10, 277–299.

Denton, C. A., Fletcher, J. M., Anthony, J. L., & Francis, D. J. (2006). An evaluation of intensive intervention for students with persistent reading difficulties. *Journal of Learning Disabilities*, 39, 447–466.

Denton, C., Foorman, B., & Mathes, P. (2003). Schools that "beat the odds": Implications for reading instruction. *Remedial and Special Education*, 24, 258–261.

Denton, C., Vaughn, S., & Fletcher, J. (2003). Bringing research-based practice in reading intervention to scale. *Learning Disabilities Research and Practice*, 18, 201–211.

Dickinson, D., & Tabors, P. O. (Eds.). (2001). *Beginning Literacy*. Baltimore: Brookes.

Dickman, E. (2017). Do we need a new definition of dyslexia? 2017 International Dyslexia Association (IDA). Available at https://dyslexiaida.org/do-we-need-a-new-definition-of-dyslexia/.

Eagle, J. W., Dowd-Eagle, S. E., Snyder, A., & Holtzman, E. G. (2015). Implementing a multi-tiered system of support (MTSS): Collaboration between school psychologists and administrators to promote systems-level change. *Journal of Educational & Psychological Consultation*, 25(2–3), 160–177. https://doi.org/10.1080/10474412.2014.929960.

Ehri, L. (2000). Learning to read and learning to spell: Two sides of a coin. *Topics in Language Disorders*, 20(3), 19–36.

Ehri, L., Cardosa-Martins, C., & Carroll, J. (2014). "Developmental Variation in Reading Words." In A. C. Stone, E. R. Silliman, B. J. Ehren, & G. P. Wallach (Eds.), *Handbook of Language and Literacy: Development and Disorders*. New York: Guilford Press, pp. 385–407.

Fletcher, J. M., Lyon, G. R., Fuchs, L. S., & Barnes, M. A. (2007). *Learning Disabilities: From Identification to Intervention*. New York: Guilford Press.

Francis, D. J., Rivera, M., Lesaux, N., Kieffer, M., & Rivera, H. (2006). Practical guidelines for the education of English language learners: Research-based recommendations for instruction and academic interventions. Center on Instruction. Available at https://www2.ed.gov/about/inits/ed/lep-partnership/interventions.pdf.

Gersten, R., & Baker, S. (2001). Teaching expressive writing to students with learning disabilities: A metaanalysis. *Elementary School Journal*, 101, 251–272.

Goldenberg, C. (2013, Summer). Unlocking the research on English learners: What we know—and don't yet know—about effective instruction. *American Educator*, 37(2), 4–11, 38 Summer. Available at https://eric.ed.gov/?id=EJ1014021.

Good, R. H., Simmons, D. C., & Kame'enui, E. J. (2001). The importance and decision-making utility of a continuum of fluency-based indicators of foundational reading skills for third-grade high-stakes outcomes. *Scientific Studies of Reading*, 5(3), 257–288.

Gough, P., & Tunmer, W. (1986). Decoding, reading, and reading disability. *Remedial and Special Education*, 7, 6–10.

Graham, S., McArthur, C. A., & Fitzgerald, J. (Eds.). (2019). *Best Practices in Writing Instruction*, 3rd ed. New York: Guilford Press.

Gutierrez-Clellan, V. F. (2000). Dynamic assessment: An approach to assessing children's language-learning potential. *Seminars in Speech and Language*, 21, 215–222.

Hart, B., & Risley, T. R. (1995). *Meaningful Differences in the Everyday Experience of Young American Children*. Baltimore: Brookes.

Haynes, C., & Jennings, T. (2006, Spring). Listening and speaking: Essential ingredients for teaching struggling writers. *Perspectives*, 32(2), 12–16.

Henry, M. (2010). *Unlocking Literacy*, 2nd ed. Baltimore: Brookes.

Hernbest, V., & Apel, K. (2017). Effective word reading instruction: What does the evidence tell us? *Communication Disorders Quarterly*, 39(1), 303–311.

Hirsch, E. D. (2001). Overcoming the language gap. *American Educator*, 25(2), 4, 6–7.

Hirsch, E. D. (2006a). Building knowledge: The case for bringing content into the language arts block and for a

knowledge-rich curriculum core for all children. *American Educator*, 30(1), 8–21, 28–29, 50–51.

Hirsch, E. D. (2006b). *The Knowledge Deficit: Closing the Shocking Education Gap for American Children*. Boston: Houghton Mifflin.

Hook, P., & Crawford-Brooke, E. (2015). "Teaching the Fundamentals of Reading: Word Identification and Fluency." In T. A. Ukrainetz (Ed.), *School-Age Language Intervention: Evidence-Based Practices*. Austin, TX: PRO-ED, pp. 493–527.

Hook, P., & Haynes, C. (2017). "Reading and Writing in Child Language Disorders." In R. Schwartz (Ed.), *Handbook of Child Language Disorders*, 2nd ed. New York: Taylor & Francis.

Hoover, W. A., & Gough, P. B. (1990). The simple view of reading. *Reading and Writing*, 2, 127–160.

Hulme, C., & Snowling, M. (2009). *Developmental Disorders of Language, Learning, and Cognition*. Oxford, England: Wiley-Blackwell.

Individuals with Disabilities Educational Act (IDEA). (2004). Available at https://sites.ed.gov/idea/.

International Dyslexia Association. (2017, February). Do we need a new definition of dyslexia? Available at https://dyslexiaida.org/do-we-need-a-new-definition-of-dyslexia/.

Joshi, M., Treiman, R., Carreker, S., & Moats, L. C. (2008, 2009). How words cast their spell: Spelling is an integral part of learning the language, not a matter of memorization. *American Educator*, 32(4), 6–16, 42–43.

Kamil, M. (2004). "Vocabulary and Comprehension Instruction: Summary and Implications of the National Reading Panel Findings." In P. McCardle & V. Chhabra (Eds.), *The Voice of Evidence in Reading Research*. Baltimore: Brookes, pp. 213–234.

Katzir, T., Kim, Y., Wolf, M., O'Brien, B., Kennedy, B., Lovett, M., et al. (2006). Reading fluency: The whole is more than the parts. *Annals of Dyslexia*, 56(1), 51–82.

Kintsch, E. (2005). Comprehension theory as a guide for the design of thoughtful questions. *Topics in Language Disorders*, 25(1), 51–64.

Kuchirko, Y. (2017). On differences and deficits: A critique of the theoretical and methodological underpinnings of the word gap. *Journal of Early Childhood Literacy*, 19(4), 533–562.

Leach, J. M., Scarborough, H. S., & Rescorla, L. (2003). Late-emerging reading disabilities. *Journal of Educational Psychology*, 95, 211–224.

Leonard, L. B. (2014). Children with specific language impairment and their contribution to the study of language development. *Journal of Child Language*, 41(S1), 38–47. https://doi.org/10.1017/S0305000914000130.

Lovett, M. W., Barron, R. W., & Frijters, J. C. (2013). "Word Identification Difficulties in Children and Adolescents with Reading Disabilities: Intervention Research Findings." In H. L. Swanson, K. R. Harris, & S. Graham (Eds.), *Handbook of Learning Disabilities*. New York: Guilford Press, pp. 329–360.

Lovett, M. W., Lacerenze, L., & Borden, S. L. (2000). Putting struggling readers on the PHAST track: A program to integrate phonological and strategy-based remedial reading instruction and maximize outcomes. *Journal of Learning Disabilities*, 33, 458–476.

Lyon, R., Shaywitz, S., & Shaywitz, B. (2003). A definition of dyslexia. *Annals of Dyslexia*, 53, 1–14.

MacArthur, C. A. (2000). New tools for writing: Assistive technology for students with writing difficulties. *Topics in Language Disorders*, 20(4), 85–100.

Masterson, J., & Apel, K. (2000). Spelling assessment: Charting a path to optimal intervention. *Topics in Language Disorders*, 20(3), 50–66.

McCardle, P., & Chhabra, V. (2004). *The Voice of Evidence in Reading Research*. Baltimore: Brookes.

Meyer, M. S., & Felton, R. H. (1999). Repeated reading to enhance fluency: Old approaches and new directions. *Annals of Dyslexia*, 49, 293–306.

Michaels, S. (1981). Sharing time: Children's narrative styles and differential access to literacy. *Language in Society*, 10, 423–442.

Moats, L. C. (2020). *Speech to Print: Language Essentials for Teachers*, 3rd ed. Baltimore: Brookes.

Moats, L. C., & Dakin, K. (2007). *Basic Facts about Dyslexia*. Baltimore: The International Dyslexia Association.

Murphey, David, PhD. (2014). *The Academic Achievement of English Language Learners: Data for the U.S. and Each of the States. Child Trends*. Office of English Language Acquisition (OCELA). (2018).

National Early Literacy Panel. (2008). Developing early literacy: Report of the National Early Literacy Panel. Washington, DC: National Institute for Literacy. Available at https://lincs.ed.gov/publications/pdf/NELPReport09.pdf.

National Reading Panel. (2000). *Teaching Children to Read: An Evidence-based Assessment of the Scientific Research Literature on Reading and its Implications for Reading Instruction*. Washington, DC: National Institutes of Health.

Olson, R. K. (2004). SSSR, environment, and genes. *Scientific Studies of Reading*, 8(2), 111–124.

Pacheco, M. B., Daniel, S. M., & Pray, L. C. (2017, November). Scaffolding practice: Supporting emergent bilinguals' academic language use in two classroom communities. *Language Arts*, 95(2).

Paradis, J., Genesee, F., & Crago, M. (2011). *Dual Language Development & Disorders: A Handbook on Bilingualism & Second Language Learning*, 2nd ed. Baltimore: Brookes.

Paul, R., Norbury, C., & Gosse, C. (2018). *Language Disorders from Infancy through Adolescence: Listening, Speaking, Reading, Writing, and Communicating*, 5th ed. Maryland Heights, MO: Elsevier/Mosby.

Pennington, B. (2009). *Diagnosing Learning Disorders*, 2nd ed. New York: Guilford Press.

Petscher, Y., Cabell, S., Catts, H. W., Compton, D., Foorman, B., Hart, S. A., et al. (2020). How the Science of Reading Informs 21st Century Education, May 10. https://doi.org/10.31234/osf.io/yvp54.

Rayner, K., Foorman, B. F., Perfetti, C. A., Pesetsky, D., & Seidenberg, M. S. (2002). How should reading be taught? *Scientific American*, 286(3), 84–91.

Roth, F. P. (2000). Narrative writing: Development and teaching with children with writing difficulties. *Topics in Language Disorders*, 20(4), 15–28.

Ruddell, R. B., Ruddell, M. R., & Singer, H. (Eds.). (1994). *Theoretical Models and Processes of Reading*, 4th ed. Newark, DE: International Reading Association.

Samuels, S. J., & Flor, R. F. (1997). The importance of automaticity for developing expertise in reading. *Reading and Writing Quarterly: Overcoming Learning Difficulties*, 13, 107–121.

Scarborough, H. S. (1998). "Early Identification of Children at Risk for Reading Disabilities: Phonological Awareness and Some Other Promising Predictors." In B. K. Shapiro, P. J. Accardo, & A. J. Capute (Eds.), *Specific Reading Disability: A View of the Spectrum*. Timonium, MD: York Press, pp. 75–119.

Scarborough, H. S. "Connecting Early Language and Literacy to Later Reading (Dis)abilities: Evidence, Theory, and Practice." In S. B. Neuman & D. K. Dickinson (Eds.), *Handbook of Early Literacy Research*. New York: Guilford Press, pp. 97–110.

Scardamalia, M., & Bereiter, C. (1986). "Research on Written Composition." In M. C. Wittrock (Ed.), *Handbook of Research on Teaching*. New York: Macmillan, pp. 778–803.

Schwirzke, K., Vashaw, L., & Watson, J. (2018). "A History of K-12 Online and Blended Instruction in the United States." In K. Kennedy & R. E. Ferdig (Eds.), *Handbook of Research on K-12 Online and Blended Learning*, 2nd ed. Pittsburgh, PA: ETC Press, pp. 7–20.

Scott, C. (1999). "Learning to Write." In H. W. Catts & A. G. Kamhi (Eds.), *Language and Reading Disabilities*. Boston: Allyn & Bacon, pp. 224–258.

Scott, C. (2000). Principles and methods of spelling instruction: Applications for poor spellers. *Topics in Language Disorders*, 20(3), 66–82.

Scott, C. (2004). "Syntactic Contributions to Literacy Development." In C. Stone, E. Stillman, B. Ehren, & K. Apel (Eds.). *Handbook of Language & Literacy*. New York: Guilford Press, pp. 340–362.

Scott, C., & Brown, S. (2001). Spelling and the speech-language pathologist: There's more than meets the eye. *Seminars in Speech and Language*, 22, 197–298.

Seidenberg, M. (2017). *Language at the Speed of Sight: How We Read, What Many Can't Read, and What Can Be Done about It*. New York: Basic Books.

Shaywitz, S. (2003). *Overcoming Dyslexia: A New and Complete Science-Based Program for Reading Problems at Any Level*. New York: Knopf.

Silliman, E. R., Jimerson, T. L., & Wilkinson, L. C. (2000). A dynamic systems approach to writing assessment in students with language learning problems. *Topics in Language Disorders*, 20(4), 45–64.

Snow, C. E., Burns, M. S., & Griffin, P. (Eds.). (1998). *Preventing Reading Difficulties in Young Children*. Washington, DC: National Academy Press.

Snow, C., Griffin, P., & Burns, S. (2006). *Knowledge to Support the Teaching of Reading*. San Francisco: Jossey-Bass.

Spear-Swerling, L. (2004). "A Road Map for Understanding Reading Disability and Other Reading Problems: Origins, Intervention, and Prevention." In R. Ruddell & N. Unrau (Eds.), *Theoretical Models and Processes of Reading*, vol. 5. Newark, DE: International Reading Association.

Spear-Swerling, L. (2008). "Response to Intervention and Teacher Preparation." In E. Grigorenko (Ed.), *Educating Individuals with Disabilities: IDEA 2004 and Beyond*. New York: Springer, pp. 273–293.

Spear-Swerling, L., & Sternberg, R. J. (2001). What science offers teachers of reading. *Learning Disabilities Research & Practice*, 16, 51–57.

Speece, D. L., & Ritchey, K. D. (2005). A longitudinal study of the development of oral reading fluency in young children at risk for reading failure. *Journal of Learning Disabilities*, 38(5), 387–399.

Stahl, K. A. D. (2004). Proof, practice, and promise: Comprehension strategy instruction in the primary grades. *Reading Teacher*, 57, 598–609.

Stahl, S. A., & Heubach, K. (2005). Fluency-oriented reading instruction. *Journal of Literacy Research*, 37, 25–60.

Stahl, S. A., & Nagy, W. E. (2006). *Teaching Word Meanings*. Mahwah, NJ: Erlbaum.

Stanovich, K. E. (2000). *Progress in Understanding Reading: Scientific Foundations and New Frontiers*. New York: Guilford Press.

Sterne, A., & Goswami, U. (2000). Phonological awareness of syllables, rhymes, and phonemes in deaf children. *Journal of Childhood Psychology and Psychiatry*, 41, 609–625.

Stone, A. C., Silliman, E. R., Ehren, B. J., & Wallach, G. (Eds.). (2014). *Handbook of Language and Literacy: Development and Disorders*, 2nd ed. New York: Guilford Press.

Tabors, P. O., & Snow, C. E. (2001). "Young Bilingual Children and Early Literacy Development." In S. B. Neuman & D. K. Dickinson (Eds.), *Handbook of Early Literacy Research*. New York: Guilford, pp. 157–178.

Torgesen, J. K. (2004). "Lessons Learned from Research on Interventions for Students Who Have Difficulty Learning to Read." In P. McCardle & V. Chhabra (Eds.), *The Voice of Evidence in Reading Research*. Baltimore: Brookes, pp. 355–381.

Trieman, R. (1993). *Beginning to Spell: A Study of First Grade Children*. New York: Oxford University Press.

Ukrainetz, T. A. (Ed.). (2015). *School-Age Language Intervention: Evidence-Based Practices*. Austin, TX: PRO-ED.

UNESCO. (2006). Education for All: A Global Monitoring Report. Chapter 6: "Understandings of Literacy," 147–159. http://www.unesco.org/education/GMR2006/full/chapt6_eng.pdf.

U.S. Department of Education, National Center for Education Statistics. (2018). The Condition of Education 2018 (2018-144), English Language Learners in Public Schools.

Vellutino, F. R., Tunmer, W. E., Jaccard, J. J., & Chen, R. (2007). Components of reading ability: Multivariate evidence for a convergent skills model of reading development. *Scientific Studies of Reading*, 11(1), 3–32.

Westby, C. E. (1994). "The Effects of Culture on Genre, Structure, and Style of Oral and Written Texts." In G. P. Wallach & K. G. Butler (Eds.), *Language Learning Disabilities in School-Aged Children and Adolescents*. Boston: Allyn & Bacon, pp. 180–218.

Westby, C. E. (2004). "A Language Perspective on Executive Functioning, Metacognition, and Self-Regulation in Reading." In C. A. Stone, E. R. Silliman, B. J. Ehren, & K. Apel (Eds.), *Handbook of Language and Literacy: Development and Disorders*. New York: Guilford Press, pp. 398–427.

Wolf, M. (2007). *Proust and the Squid: The Story and Science of the Reading Brain*. New York: Harper Collins.

Wolf, M., & Bowers, P. G. (1999). The double-deficit hypothesis for the developmental dyslexias. *Journal of Educational Psychology*, 91, 415–438.

Wong, B. Y. L. (2000). Writing strategies instruction for expository essays for adolescents with and without learning disabilities. *Topics in Learning Disorders*, 20(4), 29–44.

Zinskie, C. D., & Rea, D. W. (2016). The Every Student Succeeds Act (ESSA): What It Means for Educators of Students at Risk. *National Youth-At-Risk Journal*, 2(1). https://doi.org/10.20429/nyarj.2016.020101.

Review Questions

1. What two processes is written language composed of?

   a. Receptive processes (reading) and expressive processes (writing).
   b. Receptive processes (listening) and expressive processes (speaking).
   c. Phonemic and phonetic processes.
   d. Orthography and morphology.

2. Which of the following is NOT involved in phonic word attack and encoding?

   a. Phonological awareness.
   b. Grapheme-phoneme correspondence.
   c. Cohesive markers.
   d. Syllable recognition.

3. Which of the following is referred to as being able to identify which words start with the same sound?

   a. Rhyme awareness.
   b. Onset-rime awareness.
   c. Mophological awareness.
   d. Word awareness.

4. What is grapheme-phoneme correspondence frequently referred to as?

   a. Sound-symbol correspondence.
   b. Phonetic-phonemic correspondence.
   c. Syntax and morphology.
   d. Onset-rime.

5. What type of reading most involves gestalt recognition?

   a. Phonemic awareness.
   b. Phonetic awareness.
   c. Sight word reading.
   d. Phonics application.

6. Which of the following is an example of the preliterate stage of spelling?

   a. A child makes scribbles on a piece of paper and announces he wrote his name.
   b. The child spells *run* as "rn" and *couch* as "cowch."
   c. The child spells *united* as "younited."
   d. The child spells *bigger, stronger, faster*.

7. In what age range does the emergent writing phase typically occur?

    a. 3–4 years.
    b. 4–6 years.
    c. 7–8 years.
    d. 10–12 years.

8. Which of the following is an example of a phonemic awareness task?

    a. Say "pants" without the /p/.
    b. Use the word *understood* in a sentence.
    c. Repeat back the following numbers: one, nine, eight, five, zero, three.
    d. Name as many words starting with the letter *B* as you can in 60 seconds. Go!

9. According to Chall's stage theory, at what stage is the student "ungluing from print"?

    a. Stage 0.
    b. Stage 1.
    c. Stage 2.
    d. Stage 3.

10. According to the Early Literacy Panel meta-analyses, which is NOT a variable that predicts later literacy performance?

    a. Age of parents.
    b. Alphabet knowledge.
    c. Rapid automatic naming.
    d. Phonological memory.

11. When conducting a literacy assessment and examining underlying spoken language skills, which of the following should be addressed?

    a. Morphology.
    b. Syntax.
    c. Semantics.
    d. All of the above.

12. Which would likely NOT be addressed when assessing automaticity/fluency?

    a. Real words.
    b. Nonwords.
    c. Oral reading of paragraphs.
    d. Reading of tongue twisters.

13. A phonological processing assessment should address which of the following?

    a. Comparison of the student's spelling of regular versus irregular words.
    b. Phonological awareness, phonological short-term and working memory, rapid naming.
    c. Speed of silent reading of a paragraph.
    d. Executive functioning and working memory.

14. When it comes to cultural factors in literacy assessments, it is important to consider which of the following?

    a. Access to reading materials and literacy practices in the home.
    b. Quantity and quality of previous literacy instructions.
    c. Both a and b.
    d. None of the above.

15. Persons with hyperlexia most often show deficits in which of the following areas?

   a. Word recognition.
   b. Spelling.
   c. Underlying language skills.
   d. Automaticity.

16. What are some frequent strengths seen in those with dyslexia?

   a. Word recognition and spelling.
   b. Phonological processing.
   c. Orthographic processing.
   d. Underlying language skills.

17. Top-down processing is also referred to as which of the following?

   a. Whole language processing.
   b. Systematic instruction.
   c. Sensory processing.
   d. Detail-oriented processing.

18. Literacy instruction for at-risk readers should:

   a. Be taught at the students' current grade level.
   b. Be hierarchically structured.
   c. Be supplemental.
   d. Introduce many skills at once.

19. The IDEA:

   a. Does not address the use of an Individual Educational Plan (IEP).
   b. Only pertains to learning disabilities exhibited by children.
   c. Does not have legal implications for the education of handicapped children.
   d. Specifically addresses individuals who struggle with reading and writing difficulties.

20. The National Reading Panel meta-analyses indicated:

   a. Moderate to large effects for systematic, structured word attack and word identification instruction.
   b. Negative effects for vocabulary instruction and summary writing to enhance reading comprehension skills.
   c. Moderate effects for orthographic awareness intervention.
   d. No effect for repeated readings to enhance text-level reading fluency.

11

Autism Spectrum Disorders

GAIL J. RICHARD, PhD

4. Early warning signs of possible ASD can be observed by 12–15 months, and a diagnosis of ASD can occur by 24 months (Table 11-8).
5. Screening instruments for ASD can be completed by health care providers and/or parents.
   a. First Year Inventory (FYI, 2003).
      (1) Purpose is to identify children at risk for ASD or related developmental disorders.
      (2) Explores two developmental domains—social communication and sensory regulatory function.
   b. Checklist for Autism in Toddlers (CHAT, 2000); Modified Checklist for Autism in Toddlers (M-CHAT, 2001); Modified Checklist for Autism in Toddlers, Revised, with Follow-up (M-CHAT-R/F, 2009).
      (1) The CHAT was designed to be used as a screening tool at an 18-month checkup.
      (2) The M-CHAT expands on the CHAT with 23 questions and targets diagnosis by 24 months.
      (3) The M-CHAT-R/F is a 20-item parent-report questionnaire designed for use at 16–30 months.
         (a) The instrument is intended to maximize sensitivity regarding the possibility of ASD.
         (b) The high number of false-positive results are the reason for the Follow-up questionnaire, intended to more carefully evaluate the risk of autism versus other types of developmental delays.

   c. Communication and Symbolic Behavior Scales Developmental Profile (CSBS DP, 2002) and Systematic Observation of Red Flags (SORF, 2004).
      (1) The CSBS DP identifies communication and symbolic play deficits that are not specific to ASD but are sensitive to the core behaviors.
      (2) The SORF rates specific "red flags" for ASD from the CSBS DP screening procedures.
   d. Social Communication Questionnaire (SCQ, 2003).
      (1) A 40-item parent questionnaire to screen for autism.
      (2) Intended for older children (i.e., 4 years and older).
   e. Earlier diagnosis allows for initiation of treatment to address differences in development.

Diagnostic Procedures in ASD

1. Procedures should include a compilation of information and an evaluation of the individual.
   a. Review background information and developmental records and reports.
   b. Interview the parent/caregiver to explore family history, the child's general health and medical background, behavior, and developmental progression in speech-language, motor, sensory, and social interaction areas.
   c. Conduct an observation, behavioral evaluation, and interaction with the individual.
   d. Administer appropriate assessment tools for a normative comparison in developmental areas, particularly communication skills.
   e. Diagnostic instruments for ASD determination.
      (1) Autism Diagnostic Observation Schedule, 2nd ed. (ADOS-2, 2012).
         (a) Considered the gold standard in the diagnosis of ASD.

Table 11-7

National Institute of Child Health and Human Development's Five Warning Behaviors for ASD Evaluation
Does not babble or coo by 12 months.
Does not gesture (point, wave, grasp) by 12 months.
Does not say single words by 16 months.
Does not say two-word phrases on his/her own by 24 months.
Has loss of language or social skills at any age.

Table 11-8

ASD Social-Communication Warning Signs		
9–12 MONTHS	**18 MONTHS**	**24 MONTHS**
Lack of response to name	Lack of response to name	Lack of responsiveness
Lack of social smile	Lack of shared joy	Lack of shared enjoyment
Poor mutual attention	Poor joint attention	Lack of facial expression
Limited gestures	Minimal pointing or gesturing	Lack of pointing to shared interest
Poor imitation	Unusual prosody to speech	Poor imitation; delayed speech
Poor eye contact	Lack of appropriate gaze	Abnormal eye contact
Limited affective range	Lack of shared interests	Limited interest in shared games
Extreme passivity	Repetitive body movements	Over- or underreaction to sensory stimuli
Poor visual orientation to stimuli	Repetitive movement with objects	Unusual visual interests; unusual play with objects

Adapted from Wetherby et al. (2004).

(b) Evaluates ASD and other pervasive developmental disorders (PDD) from early childhood to adult ages.

(c) Four modules to evaluate:
- Communication.
- Reciprocal social interaction.
- Stereotypic behaviors and interests.
- Play.

(2) Autism Diagnostic Interview—Revised (ADI-R, 2003).

(a) Evaluates three domains of autism:
- Language/communication.
- Reciprocal social interaction.
- Restricted, repetitive, stereotyped behaviors.

(b) Interview caregivers to probe for ASD behaviors.

(c) Assesses children through adult ages.

(3) Childhood Autism Rating Scale, 2nd ed. (CARS-2, 2011).

(a) Evaluates ages 2 years and older, using an observation instrument.

(b) Determines the severity of ASD symptoms using a rating scale to evaluate presenting behaviors.

(4) Gilliam Autism Rating Scale, 3rd ed. (GARS-3, 2014).

(a) Checklist normed from ages 3–22 years.

(b) Categorizes observed behavioral deficits into stereotyped behaviors, communication, and social interactions.

(c) Results in an autism quotient that designates the risk of ASD.

Treatment

National Research Council

1. The National Research Council's (NRC, 2001[RC11]) review of evidence resulted in recommendations for essential aspects of intervention for children with ASD.
   a. Identify ASD and begin intervention as early as possible. Intervention initiated by age 3 years significantly improves outcomes.
   b. Provide intensive intervention that promotes active engagement (i.e., minimum of 5 hours a day, 5 days a week) through collaboration with family and teachers to structure teaching opportunities in natural learning environments.
   c. Provide systematic, repeated, instructional activities in brief, focused time intervals.
   d. Train family members to implement teaching strategies to reinforce learning and minimize disruptive behaviors.
   e. Individual instruction and low student-to-teacher ratio improves the efficacy of instructional strategies.
   f. Maintain ongoing assessment data to prompt modifications in program objectives, based on regular review of client progress.
   g. Instructional priorities for individuals with ASD, specified by NRC.
      (1) Functional, spontaneous communication.
      (2) Social skills addressed in various environments.
      (3) Peer interaction and play skills.
      (4) New skills generalized and maintained in natural contexts.
      (5) Functional assessment and support to address problematic behaviors.
      (6) Functional academic skills.

Intervention Goals

1. Intervention goals should be derived from multiple assessment procedures.
   a. Avoid criterion referencing in interpretation of results.
   b. Carefully evaluate validity of performance results.
   c. Consider the clinical impressions during assessment as well as resulting scores.
2. Impressions from informal observation and interaction.
   a. Core features of social pragmatic competence are difficult to assess in formal procedures.
   b. Consider the strengths and weaknesses, as well as adaptive and maladaptive behaviors.
   c. Evaluate communication in different settings and with different people.
   d. Include both verbal and nonverbal communication impressions.
3. Reports from parents, caregivers, and teachers.
   a. Identify learning objectives designated by the classroom curriculum.
   b. Identify family priorities, typical environments, and communication partners.
   c. Be sensitive to cultural expectations and concerns.

Language Impairments within ASD

1. The American Speech-Language-Hearing Association (ASHA) has generated guidelines (2006a, 2006b) that specify major domains and sample goals for SLP intervention with ASD (see Tables 11-6 and 11-9).
   a. Joint attention.
   b. Social reciprocity.
   c. Language and related cognitive skills.
   d. Behavior and emotional regulation.
2. Pragmatic language (use of language in social contexts) is the primary impairment in all types and severity levels of ASD.
   a. Young children require basic pragmatic skill instruction (e.g., turn-taking, sharing, joint attention, polite requests and responses).
   b. School-age children require pragmatic skills consistent with peer interaction (e.g., considering others' feelings, sharing interests, politely expressing preferences, shared attention).
   c. Adolescents and adults require more complex pragmatic skills involved in executive functions and nonverbal messages (e.g., reading others' intentions, making decisions, problem-solving, determining appropriate verbal questions and responses, understanding others' feelings and perspectives).
3. Semantic language (word meanings) is usually impaired in all types of ASD.
   a. Young children limit vocabulary to items of interest and words gained through functional experience. Goals should address conceptual terms necessary for academic learning, such as quantity, quality, and positional prepositions.
   b. School-age children need to transition from literal to abstract and metalinguistic aspects of semantics, such as multiple meanings, idiomatic expressions, and figurative language.
   c. Adolescents and adults lack comprehension of semantic nuances, such as inferred meaning, humor, sarcasm, discourse/conversational rules, as well as vocabulary consistent with adult independent living expectation (e.g., hygiene, health, banking, transportation).
4. Syntax and morphology (grammar rules for word and sentence construction) are impaired when language deficits are present.
   a. Young children speak telegraphically and omit articles, verb conjugations, and small connective words.
   b. School-age children struggle with pronouns, preferring to use concrete reference and proper nouns, as well as morphological markers, such as plurals, possessives, verb conjugations, and conjunctions.
5. Phonology (rules of sound combinations) and articulation (oral motor sound production) are impaired when childhood apraxia of speech or significant expressive speech delays are present.
   a. Young children may produce jargon and echolalia but may not be able to program or produce spontaneous voluntary speech.
   b. Goals should establish basic power words for immediate environmental impact, such as *no, stop, help, want,* and so on.
   c. Augmentative and alternative communication (AAC) techniques supplement and facilitate speech production attempts.

Table 11-9

Description of Intervention Approaches for ASD

INTERVENTION TYPE	DESCRIPTION/EXAMPLE
Environmental arrangements and structure	Use preferred materials, sabotage to promote interaction, space designed for visual clarity.
Picture schedules and visual supports	Picture sequences for activity, steps to complete, pictured choices, visual prompts.
Written scripts and social stories	Cue cards, prompts for initiation, practice script until generalized, identification of relevant aspects of activity, thought bubbles.
Video modeling	Recorded highlight of critical features within situation, visual feedback and example of desired behavior, relate better to video/object.
Computerized instruction	Teach focused communication aspects; nonsocial nature of computer beneficial.
Previewing learning context and activity	Prepare for coming events, decrease anxiety behaviors.
Strategies to promote generalization	Transfer new skill to natural environment, use parents, caregivers, field trips.
Strategies to promote self-generalization	Increase control and independence, make decisions, express preferences.

Adapted from American Speech-Language-Hearing Association (2006a).

Guidelines for Goal Prioritization

1. Establish a functional, meaningful, independent vehicle for communication.
   a. Allow the individual to express basic wants and needs.
   b. Alleviate frustration and decrease behavioral outbursts.
   c. Can be expressive, gestural, or augmented (AAC).
2. Continually evaluate receptive comprehension of language.
   a. Facilitate determination of educational curriculum expectations.
   b. Provide parents and teachers with guidance for expressive language input that the individual can understand.
   c. Revise treatment goals to progressively increase functional comprehension.
3. Focus on increased appropriate social engagement and interaction (Table 11-10).
   a. Joint attention and social engagement are critical features for learning.
   b. Appropriate social behavior improves access to diverse environments and opportunities for learning.
   c. Future vocational and occupational options are increased with appropriate reciprocal social communication skills.

Table 11-10

Sample Goal Hierarchy for Social Pragmatics
Joint attention
Turn-taking/reciprocity
Initiation
Play
Topicalization
Communicative functions
Conversational discourse
• Negotiation • Persuasion • Narration • Humor • Empathy
Nonverbal communication
• Facial expression • Body language/gesture • Paralinguistics • Proxemics
Presupposition

Adapted from Richard & Veale (2009).

4. Adjust treatment goals to level of language competence and potential.
   a. Initiate goals with objectives to establish functional, concrete competence.
   b. Progress in goal areas, guided by treatment data, to complex abstract levels.

▶ Intervention Methodologies

Variety of Intervention Methodologies

1. The SLP must consider several factors when choosing a treatment method.
   a. Review the research to explore the evidence base to support efficacy.
   b. Consider the unique needs and characteristics of the individual with ASD.
   c. Critically evaluate the advantages/disadvantages and core features of the intervention method.
   d. Reconcile philosophical beliefs with realistic parameters for best practice principles.
   e. Categorize treatment methodologies by primary emphasis:
      (1) Behavioral.
      (2) Developmental.
      (3) Naturalistic.
      (4) Affective or relationship-based.
   f. Maintain focus on the core characteristics of ASD and essential outcomes.
2. ASHA Guidelines (2006a, 2006b) present several types of intervention strategies that capitalize on strengths within ASD (see Table 11-9).

Classification System for Intervention

1. Proposed by the National Standards Project (National Autism Center, 2009a, 2009b, 2015).
   a. Reviewed research to establish an evidence base for intervention decisions in ASD.
   b. Created a merit-based rating scale to evaluate treatment effects reported in research articles.

Table 11-11

Treatment Techniques in Efficacy Categories

ESTABLISHED INTERVENTIONS	EMERGING INTERVENTIONS	UNESTABLISHED INTERVENTIONS
• Behavioral • Cognitive behavioral package • Comprehensive behavioral treatment for young children • Language training (production) • Modeling • Natural teaching strategies • Parent training • Peer training • Pivotal response • Schedules • Scripting • Self-management • Social skills package • Story-based	• Augmentative and alternative communication • Developmental relationship-based treatment • Exercise • Exposure package • Functional communication • Imitation-based • Initiation training • Language training (production & comprehension) • Massage/touch therapy • Multicomponent package • Music therapy • Picture exchange communication system • Reductive package • Sign instruction • Social communication • Structured teaching • Technology • Theory of mind	• Animal-assisted therapy • Auditory integration training (AIT) • Concept mapping • DIR/floor time • Facilitated communication (FC) • Gluten- and casein-free diets • Movement-based • SENSE Theatre • Sensory integration • Shock therapy • Social behavioral learning strategy • Social cognition • Social thinking

Adapted from National Autism Center (2015).

c. Classification system placed treatment methods in efficacy categories in regard to ASD (Table 11-11).
  (1) Established: sufficient research evidence to suggest a favorable outcome.
  (2) Emerging: appears favorable, but not consistently showing research-based conclusive evidence.
  (3) Unestablished: little or no evidence to form conclusion on treatment effectiveness; may be effective, ineffective, or harmful.
d. The classification system is a beneficial effort to guide ASD intervention, but there are some limitations.
  (1) Behavioral treatments show the strongest efficacy.
    (a) Concrete, measurable, clean administration.
    (b) Able to quantify results using research standards.
  (2) Nonbehavioral treatments are valuable, despite weak support.
    (a) Difficult to quantify in measurable research terms.
    (b) Individualized functional outcomes are important.
    (c) More research is needed on this type of intervention.

Description of Selected ASD Intervention Techniques

1. Applied behavioral analysis (ABA) and discrete trial teaching (DTT).

  a. Principle of behavior modification through operant conditioning.
  b. Teach skills through carefully sequenced steps of objectives.
  c. Intense focused training with prompts and rewards.
  d. Present one-on-one teaching segments with three primary components.
    (1) Antecedent: instruction or request for specific action.
    (2) Behavior: response from the individual.
    (3) Consequence: trainer's reaction (e.g., reinforcement, praise).
2. Augmentative and alternative communication (AAC).
  a. Improvement noted in three areas:
    (1) Behavior and emotional regulation.
    (2) Speech, expressive language, and social communication.
    (3) Receptive language development and comprehension.
  b. Low-tech (pictures, graphic symbols, written cues) to high-tech options (computer, AAC devices, voice output).
3. Floor time.
  a. Engage in spontaneous, interactive, pleasurable activity with the child.
  b. Follow the child's interest while providing semi-structured play.
  c. Natural learning situation tailored to the child's developmental level.
4. Peer and play mediation.
  a. Promote natural interaction and carryover.

b. Peers provide a model to imitate.

c. Social interaction opportunities are increased.

d. Incorporate items of interest to motivate social engagement.

e. Responsive teaching in a play setting.

5. Picture exchange communication system (PECS).

a. Establish a functional reciprocal picture communication system within a social context.

b. A picture of a desired item is exchanged with a communication partner.

c. A form of AAC that also incorporates ABA principles with focused teaching, motivation, and reinforcement.

6. Social stories.

a. Teach social skills through a story format.

b. Specific to the child and problem situation.

c. Story sequence describes relevant aspects of the situation and appropriate social responses, both verbal and nonverbal.

d. Consistently introduce the story until it becomes a routine social response.

7. Theory of mind.

a. Teach the individual to understand mental states—how others think and feel.

b. Mindblindness: inability to understand perceptions and beliefs from another person's perspective.

c. Associated with executive function deficits evidenced in Asperger's disorder.

Related Services

Interdisciplinary Approach

1. A collaborative effort among professionals and parents is required to successfully address ASD (Table 11-12).

2. The team focus should be on the whole child, not isolated skill deficits.

3. Multidisciplinary intervention enhances progress and future prognosis.

4. Consistent cross-disciplinary reinforcement of treatment objectives is critical for generalization of goals.

Table 11-12

Other Professionals and Their Role in ASD	
PROFESSIONAL TEAM MEMBER	**PRIMARY RESPONSIBILITIES**
Administrator	• Liaison among team members and family • Funding/paperwork oversight
Behavior consultant	• Evaluate dysfunctional behavior patterns • Coordinate replacement/modification of problematic behaviors
Occupational therapist	• Sensory integration assessment and treatment • Fine motor skills (e.g., handwriting, self-help)
Physical therapist	• Gross motor skills • Motor movement and strength
Physician	• General overall health • Prescribe and monitor medications
Psychologist	• Cognitive assessment • Psychometric achievement assessment • Monitor mental health and well-being
Social worker	• General background information and health history • Support network for the family • Investigate funding options for the family
Speech-language pathologist	• Assessment and treatment of communication and social skills • Integration of treatment goals into classroom and home environments
Teacher	• Academic achievement assessment • Curricular teaching • Integration of social and communication skills

Adapted from Richard (2019).

References

American Psychiatric Association. (1994). *Diagnostic and Statistical Manual of Mental Disorders*, 4th ed. Washington, DC: APA.

American Psychiatric Association. (2000). *Diagnostic and Statistical Manual of Mental Disorders*, 4th ed., text revised. Washington, DC: APA.

American Psychiatric Association. (2013). *Diagnostic and Statistical Manual of Mental Disorders,* 5th ed. Washington, DC: APA.

American Speech-Language-Hearing Association. (2006a). *Guidelines for Speech-Language Pathologists in Diagnosis, Assessment, and Treatment of Autism Spectrum Disorders Across the Life Span.* Rockville, MD: ASHA. Available from http://www.asha.org.

American Speech-Language-Hearing Association. (2006b). *Roles and Responsibilities of Speech-Language Pathologists in Diagnosis, Assessment, and Treatment of Autism Spectrum Disorders Across the Life Span: Position statement.* Rockville, MD: ASHA. Available from http://www.asha.org.

Baron-Cohen, S. (1995). *Mindblindness: An Essay on Autism and Theory of Mind.* Cambridge, MA: MIT Press.

Centers for Disease Control and Prevention. (2016). *Autism Spectrum Disorder.* Available at www.cdc.gov/ncbddd/autism/index.html.

Coleman, M., & Gillberg, C. (2012). *The Autisms,* 4th ed. New York: Oxford University Press.

Fahy, J., & Richard, G. (2017). *The Source: Development of Executive Functions,* 2nd ed. Austin, TX: Pro Ed.

Kanner, L. (1943). Autistic disturbances of affective contact. *Nervous Child, 2,* 217–250.

National Autism Center. (2009a). *Evidence-Based Practice and Autism in the Schools: A Guide to Providing Appropriate Interventions to Students with Autism Spectrum Disorders.* Randolph, MA: National Autism Center.

National Autism Center. (2009b). *Findings and Conclusions of the National Standards Project: Addressing the Need for Evidence-Based Practice Guidelines for Autism Spectrum Disorders.* Randolph, MA: National Autism Center.

National Autism Center (2009c). *National Standards Report: National Standards Project—Addressing the Need for Evidence-Based Practice Guidelines for Autism Spectrum Disorders.* Randolph, MA: National Autism Center.

National Autism Center. (2015). *Findings and Conclusions: National Standards Project, Phase 2.* Randolph, MA: National Autism Center.

National Research Council. (2001). *Educating Children with Autism.* Committee on Educational Interventions for Children with Autism. Catherine Lord and James P. McGee, eds. Division of Behavioral and Social Sciences and Education. Washington, DC: National Academy Press.

Powers, M. (2000). *Children with Autism: A Parent's Guide,* 2nd ed. Bethesda, MD: Woodbine House.

Prelock, P. (2009). Assessment and intervention in autism spectrum disorders: The role of the SLP. ASHA autism online conference.

Richard, G. (2019). *The Source for Autism,* 2nd ed. Indiana, PA: Dynamic Resources.

Richard, G., & Veale, T. (2009). *The Autism Spectrum Disorders IEP Companion.* East Moline, IL: LinguiSystems.

U.S. Department of Education (2004). Individuals with Disabilities Improvement Act of 2004, Pub.L. 108–466. *Federal Register, 70*(118): 35802–35803.

Wetherby, A., Woods, J., Allen, L., Clearly, J., Dickinson, H., & Lord, C. (2004). Early indicators of autism spectrum disorders in the second year of life. *Journal of Autism and Developmental Disorders, 34,* 473–493.

World Health Organization. (1990). *International Statistical Classification of Diseases and Related Health Problems,* 10th rev. Geneva, Switzerland: WHO.

Review Questions

1. What was the original term for autism spectrum disorder?

   a. Autistic disturbances of affective contact.
   b. Asperger's syndrome.
   c. Pervasive developmental disorder.
   d. Autism spectrum disorders.

2. Which of the following is NOT one of the primary symptoms in autism spectrum disorders?

   a. Impaired development of reciprocal social interaction.
   b. Abnormal behavioral patterns and interactions with objects.
   c. Typical attention span.
   d. Deficits in social communication.

3. Autism spectrum disorders are described using different severity levels. Which severity level requires substantial support, such as marked deficits in verbal and nonverbal social interaction?

   a. Level 1.
   b. Level 2.
   c. Level 3.
   d. Level 4.

4. Which of the following is an example of a reciprocal social interaction deficit?

   a. Poor conversational turn-taking.
   b. Repetition of utterances spoken by others.
   c. Hand flapping.
   d. Obsessive preoccupation with cars.

5. Which of the following is the leading theory regarding the etiology of autism?

   a. Vaccinations.
   b. Lack of parental/ environmental stimulation.
   c. Genetic predisposition.
   d. Delayed language development.

6. Which of the following are warning signs of autism in a young child?

   a. Difficulty with pronouncing their name, difficulty following directions.
   b. Noticeable gross motor delays, not yet potty trained.
   c. Lack of response to name, repetitive body movements.
   d. Unable to understand *first/then* phrases, poor concept development.

7. Which therapy method focuses on spontaneous, interactive pleasurable activity with the child?

   a. Applied behavior analysis.
   b. Augmentative and alternative communication.
   c. Floor time.
   d. Social stories.

8. Which therapy method focuses on promoting natural interaction and carryover and utilizes peers to provide a model to imitate?

   a. Peer and play mediation.
   b. Floor time.
   c. Social stories.
   d. Theory of mind.

9. Which of the following assessments might a parent and pediatrician fill out if they are concerned a young child has an autism spectrum disorder?

   a. First Year Inventory.
   b. Clinical Valuation of Language Fundamentals.
   c. Hodson Assessment of Phonological Patterns.
   d. Preschool Language Scales.

10. A client who is described as speaking telegraphically is most likely speaking in which way?

    a. Client may use short phrases and omit articles and verb conjugations.
    b. Client may not produce past tense when speaking.
    c. Client has difficulty with conversational turn-taking.
    d. Client may have difficulty with pronouns.

11. Hyper- or hyposensitivities to input would be considered part of which diagnostic criteria for autism spectrum disorder?

    a. Deficits in socioemotional reciprocity.
    b. Restricted, repetitive patterns of behavior, interests, or activities.
    c. Delayed expressive verbal communication.
    d. Clinically significant impairment in social communication.

12. According to the IDEA, autism:

    a. Cannot be diagnosed if there is a delay in cognitive development.
    b. Is a developmental disability that affects verbal and nonverbal communication.
    c. Does not need to be treated using a team-based approach.
    d. Is not a spectrum disorder.

13. Which of the following is true, according to environmental theories regarding autism prevalence?

    a. Toxins present in the environment may cause autism spectrum disorder in some individuals.
    b. Chromosomal abnormalities may cause autism spectrum disorder.
    c. Brain inflammation may be a factor in autism symptoms.
    d. Vaccinations may cause autism spectrum disorders.

14. Which of the following is an example of echolalia?

    a. Clinician says, "cookie," and client says, "kee kee."
    b. Clinician says, "cookie," and client says, "cookie cookie."
    c. Clinician says, "cookie," and client says, "/k/ /k/ /k/ /k/ cookie."
    d. Clinician says, "cookie," and client says, "tootie."

15. Which of the following best describes a child who dislikes being touched?

    a. Auditory sensitivity.
    b. Hyperlexia.
    c. Tactile defensiveness.
    d. Kinesthetic incoordination.

16. Difficulties in what area may lead to a client not being able to modulate their speaking volume in different locations?

    a. Self-regulation in response to tactile stimuli.
    b. Self-regulation in response to sensory stimuli.
    c. Motor deficits.
    d. Hyperacusis.

17. Which of the following defines criterion referencing?

    a. Discrepancy between cognitive ability and motor functioning level.
    b. Discrepancy between cognitive ability and cognitive performance.
    c. Discrepancy between expressive language and receptive language.
    d. Discrepancy between cognitive ability and language functioning level.

18. A pediatrician might indicate further evaluation for autism is needed for a 10-month-old if they see which of the following?

    a. Inability to roll from back to front, limited pointing, low tone.
    b. Lack of turn-taking.
    c. Lack of response to name, limited gestures, poor visual orientation to stimuli.
    d. Limited word production, poor orientation to sound.

19. Which of the following is an example of working on theory of mind?

    a. Teaching a student to play using peer modeling.
    b. Teaching a student to recognize emotions in their classmates.
    c. Teaching a student a specific behavioral response using a story.
    d. Teaching a student to communicate using pictures and photographs.

20. Which of the following is NOT typical of Applied Behavioral Analysis (ABA) treatment design?

    a. Skills taught using a carefully sequenced progression of steps.
    b. Clearly identified antecedent, target behavior, and consequence.
    c. Behavior modification using operant conditioning.
    d. Behavior modification using natural, spontaneous interaction.

12

Stuttering and Other Fluency Disorders

DEREK E. DANIELS, PhD
ALEX F. JOHNSON, PhD

▶ Aphasia and Related Terms

Aphasia Defined

1. Aphasia is a language disorder caused by acquired brain damage.
2. *Important:* it is language impairment—not speech impairment—that is the critical feature of aphasia.
3. Motor speech disorders such as dysarthria or apraxia of speech may accompany the aphasia but are separate from the aphasia.
4. Other cognitive disturbances may accompany aphasia, but generally it is the language impairment that most affects communication.
   a. Many persons with aphasia (PWA) have intact nonverbal cognition, and their thinking abilities and intelligence are for the most part intact.
   b. Other PWA may have additional deficits in selected areas of cognition that will impact their ability to use language and perhaps may limit their response to treatment.

Components of Language Affected by Aphasia

1. *Lexical retrieval* refers to the ability to access the words within one's lexicon for communicating content.
   a. Lexical retrieval deficits will affect both verbal expression and writing.
   b. Anomia is difficulty finding words, and it is a core feature of every aphasia syndrome.
   c. Anomia comes in many severity levels, from total inability to retrieve desired words for verbal expression or writing to mild, occasional failures to retrieve a desired word during conversation.
2. *Grammatical competence* refers to the expression and comprehension of the formal grammatical aspects of language (syntax and morphology).
   a. Agrammatism is difficulty with the expression or comprehension of the grammatical units of language.
   b. Patterns of agrammatism are variable depending on the characteristics of the language used by the PWA, but there are patterns that are consistent across languages.
   c. In English, agrammatism in PWA manifests by:
      (1) Omission of functor words such as articles, prepositions, auxiliary verbs, and pronouns when speaking.
      (2) Omissions or errors on grammatical markers in affixes such as the plural –s, past tense –ed when speaking.

   (3) Inability to comprehend passive constructions and other noncanonical, less frequent grammatical structures.
3. Auditory comprehension (A/C) of single words or longer linguistic units refers to the ability to attach meaning to the words spoken by others.
   a. Impairments of A/C are common in aphasia and help to distinguish among the varieties of aphasia.
   b. A/C impairments range in severity from near total inability to understand spoken language to a mild comprehension difficulty that barely impacts functional communication.
4. Verbal repetition of words spoken by the examiner is used to differentiate the aphasia syndromes and may be relatively preserved or relatively impaired compared to other language skills.
   a. *Verbal short-term memory* and *verbal working memory* are terms used to describe functions that are also required in the repetition task.
5. Reading and writing deficits are also common in aphasia.
   a. Alexia is an aphasic reading disorder.
   b. Deep dyslexia.
      (1) A person with deep dyslexia cannot access grapheme-to-phoneme (letter-to-sound) conversion rules, so they cannot "sound out" words from written form.
      (2) They are only able to use the "whole-word," also known as "lexical," reading route.
      (3) They produce semantic paralexic errors in oral reading, substituting a semantically related word for the target word (e.g., reading *doctor* as "nurse").
      (4) They cannot read nonwords (e.g., *flamp*) or semantically empty functor words (e.g., *for, by, to*).
   c. Surface dyslexia.
      (1) Surface dyslexia is a syndrome that is almost the reverse of deep dyslexia.
      (2) People with surface dyslexia have limited access to meaning on a whole-word basis and are only able to use the grapheme-to-phoneme mapping route.
      (3) This strategy works for words with regular spelling but not for irregular words.
      (4) People with surface dyslexia attempt to understand words by sounding out the letters (e.g., the irregularly pronounced word *pint* would be read aloud as /pɪnt/, rhyming with the word *mint*).
      (5) They have good ability to read aloud pseudowords (e.g., *blix*).

d. Pure alexia without agraphia.
   (1) People with this disorder have a complete inability to read aloud; they cannot recognize letters or words.
   (2) They can write normally, yet cannot read back what they wrote.
   (3) They are able to understand tactile spelling on their skin and may be able to access letter information by tracing letter forms with their fingers.
   (4) Pure alexia is caused by a loss of specifically visual input into the language areas due to a disconnection of bilateral occipital pathways into the language areas of the left hemisphere.
e. Letter-by-letter (LBL) reading.
   (1) LBL reading is a less severe form of a visual-input-based reading disorder.
   (2) There is preservation of individual letter reading, but LBL readers cannot read words as a whole.
   (3) LBL readers tend to read each letter aloud and then construct internally what the word is by using their comprehension of oral spelling (e.g., "f-a-t-h-e-r . . . oh, it's *father*").
f. Agraphia is an aphasic writing disorder.
   (1) Typical aphasic agraphia is characterized by difficulty retrieving words for writing and by various spelling errors.
      (a) The severity and form of agraphic errors often mirrors the characteristics of spoken output in PWA.
      (b) Agraphia is caused by the linguistic disorder, not by the fact that the PWA may be using their nondominant hand.
      (c) Agraphia can be seen when writing with pen/pencil on paper or when using a keyboard.
   (2) Pure agraphia is a rare syndrome characterized by inability to write but no other language problems.
      (a) In this disorder, the PWA seems to have lost the memories of the motor engrams needed for writing letters and words.

Other Disorders Commonly Accompanying Aphasia

1. Perseveration is the inappropriate repetition of a response or continuation of a behavior when it is no longer required or appropriate. Perseveration is common in PWA and can take several different forms.
   a. Recurrent perseveration is the production of a previously made response after a filled delay (e.g., carrying over some of the phonemes from a previous response on a naming test into a subsequent response, or a complete repetition of an entire previous response).
   b. Continuous perseveration is the immediate repetition of the same response that was just made; the person cannot stop making the same response.
   c. Stuck-in-set is an inability to shift response set when it is required (e.g., the PWA continues to count when asked to recite the alphabet after having just completed a counting task).
2. Apraxia is a disorder of the execution of learned movement that is not caused by motor weakness, incoordination, or sensory loss and is not due to failure to understand the command.
   a. The most common form of apraxia, known as *ideomotor apraxia*, is particularly seen in left-hemisphere strokes.
      (1) Ideomotor apraxia may affect limb or orofacial movements, or both.
      (2) It refers to difficulty with the selection, sequencing, and spatial orientation of movements for gestures.
      (3) Hugo Liepmann wrote about apraxia in the early 1900s and described it as if the person with apraxia knows the idea of the movements they want to perform (ideo) but cannot get the body (motor) to perform them correctly due to a disconnection in neuroanatomical pathways.
   b. Apraxia of speech (AOS) is a sensorimotor speech disorder with symptoms of impaired volitional production of articulation and prosody that does not result from abnormal muscle strength, tone, or timing; nor does it arise from aphasia, confusion, generalized intellectual impairment, or hearing loss.
      (1) AOS results from impairment of neural programming of skilled movements.
      (2) AOS may also be seen in PWA. Some people believe that AOS is necessarily part of the nonfluent syndrome of Broca's aphasia.
      (3) See Chapter 14 on motor speech disorders for further information on AOS.
3. Agnosias are disorders of recognition of objects, people, sounds, colors, and so on, that are not a result of primary sensory deficits.
   a. Agnosias are generally associated with cortical brain damage in regions of the parietal, temporal, and occipital lobes.
   b. Visual agnosia is the inability to recognize what visual objects or pictures of objects are. It is not simply a failure to name them but rather to understand the "meanings" of them.
   c. Prosopagnosia is the inability to recognize faces.
   d. Anosognosia is the inability to recognize one's own illness, to be aware that one has an illness.
4. Nonverbal cognitive impairments are also common in some PWA. Frontal lobe lesions are likely to result in some degree of executive system impairment, causing problems in numerous cognitive functions.

History of Modern Aphasiology

1. The history of modern aphasiology is generally acknowledged as beginning in the latter half of the 19th century.
2. Paul Broca was a French neurologist who studied PWA in life and subsequently examined their brains postmortem.
   a. In 1861, he reported that a region of the frontal lobe (third frontal convolution, now called *Broca's area*) was implicated in disorders of speech production.
   b. In 1865, Broca established the association between language disorders and damage, specifically to the left hemisphere of the brain.
      (1) Marc Dax had discovered the relationship between language disorders and damage to left-hemisphere brain regions 30 years earlier in 1836.
      (2) However, Broca publicized this to the scientific community.
      (3) Broca also suggested the possibility that the right hemisphere could take over function in the recovery process.
3. Carl Wernicke (1874) was a German neurologist who also studied PWA and together with Hugo Lichtheim wrote about many other forms of aphasia. The Wernicke-Lichtheim model is the basis for many classification systems that are still in use today.
   a. Wernicke wrote about a second major variety of aphasia (now known as *Wernicke's aphasia*) that was characterized by auditory comprehension deficit and was associated with lesions in an area of the temporal lobe now called Wernicke's area.
   b. He also wrote about what are now termed *classic connectionist models* and suggested that information could be transmitted within the brain from one region to another.
   c. He predicted the existence of a third form of aphasia called *conduction aphasia*.
      (1) Conduction aphasia would be caused by a disconnection in the neural pathways between the auditory comprehension area in the temporal lobe and the verbal expression area in the frontal lobe.
      (2) He predicted that verbal repetition would be particularly poor in this form of aphasia because of this disconnection.

▶ Neuroanatomical Bases of Aphasia

Language Zone Region of the Brain

1. The language zone region of the left hemisphere is depicted in Figure 13-1. Brain damage to structures within this region is likely to result in some degree of language impairment.
2. The language zone includes cortical and subcortical regions in the frontal, parietal, and temporal lobes of the left hemisphere.
3. The region of the language zone is fed almost entirely by the left middle cerebral artery (MCA); therefore, aphasia is typically caused by a stroke within the territory of the left MCA (Fig. 13-2).
4. The language zone includes Broca's area in the left frontal lobe, which is important for the verbal expression of language and for grammatical competence.
5. The language zone includes Wernicke's area in the left temporal lobe, which is important for the auditory comprehension of language.

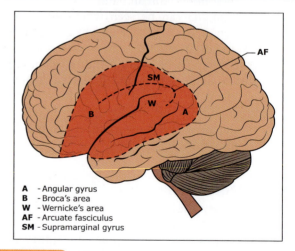

A - Angular gyrus
B - Broca's area
W - Wernicke's area
AF - Arcuate fasciculus
SM - Supramarginal gyrus

Figure 13-1 The language zone of the left hemisphere, showing Broca's and Wernicke's areas, the angular and supramarginal gyri, and the arcuate fasciculus.

Based on *Manual of Aphasia and Aphasia Therapy*, 2nd ed., by Nancy Helm-Estabrooks and Martin L. Albert, Austin, TX: Pro-ed., 2004.

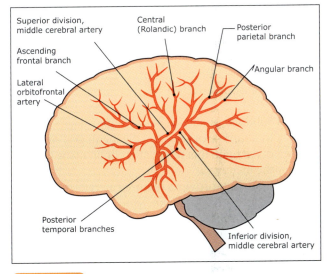

Figure 13-2 **The middle cerebral artery territory.**

Based on *Manual of Aphasia and Aphasia Therapy,* 2nd ed., by Nancy Helm-Estabrooks and Martin L. Albert, Austin, TX: Pro-ed., 2004.

6. The language zone also includes the left angular gyrus and the supramarginal gyrus in the border zone regions between the parietal and temporal lobes.
7. The language zone also includes white matter pathways beneath these regions, particularly the arcuate fasciculus and the superior longitudinal fasciculus.

Neuroanatomy and Aphasia

1. Classification of aphasia syndromes is discussed in a later section, but basic facts related to lesion location and aphasia include the following:
   a. Anterior lesions lead to nonfluent aphasias. In general, if a PWA has had a stroke or brain injury affecting only anterior structures of the language zone in the left hemisphere (i.e., anterior to the central sulcus), the PWA will most likely have a nonfluent type of aphasia.
      (1) In general, if the brain damage involves the left precentral sulcus, also called the *motor strip*, or subcortical regions deep to this area, the PWA is likely to have some degree of right hemiparesis.
         (a) Right hemiparesis is impairment of motor functioning on the right side of the body, ranging from mild to severe, affecting various regions of the foot, leg, arm, and face, depending on the location of the damage to the motor strip.
         (b) Right hemiplegia is paralysis on the right side of the body.

b. Posterior lesions lead to fluent aphasias. In general, if a PWA has had a stroke or brain injury that is restricted to the posterior structures of the language zone in the left hemisphere (i.e., posterior to the central sulcus), he/she will most likely have a fluent type of aphasia.
   (1) There will *not* be any concomitant motor impairment.
   (2) If the brain damage affects the postcentral sulcus in the parietal lobe, also called the *sensory strip*, the PWA is likely to have some sensory impairment on the right side of the body.
c. Brain damage that affects both anterior and posterior regions of the language zone of the left hemisphere is likely to result in a severe aphasia with a concomitant right hemiparesis.

Cerebral Dominance for Language

1. *Cerebral dominance* refers to the fact that, for most people, the left hemisphere is dominant for language processing.
2. Among right-handers, 99% are left-hemisphere-dominant for language. Approximately 70% of left-handers are also left-hemisphere-dominant for language.
3. Only about 1% of right-handers and 30% of left-handers do not show the typical pattern; this is referred to as *anomalous dominance.*
   a. Right-handed people who develop aphasia from a right-hemisphere stroke are given the label *crossed aphasia* because the condition is so rare.
4. *Anomalous dominance* may mean that the right hemisphere is dominant for language (a reverse or mirror-image pattern of the typical), or it may mean that language is controlled by both hemispheres (i.e., no single hemisphere is dominant).
5. People with anomalous dominance may show better or atypical patterns of recovery from aphasia if they have had a left-hemisphere stroke.

Common Etiologies of Aphasia

1. Cerebrovascular disease that damages the language zone of the left hemisphere.
2. Traumatic brain injuries that damage the language zone of the left hemisphere.
3. Brain tumors that affect the tissue or functioning of the language zone.
4. Neurodegenerative disorders that affect the left hemisphere.

5. Cerebrovascular disease is the leading cause of aphasia and is responsible for approximately 50% of the cases of aphasia.
   a. Risk factors for cerebrovascular disease include high cholesterol, diabetes, smoking, hypertension, and heart disease.
   b. A transient ischemic attack (TIA) is a temporary loss of neurological function caused by an interruption of blood flow to a brain region.
      (1) A TIA is viewed as a "warning sign" for stroke, and the person should be thoroughly evaluated by a neurologist if a TIA is suspected.
      (2) Symptoms of a TIA are variable and include difficulty speaking (dysarthria or word-finding blocks), clumsiness in one hand or arm, numbness or tingling in a limb or on one side of the face, and visual disturbances.
      (3) The FAST (face, arm, speech, time) acronym is a way for the layperson to remember the warning signs of stroke (facial droop, arm motor difficulties, speech abnormalities) and that emergency medical attention should be obtained immediately (time).
   c. Cerebrovascular accident (CVA), or stroke, is the most common cause of aphasia.
      (1) An occlusive stroke may be caused by an embolus or a thrombosis or a combination of the two.
         (a) Embolus is a clot formed in another body area (often the heart) that can travel up to the brain and then interrupt blood flow.
         (b) Thrombosis is a clot that can form in the blood vessels of the brain and results in a blockage but has not traveled from another region.
         (c) Thromboembolic stroke is a combination of an embolus and a thrombus or a stroke that could possibly be caused by either.
      (2) Occlusive strokes may be treated emergently with "clot-busting" drugs such as a tissue plasminogen activator (TPA) to prevent long-term brain damage.
         (a) The individual must be medically evaluated within a short window of time post-onset—approximately 3–5 hours.
         (b) Cerebral hemorrhage must be ruled out first, usually via neuroimaging studies prior to administration of TPA.
         (c) Administration of TPA may prevent permanent neurological damage from the stroke or may reduce the severity of the stroke.
   d. A hemorrhagic CVA results when there is a rupture of the vessels in the brain rather than a blockage of blood flow.
      (1) A ruptured aneurysm is a ballooned-out area of a blood vessel wall that becomes very thin and subsequently breaks.
      (2) An arteriovenous malformation (AVM) is a tangled mass of brain blood vessels that is often congenital and that subsequently ruptures or leaks.
      (3) An intracerebral hemorrhage is caused by a rupture of a vessel within the neural tissue of the brain.
      (4) Subdural or subarachnoid hemorrhage is caused by a rupture of vessels in the meningeal coverings of the brain that might affect brain tissue beneath the meninges.
      (5) Brain hemorrhages require emergency intervention to prevent an increase of pressure within the brain that can result in death.
         (a) Craniotomy is opening up the skull to relieve pressure and to drain excess blood resulting from the hemorrhage.

6. Traumatic brain injuries (TBI) that damage the language zone of the left hemisphere are the second most common cause of aphasia in adults.
   a. The specific linguistic and cognitive symptoms seen in TBI will depend on the brain regions affected and may be somewhat different from symptoms seen in aphasia from stroke.
   b. Symptoms may arise from either focal (localized to a specific area) or diffuse (widespread) injury or a combination of both focal and diffuse brain damage.
      (1) Focal injuries sometimes have both coup (site of impact) and contrecoup (opposite the site of impact) components, caused by the brain impacting different areas of the skull, depending on how the TBI occurs.
      (2) Diffuse damage includes diffuse axonal injury (DAI), often occurring in high-speed motor vehicle accidents, where many long branches of axons within the brain become damaged, often resulting in significant motor and cognitive difficulties.
   c. TBI may result in damage to subcortical structures in the limbic system, causing significant memory problems and emotional regulation difficulties.
   d. A common site of damage in TBI is either unilateral or bilateral prefrontal damage resulting in significant problems with emotional and behavioral regulation and executive functioning impairments.
   e. Causes of TBI.
      (1) Motor vehicle accidents are a common cause of TBI, particularly in young adult males.
      (2) Falls resulting in brain injuries are more common in young children and elderly adults.
      (3) Blows to the head causing injury to the brain, such as in assaults, are also more common in young adult males.
      (4) Chronic traumatic encephalopathy (CTE) is the name given to multiple concussions and more

serious head injuries sustained primarily by professional and amateur athletes such as boxers, football players, and soccer players.

(5) Blast injuries from improvised explosive devices (IEDs) resulting in brain injuries, such as those sustained by soldiers and civilians in war-torn areas, have become much more numerous in recent years due to the Iraq and Afghanistan wars.

(6) Gunshot wounds and stab wounds to the head (i.e., penetrating head injuries) that affect the left hemisphere may also result in aphasia.

(7) Closed head injuries (CHI): many head injuries do not involve the penetration of an object through the skull or the breakage of the skull itself.

7. Brain tumors that affect the tissue of the language zone may also result in aphasia.

a. Specific linguistic and cognitive symptoms will depend on the region affected by the tumor and may be different from symptoms seen in aphasia from stroke.

b. Tumors may arise from the neural tissues of the brain itself, such as a glioma, or from the protective meninges, such as a meningioma.

c. Tumors may also originate elsewhere in the body as a metastatic tumor.

d. Aphasia may worsen as the tumor grows or may improve if the tumor is removed or treated via medication or surgery to decrease its size.

e. Cognitive and linguistic processing may also be affected by medical treatments for the brain tumor (chemotherapy, surgical resections) and the speech-language pathologist (SLP) needs to consider this when planning the assessment or treatment for a person with a brain tumor.

8. Neurodegenerative disorders that affect the left hemisphere may also result in aphasia. (*Note:* See the later section on dementia syndromes in this chapter.)

a. Dementia is a progressive neurodegenerative brain disorder affecting multiple domains of cognition, including memory, language, visuospatial skills, and behavior.

b. Dementia syndromes that also have significant language deficits as part of the behavioral profile include:

(1) Alzheimer's disease (AD).

(2) Frontotemporal dementia (FTD) and the subtypes of FTD known as primary progressive aphasia (PPA).

(3) Vascular dementia (VaD).

(4) Dementia with Lewy bodies (DLB).

Assessment of Aphasia

Thorough Examination of All Language Components

1. Language assessment of aphasia by an SLP requires a thorough examination of all components of language, including auditory comprehension and many aspects of speaking, reading, and writing.

2. Standardized formal measures that can be used to evaluate language and communication include (among others not listed):

a. Boston Diagnostic Aphasia Examination, 3rd edition (BDAE-3; Goodglass, Kaplan, & Barresi, 2001a, 2001b).

(1) The BDAE provides an aphasia profile on the Rating Scale Profile of Speech Characteristics that can be compared to profiles consistent with one of the seven aphasia syndromes.

(2) The examiner also assigns a "subjective" Aphasia Severity Rating (ASR) from 0 to 5.

(3) The BDAE is a comprehensive assessment tool that includes both standard and extended testing subtests.

(4) Depending on the individual, it may take 2–6 hours to administer the test in its entirety.

b. Boston Naming Test (BNT), published as part of the BDAE, is a 60-item test of picture confrontation naming ability.

c. Western Aphasia Battery-Revised (WAB-R; Kertesz, 2006).

(1) The WAB subtests assess similar language abilities as the BDAE, but it is somewhat quicker to administer than the BDAE.

(2) Test scores result in an Aphasia Quotient, a Cortical Quotient, an Auditory Comprehension Quotient, a Verbal Expression Quotient, a Reading Quotient, and a Writing Quotient.

d. Aphasia Diagnostic Profiles (ADP; Helm-Estabrooks, 1992) result in diagnostic profiles similar to BDAE or WAB.

(1) Profiles that can be analyzed from results include the Aphasia Classification Profile, the Aphasia Severity Profile, the Alternative Communication Profile, Error Profiles, and the Behavioral Profile.

e. Cognitive Linguistic Quick Test Plus (CLQT+; Helm-Estabrooks, 2017) provides assessment of language ability and nonverbal cognitive abilities in attention, memory, executive functioning, and visuospatial skills.

f. Quick Aphasia Battery (QAB; Wilson et al., 2018).
   (1) Comprehensive assessment that's quicker to administer than other assessments for aphasia and has three alternate forms for retesting.
   (2) Multidimensional assessment with eight subtests: Level of Consciousness/Orientation, Connected Speech, Word Comprehension, Sentence Comprehension, Picture Naming, Repetition, Reading Aloud, and Motor Speech.
   (3) Open access article describes this free test and provides scoresheets and stimulus cards. See https://aphasialab.org/qab/.

3. Nonstandardized assessments are also commonly conducted by SLPs in many settings, but an attempt to evaluate verbal expression, auditory comprehension, reading comprehension, and writing should be part of every aphasia examination.

4. The assessment provides a detailed profile of the individual's strengths and weaknesses within each language modality.

5. These profiles are subsequently used to develop personalized treatment plans and to aid in determining an aphasia diagnosis (i.e., an aphasia syndrome label) if desired.

6. Functional communication: formal tools also exist to specifically measure functional communication. Some of the more commonly used tools include the following:

a. Communication Activities of Daily Living, 2nd edition (CADL-2; Holland, Frattali, & Fromm, 1999).
   (1) Assesses communication activities in seven areas: reading, writing, and using numbers; social interaction; divergent communication; contextual communication; nonverbal communication; sequential relationships; and humor/metaphor/absurdity.

b. Functional Assessment of Communication Skills for Adults (ASHA FACS; Frattali et al., 2003).
   (1) ASHA FACS is a 43-item test completed by interviewing the PWA and family members/caregivers to determine functional communication in several domains.
   (2) Items are rated on a seven-point scale of independence.

c. Communicative Effectiveness Index (CETI; Lomas et al., 1989) is a checklist filled out by caregivers that asks questions referring to 16 different communication situations.

d. Boston Assessment of Severe Aphasia (BASA; Helm-Estabrooks et al., 1989).
   (1) The BASA is a 60-item assessment tool specifically for people with severe aphasia that is designed to capture islands of preserved ability.
   (2) The scoring system captures both verbal and nonverbal (gestural) responses to a variety of stimuli.

7. Process approach: Many clinicians use a process approach to assessment associated with neuropsychologist Edith Kaplan and SLP Nancy Helm-Estabrooks.

a. A process approach allows for a more thorough understanding of the PWA than simply recording right or wrong on the test booklet.

b. An examiner following the process approach should:
   (1) Record exact error responses and behaviors made by the PWA during the assessment.
   (2) Note and record all off-task behaviors produced by the PWA during the assessment, such as noting whether the PWA was distracted by activities in the environment.
   (3) Note any self-cueing attempts as well as responses to cues provided by the examiner.
   (4) Conduct a qualitative analysis of error responses after the completion of the test.
   (5) Analyze data obtained from this assessment approach to form hypotheses about the cognitive processes that might underlie partially or fully incorrect responses and associated observed behaviors.
   (6) Use these hypotheses to determine the best approaches to remediation.

Components of a Standardized Language Examination

1. Verbal expression should be evaluated to establish strengths and weaknesses using the following types of tasks:

a. Spontaneous narrative expression, in response to open-ended questions such as "Tell me what happened to you," or "What kind of work do you do?"

b. Complex picture description tasks in which expected content words are specified by the picture.

c. Retelling a story such as a fable.

d. Responses to simple social greetings such as "What is your name?"

e. Naming of items presented (pictures or objects); may include naming of items in specific categories such as body parts, animals, colors, letters, numbers, tools, or actions.

f. Responsive naming (e.g., in response to a question such as "What do we tell time with?").

g. Word list generation (e.g., "Tell me the names of as many animals as you can think of in a minute").

h. Repetition of single words, phrases, and sentences that are first spoken by the examiner.

i. Oral reading of single words and longer phrases.

j. Production of automatic overlearned sequences such as the alphabet, counting from 1 to 10, the days of the week, the months of the year, and nursery rhymes.

k. Singing familiar songs such as "Happy Birthday."

2. Evaluation of verbal expression task responses. At the completion of the assessment, the examiner should seek to answer the following questions:

a. Is the verbal output primarily fluent or nonfluent, and what is the typical phrase length produced by the individual?

(1) Fluent is verbal expression in which the amount of words produced per utterance is similar to or greater than a nonaphasic individual regardless of whether the words make sense or not.

(a) Generally, seven words or more are produced in the occasional longest phrase.

(b) Some PWA are hyperfluent, producing more words than typical. This is referred to as *logorrhea* or *press of speech*.

(2) Nonfluent is verbal expression in which the amount of words produced per utterance is less than a typical nonaphasic individual.

(a) Severely nonfluent would be 1–2 words or fewer per phrase.

(b) Moderately nonfluent would be approximately 3–5 words per phrase.

(c) People who say exclusively verbal stereotypes such as repeating words or syllables (e.g., "si si wa wa . . . si si . . . wa wa") are not considered to be fluent; rather, this is considered a severe form of nonfluency, and phrase length cannot be calculated for these individuals.

b. Is there evidence of agrammatism, such as omissions of functor words and simplified syntax within phrases or sentences?

c. Is there evidence of a word-finding problem with lack of content words or overuse of indefinite terms like *thing* or *that one*?

d. Are there any obvious category-specific deficits in naming, such as the inability to name animals but good ability to name tools?

e. How intelligible is the verbal output? Is there evidence of a concomitant dysarthria or apraxia of speech?

f. What is the prosodic contour or melodic line of the verbal output? Does it sound like normal prosody or is it restricted and spoken in a monotone, word-by-word fashion?

g. Are there paraphasic errors in the verbal output? Paraphasias are word-substitution errors and may be of several types:

(1) Semantic paraphasias share elements of meaning with the target word, such as saying "lion" for the target word *tiger*.

(2) Phonemic paraphasias share elements of phonology with the target, such as saying "piger" for the target word *tiger*.

(3) Verbal paraphasia unrelated: another real-word substitution that is not semantically or phonemically related, such as saying "auto" for the target word *tiger*.

(4) Neologism: a nonword with no apparent relation to the target, such as saying "palipon" for the target word *tiger*.

(5) Mixed paraphasias may be both semantically and phonemically related.

h. Is repetition relatively preserved or particularly poor compared to narrative expression?

i. Can the individual produce words better when singing rather than when speaking?

j. Is there preservation of overlearned verbal sequences, such as counting and saying the days of the week?

k. Is there evidence of perseveration? In which tasks? What types of perseverative errors are made?

l. Does the individual use other communicative modalities, such as gesturing, drawing, or writing when verbal expression fails?

3. Auditory comprehension should be evaluated, taking care to use tasks that are as "pure" as possible (i.e., they do not require other language skills such as talking, reading, or writing). Typical tasks used to evaluate auditory comprehension include:

a. Word discrimination: pointing to pictures or objects named by the examiner.

b. Following commands: using a variety of different commands from short and simple (e.g., "Close your eyes") to complex (e.g., "Tap your shoulder with two fingers keeping your eyes shut").

c. Answering yes/no questions presented in pairs.

(1) Because there is a 50% chance of answering a yes/no question correctly, questions should be presented in pairs and the evaluation of correctness should be for the pair only.

(2) Personally relevant biographical questions are most likely to be comprehended well (e.g., "Is your name Bob?" paired with "Is your name Greg?").

(3) Questions related to the current time and place should also be asked (e.g., "Are we at the VA hospital?" "Is it summer now?").

(4) Yes/no questions related to a short story that is read to the PWA will be more difficult and are dependent on verbal memory. Take care to

create questions that could not be answered unless the PWA had comprehended the story.

d. Comprehension of grammatical forms and complex syntactic constructions such as:
   (1) Reversible possessives (e.g., "Point to the ship's captain").
   (2) Embedded sentences (e.g., "Which picture shows the man wearing the hat holding the pizza?").

e. Comprehension of geographical place names by pointing to locations named by the examiner on a map.
   (1) Comprehension of geographical place names tends to be relatively preserved even in severe aphasia.

f. Comprehension of typical conversational discourse.
   (1) Many PWA may appear to comprehend language in conversational discourse better than on standardized testing.

4. Reading comprehension should be assessed to evaluate if the PWA is able to understand written language. Care should be taken to use tasks that are "pure" measures of reading comprehension and do not require speaking, auditory comprehension, or writing. Typical tasks to evaluate reading comprehension include the following:

a. Word-picture matching: present a picture and a choice of single words from which the PWA must select.

b. Sentence-picture matching: present a picture and a choice of sentences that describe the picture.

c. Lexical decision: point to the words that are real words from a selection of both real words and nonwords.

d. Sentence and paragraph comprehension: read a sentence or a paragraph and answer follow-up written questions about the content.

e. Functional reading of newspapers, written instructions, forms, and so on.
   (1) Note: Oral reading and reading comprehension can be differentially impaired or spared. Poor ability to read aloud does not necessarily imply poor comprehension of written words.
   (2) PWA may also have modality-specific comprehension deficits (e.g., poor auditory comprehension and good reading comprehension or vice versa).

f. Writing should be assessed in every PWA.

g. Note: A right-handed PWA who has a hemiparetic right arm and hand should be tested with their nondominant left hand for writing.
   (1) Using the nondominant hand will result in slower and perhaps less legible written output but will not affect the linguistic nature of the writing.
   (2) Spelling errors and word-selection errors in writing are attributable to the aphasic writing disorder alone.
   (3) Aphasic writing disorder = agraphia.

h. Signature: signing one's name tends to be preserved even in severe agraphia.

i. Writing overlearned sequences such as the alphabet or the numbers from 1 to 10.

j. Writing to dictation of primer-level words (e.g., *cat, boy, run*) and longer phrases and sentences.
   (1) *Note*: This is not a "pure" task of writing. Poor performance may also be caused by deficits in auditory comprehension of the spoken stimulus.

k. Written confrontation naming: present pictures and ask the PWA to write the names for them.

l. Written narrative description either to describe a picture or to write a short story or narrative on a topic.

m. Functional writing tasks such as writing one's address, telephone number, or family members' names.

n. Written production should be evaluated similarly to the way verbal expression was evaluated.
   (1) Is there evidence of lexical retrieval difficulty?
   (2) What types of spelling errors are made?
   (3) Is there evidence of agrammatism in the writing (e.g., omitted functor words, lack of morphological endings, poor syntax)?
   (4) Are there paragraphic errors (written paraphasias)? What types (semantic, phonological, orthographic)?
   (5) Is writing particularly worse or better than oral-verbal expression?

Cognitive Assessment of PWA

1. Cognitive assessment of PWA should also be part of the overall evaluation, and a comprehensive assessment of cognition is usually conducted by a psychologist or neuropsychologist or behavioral neurologist, not by an SLP.

2. Language is an important part of cognition, and it also interacts with other nonlinguistic cognitive functions such as memory, attention, executive functioning, and visuospatial functioning.

3. Therefore, assessment of these other areas will greatly enhance understanding of the behavior of a PWA, particularly because, in many instances, PWA also show degrees of impairment in these other areas.

4. Formal measures for the assessment of cognition include the Wechsler Adult Intelligence Scale, 4th edition (WAIS-IV; Wechsler, 2008); the Wechsler Memory Scale, 4th edition (WMS-IV; Wechsler, 2009); the Cognitive Linguistic Quick Test Plus (CLQT+; Helm-Estabrooks, 2017); the Ravens Coloured Progressive Matrices (Raven, Raven, & Court, 2004); and many others.
   a. Many of these formal measures, such as the WAIS, are available only to psychologists.

b. The CLQT+ was designed to be used by SLPs and other professionals.

5. Patterns of impairments in nonlinguistic functions assessed by these formal measures are highly variable across individuals and depend on numerous factors, including lesion location, additional medical factors or preexisting conditions, personal history of premorbid learning disabilities, and so on.

6. Nevertheless, some common patterns of nonlinguistic cognitive impairments and areas of preservation in PWA may be seen:
   a. Some degree of impairment in executive functioning, particularly in those with lesions affecting the frontal lobe.
   b. Relatively intact nonverbal memory functions, although verbal memory may appear to be impaired due to the aphasia.
      (1) PWA often show reduced working memory capacity, particularly for verbal material but also sometimes for visual material.
      (2) Working memory (WM) requires the individual to hold information in memory for a short time period and to perform some manipulation of the information.
         (a) A standard working memory task is "digits backward," where the individual must listen to a series of digits spoken by the examiner and then tell them back in the reverse order.
         (b) PWA may have difficulty with this task due to their verbal expression deficits separate from a deficit in WM.
   c. Visuospatial functioning is relatively preserved but shows a characteristic pattern in visuoconstruction tasks such as drawing.
      (1) Drawings display good outer configurations but may be lacking in internal details (opposite of the pattern seen in those with right-hemisphere strokes).
      (2) PWA who have posterior involvement of visual pathways in the left hemisphere may have either a hemianopsia (right visual field cut) or some degree of visual inattention to the right side of space.

Limb and Orofacial Praxis Assessment

1. Assessment of limb and orofacial praxis should be part of the comprehensive examination because presence of limb or oral apraxia may affect performance on numerous tasks, especially if the PWA is asked to follow commands.
2. Modalities of assessment.
   a. Verbal command of the examiner (e.g., "Show me how you would wave goodbye").
   b. Imitation of the movement made by the examiner.
   c. Performing the action to command with an actual object.
3. Body regions to assess.
   a. Limb movements involving the arm and hand.
   b. Orofacial (e.g., "Stick out your tongue"; "Show me how you would blow out a match"; "Show me how you would cough").
   c. Axial (midline or whole-body postures) (e.g., "Lean forward"; "Stand up"; "Stand like a boxer").
      (1) Axial movements tend to be better preserved than other types of movements to command.
4. PWA may have limb apraxia and not orofacial apraxia or vice versa.
5. The left hemisphere is dominant for praxis just as it is dominant for language; therefore, it is common for PWA to have limb or orofacial apraxia.

Multicultural Considerations for Assessment of Aphasia

1. Approximately 45,000 new bilingual aphasia cases are expected per year in the United States.
2. When working with multilingual PWA, SLPs need to determine what language(s) was their dominant language pre-aphasia.
   a. Ask the PWA to indicate their self-perception of their facility with each language.
   b. Determine what language(s) were used for various daily life activities such as at work, at school, socializing at home, for reading and writing.
   c. If possible, use a formal assessment such as the Bilingual Aphasia Test (BAT) (see below) to ensure an accurate picture of the strengths and weaknesses within each language (Paradis et al., n.d.).
      (1) PWA may be unaware of which of their languages is more impaired after onset of aphasia.
      (2) If the SLP speaks only one of the languages of the PWA, the SLP may wrongly perceive that the other language(s) is either less or more impaired than it really is.
      (3) SLPs should not attribute differences between the languages to brain damage, as they may already have differed premorbidly.
      (4) SLPs need to understand relative deficits across languages to determine which languages to include in therapy and to identify specific goals within each language.
      (5) Treatment should be provided in the language requested by PWA and their family.
   d. Ideally, an SLP who is fluent in the language being assessed will conduct the assessment.
      (1) Interpreter services may be used in some clinical settings if available.

(2) It is not recommended that family members be used as language testers, but family impressions of the language of the PWA and reports of language behaviors are valuable.

e. The Bilingual Aphasia Test was developed by Michel Paradis and colleagues (2001) and is available in many different languages at www.mcgill.ca/linguistics/research/bat/.

(1) The BAT consists of three main parts:

(a) Part A: evaluation of the PWA's multilingual history.

(b) Part B: systematic and comparable assessment of the language disorder in each language known by the subject.

(c) Part C: assessment of translation abilities and interference detection in each language.

(2) The BAT is currently available in 65 languages (Part B) and 160 language pairs (Part C).

(3) Parts B and C of this test have not simply been translated into different languages, but rather adapted across languages.

f. Versions of other standardized aphasia tests such as the BDAE and the WAB also are available in other languages.

g. Caution should be observed in simply translating a standardized test from one language to another. Language and content need to be culturally appropriate as well.

3. Besides multilingualism, the SLP should remain sensitive to other cultural differences in PWA who are being assessed, such as differences in ethnic background, religion, place of origin, sexual orientation, and so on.

4. Adaptations to assessment protocols and procedures may be necessary to address cultural differences.

Classification of Aphasia

The Boston Classification System

1. Numerous classification systems exist for describing the various common syndromes of aphasia. Perhaps the best-known system is the Boston classification system that is described in the BDAE by Goodglass and colleagues (2001a; 2001b).

2. The Boston classification system has seven aphasia syndromes, each determined by a unique profile of three language characteristics: (1) fluency of verbal output (fluent or nonfluent), (2) auditory comprehension (relatively impaired or relatively spared),

and (3) verbal repetition abilities (relatively impaired or relatively spared). See Table 13-1 for each of these profiles.

a. *Important*: the seven syndromes are *not* based on lesion location; rather, they are determined by the linguistic profiles.

b. There are three nonfluent syndromes: Broca's aphasia, transcortical motor aphasia, and global aphasia.

c. There are four fluent syndromes: Wernicke's aphasia, transcortical sensory aphasia, conduction aphasia, and anomic aphasia.

d. Detailed profiles of the seven syndromes, including typical lesion location and other associated features, are presented in Table 13-2.

Table 13-1

Language Profiles of the Seven Aphasia Syndromes of the Boston Classification System			
SYNDROME	FLUENT (F) OR NONFLUENT (NF)	AUDITORY COMPREHENSION	REPETITION
Broca's aphasia	NF	+	−
Transcortical motor aphasia	NF	+	+
Global aphasia	NF	−	−
Wernicke's aphasia	F	−	−
Transcortical sensory aphasia	F	−	+
Conduction aphasia	F	+	−
Anomic aphasia	F	+	+

Plus symbol = relatively preserved; minus symbol = relatively impaired.

Table 13-2

Detailed Profiles of the Seven Aphasia Syndromes of the Boston Classification System

	APHASIA SYNDROME	LANGUAGE FEATURES	COMMON LESION LOCATION AND ASSOCIATED NEUROLOGICAL DEFICITS
Nonfluent	**Broca's aphasia**	Nonfluent, effortful, sparse verbal output with short phrase length; agrammatism, telegraphic, omission of functor words; impaired articulation, prosody, and melodic line; relatively preserved auditory comprehension but difficulty with complex syntax; deep dyslexia; poor repetition; aware of errors; range of severities.	A large frontal lobe lesion affecting Broca's area and surrounding cortical regions as well as white matter deep to Broca's area. Often a right hemiparesis. Often has apraxia of speech; may have dysarthria.
	Transcortical motor aphasia	Nonfluent, sparse output; difficulty initiating and organizing verbal responses; fair to good articulation; few paraphasias; relatively preserved auditory comprehension; strikingly preserved repetition.	A frontal lobe lesion often anterior and/or superior to Broca's area, sometimes in the territory of the ACA or in border zone between MCA and ACA; may involve supplementary motor area. Motor inertia for nonspeech activities also.
	Global aphasia	Nonfluent, severely restricted output, phrases of one word or less or verbal stereotypy; may use "swear" words; preservation of vocal intonation for affective expression; poor auditory comprehension; all language modalities impaired; may have no ability to read or write.	A large lesion affecting the frontal, parietal, and temporal lobes, or a smaller deep lesion affecting pathways from both anterior and posterior language regions. Usually a right hemiparesis. May have visual deficits if occipital lobe pathways are affected.
Fluent	**Wernicke's aphasia**	Fluent, well-articulated, paraphasic, circumlocutory, anomic verbal output results in empty speech; may have neologistic jargon; may have excess (press of) speech; poor auditory comprehension (A/C); may show better reading comprehension (R/C) than A/C; letter-by-letter oral reading; exceedingly poor repetition.	A lesion affecting Wernicke's area in the temporal lobe, often with extension into other temporal regions and parietal lobe. Usually no motor deficits. May have visual deficits if occipital lobe pathways also affected.
	Conduction aphasia	Fluent, paraphasic output, with primarily phonemic paraphasias; strings of successive attempts to self-correct (conduit d'approche); may seem hesitant and sometimes not fluent as a result; relatively good auditory comprehension; strikingly poor repetition.	Lesion in the supramarginal gyrus region of parietal/temporal lobe junction or deep to it, or in arcuate fasciculus.
	Transcortical sensory aphasia	Verbal output similar to Wernicke's except repetition is preserved; fluent, paraphasic, neologistic output; poor auditory comprehension; strikingly preserved repetition; echoes examiner's words; preservation of overlearned material such as Lord's Prayer; rare syndrome.	Border zone regions of the middle cerebral artery-posterior cerebral artery territories, sparing Wernicke's area.
	Anomic aphasia	Fluent, well-articulated, but anomic output; empty speech with lack of content words; overuse of indefinite terms like *thing* and *place*; relatively preserved auditory comprehension; preserved repetition.	A variety of lesion locations, often in posterior language regions, but sometimes in frontal lobe.

e. An eighth syndrome, known as *mixed nonfluent aphasia*, refers to a severe nonfluent syndrome in which auditory comprehension has improved beyond the level of global aphasia but is not good enough to qualify as relatively preserved, as in Broca's aphasia.

f. Subcortical aphasia syndromes have also been identified. Unlike the seven cortical syndromes, the subcortical syndromes are named for their lesion locations. Table 13-3 provides more detailed profiles of these four syndromes:

(1) Anterior capsular-putaminal aphasia.
(2) Posterior capsular-putaminal aphasia.
(3) Global capsular-putaminal aphasia.
(4) Thalamic aphasia.

Table 13-3

The Four Subcortical Aphasia Syndromes

APHASIA SYNDROME	LANGUAGE FEATURES	COMMON LESION LOCATION AND ASSOCIATED NEUROLOGICAL DEFICITS
Anterior capsular-putaminal aphasia	Features of both Broca's aphasia and TCM; sparse output, reduced phrase lengths, severely reduced articulation (like Broca's aphasia); agrammatism is *not* prominent, relatively good syntax, and preserved repetition (these like TCM); hypophonic (low volume) speech; good auditory comprehension.	Lesion in anterior part of the internal capsule and putamen. Frequently a hemiplegia.
Posterior capsular-putaminal aphasia	Features of both anterior and posterior aphasias because some pathways from cortex of Wernicke's area and motor pathways from motor cortex are interrupted; fluent, poor repetition, poor A/C; good articulatory agility (these features like a posterior aphasia case). Therefore, if PWA comes in with a fluent type of aphasia and yet they are hemiplegic and in a wheelchair, you might suspect a subcortical lesion site in the posterior internal capsule/putamen.	Lesion in the posterior part of the internal capsule and the putamen. Frequently hemiplegia (like an anterior aphasia case).
Global capsular-putaminal aphasia	Global type of aphasia with severe impairments in all language modalities; poor A/C; little or no verbal output. Pathways interrupted from both anterior and posterior cortical language areas.	Lesion in both the anterior and posterior portions of the internal capsule and the putamen. Often hemiplegia (but not always, if motor pathways happen to be spared).
Thalamic aphasia	Features of transcortical sensory or Wernicke's aphasia; generally fluent; repetition relatively good; sometimes see echolalia; semantic paraphasia; way off-target paraphasias as in extended English jargon.; poor word-finding; perseveration; attention deficits. Quick tip: May look like Wernicke's or TCS but with better A/C.	Lesion in the thalamus; more likely a hemorrhage than an occlusive infarct. With or without hemiplegia, depending on specific pathways affected.

Expressive Aphasia and Receptive Aphasia

1. An earlier classification system that originated in the 1930s used the dichotomy of expressive aphasia and receptive aphasia. Some professionals still use this terminology, but for SLPs, use of these terms is *not* preferred for these reasons:
   a. Most individuals with aphasia have linguistic deficits involving both expression and reception (comprehension of language).
   b. Two individuals given the label of "expressive aphasia" may be exceedingly different (e.g., the expressive difficulties associated with Broca's aphasia are very different from the expressive difficulties associated with Wernicke's aphasia, yet both involve significant problems in expression of language).
   c. Likewise, two individuals given the label "receptive aphasia" may be exceedingly different.
   d. Thus, these terms tend to obscure rather than clarify the deficit.

Neuropsychological Models Classification

1. In recent years, use of the "syndromes" approach to classification of aphasia described above in the section

on the Boston Classification system has received criticism. Why?
   a. Grouping together characteristics of PWA and labeling these as a "syndrome" does not help to explain the underlying cognitive mechanisms of the linguistic disorder.
   b. PWA all grouped under the heading of one syndrome (e.g., Broca's aphasia) may have widely variable profiles of strengths and weaknesses, as well as severities.
   c. Treatment approaches might be individualized in a more meaningful way if the examiner was able to obtain a more thorough understanding of the cognitive processes underlying task performances.

2. Therefore, some clinical and research SLPs have begun using an approach based on cognitive neuropsychological models such as the one in Figure 13-3.
   a. The aim of the assessment is thus to determine which of the cognitive processes depicted in the "boxes" and "arrows" of the model seem to be relatively intact or impaired in the PWA.
   b. If this can be clarified, then there is a rationale for which processes the SLP would target for treatment.
   c. In general, this approach is more successful for individuals with less severe impairments or those who have isolated impairments than it is for those with severe forms of aphasia and multiple impaired cognitive processes.

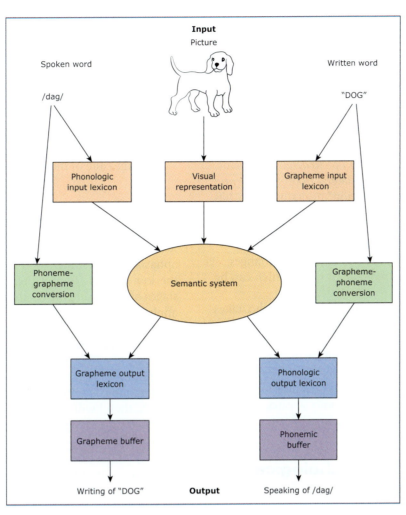

Figure 13-3 Sample neuropsychological model of lexical processing used for tasks of writing to dictation, picture naming and reading aloud in PWA.

Based on Beeson and Hillis, in Chapey, 2001, p. 573.

Psychosocial Effects of Aphasia on the Individual and the Family

Alleviating Havoc Wrought by Aphasia

1. Helping to alleviate some of the havoc wrought by aphasia in the psychosocial sphere needs to be a priority of every clinician.
2. Psychosocial effects may arise from:
   a. Organic causes: the brain damage that causes aphasia also has characteristic effects on emotional/psychological behavior.
      (1) Left-frontal lesions are associated with depression, catastrophic reactions, and sometimes indifference/apathy (from prefrontal lesions).
      (2) Left-posterior lesions are associated with unawareness, agitation, occasionally paranoia, and very rarely euphoria.
      (3) Left-hemisphere lesions are also associated with catastrophic reactions:
         (a) A behavioral state in which the PWA switches suddenly, and often violently, into a state of intense negativity.
         (b) Catastrophic reactions are not under voluntary control.
         (c) Usually last no more than a few days and are somewhat rare.
         (d) Goldstein (1948) associated catastrophic reactions with a "loss of the abstract attitude" that was seen in PWA.

b. Reactive causes: people with acute onset of illness have emotional/behavioral reactions to their newly acquired disorders.
   (1) Increased egocentrism and what appears to be reduced concern for others.
   (2) Increased concretism and need for routine.
   (3) Withdrawal from social contact that leads to social isolation.
   (4) Emotional lability such that the threshold for emotional spillover may be lowered. If extreme, this may be a sign of bilateral brain damage and is not part of the "reaction" but rather likely has an organic cause.
   (5) Anxiety and fear about having another stroke.
   (6) Frustration, anger, or embarrassment.
   (7) Guilt because of life and family role changes.
      (a) Involuntary removal of work, which can be devastating.
      (b) Familial roles may be shifted—who takes care of finances, caretaking, cooking, driving, and so on.
      (c) Loss of a conversational partner to talk over events of the day.
      (d) Changes in parent–child relationships. Children may be forced into a caregiver role, rather than being recipients of care.

Assessment of Psychological State in PWA

1. It is often difficult to assess psychiatric and emotional disturbances in people with significant communication disorders because talking and answering questions is often integral to psychological assessment.

2. Visual analog mood scales for different emotions (e.g., sad, happy, angry) have been created to accommodate some of these difficulties.
   a. The scales have a "neutral" schematic face (and accompanying word) at the top of a 100-mm vertical line and a specific "mood" face (and word) at the bottom of the line.
   b. People are asked to indicate how they are feeling by placing a mark on the line, which provides a quantitative measure of the emotional state in millimeters.

Reactions to Aphasia

1. Reactions to a major change such as a stroke and aphasia may be understood as a period of mourning the loss of one's former life. Elisabeth Kübler-Ross's stages of mourning the death of a loved one may also apply to PWA as they adjust to their new life.
   a. Denial: the PWA and family members are in shock and often feel numb.
   b. Anger: the PWA feels anger about the events and questions, "Why me?"
   c. Bargaining: the PWA attempts to bargain, "If I just do X, then I will recover."
   d. Depression: denial and anger have subsided and the reality of the situation sets in.
   e. Acceptance: the PWA is able to acknowledge the reality of the situation and can go on with life.
      (1) The SLP is an important part of the support system to help the PWA and family members reach the acceptance stage.
      (2) Referrals to psychological professionals may be required, however, if there appears to be a persistent depression or other psychological disturbance.

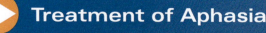

Treatment of Aphasia

General Treatment Considerations

1. Impairment-based versus non-impairment-based treatment.
   a. Impairment-based treatments are those that target a specific impairment of language and attempt to improve the language skill, thereby lessening the impairment. The majority of treatments for aphasia are of this type (e.g., using melodic intonation therapy [MIT] to increase phrase lengths and word production).
      (1) Some treatment approaches attempt to fix the underlying deficit leading to the communication problem (e.g., directly working on verbal expression of grammatical forms).
      (2) Other treatment approaches compensate for the deficit either because it is unlikely to be "fixable" or a compensatory means to communicate is preferable (e.g., learning to use a system of manual gestures to communicate).

(3) Both of these are still focused on the impairments associated with the aphasia.

(4) Both fix-it and compensatory approaches may be simultaneously implemented as elements of a treatment plan.

b. Non-impairment-based treatments seek to improve the communication environment of PWA and their quality of life without directly addressing the language deficits leading to the impairments. (See "Treatments for Other Language Modalities," section 5.)

(1) Non-impairment-based treatments have gained in popularity over the last 20 years.

(2) They may also be referred to as *indirect treatments*.

c. The A-FROM (Aphasia-Framework for Outcome Measurement) model, developed by Aura Kagan and colleagues (2008), has gained increasing acceptance as a basis for treatment considerations in aphasia.

(1) A-FROM has four domains and is based on the WHO ICF (International Classification of Functioning) model used in many rehabilitation fields.

(2) The four domains are impairment, participation, person, and environment.

(a) Impairment: refers to disorders of language and related impairments that affect communication.

(b) Participation: refers to how well people are able to participate in life activities they want to do that require communication.

(c) Person: refers to internal characteristics of the person's emotional health and self-identity that interact with communication.

(d) Environment: refers to external barriers and supports that may hinder or help communication.

(3) The purpose of the model is to encourage clinicians and researchers to focus less on the impairment domain and to consider assessments, treatments, and outcome measures within the other domains as well, particularly the participation domain.

(4) Grew from the core values of the Life Participation Approach to Aphasia (LPAA), stating that enhancement of participation in desired life activities should be the aim of intervention, not just "fixing" impairments.

2. General goals for treatment of aphasia.

a. Improve communication skills either by fixing the deficit, compensating for it, or both.

b. Maintain achievements once improvements have been achieved.

c. Facilitate the PWA's psychosocial and emotional adjustment to the new onset of aphasia.

3. When should therapy begin?

a. For PWA who have just developed aphasia and are in the acute stage, therapy can begin as soon as they are medically stable.

b. Keep in mind that diaschisis is operating in the acute phase.

(1) Diaschisis is a temporary loss of function and electrical activity in brain regions remote from the lesion but connected via neural networks (i.e., not actually damaged but temporarily dysfunctional).

(2) Deficits in some functions may appear worse than they will be within a few weeks, after diaschisis is over.

c. Clinicians often try to "harness" spontaneous recovery by treating vigorously in the first 6-month period post-onset.

(1) Spontaneous recovery starts to take place after diaschisis fades.

(2) Spontaneous recovery implies that most PWA will show some natural recovery of functions even without treatment.

d. However, research evidence shows PWA will respond to treatment regardless of time post-onset (even after many years) if the treatment is appropriately selected and administered (Robey, 1998).

4. Measuring treatment effectiveness.

a. SLPs follow the principles of evidence-based practice (EBP) when working with PWA.

(1) They carefully select which treatments to administer based on prior research evidence, the concerns of the PWA and their family, and their own clinical experiences. See Chapter 5 on evidence-based practice.

(2) They carefully and objectively measure the effects of the treatment they provide to each PWA.

(3) SLPs measure performance at baseline, during treatment, and at the completion of treatment using appropriate measures of the desired outcome variables.

5. General descriptions of direct impairment-based treatment approaches.

a. Multimodality stimulation and response approaches.

(1) Multimodality input with pairing of two modalities followed by fading out of one. The clinician presents a stimulus in two modalities (e.g., spoken and written), then gradually fades out one of the modalities (e.g., written) as performance improves on the other modality.

(2) Multimodality output requiring multiple functions per word. The task requires the PWA to produce a response in multiple modalities with the expectation that one modality may stimulate performance in another (e.g., drawing a

picture of an item while also attempting to say the name of it).

    (3) Deblocking: an unblocked modality is used to deblock a blocked modality (e.g., asking the PWA to complete a verbal repetition task first, and then asking the patient to name the same items, in the hope that naming may be achieved more easily).

b. Intersystemic reorganization is a notion from the Russian aphasiologist A. R. Luria (1970) in which an intact function, which is not normally involved in the impaired function, is introduced into the operation of the function.

    (1) Using a written scaffold of three columns on a piece of paper to help a PWA create sentences with a subject (first column), plus a verb (second column) and an object (third column).

    (2) Melodic intonation therapy is another example of intersystemic reorganization because it uses intoning and hand tapping to assist verbal expression.

c. Divergent therapies involve zeroing in on or converging on a specific target word in a treatment task item. Divergent therapies allow the PWA to come up with their own words.

    (1) In a divergent therapy approach, the SLP accepts a wider range of responses from the PWA's own verbal repertoire.

    (2) Research has shown this approach may result in better generalization of treatment effects than convergent therapies.

    (3) Response elaboration therapy (RET), for example, by Kearns (1985) and Kearns and Scher (1989) includes the following:

        (a) Targets verbal expression with the goal of increasing phrase lengths and lexical retrieval.

        (b) Clinician shows a picture and asks for any related response from the PWA.

        (c) Follow-up with a series of *wh-* questions to probe for longer and longer chaining of phrases (Table 13-4).

d. Pragmatic approaches: a variety of treatment approaches fall under the heading of pragmatic approaches.

    (1) Overall communication is the goal; therefore, encourage any modality of expression by the PWA.

    (2) Compromise on linguistic accuracy if the idea was communicated successfully.

    (3) Change the environment to make communication more successful.

    (4) Concern for transfer outside the clinic is built into the treatment.

Table 13-4

An Example from the Verbal Expression Treatment Method Called Response Elaboration Therapy (RET)

Present a stimulus picture; for example, a line drawing of a figure kicking a ball.

Clinician:	Tell me what you can about this picture. What does it make you think of?
PWA:	Soccer.
Clinician:	Right! Who is playing soccer?
PWA:	My son . . . soccer.
Clinician:	Your son played soccer? Tell me more. When was that?
PWA:	High school.
Clinician:	Your son played soccer in high school. Where was his high school?
PWA:	Weymouth.
Clinician:	Oh, your son played soccer in high school in Weymouth. Can you try to say that whole thing?
PWA:	Son . . . soccer . . . in high school . . . Weymouth.

Present the next stimulus picture and continue in this fashion.

    (5) Set up tasks so that they adhere to the four PACE principles: Promoting Aphasics' Communicative Effectiveness (Davis & Wilcox, 1981).

        (a) The clinician and PWA participate equally as senders and receivers of messages.

        (b) There is an exchange of new, previously unknown information by both parties.

        (c) The PWA has a free choice of communication modalities to use for expression (speaking, writing, gesturing, drawing, or using a communication assistive device).

        (d) The clinician provides feedback as a receiver that lets the PWA know whether the message was adequately conveyed.

Multicultural Considerations for Treatment of Aphasia

1. Treatment of PWA who are bilingual or multilingual.

    a. Generally treatment should be provided in the language desired by the PWA and his/her family, not simply the SLP's most proficient language.

    b. Cross-language generalization of effects from the treated language to untreated language(s) has been seen in research studies.

    c. Future investigations are needed to define, more precisely, factors promoting or inhibiting generalization from one language to another.

d. In general, SLPs can be reassured that they are not hampering bilingual recovery when providing direct treatment in only one language.

2. Recovery patterns seen in bilingual and multilingual PWA.

   a. Parallel recovery: the pattern seen in approximately 40% of bilingual aphasia cases; the extent to which languages recover is consistent with their premorbid patterns: If one language was stronger premorbidly, it would recover to being stronger.

   b. Differential recovery: the pattern in which one language recovers to a much greater extent than the other compared to premorbid abilities with the languages.

   c. Antagonistic recovery: a pattern in which one language is initially available, yet as the other language recovers, the initially available language becomes less accessible.

   d. Blending recovery: a pattern in which there is uncontrolled mixing of words and grammatical constructions of two or more languages when attempting to speak in only one language.

   e. Selective aphasia: the rare pattern in which there is language loss in one language with no measurable deficit in the other.

3. Using interpreters in treatment is often required when working with bilingual or multilingual PWA.

   a. An interpreter is a person specially trained to transpose oral or signed text from one language to another.

   b. Good interpreters must be able to say the same things in different ways, shift styles easily, retain chunks of information while interpreting, and have familiarity with medical, educational, and professional terminology.

   c. Ideally, professional interpreters should be used rather than friends or family members. Professional interpreters are expected to maintain neutrality, respect confidentiality, interpret faithfully, and participate in ongoing learning.

   d. Before working with the PWA, the SLP should meet with the interpreter.

      (1) Both parties should discuss the purpose of the session, the nature of the case, and the format and goals for the session.

      (2) They should agree on the best physical arrangement for the session.

      (3) The interpreter should be made familiar with the test protocols and treatment tasks to be presented and the need to interpret verbal output as close to the original as possible (e.g., identifying phonological errors or instances of agrammatism).

      (4) The clinician should plan for a longer session with the PWA so as to allow time for the interpreting process and subsequent meeting with the interpreter.

      (5) The clinician should brief the interpreter on the different types of communication impairments that may be present.

      (6) When using an interpreter, the SLP should talk directly to the PWA, not the interpreter.

         (a) The SLP should maintain eye contact and use the second person (e.g., "Tell me what problems you are having" rather than "Ask them what problems they are having").

         (b) The SLP should explain to the PWA the reason for using an interpreter in the session.

4. The National Aphasia Association (NAA; www .aphasia.org) has several resources from its Multicultural Task Force available on its website.

Specific Treatments for Improving Verbal Expression

1. Response elaboration therapy (RET) (see Table 13-4).

2. Voluntary Control of Involuntary Utterances (VCIU) is a method that uses oral reading to improve production of single words to communicate ideas in people with severe aphasia (Helm-Estabrooks, Albert, & Nicholas, 2013).

   a. Candidacy for VCIU.

      (1) People with severe nonfluent aphasia who have at least a few real words that they produce spontaneously.

      (2) It is not appropriate for totally nonverbal PWA or those with moderate or mild nonfluent aphasia.

      (3) The PWA can read at least one or two words aloud during the assessment and have some limited preservation of reading comprehension as seen in their ability to match written words to pictures.

   b. Procedures used for VCIU.

      (1) Use words the PWA has been heard to utter as the starting set of stimuli; expand with personally relevant names and emotional words.

      (2) Present a written stimulus word on a card and ask the PWA to try to read it. If the response is correct, keep that word in the VCIU "deck."

      (3) If the response is an error but it is a real word, write down that error and use that as the next stimulus (Table 13-5).

      (4) Continue to expand the list by repeated trials of new words.

      (5) After the PWA has mastered a set of words, change the task to a confrontation naming task by putting pictures on the back sides of the

Table 13-5

Sample Initial Session of Voluntary Control of Involuntary Utterances (VCIU)

Task: Present a written word on a card and ask the PWA to read what it is.

WRITTEN STIMULUS	PWA'S RESPONSE	ACTION
man	"mom"	Discard "man" card
Mom	"mom"	Keep card
hi	"hi"	Keep card
baby	"boy"	Discard "baby" card
boy	"boy"	Keep card
two	"two"	Keep card
love	"two"	Discard "love" card
Boston	"Boston"	Keep card
beer	"beer"	Keep card
OK	"OK"	Keep card
baseball	"Red Sox"	Discard "baseball" card
Red Sox	"Red Sox"	Keep card

Continue in this fashion, trying different words to get a set that the PWA is consistently able to read correctly, while using any real word "errors" produced by the PWA as the next stimulus item.

word cards in the VCIU deck and ask the PWA to name them.

(6) Build up to a vocabulary set of 100 to 200 words that can be consistently orally read and named to confrontation.

(7) Proceed to more conversational tasks with the words on the list, and, if possible, work on production of two- to three-word phrases using words on the list.

3. MIT is a method that uses a combination of intoning of phrases, hand tapping, and verbal repetition to improve verbal output. Albert, Spark, and Helm (1973) were the originators of the method.

a. MIT is based on clinical observations that some PWA could articulate words much better while singing over learned songs than when they tried to speak conversationally.

b. MIT is based on the hypothesis that singing and melody production are primarily controlled by the right hemisphere, which is not damaged, and therefore perhaps this nondamaged function of singing could be exploited to assist the production of meaningful verbal output.

c. Although specific target words and phrases are used, the aim of MIT is not to train production of just those specific stimulus items but rather to stimulate the language system for verbal expression in general.

d. MIT has been the subject of numerous research studies, many of which have shown it to be an effective method for improving verbal output in PWA (Helm-Estabrooks, Nicholas, & Morgan, 1989).

e. Candidacy for MIT. Research has indicated that good candidates have the following characteristics:

(1) Etiology of stroke and nonfluent aphasia or severely restricted verbal output such as a verbal stereotypy only.

(2) Relatively good auditory comprehension, poor verbal repetition, and poor articulatory agility (i.e., people with Broca's aphasia).

(3) No lesion in the right hemisphere.

f. Selection of target stimuli.

(1) High-probability words and phrases as well as emotional words.

(2) Functionally useful words and phrases (e.g., family names, places).

(3) Phonologically simple at first (e.g., no consonant clusters, at most two-syllable words).

g. Procedures for initial stimulus presentation.

(1) Present each target phrase with continuous voicing, using a simple high-note and low-note pattern (two tones only), presented with the stress pattern of normal speech (i.e., the higher tone should be used for stressed syllables).

(2) Pick up the PWA's left hand and tap it once on the table for each syllable.

(3) Control the PWA's behavior with your other hand to let them know when to speak and when to wait.

h. The complete levels and steps of the MIT program are presented in Table 13-6.

4. Treatments for agrammatism in aphasia.

a. Treatment of Underlying Forms (TUF; Thompson & Shapiro, 2007) is based on the idea that treatment of grammatical deficits should focus on remediation of the underlying linguistic deficit.

(1) Developed from linguistic theories explaining how surface sentences are derived from underlying "deep" structures.

(2) Thompson's research shows that if more complex forms are treated first, generalization to simpler forms will be achieved without having to directly treat them.

(a) This is known as the Complexity Account of Treatment Effectiveness (CATE).

(b) For example, linguistic theory states that *what* questions and *who* questions share certain features. Therefore, if *what* questions are treated, generalization to *who* questions will automatically occur.

(3) The TUF procedure trains production of *wh*-question forms and other syntactic structures by

Table 13-6

Melodic Intonation Therapy Levels and Steps

ELEMENTARY LEVEL*	USE SHORT, PHONOLOGICALLY SIMPLE PHRASES	POSSIBLE SCORE
Step 1: Humming	C** hums the phrase using only two tones while lifting up and tapping P's hand once for each syllable. P just listens.	Not scored
Step 2: Unison singing	C intones the phrase and asks P to join in; may require a few trials until P produces most of the phrase.	1
Step 3: Unison with fading	Once P has been able to produce the phrase by intoning it, C fades out and asks P to continue the phrase.	1
Step 4: Immediate repetition	C intones the phrase while P just listens. Then P immediately intones it.	1
Step 5: Response to a question	C asks a question such as "What did you say?" and P replies with the intoned target phrase.	1
INTERMEDIATE LEVEL	USE SLIGHTLY LONGER PHRASES AND IMPLEMENT DELAYS BETWEEN STIMULUS AND RESPONSE	POSSIBLE SCORE
Step 1: Introducing the item	C intones the phrase and asks P to join in; may require a few trials until P produces most of the phrase.	Not scored
Step 2: Unison with fading	Once P has been able to produce the phrase by intoning it, C fades out and asks P to continue the phrase.	1
Step 3: Delayed repetition	C intones the phrase while P just listens. After a delay of 6 seconds of silence, P is asked to intone the phrase.	2 or 1 if a backup to the previous step is required.
Step 4: Response to a question	C waits 6 seconds in silence and then asks a question such as "What did you say?" P replies with the intoned target phrase.	2 or 1 if a backup to the previous step is required.
ADVANCED LEVEL	USE LONGER PHRASES WITH SOME PHONOLOGICAL COMPLEXITY. RETURN TO NORMAL SPEECH PROSODY VIA THE TRANSITIONAL SPRECHGESANG TECHNIQUE.	POSSIBLE SCORE
Step 1: Delayed repetition	C intones the phrase while P just listens. After a delay of 6 seconds of silence, P is asked to intone the phrase.	2 or 1 if a backup to the previous step is required.
Step 2: Introducing sprechgesang, "Speech Song"	C presents the phrase with exaggerated prosody and continuously changing pitch as in choral speaking. P just listens.	Not scored.
Step 3: Sprechgesang with fading	C presents the phrase in sprechgesang and asks P to join in; once P has mastered the phrase in unison, C fades out and P continues the phrase.	2
Step 4: Delayed spoken repetition	C speaks the phrase using normal intonation and makes P wait 6 seconds before P attempts to repeat the phrase also using normal spoken intonation.	2
Step 5: Response to a question	C waits 6 seconds in silence and then asks a question such as "What did you say?" P replies with the spoken target phrase.	2

* If P is unable to complete a step at any level, the item is dropped and a new item is attempted at Step 1 of the current level.
** C = Clinician; P = PWA

bringing to conscious awareness the linguistic transformations that derive the sentences from underlying forms to surface structures.

(4) Table 13-7 outlines the procedures used for a sample target item for TUF.

(5) In 2010, Thompson and colleagues created a computer-automated version of this method called *Sentactics*.

b. Sentence Production Program for Aphasia (SPPA; Helm-Estabrooks & Nicholas, 2000) is for nonfluent PWA who also present with a prominent agrammatism.

(1) SPPA is based on an earlier research study that looked at the ease of production of 14 different sentence types by PWA.

(2) Easier sentence types are treated first, before more difficult types.

(3) SPPA is a structured treatment method to simulate production of sentence-level verbal output and to increase use of selected syntactic constructions.

(4) Target sentences are presented in story scenarios and elicited first with direct repetition probes and then from memory.

Table 13-12

Communication and Cognitive Symptoms Associated with Right-Hemisphere Brain Damage

AREA OF FUNCTION	SYMPTOMS
Language	Difficulty understanding nonliteral or figurative meanings of language
	Characteristic perseveration seen in writing: repeated individual letters, overwriting, and poor spatial organization
Music	Poor ability to carry a tune
	Poor ability to recognize melodies produced by others
Emotion and affect	Difficulty expressing emotion via facial expression or vocal intonation
	Difficulty recognizing emotion in facial expressions or vocal intonation of other people
	Flat affect or inappropriate affect
	Gallows (inappropriately negative) humor
General cognition	Poor theory of mind—cannot understand perspective of others' minds
Attention	Neglect of left side of space or lesser degrees of left hemi-inattention
	General inattention and distractibility
Visuospatial	Impaired visuoconstructive abilities, fragmented drawings
	Lack of overall gestalt in drawings
	Drawings, writing, reading show visual neglect of left side
Awareness	Anosognosia—denial or unawareness of illness or deficit
Personality	Taken together, these symptoms may result in a different personality style than prestroke.

c. Poor ability to carry a tune and sometimes to recognize melodies.

d. Difficulty expressing emotional states via facial expression or vocal intonation.

e. Difficulty recognizing emotional states in others' facial expressions or vocal intonations.

f. Flat affect, sometimes inappropriate affect, or inappropriate "gallows" humor.

g. Left neglect of space or lesser degrees of left hemi-inattention.

(1) The spatial neglect seen in right-hemisphere brain damage (RBD) is usually more severe than the spatial neglect or inattention to the right visual field that is seen in people with left-hemisphere strokes.

(2) This may impact the ability of a person with RBD to read written words even though they may not be alexic.

h. Impaired visuoconstructive abilities: the drawings produced by a person with RBD are often fragmented and lack an outer configuration or gestalt.

i. General inattention and distractibility; worse than is seen in those with left-hemisphere lesions.

j. Characteristic style of perseveration seen in writing: repeated individual letters, overwriting, and poor spatial organization.

k. Taken together, all these symptoms often result in a very different personality style than prestroke.

l. Anosognosia—denial or unawareness of illness or deficit—is sometimes seen, usually in the acute period post-onset.

(1) Anosognosia tends to be seen only early post-onset in RBD.

(2) Anosognosia is extremely rare in LBD.

(3) Anosognosia implies that the intact right hemisphere is perhaps more important to self-awareness than is the left hemisphere.

Assessment and Treatment

1. Assessment of individuals with RBD may be conducted with any of the assessment tools for language and cognition mentioned in the section on aphasia. Some specialized assessment tools for people with RBD that are used by SLPs include:

a. *The Mini Inventory of Right Brain Injury*, 2nd edition (MIRBI-2; Pimental & Knight, 2000).

b. *The Ross Information Processing Assessment*, 2nd edition (RIPA-2; Ross-Swain, 1996).

2. Treatment of people with RBD.

a. SLPs often work with people who have RBD in rehabilitation settings.

b. The focus of treatment may be on any one or a multiple of the symptoms listed in the "Cognitive and

Communication Symptoms" section. Multicultural considerations for assessment of RBD.

(1) Left neglect of space or inattention to stimuli in the left visual field can be quite debilitating and is often a focus of intervention by multiple rehabilitation clinicians (physical therapist [PT], occupational therapist [OT], or SLP).

(2) Lessening of the left neglect or left inattention may be required prior to attempting other interventions, particularly when working on communication modalities such as reading.

(3) Deficits in the comprehension of figurative language are also often a focus of treatment.

(4) Impaired comprehension and expression of emotional states via facial expression or vocal intonation also greatly affects interpersonal communication and relationships and is often a target of intervention.

(5) Treatment may also focus on improving speech intelligibility if dysarthria is present. See Chapter 14 on motor speech disorders.

Neurodegenerative Syndromes Affecting Language and Cognition

Note: For information on neurodegenerative disorders such as amyotrophic lateral sclerosis (ALS) or multiple sclerosis (MS) that primarily affect motor speech and not language, see Chapter 14 on motor speech disorders.

Normal Aging

1. Awareness of the language and cognition changes seen in normal aging is important to the SLP as a basis for comparison when evaluating those who may have the beginnings of a dementia syndrome.

2. Because the range of performances expected in normal aging is somewhat broad, the boundary between what is considered "normal" and what is considered as possible dementia is somewhat fuzzy.

   a. In recent years, a category called *mild cognitive impairment* (MCI) has emerged that encompasses this fuzzy boundary area (see the "Mild Cognitive Impairment" section).

3. Language and cognitive changes observed in normal aging are variable across individuals but include some common patterns relative to younger adults.

   a. Lexical retrieval ability on tests of naming and in conversation declines.

   (1) For example, for people in their mid-80s, Boston Naming Test (BNT) scores are 2.5 standard deviations below the mean scores of 30-year-olds.

   (2) Naming errors produced by elders are primarily categorized as circumlocutions (i.e., they are able to give appropriate semantic information but have difficulty retrieving the specific name).

   (3) This pattern has been described as the tip-of-the-tongue phenomenon, and people are able to say the target word when given phonemic cues.

   (4) Proper noun retrieval (e.g., the names of people and cities) may also be particularly poor in normal aging.

   b. Discourse production generally shows no impairment, with only subtle differences as people age.

   c. Auditory comprehension of language shows some clear patterns of mild deficit, including increased difficulty with measures of inferencing, syntactic processing of certain embedded structures, and semantic processing (e.g., of implausible sentences).

   (1) Most explanations of these patterns suggest that because working memory is vulnerable to aging, tasks that are dependent on WM will show deficits.

   d. A discrepancy is seen in the Performance IQ (PIQ) versus the Verbal IQ (VIQ) on the WAIS.

   (1) PIQ declines more steeply with increasing age than VIQ.

   (2) This reflects that visuoperceptual and visuoconstructional skills decline with increasing age on tasks such as block design, object assembly, drawing, and copying tasks.

   e. Memory functioning shows declines in working memory and free recall of word lists, but long-term memory is relatively resistant to aging.

   f. On tasks of executive functioning, many skills remain unimpaired, but impairments are seen on tasks of divided attention.

4. Neuroanatomical changes seen in normal aging.

   a. Decreased brain weight, gyral atrophy, and loss of myelin.

   b. Dilation of the cerebral ventricles.

c. Neuronal cell loss in hippocampus, amygdala, brainstem nuclei, and cerebellum.

d. Neurofibrillary tangles, particularly in medial temporal lobe, and neuritic plaques in the frontal and parietal lobes.

e. Dopamine receptor density declines.

f. Auditory system changes peripherally and centrally.

   (1) Hearing and vision changes are common in normal aging and need to be considered when evaluating language and cognitive performance of people who are elderly.

Mild Cognitive Impairment

1. *Mild cognitive impairment* (MCI) is a term most commonly used to describe a subtle but measurable cognitive disorder.

2. A person with MCI has memory problems greater than normal for his/her age but does not show other symptoms of dementia, such as impaired judgment or reasoning, and their daily functioning is unimpaired.

3. The definition of MCI continues to evolve, and many people view it as a prodrome state (presyndrome) to Alzheimer's dementia or another form of dementia.

Dementia

1. A general broad definition of dementia states that it is a progressive neurological disorder affecting multiple cognitive domains, including memory, language, visuospatial skills, executive functions, and behavior.

2. The *Diagnostic and Statistical Manual*, 5th edition (*DSM-V*), contains definitions and descriptions of both mild and major neurocognitive disorders, including Alzheimer's disease and many others. For Alzheimer's disease, the definition includes these elements:

a. Memory must be impaired.

b. At least one of the other cognitive domains must also be impaired.

c. The disorder must impair work or social functioning.

d. The disorder must be progressive, showing a worsening of symptoms over time.

3. SLPs may be involved in the assessment and treatment of people with dementia seen in a variety of settings, including acute care, rehabilitation, and long-term-care hospitals; skilled nursing facilities; private practice clinics; and more.

4. Treatment provided by an SLP to a person with dementia often involves treating cognition and language in early and middle stages and swallowing in later stages. See Chapter 17 on dysphagia.

5. Assessment and intervention by an audiologist is also often required given the association of neurodegenerative syndromes and presbycusis (age-related hearing loss) with advancing age.

Assessment of Language and Cognition in People with Neurodegenerative Syndromes

1. The Mini-Mental State Exam (MMSE; Folstein, Folstein, & McHugh, 1975) is one of the most commonly used screening tests for cognitive dysfunction in adults.

a. It includes items to measure orientation to time and place, concentration, memory, and language.

b. The maximum score on the MMSE is 30.

   (1) A score between 24 and 30 indicates "uncertain cognitive impairment."

   (2) A score between 18 and 23 indicates "mild to moderate cognitive impairment."

   (3) A score between 0 and 17 indicates "severe cognitive impairment."

   (4) Research studies on normal aging often use a score of ≥27 as a cutoff to ensure their participants are not showing signs of dementia.

2. The Montreal Cognitive Assessment (MoCA) is now the most commonly used screening tool for dementia.

a. It is available free at www.mocatest.org/.

b. Items on the one-page scoresheet include Visuospatial/Executive Tasks (Trails, Copy a Cube, and Clock Drawing), Naming of Pictured Animals, Memory (recall of word lists), Attention, Language, Abstraction, Delayed Recall, and Orientation.

c. The MoCA validation study (Nasreddine et al., 2005) is one of the most cited papers in the research area of MCI.

3. The Arizona Battery for Communication Disorders of Dementia (ABCD; Bayles & Tomoeda, 1993) is a comprehensive assessment tool specifically for people with dementia.

a. Table 13-13 lists the subtests of the ABCD.

4. SLPs often use standardized language assessments such as the BDAE or the WAB or a similar comprehensive language battery with selected additional measures to evaluate nonverbal cognition.

a. However, care should be taken when evaluating performance not to use the norms that are available for PWA when using these tests with people who have dementia.

b. Norms for people with dementia are not available on the BDAE or the WAB.

Table 13-13

The Subtests of the Arizona Battery for Communication Disorders of Dementia (ABCD)
Mental Status
Story Retelling—Immediate
Following Commands
Comparative Questions
Word Learning—Free Recall
Word Learning—Total Recall (free & cued)
Word learning—Recognition
Repetition
Object Description
Reading Comprehension—Word
Reading Comprehension—Sentence
Generative Naming
Confrontation Naming
Concept Definition
Generative Drawing
Figure Copying
Story Retelling—Delayed

5. The Cognitive Linguistic Quick Test (CLQT; Helm-Estabrooks, 2017) has both verbal and nonverbal subtests (clock drawing, mazes, trails, design memory, symbol cancellation, and design generation), so it is an appropriate measure for people with suspected linguistic and nonlinguistic impairments.
6. There are several other dementia rating scales that have been developed for both clinical and research purposes, including the Clinical Dementia Rating (CDR) scale, the Dementia Rating Scale (DRS), and the Alzheimer's Disease Assessment Scale—Cognitive Subscale (ADAS-COG).

Characteristics of the Neurodegenerative Syndromes

1. Alzheimer's dementias (AD).
   a. AD is a common dementia syndrome named after researcher Alois Alzheimer. It is the leading cause of dementia in adults and affects approximately 2%–4% of people over age 65.
   b. Many people believe that AD is actually a family of neurodegenerative brain disorders, not a single disease entity.
      (1) AD may have variable presentations, such as AD with visuospatial impairments (visuospatial subtype).
      (2) A familial variant of AD has been identified that has a strong genetic component, which generally presents at younger ages and has a more rapid course of deterioration.
   c. Onset of AD usually begins when people are in their late 60s or 70s, and prevalence increases dramatically with increasing age, such that up to 50% of people over age 85 may have AD.
   d. More women than men are affected, primarily because women have longer life expectancies than men.
   e. There is a somewhat higher risk for AD in African Americans than in Caucasians; believed to be the result of a combination of biological risk factors and health care disparities.
   f. Behaviorally, it is diagnosed by physicians as "probable AD" by a history of a progressive memory impairment of insidious onset.
   g. AD also presents with language deficits and eventually a behavioral comportment problem, but at first, social graces are well preserved.
   h. Average duration from onset of the disorder to death is 8 to 15 years.
   i. AD as a neuropathological entity is diagnosed definitively only postmortem by examining brain tissue and seeing both neurofibrillary tangles within neurons and amyloid plaques outside the neurons.
   j. AD is known as a disorder of the protein tau (tauopathy).
   k. Changes in brain functioning in AD are thought to be the result of the amyloid cascade, in which amyloid-beta proteins are deposited in the brain that eventually lead to fibril and plaque formation, death of neurons, and finally mental impairment.
      (1) These changes start many years prior to any apparent symptoms of mental impairment.
      (2) The neurophysiological mechanisms precipitating the start of the cascade are not fully understood but are believed to be a combination of genetic risk factors, general health, cerebrovascular factors, and environmental factors.
         (a) The apolipoprotein E (apoE-4) genotype has been identified as an important risk factor for the development of AD.
         (b) Many additional genetic risk factors have also been identified.
         (c) Diabetes and insulin resistance have also been associated with increased risk of AD.
      (3) Neuropathological changes in AD are first seen in medial temporal lobe structures, including the hippocampus and entorhinal cortex, explaining why memory impairments are usually the first sign.
      (4) As AD progresses, neuropathological changes proceed in a lateral direction to include the frontal lobe, lateral temporal lobe, and parietal cortex, explaining why language and other cognitive changes become more pronounced over time.

(5) Mild to moderate pronounced atrophy is seen on neuroimaging.

l. The 10 warning signs of AD published by the Alzheimer's Association (www.alz.org) are presented in Table 13-14.

m. Language and communication symptoms in AD change over the course of the disorder; many clinicians divide the progression into at least three stages:

(1) Mild or early AD.

   (a) Verbal output is fluent, well-articulated, and grammatical but shows a mild word-finding problem and is slightly empty and circumlocutory.

   (b) BNT scores are slightly to moderately reduced over age-matched norms, and more naming errors are due to misperceptions than are seen in normal aging.

   (c) Auditory comprehension problems may be seen in formal testing but may be secondary to reduced attention.

   (d) Oral reading is preserved but reading comprehension deficits are seen in formal testing.

   (e) Writing resembles verbal output (i.e., somewhat rambling, but often shows preservation of spelling and good syntax).

   (f) Awareness of the disorder may still be present.

(2) Moderate or midstage AD.

   (a) Language changes are more obviously different from normal elderly, as spontaneous speech becomes profoundly anomic, circumlocutory, and tangential; however, syntactic aspects of language remain intact.

   (b) Paraphasias of many types, including neologisms, may be present.

   (c) There is marked perseveration of individual phrases and of ideas.

   (d) Auditory comprehension deficit is more obvious in conversation.

   (e) The memory impairment interacts with the linguistic disorder so that the individual frequently repeats questions and is unable to retain information in answers that were given.

   (f) Awareness of deficits is quite poor.

(3) Severe or late-stage AD.

   (a) All language abilities show severe impairment, and it is nearly impossible to conduct neuropsychological assessment.

   (b) Eventually the person with dementia stops talking and becomes mute.

   (c) There may be some preservation of repetition skills seen in echolalia; the individual may echo words spoken by others without apparent comprehension.

2. Vascular dementia (VaD) is a syndrome with diagnostic criteria that are currently in flux, but it generally refers to a dementia syndrome in which the cause is cerebrovascular disease of sufficient severity that multiple cognitive domains become impaired.

a. *Important:* It is not necessarily progressive.

b. Described as a subtype of a larger syndrome called *vascular cognitive impairment* (VCI).

(1) If cognitive impairment affects only one domain of cognition, the individual may be labeled as having aphasia, apraxia, amnesia, and so on, depending on what is affected, rather than VaD.

(2) VCI is important to recognize because cerebrovascular disease can be treated and thus prevent the development of VaD.

c. VaD may be the second most common form of adult dementia.

d. The typical onset is between age 60 and 75, and more men than women are affected.

e. Life expectancy after diagnosis is not as long as AD due to vascular disease and its association with other medical conditions.

f. Risk factors for VaD are similar to those for other dementia syndromes and include hypertension as the most important risk factor, diabetes, and increased age.

g. The *DSM-V* criteria for VaD are similar to those for AD.

(1) One or more cognitive domains are impaired.

(2) There must be impairment of social or occupational functioning.

(3) Changes must represent significant decline of functioning over baseline.

(4) Additionally, there must be neurological signs or symptoms or laboratory evidence of cerebrovascular disease that is judged to be etiologically related to the disturbance.

h. Different etiologic subtypes of VaD have been recognized.

Table 13-14

The 10 Warning Signs of AD from the Alzheimer's Association Website (www.alz.org)
1. Memory loss that disrupts daily life
2. Challenges in planning or solving problems
3. Difficulty completing familiar tasks at home, at work, or at leisure
4. Confusion with time or place
5. Trouble understanding visual images or spatial relationships
6. New problems with words in speaking or writing
7. Misplacing things and losing the ability to retrace steps
8. Decreased or poor judgment
9. Withdrawal from work or social activities
10. Changes in mood or personality

(1) Lacunar state results from multiple small infarcts primarily in subcortical regions of the basal ganglia, thalamus, midbrain, or brainstem.

(2) Multiple cortical infarcts caused by a series of strokes affecting arteries feeding the cortex.

(3) Binswanger's disease is a rarer disorder in which there are multiple small infarcts in subcortical white matter, usually related to severe hypertension.

(4) Cerebral autosomal dominant arteriopathy with subcortical infarcts and leukoencephalopathy (CADASIL) is an inherited form of VaD.

i. Symptoms seen in VaD.

(1) Symptoms are highly variable because the exact symptoms depend on the region of the brain that is affected by the cerebrovascular disease.

(2) Reported symptoms include confusion, problems with recent memory, wandering or getting lost, loss of continence, pseudobulbar affect, difficulty following instructions, and problems handling money.

(3) If cortical regions are damaged, there are likely to be cortical impairments such as aphasia, apraxia, dysarthria, agnosia, hemiparesis, hemisensory deficits, and so on.

(4) If extensive subcortical regions of the brainstem or cerebellum are involved, dysphagia may be present.

(5) Many reports stress the common appearance of executive system impairments due to disruption of frontal-subcortical circuits.

j. Differentiating VaD from AD.

(1) Memory is always impaired in AD; only sometimes in VaD.

(2) The course of the disorder always shows an insidious progression in AD; only sometimes is it progressive in VaD.

k. Importance for SLP.

(1) VaD may be present in addition to other dementias (e.g., it is not uncommon for people to receive diagnoses of both AD and VaD).

(2) VaD may not always be recognized or labeled as VaD if focus is on the aphasia (i.e., some people with global aphasia could, by the criteria presented for VaD, be appropriately labeled as having VaD).

(3) Some people with VaD may be able to respond to treatment for their communication impairments if other cognitive domains are only mildly affected.

(4) The label of dementia may imply to family members that there will be relentless decline over time; SLPs may need to explain that VaD is not necessarily always progressive.

3. Frontotemporal dementias (FTD) are a group of neurodegenerative disorders that includes the primary progressive aphasias (PPA) and a nonaphasic, behavioral, or "frontal" dementia syndrome.

a. FTD is a somewhat rarer type of dementia than AD and is the label currently given to a group of dementia syndromes, including what used to be called Pick's disease and the Pick's complex of disorders.

b. Additional dementias now included in this complex of disorders include circumscribed cerebral atrophy, lobar atrophy, progressive subcortical gliosis, corticodentatonigral degeneration, frontal lobe degeneration, semantic dementia, corticobasal degeneration, dementia lacking distinctive histopathology (DLDH), dementia with motor neuron disease (MND), primary progressive apraxia, and others.

c. The onset for this group of disorders is typically younger than for AD (mean age approximately 55 years), and the progression is somewhat more rapid than in AD (between 6 and 8 years in FTD).

d. There is extensive brain atrophy visible in the frontal and temporal lobes in particular, which is the reason for the label FTD.

e. FTD is characterized by a significant decrease in brain weight and by a variety of other neuropathologies.

f. Most FTDs are known to be disorders of various proteins (tau, TDP-43), and a recent familial variant has been discovered that is related to a specific genetic mutation.

g. General symptoms of FTD and differentiation from AD.

(1) Decrease in spontaneous output and mutism earlier than in AD.

(2) Communication deficits more pronounced than memory deficits.

(3) Parietal lobe functions often preserved (visuospatial construction, R-L orientation, calculations).

(4) More common in men than in women.

(5) Approximately one-third of cases have a positive family history of FTD.

(6) A subset of individuals develops motor neuron disease (ALS) with weakness and muscle wasting.

h. Major clinical variants of FTD have been recognized, including frontal dementia and three types of primary progressive aphasias (PPA): semantic dementia, progressive nonfluent aphasia, and logopenic PPA.

(1) Frontal variant FTD is also known as the behavioral variant of FTD and does *not* include aphasia. It is characterized by disinhibition, poor impulse control, apathy, and antisocial behavior.

(2) Executive function deficits in planning and organization.

(3) Memory is relatively spared.

(4) Spontaneous conversation is reduced but language may be unimpaired on naming tests and other formal measures.

(5) Stereotypical or ritualized behaviors—insisting on a routine.

(6) Using a "catchphrase" or stereotypy.

(7) Significant increase in food preference toward sweet things.

(8) Elements of Klüver-Bucy syndrome late in course of FTD.

   (a) Increased sexual activity.

   (b) Hyperorality (oral exploration of objects).

   (c) Apathy and placidity.

i. Primary progressive aphasia (PPA): semantic dementia, progressive nonfluent aphasia, and the logopenic variety are termed PPA because progressive language disturbance is the main clinical finding in the absence of a more global dementia.

(1) To be diagnosed as having PPA, only language is impaired and this must be the case for the past 2 years.

(2) Other causes of the language disturbance such as acute CVA must have been ruled out.

(3) Eventually, most people diagnosed with PPA will develop a more global dementia syndrome within about 5 years of onset.

(4) Semantic dementia is characterized by a loss of information in semantic memory that results in a variety of linguistic disturbances.

   (a) Anomia in discourse with frequent use of circumlocutions, indefinite terms, and word-finding pauses in conversation.

   (b) Naming is impaired on formal testing, and there is reduced ability to generate category exemplars on word list-generation tasks.

   (c) Both verbal and nonverbal semantic knowledge about things and words is impaired.

   (d) Auditory comprehension is impaired, and there is sometimes alienation of word meaning (e.g., "I hear you saying 'cork' but I just can't recall what cork means").

   (e) Surface dyslexia and surface dysgraphia are seen with overreliance on phonetic rules in reading such that only the grapheme-phoneme route is used, not whole-word reading.

   (f) Grammar and phonological aspects of language remain intact.

   (g) Relatively preserved cognitive abilities include visuoperceptual and spatial skills, working memory, problem-solving, day-to-day or episodic memory, and autobiographical memory.

   (h) If temporal atrophy is bilateral, there may be prosopagnosia (difficulty recognizing faces), which gets progressively worse.

   (i) Behavioral changes only slight at first but may emerge over time as in the frontal variant.

   (j) The progression of the neuropathology in semantic dementia is the reverse of the pattern seen in AD.

     • It starts laterally in the temporal lobe and progresses to include medial temporal structures over time.

     • Symptoms mirror this progression: language is impaired at first, and over time, memory becomes more impaired (this is the opposite of the pattern seen in AD).

(5) Nonfluent progressive aphasia is characterized by significant nonfluency of verbal output as a presenting symptom.

   (a) People with nonfluent progressive aphasia may appear to have a syndrome similar to Broca's aphasia.

   (b) Nonfluency gets progressively worse over time, and eventually spontaneous verbal output deteriorates to mutism.

   (c) Auditory comprehension is preserved initially and for a while, in contrast to semantic dementia.

(6) Logopenic or phonological PPA has more recently been recognized (Ogar, 2010).

   (a) Shares some features with both the nonfluent and fluent variants of PPA.

   (b) There is a significant difficulty in word retrieval, but grammar and motor speech are relatively intact.

   (c) There is an obvious deficit in repetition, and phonemic paraphasic errors are interpreted as being caused by a deficit in the function of the "phonological loop" component of verbal working memory.

   (d) Thus, this variant shares features with conduction aphasia.

(7) Table 13-15 summarizes the three PPA syndromes (semantic dementia, nonfluent PPA, and logopenic PPA).

(8) Primary progressive apraxia of speech (PPAOS) has also been recognized as a motor speech disorder that has a nonacute presentation and is progressive in nature. See Chapter 14 on motor speech disorders.

4. Parkinson's disease (PD) and dementia with Lewy Bodies (DLB) are disorders caused by dysfunctions in brain regions that produce the neurotransmitter dopamine and the brain networks that rely on it.

a. Parkinson's disease (PD).

(1) PD is characterized by a significant movement disorder, often including a motor speech

Table 13-15

Characteristics of the PPA Syndromes

	NONFLUENT VERBAL EXPRESSION	FLUENT VERBAL EXPRESSION	AUDITORY COMPREHENSION	PHRASE LENGTH	GRAMMAR	ARTICULATION	READING	WRITING
Nonfluent PPA	+	–	+	1–4 words	–	–	+	+
Fluent PPA/Semantic Dementia	–	+	–	5+ words	+	+	–	–
Logopenic/ Phonological PPA	–	+	–	5+ words	+	+	+	+

plus = relative strength; minus = relative weakness.
Summarized from Helm-Estabrooks, Albert, & Nicholas, 2013.

disorder known as *hypokinetic dysarthria*, and not infrequently a dementia later in the course of the disease. See Chapter 14 on motor speech disorders.

(2) PD is a neurodegenerative disorder of middle and late life. Average age of onset is typically over the age of 50, but early onset PD may be on the rise.

(3) Idiopathic PD has no known cause, but it does have a well-defined anatomical site of dysfunction and a specific pattern of biochemical pathology.

(a) Dopamine-producing cells in the substantia nigra of the brainstem and other cells in the pons, medulla, and midbrain start to die off, resulting in less dopamine available to the projection sites of these cells in the basal ganglia.

(b) Severe neuronal loss in these regions is seen in PD, but approximately 50%–75% of dopamine stores must be depleted before symptoms first appear.

(c) Another major pathological marker is Lewy body inclusions in subcortical brain regions.
  • In DLB, Lewy bodies are seen in both subcortical and cortical regions.

(4) Slightly more men than women are affected.

(5) The time course of progression is highly variable across individuals.

(6) PD and DLB are synucleinopathies (i.e., disorders of the protein αsynuclein), in contrast to AD and FTD, which are tauopathies.

(7) Motor symptoms at the typical onset of PD that people complain of:

(a) Resting tremor in one hand.

(b) Generalized slowing of movement, stiffness of muscles, and fatigue with motor activity.

(c) Shortened stride length when walking.

(d) Micrographia or writing much smaller than premorbid writing.

(8) Cardinal motor signs of PD are termed *extrapyramidal signs*, since they represent functions of the extrapyramidal motor system rather than the primary pyramidal motor system.

(a) Resting tremor.

(b) Cogwheel rigidity in motor tone.

(c) Bradykinesia and akinesia, including "masked face," reduced arm swing, and reduced eye blinking.

(d) Postural instability, shuffling, and freezing of motor function, often leading to falls.

(9) Depression occurs in approximately half of the cases of people with PD.

(10) Hypokinetic dysarthria that significantly affects speech intelligibility is common in PD and is characterized by low volume of speech (hypophonia), monopitch, reduced stress, monoloudness, imprecise consonants, inappropriate silences, short rushes of speech, sometimes a harsh voice quality, and breathy voice quality. See Chapter 14 on motor speech disorders.

(11) Significant dementia develops in up to one-third of cases of PD.

(a) PD with dementia may differ from DLB only in terms of the time course of the onset of motor symptoms versus cognitive symptoms.

(b) The dementia syndrome in PD is characterized by bradyphrenia (slowness of cognitive processing), executive system dysfunction, some naming problems, and difficulty retrieving recently stored memories rather than encoding new memories.

(c) The presence of these neuropsychological deficits may have a significant effect on response to treatment for the dysarthria associated with PD, and SLPs must consider this in designing treatment plans and making treatment decisions.

Treatment of Communication in People with Neurodegenerative Syndromes

1. Common pharmacological and medical treatments for people with dementia.
   a. Many people diagnosed with dementia will receive pharmacological treatment for their dementia, and the SLP should be familiar with some of the more common medications that people may be receiving.
   b. Medications for people with AD.
      (1) Research is ongoing with many of these medications; in general, they have limited effects on cognition, and at most may delay progression of the disorder for up to, but usually not more than, 6 months.
      (2) Cholinesterase inhibitors may be prescribed.
         (a) These prevent the breakdown of acetylcholine, thus making it more available to neurons.
         (b) Common medications of this type include donepezil (Aricept), rivastigmine (Exelon), and galantamine (Reminyl).
      (3) Memantine (Namenda) was approved for treatment of moderate and severe AD and works with the neurotransmitter glutamate.
   c. For people with VaD, treatment will involve medications for the underlying cerebral vascular disease to prevent any further infarcts from occurring.
      (1) Medications such as those that control hypertension or prevent the development of blood clots may be prescribed.
      (2) In some cases, if no further vascular events occur, the symptoms may improve or plateau, unlike in most other dementia syndromes.
      (3) If the underlying cerebral vascular disease is not well controlled or is impossible to control, then the disorder will progress and symptoms will worsen.
   d. For people with PD, Sinemet, which provides a form of dopamine (levodopa or L-dopa), is the most widely prescribed medication.
   e. For people with one of the FTD syndromes, there is no evidence that cholinesterase inhibitors like those given to people with AD or that dopamine medications like those given to people with PD are useful; nevertheless, many people may be prescribed these medications.
   f. Deep brain stimulation (DBS) is a surgical approach that has had great success in treating the motor disorder associated with PD.
      (1) DBS involves implantation of electrodes in the subthalamic nucleus.
      (2) Implantations may be unilateral or bilateral.
      (3) Stimulation of the electrodes is turned on or off by a pacemaker-like device under the clavicle.
      (4) However, some studies have shown no improvement or worsening of dysarthria in people who have been treated with DBS; others have found psychiatric side effects and worsening of performance on neuropsychological measures post-surgery.
      (5) DBS is considered as a treatment option usually after people with PD find that their prescribed medications are less effective in controlling symptoms.
   g. People with DLB are sensitive to neuroleptic medications (such as those used for people with agitation and psychoses) and may exhibit even more Parkinsonian symptoms if treated with them.
      (1) Prior to the current understanding of DLB, the hallmark symptom of visual hallucinations was interpreted as indicative of a psychosis and therefore treated with antipsychotic medications.
      (2) These medications deplete dopamine, resulting in worsening of Parkinsonian symptoms.
2. Cognitive-communicative interventions for people with dementia.
   a. For people with dementia syndromes, the same array of treatment options, as in stroke-caused aphasia, may be tried in early stages, but expectations will differ because symptoms will worsen, not improve, over time.
   b. Therefore, clinicians will change their focus over the course of working with individuals with dementia, from maintaining optimal function to compensating for deficits, for example, using alternative and augmentative communication (AAC) approaches.
   c. AAC approaches may be introduced early before they are needed, in a manner similar to the approach for working with the speech disorder associated with neurodegenerative disorders such as ALS.
      (1) AAC approaches may be particularly useful for those with PPA who have not yet developed a significant dementia affecting other cognitive functions besides language.
      (2) However, in many cases, by the time the aphasic disorder of PPA has progressed to the point that AAC approaches are needed, symptoms of a more global dementia may be evident.
      (3) Deficits in executive functioning and memory may thus interfere with the ability of the person with PPA to independently or functionally use the AAC strategy.
      (4) Memory books are common compensatory aids used with people who have dementia.
         (a) These are often albums containing photos of family members, important familiar

locations, and other important information that the person with dementia, their family members, and other caregivers may wish to converse about.

    (b) Photos and pictures are captioned with text and names so that the person with dementia may be able to use these words to aid in recall during the discussions.

d. Practice guidelines for treatment of people with cognitive-communicative disorders associated with dementia have been developed by the Academy of Neurologic Communication Disorders and Sciences (ANCDS); reports on seven different types of approaches are available at www.ancds.org. Complete references for these are also at the end of the chapter.

e. The following are brief descriptions of these seven approaches that have been used successfully in people with dementia:

    (1) Simulated presence therapy consists of treatments in which clinicians attempt to reduce agitation and other negative behaviors by simulating the presence of loved ones via pretaped messages or phone calls played to the person with dementia.

        (a) A family member or friend records a one-person "conversation" about enjoyable past events they had experienced with the person with dementia.

        (b) The recording is played for the person with dementia when they are agitated or experiencing negative emotions.

        (c) Recordings may be played on an audiotape or accessed by dialing a telephone number to simulate an actual telephone call with a loved one.

        (d) Listening to the prerecorded tape of their loved one's voice may result in improvement of mood and lessening of agitation.

    (2) Group reminiscence therapy consists of treatments in which groups of people with dementia are involved in discussions facilitated by professional clinical staff on topics from their pasts that they are still able to reminisce about, such as high school graduation.

        (a) Reminiscence therapy activates cognitive and linguistic abilities to promote increased life participation and decrease social isolation.

        (b) It focuses on discussion of the types of memories that many people with dementia are still able to recall—autobiographical memories from one's youth, for example.

        (c) Visual and auditory props (e.g., popular songs from an earlier era) may be used in the discussions to help stimulate memories and positive emotions.

    (3) Spaced-retrieval training (SRT) is a treatment for those with memory dysfunction that introduces new memory associations via repeated stimulus-response trials over increasingly longer intervals.

        (a) Potential targets for SRT are face-name or object-name associations, associations between an external cue and a desired new behavior, and instilling positive alternatives to problem behaviors.

          • For example, SRT might be used to help establish a memory for where an important item was located, such as a wallet.

          • If successful, the individual with dementia would not be repeatedly asking staff where the wallet was located.

        (b) When successful, SRT is hypothesized to rely on procedural memory systems rather than declarative memory systems, which are usually impaired in dementia.

    (4) Caregiver-administered active cognitive stimulation for individuals with AD is a series of treatments administered by the caregiver, usually in the home environment, that are designed to engage the person with dementia in cognitively stimulating activities, such as playing card games, completing puzzles, and discussing films or events.

        (a) Research has indicated that these activities may be more beneficial to maintenance of cognitive function than such passive activities as simply watching television shows.

        (b) This approach may require some education and training for the caregivers as well as effort on their part to make sure cognitively stimulating activities are available on a regular basis.

    (5) Educating caregivers on Alzheimer's disease and training communication strategies are treatments designed to improve the communication environment by educating caregivers about what is expected in AD as it progresses and about the types of communication strategies that are most successful.

        (a) Research on this approach showed increases in success of conversational interchanges, improved quality of life for the person with dementia, and reduced caregiver burden (in most cases).

        (b) Examples of strategies include asking yes/no questions rather than open-ended questions that are too difficult for the person with dementia due to memory deficit, use

of memory books, and use of simultaneous nonverbal cues by the caregiver.

(6) Computer-assisted cognitive interventions (CACIs) include treatments presented via computer that may assist people with dementia with their memory and problem-solving deficits.

    (a) Examples include programs that provide a virtual representation of a person's home or the local area so that locations of objects or routes to area locations can be learned and practiced ahead of time on a computer.

    (b) CACIs are appropriate for those with mild to moderate dementia who have preserved motor learning and procedural memory skills and who have prior exposure to using computers.

(7) Montessori-based interventions are treatments based on Maria Montessori's principles of education and are designed to result in improvements in behavior, cognitive function, and mood.

    (a) Montessori principles:
- Learning within the context of purposeful and meaningful activities.
- Breaking activities down into their component parts and training parts in a sequential, structured manner.
- Incorporating multisensory materials.
- Learning in stages from observation to recognition to recall and finally to demonstration to others.

    (b) Research on this approach used with people with dementia found improvements in engagement levels, in social interaction, and on some cognitive measures.

Multicultural Considerations in Working with People with Dementia

Cultural Viewpoint and Clinical Decision-Making

1. Significant disparities have been identified in incidence and prevalence rates of dementia syndromes in ethnic and racial groups (e.g., Chin, Negash, & Hamilton, 2011).

    a. African Americans and other non-white groups may be up to twice as likely to develop some dementias such as Alzheimer's disease.

    b. Research suggests this is due to an interaction of factors related to ethnic and racial social inequalities combined with biological risk factors (higher risk of cerebrovascular disease).

2. In many cultures, dementia is viewed differently from the "Western medical model" that prevails in the United States and that has been presented in this chapter.

3. Some cultures do not view dementia as a "disease" but rather as a natural consequence of aging.

    a. A person with dementia may be cared for within the context of the family without ever being evaluated by physicians.

    b. A person with dementia who develops other medical problems for which no medical intervention is sought may not want assessment or treatment for the dementia condition.

4. Some cultures view those with dementia as being possessed by demons or suffering from a mental illness rather than suffering from a neurological disorder.

5. Caregiving, in terms of who the primary caregivers are and what is expected of caregivers, is also variable across cultures.

6. Therefore, SLPs should not assume that the person with dementia they may be treating or the person's family members possess the same beliefs they have about the causes of dementia or how best to treat and care for the person with dementia.

7. SLPs should remain open and sensitive to cultural differences that will affect their clinical decision-making when working with people with dementia and their families.

References Cited

Albert, M. L., Spark, R. W., & Helm, N. (1973). Melodic intonation therapy for aphasia. *Archives of Neurology, 29*, 130–131.

Bayles, K., & Tomoeda, C. (1993). *The Arizona Battery for Communication Disorders of Dementia (ABCD).* Austin, TX: Pro-Ed.

Beeson, P. M., & Hillis, A. E. (2008). "Comprehension and Production of Written Words." In R. Chapey (Ed.), *Language Intervention Strategies in Aphasia and Related Neurogenic Communication Disorders*, 5th ed. Philadelphia: Lippincott, Williams, and Wilkins.

Chapey, R., Duchan, J. F., Elman, R. J., Garcia, L. J., Kagan, A., Lyon, J. G., & Simmons-Mackie, N. (2001). "Life Participation Approach to Aphasia: A Statement of Values for the Future." In R. Chapey (Ed.), *Language Intervention Strategies in Aphasia and Related Neurogenic Communication Disorders*, 4th ed. Philadelphia: Lippincott, Williams, and Wilkins.

Cherney, L. R. (1995). Efficacy of oral reading in the treatment of two patients with chronic Broca's aphasia. *Topics in Stroke Rehabilitation, 2*(1), 57–67.

Cherney, L. R., Babbitt, E. M., & Oldani, J. (2004). Cross-Modal Improvements during Choral Reading: Case Studies. Presented at the Clinical Aphasiology Conference, Park City, Utah, May, 2004.

Cherney, L. R., Babbitt, E., Oldani, J., & Semik, P. (2005). Efficacy of Repeated Choral Reading for Individuals with Chronic Nonfluent Aphasia. Paper presented at the Clinical Aphasiology Conference, Sanibel, FL, June, 2005.

Cherney, L. R., Halper, A. S., Holland, A. L., & Cole, R. (2008). Computerized script training for aphasia: Preliminary results. *American Journal of Speech-Language Pathology, 17*, 19–35.

Cherney, L. R., Patterson, J. P., Raymer, A., Frymark, T., & Schooling, T. (2008). Evidence-based systematic review: Effects of intensity of treatment and constraint-induced language therapy for individuals with stroke-induced aphasia. *Journal of Speech, Language, and Hearing Research, 51*, 1282–99.

Chin, A. L., Negash, S., & Hamilton, R. (2011). Diversity and disparity in dementia: The impact of ethnoracial differences in Alzheimer's disease (Review article). *Alzheimer Disease and Associated Disorders, 25*(3).

Davis, G. A., & Wilcox, M. J. (1981). "Incorporating Parameters of Natural Conversation in Aphasia Treatment." In R. Chapey (Ed.), *Language Intervention Strategies in Adult Aphasia*. Baltimore: Williams and Wilkins.

Edmonds, L. A., Nadeau, S., & Kiran, S. (2008). Effect of verb network strengthening treatment (VNeST) on lexical retrieval of content words in sentences in persons with aphasia. *Aphasiology, 23*(3), 402–424.

Folstein, M. F., Folstein, S. E., & McHugh, P. R. (1975). "Minimental state." A practical method for grading the cognitive state of patients for the clinician. *Journal of Psychiatric Research, 12*(3), 189–198.

Frattali, C., Holland, A., Thompson, C., Wohl, C., & Ferketic, M. (2003). *Functional Assessment of Communication Skills for Adults (ASHA FACS)*. Rockville, MD: American Speech-Language Hearing Association.

Goldstein, K. (1948). *Language and Language Disturbances: Aphasic Symptom Complexes and Their Significance for Medicine and Theory of Language.* New York: Grune & Stratton.

Goodglass, H., Kaplan, E., & Barresi, B. (2001a). *Boston Diagnostic Aphasia Examination (BDAE)*, 3rd ed. Austin, TX: Pro-Ed.

Goodglass, H., Kaplan, E., & Barresi, B. (2001b). "Interpretive Summary: The Major Aphasic Syndromes." In *The Assessment of Aphasia and Related Disorders*, 3rd ed. Philadelphia: Lippincott Williams & Wilkins.

Helm-Estabrooks, N. (1992). *Aphasia Diagnostic Profiles (ADP)*. Austin, TX: Pro-Ed.

Helm-Estabrooks, N. (2017). Cognitive Linguistic Quick Test Plus (CLQT +). San Antonio, TX: Pearson.

Helm-Estabrooks, N., Albert, M. L., & Nicholas, M. (2013). *Manual of Aphasia and Aphasia Therapy*, 3rd ed. Austin, TX: Pro-Ed.

Helm-Estabrooks, N., Fitzpatrick, P., & Barresi, B. (1982). Visual action therapy for global aphasia. *Journal of Speech and Hearing Disorders, 44*, 385–389.

Helm-Estabrooks, N., & Nicholas, M. (2000). *Sentence Production Program for Aphasia (SPPA)*. Austin, TX: Pro-Ed.

Helm-Estabrooks, N., Nicholas, M., & Morgan, A. (1989). *Melodic Intonation Therapy*. Austin, TX: Pro-Ed.

Helm-Estabrooks, N., Ramsberger, G., Morgan, A., & Nicholas, M. (1989). *Boston Assessment of Severe Aphasia (BASA)*. Austin, TX: Pro-Ed.

Holland, A., Frattali, C., & Fromm, D. (1999). *Communication Activities of Daily Living*, 2nd ed. (CADL-2). Austin, TX: Pro-Ed.

Hux, K., Buechter, M., Wallace, S., & Weissling, K. (2010). Using visual scene displays to create a shared communication space for a person with aphasia. *Aphasiology, 24*(5), 643–660.

Kagan, A. (1998). Supported conversation for adults with aphasia: Methods and resources for training conversational partners. *Aphasiology, 12*, 851–864.

Kagan, A., Simmons-Mackie, N., Rowland, A., Huijbregts, M., Shumway, E., McEwen, S., Threats, T., & Sharp, S. (2008). Counting what counts: A framework for capturing real-life outcomes of aphasia intervention. *Aphasiology, 22* (3), 258–280.

Kearns, K. P. (1985). "Response Elaboration Training for Patient Initiated Utterances." In R. H. Brookshire (Ed.), *Clinical Aphasiology*. Minneapolis, MN: BRK Publishers, pp. 196–204.

Kearns, K., & Scher, G. P. (1989). The generalization of response elaboration training effects. *Clinical Aphasiology, 18*, 223–245.

Kertesz, A. (2006). Western Aphasia Battery–Revised (WAB-R). San Antonio, TX: Pearson.

Kiran, S. (2016). How does severity of aphasia influence individual responsiveness to rehabilitation? Using big data to

understand theories of aphasia rehabilitation. *Seminars in Speech and Language, 37*(1), 48–59. doi:10.1055/s-0036-1571358.

Learning Corp. (n.d.). Constant Therapy. Available at https://thelearningcorp.com/constant-therapy/.

Lomas, J., Pickard, L., Bester, S., Elbard, H., Finlayson, A., & Zoghaib, C. (1989). The Communicative Effectiveness Index: Development and psychometric evaluation of a functional communication measure for adult aphasia. *Journal of Speech and Hearing Disorders, 54*, 113–124.

Luria, A. R. (1970). *Traumatic Aphasia.* The Hague, Netherlands: Mouton and Co.

McKelvey, M. L., Dietz, A. R., Hux, K., Weissling, K., & Beukelman, D. R. (2007). Performance of a person with chronic aphasia using personal and contextual pictures in a visual scene display prototype. *Journal of Medical Speech-Language Pathology, 15*(3), 305–317.

Morgan, A., & Helm-Estabrooks, N. (1987). "Back to the Drawing Board: A Treatment Program for Nonverbal Aphasic Patients." In R. Brookshire (Ed.), *Clinical Aphasiology Conference Proceedings.* Minneapolis, MN: BRK Publishers, pp. 64–72.

National Aphasia Association. Aphasia apps. Available at www.aphasia.org/aphasia-resources/aphasia-apps/.

Nasreddine, Z., et al. Montreal Cognitive Assessment (MoCA). Available at https://www.mocatest.org/

Nasreddine, Z. S., Phillips, N. A., Bédirian, V., Charbonneau, S., Whitehead, V., Collin, I., Cummings, J. L., & Chertkow, H. (2005). The Montreal Cognitive Assessment, MoCA: A brief screening tool for mild cognitive impairment. *Journal of the American Geriatric Society, 53*(4), 695–699. doi.org/10.1111/j.1532-5415.2005.53221.x

Ogar, J. M. (2010). Primary progressive aphasia and its three variants. *Perspectives on Neurophysiology and Neurogenic Speech and Language Disorders, 20,* 5–12.

Paradis, M. (Ed.) (2001). *Manifestations of Aphasia Symptoms in Different Languages.* Oxford, UK: Pergamon Press.

Paradis, M., et al. (n.d.). Bilingual Aphasia Test (BAT). Montreal: McGill University. Test versions in many languages are available at www.mcgill.ca/linguistics/research/bat/.

Pimental, P. A., & Knight, J. A. (2000). *MIRBI-2: The Mini Inventory of Right Brain Injury,* 2nd Ed. Austin, TX: Pro-Ed.

Rao, P. R. (1994). "Use of Amer-Ind Code by Persons with Aphasia." In R. Chapey (Ed.), *Language Intervention Strategies in Adult Aphasia.* Baltimore: Williams and Wilkins.

Raven, J., Raven, J. C., & Court, J. H. (2003, updated 2004). *Manual for Raven's Progressive Matrices and Vocabulary Scales.* San Antonio, TX: Harcourt Assessment.

Rehabilitation Institute of Chicago. (2007). AphasiaScripts [Computer software]. Chicago: Author.

Robey, R. R. (1998). A meta-analysis of clinical outcomes in the treatment of aphasia. *Journal of Speech, Language, and Hearing Research, 41,* 172–187.

Ross-Swain, D. (1996). *The Ross Information Processing Assessment,* 2nd ed. (RIPA-2). Austin, TX: Pro-Ed.

Skelly, M. (1979). *Amer-Ind Gestural Code Based on Universal American Indian Hand Talk.* New York: Elsevier.

Sohlberg, M. M., & Mateer, C. A. (2010). *Attention Process Training-3.* Youngsville, NC: Lash & Associated Publishing/Training.

Sparks, R., Helm, N., & Albert, M. (1973). Aphasia rehabilitation resulting from melodic intonation therapy. *Cortex, 10,* 303–316.

Thompson, C. K., Choy, J. J., Holland, A., & Cole, R. (2010). Sentactics®: Computer-automated treatment of underlying forms. *Aphasiology, 24*(10), 1242–1266.

Thompson, C. K., & Shapiro, L. (2007). Treating agrammatic aphasia within a linguistic framework: Treatment of underlying forms. *Aphasiology, 19* (10–11), 1021–1036.

Wechsler, D. (2008). *Wechsler Adult Intelligence Scale,* 4th ed. (WAIS-IV). San Antonio, TX: Pearson.

Wechsler, D. (2009). *Wechsler Memory Scale,* 4th ed. (WMS-IV). San Antonio, TX: Pearson.

Wilson, S. M., Eriksson, D. K., Schneck, S. M., & Lucanie, J. M. (2018). A quick aphasia battery for efficient, reliable, and multidimensional assessment of language function. *PLoS One, 13*(2), e0192773. https://aphasialab.org/qab/.

References from the ANCDS: Guidelines for Treatment of Cognitive-Communication Disorders of Dementia

Bayles, K., Kim, E., Chapman, S., Zientz, J., Rackley, A., Mahendra, N., Hopper, T., & Cleary, S. (2006). Evidence-based practice recommendations for working with individuals with dementia: Simulated presence therapy. *Journal of Medical Speech-Language Pathology, 14*(3), xiii–xxi.

Hopper, T., Mahendra, N., Kim, E., Azuma, T., Bayles, K., Cleary, S., & Tomoeda, C. (2005). Evidence-based practice recommendations for working with individuals with dementia: Spaced-retrieval training. *Journal of Medical Speech-Language Pathology, 13*(4), xxvii–xxxiv.

Kim, E., Cleary, S., Hopper, T., Bayles, K., Mahendra, N., Azuma, T., & Rackley, A. (2006). Evidence-based practice recommendations for working with individuals with dementia: Group reminiscence therapy. *Journal of Medical Speech-Language Pathology, 14*(3), xxiii–xxxiv.

Mahendra, N., Hopper, T., Bayles, K., Azuma, T., Cleary S., & Kim, E. (2006). Evidence-based practice recommendations for working with individuals with dementia: Montessori-based interventions. *Journal of Medical Speech-Language Pathology, 14*(1), xv–xxv.

Mahendra, N., Kim, E., Bayles, K., Hopper, T., & Azuma, T. (2006). Evidence-based practice recommendations for working with individuals with dementia: Computer-assisted cognitive interventions (CACIs). *Journal of Medical Speech-Language Pathology, 13*(4), xxxv–xliv.

Zientz, J., Rackley, A., Chapman, S., Hopper, T., Mahendra, N., & Cleary, S. (2007). Evidence-based practice recommendations: Caregiver-administered active cognitive stimulation for individuals with Alzheimer's disease. *Journal of Medical Speech-Language Pathology, 15*(3), xxvii–xxxiv.

Zientz, J., Rackley, A., Chapman, S., Hopper, T., Mahendra, N., Kim, E., & Cleary, S. (2007). Evidence-based practice recommendations: Educating caregivers on Alzheimer's disease and training communication strategies. *Journal of Medical Speech-Language Pathology, 15*(1), liii–lxiv.

Chapter 13 ALD

Review Questions

1. What is a language disorder caused by brain damage?

   a. Apraxia.
   b. Dysphagia.
   c. Aphasia.
   d. Dysarthria.

2. Which aphasia syndrome is associated with fluent verbal expression, adequate auditory comprehension, and poor repetition?

   a. Wernicke's aphasia.
   b. Conduction aphasia.
   c. Anomic aphasia.
   d. Transcortical motor aphasia.

3. What areas of the left hemisphere make up the language zone?

   a. Frontal, occipital, and insular lobes.
   b. Parietal, temporal, and occipital lobes.
   c. Frontal, parietal, and temporal lobes.
   d. Insular, cerebellar, and frontal lobes.

4. Aphasia is *typically* caused by brain damage in the territory of which artery?

   a. Right anterior communicating artery.
   b. Left middle cerebral artery.
   c. Left internal carotid artery.
   d. Right posterior communicating artery.

5. According to the Boston classification system, what language characteristics are used to determine aphasia syndromes?

   a. Verbal fluency, written expression, auditory comprehension.
   b. Reading fluency, repetition skills, verbal fluency.
   c. Verbal fluency, auditory comprehension, repetition skills.
   d. Verbal fluency, reading fluency, written expression.

6. Who would be a good candidate for the use of voluntary control of involuntary utterances (VCIU)?

    a. A person with fluent aphasia who presents with excessive jargon.
    b. A person with nonfluent aphasia who produces a few single words.
    c. A person with nonfluent aphasia who is totally nonverbal.
    d. A person with fluent aphasia who has few episodes of anomia.

7. A person who shows signs of memory decline but continues to have intact judgment and reasoning skills is most closely associated with which diagnosis?

    a. Traumatic brain injury.
    b. Mild cognitive impairment.
    c. Dementia.
    d. Right-hemisphere aphasia.

8. How are subcortical aphasia syndromes named?

    a. Based on lesion location.
    b. Based on presentation of physical deficits.
    c. Based on presentation of language deficits.
    d. Based on results of EEG.

9. What is the underlying principle for the use of constraint-induced language therapy (CILT)?

    a. Constraining the person with aphasia to use only written expression methods to communicate.
    b. Constraining the person with aphasia to use only their weakest expression method to improve their communicative function in this method.
    c. Constraining the person with aphasia to use only verbal expression methods to communicate.
    d. Constraining the person with aphasia to use only gesturing to communicate.

10. What is the term for aphasia resulting from a right-hemisphere stroke in a right-handed person?

    a. Mixed aphasia.
    b. Crossed aphasia.
    c. Switched aphasia.
    d. Reversed aphasia.

11. What is an appropriate example of a cognitive/communication symptom that may be seen in a person with right-hemisphere brain damage?

    a. Difficulty orienting to time and space.
    b. Poor ability to use correct grammatical constructions.
    c. Difficulty recognizing emotional states in others.
    d. Difficulty naming pictures.

12. What is an example of language change associated with normal aging?

    a. Impaired discourse production.
    b. Moderate decline in auditory comprehension.
    c. Lexical retrieval deficits.
    d. Impaired executive functioning.

13. Which aphasia syndrome is classified by fluent verbal expression, adequate auditory comprehension, and adequate repetition?

    a. Global aphasia.
    b. Wernicke's aphasia.
    c. Transcortical sensory aphasia.
    d. Anomic aphasia.

14. A dementia syndrome that is caused by a significant amount of cerebrovascular disease leading to impairment of multiple cognitive domains is called:

    a. Frontotemporal dementia.
    b. Vascular dementia.
    c. Alzheimer's dementia.
    d. Lewy body dementia.

15. What is an appropriate treatment strategy to utilize in order to reduce agitation and other negative behaviors in a person with dementia?

    a. Simulated presence therapy.
    b. Group reminiscence therapy.
    c. Caregiver-administered active cognitive stimulation.
    d. Computer-assisted cognitive interventions.

16. What is the life participation approach to aphasia (LPAA)?

    a. A treatment approach to aphasia that includes targeting multiple areas of language deficit in order to improve communication of persons with aphasia.
    b. A treatment approach to aphasia targeted at improving participation and quality of life for persons with aphasia, rather than targeting language deficits.
    c. A treatment approach to dementia that allows persons with dementia to better communicate about their favorite activities.
    d. A pragmatic treatment approach to right-hemisphere language disorders that trains persons to better interact within their social environments.

17. When assessing a bilingual person with aphasia, what is the most appropriate means of assessment?

    a. Having a bilingual SLP translate a standardized assessment into both languages.
    b. Having an interpreter translate a standardized assessment into both languages.
    c. Using standardized language assessments for both languages.
    d. Assessing only the person with aphasia's self-selected dominant language.

18. Which aphasia syndrome is classified by nonfluent verbal expression, adequate auditory comprehension, and poor repetition?

    a. Broca's aphasia.
    b. Transcortical motor aphasia.
    c. Wernicke's aphasia.
    d. Global aphasia.

19. What are typical components of a standardized language assessment?

    a. Verbal expression, auditory comprehension, reading comprehension, written expression.
    b. Verbal expression, reading comprehension, writing ability, apraxia assessment.
    c. Auditory comprehension, executive function assessment, verbal expression, speech production.
    d. Oral reading, written expression, apraxia assessment, verbal expression.

20. What is the appropriate label for a temporary loss of neurological function caused by an interruption of blood flow to a brain region?

    a. Cerebrovascular accident (CVA).
    b. Transient ischemic attack (TIA).
    c. Traumatic brain injury (TBI).
    d. Mild cognitive impairment (MCI).

14

Motor Speech Disorders

GREG TURNER, PhD

Motor Speech Disorders

Relevant Terms

1. The general label of "speaker" will refer to a speaker with a motor speech disorder, including a speaker with dysarthria or a speaker with apraxia of speech.
2. The acronym *MSD* is used to refer to the generic label *motor speech disorder*.
3. *Childhood motor speech disorders* is the term used to depict an MSD originating during childhood.
4. The acronym *AOS* is used to refer to the generic label *apraxia of speech*.
5. The acronym *CAS* refers to *childhood apraxia of speech*.
6. *Developmental dysarthria*, or DD, is used when dysarthria occurs prior to acquisition of speech.
7. The term *childhood dysarthria* (CD) is used to depict the onset of dysarthria during childhood, including both DD and acquired dysarthria after speech development is complete.

Dysarthrias

1. Definition.
   a. A group of speech disorders associated with an impairment to motor speech control and execution processes resulting from damage to the peripheral nervous system (PNS) or central nervous system (CNS).
   b. Individuals exhibiting dysarthria are able to verbalize to speak, and for some individuals, to a limited extent.
   c. Anarthria or dysarthric mutism is the inability to speak due to the severe loss of speech motor control and execution processes.

2. General features of dysarthria for both children and adults.
   a. Onset: based on a developmental delay or acquired at any point across the lifespan.
   b. Neurological disease can impair the strength, speed, range, steadiness, tone, and/or accuracy of movements.
   c. Can influence the respiratory, phonatory, resonatory, and the articulatory components of speech production, resulting in both segmental and suprasegmental errors.
   d. A variety of different categories of disease influencing the nervous system can lead to dysarthria (e.g., toxins, tumors, vascular disease, and trauma).
   e. Neurological disease influences not only speech but also nonspeech activities such as feeding/swallowing and saliva management.
   f. Besides the presence of impairment in the execution of speech motor control, associated limitations include speech activity (e.g., reductions in speech intelligibility and naturalness) and restrictions in participation.
   g. Various types of dysarthria exist, resulting from differences in lesion location and underlying pathophysiology (Table 14-1).
   h. Each dysarthria type may be associated with a set of distinct perceptual features. Table 14-2 shows specific characteristics associated with each type of dysarthria.
   i. Both neurological disease and typical delays in speech-language development can influence the acquisition of speech in children with DD.
   j. The character of the speech disorder may change as the child naturally matures.

Table 14-1

Dysarthria Types, Lesion Locations, and Predominate Underlying Pathophysiology

DYSARTHRIA TYPE	LESION LOCATION	NEUROMUSCULAR CONDITION
Flaccid	Lower Motor Neuron	Weakness
Spastic	Bilateral Upper Motor Neuron	Spasticity
Ataxic	Cerebellum	Incoordination
Hypokinetic	Basal Ganglia	Rigidity
Hyperkinetic	Basal Ganglia	Involuntary movements
Unilateral Upper Motor Neuron	Unilateral Upper Motor Neuron	Weakness, incoordination and spasticity
Mixed	More than one location	More than one neuromuscular condition

Based on Duffy, J. (2020).

Table 14-2

Perceptual Features Found in Dysarthria Types

DYSARTHRIA TYPE	PHONATORY DEFICITS	RESONATORY DEFICITS	RESPIRATORY DEFICITS	ARTICULATORY DEFICITS	PROSODIC DEFICITS
Flaccid Dysarthria	• Breathy vocal quality • Harsh vocal quality • Monopitch	• Hypernasality • Nasal emission	• Audible inspiration • Monoloudness • Short phrases	• Imprecise consonants	
Spastic Dysarthria	• Breathy vocal quality • Harsh vocal quality • Low pitch • Monopitch • Pitch breaks • Strained-strangled vocal quality	• Hypernasality	• Monoloudness • Short phrases	• Distorted vowels • Imprecise consonants • Slow rate of speech	• Excess and equal stress • Reduced stress
Ataxic Dysarthria	• Harsh vocal quality • Monopitch • Voice tremor		• Excess loudness variations • Monoloudness	• Distorted vowels • Irregular articulatory breakdowns • Prolonged phonemes • Slow rate of speech	• Excess and equal stress • Prolonged intervals
Hypokinetic Dysarthria	• Breathy vocal quality • Harsh vocal quality • Low pitch • Monopitch		• Monoloudness	• Imprecise consonants • Repeated phonemes • Short rushes of speech • Variable rate of speech	• Inappropriate silences • Overall increased rate of speech • Reduced stress
Hyperkinetic Dysarthria	• Harsh vocal quality • Monopitch • Strained-strangled vocal quality • Transient breathy vocal quality • Voice stoppages	• Hypernasality	• Excess loudness variations • Monoloudness • Short phrases • Sudden forced inspiration	• Distorted vowels • Imprecise consonants • Irregular articulatory breakdowns • Prolonged phonemes • Variable rate of speech	• Excess and equal stress • Inappropriate silences • Prolonged intervals • Reduced stress
Unilateral Upper Motor Neuron (UUMN) Dysarthria	• Harsh vocal quality • Hoarse vocal quality	• Hypernasality • Nasal emission	• Decreased loudness	• Imprecise consonants • Irregular articulatory breakdowns • Slow rate of speech	

k. The symptom complex associated with DD, such as found with cerebral palsy or Down syndrome, can lead to a variety of other areas of concern (e.g., visual, attention, cognitive deficits).

l. Language and literacy are a concern for children with MSD, especially if neurological disease occurs prior to speech and language development.

Apraxia of Speech

1. Definition.
   a. Neurogenic speech disorder associated with impairment to motor planning or programming.
2. General features of acquired apraxia of speech in adults.
   a. Most common etiology is stroke; however, neurodegenerative disease can be associated with AOS.

b. Often the result of a lesion to the frontal or parietal lobe of the left cerebral hemisphere.

c. Reflects a disruption in the process of the translation of correctly selected sounds to previously learned articulatory-kinematic parameters; parameters may be lost or an interruption in access may occur.

d. Historical controversy between AOS being a language (phonological) or motoric (phonetic) disorder; this controversy still exists for the following reasons:
   (1) High frequency of co-occurrence of aphasia and AOS.
   (2) Some overlapping sites of lesion between the two disorders.
   (3) Limitations in models of phonological processing and speech planning/programming used to understand the underlying mechanisms of the two disorders.

e. Lack of neuromuscular impairment (e.g., paralysis, ataxia, involuntary movements); however, can co-occur with unilateral upper motor neuron dysarthria.

f. Difficulty with sequential movements for volitional speaking tasks while automatic verbal tasks such as counting or greetings can be spared.

g. Oral nonverbal apraxia frequently presents; limb apraxia may occur.

h. Right lower face and right lingual weakness may occur but fails to account for limitations in speech activity (i.e., speech sound errors).

i. Exhibits deficits in articulation, rate, prosody, and fluency; speakers with AOS are influenced by a number of task variables (Table 14-3).

j. Severity ranges from a total inability to speak (severe AOS), to a few inconsistent articulation errors (mild AOS).

k. No accepted diagnostic protocol and guidelines for identifying and specifying severity of AOS.

l. Table 14-4 provides examples of clinical characteristics associated with AOS.

3. Definition of childhood apraxia of speech.

a. Childhood apraxia of speech (CAS) is a neurological childhood (pediatric) speech sound disorder in which the precision and consistency of movements underlying speech are impaired in the absence of neuromuscular deficits (e.g., abnormal reflexes, abnormal tone). The core impairment in planning and/or programming spatiotemporal parameters of movement sequences results in errors in speech sound production and prosody.

b. CAS is estimated to account for 3%–5% of all speech sound disorders in children.

c. Can result from a known neurological impairment, in association with complex neurobehavioral disorders of known or unknown origin, or as an idiopathic neurogenic speech sound disorder.

d. Most often occurs as a congenital/developmental onset but can also be acquired.

e. Subtle differences in the anatomy and functioning of the brain but currently no widely accepted notion of localized deficits in brain functioning.

f. No universally accepted theory or model of the nature of CAS exists but evidence views disorder as a symptom complex that adversely influences not only sequencing speech movements but implicates comorbidity in nonverbal sequential domains of functioning (i.e., a broader deficit in sequential processing beyond speech).

Table 14-3

Perceptual Characteristics of AOS
Articulation
• Errors often reflect simplification of target sounds
• Imprecise articulation, mostly consonant distortions
• Sound substitutions
• Perseverative substitution (e.g., saseball/baseball)
• Anticipatory substitutions (e.g., gagebo/gazebo)
• Consonant additions
• Distorted sound prolongations
• Voiced-voiceless boundary inaccuracies
• Trial-to-trial production variations
Rate and Prosody
• Slow rate especially for multisyllabic productions
• Prolonged vowel duration
• Syllable segregation
• Equal stress across syllables/words
• Decreased production accuracy as rate increases
• Stress changes can appear to be a foreign accent
Fluency
• Attempts to self-correct articulator errors
• False articulatory starts and restarts
• Effortful groping for articulatory posture
• Temporary pause of articulatory movement during speech
• Sound and syllable repetitions
Task Variables
• More errors on complex words with more syllables
• More errors on two syllable words when there is an unstressed initial syllable
• Increase of errors for purposeful compared with automatic utterances
• More errors on infrequent or complex syllables, or nonsense syllables/words, than for meaningful words
• Consonant cluster errors more than singleton errors
• Initiation of utterances may be difficult
• Similar errors for both imitative and spontaneous speech tasks

Based on Duffy (2020).

Table 14-4

Examples of Clinical Characteristics Used to Diagnose Acquired Apraxia of Speech		
SPEECH CHARACTERISTICS	**SEQUENCING/RATE CHARACTERISTICS**	**OTHER CHARACTERISTICS**
• Consonantal distortions • Vowel distortions • Lengthened speech segments • Speech sound substitutions • Articulatory groping behaviors • Initiation difficulties	• Slow rate of speech • Lengthened intersegmental durations • Increase errors with increased utterance length or complexity • Consistent errors in repeated utterances	• Abnormalities in prosody • Awareness of speech difficulties • Better automatic speech

Summarized from Waumbaugh, Duffy, McNeil, Robin, & Rogers (2006).

Table 14-5

Consensus Diagnostic Characteristics (ASHA, 2007) for Childhood Apraxia of Speech and Additional Features Found in the Literature

ASHA CONSENSUS FEATURES (2007)	SPECIFIC FEATURES
Inconsistent errors on consonants and vowels in repeated productions of syllables and words.	• Consonantal errors: omissions more frequent than substitutions • Vowel errors: distortions and vowel reductions • Errors can be nonphonemic and difficult to transcribe even using narrow transcription
Lengthened and disrupted coarticulatory transitions between sounds and syllables.	• Difficulty initiating or transitioning between articulatory gestures
Inappropriate prosody, especially in the realization of lexical and phrasal stress.	• Lack of differentiating stressed and unstress syllables • Mis-stressing syllables
	Other features in addition to the ASHA features: • Groping or searching articulatory behavior • Slow maximum alternate motion rates • Syllable segregation • Schwa insertion • Voicing errors • Slow speaking rate • Increased difficulty with multisyllabic words

Adapted from American Speech-Language-Hearing Association (2007).

g. Often co-occurs with a delay in language, less often with dysarthria.

h. Presence of CAS will interact with phonological and literacy development, especially when apraxia is present prior to speech acquisition.

i. A validated list of diagnostic markers do not exist for the identification of CAS; however, based on the *Childhood Apraxia of Speech: Technical Report* (AHSA, 2007), consensus indicated that the most frequently occurring behavioral features of CAS include:

(1) Inconsistent errors on consonants and vowels in repeated productions of syllables and words.

(2) Lengthened and disrupted coarticulatory transitions between sounds and syllables.

(3) Inappropriate prosody, especially in the realization of lexical and phrasal stress. (See Table 14-5 for additional frequently shared features of children with CAS.)

j. The relevant number of identifying characteristics present in a child with CAS will depend on the linguistic and motoric complexity of a task, severity of involvement, and the age of the child.

k. The disorder is often viewed as being resistant to change given the best therapeutic efforts; however, promising increase in evidence involving adoption of specific treatment methods (linguistic and/or motoric) in tandem with motor learning principles.

Assessment of Motor Speech Disorders

Overview

1. Variety of possible reasons for assessment (Table 14-6).
2. Reasons dependent on place of employment and phase of service delivery (e.g., screening, assessment, intervention).
3. One of the overall goals of assessment is clarifying the contributions of cognitive, linguistic, motor planning and programming, and motor execution impairment to the overall communication disorder.

4. Organization of the acquisition of assessment information for a speaker with MSD can occur within the International Classification of Functioning, Disability and Health (ICF) framework. Information is obtained in the following areas: health conditions (i.e., impairment in body function and structures), activity limitations, participation restrictions, and contextual factors (e.g., environmental factors and personal factors) (Table 14-7).
5. Typical clinical examination for MSD.
   a. History.
   b. Identifying coexisting disorders.

c. Motor speech examination.
   (1) Dysarthria.
   (2) Apraxia.
d. Evaluation of physical impairment.
e. Differential diagnosis.
f. Trial therapy.
g. Development of long- and short-term goals.

Obtain the Historical Information

1. Purpose: identify and organize information based on ICF framework categories.
2. Obtain history information (e.g., medical records, case history, and speaker/caregiver interviews/questionnaires).
3. Identify and organize historical information associated with MSD.

Table 14-6

Reasons for Assessment of Motor Speech Disorders (MSDs)

Screening
- Confirming presence or absence of motor speech disorder
- Refer for further assessment

Diagnostic Assessment
- Determine which motor speech disorder is present, including subtype (if applicable)
- Determine profile of patient strengths and weaknesses (e.g., treatment targets and scaffolds)
- Reevaluation for progress measurement

Adapted from McNeil & Kennedy (1984).

a. Nature (i.e., presence and location within the speech production system) and course of impairment.
b. Type and frequency of activity limitations (e.g., articulation, speech intelligibility, prosody).
c. Perceived disabilities and restriction in participation.
   (1) Identify the communication needs.
   (2) Identify restrictions in meeting needs through self-report surveys (e.g., the Communication Effectiveness Survey, Communicative Participation Item Bank).
d. Consider relevant environmental (i.e., physical, social, and attitudinal) and personal factors (e.g., education, age, ethnicity, gender identity).
4. Document observations during interactions with the speaker (e.g., perceptual observations of speech and language).
5. Identify and organize information identifying impairment in other areas (e.g., hearing, cognition, feeding/swallowing, language, literacy) for screening or referral.

Identify the Presence of MSD and Other Associated Disorders

1. Based on the information from the "History" section, hypothesize about the type of non-MSD communication disorder(s) present.
2. Complete appropriate informal and formal testing to evaluate hypotheses (see appropriate chapters in this text for evaluating such areas as language, cognition, feeding/swallowing, and literacy skills in both children and adults).

Table 14-7

Application of the ICF Model (WHO, 2014) to the Assessment of Motor Speech Disorders

ICF MODEL COMPONENT	PURPOSE OF ASSESSMENT	ASSESSMENT PROCEDURES
HEALTH CONDITIONS		
Body structure and function	Identify presence of impairment in the subsystems of the speech production system	Examination of structure and function of respiration, phonation, resonance, and articulation, along with supplemental acoustic and physiological measures
Speech activity	Identify limitation in speech activity (i.e., articulation, speech intelligibility, prosody)	Evaluation through perceptual and acoustic measures of articulation, speech intelligibility, and prosody
Participation	Identify participation restrictions	Interview of client, care providers, and other relevant individuals in the client's environment, along with completion of questionnaires
CONTEXTUAL FACTORS		
Environmental	Identify the influence of physical, social, and attitudinal factors (client and others) on communication	Interview of client, care providers, and other relevant individuals in the client's environment, along with completion of questionnaires
Personal	Identify influence on communication for factors internal to the client (e.g., age, culture, resilience)	Chart review and interview of client

Adapted from World Health Organization (2014).

3. As testing proceeds for both children and adults, contributions of dysarthria and/or apraxia of speech, along with other cognitive/linguistic deficits (e.g., phonological disorders, aphasia, language delay, dementia), need to be thoroughly assessed to identify the correct direction for treatment.
4. Make referrals to other professionals as needed.
5. If either dysarthria (i.e., motor execution disorder) or apraxia of speech (i.e., motor planning and programming disorder) is suspected based on historical information, complete the motor speech examination.

Motor Speech Examination

1. Purpose: identify information supporting speech activity limitations.
2. Complete a detailed perceptual analysis.
   a. Obtain a speech sample, adopting methods that take into account the speaker's age.
   b. For a speaker with dysarthria, identify the perceptual features of dysarthria (see Table 14-2).
   c. For speakers with apraxia of speech, perceptual features of the disorder are largely related to articulation and prosody (see Table 14-4).
   d. For CAS, identify features noted in Table 14-5.
3. Document speech activity limitations for dysarthria.
   a. Naturalness.
      (1) Definition: overall adequacy of prosody.
      (2) Prosody is divided into:
         (a) Stress patterning.
         (b) Intonation.
         (c) Rate-rhythm.
      (3) Table 14-8 shows specific prosodic features that are often disrupted in motor speech disorders.
      (4) Some options for documenting activity limitations in the area of naturalness.
         (a) Overall judgment via a Likert scale.
         (b) Identifying type and number of speech dimensions noted in Table 14-8.
         (c) Percentage of speech dimensions noted out of the total number of speech dimensions associated with naturalness in Table 14-8.
   b. Speech intelligibility.
      (1) Definition: extent of understanding of a speaker based on the acoustic signal.
      (2) Used often as a measure of severity; however, comprehensibility and efficiency can also be measured.
      (3) Methods of evaluation.
         (a) Word intelligibility measures may include the Speech Intelligibility Test (SIT) or the Test of Children's Speech (TOCS+) Intelligibility Measures (2–7 years of age).
         (b) Sentence intelligibility measures include the SIT and the TOCS+ Intelligibility Measures.

Table 14-8

Prosodic Impairments of Motor Speech Disorders
• Alternating pitch levels
• Alternating vocal loudness
• Excess and equal stress patterning
• Inappropriate silences (pauses)
• Increased intersegmental durations
• Increased rate of speech
• Monoloudness
• Monopitch
• Prolonged intervals during connected speech
• Reduced stress patterning
• Short rushes of speech
• Shortened phrase length
• Vocal loudness decay
• Vocal loudness variation

Adapted from Yorkston, Beukelman, Strand, & Hakel (2010).

         (c) Subjective measures of speech intelligibility through equal-appearing interval scales, magnitude estimation, or visual analog scales.
      (4) The clinician needs to be cautious when evaluating speech intelligibility because he/she can be influenced by many factors (e.g., listener familiarity, closed or open set, mode of listening—audio versus visual plus auditory, education of the listener).
      (5) Another measure related to intelligibility is comprehensibility. Comprehensibility refers to a listener's understanding of the speech of a speaker based not only on the acoustic signal but also on the acoustic signal plus other information available to the listener during the communication interaction (e.g., gestures, semantic and syntactic context, and props within the communication environment).
      (6) Standardized measures of comprehensibility do not exist, but informal measures may be adopted with caution.
   c. Speaking rate.
      (1) Definition: rate at which speech units are produced within a given period of time (e.g., syllables or words per minute).
      (2) Conversational speaking gradually increases from 116 to 163 syllables per minute at age 3 to 162 to 220 syllables per minute by the age of 12, which is the typical speaking rate for adults.
      (3) An objective measure of speaking rate is calculated by dividing the number of words/syllables spoken by the duration of the speech sample. This measure can be calculated with and without pauses. The sample must be long enough to provide the best representation of the speaker's rate. Reading, monologue, and conversation can be used.

d. Efficiency.
  (1) Definition: rate of conveyance of intelligible or comprehensible speech.
  (2) Also useful as a severity measure and is often related to participation restrictions.
  (3) Efficiency rate (ER) is calculated by dividing the rate of intelligible words per minute (IWPM) by the mean rate of intelligible words per minute for a group of normal controls. Increased efficiency is associated with values closer to 1.
  (4) A subjective measure involving efficiency, Intelligibility Rating Scale for Motor Speech Disorders, is based on comprehensibility.
e. Articulation.
  (1) Definition: perceptual adequacy of consonant and vowel production.
  (2) Children with MSD.
    (a) Standardized sound inventory tests (e.g., Goldman-Fristoe Test of Articulation) provide valuable information but should be supplemented with a spontaneous speech sample to capture the influence of the segmental and prosodic complexity associated with connected speech.
    (b) Obtain a phonetic repertoire using stimuli within the child's language abilities.
    (c) For young children, obtain a spontaneous speech sample, have children name objects and pictures (imitative or spontaneous) and parent report of phonetic skills (e.g., inventory of speech sounds, syllable shapes).
    (d) For older children with a 200+ word vocabulary, obtain a 75- to 100-utterance sample and a single word task, sampling production of all vowels and consonants of a language (i.e., standardized sound inventory test), as well as both monosyllabic and multisyllabic words.
    (e) Analysis of phonology and articulation for both age groups (use transcription as needed for better description).
      • Inventory of all sounds, classes of sounds, and syllable and word shapes.
      • Inventory of errors based on sounds, classes of sounds, and syllable and word shapes associated with errors relative to adult form.
      • Measure of error consistency in repeat production of syllables and words.
      • Inventory of syllable shapes not in repertoire.
      • Results of stimulability testing.
  (3) Older children and adults with MSD.
    (a) Complete a word intelligibility assessment (e.g., SIT) to capture perceptual distinctiveness between phonemes.

• A single word or phrase reading test containing target sounds.
• Unfamiliar listener identifies each word within a forced choice format of words differing typically by one phoneme.
• Overall percent accuracy, percent of accurate vowels, and percent of accuracy of overall consonants is calculated along with breakdown charts of percent correct for consonant manner.
• Analysis of error patterns provides guidance for direction for treatment.

4. Documenting speech activity limitations in apraxia of speech.
  a. Considerations for making a diagnosis.
    (1) Currently, no accepted diagnostic criteria and guidelines for making a clinical decision for identifying the presence of AOS and CAS and deciding on level of severity for both disorders.
    (2) Diagnostic decision-making for AOS and CAS should take on an evidence-based practice perspective, adopting the best evidence (or test) available along with clinical knowledge and experience.
  b. Adults with AOS.
    (1) Standardized measures.
      (a) *Apraxia Battery for Adults-2 (ABA-2)*.
        • Consists of five subtests involving speech tasks, and one subtest identifying the presence of limb apraxia and nonverbal oral apraxia.
        • Purpose of the test is to verify the presence of AOS along with making a judgment of severity.
        • Differentiates performance between AOS, aphasia, and dysarthria.
        • Offers guidance for designing treatment and documenting progress.
      (b) *Apraxia of Speech Rating Scale (ASRS)*.
        • Documents the presence and frequency of behavioral features of AOS in adults.
        • Initial psychometric evaluation of reliability and validity were promising and the ASRS provides a cutoff score for identifying the presence verses absence of AOS.
        • In early stages of development but can be used with a level of caution.
    (2) Nonstandarized measures (a couple examples).
      (a) Wertz, LaPointe, and Rosenbek (1984) provide an informal set of tasks based on their clinical expertise along with a coding system to identify behavioral features the authors feel are unique to the diagnosis of AOS. The authors use a series of tasks (i.e., evaluating increasing word length, diadochokinesis,

automatic speech, conversation, and narrative) to elicit the informative features.

(b) Motor Speech Exam for AOS (Yorkston et al., 2010) assesses three areas the authors view as crucial to uncovering the motor planning and program deficits in AOS and designing appropriate treatment:
- Linguistic load.
- Length and complexity of utterances.
- Temporal relationship between the stimulus and response.
- Influence of cueing on performance.

c. Children with CAS.

(1) Standardized measures.

(a) *Dynamic Evaluation of Motor Speech Skills (DEMSS).*
- Assist in identifying the presence and severity of motor planning and programming deficits in children age 3 or older with speech sound disorders, especially children with limited verbal output.
- Based on the scale performance value given to imitative productions of individual words and utterances varying in length and complexity, overall articulatory accuracy, vowel accuracy, prosodic accuracy, consistency, and a total score are calculated and compared to peer performance.
- Besides providing a diagnosis and severity measure, results inform prognosis and guide direction of treatment based on an analysis of errors relative to utterance complexity and the influence of cueing.

(b) *Kaufman Speech Praxis Test for Children (KSPT).*
- Aid in the diagnosis, treatment planning, and reassessment for children between the ages of 2 and 6 years suspected of CAS.
- Performance on different tasks compared to normative charts.
- Diagnosis and severity based on a checklist and rating scale.

(c) *Screening Test for Developmental Apraxia of Speech (STDAS-2).*
- Screen for the presence of CAS in children between the ages of 4 and 12 years (not diagnose), provide guidance for treatment, use for reassessment, and use as a research tool.
- Considers receptive/expressive language discrepancy and normative data for three subtests to calculate a likelihood level of CAS.

(d) *Verbal Motor Production Assessment for Children (VMPAC).*
- Identify the presence of disruptions in the motor control system used for speech in children 3–12 years of age, identify the level of disruption, and identify modalities (i.e., visual, tactile, and auditory) useful in the intervention process.
- The test provides assistance in identifying the presence of developmental dysarthria or CAS.
- Speaker motor control plots are compared to normative plots for comparison.

(e) *The Apraxia Profile.*
- Aid in the differential diagnosis of CAS in children between the ages of 3 and 13 years, diagnose the presence of nonverbal oral apraxia, document change, and provide guidance for planning intervention.
- A separate form for preschool and school-aged children.
- Decision about presence of CAS based on 10 characteristics thought to be unique to CAS.

(2) Nonstandardized measures.

(a) Motor Speech Examination for Children.
- Due to similarity in the procedures, refer to the description of Motor Speech Examination for Apraxia. (Note: The DEMSS was conceptualized based on the MSE.)

(b) Assessment of Children with Developmental Apraxia of Speech.
- Used to obtain information regarding the presence and character of speech motor planning and programming deficits to use for diagnosis and treatment planning.
- Tasks involve spontaneous speech sample, elicited speech (phonetic repertoire), and nonspeech behaviors.
- Evaluate the productive phonetic repertoire of the speaker through spontaneous production or imitation, including isolated sounds, different monosyllable syllabic structure, multisyllabic words of differing length, and motorically challenging words and utterances.
- Note where breakdown in articulation occurs; also evaluate the benefit of using different levels of auditory, visual, and tactile cueing when errors occur; evaluate the ability of the child to self-correct.
- Evaluate the ability to sequence nonspeech and monosyllabic and multisyllabic sequences; evaluate the latency, completeness, and accuracy of tasks along with benefit of cueing if needed.

Evaluation of Physical Impairment (Body Function and Structure)

1. Identification of the presence/absence of neuromuscular impairment; may be explanatory of speech deficit and may support neurological evaluation (e.g., identify specific cranial nerve impairment).
2. Examination involves predominant use of nonspeech tasks (e.g., instructions to protrude the tongue) as would occur for a standard oral-peripheral examination, making sure to include measurement tasks for all four subsystems (e.g., the Frenchay Dysarthria Assessment).
3. Evaluate parameters of impairment (size, strength, symmetry, speed, range of movement, tone, steadiness, accuracy, and coordination).
4. Parameters measured at rest, during sustained postures, and during movement.
5. Aerodynamic (e.g., vital capacity, nasal airflow during sustained vowels) and acoustic (e.g., speaking fundamental frequency, speaking intensity) measures can also be adopted as supplemental measures to evaluate impairment.
6. A traditional model of treatment for dysarthria involves identifying the physiological deficits in the four subsystems of speech production (i.e., respiration, phonation, resonation, articulation), uncovering negative influence on speech activity and target-reducing or compensating for the impairment.
7. If apraxia of speech is suspected, evaluate presence of oral and limb apraxia, and rule out neuromuscular impairment across subsystems as accounting for deficit in speech activity, or a co-occurring dysarthria.

Differential Diagnosis

1. Individuals who are nonverbal or who present with limited speech are more difficult to diagnose.
2. Differential diagnosis for adults.
   a. Dysarthria from AOS.
      (1) The predominant lesion for AOS appears in the frontal and parietal lobes of the hemisphere dominate for language.
      (2) Speakers with apraxia typically do not exhibit neuromuscular conditions noted in dysarthria (e.g., hypertonicity, incoordination, weakness, hyperkinesia).
      (3) Speakers with apraxia typically do not exhibit feeding/swallowing deficits frequently present in dysarthria.
      (4) Nonverbal oral apraxia often presents in AOS but is uncommon in dysarthria.
      (5) Only articulation is adversely affected in AOS, while for dysarthria, deficits can be present in any of the four component systems of speech production.
      (6) Inconsistent speech sound errors greater for AOS than dysarthria.
      (7) Volitional phonation can be impaired at times in apraxia. For persons with dysarthria, both volitional and reflexive behaviors are impaired.
      (8) Speech sound errors are influenced by context (i.e., utterance length and phonetic complexity) for speakers with AOS (see other variables influence speech performance in AOS in Table 14-3) compared with speakers with dysarthria.
      (9) Well-practiced tasks will be easier to perform for speakers with AOS than less familiar tasks.
   b. Dysarthria from aphasia.
      (1) Speakers with dysarthria typically fail to exhibit language deficits in the areas of speaking, listening, reading, and writing.
      (2) Speech production subsystem functioning is typically impaired with speakers with dysarthria but not speakers with aphasia.
      (3) Speakers with aphasia may exhibit a variety of speech sound errors compared to largely distortion errors for individuals with dysarthria.
      (4) Dysarthria results from subcortical, cerebellar, and cortical lesions, while the lesions for aphasia occur in the cortical areas of the hemisphere dominant for language, often the left.
   c. AOS from aphasia.
      (1) A speaker with apraxia:
         (a) Exhibits more errors in prosody.
         (b) Exhibits sound distortions.
         (c) Has difficulty initiating speech.
         (d) Attempts to self-correct.
         (e) Gropes in search of articulatory configurations.
         (f) Speech sound errors more influenced by phonetic complexity.
      (2) Literal paraphasias (aphasic error) can be distinguished from errors produced by speakers with apraxia.
         (a) Aphasic errors are less predictable than apraxic errors.
         (b) Literal paraphasias always involve real English sounds, where some errors produced by speakers with apraxia may sound like a non-English sound.
         (c) Aphasic errors are more often "off target" in terms of place and manner.
3. Differential diagnosis for children.
   a. General considerations.
      (1) Extreme caution must be taken when attempting to diagnose children with limited experience or a limited repertoire of speech behaviors.

(2) The motor limitations associated with child-hood motor speech disorders (CMSD) can influence language development, including phonological development.

(3) The character of speech sound errors for CMSD as well as articulation and phonological disorders may be similar, suggesting applying extreme caution when considering such errors to the differential diagnosis process.

(4) CMSD and articulation and phonological disorders can co-occur.

b. Differentiating childhood dysarthria (CD) from an articulation (A) or phonological disorder (PD) (Table 14-9).

c. Differentiating CAS from A and PD (Table 14-10).

d. Differentiating CD from CAS (Table 14-11).

4. Differential diagnosis across the dysarthrias (all ages).

a. Informal assessment.

Table 14-9

Differentiation of Childhood Dysarthria, Articulation Disorders, and Phonological Disorders

CHILDHOOD DYSARTHRIA (CD)	ARTICULATION DISORDER (A)	PHONOLOGICAL DISORDER (PD)
Neurological diagnosis or site of lesion for speaker	Absence of neurological diagnosis or site of lesion	Absence of neurological diagnosis or site of lesion
Presence of neuromuscular impairment	Absence of neuromuscular impairment	Absence of neuromuscular impairment
Distortion errors (related to neuromuscular condition)	Distortion errors	No distortion errors
No substitution errors	No substitution errors	Substitution errors
Omission errors (related to neuromuscular condition)	Omission errors	Omission errors
Impaired prosody	Prosody intact	Prosody intact

Table 14-10

Differentiation of Childhood Apraxia of Speech, Articulation Disorders, and Phonological Disorders

CHILDHOOD APRAXIA OF SPEECH (CAS)	ARTICULATION DISORDER (A)	PHONOLOGICAL DISORDER (PD)
Inconsistency of speech sound errors	Consistency of speech sound errors	Consistency of speech sound errors
Deficits in lexical and phrase stress	No deficits in lexical and phrase stress	No deficits in lexical and phrase stress
Difficulty transitioning between sounds	No difficulty transitioning between sounds	No difficulty transitioning between sounds
Unusual errors (additions, prolongations, repetition of syllables)	No unusual errors	No unusual errors
Greater number of omission errors	Omission errors	Omission errors
Vowel and diphthong errors	No vowel or diphthong errors	No vowel or diphthong errors
Increased difficulties with longer and more phonetically complex utterances	Relatively similar difficulty with increased length and complexity of utterances	Relatively similar difficulty with increased length and complexity of utterances
Groping behaviors and silent postures	No groping behaviors or silent postures	No groping behaviors or silent postures

Table 14-11

Differentiation of Childhood Dysarthria and Childhood Apraxia of Speech

CHILDHOOD DYSARTHRIA (CD)	CHILDHOOD APRAXIA OF SPEECH (CAS)
Neuromuscular conditions (hypertonicity, incoordination, weakness)	No neuromuscular conditions present
Frequent feeding/swallowing deficits	Atypical feeding/swallowing deficits
Frequently exhibit impairments to all speech subsystems and prosody	Impairments to articulation and prosody only
Speech sound errors are not influenced by context	Speech sound errors are influenced by context (i.e., utterance length and phonetic complexity)
Distortions most frequent	Variety of errors
Consistency in errors	Inconsistency in errors
No groping behaviors or silent postures	Groping behaviors and silent postures

(1) The following information can be used to differentiate among speakers with dysarthria. The greater number of categorical information that are available, the more valid the differential diagnosis.
  (a) Speaker complaints.
  (b) Auditory-perceptual features.
  (c) Site of lesion.
  (d) Common neurological signs.
  (e) Movement deficits.
  (f) Common subsystem impairment.
  (g) Clusters of auditory-perceptual characteristics.

Trial Therapy (Identifying Compensatory Strategies)

1. In treatment planning, limitations may exist in the elimination or reduction of neuromuscular impairment on the influence on speech activity.
2. In such cases, compensatory treatment methods will be attempted as appropriate in the assessment process (i.e., trial therapy) to identify treatment strategies positively influencing speech intelligibility, articulation, and prosody.
3. Compensatory strategies will focus on:
  a. Subsystem-specific strategies (e.g., improve respiratory support to increase breath group length and therefore prosody).
  b. Across subsystem strategies (e.g., altering rate, loudness, clarity of speech).
4. Choose evidence-based methods and test for stimulability of instructions for changing targeted behavior for improvement as appropriate.
5. Document the influence and willingness of the speaker to adopt the trial therapy method and consider in treatment planning.
6. For apraxia of speech, one aspect of trail therapy can involve understanding the contributions of levels of cueing (auditory, visual, tactile) to improve speech sound production

Developing the Direction of Therapy

1. At the completion of the assessment process, organize information based on the ICF.
  a. Impairment (body structure and function).
  b. Limitation in speech activity.
  c. Restrictions in participation.
  d. Environmental and contextual factors.
2. What type of MSD is present? Provide supporting evidence.
3. Decide on prognosis based on cognitive function, receptive language, motivation, willingness to participate, severity, trial therapy results, and so on.
4. Consider the long-term and short-term goals and procedures that should be targeted for treatment.

▶ General Principles of Treatment of MSD

General Principles

1. Treatment planning must take into account not only the communication disorder but also other associated conditions (e.g., cognitive impairment, depression).
2. Treatment should be personalized for each individual with a motor speech disorder.
3. Treatment planning for MSD is broken down into developing goals and deciding on the treatment approaches to use.
  a. Treatment approaches involve behavioral, medical, or prosthetic management.
4. The overall goal of therapy is to improve the ability to communicate through restoring lost function or to compensate by helping individuals adjust to the loss of normal speech.
  a. Treatment does not solely target the speaker with an MSD, but also targets the communication partners.

5. Goals are driven by the severity of the speech activity limitations and the restrictions to participation.

Neuroplasticity

1. Reorganization of nervous system through transfer of restored or new behavior to spared parts of system.
2. Change can be positive (adaptive) or negative (maladaptive) and can occur immediately or slowly over time.
3. Neuroplasticity is influenced by type of experience.
  a. Therapeutically enriched environments (e.g., targeting the needs of client inside and outside the therapy room) are more likely to enhance plasticity.
  b. Plasticity may be task-specific (e.g., neural change only associated with specific task; nonspeech may not target plasticity for speech task).
  c. Progressively demanding treatment goals may lead to greater plasticity.

d. Relevant, intensive, and extended training more likely to induce plasticity.

4. Neuroplasticity is influenced by timing of experience.
   a. Neural change more likely early in recovery, but amount of surviving brain tissue can limit this change.
   b. Older nervous systems less plastic than younger.

Motor Learning Principles

1. General principles.
   a. Motor learning involves the adoption of a set of processes or principles associated with practice and experience resulting in retention and generalization of the motor behavior.
   b. The principles evolved from research in the limb motor learning literature.
   c. The principles are being applied with some success to individuals with motor speech disorders; however, the research base is limited but growing.
   d. Specific principles include:
      (1) Prepractice (considerations to prepare the learner for practice session).
      (2) Structure of practice (principles used within the practice session).
   e. Following information shared is based on application to the adult population only.

2. Prepractice considerations.
   a. Prepractice.
      (1) Establish motivation for learning by working with the client to identify specific and meaningful goals aimed at improving speech activity and communicative participation.
      (2) Sharing rationale for practice task(s) to achieve goals.
      (3) Clinician provides instruction (neither lengthy nor complex) for the treatment methods, clear modeling of correct/incorrect target behaviors, and practice achieving the target behaviors.

3. Practice principles.
   a. Massed and distributed practice schedules.
      (1) Mass practice involves less time between trials or sessions.
      (2) Distributed practice involves more time between trials or sessions.
      (3) Distributed practice schedule suggested to be the most effective for generalization, while mass practice leads to enhanced acquisition.
   b. Blocked and random practice schedule.
      (1) Blocked practice involves treatment targets produced in groupings or blocks (i.e., aaaaa, bbbbb).
      (2) Random practice involves randomly intermixing targets.

      (3) Random practice schedule may lead to greater generalization while block practice enhances acquisition.
   c. Constant and varied practice schedule.
      (1) Constant practice involves target produced in the same context (e.g., reading).
      (2) Varied practice involves target practice in different contexts (e.g., reading, spontaneous speech).
      (3) Varied practice suggested to lead to generalization and constant practice supports acquisition.
   d. Type of feedback.
      (1) Knowledge of results (KR) is feedback targeting the degree of success in achieving a motor behavior following a practice trial (e.g., "The /sh/ needs to be more distinct").
      (2) Knowledge of performance (KP) consists of specific feedback provided following practice regarding the quality of the motor behavior (e.g., "You need to round your lips more during the production of the /sh/").
      (3) KP can lead to improved acquisition, while KR is associated with improved retention.
   e. Amount of feedback.
      (1) Excessive feedback (e.g., feedback after every trial) may be less effective compared to a reduced or variable feedback schedule (e.g., feedback after every five trials).
      (2) Excessive feedback may be especially detrimental to motor learning in children.
      (3) Delaying the presentation of feedback after a trial may also improve motor learning (e.g., wait 3–5 seconds before giving feedback).
   f. Implicit and explicit learning.
      (1) Implicit learning involves acquisition of abstract knowledge without being aware of learning.
         (a) Neural substrates include prefrontal and motor areas, basal ganglia, and the cerebellum.
      (2) Explicit learning involves learning for memory or facts.
         (a) Neural substrates include parietal and temporal cortices, the hippocampus, and the thalamus.
      (3) Depending on the lesion site(s) noted for a given speaker, implicit or explicit learning will be more or less effective in the learning process.
   g. Specificity of training.
      (1) Practice should approximate the movement of the targeted skill and the environmental conditions under which the skill is intended to be produced.
   h. Intensive practice.
      (1) Motor learning occurs as a result of intensive practice.
      (2) Training sessions should be frequent, more than twice a week.

(3) Shorter sessions (e.g., 30 minutes).

(4) Maximize the number of practice trials within a session.

    (a) Avoiding reinforcements taking too much time to administer.

    (b) Limiting clinician talking time.

    (c) Assigning practice outside of therapy session.

(5) Children require a longer period of cumulative practice compared to adults because children exhibit:

    (a) Shorter attention spans.

    (b) Reduced short-term memory.

i. Other considerations.

(1) Self-learning by a speaker to achieve a targeted goal in treatment may lead to enhanced retention and generalization.

(2) In choosing tasks, consider the performance level of a task (e.g., error rate), as it can influence motivation and success.

(3) Consider the ordering of tasks based on the difficulty level of each task when organizing a treatment session (e.g., beginning and ending a session with the successful completion of an easier task may benefit motor learning).

(4) Fatigue brought on by physical activity may adversely influence speaker performance within a therapy session.

(5) Always allow time for a speaker to practice communicating within a session.

Candidacy for Treatment

1. A number of factors should be considered when deciding if a speaker will benefit and therefore should receive treatment.

    a. Motor, sensory, or cognitive deficits.

    b. Medical diagnosis and prognosis.

c. Limitations in speech activity.

d. Presence of participation restriction.

e. Limits of the health care system.

f. Communication partners.

g. Environmental and personal factors.

Approaches to Treatment

1. Consideration of the contributions of the following factors on restrictions on participation is central to developing a treatment plan.

    a. Impairment.

    b. Activity limitations.

    c. Environmental factors (e.g., physical, social, and attitudinal).

    d. Personal factors (e.g., age, social background, mental health, family support).

2. Within dysarthria, different strategies exist (e.g., speaker-oriented, communication-oriented, augmentative, and alternative).

3. A variety of approaches exist for treating AOS (e.g., articulatory, rate and rhythm, intersystemic facilitation and reorganization).

4. Similarities exist between treatment for children and adults; however, less systematic treatment research noted for children.

5. When natural speech alone does not meet communication needs, augmentative and alternative approaches to communication are adopted.

6. Counseling and family education.

    a. Provide information (e.g., nature of the disorder, assessment process, direction for treatment, resource information).

    b. Provide both speaker and family the appropriate counseling for psychological and emotional adjustment to communication disorder/neurological condition.

    c. Refer to mental health care professional as needed.

Treatment of Dysarthria

Principles of Treatment of Dysarthria in Children and Adults

1. General comments.

    a. Individualized treatment plan due to heterogeneity of the disorder.

    b. Focus of treatment based on severity.

      (1) Mild: maintain intelligibility while maximizing efficiency and naturalness.

      (2) Moderate: improve speech intelligibility.

(3) Severe: supplement distorted speech and adopt a functional communication system.

c. Organization of treatment strategies.

    (1) Speaker-oriented strategies.

      (a) Maximize physiological functioning of subsystems (i.e., reduce impairment of subsystems responsible for limitations in speech activity) or between subsystems (i.e., improve valving of the velopharyngeal subsystem to improve function of other subsystems).

(b) Compensate in the continued presence of impairment (e.g., increase speech intensity to improve clarity of articulation and speech intelligibility).

(2) Communication-oriented or speech supplementation strategies (see section on strategies based on severity).

    (a) Speaker approaches.

    (b) Communication partner approaches.

    (c) Combined speaker/communication partner approaches.

(3) Augmentative and alternative approaches.

d. Specific treatment technique adopted will depend on:

(1) Dysarthria type.

(2) Presence of linguistic and cognitive deficits.

(3) Potential for improvement of speech motor control.

Considerations for Children with Dysarthria

1. General considerations.

  a. Family members should be educated regarding the nature of the motor speech disorder, as well as effective ways to communicate with their child.

  b. Intervention should include targeting of both receptive and expressive language skills through the spoken and written language modalities as appropriate.

2. Teaching communicative effectiveness.

  a. Communicative effectiveness and communicative repair strategies should be taught to the child as a means of enhancing their overall communicative effectiveness.

  b. Assist the child in appropriate word choice and sentence structure to aid in the comprehension of the listener.

  c. Communicative effectiveness and communicative repair strategies should be generalized to outside intervention sessions while increasing the child's confidence in his/her ability to use these strategies.

3. Speech ability and phonological knowledge.

  a. The child's phonological and phonetic repertoires and word and syllable shape repertoires should be expanded to his/her level of development.

  b. The child's length of utterance may be expanded through phonological training and multiple practice opportunities.

  c. Vocal loudness, vocal quality, and prosody may be targeted to increase the child's intelligibility.

  d. Phonological awareness and literacy skills should be targeted early in intervention.

Treatment of the Respiratory/ Phonatory Subsystem

1. Improving respiratory support.

  a. Nonspeech treatment techniques.

    (1) Adopted for individuals unable to develop adequate subglottal pressure for phonation.

    (2) Behavioral techniques, examples of which are as follows:

      (a) Breathing against a resistive device (e.g., water manometer, resistive device).

      (b) Pushing/pulling techniques.

      (c) Providing visual feedback on a computer screen of acoustic and aerodynamic measures.

      (d) Maximum inhalation and exhalation tasks.

  b. Postural adjustment treatment techniques.

    (1) Rationale.

      (a) Body position influences respiratory functioning; therefore, positioning an individual, especially someone wheelchair bound, can maximize respiratory support.

      (b) Training of speech breathing outside the typical upright position may not generalize.

    (2) Positioning techniques.

      (a) Upright position used with individuals with greater inspiratory than expiratory weakness, to assist the lowering of the abdominal content and the diaphragm via gravity (e.g., amyotrophic lateral sclerosis).

      (b) Supine position used with individuals exhibiting greater expiratory versus inspiratory weakness as gravity and abdominal content move the diaphragm into the thoracic cavity (e.g., spinal cord injury).

  c. Prosthetic treatment techniques.

    (1) Rationale.

      (a) Less-frequently adopted techniques.

      (b) Important to consult with physician and/or physical therapist prior to use.

      (c) Used to counter expiratory weakness and assist in creation of expiratory force for the generation of subglottal pressure during expiration.

      (d) Use on short-term basis until respiratory support improves or use on long-term basis if improvement of respiratory support does not occur.

    (2) Techniques.

      (a) Respiratory board or paddle.

      (b) Abdominal trussing.

  d. Speech treatment techniques.

    (1) Rationale.

(a) Manipulation of breathing patterns involves instruction to achieve more normal respiratory function.

(b) Biofeedback is based on the premise that change in the functioning of the respiratory system can occur when a speaker is provided with feedback of acoustic or physiological measures of respiratory functioning; by receiving such feedback, the speaker can make adjustments to improve functioning.

(2) Technique.

(a) Manipulation of breathing patterns.

- To increase and maintain subglottal pressure over a longer period of time, the speaker is instructed to inhale more deeply, exhale with greater muscular force, and use diaphragmatic (or abdominal) breathing.

(b) Biofeedback.

- Focuses on providing feedback to the speaker on aspects of respiratory functioning (e.g., airflow, chest wall or abdominal movement).

2. Improving coordination of respiration/phonation.

a. Nonspeech treatment techniques.

(1) Only use nonspeech tasks if speakers are unable to produce speech and include speech stimuli as soon as possible.

(2) Possible tasks.

(a) Practicing speech-like breathing patterns (e.g., short inhalation followed by a long exhalation phase).

(b) Practicing "inspiratory checking" without speaking by inhaling to about 50% of vital capacity and slowly exhaling via control of the chest wall and the abdomen, and not valving at the lips (i.e., not pursing the lips to control the airflow).

(c) Support for use with individuals with cerebral palsy and traumatic brain injury, and also individuals with ataxic, spastic, and mixed dysarthria.

b. Speech treatment techniques.

(1) Possible tasks.

(a) Bring to speaker's awareness the speech breathing pattern (i.e., quick inhalation, long exhalation).

(b) Apply different biofeedback methods for visualizing and sensing movement of the chest wall and abdomen while speaking (e.g., the clinician places his/her hands on the speaker's abdomen and has the speaker inhale to appropriate size for the speaking task).

(c) Identify optimal breath group (i.e., number of syllables produced comfortably in one breath) and target a gradual increase in the optimal breath group length.

3. Improving phonatory function.

a. Treating hypoadduction.

(1) Physical strategies.

(a) Effortful closure.

- Results in improved adduction and strength of vocal folds, increased loudness, and reduced breathy/hoarse voice quality (outcome measures).

(b) Postural adjustments.

- Involves turning head to left or right during phonation for individuals with paretic/paralyzed vocal folds.
- Frequent use of strategy may be viewed as pragmatically undesirable; however, selective use in situations demanding increased loudness may be more palatable (compensatory strategy).

(c) Physical manipulation.

- Involves the clinician gently applying pressure to the thyroid lamina on the side of the paretic/paralyzed vocal fold while the speaker phonates.
- If physical manipulation results in improvement of the voice in chronic conditions, surgical treatment (e.g., medialization) should be considered.

(2) Lee Silverman Voice Treatment (LSVT).

(a) Application of high-effort tasks to increase loudness and improve vocal fold function.

(b) Originally targeted individuals with the hypokinetic dysarthria associated with idiopathic Parkinson's disease (IPD) (applied to other neurological conditions such as multiple sclerosis, but greatest evidence for IPD).

(c) Program.

- Targets vocal loudness, breathiness, intonation, and vocal stability.
- Involves multiple repetitions of speech stimuli.
- Adopts high-effort activities (e.g., maximum sustained phonation).
- Intensive intervention schedule (four times a week for 1 month) but some support for reduced dosage frequency.
- Heighten sensory awareness of increased loudness and effort through self-monitoring activities (i.e., recalibration).
- Daily practice required along with group practice.

(d) Outcomes.

- Improvement in a variety of perceptual, acoustic, and physiological measures of the voice (e.g., vocal quality, intensity, fundamental frequency variation, vocal fold adduction).
- Improvements also noted in participation.

- Shown to indirectly improve performance in other subsystems (i.e., articulation) and slow speaking rate.
- Maintenance of improvement out to 24 months.

(e) Candidate criteria.
- Exhibit hypoadduction of vocal folds, reduced loudness, and vocal fatigue.
- Poor respiratory support/effort.
- Highly motivated to participate in intensive program (however, other forms of delivery continue to be evaluated).
- Stimulable to cues to improve vocal performance.
- Normal cognition, but benefit seen in those with mild/moderate deficits.

b. Treating hyperadduction.
(1) Behavioral treatment of vocal quality resulting from hyperfunctioning in dysarthria is not typically undertaken due to lack of success (i.e., very limited evidence supporting success for any of the techniques discussed below).
(2) Nonspeech treatment techniques.
  (a) Relaxation strategies.
    - Relaxation strategies result in inconsistent effects on hyperfunctioning.
  (b) Biofeedback of airflow or laryngeal muscle activity.
    - Biofeedback of nonvocal airflow.
    - Use of electromyography and videoendoscopic biofeedback for the control of laryngeal tension.
(3) Speech treatment techniques.
  (a) Traditional tension-reducing strategies.
    - Based on the hypothesis that reduced laryngeal tension will be facilitated in the context of reflex-like or continuous phonation responses.
    - Initially the voice facilitating techniques (e.g., yawn/sigh) are applied to isolated vowels and then extended to utterances of increasing length.
  (b) Biofeedback-enhanced relaxation.
    - Monitoring of physiological or acoustic variables associated with phonation, typically through visual feedback, may allow a speaker to reduce hyperadduction.
    - Feedback variables include electromyographic, aerodynamic, and videoendoscopic therapies.
  (c) Head positioning and miscellaneous instruction.
    - Altering head positioning (e.g., forward-backward and/or side to side) during quiet, short duration phonations may lead to reduced hyperadduction for

individuals with spastic cerebral palsy; inability to maintain reduced laryngeal tension may diminish as lung volume decreases as an utterance progresses; can become counterproductive.

c. Improving phonatory coordination impairments.
(1) Phonatory coordination impairments lead to reduction or loss of distinctiveness of two specific phonetics contrasts (e.g., voice-voiceless).
(2) Apply contrastive production drills, a technique found in the section on treating the articulatory system to target phonatory coordination impairments.

d. Augmentative and alternative communication (AAC).
(1) If significant reductions in speech activity and participation still exist after attempts to reduce impairment or adopt compensatory strategies, AAC technique must be considered.
(2) AAC devices targeting individuals with deficits in respiration/phonation.
  (a) Vocal intensity controller.
    - Acts to monitor vocal intensity and inform the speaker if intensity falls below a targeted level.
  (b) Portable amplifier.
    - Use with individuals with intact articulation skills but still indicate difficulty being heard in different speaking situations after implementing behavior treatment aimed at improving loudness.
  (c) Electrolarynx.
    - May be useful for speaker with aphonia or severe breathiness to enhance voicing.

Treatment of the Velopharyngeal Subsystem

1. Surgical management.
  a. Pharyngeal flap surgery (superiorly based flap).
  b. Injection of Teflon or surgical implants into the posterior pharyngeal wall.
2. Prosthetic management.
  a. Palatal lift.
  (1) General comments.
    (a) Viewed as an effective treatment for *selected* speakers with dysarthria who exhibit significant velopharyngeal weakness, most often those with flaccid dysarthria.
    (b) Results in a reduction in nasal airflow and an increase in intraoral pressure, leading to potential improvements in intelligibility and articulation, along with communication efficiency.

(2) Design and function of the palatal lift.
  (a) A rigid acrylic appliance fabricated by a prosthodontist.
  (b) Consists of a retentive (palatal) portion covering the hard palate and a lift portion, which contacts the oral surface of the soft palate and pharyngeal walls.
(3) Construction/fitting of the palatal lift.
  (a) The prosthodontist and the speech-language pathologist collaborate during the construction/fitting process.
(4) Candidacy criteria.
  (a) Different candidacy criteria depending on whether progressive or stable-recovering dysarthria exist (Tables 14-12 and 14-13).
  (b) Often the final decision to fit is based on clinical judgment (i.e., weighing all clinical factors).

Table 14-12

Characteristics of Good Candidates for Palatal Lift Fitting
• Able to inhibit gag reflex.
• Adequate functioning of the speech subsystems (i.e., articulation, phonation, prosody, respiration, and resonance).
• Adequate or improving articulatory abilities for speech production.
• Cognitive abilities are within functional limits, or mild deficits are noted.
• Diagnosis of flaccid dysarthria (either recovering or progressive).
• Enough manual dexterity to independently operate palatal lift.
• Pressure consonants are significantly more unintelligible than other consonant types.
• Slow progression of symptoms (i.e., progressive dysarthria) or slow improvement of symptoms (i.e., recovering dysarthria).
• No presence of dysphagia.
• Occlusion of the nares improves resonance.
• Patient is motivated to maintain or improve speech abilities.

Adapted from Yorkston, Spencer, Duffy, et al. (2001).

Table 14-13

Characteristics of Poor Candidates for Palatal Lift Fitting
• Not able to inhibit gag reflex.
• Poor functioning of the speech subsystems (i.e., articulation, phonation, prosody, respiration, and resonance).
• Declining articulatory abilities for speech production.
• Moderate to severe cognitive deficits, particularly in executive functioning.
• Diagnosis of spastic dysarthria (either recovering or progressive).
• Not enough manual dexterity to independently operate palatal lift.
• All consonant types are equally unintelligible.
• Rapid progression of symptoms (i.e., progressive dysarthria) or rapid improvement of symptoms (i.e., recovering dysarthria).
• Presence of dysphagia, or difficulty managing saliva.
• Occlusion of the nares does not improve resonance.
• Patient is unmotivated to maintain or improve speech abilities.

Adapted from Yorkston, Spencer, Duffy, et al. (2001).

(5) Minor devices.
  (a) Useful for some speakers who would benefit, but for various reasons (e.g., lack of acceptance, poor dentition, hyperactive gag reflex) cannot be fitted with a palatal lift.
  (b) Nose clip or pinching the nose.
    • Consider if nasal occlusion results in significant improvement in speech activity (e.g., speech intelligibility).
    • Typically pragmatically unacceptable; however, may be used on a temporary basis.
  (c) Nasal obturator or plug.
    • A fabricated device placed in the nares for the purpose of impeding nasal airflow and allowing a speaker to increase intraoral air pressure.
3. Behavioral management.
  a. General comments.
    (1) Behavioral management techniques appropriate for those who can compensate or will have the ability to compensate as medical status of speaker improves.
    (2) Evaluating the ability to compensate is completed through stimulability testing.
    (3) For each condition, the clinician will provide instructions and evaluate if the speaker performed the instructions as specified and indicate if improvement in target speech outcome measure occurred.
    (4) A clinically significant change in the outcome measure (e.g., reduced nasality, improved pressure consonants, and intraoral pressure) toward more normative values for a given condition would support compensation.
  b. Techniques.
    (1) Modifying speaking patterns.
      (a) Speak with increased effort.
      (b) Speak a slower than normal speaking rate.
      (c) Speak more precisely through the use of overarticulate speech.
    (2) Resistance treatment while speaking.
      (a) Involves speaking against airway resistance developed via a continuous positive airway pressure (CPAP) device.
    (3) Biofeedback.
      (a) Possible forms of feedback include visualization of nasal airflow or visualization of the pharyngeal walls.
    (4) Nonspeech techniques.
      (a) Evidence and expert opinion do not support effectiveness of nonspeech techniques (e.g., blowing bubbles, sensory inhibition tasks).

Treatment of the Articulatory Subsystem

1. General comments.
   a. Speech sound errors (i.e., vowel and consonant distortions) in dysarthria are not always related to neuromuscular impairment to the articulators (i.e., tongue, lips, or jaw) but can be the result of impairment to other subsystems (e.g., velopharyngeal) or a combination of subsystem impairment.
   b. Treat subsystems in the order of the magnitude of their contributions to speech activity limitations; if multiple subsystems are impaired, typically the articulatory system is the last to be treated.
   c. Best practices suggest that the implementation of compensatory treatment techniques should not wait until the completion of treatment to reduce impairment.
2. Strategies for normalizing function (i.e., reduced impairment).
   a. Strengthening.
      (1) Assumes reductions in strength of articulatory structures (e.g., tongue), clearly contributes to deficits in articulation, but potentially also to reductions in speech intelligibility and limitations in participation.
      (2) Strength training can be completed with and without resistance and with and without biofeedback for a variety of movements of the tongue, lips, and jaw.
      (3) Strengthening should lead to increased muscle tension, force, or endurance and improve range of motion and speed of movement of the articulators.
      (4) Controversy regarding the use of oral-motor or nonspeech exercises to improve speech performance, including strengthening exercises.
         (a) Limited data regarding effectiveness of strength training.
         (b) Weak correlations between measures of strength and speech deficits in speakers with dysarthria.
      (5) Considerations.
         (a) Most useful for speakers with flaccid dysarthria; however, some individuals with spastic, hypokinetic, and unilateral upper motor neuron dysarthria may benefit.
         (b) During speaking, individuals use only 10%–20% of the maximum force of the lips and tongue, so in general a speaker needs to be extremely weak for therapy to be considered.
      (6) Organization of treatment.
         (a) Treatment should involve multiple repetitions, sets, and practice periods within and outside the therapy room.
   b. Reducing muscle tone.
      (1) Use of auditory or visual feedback of magnitude of muscle activity to reduce level of hypertonicity.
   c. Traditional approaches.
      (1) Integral stimulation.
         (a) Clinician models production of utterance.
         (b) The speaker is asked to watch and listen, and then say the target utterance after the clinician.
      (2) Phonetic placement.
         (a) Clinician describes or provides pictures of the articulator placement for targeted phoneme.
         (b) Clinician physically positions or provides touch cues on where the articulator contact is in oral cavity.
      (3) Phonetic derivation.
         (a) Clinician uses an intact nonspeech movement (e.g., whistling) as an initial movement from which to build or mold into the production of a target sound.
   d. Surgical management.
      (1) Neural anastomosis.
         (a) Neural anastomosis involves surgically attaching a healthy functioning nerve to a damaged nerve.
         (b) A side effect of hypoglossal-facial surgery may lead to impaired lingual articulation due to surgery-induced lingual weakness.
   e. Pharmacological management.
      (1) Botulinum toxin injections.
         (a) Botox has the potential to be an effective treatment for a number of hyperkinesias; especially effective for spasmodic dysphonia.
3. Strategies for compensating for impairment.
   a. Compensatory articulatory movements.
      (1) Through self-exploration or training, a speaker can learn to make compensatory adjustments to achieve adequate production of erred phonemes.
      (2) Type of compensatory strategy will be unique to the speaker's impairment profile.
   b. Minimal contrasts or contrastive production drills.
      (1) Used for practice to make contrasting sounds perceptually distinct.
      (2) The clinician instructs the speaker to make the two words as distinct as possible.
      (3) The contrastive production drills can be applied to utterances beyond words (e.g., "The word is sent. The word is tent").
   c. Intelligibility drills.
      (1) Speaker produces an unfamiliar utterance (e.g., words, phrases, sentences) to the clinician-listener for identification.
      (2) If the listener identifies the correct utterance, then the speaker produces a new utterance; otherwise, the speaker is asked to produce the utterance a second time, making it more distinct.

(3) The drills.
  (a) Promote self-discovery on how to make speech more intelligible, a primary goal of treatment.
  (b) Provide both the speaker and listener experience with strategies to repair breakdowns in intelligibility.
d. Exaggeration of consonant production (clear speech).
  (1) Articulatory precision may be enhanced by instructing the speaker with dysarthria to speak clearly by exaggerating speech sound production.
  (2) Instructions can lead to improved articulation and speech intelligibility, increased loudness, more varied pitch inflection, slightly louder speech, and a slow rate.
e. Prosthetic management.
  (1) Bite block.
    (a) Consists of a small piece of acrylic or hard putty placed unilaterally between the lower and upper teeth.
    (b) When the speaker bites down on the block while speaking, abnormal jaw movement is stabilized.
    (c) May be helpful if jaw control is impaired to a greater extent than tongue or lower lip control and adversely influences their functioning due to anatomical connections.
  (2) Other prosthetic devices influencing articulation.
    (a) Prosthetic devices used to compensate for impairments in other parts of the speech production system can benefit articulation (e.g., palatal lift).
    (b) Devices used to slow speaking rate (e.g., pacing and alphabet boards, delayed auditory feedback unit) can benefit precision of speech sound production and enhance speech intelligibility for some speakers with dysarthria.

Treatment of Prosody

1. General comments.
  a. Prosodic therapy focuses on naturalness for the mildly impaired speaker (i.e., intelligibility 90% or greater) and alters aspect of prosody for improvement of speech intelligibility for the speaker with moderate to severe dysarthria.
  b. The clinician must be aware of the trade-off between naturalness and speech intelligibility when planning treatment (e.g., increasing breath group length may improve naturalness but decrease speech intelligibility).

c. Methods for improving prosody based on unique prosodic deficits in any of the three aspects of prosody (i.e., stress patterning, intonation, and rate-rhythm; see Table 14-8).
d. When targeting monotonicity, focus on the use of prosody to express emotion and linguistic emphasis (e.g., syllabic and emphatic stress).
e. In treatment planning, improving respiratory support may lead to improvements in features of prosody.
f. Treating prosody moves from highly structured tasks (e.g., contrastive stress tasks), to less structured tasks (e.g., marked and unmarked reading passages and conversational scripts), to spontaneous speech.
g. Visual feedback of prosodic acoustic parameters (e.g., fundamental frequency, pause locations) can supplement and clarify perceptual judgments for both the clinician and speaker.
h. For some speakers, prosodic features of emotional expression need to be considered in treatment.
i. Initiate self-monitoring activities early in the treatment process.
2. Treatment methods for use within breath groups.
  a. Techniques for treating reduced prosody.
    (1) Referential tasks.
      (a) Training material premarked for targeted prosodic feature (e.g., lexical stress, intonation).
      (b) The speaker is instructed to produce the targeted feature and the clinician/listener indicates the feature they heard (e.g., syllable receiving lexical stress or intonation pattern).
      (c) If the speaker is less consistent at marking prosodic features, the clinician should increase times the speaker is successful and train speaker to use method more consistently.
    (2) Contrastive stress tasks.
      (a) Classical application of a contrastive stress task involves a scripted response where the response utterances do not vary but the stress pattern does.
      (b) The stress pattern or prominence is placed on a specific syllable or word within the scripted response.
      (c) The clinician asks a series of questions for which the speaker is to respond using the core sentence with appropriate prosodic emphasis.
    (3) Modification of only one parameter to signal stress.
      (a) Targeting one prosodic feature (e.g., pitch, loudness, duration) compared to several can be more effective.
      (b) The feature of choice would be the feature the speaker appears to have most control

over based on clinical observation; however, if this feature does not exist, duration should be targeted.

   b. Techniques for treating excessive prosody.
      (1) Reduce number of suprasegmental features signaling stress.
         (a) Speakers exhibiting excessive and equal stress or exaggerated signaling of stress (or another prosodic feature) may benefit using only one prosodic feature.
         (b) Altering duration to signal stress (e.g., insertion of a short pause) typically sounds more natural than alterations of fundamental frequency and intensity.

3. Treatment methods for use across breath groups.
   a. Limit breath group length and range.
      (1) If results from maximum phonation or counting tasks suggest a sufficient air supply for the production of longer breath groups, training should focus on increasing breath group lengths through the use of stimuli conducive to longer utterances.
      (2) If results from the two tasks suggest insufficient air supply, supportive of shorter breath groups, treatment should focus on factors leading to short breath groups (e.g., decreased respiratory support, poor valving of phonatory system).
      (3) If the flexibility of breath groups is not enhanced through treatment of other factors, then compensatory methods (e.g., better linking pauses to syntactic units) must be taught.
   b. Using both breath and nonbreath pauses.
      (1) Evaluate the number of words the speaker can produce on one breath.
      (2) If limited, work on increasing breath group length as noted previously.
      (3) If breath group length is adequate or became adequate after treatment, increase the use of nonbreath pauses.

Global Management Techniques

1. Global management techniques reduce speech activity limitations through influencing multiple speech production subsystems.
2. Techniques.
   a. Treatment of speaking rate.
      (1) Rationale.
         (a) Altering speaking rate (usually reducing rate) generally leads to improvement in sentence intelligibility and comprehensibility but not phoneme intelligibility.

      (b) Overall, slower rate may help to compensate for impairment across subsystems and also enhance speech perception by communication partners.
      (2) Candidacy criteria.
         (a) Lack of specific candidacy criteria predicting who will benefit and to what extent, but typically used with individuals with reduced speech intelligibility.
      (3) Treatment strategies.
         (a) Rigid rate techniques.
            • Techniques.
               – Alphabet supplementation.
               – Hand and finger tapping or pacing board.
               – Using a metronome to produce a syllable or a word in time with a beat.
            • Advantages of rigid rate techniques.
               – Slows speaking rate.
               – Improves intelligibility for some speakers.
               – Simple and inexpensive devices.
               – Require minimal training.
               – Allows for practice outside of therapy room.
            • Disadvantages of rigid rate techniques.
               – Disrupt naturalness.
               – Device cosmetically unacceptable by some speakers.
               – Technique can be overlearned and lose effect.
         (b) Rate techniques that preserve prosody.
            • Delayed auditory feedback (DAF).
            • Rhythmic cueing.
            • "Backdoor" approaches.
               – Phrasing and breath patterning.
               – Pitch variation.
               – Loudness control.
               – Word and stress patterns.
            • Visual feedback.
            • Advantages of prosody preserving rate techniques.
               – Slows speaking rate.
               – Improves intelligibility for some speakers.
               – Speech sounds more natural.
               – Does not involve use of prosthetic device.
            • Disadvantages of prosody preserving rate techniques.
               – Requires extensive training.
               – Speaker must be highly motivated and physically capable of altering speaking rate in a relative natural fashion.
               – Speaker less easily able to practice outside therapy initially.

b. Treatment of loudness: use with speakers who have reduced loudness and poor respiratory support; results in increased loudness and vocal inflexion; secondary benefits include precision of articulation; often used with hypokinetic dysarthria; however, can benefit other types.
   (1) Refer to the "Treatment of the Respiratory/Phonatory Subsystem" section for details on LSVT.
c. Treatment of prosody: treatment of stress patterning, intonation, and rate-rhythm includes functioning of a variety of subsystems; influences acoustic (e.g., F0 contours) and perceptual measures (e.g., precision of articulation, naturalness); often use with ataxic dysarthria but can benefit other dysarthria types.
   (1) Biofeedback (i.e., F0 or intensity contours).
   (2) Behavior instruction (training linguistic aspects of prosody, such as contrastive stress or pause usage).
d. General instructions: influences intelligibility, precision in articulation, loudness, speaking rate; often used with mixed dysarthria but can benefit other dysarthria types; in general, feedback about adequacy of productions results in greater improvement than instructions to talk clearly (refer to treatment of the Articulatory Subsystem).
   (1) Provide instructions to produce clear speech.
   (2) Provide feedback about adequacy of production (i.e., feedback about clarity of an utterance or in repairing a misunderstood utterance).

Strategies to Enhance Participation

1. Intent of participation strategies is to increase participation by improving communication in the presence of impairment; consists of environmental modifications, extra information (acoustic signal independent) to enhance understanding of distorted speech and improve comprehensibility, and repair strategies for communication breakdowns; strategies adopted dependent on the severity of dysarthria.
   a. Strategies used when limitations in speech activity (e.g., reduced speech intelligibility) still exist after adoption of speaker-oriented approaches for treatment.
   b. Strategies adopted differ based on severity of dysarthria (e.g., from normal-sounding speech to limited natural speech).
   c. Consider both contextual factors in the ICF model (environmental and personal factors) when planning treatment.
   d. Speech sounds normal.
      (1) Treatment: counsel speaker on how to best compensate for barriers to communication. Organize communication interactions around times when he/she exhibits the least amount of fatigue or enhances/compensates for mobility limitation that causes a barrier to communication.
   e. Intelligible but unnatural sounding speech.
      (1) Treatment: identify communication barriers through use of communication diaries; analyze with the speaker factors associated with communication failures and successes; adjust communication style and environment to minimize communication breakdown and target communication success. Consider facilitators and barriers associated with social and attitudinal environments; adjust as appropriate.
   f. Reduced intelligibility.
      (1) Treatment: enhance comprehensibility by adopting strategies aimed at providing extra or signal-independent information. Strategies are categorized into those used by the speaker with dysarthria, those used by his/her communication partner (listener), and interaction strategies used together by both speaker and listener. Continue to consider context and personal factors when identifying facilitators and barriers for those speakers with intelligibility deficits.
   g. Strategies used specifically by speakers with dysarthria.
      (1) Obtain listener attention and choose a communicative enhancing environment (e.g., well-lit, quiet settings; minimal distractions; close approximation with communication partner).
      (2) Use semantic cues when initiating a topic or changing topic.
      (3) Enhancement of the message through use of complete, simple, and predictable sentences.
      (4) Use gestures (e.g., eye gaze, pantomime) and props to initiate and maintain turn-taking and for repairing of communication breakdowns.
      (5) Conserve energy for the most important communication exchanges to maximize comprehensibility.
      (6) Monitor communication partner comprehension through direct query and observation, and strive to maintain that comprehension.
   h. Strategies used specifically by the communication partners of speakers with dysarthria.
      (1) Maintain topic knowledge by monitoring message and querying to verify understanding; if communication breakdown occurs, immediately pursue repair strategies such as asking multiple questions, beginning from broad to more narrow topics.
      (2) Maximize the communication environment by communicating in a well-lit and quiet

environment, devoid of distractions. Watch the speaker's face (maintain eye contact) and pay attention to nonverbal cues associated with communication of a message.

(3) Combine clues to achieve comprehension.

(4) Monitor and integrate all cues toward comprehension.

(5) Maximize visual and hearing acuity: wear hearing aids and/or glasses/contacts.

(6) Train significant others through targeted listening practice to improve comprehensibility.

i. Interaction strategies used by both speakers of dysarthria and their communication partners.

(1) Manage communication breakdown by adopting repair strategies; repair strategies are the responsibility of both speaker and listener.

(2) Communication partners should develop agreed-upon rules and cues used while communicating.

2. Limited natural intelligible speech.

a. Treatment for speakers when natural speech alone is inadequate to meet communication needs and augmentative and alternative strategies are necessary; alphabet supplementation is one augmentative strategy used frequently. Refer to Chapter 18 in this text for application of other AAC methods.

(1) Description of alphabet supplementation.

(a) Typically, speakers are trained to say each word of a message while simultaneously pointing to the first letter of the word located on the board.

- Limits range of possible words spoken.
- Adds short pause between words to enhance lexical segmentation during connected speech.

(b) Slows the rate of production.

(c) Used to repair communication breakdowns (e.g., spelling out words not understood).

(2) Additional candidacy criteria beyond general requirements.

(a) Consistent voluntary phonation.

(b) Minimal literacy skills.

(c) Reliable method for highlighting letters (typically touch letter with finger).

(d) Adequate cognitive and linguistic skills (e.g., pragmatic).

(3) Advantages.

(a) Improves comprehensibility; some speakers exhibit improved articulatory precision.

(b) Faster than spelling out entire word.

(c) Minimal cost.

(d) Often minimal training involved.

(4) Disadvantages.

(a) Slow rate adversely influences naturalness and communication efficiency.

(b) For the most severe speakers, comprehensibility will fail to reach beyond 80%.

(c) Possible future adaptation to technique (e.g., loose benefit).

(d) Need to physically have board present during communication interactions.

Treatment of Apraxia of Speech

Treatment of Apraxia of Speech in Adults

1. Overview.

a. Major goal to improve naturalness, effectiveness, and efficiency, with a focus on articulation and prosody.

b. Target reestablishing motor planning and programming or improving the ability to assemble, retrieve, and execute planning and programming for speech.

c. Based on the treatment literature on AOS, overall treatment can be successful, even with chronic cases; however, limited data exist for guiding decisions on a specific treatment for a specific speaker with AOS and predicting outcomes.

d. Begin therapy with maximum cueing, with gradual fading of cues with success.

e. Manipulate utterance length and phonetic complexity to maximize performance.

f. Adopt principles of motor learning.

2. Treatment planning.

a. Choose a motor, linguistic, or combination approach to treatment.

(1) Decide on the separate contributions of the motor deficits of AOS (e.g., motor planning and programming disorder) and any co-occurring linguistic deficits (e.g., aphasia) to the communication disorder.

(a) For some speakers, separating contributions is nearly impossible and combining motor and linguistic approaches of treatment must occur.

(2) Significant contribution of AOS, use motor approach.

(3) Significant contributions of aphasia, adopt melding of linguistic (e.g., target language deficits) and motor approaches.

b. Considerations when choosing a specific motor approach.

(1) Severity (e.g., articulatory kinematic methods used with more severely affected speakers).

(2) Lack of prerequisite skills by speaker for specific motor approach (e.g., upper limb motor disabilities may rule out methods using hand tapping).

(3) Training/experience of clinician.

c. Selecting treatment targets.

(1) Target meaningful sound combinations and not sound production to support daily communication.

(2) Identify factors influencing communication (i.e., facilitators and barriers).

(a) Articulatory deviations, prosodic deviations, and speech intelligibility.

(b) Communication participation restrictions.

(c) Social, attitudinal, and environmental factors resulting in facilitators/barriers to communication.

(d) Counseling.

(3) Refer to treatment information for reducing participation restriction and environment barriers in sections targeting individuals with dysarthria.

d. Choosing speech stimuli.

(1) General comments.

(a) Use informal and formal testing to obtain:
  • An inventory of the nature of both accurate and inaccurate articulatory behaviors.
  • Factors influencing the articulatory behaviors (e.g., syllable shape, phonetic context, utterance length, cueing effects).

(b) Therapy success dependent on selection and ordering of stimuli.

(c) Don't target individual phonemes unless for a very severe disorder.

(2) Type of stimuli.

(a) Choose functional stimuli with help of speaker and significant others (e.g., useful in meeting communication needs).

(b) Initial stimuli should involve visible movements (e.g., anterior production) and movements that may benefit from tactile cueing.

(c) The less severe the impairment, the greater the length and articulatory and/or linguistic complexity of stimuli.

(d) Typically, speech stimuli are chosen; however, nonspeech targets (e.g., movements closely associated with speech sound positions) may be chosen for severe cases as initial building blocks to speech production.

(e) Often high-frequency, real words chosen over nonreal words and lower-frequency real words.

(f) Treating nonstimulable sounds and sounds with shared phonetic features may lead to better generalization.

(g) Speech sounds exhibiting low error rates should be targeted for more immediate success, but some support for improved generalization for targeting phonemes with high error percentages.

(h) Treatment typically targets more difficult end of the continuum (vowels, nasals, glides, plosives, fricatives, affricates, consonant clusters).

(i) Phonetic contrasts from least to most difficult.
  • Oral/nasal.
  • Voicing.
  • Manner.
  • Place.

(j) Stimuli may need to be chosen based on lack of certain sound contrast distinctions.

(k) Be cognizant of the influence prosody may have on articulation errors. If segmental distortion exists as a result of slow rate (e.g., exaggerated duration), target both prosodic and articulatory features. If place, manner, or voicing errors are present, articulatory features should be targeted directly.

(3) Number of stimuli per session.

(a) Severity increases, set size decreases.

(b) Guiding factor: balance between mass and distributed practice.

(c) Target some stimuli for mass practice and others for distributed practice.

(d) As motor skills improve for certain stimuli, move those stimuli to distributed practice and add new stimuli, starting initially with mass practice.

(e) When stimuli receiving distributed practice meet accuracy criterion, shift to practice outside therapy room.

(f) Targeting more than one sound at a time can allow variable practice to occur (hypothesized to benefit generalization); however, may want to limit number of phonemes treated simultaneously (less than three).

e. Intensity of treatment.

(1) Frequent sessions (e.g., four times per week).

(2) Length of session decreases with severity.

3. Motor approaches to treatment.

a. Articulatory kinematic.

(1) Key features.

(a) Treatment focuses on improving spatial and temporal aspects of articulatory movement as a means to improve speech production.

(b) Repeated, motoric practice of speech targets.

(c) Facilitate articulatory accuracy through various forms of additional stimulation.

(d) Provide movement information thought to be lacking or incorrect.

(e) Involves conscious processing of various cues related to speech production.

(f) Majority of evidence for more severe speakers with AOS.

(2) Treatment targets.

(a) Words (containing target sounds).

(b) Short sentences or phrases.

(3) Candidacy criteria.

(a) Good auditory comprehension.

(b) Aberrant speech sound production.

(c) Motivated to improve speech.

(d) Moderate to severe AOS.

(4) Various techniques associated with the articulatory/kinematic category of treatment.

(a) Modeling and repetition.

(b) Integral stimulation.

(c) Phonetic placement.

(d) Phonetic derivation.

(e) Key-word technique.

(5) Overall results of articulatory kinematic treatment.

(a) Improvement in the accuracy of trained sounds.

(b) Training of an adequate number of exemplars for a given sound leads to accuracy improvements for untrained exemplars of the given sound.

(c) Generalization to untrained sound typically does not occur.

b. Rate and/or rhythm.

(1) Key features.

(a) Therapy techniques aimed to restore temporal control of speech production.

(b) Assumes an underlying deficit in the timing of speech production (e.g., damaged central pattern generators) in individuals with AOS.

(c) Rate and/or rhythm techniques focusing on slowing rate are hypothesized to benefit speech production by allowing additional time for (1) planning and programming processes and (2) processing of feedback.

(d) Other techniques (e.g., metronome or hand tapping) may positively influence internal oscillatory mechanisms associated with speech production through entrainment or may refocus attention toward speech production processes.

(2) Treatment targets.

(a) Varied types of targets.

(b) Individual targets range from isolated vowels and vowel combinations to oral reading.

(c) Targets within a given treatment program often involved a gradual increase in complexity with increasing treatment success.

(3) Candidacy criteria.

(a) No specific restrictive criteria except for motivation to change behavior.

(4) Techniques.

(a) Pacing via a metronome.

(b) Hand tapping.

(c) Utilization of a pacing board.

(5) Overall results for rate or rhythm treatment.

(a) Improved articulation and fluency, a decrease in overall AOS symptoms, and reduced rate for trained material and mixed results for untrained material.

c. Alternative/augmentative communication (AAC).

(1) Key features.

(a) AAC techniques aimed at substituting or supplementing verbal communication.

(b) Verbal communication is viewed as less than adequate, and an alternate or supplemental form of communication is implemented.

(2) Treatment targets.

(a) Range from skill training associated with the AAC system (e.g., acquisition of symbols) to application and acceptance by communication partners.

(3) Candidacy criteria.

(a) Severe AOS.

(b) Motivated to use AAC.

(c) Adequate motor, visual, literacy, and linguistic skills needed for the specific AAC system adopted.

(4) Techniques.

(a) Comprehensive communication system.

(b) Single systems involving pictures and symbols.

(c) Voice output communication aid.

(5) AAC methods can be appropriate for some individuals with AOS who exhibit limited verbal output, but given the limited number of clinical research studies on this category of treatment, a prediction could not be made about success of treatment.

d. Intersystemic facilitation/reorganization.

(1) Key features.

(a) Facilitate the function of an impaired system/modality (e.g., speaking) through a relatively intact system/modality (e.g., limb movement).

(b) Hypothesized reasons for facilitating effects.

• Provides additional sensory cues for speech production.

• Use of limb gestures provide organizational framework for speech production.

(2) Treatment targets.
  (a) Words containing specific phonemes and sentences.
  (b) Accuracy of phonemes and word production and accuracy of gestures.
(3) Candidacy criteria.
  (a) Severe AOS.
  (b) Free of limb apraxia for use of meaningful gestures.
  (c) Ability to produce words, phrases, or sentences for receiving nonmeaningful gestures.
(4) Techniques.
  (a) Gestural reorganization.
  (b) Singing.
  (c) Vibrotactile stimulation.
(5) Overall results for intersystemic facilitation/reorganization treatment.
  (a) Gestural reorganization.
    • Improvement in articulation and some improvement in gestures; however, uncertain about maintenance of gains.
    • Some generalization for gestures to untrained gestures.
  (b) Improvements for both vibrotactile stimulation and singing.
  (c) Improvements with intersystemic techniques.

Treatment of Childhood Apraxia of Speech

1. Overview.
   a. Treatment decision typically guided by understanding of disorder, but no universally accepted theory or model of CAS on which to base treatment.
   b. The predominant focus of therapy for CAS is to develop/improve motor planning and/or programming skills for speech sound production and prosody; however, other deficit areas may need attention (e.g., language, phonology, phonological awareness, literacy).
   c. Consider other processing deficits (e.g., cognition, attention) in treatment planning.
   d. A treatment plan should take into account *all* factors influencing communication (i.e., receptive/expressive language, phonological concerns, and literacy).
2. Basic principles of treatment.
   a. Goals.
      (1) Establish motor plans and programs for speaking.
      (2) Store the plans and program.
      (3) Habituate use of plans and programs to the level of automaticity.
   b. Treatment should incorporate motor learning principles (see the "General Principles of Treatment of MSD" section).
   c. Session characteristics.
      (1) Intensive and individualized treatment.
      (2) A clinician should maximize production practice during each practice session.
      (3) Adopt more frequent sessions (e.g., three to five per week) compared to traditional one to two sessions per week.
      (4) Length of session based on the attention/learning capabilities of child; however, 30-minute session appropriate for younger child.
   d. Practice stimuli.
      (1) Stimuli should typically include combinations of sounds.
      (2) Include a few words or phrases the child can use in daily communication (i.e., functional utterances); however, some treatment programs adopt nonsense words.
      (3) In general, begin with less phonetically complex sounds and gradually increase in complexity as the child becomes more successful. For more severe speakers, may need to begin with nonmeaningful syllables in order to achieve building blocks of speech movement.
      (4) Choose stimuli the child can successfully imitate with cuing (e.g., auditory, visual, or tactile) or through simultaneous repetition with clinician (integral stimulation procedures).
      (5) Build within the treatment hierarchy the gradual removal of forms of cueing (e.g., tactile, visual, auditory) or suprasegmental facilitator (e.g., slowing rate, stress) until achievement of spontaneous production of utterance.
      (6) Begin with smaller set of training words and increase in size with success; larger beginning set size with decreasing severity of the disorder.
      (7) After accomplishing correct production for a word in a set, begin practicing the word in a short sentence or phrase; add new word to original set.
   e. Use a multisensory approach to treatment (e.g., visual prompts, tactile cues, AAC).
   f. Teach the speaker to self-monitor.
   g. Auditory training typically not part of treatment program for CAS.
   h. Select some easily obtainable goals to ensure success and maintain motivation.
   i. May need to teach compensatory strategies (e.g., intrusive schwa for consonant clusters).
   j. Carryover and generalization of skills can be maximized through treating speakers within naturalistic environments.

3. Motor-based treatment methods.
   a. General comments.
      (1) A variety of different motor-based methods used to treat CAS.
      (2) Often methods are adoptions of techniques originally used with adults but take into account lack of experience with speaking in children.
      (3) Evidence supporting effectiveness is evolving but limited for any one method of treatment.
   b. Factors to consider when choosing a specific motor-approach to treatment.
      (1) Severity (e.g., prosodic methods more appropriate for mild cases).
      (2) Presence of oral apraxia (may interfere with effective cueing within some articulatory-based treatment methods).
      (3) Training/experience of clinician with method.
   c. Treatment methods.
      (1) Articulatory.
         (a) Key features.
            • Similar to the articulatory kinematic approach for adults with AOS.
            • The majority of articulatory treatment methods for CAS adopted features of integral stimulation (IS).
         (b) Specific methods.
            • Dynamic temporal and tactile cueing for speech motor learning.
               – Targets individual utterances within set of utterances chosen for client.
               – Utilizes motor learning principles such as mass and distributed practice and feedback schedules.
               – Adds and subtracts cueing to support successful planning and programming.
               – End result spontaneous productions with normal rate and prosody without cueing.
            • Nuffield Centre Dyspraxia Programme.
               – Based on a hierarchy, starting with core isolated sounds and consonant-vowel syllables, and gradually increasing the complexity of phonotactic structures and utterance length until reaching conversational speech.
               – Controlling the phonotactic structure of utterances leads to the development of linguistic contrast.
               – Visual materials supportive of literacy practice.
            • Rapid Syllable Transition Treatment (ReST)
               – Involves intensive practice of multisyllabic pseudo-words to target speech sound accuracy, transitions between phonemes, and prosody in children with CAS.

– The treatment method contains both prepractice and longer practice.
– Prepractice uses knowledge of performance to increase awareness of speech targets the client needs to achieve during the longer practice session.
– The treatment method uses modeling, phonetic placement cues, segregation of syllables and rejoining of syllables, reduced speed of production, and visual representation of relative syllable length.
      (2) Rhythm and rate.
         (a) Key features.
            • Provides speaker more time to evoke motor program or provide speaker with a longer time to process tactile and kinesthetic feedback information for positioning of articulators.
            • Hypothesized impaired prosody in CAS and rhythmic methods help to lay the groundwork for more improved speech rhythm, an important aspect of speech development.
            • Finally, the melody or intonation of speech along with hand tapping or signing can enhance speech production skills in speakers with CAS.
         (b) Specific methods.
            • Different rhythm and/or rate methods.
            • Pairing movement of the body (e.g., foot or hand tapping for each syllable of a word) with speech production.
            • Melodic intonation therapy (MIT); refer to Chapter 13.
      (3) Tactile/gestural.
         (a) Key features.
            • Provide multisensory input through both visual and kinesthetic cues.
            • Such cues thought to facilitate/enhance sequential speech movements.
         (b) Treatment methods.
            • Prompts for restructuring oral muscular phonetic targets.
               – Adoption of tactile cues to face and neck via hands to aid movement for syllable/word production.
               – Cues manner and place; presented in sequential order.
               – Targets meaningful utterances, moving from least to most motorically difficult.
            • Touch cues.
               – Utilized tactile cues on neck and face, plus auditory and visual cues.

6. What is true of childhood apraxia of speech (CAS)?

a. It is usually associated with a lesion in the frontal lobe.
b. It often co-occurs with childhood dysarthria.
c. It is often associated with length and disruptive coarticulatory transitions between sounds and syllables.
d. It usually does not impact literacy development.

7. What is intelligibility?

a. The overall adequacy or prosody.
b. The extent of understanding of a speaker.
c. The rate at which speech units are produced.
d. The perceptual adequacy of speech sound production.

8. According to principles of motor learning, which practice schedule type leads to best generalization?

a. Massed practice schedule.
b. Excessive practice schedule.
c. Low frequency practice schedule.
d. Delayed practice schedule.

9. Which type of dysarthria is associated with distorted vowels, monoloudness, voice tremor, and damage to the bilateral cerebral hemispheres?

a. Spastic dysarthria.
b. Ataxic dysarthria.
c. Hyperkinetic dysarthria.
d. Hypokinetic dysarthria.

10. Which is typically a treatment method used to improve the articulatory subsystem?

a. Lee Silverman Voice Treatment (LSVT).
b. Integral stimulation.
c. Expiratory muscle strength training.
d. Contrastive stress.

11. What best describes the motor learning principle of "type of feedback"?

a. Knowledge of results (KR) is feedback regarding the quality of motor behavior.
b. Knowledge of performance (KP) is feedback regarding the success in achieving a motor behavior.
c. Knowledge of results (KR) leads to improved acquisition.
d. Knowledge of performance (KP) leads to improved acquisition.

12. Which is typically a treatment method used to improve the respiratory and phonatory subsystems?

a. Lee Silverman Voice Treatment (LSVT).
b. Integral stimulation.
c. Expiratory muscle strength training.
d. Contrastive stress.

13. Which clinical characteristic most closely represents a diagnosis of childhood apraxia of speech?

a. Consonantal distortions with adequate vowel production.
b. Adequate vowel production with vowel distortions.
c. Slow rate of speech with initiation difficulties.
d. Inconsistency of speech sound errors for a given phoneme.

14. Which of the following types of treatment for apraxia of speech involves improving spatial and temporal aspects of articulatory movement?

   a. Articulatory kinematic.
   b. High frequency of practice.
   c. Rate and/or rhythm.
   d. Alternative/augmentative communication (AAC).

15. What is apraxia of speech (AOS)?

   a. A motor speech disorder characterized by phonological deficits.
   b. A motor speech disorder characterized by motor planning deficits.
   c. A motor speech disorder characterized by motor execution deficits.
   d. A motor speech disorder characterized by consistent speech errors.

16. Which can help distinguish between childhood dysarthria (CD) and childhood apraxia of speech (CAS)?

   a. In CD, there are frequent groping behaviors for speech postures, whereas in CAS there are not.
   b. In CAS, there are typically impairments to only articulation and prosody, whereas in CD there are typically impairments to all speech subsystems.
   c. In CAS, there are additional neuromuscular conditions, whereas in CD there are not.
   d. In CD, there are a variety of speech errors, whereas in CAS, distortions are most frequent.

17. As a treatment for childhood apraxia of speech (CAS), which speech subsystem is targeted through use of Dynamic Temporal and Tactile Cueing?

   a. Articulation.
   b. Respiration.
   c. Phonation.
   d. Prosody.

18. Which is typically a treatment method used to improve the respiratory subsystem?

   a. Expiratory muscle strength training.
   b. Effortful closure.
   c. Phonetic placement.
   d. Relaxation strategies.

19. Which type of dysarthria is associated with imprecise consonants, decreased loudness, harsh vocal quality, and one cerebral hemisphere?

   a. Hypokinetic dysarthria.
   b. Spastic dysarthria.
   c. Unilateral upper motor neuron dysarthria.
   d. Flaccid dysarthria.

20. What is considered a type of prosodic impairment in motor speech disorders?

   a. Excess and equal stress.
   b. Palilalia.
   c. Diplophonia.
   d. Audible inspiration.

Structural Communication and Swallowing Disorders

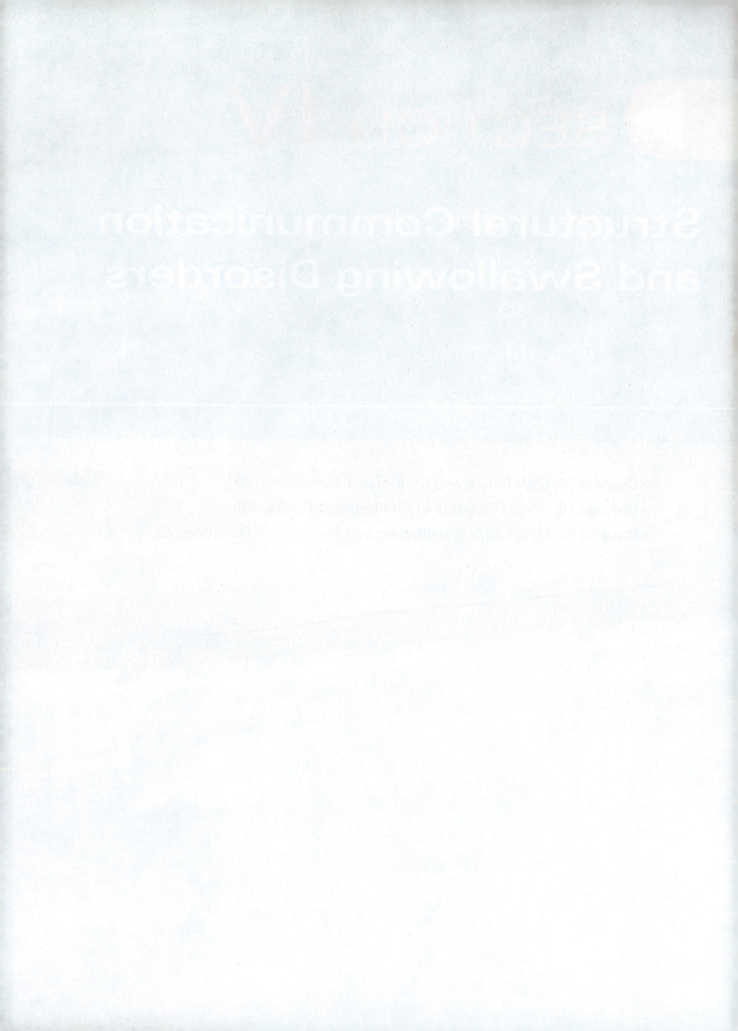

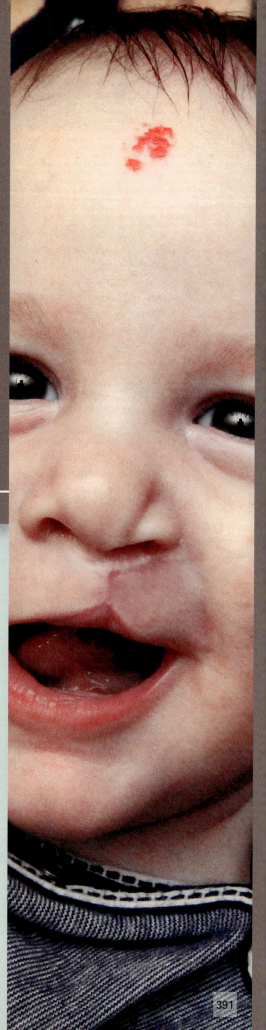

15

Cleft Palate and Craniofacial Conditions

ANN W. KUMMER, PhD
MARGARET WILSON, MA

Chapter Outline

Anatomy of the Face and Oropharyngeal Structures

Nose, Nasal Cavity, and Upper Lip

1. Outer nasal structures.
   a. Nasal bridge: the upper bony structure of the nose.
   b. Columella: structure between the nostrils that supports the nasal tip.
   c. Ala nasi: the outside curved part around the nostril.
   d. Naris (plural nares): nostril.
2. Nasal septum: divides the nasal cavity into two sections.
   a. Vomer bone: trapezoidal-shaped bone in the nasal septum that is perpendicular to the palate.
   b. Perpendicular plate of the ethmoid.
   c. Quadrangular cartilage.
   d. Turbinates (also called *conchae*): small structures that project inside the nose that cleanse and humidify air that passes through the nose.
      (1) Superior turbinate.
      (2) Middle turbinate.
      (3) Inferior turbinate.
   e. Meatus (pl. meatuses): passage in the nasal cavity that lies directly under a nasal turbinate.
      (1) Superior meatus.
      (2) Middle meatus.
      (3) Inferior meatus.
3. Upper lip.
   a. Philtrum: long dimple or indentation that courses from the columella down to the upper lip.
   b. Cupid's bow: the shape of the upper lip.
   c. Labial tubercle: prominent projection on the inferior border of the midsection of the upper lip.
   d. Vermillion: red tissue of the lips.

Oral Structures

1. Tongue.
   a. Dorsum of tongue (dorsal surface): top surface of tongue.
   b. Ventrum of tongue (ventral surface): under surface of tongue.
2. Faucial pillars and tonsils.
   a. Anterior and posterior faucial pillars: paired curtain-like structures in the back of the oral cavity on each side.
   b. Palatine tonsils: lymphoid tissue found between the anterior and posterior faucial pillars on both sides.
   c. Lingual tonsils: masses of lymphoid tissue that are located at the base of the tongue and extend to the epiglottis.
3. Bones of the oral cavity.
   a. Alveolar ridge: outer surface of the hard palate that forms the bony support for the teeth and a surface for lingual-alveolar sound production.
   b. Incisive foramen: hole through the bone located in midline just behind the alveolar ridge of the maxillary arch.
   c. Premaxilla: triangular-shaped bone bordered on either side by the incisive suture lines and at the point by the incisive foramen.
   d. Hard palate: bony structure that separates the oral cavity from the nasal cavity.
   e. Pterygoid process of the sphenoid bone: provides attachments for velopharyngeal muscles. Contains:
      (1) Medial pterygoid plate.
      (2) Lateral pterygoid plate.
      (3) Pterygoid hamulus.
4. Velar structures.
   a. Velum (soft palate): soft, muscular structure, just posterior to the hard palate.
   b. Median palatine raphe: white suture line that can be seen coursing down the midline of the velum on the oral surface.
   c. Uvula: a teardrop-shaped structure that hangs freely from the posterior border of the velum.

Pharyngeal Structures

1. Pharynx.
   a. Includes the throat area between the esophagus and the nasal cavity.
   b. Oropharynx: part of the pharynx that is at the level of the oral cavity or just posterior to the mouth.
   c. Nasopharynx: part of the pharynx that is above the oral cavity and just posterior to the nasal cavity and velum.
   d. Hypopharynx: part of the pharynx that is below the oral cavity and extends from the superior edge of the epiglottis inferiorly to the area of the esophagus and larynx.
   e. Posterior pharyngeal wall (PPW): back wall of the throat.
   f. Lateral pharyngeal walls (LPW): side walls of the throat.

2. Adenoids (also called *pharyngeal tonsils*): lymphoid tissue on the posterior pharyngeal wall of the naso-pharynx, just behind the velum.
   a. Children often have velo-adenoidal closure during speech.
   b. Removal of the adenoids can affect velopharyngeal function.

3. Eustachian tube: membrane-lined tube that is lateral and slightly above the velum during phonation.
   a. Connects the middle ear with the pharynx on each side.
   b. Is responsible for middle ear function.

▶ Physiology of the Velopharyngeal Valve

Velopharyngeal Function

1. Velar movement.
   a. During nasal breathing, the velum rests against the base of the tongue, creating a patent airway.
   b. During speech, the velum elevates in a superior and posterior direction to contact the posterior pharyngeal wall or, in some cases, the lateral pharyngeal walls.
   c. "Knee action": the velum bends (like a knee) to provide contact with the posterior pharyngeal wall.
   d. "Velar dimple": indentation in the velum noted on the oral surface of the velum during phonation.
      (1) Formed by the contraction of the levator muscles where they interdigitate.
      (2) Usually located at a point that is about 80% of the distance from the hard palate to the uvula.
2. Lateral pharyngeal wall movement.
   a. Both walls move medially to close against the velum or, in some cases, to meet in midline behind the velum.
   b. There is variability as to the extent of movement in individuals.
   c. From the oral cavity, the lateral pharyngeal walls may appear to bow outward during movement for speech, which is normal.
3. Posterior pharyngeal wall movement.
   a. Moves forward to assist in achieving contact against the velum, though this forward movement may be slight.
   b. Contributes minimally to closure.
4. Passavant's ridge.
   a. A shelf-like projection from the posterior pharyngeal wall that occurs inconsistently in some individuals during velopharyngeal activities, such as speech, whistling, and blowing.
   b. Not a permanent structure, but a dynamic structure that occurs during velopharyngeal movement and disappears when velopharyngeal activity ceases.
   c. Thought to be formed by contraction of the superior constrictor muscles.
   d. Usually occurs below velopharyngeal closure so it does not assist with closure.
   e. Does not indicate an abnormality and is not relevant when considering appropriate treatment.
5. Muscles of the velopharyngeal valve.
   a. All are paired muscles on each side of midline.
   b. Velopharyngeal sphincter requires the coordinated action of several different muscles.
      (1) Levator veli palatini muscles: provide the main muscle mass of the velum.
         (a) Responsible for velar elevation in a 45-degree angle to close the posterior pharyngeal wall again.
         (b) Contraction is responsible for the "knee action" and also forms the velar dimple.
      (2) Superior constrictor muscles: responsible for constriction of the lateral and posterior pharyngeal walls to close around the velum.
      (3) Palatopharyngeus muscles: associated with the medial movement of the lateral pharyngeal walls.
      (4) Palatoglossus muscles: depresses the velum for production of nasal consonants in connected speech.
      (5) Musculus uvulae muscles: only intrinsic muscles of the velum.
         (a) Contracts during phonation to create a bulge on the superior and posterior part of the nasal surface of the velum.
         (b) Provides additional stiffness to the nasal side of the velum during velopharyngeal closure.
      (6) Tensor veli palatini muscles: open the eustachian tubes during swallowing or yawning; enhances middle ear aeration and drainage.
6. Motor and sensory innervation.
   a. Innervation arises from cranial nerves in the medulla.

b. Motor and sensory innervation.
   (1) Pharyngeal plexus: a network of nerves that lies along the posterior wall of the pharynx.
   (2) Many cranial nerves provide motor and sensory innervation for the velopharyngeal complex.
      (a) Trigeminal (CN V).
      (b) Facial (CN VII).
      (c) Glossopharyngeal (CN IX).
      (d) Vagus (CN X).
      (e) Hypoglossal (CN XII).
7. Variations in velopharyngeal closure among speakers (normal and abnormal).
   a. Coronal.
      (1) Most common pattern.
      (2) Posterior movement of the soft palate closes against a broad area of the posterior pharyngeal wall.
      (3) There is little contribution from lateral pharyngeal walls.
      (4) When closure is complete, there is a coronal slit.
   b. Circular.
      (1) Second-most common pattern.
      (2) Soft palate moves posteriorly, the posterior pharyngeal wall moves anteriorly, and the lateral pharyngeal walls move medially.
      (3) Closes like a true sphincter.
      (4) When closure is complete, there is a circular slit.
      (5) Passavant's ridge is commonly seen with this type of closure.
   c. Sagittal.
      (1) Least common pattern.
      (2) The lateral pharyngeal walls move medially to meet in midline behind the velum.
      (3) There is minimal posterior displacement of the soft palate for closure.
      (4) When closure is complete, there is a sagittal slit.

d. The patient's basic pattern of closure can affect surgical treatment decisions for velopharyngeal insufficiency.
8. Variations with type of velopharyngeal activity.
   a. Nonpneumatic activities do not involve air pressure.
      (1) Includes gagging, vomiting, and swallowing.
      (2) Gagging and vomiting: velum rises very high in the pharynx and the lateral pharyngeal walls close tightly along their entire length; closure is exaggerated and very firm.
      (3) Swallowing: velum is pushed upward by the back of the tongue rather than elevating independently.
   b. Pneumatic activities involve air pressure.
      (1) Positive pressure activities: blowing, whistling, singing, and speech.
      (2) Negative pressure activities: sucking and kissing.
      (3) Closure occurs lower and is less exaggerated than with nonpneumatic activities.
   c. There is a different neurophysiological mechanism for different activities, which is why blowing and sucking exercises do not improve velopharyngeal function for speech (or even blowing and sucking).
   d. Other causes of variations in velopharyngeal closure.
      (1) Phonemic content.
      (2) Length of the utterance.
      (3) Rate and fatigue.
      (4) Changes with growth and age.
9. Physiological subsystems for speech.
   a. Respiration.
   b. Phonation.
   c. Stress and intonation.
   d. Velopharyngeal function.
   e. Articulation.

▶ Clefts, Craniofacial Anomalies, and Syndromes

Cleft Lip and Palate

1. Primary palate.
   a. Structures are located anterior to the incisive foramen.
   b. Includes lip and alveolar ridge.
   c. Develops at 7 weeks' gestation.
   d. Embryological path is from the incisive foramen to the lip.

2. Primary palate clefts.
   a. "Complete" clefts of the primary palate extend through the lip and alveolus to incisive foramen.
   b. Incomplete clefts do not extend all the way to the incisive foramen and can include:
      (1) A "forme fruste," or slight notch of the lip.
      (2) A cleft of the lip only.
      (3) A cleft of the lip and just part of the alveolus.
   c. Cleft location: unilateral or bilateral.
   d. Sutures affected: incisive sutures.

3. Secondary palate.
   a. Structures are located posterior to incisive foramen.
   b. Includes hard palate, velum, and uvula.
   c. Develops at 9 weeks' gestation.
   d. Embryological path is from the incisive foramen to the uvula.
4. Secondary palate clefts.
   a. "Complete" clefts of the secondary palate extend from the uvula to incisive foramen.
   b. Incomplete clefts do not extend all the way to the incisive foramen and can include:
      (1) A bifid uvula.
      (2) A cleft of velum only.
      (3) A cleft of the velum and just part of the hard palate.
   c. Cleft location: midline only.
   d. Suture affected: median palatine suture.
5. Effects of cleft lip and palate on speech.
   a. Dental and occlusal anomalies, particularly crossbites and skeletal malocclusion.
   b. Hearing loss due to eustachian tube malfunction.
   c. Velopharyngeal insufficiency (VPI) (see "Velopharyngeal Dysfunction").
6. Effects of cleft lip and palate on feeding.
   a. Cleft lip usually does not affect feeding, but there can be initial difficulties latching on to the nipple.
   b. Cleft palate causes the inability to build up suction, due to the open cleft.
   c. Breastfeeding is usually not possible with cleft palate due to inability to suck.
   d. With use of special nipples and bottles, most babies with clefts are able to feed well until the palate is repaired.

Sequence Associated with Cleft Palate

1. Pierre Robin sequence.
   a. Sequence caused by micrognathia (small mandible).
      (1) Mandible does not grow down and forward during embryological development.
      (2) Tongue does not move down and forward from its position in the pharynx.
      (3) Palate forms around the back of the tongue, resulting in a cleft palate.
   b. Type of cleft: usually a wide, bell-shaped cleft palate.
   c. Craniofacial features: micrognathia, glossoptosis (posterior tongue position).
   d. Functional concerns.
      (1) Airway and feeding problems, particularly at birth, due to the micrognathia and glossoptosis.
      (2) Speech issues secondary to velopharyngeal insufficiency.

Craniofacial Syndromes

1. 22q11.2 deletion syndrome (also called velocardiofacial syndrome).
   a. Type of cleft: usually occult submucous cleft palate or velopharyngeal hypotonia.
   b. Craniofacial features.
      (1) Velo: often velopharyngeal dysfunction causing hypernasality.
      (2) Cardio: minor cardiac and vascular anomalies.
      (3) Facial.
         (a) Microcephaly: long face with excess vertical growth of the maxillae.
         (b) Micrognathia (small mandible) or retruded mandible: often with a Class II malocclusion.
         (c) Nasal anomalies: including wide nasal bridge, narrow alar base, and bulbous nasal tip.
         (d) Narrow palpebral fissures (slit-like eyes).
         (e) Malar (cheekbone) flatness.
         (f) Thin upper lip.
         (g) Minor auricular anomalies.
         (h) Abundant scalp hair.
      (4) Other abnormalities: long, slender fingers; short stature.
      (5) Functional concerns: early feeding problems, hypotonia, hypernasality, high-pitched voice, speech sound errors, apraxia, language delay, learning problems, and risk for psychiatric problems in adolescence.
2. Fetal alcohol syndrome (FAS).
   a. Type of cleft: cleft palate, and cleft lip.
   b. Craniofacial features.
      (1) Pierre Robin sequence with micrognathia, glossoptosis, and wide, bell-shaped cleft palate.
      (2) Short palpebral fissures.
      (3) Short nose, flat philtrum, and thin upper lip.
      (4) Microcephaly.
   c. Functional concerns: developmental disabilities, behavior problems, speech disorders, and language disorders.
3. Opitz G syndrome.
   a. Type of cleft: laryngeal cleft, cleft lip, cleft palate.
   b. Craniofacial features: hypertelorism, flat nasal bridge, thin upper lip, and low-set ears.
   c. Functional concerns: voice and swallowing problems if there is a laryngeal cleft.
4. Orofaciodigital syndrome type 1 (OFD1).
   a. Type of cleft: cleft lip, cleft palate, and midline cleft lip.
   b. Craniofacial features.
      (1) Hypertelorism.
      (2) Lobulated tongue.
      (3) Multiple hyperplastic oral frenula.

(4) Notching in alveolar ridge.

(5) Broad nose.

(6) Hydrocephalus.

(7) Absence of corpus callosum.

  c. Functional concerns: developmental disabilities and speech and language disorders.

5. Stickler syndrome.

  a. Type of cleft: cleft palate only.

  b. Craniofacial features.

    (1) Pierre Robin sequence with micrognathia, glossoptosis, and wide, bell-shaped cleft palate.

    (2) A wide, flat face with midface hypoplasia.

  c. Functional concerns.

    (1) Sensorineural hearing loss.

    (2) High myopia and risk for retinal detachments.

    (3) Risk for velopharyngeal insufficiency.

6. Van der Woude syndrome.

  a. Type of cleft: cleft lip and palate.

  b. Craniofacial features: bilateral lip pits on the lower lip; missing teeth.

  c. Functional concerns: speech disorders related to cleft lip and palate.

  d. Recurrence risk: 50% because it is an autosomal dominate condition.

Craniosynostosis Syndromes

1. Craniosynostosis: a condition in which one or more of the cranial sutures close too early, causing abnormal growth of the skull and facial bones.

  a. Apert syndrome.

    (1) Type of cleft: cleft palate occurs infrequently.

    (2) Craniofacial features: similar to Crouzon syndrome, including a prominent forehead with a flat occiput, exophthalmos, hypertelorism, antimongoloid slant, strabismus and midface hypoplasia/retrusion, Class III malocclusion, low-set ears.

    (3) Functional concerns: developmental disabilities, speech and language disorders, upper airway obstruction.

  b. Beckwith-Wiedemann syndrome.

    (1) Type of cleft: none.

    (2) Craniofacial features: hypertrophic facial features, macroglossia.

    (3) Functional concerns: airway, feeding, and speech disorders.

  c. CHARGE syndrome.

    (1) Type of cleft: cleft palate.

    (2) Primary features.

      (a) Coloboma.

      (b) Heart disease.

      (c) Atresia of the choanae.

      (d) Retarded growth and development.

      (e) Genital anomalies, cryptorchidism, micropenis, hypogonadism, delayed puberty.

      (f) Ear anomalies, hearing loss and deafness.

    (3) Functional concerns: hearing loss or deafness, developmental disabilities, speech and language disorders.

  d. Crouzon syndrome.

    (1) Type of cleft: cleft palate or submucous cleft palate occur infrequently.

    (2) Craniofacial features: similar to Apert syndrome, including a broad forehead, flat occiput, exophthalmos, hypertelorism, antimongoloid slant, strabismus and midface hypoplasia/retrusion, Class III malocclusion, low-set ears.

    (3) Functional concerns: risk for developmental disabilities if not treated and upper airway obstruction.

  e. Hemifacial microsomia (oculoauriculovertebral dysplasia).

    (1) Type of cleft: cleft palate in about 15% of cases.

    (2) Craniofacial features.

      (a) Facial asymmetry due to unilateral hypoplasia of the face, malar, maxillary, and/or mandibular processes.

      (b) Cleft-like extension of corner of mouth.

      (c) Ear anomalies, including microtia or anotia and preauricular tags or pits.

      (d) Eye anomalies, including colobomas of upper eyelid, epibulbar lipodermoids, microphthalmia.

      (e) Dysplasia or aplasia of temporomandibular joint, affecting the opening of the mouth and excursion of mandible.

    (3) Functional concerns: hearing loss, occasional velopharyngeal insufficiency or incompetence due to unilateral velar paralysis or paresis.

  f. Pfeiffer syndrome.

    (1) Type of cleft: cleft palate is rare.

    (2) Craniofacial features.

      (a) Coronal craniosynostosis.

      (b) Midface hypoplasia.

      (c) Shallow orbits with exophthalmos.

      (d) Hypertelorism.

      (e) Tracheal anomalies.

      (f) Upper airway stenosis.

    (3) Functional concerns: hearing loss, developmental disabilities in Pfeiffer type 2 and type 3, and upper airway obstruction.

  g. Saethre-Chotzen syndrome.

    (1) Type of cleft: cleft palate or submucous cleft palate.

    (2) Craniofacial features: oronasal synostosis, ptosis of the eyelids, midface hypoplasia, external ear anomalies.

    (3) Functional concerns: risk for developmental disabilities.

h. Treacher Collins syndrome.
  (1) Type of cleft: clefts occur infrequently, despite Pierre Robin sequence with pronounced micrognathia.
  (2) Craniofacial features.
    (a) Downward slanting of the palpebral fissures.
    (b) Coloboma (notching) of the lower eyelids.
    (c) Microtia or middle ear anomalies.
    (d) Hypoplastic zygomatic arches and malar hypoplasia.
    (e) Macrostomia or microstomia.
    (f) Micrognathia.
    (g) Glossoptosis.
  (3) Functional concerns: hearing loss.

Resonance Disorders and Velopharyngeal Dysfunction

Normal Resonance and Velopharyngeal Function

1. Normal resonance.
   a. Determined by the function of the velopharyngeal valve.
   b. Affected by the size and shape of cavities of the vocal tract (pharynx, oral cavity, nasal cavity).
2. Velopharyngeal structures.
   a. Velum (soft palate).
   b. Lateral pharyngeal walls (LPW).
   c. Posterior pharyngeal walls (PPW).
   d. See anatomy section for more information.
3. Normal velopharyngeal function is dependent on:
   a. Normal anatomy (structure).
   b. Normal neurophysiology (function).
   c. Normal speech sound learning (articulation).

Velopharyngeal Dysfunction

1. Velopharyngeal dysfunction refers to any situation in which an individual is unable to completely close the velopharyngeal valve during oral speech sound production.
   a. The acronym VPI can be used for both velopharyngeal insufficiency and for velopharyngeal incompetence.
2. Velopharyngeal insufficiency.
   a. Due to abnormal structure.
     (1) History of cleft palate or submucous cleft (overt or occult).
     (2) Short velum.
     (3) Deep pharynx due to cervical spine or cranial base abnormalities.
     (4) Irregular adenoids.
     (5) Enlarged tonsils that intrude into nasopharynx and affect closure.
   b. Surgical or intervention causes.
     (1) Adenoidectomy.
     (2) Maxillary advancement (Le Fort I surgical advancement or distraction).
     (3) Treatment of nasopharyngeal tumors (surgery or radiation).
     (4) Cervical spine surgery through the mouth.
   c. Treatment: always requires physical management (i.e., surgery or a prosthetic device if surgery is not an option). Postoperative speech therapy is often required to change compensatory productions that developed as a result of the VPI.
3. Velopharyngeal incompetence.
   a. Due to a congenital or acquired neurophysiological disorder.
     (1) Velar and/or pharyngeal hypotonia.
     (2) Velar paralysis or paresis due to brainstem or cranial nerve injury.
     (3) Neuromuscular disorders.
       (a) Myasthenia gravis.
       (b) Muscular dystrophy.
       (c) Cerebral palsy.
     (4) Often associated with dysarthria.
     (5) Can occur as apraxia.
   b. Treatment: with the exception of apraxia, which requires speech therapy, usually requires physical management (i.e., palatal lift or even surgery in select cases).
3. Velopharyngeal mislearning.
   a. Caused by faulty articulation learning, resulting in abnormal placement for specific speech sounds.
     (1) Substitution of a pharyngeal placement for one or more of the sibilant sounds results in phoneme-specific nasal emission.
     (2) Substitution of a nasal sound for oral sound results in phoneme-specific hypernasality.
   b. Severe hearing loss or deafness causes abnormal resonance due to a lack of auditory feedback, which is a type of mislearning.

c. Treatment: always requires speech therapy; never requires surgery.

4. Effects of velopharyngeal dysfunction on speech.
   a. Hypernasality (see description under "Resonance Disorders" below).
   b. Nasal air emission resulting in:
      (1) Weak or omitted consonants due to the lack of adequate air pressure.
      (2) Short utterance length, due to the need to take frequent breaths to replenish the lost airflow through the nose.
      (3) Dysphonia, due to associated laryngeal anomalies or due to strain in the entire vocal tract in efforts to achieve velopharyngeal closure.
      (4) Compensatory articulation productions: abnormal articulation placement in an attempt to compensate for the lack of airflow in the oral cavity; usually produced in the pharynx where there is airflow.
      (5) Obligatory distortions: distortions due to abnormal structure only (i.e., VPI), despite normal articulation placement; speech therapy is not indicated for these distortions because articulation placement is normal.

Resonance Disorders

1. Hypernasality.
   a. Too much sound resonating in the nasal cavity during speech.
   b. Most perceptible on vowels (because vowels are voiced).
   c. Voiced consonants may be nasalized (e.g., m/b, n/d).
   d. Does not affect voiceless consonants, because resonance affects sound vibration.
   e. Causes: VPI or a fistula (hole in the palate due to a palate repair breakdown); can even be caused by keeping the back of the tongue too high when articulating vowels.

2. Hyponasality.
   a. Not enough sound resonating in the nasal cavity during speech.
   b. Most perceptible on nasal consonants (/m/, /n/, /ŋ/).
   c. Can also be noted on vowel sounds.
   d. Cause: upper airway obstruction due to adenoid hypertrophy or nasal blockage.

3. Cul-de-sac resonance.
   a. Occurs when the sound is blocked from exiting one of the cavities of the vocal tract (e.g., pharyngeal cavity, oral cavity, or nasal cavity).
   b. Causes low volume with a muffled quality and indistinct articulation; commonly described as "mumbling."
   c. Commonly caused by enlarged tonsils, which block the entrance to the oral cavity, causing pharyngeal cul-de-sac resonance.

4. Mixed nasality.
   a. Occurs when there is hypernasality or nasal air emission on oral consonants and hyponasality on nasal consonants.
   b. Caused by apraxia or a combination of velopharyngeal dysfunction and upper airway obstruction.

Evaluation and Treatment of Resonance and Velopharyngeal Function

Evaluation of Resonance and Velopharyngeal Dysfunction

1. Perceptual evaluation.
   a. Determine type of resonance (normal balance of oral and nasal resonance, hypernasality, hyponasality, cul-de-sac resonance, or mixed resonance); rating of severity is not necessary, as it usually doesn't affect treatment decisions.
   b. Determine if there is nasal emission, and if so, whether it is consistent or phoneme-specific.
   c. Determine if there are compensatory errors or obligatory distortions.

2. Oral examination.
   a. Evaluate oral structures and function.
      (1) Palatal arch and presence of fistula (if there is a history of cleft palate).
      (2) Evidence of submucous cleft palate, including a bifid or hypoplastic uvula, an upside-down V shape of the velum during phonation, or a zona pellucida (thin, bluish area in the soft palate). Occasionally you can palpate a notch in the midline of the posterior border of the hard palate.
      (3) Position of uvula during phonation.
      (4) Size of tonsils.
      (5) Dental occlusion and teeth that may interfere with tongue tip movement.
      (6) Signs of oral-motor dysfunction.
      (7) Signs of upper airway obstruction.

b. Can't evaluate velopharyngeal function because it is above the oral level.

3. Instrumental assessment.
   a. Nasometer.
      (1) Uses a handheld plate with microphones to capture acoustic energy from the nasal cavity and oral cavity during the production of speech.
      (2) Gives a ratio of oral energy over total energy for a nasalance score, which can be compared to normative data.
   b. Videofluoroscopy.
      (1) A radiographic procedure of the velopharyngeal valve.
      (2) Requires multiple views, usually a lateral, frontal, and base view, to assess velopharyngeal closure during speech.
   c. Nasopharyngoscopy.
      (1) An endoscope is passed through the nasal cavity to the nasopharyngeal port.
      (2) Allows the examiner to view the nasal surface of the velum and the entire velopharyngeal port during speech.

Treatment of Resonance and Velopharyngeal Dysfunction

1. Surgery for velopharyngeal insufficiency or incompetence (VPI).
   a. Velopharyngeal insufficiency or incompetence requires physical management, preferably surgical intervention.
   b. Speech therapy cannot correct hypernasality or nasal emission due to VPI.
   c. Common surgical procedures.
      (1) Pharyngeal augmentation: injection or implantation of a substance in the posterior pharyngeal wall or velum to fill in an opening.
      (2) Furlow Z-plasty: technique to repair or re-repair the velum in an attempt to lengthen it.
      (3) Sphincter pharyngoplasty: technique to narrow the sides of the pharyngeal port while leaving a midline port open for nasal breathing and production of nasal sounds.
         (a) The posterior faucial pillars (which include the palatopharyngeus muscles) are released at the base, rotated backward, and overlapped on the posterior pharyngeal wall.
         (b) This closes the lateral aspects of the pharynx, so it works well for lateral gaps, as in hemifacial microsomia.
      (4) Pharyngeal flap: technique to close midline velopharyngeal openings while leaving lateral ports for nasal breathing and production of nasal sounds.
         (a) A flap is elevated from the posterior pharyngeal wall and sutured into the velum to partially close the nasopharynx in midline.
         (b) This closes the midline so it is the best for cleft palates that have a midline opening.
      (5) Buccal flap: technique to lengthen the velum without obstructing the airway.
         (a) Buccal flaps are created from the inside of each cheek and inserted between the hard palate and velum to push the velum, along with the levator muscles, backward.
         (b) This pushes the entire velum back, so it is effective for all types of openings.

2. Prosthetic devices.
   a. Prosthetic devices are used either on a temporary basis or when surgery is not an option.
   b. Prosthetic device types.
      (1) Palatal obturator: to close or occlude an open cleft or fistula.
      (2) Palatal lift: to raise the velum when velar mobility is poor or to extend the velum beyond the velar eminence.
      (3) Speech bulb obturator: to occlude nasopharynx when velum is short.

3. Speech therapy.
   a. Speech therapy cannot correct hypernasality or nasal emission due to VPI.
   b. Speech therapy is appropriate after repair of the structure to address:
      (1) Compensatory articulation errors due to VPI.
         (a) Pharyngeal plosive.
         (b) Glottal stop (plosive).
         (c) Pharyngeal fricative.
         (d) Posterior nasal fricative.
         (e) Glottal fricative (/h/).
      (2) Compensatory productions due to a fistula.
         (a) Velar fricative.
         (b) Generalized backing.
      (3) Compensatory productions due to abnormal dental occlusion.
         (a) Palatal-dorsal productions.
      (4) Phoneme-specific nasal emission, where nasal emission is due to faulty articulation. This occurs most commonly on sibilant sounds (/s/, /z/, /ʃ/, /ʒ/, /tʃ/, /dʒ/).
      (5) Variable resonance due to apraxia of speech.
      (6) Hypernasality or nasal emission following surgical correction.
         (a) Changing structure does not change function.
         (b) Patient needs to learn to use the corrected valve through auditory feedback.
   c. Techniques.
      (1) Auditory awareness and auditory feedback.
      (2) Articulation techniques to correct placement.
      (3) Drills and frequent practice (as is consistent with motor learning evidence).

(4) Oral-motor exercises (i.e., blowing, sucking, and velar exercises) are NOT effective and are inappropriate.

d. Timeline for intervention and assessment for children with history of cleft lip and palate.

(1) Birth to 3 years: should monitor early feeding and language development and start therapy, if needed.

(2) Three years: should evaluate speech, resonance, and velopharyngeal function and:

(a) Should recommend surgical correction for VPI.

(b) Should start speech therapy, if needed.

References

American Cleft Palate–Craniofacial Association (ACPA). (2009). Parameters for evaluation and treatment of patients with cleft lip/ palate or other craniofacial anomalies. *Cleft Palate-Craniofacial Journal, 30* (Suppl.), 1–16.

Kummer, A. W. (2009). "Assessment of Velopharyngeal Function." In J. E. Lossee & R. E. Kirschner (Eds.), *Comprehensive Cleft Care*. New York: McGraw-Hill.

Kummer, A. W. (2011a). Disorders of resonance and airflow secondary to cleft palate and/or velopharyngeal dysfunction. *Seminars in Speech and Language, 32*(2), 141–149.

Kummer, A. W. (2011b). Perceptual assessment of resonance and velopharyngeal function. *Seminars in Speech and Language, 32*(2), 159–167.

Kummer, A. W. (2011c). Speech therapy for errors secondary to cleft palate and velopharyngeal dysfunction. *Seminars in Speech and Language, 32*(2), 191–198.

Kummer, A. W. (2011d). Types and causes of velopharyngeal dysfunction. *Seminars in Speech and Language, 32*(2), 150–158.

Kummer, A. W. (2014a). Speech evaluation for patients with cleft palate. *Cleft Lip and Palate: Modern Surgical Management, Clinics in Plastic Surgery, 41*(2), 241–251.

Kummer, A. W. (2014b). Speech and resonance disorders related to cleft palate and velopharyngeal dysfunction: A guide to evaluation and treatment. *Perspectives on School-Based Issues, 15*(2), 57–74.

Kummer, A. W. (2020). *Cleft Palate and Craniofacial Conditions: A Comprehensive Guide to Clinical Management,* 4th ed. Burlington, MA: Jones & Bartlett Learning.

Perry, J. L. (2011). Anatomy and physiology of the velopharyngeal mechanism. *Seminars in Speech and Language, 32*(2), 83–92.

Peterson-Falzone, S. J. (2011). Types of clefts and multianomaly craniofacial conditions. *Seminars in Speech and Language, 32*(2), 93–114.

Peterson-Falzone, S. J., Hardin-Jones, M. A., & Karnell, M. P. (2010). *Cleft Palate Speech,* 4th ed. St. Louis, MO: Elsevier.

Smith, B. E., & Kuehn, D. P. (2007). Speech evaluation of velopharyngeal dysfunction. *Journal of Craniofacial Surgery, 18*(2), 251–260.

Review Questions

1. The philtrum is:

   a. Also called Cupid's bow.
   b. Part of the naris.
   c. The middle meatus.
   d. The indentation from the columella down to the upper lip.

2. Complete clefts of the primary palate:

   a. Involve the lip and part of the alveolus.
   b. Extend through the lip and alveolus to the incisive foramen.
   c. Extend from the uvula to incisive foramen.
   d. Has no lip involvement.

3. A bifid uvula:

   a. Is a type of secondary incomplete cleft.
   b. Indicates a complete cleft palate.
   c. Will develop normally at 7 weeks' gestation.
   d. Hinders closure of the velopharyngeal complex.

4. During speech, which of the following rises in a superior and posterior direction to contact the posterior pharyngeal wall?

   a. Eustachian tube.
   b. Velum.
   c. Uvula.
   d. Incisive foramen.

5. The premaxilla is:

   a. A triangular bone that contains the upper incisors.
   b. Part of the soft palate.
   c. Soft tissue of the faucial pillars.
   d. Connected to the columella.

6. For children with cleft palate, breastfeeding:

   a. Causes no issues.
   b. Usually is not possible.
   c. Is highly recommended.
   d. Is considered dangerous.

Chapter 15 CPC

7. Another name for the pharyngeal tonsils.

   a. Adenoids.
   b. Pharynx.
   c. Velopharynx.
   d. Middle turbinate.

8. Which of the following is caused by micrognathia?

   a. Fetal alcohol syndrome.
   b. Pierre Robin sequence.
   c. Stickler syndrome.
   d. Velocardiofacial syndrome.

9. Velopharyngeal insufficiency:

   a. Is caused by faulty learned speech patterns.
   b. Is due to abnormal structures.
   c. Is the same thing as velopharyngeal incompetence.
   d. Results in speech with frequent nasal snorts.

10. Which of the following is most perceptible on vowels?

    a. Hypernasality.
    b. Hyponasality.
    c. Cul-de-sac resonance.
    d. Nasal emission.

11. A fistula:

    a. Is a bunching of muscles in the pharynx.
    b. Is a hole in the palate due to surgical repair breakdown.
    c. Typically causes hyponasality.
    d. Is identified by an articulation test.

12. Pneumatic activities involve:

    a. Swallowing.
    b. "Velar dimple."
    c. Air pressure.
    d. Gagging.

13. A pharyngeal flap is:

    a. A technique to lengthen the velum.
    b. A prosthetic device.
    c. A technique to close midline velopharyngeal openings.
    d. Always used in conjunction with speech therapy.

14. The main muscle mass of the velum is the:

    a. Inferior constrictor.
    b. Palatopharyngeus.
    c. Superior constrictor.
    d. Levator veli palatini.

15. Which is NOT a compensatory articulation error due to VPI?

    a. Pharyngeal plosive.
    b. Glottal stop.
    c. Distortion of "sh" sound.
    d. Posterior nasal fricative.

16. Craniosynostosis:

    a. Is premature fusion of the sutures, which causes abnormal growth of the skull and facial bones.
    b. Causes a Class II malocclusion.
    c. Causes minor cardiac and vascular anomalies.
    d. Is a characteristic of orofaciodigital syndrome type 1.

17. Treatment of VPI:

    a. Consists of intensive speech therapy.
    b. Requires physical management.
    c. Rarely involves surgery.
    d. Typically uses nonspeech oral motor exercises to strengthen the pharyngeal structures.

18. Which muscles open the eustachian tubes during swallowing?

    a. Palatopharyngeus.
    b. Tensor veli palatini.
    c. Superior constrictor.
    d. Musculus uvulae.

19. Passavant's ridge:

    a. Is not a permanent structure.
    b. Is a clefted alveolar ridge.
    c. Must be evaluated during the oral mechanism examination.
    d. Is a contributor to normal velopharyngeal function.

20. Why is it important to understand a patient's basic pattern of velopharyngeal closure?

    a. It will indicate the success of speech therapy treatment.
    b. It will help differentiate between hyponasality and hypernasality.
    c. It can affect surgical treatment decisions for VPI management.
    d. It allows a nasalance score to be compared with normative data.

16

Voice Disorders in Children and Adults

AARON ZIEGLER, PhD
CARA BRYAN, MA

▶ Anatomy and Physiology of the Vocal Mechanism

Laryngeal Anatomy and Physiology

1. Larynx.
   a. Supportive framework, comprised of bone and cartilages (see Table 16-1).
   b. Houses the true vocal folds (VFs), comprised of muscular and nonmuscular tissues.
2. Other muscles and tissues (see Table 16-2).
   a. Ventricular folds and aryepiglottic folds.
   b. Membranes include quadrangular membrane, conus elasticus, cricothyroid membrane.
   c. Ligaments and connective tissue include vocal ligament, cricothyroid ligament, and macula flava.
3. Extrinsic laryngeal and supplementary muscles (see Table 16-3).
   a. Suprahyoid muscles move the larynx superiorly and anteriorly, or superiorly and posteriorly.
   b. Infrahyoid muscles lower and stabilize the larynx.
4. Intrinsic laryngeal muscles (see Table 16-3).
   a. Abductors open the VFs.
   b. Adductors close the VFs.
   c. Tensors stiffen or lengthen the VFs.

5. Associated anatomical features.
   a. Several spaces are defined by structures of the larynx. The vestibule, or the region between the false VFs, and aditus (see Figure 16-1).
6. VF histology shows that the structure of the adult true VFs consists of five layers (see Figure 16-2).
   a. VF tissue contains interstitial proteins, elastin, and collagen.
   b. Basement membrane zone.
      (1) Complex layer of proteins.
      (2) Between the deepest layer of squamous cells and the superficial layer of the lamina propria
   c. Extracellular matrix.
      (1) Consists of interstitial proteins, including hyaluronic acid, that fill spaces between cells.
      (2) Important in wound repair and regeneration of tissues.
   d. Vocal ligament includes both elastic and collagenous fibers.

Neuroanatomy of Phonation

1. Cranial nerve input to larynx (see Figure 16-3).
   a. Through the vagus nerve (CN X), which arises in the nucleus ambiguous.
   b. Three branches of the vagus nerve travel to pharynx and larynx.
   c. Right and left branches of the recurrent laryngeal nerve (RLN) differ in length; both enter larynx through thyroid gland.
   d. Left RLN branch is longer because it wraps around the aorta before coursing upward.
   e. Right branch wraps around the subclavian artery before entering larynx.
   f. RLN susceptible to trauma from surgery involving neck and chest.

Table 16-1

Paired and Unpaired Cartilages of the Larynx

	PAIRED	UNPAIRED
Hyoid bone		•
Epiglottis		•
Cricoid cartilage		•
Thyroid cartilages	•	
Arytenoid cartilages	•	
Corniculate cartilages	•	
Cuneiform cartilages	•	

Table 16-2

Other Structures and Tissues of the Larynx

STRUCTURE	FUNCTION	CONNECTIONS
Aryepiglottic folds	Tissue that helps in laryngeal closing/folding protective mechanism	Connects arytenoid cartilages and epiglottis, contains cuneiform cartilages
Macula flava	Dense tissue at anterior and posterior ends of true VF	Connects true VFs to cartilages at anterior commissure and vocal processes
Conus elasticus	Membrane lining infraglottal region • Cricothyroid ligament • Cricothyroid membrane	Connects the thyroid, cricoid, and arytenoid cartilages • Connects cricoid and thyroid cartilages at anterior midline • Connects cricoid and thyroid cartilages lateral to cricothyroid ligament
Quadrangular membrane	Membrane lining supraglottal region	Covers and protects underlying tissue

Table 16-3

Intrinsic and Extrinsic Muscles of the Larynx

MUSCLE	ORIGIN	INSERTION	MOVEMENT	ACTION
Intrinsic Laryngeal Muscles: muscles that attach to and within the larynx itself				
Posterior cricoarytenoid	Cricoid cartilage	Arytenoids	Abductors	Opens VFs
Lateral cricoarytenoids	Cricoid cartilage	Arytenoids	Adductors	Closes membranous VFs
Interarytenoids			Adductors	Closes posterior VFs/ respiratory glottis
• Oblique interarytenoid	Arytenoids	Arytenoids		
• Transverse interarytenoid	Arytenoids	Arytenoids		
Thyroarytenoids			Tensors	Changes VF stiffness; under some circumstances acts as relaxer
• Medial/internal (thyrovocalis)	Thyroid cartilage	Arytenoid vocal process		
• Lateral/external (thyromuscularis)	Thyroid cartilage	Arytenoid muscular process		
Cricothyroid	Cricoid cartilage	Thyroid cartilage	Tensors	Changes VF length and stiffness
• Pars recta				
• Pars oblique				
Extrinsic Laryngeal Muscles: attachments to muscle outside of the larynx in addition to their laryngeal attachments				
Suprahyoid muscles			Move larynx within neck	Move larynx superiorly and anteriorly or superiorly and posteriorly
• Mylohyoid	• Mandible	• Hyoid bone		
• Geniohyoid	• Mandible	• Hyoid bone		
• Anterior belly of digastric	• Mandible	• Hyoid bone		
• Hyoglossus	• Hyoid bone	• Tongue		
• Stylohyoid	• Styloid process	• Hyoid bone		
Infrahyoid muscles			Move larynx within neck	Lower and stabilize larynx
• Thyrohyoid	• Thyroid cartilage	• Hyoid bone		
• Sternohyoid	• Sternum	• Hyoid bone		
• Sternothyroid	• Sternum	• Thyroid cartilage		
• Omohyoid	• Scapula	• Hyoid bone		
• Inferior constrictor	• Thyroid/cricoid cartilages	• Pharyngeal raphe		

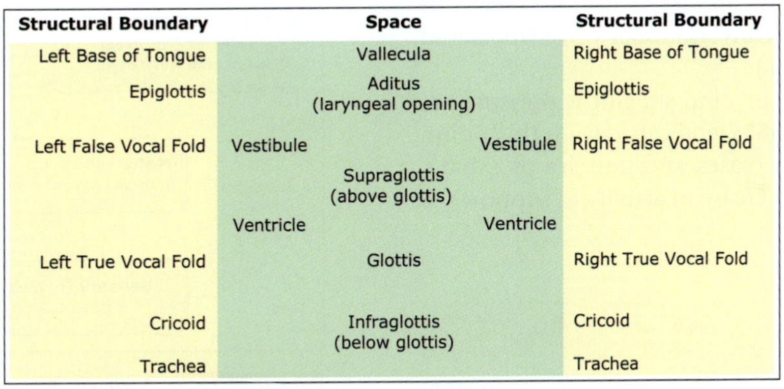 Structural Boundary	Space	Structural Boundary
Left Base of Tongue	Vallecula	Right Base of Tongue
Epiglottis	Aditus (laryngeal opening)	Epiglottis
Left False Vocal Fold	Vestibule — Vestibule	Right False Vocal Fold
	Supraglottis (above glottis)	
	Ventricle — Ventricle	
Left True Vocal Fold	Glottis	Right True Vocal Fold
Cricoid	Infraglottis (below glottis)	Cricoid
Trachea		Trachea

Figure 16-1   Anatomical Structures of the Upper Airway and Associated Spaces

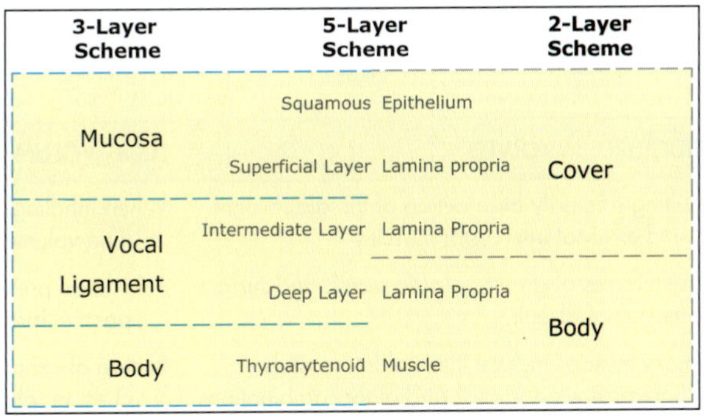

3-Layer Scheme	5-Layer Scheme	2-Layer Scheme
Mucosa	Squamous Epithelium	Cover
	Superficial Layer Lamina propria	
Vocal Ligament	Intermediate Layer Lamina Propria	
	Deep Layer Lamina Propria	Body
Body	Thyroarytenoid Muscle	

Figure 16-2   Classification of the Layers of the VFs

Chapter 16 VDC

Processes of Speech

Breathing for Speech

1. Resting expiratory level (REL).
   a. The volume level in the lungs at the end of exhalation in tidal breathing, when no respiratory muscles are active.
   b. Volume level where the forces of contraction of the lungs are balanced by the forces of expansion of the chest wall.
2. Relaxation pressure.
   a. Equals zero at resting expiratory level; increases when lung volume is above or below REL.
      (1) Relaxation pressure is positive above REL and negative below REL.
      (2) Expiratory pressure is positive.
      (3) Inspiratory pressure is negative.
3. Checking action (see Table 16-4).
   a. Activity of inhalatory muscles to control passive forces of exhalation in order to maintain steady subglottic pressure and airflow needed for speech production.
   b. These inhalatory muscles, primarily the external intercostals, stay activated until relaxation pressure equals subglottic pressure.
      (1) Average subglottic pressure during speech is 4–6 cm H_2O in conversational voice (increased for louder voices).
      (2) Relaxation pressure and subglottic pressure are equal at about 55% vital capacity. At this point, checking action ceases and muscles of exhalation gradually increase in activity to support the outflow of air.

VF Vibration

1. Aerodynamic myoelastic theory of phonation (ADMET): the aerodynamic myoelastic theory of phonation.

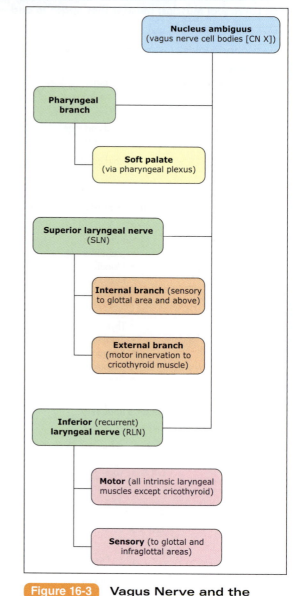

Figure 16-3 **Vagus Nerve and the Branches of Cranial Nerve X**

Table 16-4

Phases of the Respiratory Cycle			
PHASE	NATURE	STRUCTURES INVOLVED	LUNG VOLUMES AND MUSCLE ACTIVITY
Inhalation	Active process	Resulting primarily from action of the diaphragm and external intercostal muscles.	When inhaling for speech, usually inhalation results in lung volumes above tidal breathing levels.
Exhalation	Passive during quiet breathing	Passive forces of gravity, elastic recoil, and surface tension of alveoli.	Relaxation pressure is pressure generated entirely by passive forces, pulling toward equilibrium at REL.
	Active during breathing	Primary muscles include internal intercostals (interosseous portions) and other combinations of chest wall and abdominal wall muscles.	Pattern of exhalatory muscle activity (i.e., degree of chest vs. abdominal muscle contraction) varies from person to person and across activities.

a. Van den Berg (1958) proposed this theory to reflect what mechanisms are involved in one cycle of glottal vibration that results in VF vibration.

(1) The adductor muscles (lateral cricoarytenoids [LCAs] and interarytenoids [IAs]) close the VFs to midline or near midline, while the tensors (cricothyroids [CTs] and thyroarytenoids [Tas]) stiffen the VFs to the desired fundamental frequency level.

(2) With the VFs in a closed position, as the person begins to exhale, subglottal pressure builds beneath the VFs. Pressure builds until it is great enough to overcome the resistance of the VFs and push the VFs open.

(3) A noise burst of air, termed a *glottal pulse*, is released, creating an acoustic shock wave traveling at the speed of sound through the vocal tract.

(4) Once the VFs have been blown open, forces of elastic recoil and the Bernoulli effect help to bring the folds back to their original position.

(a) The Bernoulli effect indicates that at a point of constriction, airflow increases in rate and lateral pressure decreases. This has the effect of a vacuum, sucking the folds back toward one another.

(b) As the VFs begin to be pulled closer and closer together, the Bernoulli effect increases since the constriction is becoming narrower and narrower.

(5) The opening and closing of the VFs during phonation is the result of the aerodynamic and muscular forces indicated above.

(a) This implies that VF vibration will continue as long as the VFs are in a closed or nearly closed position and air is flowing, building up sufficient pressure below the VFs to blow them apart.

(b) The VFs do not open and close during voicing because of separate muscle contractions.

Cover-Body

1. Cover-body theory of vocal cord vibration.

a. Proposed by Hirano and Kakita in 1985, this theory posits that the VF cover moves independently of the body.

b. The body of the VFs (i.e., the TA muscle) participates very little in vibratory movement.

c. Movement of the vocal ligament, called the *transition*, falls in between the significant movement of the cover and the minimal movement of the body.

d. This theory suggests that anything that interferes with the movement of the cover will affect the resulting voice quality (see Figure 16-4).

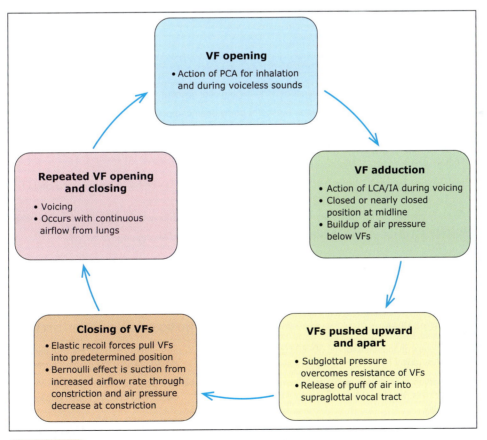

Figure 16-4   **Process of Self-Sustained VF Vibration**

Phonation Type

1. Definition: the degree of VF opening during speech production (see Table 16-5).

Registers

1. Definition: a register is a series or range of consecutively phonated frequencies that can be produced with nearly identical voice quality and that ordinarily do not overlap.
2. An individual's phonation range can be divided into three registers (see Table 16-6).

▶ Measures of Voice Production (Acoustic, Aerodynamic, Perceptual)

1. Normative values of many of the following measures are related to the age, gender identity, and health status of the speaker.

2. Normative values also vary with the methodology used to elicit and extract them (see Table 16-7).

▶ Development of the Vocal Mechanism

Growth, Development, and Age-Related Changes

1. More is known about age-related changes in men.

2. Some gender differences seem to be present, though data are limited (see Figure 16-5).

Table 16-5

Types of Phonation and VF Closure

PHONATION TYPE	PERCEPTUAL QUALITY	PHYSIOLOGICAL CHARACTERISTICS
Normal	Normophonic	Regular bursts of air through glottal opening with full opening and closing of VFs with vibration.
Breathy	Noisy airflow with some voicing	Noise plus air burst; VFs partly open and partly close; closed phase vibrates.
Whisper	Noisy friction airflow	Narrow VF opening and no vibration.
Voiceless	Noiseless airflow	VFs are open and no vibration.
Strained	Pushed voice quality	Irregular bursts of air through vibrating VFs with full VF opening and closing with increased medial compression.
Glottal fry	Gravelly quality	Low-frequency, irregular air bursts in which only a small portion of the VF margin opens and closes.
Glottal stop	Audible stop of sound	VFs fully adduct with no vibration; a complete stoppage of airflow.

Table 16-6

Types of Registers and Phonation Ranges

REGISTER	FREQUENCY RANGE	PHYSIOLOGICAL CHARACTERISTICS
Pulse	Lowest of one's phonational range, 30–80 Hz; sometimes heard as glottal fry.	VFs are relaxed and vibrate with minimal subglottic pressure; closed phase is the greatest portion of the glottal cycle.
Modal/chest	Largest portion of one's frequency range, comprises about 1.5 octaves; vocal quality has the greatest timbre and flexibility.	Normal periodic movement of the VFs; nearly equal closing/closed and opening/open phases.
Loft/falsetto	Occurs at about 300–350 Hz in both men and women.	VFs are stretched and tense/stiff, vibrating at their medial edges. Airflow rate is increased.

Table 16-7

Measures Contributing to Multidimensional Voice Assessment

ACOUSTIC MEASURES	DEFINITIONS	CORRELATES
Frequency (Hz)	Number of times per second the VFs open and close during voicing; determined by VF mass and stiffness. Frequency is the inverse of period length. A glottal period is the time for the VFs to open and close one time, consisting of one glottal cycle.	Pitch
Intensity (dB)	Sound pressure level generated by the acoustic shock wave traveling through the vocal tract; determined by subglottic pressure required to push the VFs open, which is related to the degree of glottal resistance of the VFs when adducted; relates to the amplitude of the acoustic waveform.	Loudness
Maximum phonation time (seconds)	The longest time a subject can produce a vowel following a deep inhalation; typically improves with practice or training.	May reflect phonation type and characteristics of breath support for speech.
Jitter (%)	The average cycle-to-cycle change in frequency from one cycle to the next; also known as *pitch perturbation* and is highly dependent on a periodic cycle; influenced by signal periodicity, which can be problematic for dysphonia that tends to be aperiodic.	Measure of frequency or "pitch" instability; normal to have small degree of instability, greater % is indicative of dysphonia or lack of control of VF vibration.
Shimmer (%)	The average cycle-to-cycle change in amplitude (intensity) from one cycle to the next; is less dependent on average intensity, so can be calculated as absolute shimmer.	Measure of amplitude instability related to intensity of sound wave.
Harmonic-noise ratio (no unit of measurement)	Quantifies the amount of additive aperiodicity in the voice signal. Long-term average spectrum is a measure that describes the spectral characteristics of speech by averaging the contribution of individual speech sounds.	Correlates to noise in vocal signal, where increasing noise compared to harmonics is indicative of dysphonia.
Long-term average spectrum (no unit of measurement)	Measure that describes the spectral characteristics of speech by averaging the amplitude across a defined frequency range of an individual's speech sounds.	Frequency-based acoustic measure up to 30–40 sec of continuous speaking is a good indicator of an individual speaker's vocal quality.
Soft Phonation Index (no unit of measurement)	An acoustic analysis parameter that provides indication of VF adduction and glottal closure during phonation.	High SPI indicates breathiness.
Cepstral peak prominence (no unit of measurement)	Measure of vocal quality. It is a relevant measure to assess effects of different treatment protocols and may be able to distinguish among laryngeal disorders.	A measurement used to assess breathiness and overall vocal quality—related to harmonics or overtones.
Voice Turbulence Index (no unit of measurement)	An average ratio of the spectral inharmonic energy between 2,800 and 5,800 Hz (breath noise) and the spectral harmonic energy between 70 and 4,500 Hz (VF vibration and associated harmonics).	A measurement that provides a quantitative index of breathiness.
Acoustic Voice Quality Index (no unit of measurement)	Quantifies dysphonia severity using sustained phonation and continuous speech.	Severity of dysphonia
Cepstral Spectral Index of Dysphonia (no unit of measurement)	Correlates with auditory-perceptual assessment of voice.	Severity of dysphonia
Dysphonia severity index (no unit of measurement)	Weighted combination of maximum phonation time, high- and low-frequency values, and percent jitter.	Severity of voice quality
AERODYNAMIC MEASURES	DEFINITIONS	CORRELATES
Mean flow rate (mL/s)	Measure of the rate of airflow through the vocal tract during phonation; associated with the efficiency of phonation.	Breathy vs. normal vs. pressed voice
Subglottic pressure (cm H_2O)	Pressure measured below VFs, usually during vibration; associated with intensity of voice produced and related to degree of medial compression of closed VFs; average subglottic pressure during speech is 4–6 cm H_2O in conversational voice (increased for louder voices).	Normal vs. pressed voice
Glottal resistance (measured in cm H_2O/LPS)	Ratio of subglottal pressure to airflow rate.	Associated with intensity (loudness) at low and middle frequencies.

(Continued)

Chapter 16 VDC

Table 16-7

Measures Contributing to Multidimensional Voice Assessment (*Continued*)

PERCEPTUAL MEASURES	DEFINITIONS	CORRELATES
GRBAS	Grade of dysphonia, roughness, breathiness, asthenia, strain.	Score 0 = none Score 1 = mild Score 2 = moderate Score 3 = severe
Consensus Auditory-Perceptual Evaluation of Voice (CAPE-V)	Overall severity, roughness, breathiness, strain, pitch, loudness, other.	0–100 visual analogue scale
Stroboscopic and visual measures	Appearance of VFs, especially color, any supraglottal constriction, and presence of mucus; description of VF edge as smooth and even, irregular, with an excrescence, etc.; glottic closure pattern (position of VFs and any space between them during most closed phases of vibration) as complete, incomplete, irregular, hour-glass-shaped, with an anterior or posterior gap; whether left and right VFs move symmetrically during vibration and are mirror images of each other; amplitude or extent of horizontal excursion of VFs during vibration. Periodicity or regularity of (apparent) successive cycles of vibration. Mucosal wave behavior or lateral movement of superior surface, or cover, of VFs during vibration.	Normal appearance is white VFs with smooth and even edges; complete glottic closure with symmetric and periodic vibration; normal amplitude of vibration at about 1/3 width of visible folds; mucosal wave traveling about half the width of VFs at typical pitch and loudness. Judgments of stroboscopic parameters may improve with training and standardized procedures.
PHYSIOLOGICAL MEASURES	DEFINITIONS	CORRELATES
Force	Measure of collision force amplitude between the vibrating VFs.	In millinewtons (mN)
Muscle activity	Activity of single motor units and muscle fibers in general.	Measured through electromyography
Vital capacity	Amount of air available for use when lungs are inflated maximally.	Measured with spirometry

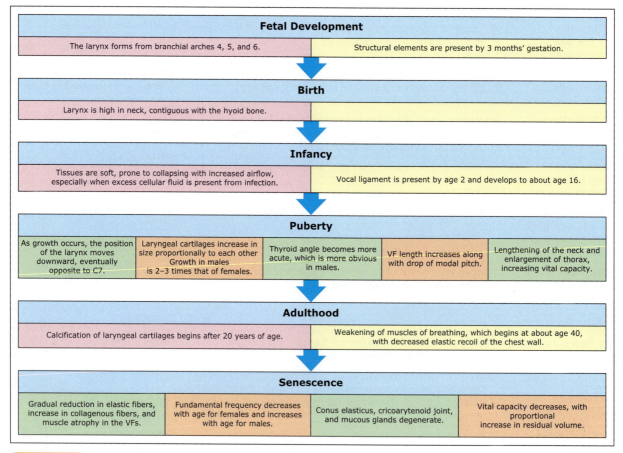

Figure 16-5   Growth, Development, and Age-Related Changes of the Vocal Mechanism

Etiologies and Characteristics of Vocal Pathologies

Voice Problems

1. A number of factors are associated with voice problems (see Table 16-8).

2. Phonotraumatic etiologic factors include occupation, personality, and vocal "style," as well as activities involving frequent shouting.
3. Other etiologic factors include laryngopharyngeal reflux (LPR), allergies, family history/genetics, and medications.

Table 16-8

Common Vocal Pathology and Voice Disorders in Adults

PATHOLOGY	ETIOLOGY	APPEARANCE	VOCAL QUALITY
Vocal nodules	Results from phonotrauma; significant impact stress and other biomechanical forces result in an increase in intracellular fluid and a buildup of hyperkeratotic tissue with underlying fibrosis arising from the superficial layer of the lamina propria. Abnormal growth forms at junction of the anterior one-third, posterior two-thirds of the VFs (i.e., the middle of the membranous VFs).	Mid-membranous, opposing lesions (i.e., bilateral) along vibratory edge, may develop into soft, fluid-filled lesions much like blisters and ultimately may become harder and more callous-like. Hallmark glottic closure: hourglass configuration.	Voice quality ranges from mild to severely impaired and can be described variously as hoarse, breathy, harsh, or raspy with phonation breaks and vocal effort. Quality usually worsens throughout the day. Fundamental frequency may vary; maximum phonation time is reduced and jitter and shimmer are often increased.
Polyps	Results from phonotrauma; impact stress from hyperfunctional VF adduction that results in wound formation arising in the superficial layer of the lamina propria; may result from periods of phonotrauma or from a single traumatic incident. Lesions may arise anywhere on the VF cover, including the inferior surface of the VFs.	Usually unilateral and may be pedunculated (attached by a stalk) or sessile (broad-based). Some may be hemorrhagic (filled with blood). Glottic closure: varied depending on location and size of polyp.	Voice quality may be minimally impaired or significantly changed. Pitch is typically lowered; jitter and shimmer are elevated. VF closure may be affected, depending on the location of the polyp. The patient may experience the sensation of something catching in the throat with heavy breathing or talking.
Polypoid degeneration "Reinke's edema"	Is most often seen in women who are heavy smokers with chronic phonotraumatic behaviors and perhaps gastroesophageal reflux disease (GERD); the superficial layer of the lamina propria (Reinke's space) reacts to trauma by increasing fluid in the submucosal lining.	It may be unilateral or bilateral and is typically asymmetrical. The edema causes a loose, floppy appearance of the surface of the VF, often pale in color. The cover of the VF becomes less stiff. Stroboscopic exam reveals decreased mucosal wave and decreased amplitude of vibration. Glottic closure: often irregular.	Fundamental frequency is noticeably reduced with a reduced phonational range.
Cyst	Benign collection of material, such as fluid, surrounded by a membrane, typically arising from the superficial layer of the lamina propria. Two common types are mucous retention cysts, which result from a plugged mucous duct, and epidermoid cysts, where epithelial cells have become trapped and encapsulated in Reinke's space. Cysts may be congenital or form as a result of phonotrauma.	Cysts vary in size and in location within Reinke's space of the VF. A cyst may be suspected whenever voice change does not resolve with conservative treatment and an adynamic portion of mucous wave on a VF suggests increased stiffness of that fold. Sometimes cysts are seen to co-occur with other benign tissue changes in the VFs. Glottic closure: varied depending on location and size of cyst.	Voice quality may vary depending on the size and location of the cyst and whether glottic closure is affected. Vocal fatigue may be reported along with some lowering of habitual pitch.

(Continued)

Table 16-8

Common Vocal Pathology and Voice Disorders in Adults (Continued)

PATHOLOGY	ETIOLOGY	APPEARANCE	VOCAL QUALITY
Human papillomavirus (HPV) infection	Infection in the larynx from types 6 and 11 results in recurrent respiratory papillomatosis. Lesions may be found anywhere in the respiratory tract, although the VFs are the most common location. Childhood onset is linked to maternal genital infection; however, adult onset of the virus does occur.	Appears as masses of nonkeratinized stratified squamous epithelium that typically are white to pink or red in color. Single, multiple, or clumps of lesions may be found. Glottic closure: irregular.	May exhibit a wide variety of changes in voice quality with frequent coughing or throat-clearing and may also experience some restriction in breathing with stridor.
Laryngitis	Laryngitis can be acute or chronic. Acute laryngitis results in short-term loss of voice or impaired voice quality due to a bacterial or viral respiratory infection. Chronic laryngitis can result from long-term vocal trauma, GERD, allergies, and other causes.	Epithelial thickening and long-standing mucosal inflammation result that are not associated with an infection; the laryngeal mucosa may appear dry, have areas of thickened secretions, and show changes in color, such as increased redness. Under stroboscopy, the folds move asymmetrically and aperiodically. Glottic closure: complete or irregular.	Voice quality is dysphonic and often described as rough, with increased spectral noise. Quality may decrease with increased talking. Phonational range is reduced; jitter and shimmer are increased. Patients may complain of dryness.
Muscle tension dysphonia (MTD)	A hyperfunctional dysphonia that is from chronic increased tension of the laryngeal musculature resulting in dysphonia that typically has multifactorial contributing etiologies. Two types of MTD: Primary MTD: MTD without laryngeal pathology Secondary MTD: presence of laryngeal pathology that causes MTD	Primary MTD: VF appearance is normal, although hypo- or hyperfunction may be seen. Secondary MTD: hyperfunction seen as a response to the presence of a laryngeal pathology. Stroboscopy may reveal vibratory symmetry and abnormal glottal closure. GERD may be a confounding finding. Larynx may be held high in the neck with pain present on palpation. Glottic closure: varies on type of MTD.	Dysphonia can range from mild to severely dysphonic, often with a rough, strained quality.
Psychogenic dysphonia/aphonia	Voice change associated with psychological causes, including anxiety or unconscious emotional distress; it may be related to a single incident. This is reported to be more common in patients who identify as female.	VF tissue and movement are determined to be normal; however, during speech, the VFs are held in a partially abducted position, may hyperadduct, or may appear bowed, all resulting in restricting normal vibration.	Aphonic or dysphonic: voice may be produced sporadically or intermittently. A normal cough is typically present, signaling an intact vocal mechanism despite the lack of normal volitional voice quality. Patients may complain of pain on talking.
Puberphonia (mutational falsetto)	Considered to be a functional voice disorder with possible psychological roots in some cases. It may be caused by the patient attempting to stabilize voicing during puberty when a "growth spurt" of the speech mechanism happens. Occurs more noticeably in males but can be found in females.	The larynx and other physical changes associated with puberty are normal. Voice will be high in pitch with the larynx held in an elevated position, and neck tension may be evident.	High pitch, pitch breaks, phonation breaks, vocal fatigue, and breathiness may also be present. Patient may not be able to shout with this voice.
Ventricular fold phonation (plica ventricularis)	Hyperadduction of the false VFs due to a psychological problem, a compensatory behavior, a component of a pattern of hyperfunction, or as an unexplained phenomenon. In rare cases, the false VFs are used as a vibratory source of sound for individuals with nonfunctioning VFs.	The false VFs adduct and obscure the view of the underlying true VFs during voicing. The true folds may remain in an open position or also close toward midline; the true folds do not appear to vibrate during attempts at phonation in most cases.	Resulting voice quality is low in pitch and loudness, monotone, rough/harsh, often diplophonic or multiphonic and has a significantly restricted pitch range.

(Continued)

Table 16-8

Common Vocal Pathology and Voice Disorders in Adults (*Continued*)

PATHOLOGY	ETIOLOGY	APPEARANCE	VOCAL QUALITY
Vocal cord dysfunction (paradoxical VF motion)	Upper airway disorder. Possible etiologies of VCD include upper airway sensitivity as a physiological response to an irritant, psychogenic as a result of anxiety, and laryngeal dystonia resulting from a neurological event or process; asthma, allergies, GERD, anxiety, and stress are comorbid factors in many patients.	A diamond-shaped posterior glottic chink can be seen endoscopically during inspiration or expiration. VFs adduct to varying degrees during quiet breathing, restricting airflow; vibration of VFs can be visualized during inhalation (stridor); pulmonary function testing shows a reduced inspiratory flow volume.	The patient feels tightness in the neck and throat and may present with a cough or throat-clear just prior to an episode of difficulty breathing. Some patients report distinct triggers, such as episodes associated with exercising or with strong odors (gasoline, perfume, coffee). Episodes of difficult breathing may vary from several episodes a day to only a few times a year. Patient's test results may be entirely within normal limits when not experiencing an episode. Dysphonia may co-occur.
Vagal nerve damage	The vagus nerve or its branches, either superior or inferior, may be damaged, leading to paresis or paralysis of the muscles of the larynx. Lesions may occur on one or both sides; a unilateral lesion is more common than bilateral lesions. Damage to the recurrent laryngeal nerve may affect all of the intrinsic laryngeal muscles except for the cricothyroid muscle. Common sources of damage include surgery (cardiac, thyroid, or cervical spine), trauma, tumors, inflammatory processes or idiopathic, where no clear cause can be determined.	Damage to the nerve results in the affected VF typically resting in the paramedian position, just lateral to midline. The thyroarytenoid muscle fibers atrophy from lack of neurostimulation. The affected fold is unable to adduct to midline for normal VF closure; under stroboscopy, the VFs will vibrate asymmetrically and aperiodically with greater than normal vibratory amplitudes. Glottic closure: incomplete.	Because of the paramedian position of the VF and its flaccidity, the voice can be breathy/hoarse and soft, and patients typically have a weak cough. Maximum phonation time is decreased.
Superior laryngeal nerve damage	Damage to the superior laryngeal nerve may result from any of the events listed for the recurrent laryngeal nerve. However, usually the etiology of a superior laryngeal nerve paralysis is unknown, especially since the effects of a unilateral paralysis to only this nerve are quite subtle. If the internal branch of the SLN is affected, then sensation to the glottal and supraglottal regions is compromised. Unilateral damage to the external branch of the superior laryngeal nerve affects only the cricothyroid muscle.	Laryngoscopic/stroboscopic signs that may be present include a rotation or tilting of the larynx toward the normal side on phonation, slightly unequal levels of the folds at closure, reduced mucosal wave movement, and reduced amplitude of vibration. Glottic closure: incomplete.	This causes an inability to lengthen the muscle on that side and results in altered pitch control and reduced pitch range. Patients may complain of vocal fatigue.
Spasmodic dysphonia (SD)	Vocal dystonia due to abnormalities in laryngeal motor control arising in the basal ganglia. The exact etiology remains unknown. Three types of SD: Adductor SD: most common, found in approximately 90% of diagnosed cases; more common in women. Abductor SD: less common; VFs remain open. Mixed SD: a mix of both adductor and abductor SD. SD may be difficult to differentially diagnose from muscle tension dysphonia, or patients may experience muscle tension dysphonia, which confounds the effects of the SD.	Adductor SD: patients experience irregular, uncontrolled, random *closing* spasms of the VFs during phonation. Abductor SD: experience irregular, random, uncontrolled *opening* movements of the VFs.	Adductor SD: strained-strangled. Abductor SD: breathy; spasms are most common in contexts with many voiced-voiceless transitions and are less noticeable or not present in a breath phrase with all voiced speech sounds. Voice quality may be near normal during singing or when speaking in falsetto or for brief periods after laughing or crying.

(*Continued*)

Table 16-8

Common Vocal Pathology and Voice Disorders in Adults (*Continued*)			
PATHOLOGY	**ETIOLOGY**	**APPEARANCE**	**VOCAL QUALITY**
Essential tremor of the voice	An organic voice tremor thought to result from a lesion in the extrapyramidal system of the central nervous system; voice tremor is also known to have a hereditary basis in some cases. Voice tremor may be accompanied by a resting tremor of the face, head, hands, or other muscles of the oral mechanism. Essential tremor of the voice may begin in late adolescence or young adulthood but more commonly manifests in the fifth or sixth decade of life.	Rhythmic oscillations of the larynx result in a voice often described as "quavering" and reminds listeners of aging. The tremor is on the order of 4–12 cycles per second, which is slower than normal tremor.	Vocal tremor; may interfere with intelligibility, although complete voice breaks are not common.

Pediatric Voice Problems

1. Pediatric voice problems can be congenital and acquired (see Table 16-9).

Table 16-9

Common Pediatric VF and Laryngeal Pathology			
PATHOLOGY	**ETIOLOGY**	**APPEARANCE**	**VOCAL QUALITY**
Laryngomalacia	Most common congenital laryngeal disorder; diagnosed after birth due to the immature development of laryngeal cartilages.	Pressure as air flows through the vocal tract results in the cartilages collapsing inward; sometimes surgery to protect the airway is performed until the problem resolves as the infant grows.	Stridor and respiratory distress.
Subglottic stenosis	The result of failure in the development of vocal tract tissue, including tracheal cartilages.	Stenosis involving the soft tissues only may resolve as the child develops; reconstruction may be required, and these children may have long-term consequences affecting speech development.	Identified at birth due to respiratory distress.
Laryngeal web	Congenital nature is thought to result from disruption in normal embryonic development.	Webs are common at anterior commissure; can vary in thickness and length; surgical removal is necessary to free entire length of VFs for vibration.	Symptoms of stridor and difficulty breathing at birth.
VF nodules	Most common acquired voice problem in children; thought to result from excessive voice use, including considerable yelling and effortful voice. GERD is also suspected to play a role.	Treatment commonly involves physiological voice modification techniques and may include family counseling; surgery for nodules is rarely recommended in children, although acid reflux management may be recommended.	Many children with bilateral vocal nodules appear to "outgrow" them during puberty, but the exact reasons for this have not been determined; patients recall first noticing hoarseness and voice breaks associated with nodules during adolescence.

Other Voice Populations

Professional Voice Users

1. This population covers a wide range of professions and activities but can be grossly divided into two categories:
   a. Individuals who need to talk a lot.
   b. Individuals who need to talk loudly.
2. Professions or activities associated with voice problems: actors, singers, cheerleaders, coaches, fitness instructors, auctioneers, ministers, teachers, call center operators, salespeople.
3. Those whose occupations require hard or frequent voice use need careful laryngologic assessment and individualized treatment plans developed with specific patient needs in mind.
4. Most professional voice users need to take a long-term view of managing their voice problems in relation to their work and life needs.

Gender-Expansive Clients

1. Voice therapy may be sought to align voice and communication with gender identity.
2. A speech-language pathologist (SLP) who works with transgender and nonbinary individuals should be culturally aware and use appropriate terminology, particularly use of pronouns.
3. The following voice and speech characteristics can be modified: pitch, intonation, resonance, vocal intensity, articulation, vocabulary, and nonverbal behaviors (body language, laughing, coughing, and audible intake of air).

Persons with Velopharyngeal Dysfunction

1. Effect on voice of velopharyngeal dysfunction is primarily resonance.
2. Research indicates an opening in the velopharyngeal port >20 mm^3 will typically result in perception of hypernasality.
3. When velopharyngeal dysfunction is consistent, patients will attempt to compensate for poor closing of that valve by excessive closing of laryngeal valve (i.e., the VFs).
   a. Repeated hyperfunction of this type may result, then, in formation of traumatic lesions on the VFs, such as vocal nodules.
   b. Resulting vocal characteristics of hoarseness, voice breaks, lowered pitch, and the like.

Persons with Hearing Loss

1. The voice quality of individuals with hearing loss may vary from that of normal, depending on:
   a. Age of onset of the loss.
   b. Extent of the hearing deficit.
2. Those with hearing impairments may have abnormal resonance characteristics and monotonous habitual pitch.
   a. Intonation patterns are likely to be disrupted.

Voice Evaluation Protocol

1. The patient should see the SLP only after a medical diagnosis has been obtained.
2. A case history is typically the first assessment procedure (see Figure 16-6).
3. Evaluation of voice is multidimensional: laryngeal imaging, auditory-perceptual, acoustics, aerodynamics, patient-reported outcome measures (PROMs) (see Figure 16-7).
4. A voice evaluation should include a hearing screening appropriate for the patient's age or otherwise note an impression of hearing ability from a functional perspective.
5. Resonance may require evaluation.
   a. Most common perceptual features may include hyponasality, hypernasality, cul-de-sac resonance, or observations of nasal emission.
6. Voice tremor may be heard.
   a. Tremor of other structures of the speech mechanism or of the head or hands may be observed.
7. Motor speech production may require evaluation.
   a. Voice problems may co-occur as part of dysarthria or apraxia symptoms.

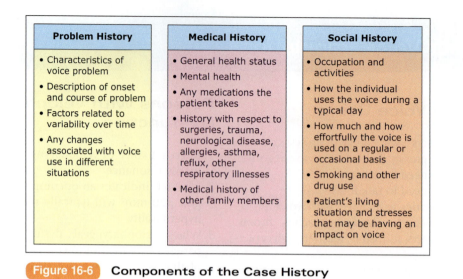

Figure 16-6   Components of the Case History

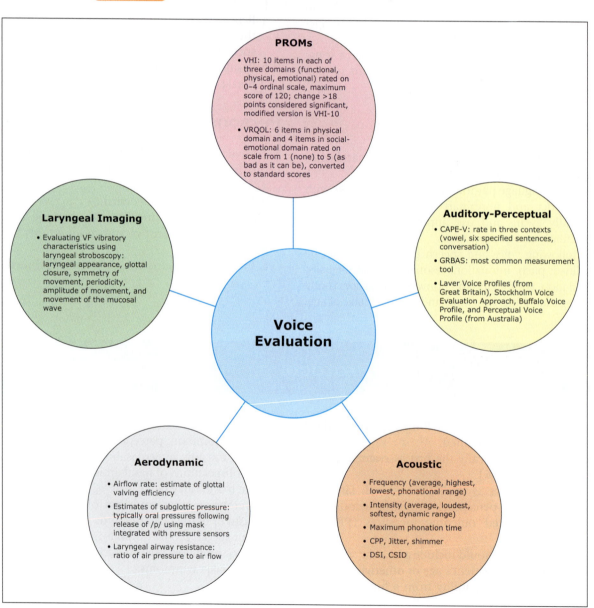

Figure 16-7   The Multidimensional Voice Evaluation and Tools of Assessment

8. Should initial observations or the patient's history warrant, each speech subsystem should be assessed: respiration, phonation, articulation, resonance, and prosody.
   a. A thorough oromotor examination would begin this assessment.
9. Should overall speech understandability be decreased, intelligibility should be assessed.
   a. Subjective judgments of how much is understood by a listener in known and unknown contexts.
   b. Standardized testing such as the Sentence Intelligibility Test.
10. Functional assessment: International Classification of Functioning, Disability, and Health (ICF).
    a. Categorizes problems with human functioning into three interconnected areas:
       (1) Impairments: problems in body function or alteration in body structure.
       (2) Activity limitations: difficulty in executing activities.
       (3) Participation restrictions: problems with involvement in any area of life.
    b. *Disability* refers to difficulties in any or all three areas of functioning and the interaction of health conditions with personal and environmental factors.
    c. ICF covers all areas of human functioning and treats disability as lying on a continuum.
11. Functional communication measure (FCM).
    a. Developed by the American Speech-Language-Hearing Association for its National Outcomes Measurement project.
    b. Voice capability and quality is assessed on a seven-point scale reflecting functional capability.

Voice Treatment Approaches

1. Evidence indicates voice therapy is effective and should be recommended as a treatment option:
   a. For a particular problem.
   b. If voice does not give a positive image.
   c. When voice does not allow one to perform normal activities of daily living, including fulfilling one's job requirements.
2. There are two broad categories of treatment approaches: indirect and direct (see Figure 16-8).

Indirect Therapy: **Encouraging Vocal Health and Wellness**	**Direct Therapy:** **Approaches and Techniques with Good Evidence**
• Reduce phonotraumatic behaviors, unnecessary coughing, and throat-clearing	• *Vocal function exercises* have shown benefit in improving vocal range, stability, flexibility, and resonance in normal and disordered populations.
• Conservative use of loud, effortful voice or shouting	• *Resonant voice therapy* focuses on optimizing voice quality by maximizing oropharyngeal resonance and reducing degree of VF compression.
• Attention to potential laryngopharyngeal reflux	• *Conversation training therapy* focuses on kinesthetic feedback of oral sensations from articulatory precision of "clear speech" within patient-driven conversation.
• Adequate hydration	• *Phonation resistance training exercises* are used to treat presbyphonia by requiring a systematic increase in a patient-specific vocal-intensity target.
• Holistic elements (good nutrition, enough rest, regular physical exercise, and good mental health)	• There are at least 25 reported facilitating approaches, though few have been studied with strong experimental controls, techniques, or approaches; these include accent method, pushing, chewing, confidential voice, chanting, respiration training, and yawn-sigh, among others. Any technique should be carefully chosen with patient characteristics and physiological mechanisms in mind.

Figure 16-8   **Indirect and Direct Voice Therapy Approaches**

▶ Management Recommendations and Referrals

Voice Therapy

1. When to recommend voice therapy.
   a. Evidence indicates voice therapy is effective for a particular problem.
   b. Voice does not give a positive image.
   c. Voice does not allow one to perform normal activities of daily living, including fulfilling one's job requirements.

2. Referrals to other professionals.
   a. Otolaryngology, neurology, psychology, singing teachers.
   b. Botox for injection into thyroarytenoid (usually) or other intrinsic muscles (less common) for treatment of spasmodic dysphonia and sometimes essential tremor of the voice.

▶ Management of Head and Neck Cancer

Surgery, Radiation, and Chemotherapy

1. Strategies to cure the disease.
   a. Surgery alone.
   b. Radiotherapy alone.
   c. Surgery followed by radiation or chemoradiation.
   d. Chemotherapy followed by surgery, radiation, or chemoradiation.
   e. Chemoradiation followed by surgery.

2. Effects related to surgery.
   a. Loss of function related to excised tissues, including effects on speech (speech distortions, voice or resonance changes) and swallowing (oral control, aspiration, residue issues).
3. Effects related to chemotherapy.
   a. Fatigue, nausea, loss of appetite, changes in taste, and potentially hair loss.
4. Effects related to radiation.
   a. Inflammatory reactions, tissue fibrosis, loss of appetite, fatigue, xerostomia, necrosis, mucositis, pain.

▶ Anatomical and Physiological Changes After Total Laryngectomy

Total Laryngectomy Procedure

1. The entire larynx is removed in situ.
   a. Hyoid bone and intrinsic laryngeal cartilages down through first tracheal ring.
2. The respiratory tract is separated from the oral/digestive tract through creation of a permanent tracheostoma in the front of the neck.
3. If cancer has spread to the lymphatic system in the neck, the neck nodes and surrounding tissues are removed in a neck dissection.
   a. A radical neck dissection involves severing the spinal accessory nerve, which affects the ability to raise one's arm straight out to the side when neck tissue and lymph glands are removed.

Breathing, Speech, Voice, and Swallowing Function After Total Laryngectomy

1. After a total laryngectomy, during respiration, air enters and leaves the pulmonary system through the open tracheostoma.
2. Following surgical healing, swallowing function typically returns to normal, unless affected by radiotherapy treatment to the neck.
3. Speech and voice production post-laryngectomy surgery can no longer use the true VFs.
   a. Most common forms of alaryngeal voice production include the use of an electronic, artificial

larynx or placement of a one-way valve (prosthesis) through a surgical puncture made between the trachea and the esophagus.

(1) This latter form of voice production is called T-E voice, for "tracheoesophageal," and is produced via a TEP, or "tracheoesophageal puncture."

(2) T-E prostheses remain in place for months at a time.

(3) When the tracheostoma is closed, either manually or by means of a two-way "speaking valve," air is shunted through the prosthesis into the upper esophagus. This airflow causes vibration of the upper esophageal or lower pharyngeal tissues. The voice produced is low in pitch and intensity with greater perturbation than normal voice.

Alaryngeal Voice Assessment Protocol

Applying the Protocol

1. Stimulability.
   a. Is the patient able to make sounds using the pharyngoesophageal segment as a voicing source?
   b. Is spontaneous belching heard?
   c. Can a good placement for the head of an electrolarynx be found on the neck?
   d. Are the patient's articulation and rate of speech conducive to good post-treatment intelligibility?
2. Insufflation testing.
   a. Air is directed into the upper esophagus to see if the air can be released into the oropharynx and if vibration of upper esophageal tissues occurs.
   b. This testing is performed to see if after a total laryngectomy, vibration of the pharyngoesophageal segment can be initiated and maintained for several seconds with relative ease.

3. Fitting of prosthesis.
   a. Most common type of prosthesis is a one-way, low-pressure valve inserted into the tissue space between the trachea and the esophagus at the back of the permanent stoma. The tissue space has been created by a surgical puncture at the time of surgery.
   b. Prostheses come in different lengths. Fit is determined by the SLP after referral from the otolaryngologist.
   c. The indwelling prosthesis typically stays in place for several months. Removal of an old prosthesis and insertion of a new one is accomplished in an office visit to the SLP or surgeon.
   d. A two-way breathing valve can be placed over the stoma opening to allow for hands-free voice production. If this valve does not work well for a particular patient, voicing is initiated by covering the stoma with a thumb to allow for the diversion of air.

Alaryngeal Voice Treatment Approaches and Considerations

TEP Voice Production and Troubleshooting

1. Improving TEP voice production.
   a. Once a prosthesis has been placed, patients must learn to coordinate breathing and voice for optimal speech production. This often involves attention to articulation, speech rate, and phrasing.
   b. Optimal speech output is typically achieved after a small number of treatment sessions with motivated patients whose health status is stable.
   c. A significant decline in performance may signal recurrent disease, other health issues, or problems with the prosthesis.

2. Troubleshooting prosthesis problems.
   a. Leakage may occur around or through a tracheoesophageal prosthesis, and these symptoms require different management strategies.
      (1) Leakage through a prosthesis often means the prosthesis needs to be changed.
      (2) Leakage around a prosthesis, on the other hand, suggests the need for a larger esophageal flange or a shorter prosthesis (but not a larger-diameter prosthesis).
   b. Patients using a TEP may be susceptible to fungal infections affecting the oropharynx, the tracheoesophageal tract, or the prosthesis.
      (1) Such infections require medical management, often with the use of antifungal medications.

Other Head and Neck Cancer Effects on Speech, Voice, and Swallowing

Partial Laryngectomy

1. *Partial laryngectomy* is a general term referring to any surgery that involves removal of part (but not all) of the voice-producing mechanism.
2. *Supraglottic laryngectomy*: the laryngeal structures and tissues above the level of the true VFs are surgically removed.
3. *Hemilaryngectomy*: a vertical (sagittal) portion of laryngeal tissue is resected. This involves part or all of one VF, and sometimes includes tissues above the fold at the same time; occasionally may extend around the anterior commissure to include portions of the opposite VF.
4. With partial laryngectomy surgery, voice, swallowing, and sometimes resonance are often affected. The effects may be temporary or long-term and are related to many factors, including how much tissue was surgically removed, other treatments the patient may have received, and the patient's general health.

Total or Partial Glossectomy

1. *Glossectomy* refers to the surgical removal of tongue tissue. In most cases, this surgery results in some degree of swallowing difficulty due to oral stage changes and altered articulatory precision with subsequent reduced intelligibility.
2. In a total glossectomy, the entire tongue is removed. Speech intelligibility is dramatically affected due to limited articulatory ability. Swallowing, too, is difficult due to limited bolus control.
3. In a partial glossectomy, only a portion of tongue muscle is removed. In general, the proportion of tissue removed is directly related to the degree of the resulting speech and swallowing difficulty.

Other Surgical Treatments

1. Head and neck tumors may occur anywhere in the upper respiratory tract. Besides the larynx and tongue, other common sites include the floor of the mouth, tonsil, and palate.
2. Treatment approaches are the same as for laryngeal cancers, involving surgery or radiotherapy alone or in combination, along with chemotherapy.

References

Boutsen, F., Cannito, M. P., Taylor, M., & Bender, B. (2002). Botox treatment in adductor spasmodic dysphonia: A meta-analysis. *Journal of Speech, Language and Hearing Research, 45*(3), 469.

Casper, J. K., Colton, R. H., & Gress, C. D. (1993). *Clinical Manual for Laryngectomy and Head/Neck Cancer Rehabilitation*. San Diego, CA: Singular Publishing Group, p. 197.

Colton, R. H., Casper, J. K., & Leonard, R. (2011). *Understanding Voice Problems: A Physiological Perspective for Diagnosis and Treatment*, 4th ed. Philadelphia: Lippincott, Williams and Williams.

Gartner-Schmidt, J., Gherson, S., Hapner, E. R., Muckala, J., Roth, D., Schneider, S., & Gillespie, A. I. (2016). The development of conversation training therapy: A concept paper. *Journal of Voice, 30*(5), 563–573.

Hirano, M. (1981). *Clinical Examination of Voice. Disorders of Human Communication*. New York: Springer-Verlag.

Hirano, M. , & Kakita, Y. (1985). *Cover-Body Theory of VF Vibration*. In *Speech Science: Recent Advances*, by Daniloff R. G. (Ed.). College-Hill Press, San Diego, CA, pp. 1–46.

Hixon, T. J., Weismer, G., & Hoit, J. D. (2008). *Preclinical Speech Science: Anatomy, Physiology, Acoustics, and Perception*. San Diego, CA: Plural Publishing.

Hogikyan, N. D., & Sethuraman, G. (1999). Validation of an instrument to measure voice-related quality of life (V-RQOL). *Journal of Voice, 13*(4), 557–569.

Jacobson, B., Johnson, A., Grywalski, C., Silbergleit, A., Jacobson, G., Benninger, M., & Newman, C. (1997). The Voice Handicap Index (VHI): Development and validation. *American Journal of Speech Language Pathology, 6*(3), 66–70.

Kahane, J. (1982). Growth of the human prepubertal and pubertal larynx. *Journal of Speech and Hearing Research, 25*, 446–455.

Kent, R. D. (1994). *Reference Manual for Communicative Sciences and Disorders: Speech and Language*. Pro-Ed: Austin, TX.

Linville, S. E. (2001). *Vocal Aging*. San Diego, CA: Singular Thomson Learning.

Mathers-Schmidt, B. A. (2001). Paradoxical vocal fold motion: A tutorial on a complex disorder and the speech-language pathologist's role. *American Journal of Speech Language Pathology, 10*(2), 111–125.

Mathers-Schmidt, B. A., & Brilla, L. R. (2005). Inspiratory muscle training in exercise-induced paradoxical vocal fold motion. *Journal of Voice, 19*(4), 635–644.

Orlikoff, R. F., & Kahane, J. C. (1996). "Structure and Function of the Larynx." In *Principles of Experimental Phonetics.* Baltimore: Mosby, pp. 112–181.

Patel, R. R. et al., (2018). Recommended protocols for instrumental assessment of voice: American Speech-Language-Hearing Association expert panel to develop a protocol for instrumental assessment of vocal function. *American Journal of Speech Language Pathology, 27*(3), 887–905.

Rousseau, B., & Branski, R. C. (2018). *Anatomy & Physiology of Speech and Hearing.* New York: Thieme Publishers.

Sapienza, C. M., & Ruddy, B. H. (2009). *Voice Disorders.* San Diego, CA: Plural Publishing Group.

Titze, I. R. (1994). *Principles of Voice Production.* Englewood Cliffs: Prentice Hall, pp. 279–306.

Titze, I. R., & Verdolini Abbott, K. (2012). *Vocology: The Science and Practice of Voice Habilitation.* Salt Lake City, UT: National Center for Voice and Speech.

Van den Berg, J. (1958). Myoelastic-aerodynamic theory of voice production. *Journal of Speech and Hearing Research, 1*(3), 227–244.

Van Stan, J. H., Roy, N., Awan, S., Stemple, J., & Hillman, R. E. (2015). A taxonomy of voice therapy. *American Journal of Speech Language Pathology, 24*(2), 101–125.

Ward, D. E. C., & van As-Brooks, C. J. (Eds.). (2007). *Head and Neck Cancer: Treatment, Rehabilitation, and Outcomes.* San Diego, CA: Plural Publishing Group.

Ziegler, A., Gillespie, A., & Verdolini Abbott, K. (2010). Review: Behavioral treatment of voice disorders in teachers. *Folia Phoniatrica et Logopaedica, 62,* 9–23.

Ziegler, A., Henke, T., Wiedrick, J., & Helou, L. B. (2018). Effectiveness of testosterone therapy for masculinizing voice in transgender patients: A meta-analytic review. *International Journal of Transgenderism, 19*(1), 25–45.

Ziegler, A., Verdolini Abbott, K., Johns, M. M., Klein, A., & Hapner, E. (2014). Preliminary data on two voice therapy interventions in the treatment of presbyphonia. *Laryngoscope, 124*(8), 1869–1876.

Acknowledgement: We would like to thank Dr. Gail Kempster who was the author of this chapter for the first edition of this book. We drew upon her organization and content for revisions for this edition.

Chapter 16 VDC

Review Questions

1. Which of the following is an extrinsic laryngeal muscle?

   a. Lateral cricoarytenoids.
   b. Mylohyoid.
   c. Posterior cricoarytenoids.
   d. Interarytenoids.

2. Which of the following is an intrinsic laryngeal muscle?

   a. Thyroarytenoid.
   b. Geniohyoid.
   c. Sternothyroid.
   d. Hyoglossus.

3. What are the three layers of the vocal folds?

   a. Cover, vocal ligament, body.
   b. Sheath, thyroid ligament, corpus.
   c. Coat, vocal ligament, body.
   d. Cover, cricoid ligament, frame.

4. Which portion of the vagus nerve innervates the glottal and supraglottal areas?

   a. Pharyngeal nerve.
   b. Internal laryngeal nerve.
   c. Superior laryngeal nerve.
   d. Inferior laryngeal nerve.

5. Which portion of the vagus nerve innervates the glottal and infraglottal areas?

   a. External laryngeal nerve.
   b. Recurrent laryngeal nerve.
   c. Pharyngeal nerve.
   d. Superior laryngeal nerve.

6. Which phonation type is best described as noise plus an air burst?

   a. Normal voice.
   b. Strained voice.
   c. Breathy voice.
   d. Glottal fry.

7. What is a modal register?

   a. The lowest portion of one's phonational range.
   b. The largest portion of one's phonational range.
   c. The highest portion of one's phonational range.
   d. The smallest portion of one's phonational range.

8. What term refers to the number of times per second the vocal folds open and close during phonation?

   a. Intensity.
   b. Fundamental frequency.
   c. Jitter.
   d. Shimmer.

9. What term refers to the average cycle-to-cycle change in amplitude from one cycle to the next?

   a. Intensity.
   b. Fundamental frequency.
   c. Jitter.
   d. Shimmer.

10. Which form of aerodynamic testing measures pressure below the vocal folds and is related to the degree of medial compression of the closed vocal folds?

    a. Airflow rate.
    b. Subglottic pressure.
    c. Glottal resistance.
    d. Maximum phonation time.

11. What term refers to the aspect of voice perceived by listeners?

    a. Fundamental frequency.
    b. Vocal intensity.
    c. Vocal quality.
    d. Symmetry.

12. What aspect of voice, assessed via stroboscopic means, refers to the regularity of successive cycles of vibration?

    a. Symmetry.
    b. Amplitude.
    c. Periodicity.
    d. Phase.

13. Which form of vocal fold excrescence is usually bilateral in nature and occurs at the junction of the anterior one-third and posterior two-thirds of the vocal folds?

    a. Polyps.
    b. Cysts.
    c. Nodules.
    d. Edema.

14. Which form of vocal fold excrescence is caused by an infection and may result in restriction of breathing and stridor?

    a. Reinke's edema.
    b. Muscle tension dysphonia.
    c. Human papillomavirus.
    d. Puberphonia.

15. Damage to which nerve will lead to difficulty with pitch control and reduced pitch range?

    a. Superior laryngeal nerve.
    b. Inferior laryngeal nerve.
    c. Pharyngeal nerve.
    d. Maxillary nerve.

16. What is the most common acquired voice problem in children?

    a. Vocal fold paralysis.
    b. Vocal fold polyps.
    c. Bilateral nodules.
    d. Sulcus vocalis.

17. The *CAPE-V* is a form of what type of assessment?

    a. Functional assessment.
    b. Perceptual assessment.
    c. Acoustic assessment.
    d. Aerodynamic assessment.

18. What is an effect of radiation therapy?

    a. Tissue fibrosis.
    b. Fatigue.
    c. Nausea.
    d. Hair loss.

19. What is the term for the permanent opening to the respiratory tract that can be found in the front of the neck following a total laryngectomy?

    a. Trachea.
    b. Stoma.
    c. Dissection.
    d. Esophagostoma.

20. What is a tracheoesophageal prosthesis?

    a. An artificial larynx that produces vibrations through the vocal tract, which is then perceived as voice.
    b. A one-way valve that allows air to pass through and vibrate esophageal tissues, which is then perceived as voice.
    c. A one-way valve through which a person who has a tracheostomy tube can redirect airflow, which is then perceived as voice.
    d. A cap that is placed at the end of a tracheostomy tube, which allows a person to have normal function of their respiratory and phonatory systems.

17

Dysphagia: Swallowing and Swallowing Disorders

BARBARA C. SONIES, PhD
R. JORDAN HAZELWOOD, PhD

(d) Reduced salivary flow also due to certain medications.

(10) Decrement in smell is pervasive and is found to be important for oral preparation phase.

(11) Taste may or may not change significantly, but it is suggested that the threshold for detection may increase, requiring the use of more tastants.

(a) Tastant: any substance capable of eliciting gustatory excitation.

▶ Dysphagia

Definition, Signs, and Symptoms

1. From Greek *phaegin*, meaning "to eat," and *dys*, meaning "disordered."
2. Difficulty moving food from the mouth to the stomach. Includes problems in oral manipulation, chewing, sucking, and suckling.
3. Signs and symptoms (Table 17-2).

Neurological Conditions

1. Stroke and Parkinson's disease are the most common neurological conditions that result in dysphagia.
   a. Other neurological causes include progressive supranuclear palsy (PSP), amyotrophic lateral sclerosis (ALS), myasthenia gravis (MG), multiple sclerosis (MS), Huntington's disease, postpolio syndrome, Guillain-Barré syndrome, dystonia, traumatic brain injury (TBI), and dementia.
   b. Any condition that impairs cortical function, cortical pathways, upper or lower motor neurons, or subcortical function can impair swallowing.
2. Classification of these conditions includes, but is not limited to, the following categories:
   a. Vascular: stroke, transient ischemic attack (TIA).
   b. Infectious: meningitis, postpolio.
   c. Traumatic: brain injury, surgical.
   d. Autoimmune: dermatomyositis, polymyositis, MS, lupus, rheumatoid arthritis.
   e. Neoplastic: intracranial or cortical tumors.
   f. Degenerative: ALS, Huntington's disease, Parkinson's disease, multisystem atrophy (MSA), dementia.
   g. Neuropathies: cranial nerves.
   h. Congenital, structural: cleft palate.
   i. Neurodevelopmental: cerebral palsy, Down syndrome.
   j. Iatrogenic medication or treatment-induced dysphagia (e.g., radiation, surgical).
3. Dysphagia symptoms.
   a. Impaired lip strength and movement and reduced lip seal needed to remove bolus from utensils.
   b. Tongue instability, incoordination, weakness, and rocking motions during oral or oral preparatory phases.
   c. Abnormal chewing and impaired rotary jaw motions.
   d. Impaired anterior-posterior tongue movements to prepare, form, or transfer a bolus over the tongue surface to the pharynx.
   e. Nasal regurgitation and/or velopharyngeal incompetence.
   f. Residue on the lingual surface and posterior pharyngeal wall.
   g. Bolus residue in valleculae and/or pyriform sinuses.
      (1) Look for unilateral residue in pharynx.
   h. Lack of epiglottal inversion.
   i. Impaired elevation of the hyolaryngeal complex.
   j. Laryngeal penetration or aspiration, backup bolus from the pyriform sinuses or dripping from valleculae.

Table 17-2

General Signs and Symptoms of Oropharyngeal Dysphagia
Patient reports feeling that something is stuck in his/her throat after eating.
Excessive coughing during eating.
Choking during eating.
Excessive drooling.
Wet, gurgling vocal quality after eating.
Poor lung sounds; rasping.
Dysphonia or loss of voice after meals.
Pocketing of food in the mouth.
Pills sticking in the throat.
Shortness of breath after swallowing.
Unexplained weight loss.
Fever or sweating following meals.
Pneumonia of unknown origin.
Voice changes (e.g., hoarseness).
Heartburn or indigestion.

k. Impaired duration (timing) or distension (expansion) of UES opening.

l. Impaired esophageal peristalsis and reflux into the pharynx.

m. Impaired sensation.

(1) Decreased sensory input for smell, taste, touch, or temperature for face, mouth, and the oropharyngeal cavity.

(2) Decreased sensation for oral and/or pharyngeal residue.

(3) Decreased or absent motor response from lack of sensory input for airway invasion.

(a) A spontaneous swallow results from penetration.

(b) A cough response results from aspiration.

4. Stroke or cerebrovascular accident (CVA).

a. Caused by vascular dysfunction (disruption of blood flow) leading to lack of oxygen to the brain and is the primary cause of dysphagia.

b. Brainstem strokes can occur with damage in the medulla or pons.

c. Bilateral damage to the pons and medulla may cause total dysphagia with poor prognosis.

(1) Pontine (pons) stroke: damage causes hypertonicity and delayed or absent swallow response.

(a) Reduced laryngeal elevation.

(b) Cricopharyngeal dysfunction.

(c) Slow recovery.

(2) Medullary (medulla) stroke.

(a) Nucleus tractus solitarius (NTS) or nucleus ambiguous (NA) lesions cause significant dysphagia.

(b) Longer pharyngeal response times.

(c) Increased duration for velar and laryngeal elevation.

(d) Longer response time for cricopharyngeal sphincter (UES) opening.

(e) If a unilateral stroke occurs, it results in a near-normal swallow with delayed triggering of pharyngeal swallow and pooling of residue in the valleculae and pyriform sinuses.

(3) Wallenberg's syndrome is a form of brainstem stroke causing pharyngeal phase problems.

(a) Due to lateral medullary infarct, caused by occlusion of the vertebral artery.

(b) Although unilateral, it causes bilateral pharyngeal dysfunction, dysarthria, vertigo, ptosis, numbness, and weakness of same side of the face.

d. Subcortical strokes.

(1) Milder symptoms, including mild oral and pharyngeal transit delays.

(2) Greater pharyngeal phase findings, resulting in possible aspiration or laryngeal penetration.

(3) Therapy directed at triggering pharyngeal swallow and tongue base movement is often successful.

e. Cortical strokes.

(1) Right hemisphere: more susceptible to pharyngeal problems, such as delayed pharyngeal stripping wave motion.

(a) Mild oral delays, longer pharyngeal delays.

(b) Aspiration before or during swallow due to incomplete laryngeal elevation.

(2) Left hemisphere: difficulty in the oral phase of the swallow.

(a) May have difficulty initiating a swallow (oral apraxia).

(b) Mild delay in triggering pharyngeal phase, which may result in aspiration or laryngeal penetration before the swallow is triggered.

(c) Better recovery of swallow function.

(3) New evidence is emerging to indicate that there may be bilateral innervation from the right hemisphere to explain the increased severity of right-hemisphere strokes.

(4) It is possible that the left hemisphere has more unilateral activation to the brainstem.

f. Persons with stroke usually respond well to dysphagia interventions, and since strokes often cause unilateral dysfunction, including lingual weakness, function can be rehabilitated (see "Treatments" section).

g. Multiple strokes usually cause more swallowing dysfunction and poorer prognosis for recovery of swallowing ability.

5. Parkinson's disease.

a. Dysphagia is found in approximately 50% of patients, especially those with disease progression.

b. PD is a movement disorder caused by dopamine depletion in the substantia nigra in the subcortical region.

c. Treated pharmacologically with Levadopa and Sinemet.

d. Primary symptoms include resting tremor, rigidity, impaired postural reflexes, and paucity of movement.

e. Swallowing abnormalities include lingual rocking, pharyngeal dysmotility, and pooling in the pharynx.

f. Silent aspiration (being unaware of bolus entry into larynx without attempt to clear airway) subsequent to sensory dysfunction of oropharynx is a major finding.

g. Tongue base sensory impairments may result in residue in the valleculae.

h. Penetration and aspiration are also noted.

i. Treatment focuses on sensory awareness and control of the oral swallow.

(1) Expiratory muscle strength training (EMST) and Lee Silverman Voice Treatment (LSVT) for voice may be helpful for treatment of oropharyngeal symptoms.

6. Progressive supranuclear palsy (PSP).
   a. A degenerative disorder of the CNS, caused by widespread neuronal degeneration in multiple systems in the brainstem and basal ganglia.
   b. PSP resembles PD but differs due to disturbed ocular motility and earlier signs of cognitive loss.
      (1) People with PSP are more aware of their dysphagia and have more coughing and choking during eating.
   c. Patients are minimally responsive to dopamine.
   d. Swallowing rehabilitation is helpful.

7. Amyotrophic lateral sclerosis (ALS).
   a. A severe and rapid progressive degeneration of UMN and LMN tracts, causing severe motor dysfunction, dysarthria, and dysphagia affecting all phases of swallow.
   b. Cognition is not impaired, and there is adequate retention of eye movement.
   c. Significant declines in respiratory function requiring total respiratory support.
   d. Patients develop severe dysphagia, leading to a need for nonoral feeding (usually percutaneous gastrostomy [PEG] tube).
   e. There is no known cure—dysphagia treatment is temporary and minimally successful.
   f. Family and patient counseling is essential in early stages.

8. Myasthenia gravis (MG).
   a. An LMN disorder in which conduction is impaired at the myoneural junction, due to a defect of acetylcholine release.
   b. Weakness that exacerbates with repeated effort is the primary symptom. Dysphagia occurs due to fatigue of the muscles of mastication.
      (1) Drooling, lingual holding of bolus.
      (2) Breathing difficulty, hoarseness.
      (3) Gagging and choking.
   c. Muscle strength evaluated by the Tensilon test.
      (1) Tensilon (edrophonium) blocks the action of the enzyme that breaks down the transmitter.
      (2) Tensilon is an acetylcholine inhibitor.
      (3) May also use EMG to evaluate muscle strength.
   d. Medical treatments include removal of the thymus gland (thymectomy) and use of medication to help facilitate muscle movement.
   e. Behavioral treatment includes energy conservation.
      (1) Small meals, increased frequency.
      (2) Modify texture so less chewing effort is needed for oral preparation.

9. Multiple sclerosis (MS).
   a. An immune-mediated demyelination of nerve fibers in the brain and spinal cord.
   b. Fluctuates and waxes and wanes in stages.
      (1) May be gradually progressive.
      (2) More common in white females.
      (3) Slight risk of other autoimmune diseases.
   c. Dysphagia occurs if corticobulbar tracts or brainstem pathways are affected.
   d. General symptoms are delays in triggering a swallow, reduced tongue base retraction, and pooling in the valleculae.
   e. Medical treatment by high-dose intravenous corticosteroids and beta-interferon has been proven effective.

10. Huntington's disease.
    a. An autosomal-dominant, neurodegenerative disease that can be detected with blood tests.
    b. There is a progressive psychiatric disturbance.
    c. Dementia will become severe.
    d. Choreatic movements: involuntary movements.
    e. Respiratory failure may be terminal.
    f. Oropharyngeal dysphagia appears with disease progression.
       (1) Rapid, excessive rate of swallow, due to poor impulse control, causing choking and gagging.
       (2) Buccal squirreling of bolus can occur, as well as premature swallowing of an unprepared bolus.
       (3) Holding the head in an extended position impairs the ability to swallow and causes airway compromise.
    g. Treatment for dysphagia is to feed patient in an uncluttered space, with seating that provides head and trunk support.
       (1) Place food and drink directly into the mouth, using single, slowly paced bolus feedings.
       (2) The purpose is to control impulsivity and rapid feeding rate.

11. Post-polio syndrome.
    a. Viral-induced degeneration of the LMN and brainstem.
    b. The syndrome is due to degeneration of existing motor neuron end plates decades after an initial polio episode.
       (1) Bulbar or spinal classification of the disease, with bulbar classifications having initial signs of swallowing difficulty.
    c. Dysphagia occurs in almost all postpolio patients decades after the initial attack due to overuse of remaining motor neurons.
    d. Dysphagia symptoms are found in all phases of the swallow.
    e. Because of oropharyngeal muscle weakness, oral exercises are minimally effective, while postural and dietary treatments appear helpful.

12. Guillain-Barré syndrome.
   a. An autoimmune disorder affecting the peripheral nervous system, resulting in demyelination of cranial nerves.
   b. Causes weakness and sensory loss of the oral cavity, pharynx, and larynx during the acute phase of the disease.
      (1) May require a feeding tube.
   c. Effects are temporary and recovery is spontaneous.
   d. Plasmapheresis or intravenous immunoglobulin are highly effective cures.
13. Dystonias and dysphagia.
   a. Generalized dystonia.
      (1) Difficulty coordinating respiration and swallowing.
   b. Neck dystonia.
      (1) Cervical spasmodic torticollis causes delayed swallow initiation and vallecular residue.
   c. Laryngeal or spasmodic dystonia.
      (1) Swallowing preserved.
   d. Oromandibular dystonia (OMD-Meige syndrome).
      (1) Premature spillage of bolus into pharynx with vallecular residue, difficulty in oral preparation. Sometimes is progressive but responds to treatment.
   e. Lingual dystonia.
      (1) Biting of tongue, expelling food from mouth.
   f. Treatments may include Botox injections or lesion surgery but effects remain inconclusive.
14. Dermatomyositis.
   a. An immune system disorder, which may appear in childhood.
   b. A serious condition in children, which appears as sun sensitivity.
   c. Begins as a skin rash of upper eyelids and periorbital region with scaly eruptions on knees, knuckles, and elbows.
   d. Weakness, stiffness, and pain in muscles in the abdominal area.
   e. Dysphagia may appear and can be treated with medication such as steroids.
   f. Prednisone or corticosteroid treatment results in improvement in a majority of patients.
15. Traumatic brain injury (TBI).
   a. The leading cause of death and disability in the United States for persons 40 years and under.
      (1) Primary cause is motor vehicle accidents.
   b. Two types: closed head injury or penetrating head injury.
   c. Usually causes memory and other cognitive impairments.
   d. Dysphagia can also be present.
      (1) Secondary effects may be due to intubation and damage to pharyngeal anatomy.
      (2) Fractures of spinal column may affect recovery.
      (3) Cervical spinal cord injuries, spinal cord fusion surgery, and effects of neck bracing may restrict swallowing.
      (4) Problems in laryngeal elevation, airway closure, and UES opening may result from trauma or surgery.
      (5) May see abnormal oral reflexes if damage is to the brainstem and may note many aspects of the complete range of possible deficits, depending on the damage to the oropharyngeal structures and the nervous system.
   e. Prognosis ranges from good to unknown, depending on location of injury.
16. Dementia.
   a. A cognitive impairment where dysphagia is not typical.
   b. Generally not associated with oral motor sensory deficits, except if there are findings of stroke, other brain injuries, or a neurological condition in addition to the dementia.
   c. If there is dysphagia, it will appear in volitional eating, transporting food to the mouth, lack of awareness of food placed in the oral cavity, and an inability to determine when to swallow.
      (1) Food agnosia: inability to recognize food.
      (2) Feeding apraxia: inability to remember how to swallow.
   d. Directed feeding and individual assistance during meals is often required.
   e. As cognition becomes more impaired, treatment may no longer be beneficial for swallowing or feeding.

Geriatric Patients

1. Treatment for geriatric patients usually focuses on tasks that center on bolus flow, posture, and diet modifications.
2. Fatigue is a factor in treating the elderly, so rigorous exercises are often not feasible.
   a. A specific treatment for elderly patients is used to increase muscle strength in the tongue.
3. Lingual strength retraining using the IOPI (Iowa Oral Performance Instrument) reverses loss of muscle mass and can increase muscle strength.
   a. Incorporates progressive resistance programs for lingual strengthening. New devices are being tested and appear to be useful for improving swallowing.
   b. *Sarcopenia* is the term for reduced muscle mass common in the elderly.
      (1) Often a major factor in causing oropharyngeal dysphagia in the elderly and in elderly stroke patients. The lingual strengthening devices can lessen the effects of sarcopenia.

Neuroplasticity and Swallowing

Central Nervous System and Dysphagia

1. Central nervous system.
   a. The central nervous system is known to have the ability to alter itself morphologically or functionally as a result of experience.
   b. This reorganization is an intrinsic property of the brain through which it is continually remodeled by experience.
      (1) Experience can take many forms, such as sensory stimulation, skill acquisition, or repetition.
      (2) Adjacent undamaged areas of the cortex or undamaged tissue in other cortical areas on the intact hemisphere may take over functions that were lost.
2. Principles of neuroplasticity.
   a. Use it or lose it.
   b. Use it and improve it.
   c. Specificity.
   d. Repetition matters.
   e. Intensity matters.
   f. Time matters.
   g. Salience matters.
   h. Age matters.
   i. Transference.
   j. Inference.
3. Neuroplasticity and dysphagia.
   a. The evidence is beginning to accumulate that some of the motor tasks, especially lingual strengthening, may induce neuroplastic effects on swallowing due to cortical reorganization.
   b. This is one of the major new areas in treatment and offers encouraging promise of recovery.
   c. The various treatments we use may affect neuroplasticity and thus improve the ability to swallow.

Head and Neck Cancer and Dysphagia

Characteristics, General Considerations, and Prevalence

1. Most cancers that affect the oropharynx, larynx, and/or esophagus will have a direct and negative impact on the ability to swallow.
   a. Due to the effects of surgical removal of tissue and fibrosis or necrosis of tissues after chemotherapy and/or radiation therapy.
2. The major post-treatment concern is swallowing and nutrition.
3. The prognosis is usually poor, with poor survival after 5 years.
   a. Most cases are smokers who consume alcohol and may not seek early medical care.
4. Risk factors for oropharyngeal cancer include:
   a. Sun exposure.
   b. Human papillomavirus (HPV).
      (1) The HPV vaccine given to children (boys and girls) ages 11 to 12 can protect from certain types of cancers.
   c. Chronic acid reflux.
   d. Laryngopharyngeal reflux (LPR).
   e. Inhalation and long-term exposure to airborne toxins.
5. Initial symptoms may include:
   a. Loose teeth.
   b. Red patches on mucosa or tongue.
   c. Bleeding.
   d. Oral candida or thrush.
   e. Ulcers.
   f. Ear pain.
   g. Feeling a mass.
6. Squamous cell cancers are the most prevalent.

Swallowing Recovery

1. Swallowing recovery is partly associated with past behaviors, such as smoking and alcohol consumption, as well as the type and grade of tumor invasion, secondary metastasis, and the amount of radiation used.
2. Surgery, radiation, and chemotherapy treatments can impair speech and swallowing function.
3. Late radiation effects include:
   a. Tissue changes.
   b. Changes in oral bacteria due to lack of saliva.
4. Mucositis, or inflammation and infection of mucous membranes, causes pain and may be a severe limitation on the ability to swallow.

5. Tumors occur indiscriminately in nerves, muscles, bone, and other tissues and can impair any and all aspects of swallowing.

Tumor Staging (TNM)

1. Relates to the size and location of the tumor(s): larger numbers indicate greater severity and poorer prognosis.
   a. T relates to tumor size and depth of invasion.
      (1) Tumor size ranges from T1 (smallest) to T4 (largest).
   b. N relates to involvement of lymph nodes.
      (1) No involvement of regional lymph nodes (N0) or involvement of regional lymph nodes (N1) is possible.
   c. M relates to presence of metastasis.
      (1) No metastasis present (M0) or distant metastasis present (M1) is possible.
   d. Clinical staging is determined from physical exam and imaging while pathological staging is determined from biopsy.
      (1) M1 would mean that there was metastasis in one other area.
2. Surgical reconstruction ranges from wound closure in small lesions to a need for a tissue flap from another bodily area to close the surgical defect to microvascular grafts for blood flow.
3. The amount of remaining muscle, innervation, sensation, and blood flow all relate to successful outcomes in dysphagia treatment.
4. Oral/dental prostheses are often important for swallowing rehabilitation.
5. Dysphagia evaluations should be conducted prior to surgery or medical intervention and after healing from acute effects postoperatively.
   a. Prior to surgery, the multidisciplinary evaluation should include a medical and drug history and a physical examination to determine if risks and symptoms of dysphagia occur.
   b. After surgery, the multidisciplinary evaluation should include determination of postsurgical effects, pain, swelling, radiation effects, xerostomia, and mucus production.
6. Treatment for dysphagia should begin after major healing.
   a. Dental evaluation is required prior to radiotherapy.
   b. The evaluation and treatment must involve a team that includes physician, oncologist, dentist, nurse, and social worker, in addition to the speech-language pathologist.
   c. Instrumental imaging techniques are used diagnostically to determine the site and size of the lesion.
      (1) CT scan of bone.
      (2) MRI of soft tissue.
      (3) Ultrasound of blood flow, soft tissue lesions, and structural functioning.
   d. Different surgical procedures will have varying effects on swallowing and may require different treatment strategies.
   e. Patients are cared for by an interdisciplinary health care team.
      (a) Head and neck surgeon.
      (b) Radiation oncologist.
      (c) Medical oncologist.
      (d) Speech-language pathologist.
      (e) Nurse.
      (f) Social worker.
      (g) Dentist/prosthodontist.
      (h) Radiologist.
      (i) Nutritionist.
      (j) Pharmacist.

Classification of Tumors

1. Some classifications are based on broad categories, such as oral, oropharyngeal, and laryngeal.
2. Other classifications are more specific to the anatomy and can include the oropharynx, nasopharynx, hypopharynx, larynx, nasal cavity, salivary glands, and esophagus.
3. Another classification system is specific to the organ itself.
4. Tongue tumors and glossectomy.
   a. Less than 50% of tissue removal typically results in only a temporary problem with a good prognosis.
   b. More than 50% of tissue removal will require more treatment.
   c. Treatments, including thermal tactile stimulation, lingual exercises, posterior bolus placement, and backward head movement, are usually successful if the main problem targeted is oral transfer to pharynx.
   d. In a total glossectomy, deficits include:
      (1) Reduced BOT motion.
      (2) Difficulty with bolus propulsion.
      (3) Reduced hyolaryngeal elevation.
5. Tonsillar, FOM, and pharyngeal tumors.
   a. Patients experience more difficulty swallowing as more structures can be involved.
   b. Anterior FOM may have adequate pharyngeal function.
      (1) If lingual suturing is used, the patient will have severe oral transfer problems and will require a method to transfer the bolus to the posterior lingual region.
      (2) Methods may include:
         (a) Head movement.
         (b) Special utensils.

c. FOM, BOT, and tonsillar resections will impair both oral and pharyngeal phases.
  (1) If the faucial arches are involved, the patient won't be able to trigger a swallow, resulting in residue in the valleculae.
  (2) Mendelsohn maneuver, sensory stimulation, and prosthesis are methods that may be used.
  (3) Problems experienced may include:
    (a) Increased oral transit.
    (b) Pooling in the lateral sulcus.
    (c) Delayed swallow, with premature bolus spillage.
    (d) Reduced pharyngeal contraction.
    (e) Reduced hyolaryngeal elevation.
d. If treatment is radiation therapy, xerostomia and reduced range of motion will result.
  (1) Radiation effects can appear months after the treatment (late effects), which will impair the swallow.
  (2) Treatment should include exercises for range of motion of the jaw and tongue mobility.
    (a) The patient may be unable to chew and will need to puree or thicken food.
    (b) Some cases will do best with liquids.
  (3) It is imperative to have the results of a modified barium swallow study (MBSS) for treatment planning.
6. Hypopharyngeal tumors.
  a. May present as a sore throat or a lack of symptoms until dysphagia appears.
7. Laryngeal tumors.
  a. Associated with a high risk of aspiration, due to reduced airway protection.
    (1) This will depend on where the tumor was located and how much of the structure was removed.
  b. Tumors can be categorized as indicated (reference is to above, at, or below the glottis):
    (1) Supraglottic.
      (a) The epiglottis, aryepiglottic folds, and false (ventricular) vocal folds may be resected.
      (b) 50%–70% of this population will aspirate and will benefit from supraglottic or safe swallow.
    (2) Glottic.
      (a) Treated either with radiation or surgery and can range from a hemilaryngectomy to a total laryngectomy, where all cartilages and pyriform sinus may be resected.
      (b) Small tumors on the true vocal folds may respond to radiation, but if the tumor is larger, treatment may be combined with surgery.
      (c) Most laryngeal tumors are glottic.

    (3) Subglottic.
      (a) The structures below the glottis and above the inferior cricoid cartilage border.
      (b) May include muscles of the cricopharynx and can cause difficulty in bolus transfer to the esophagus.
      (c) Rare in the United States.

Surgical Procedures

1. Laryngectomy: surgical removal of all or part of the larynx.
  a. Partial laryngectomy (hemilaryngectomy).
    (1) Will spare portions of the laryngeal structure.
      (a) Organ preservation is the main focus.
    (2) Spares hyoid and epiglottis with good swallowing recovery.
    (3) Compensatory techniques include tilting the head forward and rotating it to the damaged side.
  b. Total laryngectomy.
    (1) Removes all of the laryngeal cartilages and separates the gastric and respiratory tracts.
    (2) Aspiration is not an issue, but this method may produce oropharyngeal swallowing problems.
  c. To achieve UES opening, one must generate force with the BOT against the PPW, producing a pumping motion of the tongue to compensate.
  d. Pseudo-epiglottis is often constructed with a tissue fold at the BOT that can cause a problem and obstruct the pharynx or collect residue.
    (1) May need surgical intervention to correct this issue.
    (2) Scar tissue may form near the esophagus and further obstruct the area, requiring dilation for passage of material into the esophagus.
    (3) The patient may become a neck breather with an altered airway and reduced moisture, loss of taste and smell, and an inability to blow the nose.
2. Any of these surgical procedures where tissue is removed and a flap is constructed from distal tissue may cause sensory and motor changes to the swallow.
  a. The effect may be backflow of a bolus into the oral cavity.
  b. Reassessment on an MBSS is required to diagnose the effect.
  c. Tracheoesophageal puncture (TEP) is a placement of a small, flexible prosthesis into a tracheal stoma to prevent backflow and aspiration.
    (1) This device also serves as a voice prosthesis.
  d. Passy-Muir speaking valve has benefits for swallowing, as it helps restore sensation, taste, and laryngeal closure.

3. Because of the great variability among patients with head and neck cancer, every person must be evaluated and individual treatment plans must be developed based on the extent of medical treatment, remaining structures, cognition, and medical complications. This requires a team effort.

4. Specific treatment may use special feeding devices, intraoral prostheses, and compensatory techniques implemented to increase the range of mandibular opening (e.g., using a device such as TheraBite).

Aspiration and Penetration

Aspiration

1. Aspiration is the entry of food or liquid into the airway, below the true vocal folds, that eventually enters the lungs. It is best assessed on videofluoroscopy with an MBSS.
2. Aspiration can occur before, during, or after a swallow.
3. Healthy, normal people aspirate saliva during sleep, with no harmful effect. Aspiration is prevalent in bronchitis, asthma, gastroesophageal reflux (GER), and in neurological conditions.
   a. Aspiration pneumonia will occur only if the material contains a respiratory pathogen (gram-negative bacteria).
      (1) Microaspiration of oropharyngeal secretions that have colonized with bacteria may occur.
      (2) Anaerobic bacteria: gram-negative, staphylococcus.
      (3) Artificial airways and intubation often cause problems due to bacterial growth on the plastic. Tube feeding may neutralize gastric acid, allowing bacteria to colonize.
4. Aspiration may occur with PEG placement, due to wicking effect, impaired sensation, and collection of material on an inflated cuff when it is deflated.
5. Methods to detect aspiration may include use of blue dye or glucose monitors, which some believe are unreliable or unsafe compared to instrumental imaging techniques such as MBSS and fiberoptic endoscopic evaluation of swallowing (FEES; see "Instrumental Dysphagia Evaluation").
6. Suggestions to reduce the risk of aspiration in intubated or hospitalized patients include:
   a. Feeding in a semirecumbent position.
   b. Feeding with the cuff deflated.
   c. Aggressive suctioning.
   d. Supervised feeding.
   e. Not overfeeding.

Aspiration Pneumonia and Pneumonitis

1. Aspiration may lead to aspiration pneumonia (or aspiration pneumonitis) and increased health care costs. It is best assessed on videofluoroscopy with an MBSS.
2. Oral hygiene is the most important predictor of aspiration pneumonia, and studies have shown that brushing the teeth and reducing oral bacteria is especially important in nursing homes.
3. Aspiration pneumonitis (Mendelson's syndrome) is a "chemical injury caused by inhalation of sterile gastric contents . . . It differs from aspiration pneumonia, which is caused by inhalation of oropharyngeal secretions colonized by pathogenic bacteria" (Mark, 2001, p. 665).
   a. Occurs in patients who have disturbed consciousness, drug overdose, seizures, CVA, or during anesthesia.
   b. Increases in severity as pH decreases (<2.5) or if food from the stomach is aspirated.

Penetration and Silent Aspiration

1. Penetration occurs when material enters the laryngeal aditus or laryngeal ventricle at some level above the true vocal folds but does not pass into the airway.
2. The neurological response to penetration is a swallow as mediated by the internal branch of the SNL (CN X).
3. In healthy older persons, penetration is often seen; however, material is ejected from the laryngeal aditus before the swallow.
   a. This is not considered a sign of dysphagia.
4. Aspiration occurs when material enters the larynx below the level of the true vocal folds and enters into the subglottic space. The neurological response to aspiration is a cough as mediated by the RLN (CN X). In silent aspiration, the individual is not aware of material entering the airway and, therefore, does not react. No effort is made to expel material from the airway (i.e., the patient does not cough).

a. Usually occurs in individuals with impaired cognition, if there is a deficit in superior laryngeal nerve innervation to the larynx (causing sensory deficit) or if the true vocal folds do not adduct protectively.

Aspiration-Penetration Scale

1. In combination with videofluoroscopic imaging, provides a quantitative method to express the occurrence of penetration or aspiration. Furthermore, it includes enough detail and is sensitive enough to describe additional aspects of swallowing events that are clinically relevant.
2. The Aspiration-Penetration Scale:
   a. Quantifies selected penetration and aspiration events during a videofluoroscopic swallow study.
   b. Does not quantify all events, such as amount and timing of penetration and aspiration.
   c. Can be included as a component of a total swallowing assessment battery.
   d. Is used to demonstrate functional change and the reduction of risk.
   e. Is the most commonly used rating scale for the MBSS.
   f. Is used to describe single swallow events.
   g. Components.
      (1) Depth of bolus invasion into the airway.

(2) Response of the client to the bolus.
   (a) Bolus material completely expelled, partially expelled, or not expelled.
(3) Severity.
   (a) Level of bolus entry.
   (b) Awareness of bolus and response to material.

The 8-Point Aspiration-Penetration Scale (PAS)

1. Material does not enter the airway.
2. Material enters the airway, remains above the vocal folds, and is ejected from the airway.
3. Material enters the airway, remains above the vocal folds, and is NOT ejected from the airway.
4. Material enters the airway, contacts the vocal folds, and is ejected from the airway.
5. Material enters the airway, contacts the vocal folds, and is NOT ejected from the airway.
6. Material enters the airway, passes below the vocal folds, and is ejected into the larynx or out of the airway.
7. Material enters the airway, passes below the vocal folds, and is NOT ejected from the trachea, despite effort.
8. Material enters the airway, passes below the vocal folds, and no effort is made to eject the material.

Esophageal Disorders

General Considerations for the SLP

1. Although the SLP does not treat esophageal disorders, which are the responsibility of the physician (gastroenterologist), they need to be familiar with the esophagus and know when to refer a patient for further study.
2. With the assistance of a radiologist, it is important to conduct a modified barium swallow and screen the esophagus for reflux, obstructions, or other signs of abnormality. Since the problems in the oropharynx are often reflected by problems of the esophagus and vice versa, the SLP cannot ignore this structure.

Motility Disorders and GERD

1. Esophageal motility disorders are common in adults, especially in the elderly.

a. Gastroesophageal reflux disease (GERD) is found in at least 2% of the population and 30% of those with oropharyngeal dysphagia.
2. One symptom of GERD is heartburn, which may occur after a meal, accompanied by acid reflux.
   a. Meals buffer gastric acid so that gastric pH rises above 5.
   b. There is a small area, the proximal cardiac/gastroesophageal junction, where acid does not get the effects of buffering.
3. Fatty meals give more buffering of the gastric acidity than a bland or spicy meal.
4. Rapid gastric emptying may cause higher postmeal gastric acidity and predispose one to reflux.
5. pH esophagogastric monitoring can determine if gastric emptying correlates with acid buffering.
6. Gastroesophageal reflux (GER) can result from inadequate relaxation of the lower esophageal sphincter, abnormal peristalsis, and hiatal hernia.
   a. Common after meals (especially spicy or acidic foods) and when lying down.

b. Risk factors include smoking, obesity, alcohol, and medications for blood pressure.

7. Backflow: when stomach acid flows back upward into the esophagus, pharynx, and oral cavity.

8. Laryngopharyngeal reflux (LPR) occurs when backflow rises to the level of the larynx, which can then accumulate in the pyriform sinuses and spill over into the larynx, causing aspiration and hoarseness.
   a. Other symptoms of GER include regurgitation, hoarseness, throat clearing, choking, or gagging.
   b. Can be caused by inflammation or damage to mucosal lining of pharynx and larynx.
   c. GER is commonly treated with antireflux medications such as proton pump inhibitors.
      (1) Medications may relax the LES and promote reflux.
      (2) Tobacco, ethanol, dopamine, nitrates, morphine, diazepam, and calcium channel blockers.

Other Esophageal Abnormalities

1. Zenker's diverticulum: a pocket or pouch that forms when the pharyngeal or esophageal muscles herniate.
   a. This usually occurs near the UES (Killian's triangle) and is seen when it fills with barium on fluoroscopy.
   b. If the diverticulum is filled, contents may drain out and spill over into the open airway after a swallow.

2. Pill-induced esophagitis: an inflammation of the wall of the esophagus produced by a pill or capsule that has lodged in the mucosa.
   a. This is often due to insufficient moisture to transfer a bolus and may become painful.

3. Obstructions in the esophagus will impair flow of the bolus and may cause pain.

4. Achalasia: absence of esophageal peristalsis and failure of the lower esophageal sphincter to relax.
   a. On barium study, a "bird's beak" or narrowing is apparent at the LES. Regurgitation and weight loss are common.

5. Strictures and webs in the esophagus will obstruct bolus flow and can be diagnosed radiographically on a barium swallow of the esophagus performed by a radiologist.
   a. Strictures are treated with dilation.

6. Scleroderma: a motility disorder of the connective tissue that affects the smooth muscle region of the esophagus (lower two-thirds), weakening the LES. It is associated with increased GERD.
   a. Symptoms include heartburn and difficulty swallowing. Diagnosed by a regular barium swallow study. Only symptoms can be treated, not the disease itself.

7. Tumors or neoplasms of the esophagus can form in the esophageal lining and obstruct bolus flow.
   a. May be more common in males with a history of drinking and smoking.
   b. Squamous cell carcinoma common in 90% of esophageal tumors.

Medications and Swallowing

Side Effects

1. Many clients with dysphagia are taking numerous medications that can affect the ability to swallow. This is especially true for the elderly and those with neurological conditions and disorders. The SLP needs to consider all medications when doing a swallowing evaluation to determine whether symptoms are medication-related.

2. A result of medication is the reduction of salivary flow (xerostomia) to the oropharynx, which reduces the ability to mix a bolus and makes bolus transfer through the pharynx and esophagus difficult.

3. Medications can interfere with the oral voluntary phase of swallowing, as many have an impact on cognition or cause sedation, confusion, and reduced alertness.
   a. Drugs include antianxiety drugs, antiepileptics, anticholinergics, antihistamines, and antihypertensives.

4. Patients should be evaluated when their symptoms are controlled by medication or when they are "on."

5. Some medications cause muscle wasting or excessive muscle relaxation of the oropharyngeal muscles or the LES.
   a. Examples are antithyroid drugs, antacids, steroids, barbiturates, calcium channel blockers, dopaminergics, and nitrates.

6. A complete drug history should be performed from chart review and in consultation with a pharmacist or nurse.

Diagnostic Procedures

Case History and Clinical Evaluation

1. An interview with the patient and caregiver is the first step in an evaluation.
   a. An assessment of function can occur at bedside or in an office setting.
   b. A complete evaluation of swallowing should include the interview, questionnaire of patient awareness of dysphagia, chart review, oral motor and feeding assessment, and an instrumental swallowing study.
   c. The purpose of the diagnostic evaluation process is to determine a treatment plan and a set of baseline performances upon which to compare change.
2. Clinical evaluation will serve as the basis for the instrumental evaluation. It will allow differentiation between normal and abnormal behavior, levels of severity, risks for aspiration, and understanding of how a patient eats.
   a. Components include physical inspection of swallow mechanism, cranial nerve assessment, medical history, nutritional and respiratory status, cognition, oral sensation, secretion, taste and smell, lingual and labial strength and movement, velar sufficiency, phonation, and oral reflexes.
   b. Observations of body tone, motor function, cough, chewing, rate of eating, mealtime discomfort, alertness, and risks for dysphagia should be noted.
3. The Yale Swallow Protocol may be used as a clinical bedside screening tool for aspiration risk.
   a. Brief cognitive screen.

b. Oral-mechanism examination.
c. Three-ounce water swallow challenge.
4. The Mann Assessment of Swallowing Ability (MASA) is a standardized clinical bedside evaluation tool.
   a. Was validated for use with stroke patients. The MASA-C was validated for use with head and neck cancer patients.
   b. The MASA provides a risk rating for aspiration and dysphagia based on a weighted score system derived from observations from the oral and pharyngeal stages of swallowing and laryngeal function.
5. Functional outcome measures can be used to determine the impact of swallowing impairment on a patient's function.
   a. The Functional Oral Intake Scale (FOIS) is a 7-point rating scale that can be completed by a caregiver or health care provider using chart review or patient interview to determine patient's intake diet level.
   b. The American Speech-Language-Hearing Association's National Outcome Measurement System Functional Communication Measures (ASHA NOMS FCM) is a 7-point rating scale that describes function over time.
6. The impact of swallowing impairment on a patient's quality of life can be included by administering patient-reported outcome measures.
   a. Eating Assessment Tool-10 (EAT-10).
   b. Swallowing Quality of Life (SWAL-QOL).
   c. Dysphagia Handicap Index (DHI).
   d. M. D. Anderson Dysphagia Inventory (MDADI).

Instrumental Dysphagia Evaluation

Definition and Purposes

1. The instrumental examination is the objective assessment of a patient's complaints that allows the clinician to plan treatment based on observed signs of dysphagia in the oropharyngeal, laryngeal, and esophageal regions.
   a. The most commonly used instrumental procedures are the modified barium swallow study (MBSS) followed by fiberoptic endoscopic evaluation of swallowing (FEES). Also used are electromyography (EMG), ultrasound, high-resolution manometry (HRM), and less common research procedures such as scintigraphy or functional MRI (fMRI).
2. Purposes of instrumental evaluation.
   a. Provide objective, visualized, dynamic, real-time documentation of anatomical and functional (physiological) causes of swallowing impairment.
   b. Visualize bolus flow and control, swallowing timing, pharyngeal residue, response to bolus misdirection, and airway protection.
   c. Determine aspiration risk, effect of modifications in body position, posture, treatment strategies,

and changes in bolus consistency on ability to swallow.

   d. Signs that require instrumental assessment include fever, pain, excessive effort, coughing, choking, or difficulty breathing during or after swallowing.

     (1) Lack of cough or throat clearing with fever, pain, or difficulty breathing may indicate silent aspiration and require assessment.

   e. Findings obtained from an instrumental evaluation include:

     (1) Oral and pharyngeal transit times.

     (2) Hyolaryngeal, epiglottic, and lingual motion.

     (3) Aspiration, laryngeal penetration.

     (4) Movement of BOT, velum, pharyngeal walls.

     (5) Opening and relaxation of UES, esophageal motility, esophageal and pharyngeal reflux, and pharyngeal backflow.

     (6) Vocal fold function, residue in pharynx.

     (7) Symmetry of structures and symmetry of bolus flow.

     (8) Impact of compensatory strategies or implementation of maneuverers on efficiency and safety of the swallow.

     (9) Changes from previous examination.

   f. Selection criteria for instrumental evaluation are intended to match the patient's clinical signs and symptoms with the most accurate, least invasive, and safest technique.

     (1) Consider comfort, side effects, compliance, age, and medical fragility and behavioral factors.

     (2) Aim for a technique that gives a complete, dynamic, and pictorial image with the possibility of imaging from various positions.

     (3) MBSS meets all of the above criteria but may not be advisable for an infant, someone with limited mobility, or persons who have allergies to barium or who have a record of high doses of radiation exposure.

Modified Barium Swallow Study (MBSS)

1. The MBSS, also known as a *videofluoroscopic swallowing study* (VFSS) (originally the cookie swallow test), is the most complete method to assess oropharyngeal swallowing behavior for treatment planning purposes and follow-up.

   a. MBSS is recommended for oral phase complaints or for initial examination of a client with dysphagia.

2. Its major flaw is radiation exposure.

   a. Recent research shows that the MBSS exposes adult patients to very low levels of radiation.

   b. Clinicians should always work to minimize radiation exposure by following the ALARA (as low as reasonably achievable) principle.

3. Small boluses are used in 3, 5, and 10 cc sizes for liquid barium while patient is upright. If patient presents with severe dysphagia, consider using 1 cc of liquid per each consistency administered.

   a. Most protocols use thin, nectar-thick, and honey-thick barium, or pudding and a cookie.

   b. Using standardized barium products provides reproducible results and it decreases infection concerns.

4. Assessment is done in both the lateral and anterior/posterior (A/P) views.

   a. In the lateral view, the nasopharynx and entire oropharynx to the upper esophagus can be scanned to determine bolus transit and flow. The velum, tongue, BOT, epiglottis, FOM, and hyoid bone are seen.

     (1) Aspiration and penetration can be best viewed from the lateral view.

   b. In the A/P view, one can image the bolus flow from the mouth, larynx, and esophagus into the stomach.

     (1) A/P view can identify asymmetries in bolus flow and unilateral residue in the pyriform sinus and valleculae.

     (2) In the A/P view, barium can be detected in the laryngopharynx and trachea.

     (3) A/P view is recommended for observing the esophagus from the UES to the LES.

   c. MBSS is the best procedure to detect aspiration, penetration, swallow duration, and oropharyngeal and esophageal function.

5. Swallowing studies must be recorded on video or digital format for replay and frame-by-frame investigation of a swallow in real time.

   a. The MBSS exam should be performed at 30 pulses per second and recorded and reviewed at a rate of 30 frames per second to ensure diagnostic accuracy.

   b. This is required, as a swallow is a dynamic event necessitating continuous fluoroscopic imaging.

6. Cautions and considerations in reviewing results include understanding that an MBSS study is not a replica of a real meal, and barium may cause a unique swallow pattern. Some caution should be used in interpretation of the study if aversion to the testing situation or lack of compliance is noted.

7. Clinicians must wear protective lead aprons and thyroid shields, and remain out of the direct radiation field, especially females of child-bearing age. Clinicians should wear dosimeter, lead gloves and glasses, and thyroid shield to minimize radiation exposure.

8. The specific findings observed regarding swallowing physiology (function) in regard to bolus flow and observed signs and symptoms of dysphagia in relation to remedial postural techniques are seen in the following tables. These summary tables contain essential observations leading to remediation and follow-up of progress after dysphagia rehabilitation. The tabular information is derived from MBSS studies (Tables 17-3 and 17-4).

Table 17-3

Swallowing Disturbances Observed on MBSS

SWALLOWING DISTURBANCE	OBSERVABLE SYMPTOMS
Impaired epiglottic function	Laryngeal penetration or aspiration (MBSS, FEES)
Laryngeal penetration or aspiration	Coughing, choking, wet/gurgly voice, harsh vocal quality related to meals
Silent aspiration	None on clinical exam but seen on instrumental study
Reduced laryngeal elevation	Penetration, aspiration, residue, effortful or incomplete swallows
Impairment in vocal fold adduction	Penetration due to reduced vocal fold closure; may cause aspiration
Mass or obstruction in pharynx	Pain when swallowing; bolus feels stuck in throat

Fiberoptic Endoscopic Evaluation of Swallowing (FEES)

1. Also known as *transnasal endoscopy*, FEES uses a flexible fiber-optic scope (or more recently, high-definition distal chip) or naso-pharyngo-laryngoscope to observe the pharynx and larynx and vocal folds before and after a swallow.
2. During the swallow, there is a "whiteout" of light reflected off pharyngeal structures during pharyngeal contraction, obliterating the view. The oral and esophageal swallow are not able to be observed.
   a. The FEES is a procedure that allows one to see laryngeal penetration and pharyngeal residue.
   b. Using green, blue, or white food dye to color a bolus, such as applesauce, improves judgment of airway invasion.
      (1) The Yale Pharyngeal Residue Severity Rating Scale is a validated metric that quantifies how much residue remains in the valleculae and pyriform sinuses following a swallow.
      (2) The Boston Residue and Clearance Scale (BRACS) is a validated metric that rates the amount and location of reside and whether or not any spontaneous swallows are effective to clear the residue.
3. There is no radiation, and the equipment is portable. In some institutions, an otolaryngologist must insert the tube into the nares.

Table 17-4

Postural Techniques Observed on VFSS/MBSS

PROBLEM OBSERVED ON MBSS	POSTURE USED	RATIONALE
Reduced posterior propulsion of bolus over tongue	Slightly tilt head backward and then move head forward quickly.	Gravity and oral pressure change helps clear oral cavity.
Delay in triggering the pharyngeal swallow	Chin down in midline.	Widens valleculae and narrows laryngeal aditus; may present bolus entry into airway.
Reduced movement of the base of tongue	Chin down in midline or hawking and throat clearing.	Pushes base of tongue closer to posterior pharyngeal wall.
Aspiration during the swallow due to unilateral vocal fold impairment	Chin down with head rotated to close off the weakened side.	Forces vocal fold closure on weaker side.
Aspiration from oropharynx during the swallow	Chin lowered with a forceful swallow or hawking and throat clearing.	May narrow laryngeal aditus and clear airway; may aid in vocal fold adduction and hyoid elevation.
Residue in the valleculae or pyriform due to paresis/paralysis on one side of the pharynx	Rotate head toward the weaker side.	Closes off the weaker side and permits bolus to flow down the stronger side.
Slowed pharyngeal contractions	Side lying or forceful swallow.	May help force bolus through the pharynx.
Combination of unilateral oral and pharyngeal stasis (residue)	Head tilt and forceful swallow.	Permits bolus to flow down the stronger side.
Impaired laryngeal elevation and impaired UES opening	Mendelsohn maneuver.	Manual manipulation raises the thyroid cartilage and may relax the UES.

4. Although the effects are controversial, the use of a topical anesthetic (lidocaine) is common for insertion of the scope to avoid discomfort.
   a. Studies have not found any difference in outcome with and without anesthetic.
5. Special training is recommended for the SLP performing this procedure.
6. FEES is used for bedridden or immobile patients and for a bedside evaluation or follow-up assessment of swallowing.
   a. FEES is often a component of a swallowing work station (e.g., Kay Elemetrics).
7. FEES provides a good assessment of laryngeal, velar, and lingua-velar valving needed for a safe swallow.
8. FEES is unable to assess hyolaryngeal movement, bolus transfer, and oral preparation and cannot visualize aspiration during a swallow. FEES is unable to make measurements of swallowing duration and structures in motion.
   a. Copious secretions may impair the view of the laryngopharynx.
   b. Length of study must be monitored, as it is often uncomfortable to swallow with the endoscope positioned in the pharynx.
9. The study can be recorded for playback and later analysis.
10. Care must be taken to sterilize the scope and to use universal precautions, as oral secretions may contain bacteria or other infectious material.
    a. FEES is considered to be an aerosol-generating procedure and should not be conducted on patients with pathogens causing acute respiratory infections (e.g. SARS, COVID-19).
11. May be a useful biofeedback technique and has value to determine food management without radiation.

Fiberoptic Endoscopic Evaluation of Swallowing with Sensory Testing (FEEST)

1. FEEST adds sensory testing of the larynx using air puffs to the laryngeal ventricle as a test of ability to swallow.
2. This is based on the theory that laryngeal or airway protection requires a cough response and that this technique is able to assess the reflexive cough.
3. It is postulated that persons with stroke or CN X problems may be silent aspirators without a cough, and this test may be able to predict that event.
4. This is a technique utilized by otolaryngologists.

Ultrasound (U/S) Imaging

1. U/S is a safe and noninvasive technique used to view the oral and pharyngeal muscles and soft tissues.
2. U/S is dynamic and can visualize real-time movements of the tongue, floor of the mouth, hyoid, and larynx during swallowing using normal foods.
   a. Sagittal and coronal planes can be seen and various postures and swallowing maneuvers can be imaged. Tumors and masses can be monitored during treatment.
3. U/S can be used as biofeedback during swallowing treatment, as ongoing images are digitized and can be played side-by-side with normal views for comparison purposes.
   a. Bolus preparation and bolus transfer can be seen along with specific movements of the tongue tip, blade, and dorsum during oral preparation for the swallow and during the swallow.
4. Measurements of timing and duration of the swallow and movement of the tongue and hyoid bone can be made from digitized images.
   a. Hyolaryngeal elevation can be measured in conjunction with bolus transfer and lingual transport into the pharynx.
   b. Hyolaryngeal elevation, epiglottal lowering, and airway protection are interrelated and can be measured objectively with U/S.
5. U/S is safe to use repeatedly and thus is advantageous for infants and children who are high risk for airway invasion or who are poor feeders.
6. U/S does not image bones and has a limited field of view, depending on the scope of the transducer that is being used. Aspiration is not visible with submental imaging.
7. The larynx can be viewed and vocal fold adduction can be seen during phonation or swallowing.

High-Resolution Manometry (HRM)

1. Manometry is a medical procedure to view the pressure changes in the esophagus and pharynx during swallowing. It may be performed under sedation to view the gastric system or without sedation to view the pharynx and esophagus.
   a. Manometry has been paired with MBSS, called *manofluorography*, to visualize and quantify the relationship between pressure changes and bolus flow.
2. HRM can be used as an assessment tool to identify impairment in swallowing physiology and as biofeedback for effective interventions.

a. HRM can be used to evaluate pressures in the pharynx and the relaxation of the upper esophageal sphincter during the swallow.

3. Pressure-generated topographic plots show color-coded maps that relate swallowing physiology to various pressure sensors embedded in the manometry catheter.
    a. Real-time biofeedback allows outcomes of timing measures, effectiveness of maneuvers and strategies, and pressure-generating swallowing components to be measured.

4. In order to use HRM as biofeedback, patients must be able to follow complex commands, have normal anatomy, no recent head/neck surgery, no obstructions, be able to tolerate the catheter in place, and be able to generate pharyngeal contraction for measurement.

Other Instrumental Procedures for Swallowing Research

1. Scintigraphy is a radiographic procedure that uses radioactive tracer T99 (technetium sulfur colloid) mixed into foods.
    a. The bolus flow and location is detected by a specialized gamma camera, or collimator, and the radiation emitted from the bolus is measured.

b. Can detect bolus volume and quantify the amount of aspiration or bolus in the system well after a swallow.

c. Does not display anatomy or the cause of abnormal bolus flow. It is an excellent, but rarely used, method to examine aspiration and gastric motility.

2. fMRI, or functional magnetic resonance imaging, is a sophisticated radiographic technique using alternating magnetic fields to delineate soft tissues and blood vessels.
    a. Gives excellent tissue resolution and will most likely become more prominent when the issue of movement artifact is better resolved. At present, rapid movement, such as in swallowing, impedes the image.
    b. Three-dimensional MRI images can be obtained and will prove invaluable in the next decade.

3. Surface electromyography (sEMG) requires the use of electrodes placed on the submental or neck region to measure muscle activation, timing, and force.
    a. The electrical signal generated by muscle contractions of the thyrohyoid muscle and FOM muscles during swallowing is produced.
    b. The signal begins at the onset of the swallow, with a peak rise and descending pattern at the end of the swallow. sEMG is often used as a biofeedback technique for swallowing.

Treatments

Direct or Indirect

1. Direct treatments use food, dietary modifications, or postural changes and maneuvers during swallowing.
    a. The purpose of direct treatment is to modify the swallow by modifying food or feeding methods.
        (1) Modify posture, bolus size, texture, smell and taste, tactile stimulation; focused on swallowing strategies.
        (2) Biofeedback with EMG or ultrasound.
        (3) Includes special swallowing techniques (e.g., supraglottic swallow, Mendelsohn maneuver, Shaker exercises).

2. Indirect, or rehabilitative, treatments do not use food during the actual exercises. More than one treatment technique is often required if a client has both oral and pharyngeal dysphagia. *Swallowing is the most effective exercise to retrain the swallow.*
    a. Treatment is undertaken to retrain the swallow phases; to prepare, collect, and transfer a bolus

over the tongue into the pharynx and into the esophagus.

b. Purpose of indirect treatment is to modify the swallow mechanism and modify the patient without the use of food or liquid. Indirect treatments may involve oral exercises and those that simulate sucking, chewing, lip and lingual movement, and a swallow.
    (1) Can include sensory stimulation of the swallowing mechanism, including use of cold or pressure.
    (2) Sour lemon bolus swallow—a frozen mixture may be used before a meal to stimulate oral or pharyngeal sensory awareness. Studies have indicated that a sour bolus will trigger a swallow.
    (3) Oral motor exercises, or neuromuscular treatments, are indirect treatments often used to strengthen and improve range of motion of the oral, facial, lingual, pharyngeal, and laryngeal muscles as a precursor to swallowing.

(a) Consensus appears to be that these exercises have to be targeted to the deficit and be intense and repeated to have a lasting effect.

Supraglottic Swallow

1. Initially for head and neck patients with cancer to protect airway in supraglottic laryngectomies; used commonly for many etiologies.
2. Hold breath, take sip, swallow, cough and clear the airway, swallow again.
3. To protect airway before the swallow and to clear the airway of penetrated material that has accumulated during or after the swallow.
4. Super supraglottic swallow is different only in the amount of effort used before the swallow in breath holding.
   a. May increase anterior laryngeal motion and tongue base movement while aiding in UES opening.
   b. Contraindicated for coronary artery disease or recent stroke.

Mendelsohn Maneuver

1. Mendelsohn maneuver is a direct technique used during a swallow to manually lift the larynx and sustain a swallow at the height of laryngeal elevation.
2. Designed for those with reduced opening of the UES and cricopharyngeal muscle dysfunction.
3. Is difficult to learn and requires intact cognition.
4. Has been demonstrated to be effective with intensive use.
5. Recent studies demonstrate that it may be learned using ultrasound biofeedback.

Masako Maneuver

1. Masako maneuver is a tongue-holding maneuver where the tongue is held outside of the mouth. This is based on the observation that during a swallow, the posterior pharyngeal wall bulges forward and at the same time contacts the base of the tongue, which creates pharyngeal pressure.
2. Assists bolus flow through the pharynx.
3. It is not recommended to be used with food and has not been thoroughly studied.

Thermal Tactile Stimulation

1. Thermal tactile stimulation is also called *thermal application*.
2. Purpose is to trigger a pharyngeal swallow with use of sensory stimulation (cold) and contact (tactile pressure) to the anterior faucial arches and surrounding tongue and posterior pharyngeal area.
3. Useful for stroke and in persons with delay in triggering of the pharyngeal swallow.
4. It is used without food to heighten sensitivity so that the swallow can be stimulated when food is introduced.
5. Uses a cold, size 00 laryngeal mirror dipped in ice, making circular motions.
6. Studies vary in results, and use of this technique is controversial.

Shaker Exercise

1. Shaker exercise (upper esophageal sphincter [UES] augmentation) is an isometric neck exercise that has improved anterior laryngeal excursion and the anterior-posterior diameter of UES opening.
2. Found to improve UES opening and bolus flow in elderly and younger adults with dysphagia.
3. Consists of repetitions of sustained head-raising in supine position.
4. Considered a rehabilitative strategy. Suprahyoid muscle strengthening exercise that can be used to treat UES opening abnormalities.
5. Not recommended if cervical spine problems or radical neck dissection.
6. May be contraindicated if coronary disease.

Effortful Swallow

1. Effortful swallow found that when subjects were able to use a hard swallow with the IOPI, they were able to increase oral-lingual pressure and duration of maximum hyoid elevation and closure of the laryngeal vestibule. This was helpful in reducing aspiration risk.

Postural Changes

1. Postural changes are compensatory techniques that are used to improve patient's safety and ability to transfer a bolus safely into the pharynx.
2. The patient must be able to understand the postural change in order to use it independently.
3. Postural maneuvers involve the body or head.
   a. Fundamental posture: seated upright or close to 45 degrees with hips flexed to 90 degrees to achieve best bolus flow and benefit of gravity on bolus transit to the esophagus. Pillows or a wedge are used. Elevate head of the bed or wheelchair (postural techniques summarized below).

b. Tilt chin downward: if there is residue in valleculae or delayed triggering of swallow. Widens valleculae and narrows entry into larynx.

c. Turn or tilt head: rotate head to damaged side (left or right) if there is unilateral paralysis or paresis. This allows bolus to flow down stronger side. Reduces pharyngeal residue and aspiration risk.

d. Turn head to damaged side and tuck chin: useful if there is unilateral paralysis or paresis and slowed triggering of the swallow. Allows bolus to flow down the undamaged or stronger side. May be the most effective posture.

e. Tilt head back: lingual transit insufficient to move bolus. Will allow gravity to assist in bolus motion. May be useful in early ALS.

f. Side lying: for oral cancer or if risk of aspiration is not severe. Head of bed should be tilted upward at least 30 degrees and pillows used for back support.

Diet Modifications

1. Diet modifications should be instituted only after an objective swallow study to determine which bolus types are safe. Modifications can range from NPO (nothing by mouth) to a mechanical soft consistency or use of thickeners or special foods.

a. Thicker liquids may help provide sensory input needed to trigger a swallow if bolus is held in the oral cavity. Thickened liquids may be appropriate for those with poor tongue or lip control.

b. Moist foods with sauces and gravy are more cohesive and easier to transfer into the pharynx. Patients/caregivers may be advised to mash table foods and add sauces, gravy, melted butter, and mayonnaise to produce a single soft, homogeneous texture.

(1) Make sure that foods are not lumpy. Should be without uneven bits or coarse, crispy, crusty surfaces or peelings that are difficult to swallow.

c. Purees may decrease choking risk or aspiration in neurologically impaired who have most difficulty with liquids due to inability to contain a bolus on the lingual surface. Steam or boil fruits and vegetables and then puree them.

d. Use natural thickeners, nectars, tomato juice, cream soups, gelatin, hot cereals, puddings, and custards.

e. Increase protein intake with custards, shakes, and milk powder.

f. Use high-energy or high-protein foods when minimal intake or low appetite. Dairy creams, whipping cream, sour cream, cream cheese, butter, ice cream, whole milk, milk powder, yogurt, tofu, and legumes.

(1) Make sure person is not lactose intolerant.

g. Assess oral hygiene and brush teeth or clean oral cavity as needed.

h. It is important that the person is adequately hydrated. Water is essential for normal metabolism.

i. Work with dietary specialists to ensure patients are receiving appropriate nutrition and hydration to support recovery.

j. NPO recommendations for those who are critically ill should be ordered by a medical professional. Patients who are comatose, unable to swallow, who aspirate over 10% of all food consistencies or whose swallow is delayed for more than 10 seconds per bite should be considered for alternative means of hydration and nutrition.

(1) Feeding tubes will be needed for these individuals and require special nutritional evaluation.

k. Oral hygiene is one of the most important treatments for patients who are in hospitals or nursing facilities or who are infirm, elderly, and unable to take proper care of themselves.

l. Oral hygiene protocols need to be individualized to meet the specific requirements of each patient. This can be done through oral hygiene consultations with dentistry, nursing, and pharmacy.

m. Simple basic oral care is often better than complicated routines. A soft toothbrush can be used for most purposes. A suction toothbrush may also be utilized. Patients with teeth need fluoride.

n. Products containing alcohol are not recommended because of its drying effect. Products containing petroleum are not recommended.

o. Water-soluble products are recommended for hydration.

p. Product ingredients should match the pH balance of the mouth (5.0 to 7.0).

2. International Dysphagia Diet Standardisation Initiative (IDDSI). International, culturally sensitive standardized framework that describes eight diet levels for drinks (Levels 0–4) and foods (Levels 3–7) using common terminology and color-coding.

a. Levels include:

0, white: drinks—thin.

1, dark gray: drinks—slightly thick.

2, magenta: drinks—mildly thick.

3, yellow: drinks—moderately thick; foods—liquidized.

4, green: drinks—extremely thick; foods—pureed.

5, orange: transitional foods—minced and moist.

6, blue: transitional foods—soft and bite-sized.

7, black: transitional foods—easy to chew/regular.

b. Drink testing methods utilize the IDDSI Flow Test, which is a gravity flow test using a 10 ml syringe.

c. Food testing methods utilize a fork drip test, fork pressure test, spoon pressure test, chopstick test, and finger test.

Neuromuscular Electrical Stimulation (NMES)

1. A controversial technique that requires the use of electrodes placed submentally to provide electrical stimulation to the muscles of the neck.
2. Numerous studies have found inconclusive results with use of this technique.
3. It does not have positive results in children, progressive neurological conditions, or in damaged tissues such as those that are often the result of radiation.

McNeill Dysphagia Therapy Program

1. A systematic, exercise-based program combined with traditional swallowing therapy and surface electromyography biofeedback.
2. Patients improved functionally and were clinically better when these combined strategies were used.

Mealtime Strategies

1. Mealtime strategies for nursing home residents and patients with dementia can enhance the feeding experience and compensate for some of the behavioral and cognitive impairments in persons with dysphagia.
   a. Providing visual cues, improving lighting, removing distractions, giving one-step directions, strategically placing food on the plate, increasing visual contrasts of the food, and modifying flatware and/or utensils can facilitate success during mealtime.
   b. Direct feeding supervision; soft foods; small, bite-sized items; one item at a time; easily chewed foods; added smell and taste enhancement to bland or pureed foods; grouping by compatibility are all helpful.

Surgical Options

1. Surgical options exist to:
   a. Improve opening of the UES (dilatation, myotomy, botulinum toxin).
   b. Enhance airway protection (laryngeal stents, tracheostomy, feeding tubes).
   c. Improve glottal closure (injection of biomaterials in the VF).
   d. Close the glottis (a serious procedure called medialization thyroplasty) to all foreign material, terminating phonation.
2. These are used only if all previous dysphagia treatments have been proven ineffective and the individual is in constant risk of aspiration pneumonia.

References

American Speech-Language-Hearing Association. (2020). Coronavirus/COVID-19 updates. www.asha.org/About/Coronavirus-Updates/.

Bass, N. H. (1997). "The Neurology of Swallowing." In M. E. Groher, (Ed.), *Dysphagia Diagnosis and Management*, 3rd ed. Waltham, MA: Butterworth-Heinemann.

Belafsky, P. C., & Rees, C. J. (2008). "Esophageal Phase Dysphagia." In R. Leonard & K. Kendall (Eds.), *Dysphagia Assessment and Treatment Planning: A Team Approach*, 2nd ed. San Diego, CA: Plural Pub.

Brown, B. P., & Sonies, B. C. (1997). "Diagnostic Methods to Evaluate Swallowing Other Than Barium Contrast." In A. Perlman & K. Schulze-Delrieu (Eds.), *Deglutition and Its Disorders*. San Diego, CA: Singular Publishing Group.

Brush, J. A., & Calkins, M. P. (2008). Environmental interventions and dementia-enhancing mealtimes in group dining rooms. *ASHA Leader, 13*(8), 24–25. https://doi.org/10.1044/leader.FTR4.13082008.24.

Brush, J. A., Slominski T., & Boczko, F. (2006). Nutritional and dysphagia services for individuals with Alzheimer's disease. *ASHA Leader, 11*(7), 8–26. https://doi.org/10.1044/leader.FTR1.11072006.8.

Buchholz, D. W., & Robbins, J. (1997). "Neurologic Diseases Affecting Oropharyngeal Swallowing." In A. Perlman & K. Schulze-Delrieu (Eds.), *Deglutition and Its Disorders*. San Diego, CA: Singular Publishing Group.

Burkhead, L. M. (2009). Applications of exercise science in dysphagia rehabilitation. *Perspectives on Swallowing and Swallowing Disorders, ASHA Division 13, 18*(2), 43–48.

Carnaby-Mann, G. S., & Crary, M. S. (2010). McNeill dysphagia therapy program: A case-control study. *Arch Physical Medicine and Rehabilitation, 91*, 743–749.

Clark, H. M. (2003). Neuromuscular treatments for speech and swallowing: A tutorial. *American Journal of Speech-Language Pathology, 12*(4), 400–415.

Coyle, J. L. (2002). Critical appraisal of a treatment publication: Electrical stimulation for the treatment of dysphagia. *Perspectives on Swallowing and Swallowing Disorders, 11*, 12–15.

Crary, M. A., Carnaby-Mann, G. D., & Faunce, A. (2007). Electrical stimulation therapy for dysphagia: Descriptive results of two surveys. *Dysphagia, 22*(3), 165–173.

Curtis, J., Perry, S., & Troche, M. S. (2019). Detection of airway invasion during flexible endoscopic evaluations of

Wheeler, K. M., Chiara, T., & Sapienza, C. M. (2007). Surface electromyographic activity of the submental muscles during swallow and expiratory pressure threshold training tasks. *Dysphagia*, *22*, 108–116.

Wilmskoetter, J., Bonilha, L., Martin-Harris, B., Elm, J. J., Horn, J., & Bonilha, H. S. (2019). Mapping acute lesion locations to physiological swallowing impairments after stroke. *NeuroImage: Clinical*, *22*, 101685. https://doi.org/10.1016/j.nicl.2019.101685.

Yoshida, M., Yoneyama, T., Akagawa, Y., Nippon, R., & Igakkai, Z. (2001). Oral care reduces pneumonia of elderly patients in nursing homes, irrespective of dentate or edentate status. *Japanese Journal of Geriatrics*, *38*(4), 48–103.

Review Questions

1. Which portion of the pharynx contains the epiglottis?

   a. Nasopharynx.
   b. Oropharynx.
   c. Tracheopharynx.
   d. Laryngopharynx.

2. Which cranial nerve controls taste from the posterior one-third of the tongue?

   a. Trigeminal nerve (CN V).
   b. Facial nerve (CN VII).
   c. Glossopharyngeal nerve (CN IX).
   d. Vagus nerve (CN X).

3. What are the four phases traditionally acknowledged as making up the swallow?

   a. Oral prep phase, lingual phase, pharyngeal phase, esophageal phase.
   b. Oral prep phase, oral phase, epiglottal phase, esophageal phase.
   c. Oral prep phase, oral phase, pharyngeal phase, esophageal phase.
   d. Oral prep phase, lingual phase, tracheal phase, epiglottic phase.

4. How many pharyngeal constrictor muscles are there?

   a. Two.
   b. Three.
   c. Four.
   d. Five.

5. During which phase of swallowing does anterior-posterior bolus transit occur?

   a. Oral prep.
   b. Oral.
   c. Pharyngeal.
   d. Esophageal.

6. What is an impact of normal aging on the swallow?

   a. Delayed pharyngeal swallow initiation.
   b. Decreased lingual pressure.
   c. Increased occurrence of aspiration.
   d. Shortened opening of the upper esophageal sphincter.

7. Which muscle has the main action of elevating the posterior tongue to cause contact with the soft palate?

   a. Hyoglossus.
   b. Styloglossus.
   c. Palatoglossus.
   d. Genioglossus.

8. Which muscle flattens and broadens the tongue?

   a. Superior longitudinal.
   b. Inferior longitudinal.
   c. Transverse.
   d. Vertical.

9. In which neurological condition are lingual rocking, pharyngeal dysmotility, and pharyngeal pooling common features?

   a. Amyotrophic lateral sclerosis.
   b. Myasthenia gravis.
   c. Parkinson's disease.
   d. Multiple sclerosis.

10. What would be the most appropriate classification for a tumor occurring on the epiglottis?

    a. Supraglottic tumor.
    b. Infraglottic tumor.
    c. Hemiglottic tumor.
    d. Glottic tumor.

11. What is the term for food or liquid entering the airway, below the true vocal folds?

    a. Penetration.
    b. Pneumonia.
    c. Aspiration.
    d. Invasion.

12. On the 8-point penetration-aspiration scale, which level is labeled "material enters the airway, contacts the vocal folds, and is ejected from the airway"?

    a. Level 2.
    b. Level 4.
    c. Level 6.
    d. Level 8.

13. What is the absence of esophageal peristalsis and failure of the lower esophageal sphincter to relax?

    a. Zenker's diverticulum.
    b. Esophagitis.
    c. Achalasia.
    d. Stricture.

14. Which diagnostic instrumentation for swallow evaluation uses radiological means to assess oropharyngeal function?

    a. Modified barium swallow study (MBSS).
    b. Fiber-optic endoscopic evaluation of swallowing (FEES).
    c. Pharyngeal manometry.
    d. Ultrasound imaging (US).

15. Which postural technique may be best suited for use when a person exhibits a delay in pharyngeal swallow initiation?

   a. Right head turn.
   b. Head tilt.
   c. Chin tuck.
   d. Side lying.

16. What is sarcopenia?

   a. Muscle rigidity.
   b. Muscle flaccidity.
   c. Muscle hypertrophy.
   d. Muscle wasting.

17. Which swallowing exercise has been found to improve anterior laryngeal excursion?

   a. Masako maneuver.
   b. Thermal tactile stimulation.
   c. Shaker exercise.
   d. Mendelsohn maneuver.

18. Which postural strategy may be most effective if a person experiences insufficient lingual transit?

   a. Chin tuck.
   b. Head tilt.
   c. Side lying.
   d. Head turn.

19. When using the Functional Oral Intake Scale (FOIS), which level indicates a total oral diet with no restrictions?

   a. Level 3.
   b. Level 5.
   c. Level 6.
   d. Level 7.

20. Which swallowing exercise has been found to increase oral lingual pressures?

   a. Thermal tactile stimulation.
   b. Oral motor exercises.
   c. Supraglottic swallow.
   d. Effortful swallow.

SECTION V

Special Considerations in Speech-Language Pathology Practice

18

Augmentative and Alternative Communication

MICHELLE L. GUTMANN, PhD

AAC Defined and Related Terms

1. *Augmentative and alternative communication* (AAC) refers to forms of communication that either supplement or replace more conventional means of communication, typically referring to speech.
2. The position statement on AAC from the American Speech-Language-Hearing Association (ASHA): "Augmentative and alternative communication (AAC) refers to an area of research, clinical, and educational practice. AAC involves attempts to study and when necessary compensate for temporary or permanent impairments, activity limitations, and participation restrictions of individuals with severe disorders of speech-language production and/or comprehension, including spoken and written modes of communication" (ASHA, 2005).
3. AAC uses a variety of techniques and tools, including picture communication boards, line drawings, speech-generating devices (SGDs), tangible objects, manual signs, gestures, and finger spelling, to help the individual express thoughts, wants and needs, feelings, and ideas. AAC is augmentative when used to supplement existing speech, and alternative when used in place of speech that is absent or not functional (ASHA Practice Portal, Retrieved 12/09/2020 from www.asha.org/Practice-Portal/Professional-Issues/ Augmentative-and-Alternative-Communication/).
   a. *Important*: AAC can be used to support receptive and expressive speech, language, and communication disorders.
   b. Anyone who cannot meet their *daily written or spoken communication needs* through natural speech or writing is a candidate for AAC.
   c. People who need or use AAC, regardless of type or severity of disability, are also referred to as people with complex communication needs (CCN).
   d. Face-to-face communication (F2F): typically refers to spoken communication.
   e. Written communication: typically refers to textual output. May be printed as hard copy. Includes text messages.

A Broader Concept: Communication Vulnerability

1. Someone is communication vulnerable, or has a communication vulnerability, if due to a disease or disorder, he/she has difficulty expressing themselves or understanding information in particular environments or situations. Their communication difficulties can be mild to severe and can be due to sensory, emotional, physical, or cognitive (dis)abilities.
2. Communication vulnerability may also be influenced by:
   a. Environmental factors (e.g., lighting, acoustics, access [or lack thereof] to technology such as a pad of paper and pen, a tablet, or a smartphone), arrangement of physical space/environment.
   b. Social factors (e.g., policies in place regarding access to interpreters, lack of information availability in a client's language or dialect, lack of time or training to engage with people with communication vulnerabilities).

Communication Disorders Associated with Need for AAC

1. Developmental disorders (may include congenital disorders) include but are not limited to:
   a. Autism spectrum disorders (ASD), cerebral palsy (CP), many and various syndromes (e.g., Down syndrome), severe and refractory speech sound disorders, childhood apraxia of speech (CAS), individuals with intellectual disability (ID), some individuals with spina bifida.
2. Acquired disorders include but are not limited to:
   a. Brain tumor; cerebrovascular accident (CVA); primary progressive aphasia (PPA); spinal cord injury (SCI); traumatic brain injury (TBI); amyotrophic lateral sclerosis (ALS); Parkinson's disease (PD); multiple sclerosis (MS); Guillain-Barré syndrome; Huntington's disease (HD); head and neck cancers (HNC); other cancers that metastasize

to the brain and affect speech, language, or cognition; and cognitive impairment associated with dementia (e.g., Alzheimer's disease, frontotemporal degeneration).

3. Temporary versus permanent need for AAC.
   a. Conditions that may necessitate temporary use of AAC.
      (1) Intubation.
      (2) Prescription of voice rest.
      (3) Phonotrauma: trauma to larynx.
   b. Conditions that may necessitate permanent use of AAC.
      (1) Total glossectomy and laryngectomy.
      (2) Severe, chronic, or progressive dysarthria.
      (3) Severe and chronic aphasia.
4. AAC across the lifespan.
   a. AAC techniques, strategies, and systems may be used across the lifespan to support both speech and language in development, as well as in dissolution.
   b. Literacy skills are not necessary to use a variety of AAC options.
   c. AAC can be helpful for people with cognitive-based deficits.
5. Types of representation.
   a. AAC systems can be symbol-based, photograph-based, or orthographically based (i.e., text-based).
      (1) Symbol-based systems: curated, commercially available collections of symbols to represent vocabulary and parts of speech.
      (2) Photograph-based representation: often comprised of photos from individual photo albums; may include some stock photos.
         (a) Use of photographs as representation facilitated by proliferation of smartphones and tablets.
      (3) Text-based systems: entirely reliant on spelling.
         (a) Text (words, phrases, sentences) may be incorporated into symbol or picture-based systems.
      (4) People may use a system comprised of one or the other types of representation or a system that combines elements of symbols, photographs, and text.
6. Types of AAC supports.
   a. Low-technology AAC supports/visual supports.
      (1) Visual supports: the name of the category of low-technology visuals used to support communication, cognition, and participation in conversation. May include pictorial Likert-type scales (e.g., pictorial pain scale) and other graphic media. May or may not be paired with text.
      (2) Types of communication boards/displays.
         (a) General communication displays: display designed to support communication across contexts and needs. May be multiple pages.
         (b) Topic/theme displays: designed to support communication for a single activity or about a designated theme (e.g., a placemat type display for mealtime).
         (c) Remnant page: a single page, often in a plastic page protector or in a binder, is composed of remnants of events, places, or occasions.
            • Purpose of a remnant page: to evoke a memory and to serve as a focus for conversation.
            • Example: a ticket stub from a movie or concert, or a cocktail napkin from a favorite restaurant, or the program from a relative's graduation ceremony.
         (d) Pragmatic organization dynamic display (PODD): developed by Gayle Porter. PODD is both a tool for AAC intervention and a method for communication. May be low-tech (paper-based and laminated) or integrated into a high-tech system on a tablet. The rationale for PODD books is to include features that facilitate consistent navigation, supports pragmatic functions, rely on efficient and predictably associated vocabulary arrangement, have a system for adding vocabulary, and support various access methods.
      (3) Visual schedules.
         (a) Use pictures or symbols sequenced to represent a person's daily schedule.
         (b) May be used to indicate order of events within a specific activity (e.g., first/then or now/later; steps within a routine such as brushing one's teeth).
      (4) Visual scene displays (VSDs).
         (a) Photographs/pictures that capture action, are highly contextualized, and are personally meaningful.
         (b) Capture a scene around which there are many options for communication (e.g., commenting, answering/asking questions, conveying information, scaffolding social closeness).
         (c) May have text associated with specific points of interest in each picture.
      (5) Whiteboards/dry-erase boards.
         (a) Used for drawing or writing.
         (b) Lightweight and portable.
         (c) Can also be used to facilitate communication breakdown repair when videoconferencing.
      (6) Electronic magic slates.
         (a) Commercially available write-on/electronically erase magic slates for drawing or writing.
         (b) Tend to be thinner and lighter than whiteboards.

(7) External memory aids (EMAs).

    (a) Group of low-tech aids that may be comprised of some combination of calendars, whiteboards, memory books, notebooks, and sticky notes, for people with memory impairments, dementia, or progressive language disorders (e.g., primary progressive aphasia).

    (b) Used to cue memory for appointments, task completion, social engagements, and so on.

    (c) EMAs are helpful for scaffolding reminiscing and conversation about pictured events.

    (d) Memory book/life history book: a life history book is a collection of pages where each page contains a picture (or pictures) and syntactically simple text that describes the picture(s).

- Often created for people with dementia or other cognitive impairment.
- Pages might be dedicated to the person's family and siblings, another to graduation from high school, another about military service, another about their wedding, and so on.
- Purpose of the life history book is to provide a visual and textual compilation of a person's life events to scaffold reminiscing and conversation.
- Can be electronic (e.g., certain apps or talking photo frames).

7. High-technology AAC supports.

    a. High-tech versions of all of the above.

    b. Mobile tablets and specialized AAC apps.

    c. Speech-generating devices (SGDs).

        (1) Mobile tablets with specialized AAC apps.

        (2) Dedicated devices designed to support communication functions.

    d. PODD (see above, low-technology AAC supports) may also be available via mobile tablets.

    e. *Important*: anyone who receives a high-technology AAC system should have a low-technology backup system, such as a paper replica of layouts used in the high-technology system, or something entirely different. The AAC team doing the evaluation and implementation should include this as part of planning for an AAC system.

    f. Consideration needs to be given to emergency preparedness (e.g., a weather event where power goes out and may be out for an indefinite period of time), as well as for everyday situations that preclude use of a high-technology system (e.g., bath or shower).

The Law and Access to AAC

1. In educational settings:

    a. Free Appropriate Public Education (FAPE; US Dept. of Education, 2010).

        (1) Educational right of children with disabilities in the United States that guarantees the right to a free and appropriate public education in the least restrictive environment (LRE).

        (2) Guaranteed by the Rehabilitation Act of 1973 and the Individuals with Disabilities Education Act (IDEA, 2004).

        (3) Requires that children with disabilities receive support free of charge, as is provided to nondisabled students.

        (4) Provides access to general education services for children with disabilities by encouraging that support and related services be provided to children in their general education settings as much as possible.

        (5) Does *not* entitle one to a tablet or other specific type of device in school.

    b. IDEA stipulates that assistive technology, of which AAC is part, must be provided if it is required as part of a child's special education, related services, *or* supplementary aids and services.

        (1) IDEA states that the Individualized Education Program (IEP) team must consider whether a child needs assistive technology devices and services to *increase, maintain, or improve functional capabilities.*

2. In the community:

    a. Assistive Technology Act Amendments of 2004 (AT Act; PL-108-364).

        (1) Mandated assistive technology (AT) centers in each U.S. state and territory.

        (2) Goal of each center is to increase availability and utilization of AT services for individuals with disabilities.

    b. Many AT centers run active loan programs that include loan of switches, switch-activated toys, and other AAC equipment (e.g., tablets).

c. Under the Americans with Disabilities Act (ADA), hospitals must provide effective means of communication for patients, family members, and hospital visitors who are deaf or hard of hearing.

d. The Joint Commission's *Advancing Effective Communication, Cultural Competence, and Patient- and Family-Centered Care: A Roadmap for Hospitals (2010)* is a resource to help health care providers learn to communicate with patients so that each understands the other, regardless of cultural or linguistic differences, sensory impairments, or limitations on ability to communicate via natural speech. The document addresses ways to improve overall patient-provider communication. Examples of recommendations include:

(1) Developing language access services for patients (or providers) who speak languages other than English (including sign language) or who have limited health literacy.

(2) Translating forms and instructional materials into other languages.

(3) Addressing the needs of patients with disabilities, including those with speech, physical, or cognitive impairments, blindness/low vision, or hearing impairments.

e. Augmentative communication strategies and assistive technologies are requisite tools for many hospitalized patients.

f. Access to AAC is mandated for all patients: those who are temporarily unable to speak (e.g., intubated and in the ICU), those in trauma bay, or those who use AAC technology daily.

g. The need to support patient-provider communication has spawned development of new low- and high-technology AAC options for use in medical settings.

Core Concepts in AAC

1. Unaided versus aided communication. (See Figure 18-1.)

a. *Unaided AAC* refers to the use of only the body's axis to communicate, without external aids or equipment.

(1) Examples of unaided AAC include gestures, manual signs, gaze, pantomime, head movements (e.g., nod/shake), facial expression, and vocalizations.

b. *Aided AAC* refers to the use of external equipment to assist with communication.

(1) Examples of aided AAC include objects, pictures, line drawings, labeled symbols, and some type of SGD.

(2) Typically, aided AAC extends beyond the body's axis.

2. Types of aided AAC: no tech versus low-/mid-tech versus high-tech.

a. Aided AAC can be further subdivided according to levels of sophistication of devices/systems.

(1) *No tech* refers to any type of AAC device/system that is nonelectronic (i.e., does not use a battery and cannot be plugged in).

(a) Examples include use of symbol systems as part of a communication board or display, pencil and paper, whiteboards.

(2) *Low-/mid-tech* refers to simple electronic devices on which a limited number of messages can be recorded and played back. These devices may not have rechargeable batteries.

(a) Examples include single or multiple message switches, or very basic communication devices with a limited number of messages/cells, electronic message slates (e.g., Boogie Board).

(3) *High-tech* refers to more sophisticated electronic devices that support speech and written output.

(a) Examples include fully functional computers or tablets that run specialized software or apps for communication, SGDs.

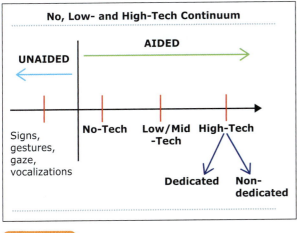

Figure 18-1   Low- and High-Tech Continuum

(b) High-tech options may have rechargeable batteries.

3. Dedicated versus nondedicated devices.

a. All high-tech AAC devices and some mid-tech AAC options can further be classified as either dedicated or nondedicated.

(1) Dedicated devices are devices whose sole purpose is to assist with communication, typically face-to-face communication, by providing speech output.

(a) Dedicated devices may be referred to as SCDs.

(b) Examples include some midtech AAC options and most high-tech AAC devices.

(2) Nondedicated devices are typically commercially available and support a range of functions in addition to speech output.

(a) Additional functions include but are not limited to access to the Internet, gaming, serving as an e-reader, and word processing.

(b) Examples include mobile tablets and laptop computers.

(c) Some nondedicated devices also support written output.

4. Types of aided AAC symbols: how messages are represented on an AAC system.

a. All symbols represent some type of referent.

b. Symbols vary with respect to both complexity and the degree of transparency relative to the referent.

c. Iconicity is a characteristic of symbols.

(1) *Iconicity* refers to the association between a symbol and its referent.

d. Symbol transparency varies along the iconicity continuum:

(1) Opaque: least transparent; symbol does not resemble referent.

(2) Translucent: more transparent than opaque; symbol bears some resemblance to referent.

(3) Transparent: most transparent with respect to referent; meaning of the symbol can be readily guessed in absence of referent.

(4) Real objects (e.g., a fork to represent "food/hungry"), partial objects (e.g., a drumstick to represent "drum/playing the drum"), and miniature objects (e.g., a mini-dollhouse to represent "house/home") may be used with no-tech AAC.

(5) Pictures (often downloaded from the web or a personal photo album on a mobile device), line drawings (black on white background or white on black background), and text (i.e., orthography) are most commonly used with no, low-/mid-, and high-tech AAC systems.

e. Depending on the individual's needs, an AAC system may be comprised of combinations of various aided AAC symbol types (e.g., pictures, symbols, and text).

5. Physical characteristics of aided AAC systems.

a. Aided AAC systems vary with respect to the following parameters:

(1) Type of symbols.

(2) Number of symbols.

(3) Colorization of symbols.

(4) Spacing between symbols.

(5) Use of white space between and around symbols or groups of symbols.

(6) Symbol size.

(7) Dimensions of display or device.

(8) Specifications of display or device (weight, size).

(9) Type of display: static or dynamic.

(a) Static: a display that doesn't change, is fixed (e.g., low-tech communication board).

(b) Dynamic: screen changes following user input (e.g., ATM machines). Input causes screen to change by branching to another page, another menu, or a specific set of applicable or predictable symbols.

6. Additional features of aided AAC systems: portability, adaptability, cosmesis, connectivity, customizability (PACCC).

a. Portability: whether or not system is lightweight enough to be portable.

(1) If system is not portable, it will need to be mounted on the person's wheelchair or walker, bed, or a desk or bedside table.

b. Adaptability: whether or not the features on a device can be adjusted according to need. Often used with respect to whether device supports alternate access.

(1) This is an especially important consideration for people with degenerative/neurodegenerative diseases.

c. Cosmesis: aesthetic appeal of device and whether it be modified (e.g., addition of user-chosen colored panels, covers, or color choice of device).

(1) Part of the appeal of tablets is they are commercially available and often nonstigmatizing since they are so commonplace.

d. Connectivity: whether the device supports connection to Internet, Bluetooth, and so on.

e. Customizability: whether features on the device can be customized to meet a user's needs and preferences.

(1) Includes customization of features such as word prediction, access method, display (e.g., background color, font size, cell size), range of synthetic voices supported, type of speech output supported (e.g., digitized vs. synthetic speech).

7. Access.

a. Physical access: how an AAC user physically accesses the AAC system in order to use it.

b. Direct selection: the user directly makes a choice on the system via touch, pointing, looking, or speaking.

(1) Touch: via finger, hand, headstick, mouth stick, stylus. Medium comes into direct contact with AAC system screen.

(2) Pointing: via finger, hand, or capacitive stylus. Medium does not come into direct contact with screen of AAC system but is directed toward a specific target.

(3) Looking: eye gaze, eye linking. Person using system makes selections via looking at targets. Eye gaze systems require careful calibration.

(4) Speaking: using speech-recognition software, person using system dictates what they wish to type.

c. Alternate access: required when the user cannot use direct selection. User must use alternate means to indicate desired target(s) and then use the device.

(1) Scanning: a method of indirect access. Choices are presented to the person using the AAC system. Person indicates, via predetermined signal (typically using a switch), when desired target is reached.

(a) Scanning involves the selection set, which is all of the messages, symbols, and codes that are available at one time to the person using the AAC system.

(b) Selection set: influenced by level of literacy, visual field constraints, and user's comprehension of symbols.

(2) Common scanning patterns used to choose from selection set. Scanning may be accomplished using a single switch or two switches. When using a single switch, it is used for both starting the scanning and making a selection. When using two switches, one switch is used to start the scanning, the second switch is used to make a selection.

(a) Row–column: scanning proceeds by highlighting each row until user selects row in which target is located. Then scanning proceeds by highlighting column by column.

- When desired target is reached, user activates switch to select target.
- Row–column scanning is the most widely used scanning pattern.

(b) Circular: device presents the selection set in a circle and scans item by item, until a selection is made. Simplest type of scanning.

(c) Linear: device highlights each item in the first row of the selection set, followed by each item in the second row, and so on, until a selection is made.

(d) Top–bottom: scanning proceeds such that the top half of the screen/display is highlighted followed by the bottom half of the screen/display. User indicates which half of the screen the target is in by using a switch. Once target area is selected, then that area (either top or bottom) is scanned using a row–column pattern.

(e) Group–item: scanning proceeds by group (e.g., color, semantically or thematically grouped items, or by quadrants) until user indicates which group the target item is in. That group is then scanned using row–column scanning.

(3) Selection control techniques: how a selection is made via scanning.

(a) Directed (inverse) scanning: the cursor begins to move when the person activates and holds the switch. When the switch is released, a selection is made. Useful for those who can sustain activation and release in a timely manner.

(b) Automatic (regular) scanning: the cursor moves automatically according to preset pattern (e.g., row–column scanning), and when person activates the switch, a selection is made. Useful for those who have difficulty sustaining pressure on switch.

(c) Step scanning: one-to-one correspondence between cursor movement and switch activation. Each switch hit advances the cursor one step. When the desired item is reached, the user stops activating the switch. Step scanning is helpful for learning to scan but can be very fatiguing.

(4) Partner-assisted scanning (or *partner-dependent scanning*).

(a) Used when person needing AAC cannot scan independently in any way.

(b) Communication partner presents choices to the AAC user, either line by line or group by group.

(c) AAC user indicates when communication partner identifies group or line containing desired target.

(d) Then communication partner points to or labels each item in the designated group or line.

(e) User indicates when communication partner reaches the desired target.

(f) This type of scanning is used with a predetermined signal such as a slight head nod or eye blink for "yes."

(g) Requires training for communication partner(s).

(h) Quite efficient when:
- Both partners trained in system use.
- System is organized to support this type of scanning.

(5) Auditory scanning: used when visual interaction with device is not possible due to visual problems (e.g., severe uncorrected vision problems, visual deficits postneurological insult, cortical visual impairment). Choices are presented to user auditorily, either out loud or privately via earbud. Person selects message to be spoken via switch activation and message is spoken publicly.

(1) The message presented to user is an abridged version or keyword related to the message. The message spoken publicly may be longer and more syntactically complex (e.g., auditory cue is "pizza"; public message is "I prefer pepperoni pizza").

(6) Switches.

(a) Scanning is accomplished using switches.

(b) Switches are pieces of hardware that open or close an electronic circuit.

(c) Multitude of switches on the market that meet a variety of user needs.

(d) Can use single switch or multiple switch scanning.

(e) When two switches are used for scanning, one is used to navigate, the other to make selection.

(7) Types of switches.

(a) Mechanical: require activation pressure; some "travel" or excursion involved during activation.

(b) Electrical: no pressure required; some travel required, provide less feedback.

(c) Pneumatic: sip and puff; use inhalation and exhalation for activation.

(d) Electronic: includes switches that work via activation of infrared, sound, sensors, or fiber-optics.

(e) Brain–computer interface (BCI).
- Does *not* require neuromuscular activation.
- Captures change in brain's electrical activity as intended activation.
- Invasive BCIs: electrodes placed directly in cortex.
- Noninvasive BCIs: recording sites at scalp or via magnetic brain forces (e.g., EEG, MEG).
- With noninvasive BCIs, must attenuate noise to enhance signal-to-noise ratio.
- As of this writing in 2020, BCIs are currently being actively researched.

(8) Switch site assessment: closely associated with number 7 above. Often conducted in conjunction with occupational or physical therapist knowledgeable about assistive technology (AT).

(a) To determine whether patient has a consistent and nonfatiguing movement that can be used to activate a switch.

(b) Must consider movement pattern: cannot be a movement that is difficult to perform or has the potential to create muscular or postural problems.

(c) Ideal switch site uses a small, isolated, volitional, controlled movement, with sustained pressure and controlled release.

(d) Switch site hierarchy: hands, head, mouth, feet, lower extremities, upper extremities, brain (BCI).

(e) Variety of rubrics for switch site assessment available.

(9) Type of communicator: emerging, contextual, and independent.

(a) Useful classification system for AAC users across both developmental and acquired disorders.

(b) Emerging AAC communicator.
- Has extreme difficulty communicating, using symbols, and responding to conversational input. May include apraxic component.

(c) Contextual AAC communicator.
- More functional communicators than emerging communicators.
- Indicate basic needs by pointing; can recognize visual symbol (e.g., photographs, labels, signs, logos).
- Is aware of daily routines and schedules.
- Does *not* have linguistic ability to independently initiate or add to a conversation.
- Can participate in conversation with assisted input to boost comprehension and with scaffolding for output.

(d) Independent AAC communicator.
- Comprehend most of what they hear without contextual support.
- Can initiate intentional communication using a variety of strategies and modalities.
- Know how to alternate among strategies and modalities to accomplish communicative goals.

8. Four main reasons for communicative interaction. (Light, 1989).

a. Communication of needs and wants.

(1) To regulate the behavior of others to get needs and wants met (e.g., "I'm thirsty" expresses to the communication partner the need for a drink).

b. Information transfer.
   (1) To share information with others; typically, novel information.
   (2) Does not require action by communication partner.

c. Social closeness.
   (1) To establish and maintain personal relationships.
   (2) Interaction is of primary importance.

d. Social etiquette.
   (1) To engage in brief interactions that conform to social conventions of politeness (e.g., saying "Good morning" as you pass a co-worker in the hall; saying "Hi, how are you?" as a greeting).

Communicative Competence for AAC Users

1. Four core competencies constitute communicative competence for an AAC user. (Light, 1989; Light & McNaughton, 2014).

2. Model is foundational for guiding both assessment and intervention.

3. Communicative competence for AAC users includes:
   a. Linguistic competence: knowledge of the linguistic code used by one's AAC system (e.g., symbols, print, icons). AAC user must also learn the language spoken/signed by members of the community so that they may receive and understand messages.
   b. Operational competence: the technical skills needed to operate the AAC system efficiently. This includes learning how to operate, program, and maintain the system. System maintenance (e.g., charging on a regular schedule) may be the responsibility of communication facilitators rather than the user themselves, depending on the user's physical ability.
   c. Social competence: skills of social interaction; the pragmatics of communication. These skills may be targeted directly in therapy to train the AAC user and may extend to training of facilitators how best to support the AAC user in social interactions.
   d. Strategic competence: the ability of people who use AAC to invoke and use compensatory strategies to circumvent the functional limitations introduced by use of AAC systems.
      (1) Examples: resolving communication breakdowns, using preprogrammed messages to indicate when a communication partner has misunderstood a message or when a communication partner should be patient while message composition is ongoing.
   e. Acronym for this model of communicative competence for an AAC user is LOSS (linguistic, operational, social, strategic).
   f. This model of communicative competence is applicable across the lifespan and cross-culturally.
   g. Cultural views of disability, and particularly severe disability such as that often associated with CCN, may influence the acceptance of AAC and the extent to which a person with CCN may achieve these four competencies, regardless of true ability.

4. Rate enhancement: strategies and techniques used by AAC users to accelerate message formulation and transmission. Cognitive demands for each rate-enhancement technique vary with respect to memory and learning requirements.
   a. Used to facilitate communication by attenuating the gap between speaking rate (typically 150 up to a maximum of 250 words per minute) and how quickly an AAC user can compose a message (approximately 15 to 25 times *slower* than rate of spoken speech, slower still for AAC users who use scanning).
   b. Types of rate enhancement.
      (1) Prediction: used in smartphone technology. System uses various algorithms to predict word or message completion based on the portion of the word or message the AAC user has already formulated.
      (2) Single letter: the probability of a letter occurring based on the previous letter (e.g., in English, *q* is often followed by *u*). Constrained by possible letter combinations/sequences allowable in the language.
      (3) Word-level: prediction of a constrained set of likely words, based on the word's frequency of use (e.g., in English, if the letters *q-u-i* are typed, the system may predict *queen, quiet, quite, quill*, in that order).
      (4) Linguistic prediction: prediction constrained and governed by the organizational patterns of the language (e.g., in English, if the user types "I" at the beginning of a sentence, the system presents only verbs that agree in tense with "I," such as "I am, I go, I want").
      (5) Phrase- or sentence-level: prediction based on units of language longer than a single word. Some high-level systems employ this type of prediction.

(6) Icon prediction: some AAC systems provide icon prediction whereby when one icon is selected, only the icons that can be paired with the original one selected are made available. Other icons are temporarily unavailable for selection. Icon prediction is a good learning tool so user learns which icons go together by decreasing the available selection set.

(7) Coding: used to represent single words.

  (a) Alpha word codes: created by either *truncation* (i.e., using first few letters of word, such as *comm* for "communication") or *contraction*, which often involves deletion of some or all of the vowels (e.g., *commctn* for "communication").

  (b) Alphanumeric word codes: use both numbers and letters to code for words or phrases. Advantage is that the same letters can be used across words or phrases; the number differentiates them (not used that frequently).

  (c) Letter-category word codes: the initial letter codes the superordinate category and the second letter is the first letter of the specific word. Example: if *F* = friends and *B* = beverages, then *FA* could refer to Adam while *FB* could refer to Brandon. Similarly, *BC* could refer to coffee and "BG" could refer to grape juice.

  (d) Numeric codes: arbitrary relation between number and word. Used when AAC user has very limited motor abilities and needs many options represented in a small selection set. The strength of this system is in the combinatorial power of words. Requires extensive learning/memory or creation of a reference glossary. Not used often.

  (e) Morse code: international system that uses dots and dashes in various combinations to represent a complete keyboard complement, including letters, punctuation, and numbers.

(8) Message coding: used to encode messages.

  (a) Many of the same strategies used for words can be used for messages.

  (b) Alpha-letter encoding: an example of this type of message encoding is *salient letter encoding*.

  (c) Capitalizes on knowledge of orthography and syntax.

  (d) The initial letters of salient content words are used to create the code.
    • Example: "Hello, how are you?" could be coded "HHY" for the salient words of the message.

  (e) Abbreviation/expansion (Abex).
    • Similar to alpha-letter encoding.
    • Use initial letters of core content words to formulate abbreviation.
    • Abbreviation can't be a real word; otherwise when the real word is typed, the system will insert the abbreviated message instead of the real word. Example: "I am tired" should not be abbreviated "it" as *it* is a real word. Rather, would need to abbreviate the phrase "ia" for "I am."

(9) Color coding.

  (a) Fitzgerald key system: left to right, color-based, semantic-syntactic coding system.
    • Example: nouns, verbs, modifiers, question words organized from left to right, with each syntactic category assigned a different color.

  (b) Originally used for hearing impaired population.

Organization and Layout of Communication Displays/Devices

1. Goals associated with organization and layout are to:
   a. Maximize efficient communication.
   b. Minimize effort expended in communication.
   c. Promote language learning, as applicable.
2. Organizational strategies: grid displays and visual scene displays.
   a. Grid displays.
     (1) Symbols, words, messages are arranged in a grid pattern.
     (2) Size of grid and number of symbols is determined during assessment.
     (3) Grid layout often reflects linear pattern(s) of written syntax (e.g., subject-verb-object [SVO] sentences).
     (4) Examples of grid-type displays include, but are not limited to:
       (a) Fitzgerald Key System (see above).
       (b) Topic boards.
         • Vocabulary organized according to topic, event, routine, or activity (e.g., going to school, circle time, work routines).

(c) Taxonomic layout: hierarchical categorical organization.
- Each page represents a single category related to a topic (e.g., people, actions, places).

(d) Schematic layout.
- Each page represents a singular aspect of the schema (e.g., getting to the supermarket, shopping at the supermarket, checking out from the grocery, going home with the groceries).

b. Pragmatic organization dynamic display (PODD).
(1) Developed to increase communicative efficiency across and within environments.
(2) Pragmatic functions purposefully added to every page.
(3) Words/phrases repeated as many times as necessary throughout the book.
(4) May be used via direct selection or via partner-assisted scanning.

c. Visual scene displays (VSDs).
(1) Highly contextualized and personally meaningful pictures that capture environmental and action/interaction aspects of the context.
(2) Used for people across levels of impairment, from children developing language to adults with acquired communication disorders (e.g., aphasia, dementia).

(3) Involve "hot spots" where vocabulary/messages are programmed for use by person with CCN.
(4) Some VSDs have navigational buttons around the main picture for ease of access to other pages/menus. This is referred to a navigational ring.
(5) When programmed thoughtfully, VSDs can be used for rate enhancement.
(6) Video clips can be embedded in VSDs to highlight specific action sequence.
(7) VSDs widely used for people with aphasia and for language development and for people with ASD.

3. Alphabet displays.
a. QWERTY or ABCD layout.
b. Frequency of use layout.
(1) Letters that are more frequently used are arranged for easiest access.
(2) These layouts vary according to language.
c. Vowels on the left, with consonants following. For example:

A B C D
E F G H
I J K L M N
O P Q R S T
U V W X Y Z

Assessment in AAC

1. Anyone can be a candidate for AAC.
2. Do not need special skills already in place to be eligible for assessment.
3. Central to the entire assessment enterprise is the person with CCN.
   a. Identified significant others (e.g., family members, spouse, primary communication facilitator) also play an important role.
4. Importance of team in assessment in AAC.
   a. Due to the multitude of skills needed for use of AAC, the input of professionals of differing backgrounds is necessary for thorough assessment.
   b. Team composition will depend on needs of person with CCN.
   c. The types of professionals involved in assessment for AAC may include, but are not limited to, speech-language pathologist, physical therapist, occupational therapist, teacher, special education teacher or resource person, biomedical engineer, vocational counselor, and assistive technology specialist.

d. All participants in the assessment process must share information regarding findings and recommendations so that a comprehensive plan can be made.
5. Identify purpose for AAC. Is it to support:
   a. Language development, communication, literacy acquisition, employment.
   b. Specify priorities for what AAC will do that the person with CCN cannot accomplish at present.
6. Skills/status/domains to be assessed (as indicated).
   a. Cognition, language (receptive and expressive), speech intelligibility (if appropriate), sensory-perceptual status (e.g., vision and hearing), physical/health status, seating and mobility/motor abilities, literacy skills.
7. Phases of assessment.
   a. Beukelman and Mirenda (2020) proposed a four-phase framework for assessment:
   (1) Phase 1: referral for AAC assessment.
   (2) Phase 2: initial assessment and intervention for today.

(a) Identify current communication skills and abilities.

(b) Identify what person wants and needs to be able to do in terms of communication.

(3) Phase 3: detailed assessment for tomorrow.

(4) Phase 4: follow-up assessment and maintenance.

b. This is an iterative process and is informed by the person with CCN's goals, needs, wants, and medical diagnosis.

8. Model of assessment.

a. Participation model (Beukelman & Mirenda, 2020).

(1) A systematic approach to assessment and intervention.

(2) Based on participation requirements of routines, activities, and interests of typically developing same-age peers of person with CCN.

(3) Conduct a participation inventory of routines, activities, interests (e.g., home, school, work, recreation, religious activities, etc.).

(4) Identify participation patterns of typically developing same-age peers of person with CCN—involves careful task analysis.

(5) Assess how well person with CCN is currently able to participate in desired task/routine/activity.

(6) Identify participation barriers: two main types:

(a) Opportunity barriers.
- Imposed by forces external to the person with CCN.
- Cannot be eliminated by provision of AAC.

(b) Access barriers.
- Imposed by limitations of individual with CCN or their current communication system.

(7) Types of opportunity barriers.

(a) Policy barriers: based on legislative decisions that govern various environments.
- Examples: restrictions on bringing AAC equipment into the ICU setting; person with CCN being placed in a nonmainstream class at school.

(b) Practice barriers: procedures or conventions that have become commonplace in the environment.
- Examples: a school district barring a person with CCN from taking home AAC system over the weekend or over the summer.

(c) Knowledge barriers: caused by a lack of information on the part of the person with CCN's facilitator/team members that result in decreased participation opportunities for person with CCN.
- Example: lack of familiarity with carry cases/second skins for AAC systems to protect from the elements. This bars the person with CCN from participating in outdoor activities with their AAC system.

(d) Skill barriers: caused by facilitator difficulty implementing AAC technique or strategy.
- Example: despite training, communication facilitator cannot adequately perform partner-assisted scanning.

(e) Attitude barriers: caused by incorrect, outdated, outmoded, and discriminatory attitudes regarding the abilities of people with CCN.
- Example: a teacher who implicitly conveys lower expectations of a student with CCN than for other students in the class.

(8) Access barriers.

(a) Involve the capabilities, attitudes, and resource limitations, perceived or otherwise, of the person with CCN versus being externally imposed by society.
- Example: a person with a neurodegenerative disease stops socializing due to changes in their ability to communicate. That person's friends want to maintain the friendship but person with CCN believes they can't participate in social activities given the changes in their functional status.

9. Assessment tools.

a. No standardized assessment batteries in AAC due to heterogeneity of populations that require AAC.

b. No norm-referenced tests for the same reason as previous.

c. Can administer standardized tests in nonstandardized ways (e.g., by varying response mode, altering instructions and time limitations, etc.) as long as it is reported that the test was administered in this way and norms were not used.

d. Criterion referenced tests and inventories are commercially available.

e. Examples of AAC skill inventories include but are not limited to:

(1) *Social networks* (Blackstone & Hunt-Berg, 2003): a communication inventory for individuals with complex communication needs and their communication partners.

(a) Comprehensive inventory of communication-related behaviors and technology use as it relates to people with CCN and their communication partners.

(b) Comes with a manual detailing how inventory should be administered.

(2) *Augmentative & Alternative Communication Profile: A Continuum of Learning* (Kovach, 2009).

(a) Based on Light's model of communicative competence.

(b) Inventories to explore skill sets across all four competencies.

(c) Provides mechanism for record-keeping across initial and follow-up assessments.

(3) Symbol assessment (e.g., *Tangible Symbol Systems*, Rowland & Schweigert, 2000).

　(a) Provides a protocol for conducting a basic symbol assessment.

　(b) Symbol assessment is especially critical to AAC assessment for persons who are nonliterate.

　(c) Typically involve 10 items that are very familiar to the person with CCN.

　(d) Also involves colored photos, black and white photos, line drawings, line drawings that are color embellished, and written words.

　(e) Different-sized versions of all the aforementioned types of representation are trialed during a symbol assessment.

　(f) Goals of symbol assessment are to determine:

　　• Most abstract level of symbol/representation that person with CCN can reliably use.

　　• Smallest size of symbol/representation that person with CCN can reliably use.

　(g) See Glennen & DeCoste (1997) or Beukelman & Mirenda (2020) references for full description of how to conduct symbol assessment.

(4) *Test of Aided-Communication Symbol Performance* (TASP; Bruno, 2007).

　(a) Commercially available test to assess symbolic skills. Results may be helpful in:

　　• Designing communication boards and establishing AAC intervention goals.

　　• Assesses the following skills with picture symbols: symbol size and number, grammatical encoding, categorization, and syntactic performance.

10. Feature matching: a critical component of assessment.

a. Process by which the skills and needs of the person with CCN are matched against the features of various AAC systems and AAC apps.

b. Iterative process while a system of best fit is found.

c. Can be used for both low- and high-tech AAC options, hardware, software, apps.

　(1) Example: a child with CP is seen for AAC assessment. After the team has conducted their assessment, it is determined that this child is not a direct selector and so options that support *scanning* must be considered. Further, child is *not yet literate* but that is an educational goal, so the AAC system must support both symbols and access to text/keyboard.

　(2) Example: a literate adult with ALS who is ambulatory and can use their hands wants a lightweight, portable AAC aid because his/her speech is severely dysarthric.

　(3) After careful assessment across domains of function (e.g., cognition, sensory status, motor ability, speech and language), the team determines that this person is presently a *direct selector*. They proceed to identify options that meet the person's current needs (i.e., are portable, lightweight, allow direct selection and ready access to speech output and text), knowing that as the disease runs its course, the feature match will likely change, which will necessitate changes in the AAC system. Initially, this person may use a tablet with communication apps (e.g., text-to-speech). When the person's mobility and physical access needs change, they may continue to use the system as long as it can be mounted on a wheelchair and support access via eye gaze.

d. Feature matching with apps. See Figure 18-2.

　(1) Many feature-matching rubrics exist for apps.

　(2) Compare features of apps.

　(3) Example: for text-to-speech-based apps, the following features would be compared:

　　(a) Availability of word prediction, ability to customize prediction, ability to customize display, storage for phrases/messages, types of voices, compatibility with messaging functions (e.g., texting, email), supports alternate access, and so on.

11. System selection.

a. Culmination of feature-matching process, typically resulting in a few options that have been identified as best meeting person's needs.

b. When possible, arranging for a short-term loan of the recommended system for person with CCN to try in real (e.g., home, work) versus clinic environments before a final decision is made.

c. If short-term loan or rental is not feasible, careful review of systems, components, training, and supports necessary for system implementation can help guide decision-making.

12. Funding of AAC systems.

a. Some insurance policies cover AAC systems/SGDs as part of durable medical equipment (DME).

b. Insurance coverage is highly variable and is constantly changing.

c. Some SGDs that support connectivity (i.e., Internet) may not be funded in their open (i.e., connected) state.

d. Medicare funding of AAC devices is variable.

e. Check the website of the device vendor/manufacturer for updates on funding issues.

Example: Patient with bulbar-onset ALS who is still fully independently ambulatory and has use of both arms and hands. Patient's speech is very mildly affected at present—mostly with fatigue and exertion. Patient wants an iOS-based system to use at work or at home, as necessary. Patient is highly literate and would like to explore text-to-speech (TTS) options. This table outlines just a few basic features of AAC TTS apps that may be considered during this hypothetical assessment.

FEATURES	APP A	APP B	APP C	APP D
Voice options available	✗	✗	✓	✓
QWERTY keyboard	✓	✓	✓	✓
Keyboard keys can be rearranged/reassigned	✗	✗	✗	✓
Word prediction (customizable?)	✓	✓	✓	✓
Linguistic prediction (customizable?)	✗	✓	✓	✓
Phrase storage	✗	Only in premium version	✓	✓
Adjustable fonts	✗	Only in premium version	✓	✓
Adjustable rate of speech	✓	Only in premium version	✓	✓
Cost	Free	Free/Premium version is $$	$$$	$$$

App A doesn't have many of the features patient wants. App B has more of the desired features but the base version, which is free, does not support most of the features patient wants. App C has most, and App D has all of the features desired by patient. Cost is comparable for Apps C and D. Since App D supports all the desired features (in this hypothetical situation), it's likely that App D would be the choice.

Figure 18-2 Sample Feature Matching Table for Text-to-Speech Apps

Intervention in AAC

1. Once assessment is complete, team focus shifts to the process of intervention, which may entail any or all of the following evidence-based techniques and steps.
   a. Vocabulary selection.
      (1) Critical component of AAC intervention.
      (2) System usage often hinges on having age-, gender-, situational-, and socially appropriate vocabulary.
      (3) Vocabulary (both expressive and receptive) information can be collected via informants who know person with CCN across contexts (e.g., family, friends, teachers, clergy, coaches can use vocabulary inventories to collect this information).
         (a) Often SLP will collate information from all sources.
         (b) Create vocabulary that will go on person with CCN's system.
   b. Two main types of vocabulary in AAC systems.
      (1) Core.
         (a) High-frequency words that are highly functional for the individual.
         (b) Comprised of verbs, pronouns, adjectives, adverbs, and function words.
         (c) Used for approximately 80% of communication.
         (d) Note: few nouns in core vocabulary.
      (2) Fringe: words (often nouns) and phrases that are specific to a particular topic/activity/individual; often are content-rich and not used that frequently.
   c. Vocabulary must be updated regularly.
   d. Additional types of vocabulary to consider:
      (1) Developmental vocabulary: words/phrases that the person with CCN does not yet know but are included on system to encourage vocabulary growth.
      (2) Coverage vocabulary: those words/phrases that the person with CCN needs to communicate essential messages. Typically relate to basic needs and are context- and age-dependent.
2. Refinement of symbol selection and placement on AAC system.
   a. Decisions regarding symbol placement informed by:
      (1) Location, location, location!
         (a) With respect to person with CCN's physical and visual access.

b. Relative importance of symbol/vocabulary item.
  (1) High-frequency, high-priority items should be placed where person with CCN can most readily access them.
  (2) Dimensions of system.
    (a) Low-tech: are there pages in a book? Or on a lap tray on wheelchair?
    (b) High-tech: can user navigate between pages/levels?
3. Training person with CCN in system use.
  a. Relates to operational competence (i.e., use and maintenance of AAC system).
  b. Person with CCN should be trained on system usage and maintenance to the fullest extent of their capability.
  c. Often a facilitator may perform maintenance such as charging and cleaning a device, although person with CCN may direct these functions with appropriate messages (e.g., "my device needs charging" or "the app needs updating").

d. Some operational features may not be introduced immediately but will be introduced later.
e. Person with CCN's functional communication goals should guide prioritization of operational features to be taught.
4. Facilitator training involves:
  a. Guiding each identified facilitator (e.g., parents, spouse, paraprofessional, siblings) in all aspects of operational competence.
  b. Teaching each new facilitator (e.g., even if system stays the same but paraprofessional changes, the new paraprofessional must be trained).
  c. Training on how to update a system (e.g., add/delete vocabulary items as needed; download system updates).
  d. Demonstrating and training in AAC strategies and techniques to encourage communication in real-life situations.
  e. Models of training have been developed and tested (e.g., IMPAACT, MASTER-PALS).

Sample AAC Strategies and Techniques

1. Augmented input/aided language stimulation.
  a. A way to model message composition on an AAC user's device.
  b. This type of modeling is important so that the person with CCN receives language input via AAC, not just via speech.
  c. Provides powerful model of AAC use as a viable and respected means of communication.
2. Expectant delay.
  a. Training facilitators to wait expectantly for a response.
  b. Can be 3–5 seconds or longer (count slowly and silently while waiting; e.g., at least 5 seconds, perhaps longer for scanners).
  c. Can even arch eyebrows to indicate that person is waiting for person with CCN to begin to respond.
3. Message co-construction.
  a. Training facilitators to encourage person with CCN to supply main content elements of message.
  b. Communication partner confirms the content words.
  c. Communication partner then expands and elaborates these components.
  d. Resulting message is co-constructed.
4. Alphabet supplementation.
  a. For people with CCN who are literate and who have severely dysarthric speech.
  b. Use an alphabet display so user points to the initial letter of each word as it is said.
  c. Combined effect of slowing speech rate (because of the need to point to the first letter of each word

spoken) and adding clarification for communication partner, which is provided by the indication of the word-initial letter, which constrains the choices of what the user might be saying (e.g., if the word is *postal*, the person would point to the letter *p* while saying the word. By knowing that the word initial letter is *p*, the listener can focus on words that start with *p* and not other letters of the alphabet).
5. Topic supplementation.
  a. For people with CCN who have severely dysarthric speech and may or may not be literate.
  b. Use of communication board/app that has lists (either written or pictorial) of their commonly discussed topics.
  c. Person with CCN selects topic/context to cue the communication partner.
  d. Having the topic/context should theoretically facilitate:
    (1) The flow of relevant conversation.
    (2) Resolution of communication breakdown.
6. Voice and message banking.
  a. Message banking.
    (1) An intervention strategy used with individuals who are likely to lose their ability to speak or for whom speech is severely compromised.
    (2) Consists of the recording of whole messages by the person in his/her own natural voice.
    (3) These messages are stored electronically for later use (e.g., uploading to an SGD or AAC app).

(4) Allows for recording legacy messages in one's own voice (e.g., "I love you," "Happy birthday," "I will miss you and want you to be happy").

(5) Its main aim is to maintain social closeness between the person whose speech will be lost and their chosen social circle.

b. Voice banking.

(1) Process whereby a large corpus of speech is collected (i.e., recorded) and a synthetic voice created that resembles the speaker's original voice.

(2) Voice banking done in anticipation of losing one's speech (e.g., in ALS or MS).

(3) Synthetic speech created from voice-banked corpus can then be uploaded and used in an SGD.

(4) A number of online options exist to guide this process.

c. Both message banking and voice banking can be used with patients with neurodegenerative diseases where loss of natural speech is part of the disease process. These options should be considered early on in the disease process so that the person's natural speech and intonation patterns have the best chance of being preserved.

Literacy

1. A critical skill for people with CCN.
2. Speech is integral for the practice of phonology and all skills associated with phonological awareness (e.g., blending, segmenting).
3. For people with CCN, literacy must be taught with special attention given to teaching phonological skills and ways to practice these skills that don't rely on speech.
4. A number of literacy programs developed for people with CCN have been developed.
5. Materials to supplement these programs are available (e.g., symbol-based storybooks).
6. Shared reading is one of the most critical activities to engage in with people with CCN to scaffold literacy skills.

Anatomy of an AAC Device

1. Device characteristics.
   a. Specifications and dimensions such as size, weight, screen size, number of keys/cells.
   b. Location of the following features:
      (1) Speakers.
      (2) Message display.
      (3) On/off keys and home button.
      (4) Adjusting volume.
      (5) Speak key.
      (6) Function keys (e.g., clear, backspace, delete).
   c. Does device support use of a keyguard?
      (1) Keyguard is a plastic or Plexiglas overlay that is made to help isolate each key/cell on device to prevent user from inadvertently activating keys/cells on the way to target.
      (2) Useful for people who use pointers or who have tremor.
      (3) Keyguards can be custom fit to devices and mobile tablets.

   d. Rate-enhancement techniques supported.
      (1) Example: word prediction, icon prediction.
      (2) Preprogrammed phrases.
   e. Message display/message bar.
      (1) Shows words or pictures/symbols or both.
      (2) Speaks each word/phrase as added or at end of message composition.
      (3) Speaks on demand.
      (4) Highlight each word as it speaks.
   f. Message keys.
      (1) Number and size of keys.
      (2) Keys can be reassigned at will.
   g. Message feedback.
      (1) Activation feedback: a specified signal that a key has been activated.
   h. Key action.
      (1) Does device zoom/enlarge each message as selected?

2. Person characteristics.
  a. Direct selector/alternate accessor.
  b. Literate/nonliterate.
  c. Ambulation.
  d. Vision and hearing status.
  e. Gross and fine motor skills.
  f. Seating and mobility.
    (1) Has wheelchair (power, manual).
    (2) If person has wheelchair, device will need to be affixed to chair using a mounting system (i.e., clamps, tubing, and plates that allow device to be attached to chair so it can be used and swung out of the way, as needed).
3. Commercially available versus dedicated device.
  a. Dedicated devices (SGDs).
    (1) Sold by manufacturers.
    (2) Insurance typically requires a doctor's prescription and comprehensive SLP report for purchase.
  b. Commercially available: widely available to all consumers.
    (1) Mobile tablets.
    (2) Laptop computers that can support special software.
4. Type of screen.
  a. Static display. Display does not change when used. Likely has fixed number of cells.
  b. Dynamic display. Display/screen that changes after a selection is made.
5. Type of input supported.
  a. Text.
    (1) Built-in or add-on keyboard.
    (2) Onscreen keyboard.
  b. Symbols.
  c. Speech.
    (1) Use of speech-to-text algorithm to convert speech to text.
6. Type of speech output.
  a. Synthesized speech.
    (1) Computer-generated speech.
    (2) May lack some prosodic contours.
    (3) Text-to-speech (TTS).
      (a) Words or messages are entered via text (e.g., typed into the device) and are converted to phonemes and allophones so they can be spoken.
      (b) Device uses stored speech data to generate digital speech signals that correspond to phonetic representations of the text.
      (c) Device converts digital signals to analog speech waveforms that are spoken by device.
      (d) Some devices do not store digital signals but use rule-based mathematical algorithms to generate speech sounds that correspond to phonetic representations entered by system user.

      (e) Now available in male, female, and child voices and in many languages.
  b. Digitized speech.
    (1) Human speech that has been recorded, stored, and reproduced.
    (2) Stored as words or messages.
  c. Hybrid: devices that support both synthesized and digitized speech.
7. Type of message formulation supported.
  a. Single utterance/message units.
  b. Sequences of words or phrases.
  c. Spelling.
8. Type of language representation supported.
  a. Phrase-based.
  b. Visual scene displays (VSDs).
  c. Core words.
  d. Minspeak icons: a branded set of icons rich in semantic associations.
  e. Orthography.
9. Type of selection methods supported.
  a. Direct selection.
  b. Alternate access: scanning (and what types of scanning).
10. Issues in AAC.
  a. Speech is default system for communication.
    (1) Buy-in to AAC can be tough.
    (2) AAC may be viewed as "method of last resort" by both clinicians and patients.
    (3) Reluctance to accept AAC.
    (4) May use speech long beyond point it is viable.
  b. Perception that AAC will impede speech development.
    (1) *No* research supports this claim.
    (2) Research indicates that use of AAC, both low- and high-tech, may promote increased communication.
    (3) Use of high-tech AAC options may provide repeated exposure to speech and language models that provide opportunity for imitation.
  c. Financial realities.
    (1) Tablets and apps are less expensive, nonstigmatizing, and commercially available.
    (2) Dedicated devices (i.e., SGDs) tend to be more expensive and not commercially available.
    (3) Insurance funding for SGDs is in flux at the time of this writing.
  d. Need for ongoing support for person with CCN and their facilitators.
    (1) Who pays?
    (2) Who provides the service?
    (3) Who advocates for this support when person with CCN either does not have an advocate or does not have consistent facilitators?

11. Mobile tablets (MTs) and AAC.
   a. Each app makes the tablet a qualitatively different device.
   b. Use feature matching to determine which apps best meet person with CCN's needs.
   c. Rubrics available to assist with app feature matching.
   d. Person with CNN must be able to touch, swipe, and tap to use MT via direct selection.
   e. More AAC apps available that support use of alternate access (e.g., Bluetooth synched switches).
   f. Switches available for use with Android and iOS tablets.
   g. Funding for MTs and AAC apps is on a case-by-case basis.
   h. Entertainment versus communication.
      (1) Use of MT as AAC device may be sidelined by MT as entertainment device.
      (2) Opinion differs with respect to needing separate MTs for communication and for entertainment.

Key Reference Texts

Beukelman, D. R., Garrett, K. L., & Yorkston, K.M. (2007). *Augmentative Communication Strategies for Adults with Acute or Chronic Medical Conditions.* Baltimore: Paul H. Brookes Publishing Company.

Beukelman, D. R., & Light, J. C. (2020). *Augmentative & Alternative Communication: Supporting Children & Adults with Complex Communication Needs*, 5th ed. Baltimore: Paul H. Brookes Publishing Company.

Binger, C., & Kent-Walsh, J. (2010). *What Every Speech-Language Pathologist/Audiologist Should Know About Augmentative and Alternative Communication.* Boston: Pearson Education.

Glennen, S. L., & DeCoste, D. C. (1997). *Handbook of Augmentative and Alternative Communication.* San Diego, CA: Singular Publishing Group.

Soto, G., & Zangari, C. (2009). *Practically Speaking: Language, Literacy, & Academic Development for Students with AAC Needs.* Baltimore: Paul H. Brookes Publishing Company.

Key Reference Articles/Tests

American Speech-Language-Hearing Association (ASHA). (2005). Roles and responsibilities of speech-language pathologists with respect to augmentative and alternative communication: position statement [Position Statement]. Available at www.asha.org/policy.

Blackstone, S. W., & Hunt Berg, M. (2003). *Social Networks: A Communication Inventory for Individuals with Complex Communication Needs and Their Communication Partners.* Monterey, CA: Augmentative Communication Inc.

Blischak, D. M., Lombardino, L. J., & Dyson, A. T. (2003). Use of speech-generating devices: In support of natural speech. *Augmentative and Alternative Communication, 19,* 29–35.

Bruno, J. (2007). Test of Aided-Communication Symbol Performance (TASP). Boardmaker.

Individuals with Disabilities Education Act, 20 U.S.C. § 1400 (2004).

Joint Commission. (2010). *Advancing Effective Communication, Cultural Competence, and Patient- and Family-Centered Care: A Roadmap for Hospitals.* Oakbrook Terrace, IL: Author. Available at www.jointcommission.org/Advancing _Effective_Communication_Cultural_Competence_and _Patient_and_Family_Centered_Care/.

Kovach, T. (2009). *Augmentative & Alternative Communication Profile: A Continuum of Learning.* East Moline, IL: LinguiSystems.

Lange, M. (n.d.). Switch Assessment: Part 1. Ablenet University. Recorded webinar. Available at www.ablenet.com.

Light, J. (1988). Interaction involving individuals using augmentative and alternative communication systems: State of the art and future directions for research. *Augmentative and Alternative Communication, 4,* 66–82.

Light, J. (1989). Toward a definition of communicative competence for individuals using augmentative and alternative communication system. *Augmentative and Alternative Communication, 5*(2), 137–144.

Light, J., & McNaughton, D. (2014). Communicative competence for individuals who require augmentative and alternative communication: A new definition for a new era of communication? *Augmentative and Alternative Communication, 30*(1), 1–18.

Light, J., Wilkinson, K. M., Thiessen, A., Beukelman, D. R., & Koch Fager, S. (2019). Designing effective AAC displays for individuals with developmental or acquired disabilities: State of the science and future research directions. *Augmentative and Alternative Communication, 35*(1), 42–55.

Millar, D. C., Light, J. C., & Schlosser, R. W. (2006). The impact of augmentative and alternative communication intervention on the speech production of individuals with developmental disabilities: A research review. *Journal of Speech, Language, and Hearing Research, 49*, 248–264.

Oosthuizen, I., Dada, S., Bornman, J., & Koul, R. (2018). Message banking: Perceptions of persons with motor neuron disease, significant others and clinicians. *International Journal of Speech-Language Pathology, 20*(7), 756–765, doi:10.1080/17549507.2017.1356377.

Rowland, C., & Schweigert, P. (2000). *Tangible Symbol Systems Manual and DVD*. Downloaded from www.designtolearn.com.

U.S. Department of Education, Office for Civil Rights, Free Appropriate Public Education for Students With Disabilities: Requirements Under Section 504 of the Rehabilitation Act of 1973, Washington, D.C., 2010.

Yamagishi, J., Veaux, C., King, S., & Renals, S. (2012). Speech synthesis technologies for individuals with vocal disabilities: Voice banking and reconstruction. *Acoustical Science and Technology, 33*, 1–5. http://dx.doi.org/10.1250/ast.33.1.

Review Questions

1. The Americans with Disabilities Act (ADA) requires that hospitals provide which of the following?

    a. There must be an effective means of communication for patients, family members, and hospital visitors.
    b. Assistive technology centers must be present in each state.
    c. Every child must have access to free and appropriate public education.
    d. Students in public schools should initially be seen through RTI.

2. Which of the following are considered low-tech tools for augmentative and alternative communication?

    a. iPad with communication applications.
    b. A button pressed to initiate a single, preprogrammed spoken message.
    c. Printed out pictures for making choices or as a visual schedule.
    d. Mac laptop with text-to-speech capabilities.

3. Which one is NOT a common scanning pattern?

    a. Linear.
    b. Eye gaze.
    c. Circular.
    d. Top-bottom.

4. Which of the following is an appropriate standardized assessment to determine an appropriate AAC system?

    a. Clinical Evaluation of Language Fundamentals.
    b. Preschool Language Scales.
    c. Boston Diagnostic Aphasia Evaluation.
    d. There are currently no standardized assessment batteries in AAC.

5. What is feature matching in augmentative and alternative communication?

    a. Matching the skills and needs of the person with communication needs with the features of various AAC systems.
    b. Matching specific vocabulary needs to an individual and making them easily accessible.
    c. Featuring specific people and phrases within a communication system to support individuals with cognitive decline.
    d. Selecting the appropriate communication device based on the SLP's familiarity with devices.

6. Which of the following is an example of a visual scene display?

    a. Two separate pictures presented, one of an orange and one of an apple.
    b. A visual schedule of five different pictures of activities that will occur throughout the day.
    c. A photograph of two kids actively engaged in playing soccer and their puppy is nipping at their feet.
    d. A grid-based communication application using pictures/photographs to help an individual communicate.

7. Which of the following is a knowledge barrier for a family or individual needing AAC?

    a. When the individual does not yet have a device due to funding.
    b. When the individual has a device but does not know how to use it.
    c. When the individual is not allowed to use the device outside of a hospital.
    d. When the individual has a device but thinks the device will stop their child from learning to speak.

8. An SLP would consider trialing eye-gaze technology to establish access to a communication system for a client that:

    a. Has two or three viable sites for switch access.
    b. Can't use any switches or any other means of access.
    c. Is a direct selector using their right index finger.
    d. is legally blind in both eyes but has good audition.

9. Which of the following conditions might require permanent AAC usage?

    a. Intubation following surgery.
    b. Prescription of voice rest.
    c. Total glossectomy.
    d. Severe laryngitis.

10. What are manual signs considered?

    a. Unaided communication.
    b. Aided communication.
    c. Temporary AAC.
    d. Permanent AAC.

11. Using a speech-generating device:

    a. Is no longer stigmatizing.
    b. May delay oral speech and language development.
    c. Is covered by insurance when recommended by a physician.
    d. May promote increased verbal communication.

12. Which of the following occurs in message co-construction?

    a. The client is able to share basic content elements of the message, which the communication partner confirms and expands.
    b. The client is able to, when given additional time, create their messages independently.
    c. The communication partner interrupts and guesses at the client's meaning.
    d. The client pantomimes and uses gestures to communicate their message.

13. Which act mandated assistive technology centers in each state and territory?

    a. Assistive Technology Act Amendments of 2004.
    b. Free Appropriate Public Education.
    c. Rehabilitation Act of 1973.
    d. Individuals with Disabilities Education Act.

14. Which of the following is NOT considered unaided AAC?
    a. Gestures.
    b. Manual signs.
    c. Pantomime.
    d. Pictures.

15. Which of the following describes a communication device that does not have access to Wi-Fi and no other applications?
    a. Low-tech device.
    b. Mid-tech device.
    c. Dedicated device.
    d. Nondedicated device.

16. Which type of symbol does NOT resemble the referent?
    a. Opaque.
    b. Translucent.
    c. Transparent.
    d. Real objects.

17. Which of the following describes a static display?
    a. When a screen changes following input.
    b. When a screen does not change when touched.
    c. When a device does not move location.
    d. When a device is considered high-tech.

18. Which of the following is an example of alternative access?
    a. When a user uses their finger to directly touch their selection.
    b. When a user uses eye gaze and looks at their selection.
    c. When a user uses linear scanning and the device highlights each item in a row individually when the row is selected.
    d. When a user uses natural speech to dictate what they wish to type.

19. When is partner-assisted scanning used?
    a. When the person who uses AAC cannot initiate the scan independently.
    b. When visual interaction with the device is not possible.
    c. When auditory interaction with the device is not possible.
    d. When the person who uses AAC uses direct selection.

20. Which of the following professionals is unlikely to be involved in an assessment for AAC?
    a. Speech-language pathologist.
    b. Vocational counselor.
    c. Biomedical engineer.
    d. Computer programmer.

19

Audiology and Hearing Impairment

SHARON A. SANDRIDGE, PhD
CRAIG W. NEWMAN, PhD
DONALD M. GOLDBERG, PhD

Chapter Outline

Anatomy and Physiology of the Auditory System

Auditory Structures

1. Anatomy of the auditory system consists of the structures of the outer ear, middle ear, and inner ear (Figure 19-1).

Outer Ear (OE)

1. Pinna (auricle).
   a. Cartilage-framed appendage covered with skin.
   b. Appears around sixth week of gestation from the first and second brachial arches.
   c. Major structures of pinna (Figure 19-2).
      (1) Helix: folded outside edge of ear.
      (2) Antihelix: Y-shaped upper part of ear.
      (3) Concha: bowl-shaped structure leading into the external auditory canal.
      (4) Tragus: triangular structure extension from face.
      (5) Antitragus: triangular structure arising from lower part of the lobe.
      (6) Lobe (lobule): fatty and fibrous structure; can be attached or free.
   d. Attaches to cranium by skin, cartilage, three extrinsic muscles, and extrinsic ligaments.
   e. Sensory innervation via trigeminal nerve (CN V).
2. External auditory meatus (EAM).
   a. S-shaped oval canal 25–35 mm in length, opening at the pinna and terminating at the tympanic membrane.
   b. Outer (lateral) one-third of canal is cartilaginous and lined with skin, glands that produce cerumen, and hair follicles (cilia) that move cerumen outward; medial two-thirds is osseous (bony).
   c. Innervated by trigeminal, facial, and vagus nerves (CN V, VII, and X).
3. Tympanic membrane (TM).
   a. Thin oval membrane that forms partition between the OE and the middle ear (ME).
   b. Layers.
      (1) Lateral epidermal layer continuous with the skin of the external auditory canal.
      (2) Intermediate fibrous layer consisting of radial and concentric fibers; provides structure to TM.
      (3) Medial mucosal layer continuous with the mucosa of the ME.
   c. The TM is a cone-shaped membrane with an area of 55 mm.
   d. The TM transduces sound—an acoustic vibration transformed into mechanical energy.

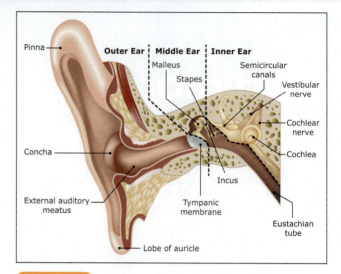

Figure 19-1   **Cross-section of the peripheral auditory system illustrating the major anatomic structures within the outer, middle, and inner ear.**

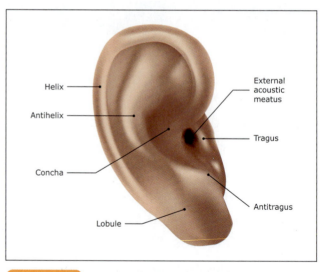

Figure 19-2   **Illustration of the major structures of the pinna**

4. Function.
   a. Auditory function: the OE collects sound and channels it to the ME.
      (1) The pinna collects sound originating from in front of listener; reflects sound (due to concave shape of pinna) coming from the back; this assists in front/back localization (especially for high-frequency sounds with short wavelengths).

(2) Serves as a natural filter enhancing or boosting higher-frequency sounds approximately 10–12 dB.

(3) Natural resonance of the concha is approximately 5,000 Hz.

(4) The EAM enhances sounds that have frequencies four times the length of canal (1/4 wavelength theory); approximately 2,500–2,700 Hz (in adults).

b. Nonauditory function is protection.

(1) Cerumen is noxious to "intruders" such as insects and provides lubrication to the EAM.

(2) The S-shape prevents foreign objects, such as cotton swabs, from reaching TM and ME.

Middle Ear (ME)

1. Six-walled, air-filled cavity within the petrous portion of the temporal bone.

a. Roof (superior wall) is formed by thin plate of bone—tegmen tympani that separates ME from dura mater.

b. Floor (inferior wall) separates ME from the internal jugular vein.

c. Lateral wall is formed by the TM.

d. Medial wall consists of the oval window, round window, and the promontory (formed by first turn of cochlea).

e. Posterior wall is the mastoid wall.

f. Anterior wall is a small wall opening into the eustachian tube.

2. Houses three ossicles (bones), five ligaments, and two muscles (tendons).

a. Ossicular chain: consists of three bones, which are the smallest in the human body, transferring the mechanical vibration from the tympanic membrane to the inner ear (IE).

(1) Malleus: the most lateral (first) ossicle, consisting of a manubrium (handle), head, neck, and lateral and anterior processes; attached to the TM (at the umbo) and the incus.

(2) Incus: the middle and largest bone in the ossicular chain consisting of a body and a short, a long, and a lenticular process.

(3) Stapes: the most medial (third) and smallest ossicle consisting of a head, footplate, and two crura. The footplate is held in the oval window by the annular ligament.

b. Ligaments: five ligaments that suspend the ossicular chain in the ME.

(1) Superior malleolar: attaches at head of malleus and the tegmen tympani.

(2) Lateral malleolar: attaches to neck of malleus and bony wall.

(3) Anterior malleolar: extends from anterior process of malleus to anterior wall.

(4) Posterior incudal: attaches to short process of incus and posterior wall.

(5) Annular ligament: attaches the stapes footplate to the oval window.

c. Muscles: two muscles that serve to hold the ossicular chain in place and to reduce intensity reaching IE by pulling against each other to stiffen the system and reduce the efficiency of the ME. The ME muscles are unique in their ability to exert the amount of force for their size.

(1) Tensor tympani: a 2-cm-long muscle attaching to the head of the malleus; innervated by trigeminal nerve; pulls malleus medially.

(2) Stapedius: the smallest muscle in the body; attached to the neck of the stapes; innervated by the facial nerve; pulls stapes posteriorly and tilts footplate in oval window.

3. Eustachian tube: mucosal-lined pathway that ventilates the ME through the connection to the nasopharynx.

4. Function.

a. The ME compensates for the impedance mismatch (loss of sound energy) between the acoustic signals from the OE and the cochlear fluids of the IE using two primary mechanisms; approximately 25–27 dB of the estimated 30-dB impedance mismatch is compensated by two primary effects.

(1) Lever ratio.

(a) The arm of the incus is shorter than the malleus, creating a lever effect that increases the force and decreases the velocity at the stapes; only accounts for gains of a few decibels.

(b) Overall, approximately 25–27 dB of the estimated 30-dB impedance mismatch is compensated for by the area ratio and lever ratio mechanism.

b. ME muscles serve to increase the sensitivity of the auditory system for speech, especially in background noise, through stiffening of the ossicular chain (reducing low-frequency noise transmission); also serves as a protective process against intense sounds by attenuating or decreasing the intensity by 15–20 dB (frequency dependent).

Inner Ear (IE)

1. Complex structure residing within the petrous portion of the temporal bone; seen anatomically as one unit but has two distinct functions—sense of hearing (cochlea) and sense of balance (semicircular canals and otolithic organs).

2. Osseous (bony) labyrinth is a complex series of excavations in the bone containing a series of communicating membranous sacs and ducts (membranous labyrinth).
   a. Semicircular canals are responsible for angular movement; consists of three canals: lateral, posterior, and superior.
   b. Vestibule is a 4-mm central chamber of the bony labyrinth housing the utricle and saccule, which are sensory organs responsible for detecting linear movement.
   c. Cochlea: a snail-shaped structure containing the end-organ of hearing.
3. Cochlear structures (Figure 19-3).
   a. A bony canal surrounds a membranous tube, about 35 mm in length, and coils around a central core (modiolus) approximately 2¾ turns (in humans).
   b. The base of the cochlea, the largest turn, sits next to the vestibule; the apex, the smallest turn at the top of the cochlea, points anteriorly (toward the eye).
   c. The membranous labyrinth is divided into three canals.
      (1) Scala vestibuli: upper canal running from the oval window to the helicotrema (tip of cochlea); contains perilymph, a fluid similar to cerebrospinal fluid.

(2) Scala tympani: lower canal running from the round window to the helicotrema (tip of cochlea); contains perilymph.
(3) Scala media: middle canal divided from the scala vestibuli by Reissner's membrane and from the scala tympani by the basilar membrane; contains the organ of Corti, the end organ of hearing; contains endolymph.
   d. Organ of Corti consists of sensory hair cells, support cells, support membranes, and ligaments (Figure 19-4).
      (1) Sensory hair cells: outer hair cells (OHC).
         (a) Approximately 13,500 per ear housed in three to four rows.
         (b) Test-tube-shaped; supported at base and apex only.
         (c) Three to five rows of stereocilia; W-shaped; graduated in length with the longest stereocilia in outside row.
         (d) Afferent and efferent nerve fibers synapse, directing to the base of the hair cell; one afferent fiber synapses with as many as 10 OHC, providing convergent information.
         (e) Serve as a biological modifier increasing or decreasing sensitivity to sounds by changing length of hair cells (as they lengthen,

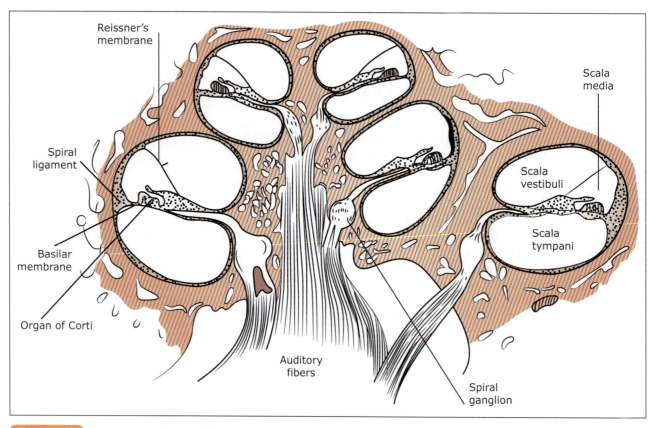

Figure 19-3   Cross-section of the cochlea illustrating the major anatomic structures within the scalae.

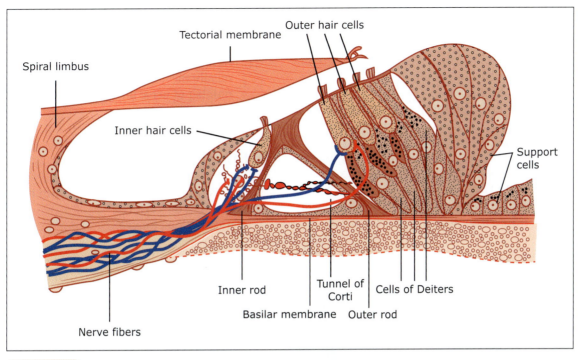

Figure 19-4   **Cross-section of the organ of Corti within the cochlea.**

the tectorial membrane is moved farther from the stereocilia of the inner hair cells, decreasing the sensitivity of the organ of Corti).

(2) Sensory hair cells: inner hair cells (IHC).
  (a) Approximately 3,500 per ear housed in one row.
  (b) Flask-shaped; completely surrounded by support cells.
  (c) Two to three rows of stereocilia; crescent-shaped; graduated in length, with the longest stereocilia in outside row.
  (d) Afferent nerve fibers synapse, directing to hair cell; as many as 10 nerve fibers synaps with 1 IHC, providing divergent information; efferent nerve fibers synapse on the afferent fibers.
  (e) Serve to process frequency and temporal (time) and intensity information to the auditory pathway.
(3) Support cells: serve as the core of the organ of Corti.
(4) Membranes.
  (a) Reissner's membrane: forms the roof of the scala media; may rupture with an active episode of Ménière's disease.
  (b) Basilar membrane: forms the floor of the scala media; the membrane becomes wider as it moves apically; as the width changes, so does the mass and stiffness, yielding

tonotopicity in which high frequencies are processed at the base (thinner and stiffer) and low frequencies at the apex (wider and more massive).
  (c) Tectorial membrane: a semitransparent, gelatinous structure that attaches medially to the spiral limbus and laterally to the top of the stereocilia of the OHCs; responsible for shearing the stereocilia of the hair cells.
4. Function.
  a. Changes the mechanical energy into hydromechanical energy and then into neural impulses.
    (1) Stapes acts like a piston, moving the fluid in the scala vestibule to create a wave—the traveling wave.
    (2) The fluid moves inward, pushing down on Reissner's membrane, which in turn creates a wave in the scala media.
    (3) The movement of the fluid causes the tectorial membrane and the basilar membrane to move, resulting in a shearing effect of the stereocilia.
    (4) The stereocilia movement causes calcium channels to open, exciting the hair cells; energy now becomes electrochemical.
    (5) The hair cells release neurotransmitter, which binds with the nerve fibers, creating neural impulses.
    (6) The neural impulses travel via CN VIII (vestibulocochlear) through the internal auditory canal to the brainstem and synapse at the cochlear

nucleus (the first nuclei in the central auditory nervous system).

b. Coding frequency.

(1) Place theory: frequencies are encoded based on place along basilar membrane; responsible for frequency coding above 5,000 Hz.

(2) Temporal theory: auditory nerve is phase-locked to stimulus pattern and the brain encodes the timing pattern of the nerve firing.

(3) Missing fundamental frequency: if the fundamental frequency is absent in a complex sound (e.g., 1,000 Hz, 1,200 Hz, and 1,400 Hz), the fundamental frequency (i.e., 200 Hz) will be heard even though it is not present in the sound.

c. Coding intensity.

(1) As intensity increases, each nerve fiber fires more often; however, this is limited.

(2) As intensity increases, a wider area of the basilar membrane is stimulated, resulting in greater number of nerve fibers activated.

Vestibulocochlear Nerve (CN VIII)

1. CN VIII is comprised of fibers from both the vestibular organs and the cochlea.

a. Inferior vestibular nerve.

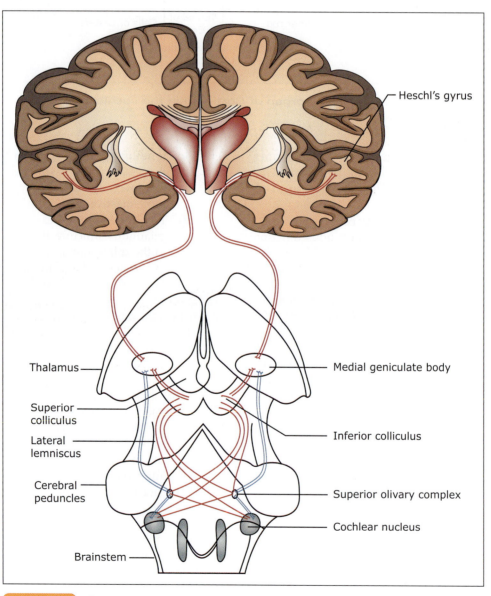

Thalamus

Superior colliculus

Lateral lemniscus

Cerebral peduncles

Brainstem

Heschl's gyrus

Medial geniculate body

Inferior colliculus

Superior olivary complex

Cochlear nucleus

Figure 19-5 Schematic of the ascending central auditory nervous system pathways.

b. Superior vestibular nerve.

c. Cochlear nerve.

   (1) Consists of both type I and II afferent fibers.

   (2) Majority (95%) of type I afferent fibers arise from the IHC; only 5% from the OHC.

   (3) Divergent pattern of nerve innervation for the IHC (one hair cell to many nerve fibers); convergent pattern for OHC (many hair cells to one nerve fiber).

   (4) Afferent fibers carry frequency and temporal and intensity information from the cochlea through the internal auditory canal to the ipsilateral cochlear nucleus (CN).

Brainstem Pathways and Cortex (Figure 19-5)

1. All cochlear nerve fibers synapse at the ipsilateral anterior ventral cochlear nucleus (AVCN). Each nerve fiber bifurcates and either synapses at the posterior ventral cochlear nucleus (PVCN) or the dorsal cochlear nucleus (DCN).

2. From the CN, fiber tracts proceed to ipsilateral and contralateral superior olivary complex (SOC). The SOC is primarily responsible for localization and the acoustic reflex.

3. From the SOC, neural impulses travel up the lateral lemniscus, primarily a sensory fiber tract, to the inferior colliculus (IC).

4. From the IC, impulses travel via the brachium of the IC to the medial geniculate body (MGB), one of the nuclei of the thalamus.

5. From the MGB, the acoustic message is relayed to various areas for auditory processing. The primary area, AI, is located in the superior temporal gyrus or in Heschl's gyrus. Surrounding association areas are located in the temporal and insular lobes.

Audiological Evaluation

Otoscopy

1. Otoscopy: a systematic visual inspection of the OE and surrounding tissue, EAM, and TM.

2. Inspection components.

   a. External ear structures for anomalies such as skin tags or pits (sinuses), tenderness, redness, or edema (swelling).

   b. EAM for obvious inflammation, growths, foreign objects, excessive cerumen, drainage.

   c. TM for presence of normal landmarks (e.g., cone of light, pearly gray translucent color) or for any inflammation, perforation, or any other obvious abnormalities in structure.

3. Pass criteria for visual inspection.

   a. Normal appearance of all structures.

   b. No complaints of pain when pinna or surrounding tissue is manipulated.

4. Referral for medical assessment.

   a. Reports of tenderness.

   b. Excessive or impacted cerumen.

   c. Sign of drainage or odor.

   d. Abnormal TM color (e.g., red/bulging).

   e. Growth/abnormality on canal wall.

   f. Foreign body.

Behavioral Assessment of Hearing

1. Psychoacoustic and measurement principles.

   a. Intensity: magnitude (amplitude) of a sound related to the perception of loudness.

    (1) Decibel (dB): unit of measurement of intensity used in acoustics and audiometric testing; one-tenth of a Bel. Decibel is a relative unit; it is logarithmic, nonlinear, and expressed in terms of various reference levels.

    (2) Sound pressure level (dB SPL): intensity level based on an absolute *pressure* measurement; reference is 20 micropascals (20 µPa).

    (3) Hearing level (dB HL): reference of normal human hearing thresholds for each audiometric frequency tested. Audiogram uses dB HL to plot thresholds; audiometric zero (dB HL) is represented as a straight line on the audiogram but based on minimal audible curve in dB SPL.

    (4) Sensation level (SL): any measurement that is made above an individual's threshold.

    (5) The *Y*-axis (ordinate) on the audiogram is expressed in dB HL.

b. Frequency: cycles per second of the signal measured in hertz (Hz) related to the perception of pitch. For example, a 2,000 Hz tone completes 2,000 cycles in 1 second.
   (1) Period: amount of time it takes for one sine wave to complete one cycle; the reciprocal of frequency (period = 1/frequency).
   (2) Pure tone: a sound consisting of a single frequency.
   (3) Periodic sounds: variations of sound that are repetitive over time and that can be both simple (pure tone) and complex (voice).
   (4) Aperiodic sounds: complex sounds that are not repetitive over time.
   (5) The X-axis (abscissa) on the audiogram is expressed in Hz.
c. Sensitivity: capacity of sense organ to detect a stimulus.
   (1) Absolute sensitivity: ability to detect a faint sound.
   (2) Differential sensitivity (acuity): ability to detect differences or changes; ability to detect differences between two frequencies or two different intensities.
   (3) Threshold: level at which a stimulus is perceived; clinical threshold defined as the lowest intensity to respond to the stimulus 50% of the time (e.g., two out of four trials using a bracketing approach).
   (4) Frequency range for hearing is 20 to 20,000 Hz at birth; intensity range is 0–140 dB.

2. Audiometer.
   a. Electronic instrument used to quantify hearing by producing sounds at calibrated intensities; sounds include pure tones, speech, and noise.
   b. Sounds can be delivered by different transducers (device that changes energy from one form to another); options include headphones, insert phones, bone oscillator, sound field speakers.
   c. The attenuator controls the intensity of the signal, usually in 5 dB steps; however, some audiometers permit dB step sizes smaller than 5 dB (e.g., 2 dB steps).
   d. The duration of the signal is controlled by the interrupter switch.
      (1) The interrupter switch is turned off for the delivery of pure tone signal.
      (2) The interrupter switch is turned on when speech signals are presented.
   e. Can produce various sounds.
      (1) Pure tone signals are produced by the oscillator; octave and interactive frequencies are 125, 250, 500, 750, 1,000, 1,500, 2,000, 3,000, 4,000, 6,000, and 8,000 Hz. Some audiometers can produce frequencies above 10,000 Hz.

   (2) Broadband signals (also known as *white noise*) are complex, aperiodic signals that contain all frequencies in the audible spectrum.
   (3) Narrowband noise is a white noise with frequencies above and below a center frequency filtered out.
   (4) Speech noise is a broadband noise containing frequencies between 300 and 3,000 Hz and is used for masking during speech audiometry.

3. Pure tone audiometry.
   a. Pure tone audiometry serves several purposes.
      (1) Determines severity of hearing loss.
      (2) Provides information to help diagnose type of hearing loss (i.e., conductive, sensorineural, or mixed).
      (3) Depicts the configuration of hearing loss (i.e., pattern of pure tone thresholds from low to high frequencies).
      (4) Determines the intensity level at which other audiological procedures will be performed.
      (5) Determines the need for further rehabilitative treatment, either hearing aid (HA) or cochlear implant (CI) candidacy.
   b. Air-conduction audiometry: stimulates the entire peripheral auditory system, including both the *conductive* (OE and ME) and *sensorineural* portions (cochlea and CN VIII).
   c. Bone-conduction audiometry: bypasses the conductive mechanism; bone vibrator placed on mastoid to directly stimulate the IE.
   d. Audiogram: graph with frequency (measured in Hz) plotted on the X-axis and intensity (measured in dB HL) on the Y-axis; denotes the assessed threshold as a function of frequency.
      (1) An audiogram is generated for each ear independently.
      (2) A standardized set of symbols is used to document air- and bone-conduction threshold results on the audiogram (Figure 19-6).

4. Audiogram interpretation.
   a. Degree of hearing loss: magnitude or severity of hearing loss.
      (1) Pure tone average (PTA): average threshold value based on thresholds obtained at 500, 1,000, and 2,000 Hz.
      (2) Fletcher average: best *two* thresholds at 500, 1,000, and 2,000 Hz, which is often a better predictor of hearing for speech than the three-frequency PTA.
      (3) Classification schemes have been developed to provide a metric of hearing loss ranging from normal hearing sensitivity to profound hearing loss (Table 19-1).

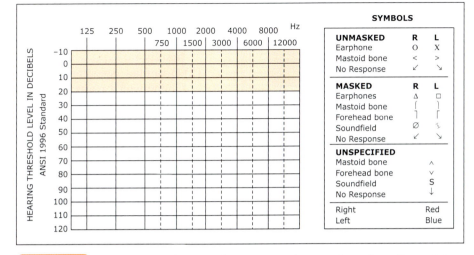

Figure 19-6   Example of an audiogram and associated audiometric symbols. Hz, Hertz.

Table 19-1

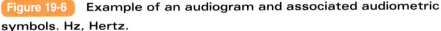

RANGE OF LOSS (IN dB HL)	DEGREE OF LOSS CATEGORY	POTENTIAL COMMUNICATION IMPACT
–10 to 15	Normal	No significant problem
16 to 25	Slight/minimal	Difficulty understanding faint speech especially in noise
26 to 40	Mild	Difficulty understanding faint or distant speech, even in quiet
41 to 55	Moderate	Hears conversational speech at a close range (approximately 3–5 feet)
56 to 70	Moderately severe	Hears loud conversational speech; significant difficulty in groups
71 to 90	Severe	Unable to hear conversational speech; able to distinguish vowels but not consonants
90+	Profound	May hear loud sounds; hearing is not primary communication mode

Hearing Loss Categories Based on Pure Tone Average (PTA; 500, 1,000, 2,000 Hz) and Associated Communication Impact

b. Types of hearing loss: determined by comparing air-conduction thresholds to bone-conduction thresholds for each ear independently (Figure 19-7).
(1) Conductive hearing loss (CHL): characterized by bone-conduction thresholds within normal range (0–20 dB HL) with air-conduction thresholds falling outside the normal limits for hearing; CHL results from problems associated with the OE and/or ME.
(2) Sensorineural hearing loss (SNHL): characterized by air-conduction and bone-conduction thresholds essentially equal (i.e., within 10 dB) and all thresholds outside normal range; SNHL results from disorders of the cochlea and/or CN VIII.
(3) Mixed hearing loss: characterized by bone-conduction thresholds outside the normal hearing range with the air-conduction thresholds poorer than bone-conduction thresholds; combination of both CHL and SNHL. Difference between the air- and bone-conduction

thresholds is known as the *air-bone gap* (ABG), reflecting the degree of conductive component contributing to the overall hearing loss.
c. Audiometric configurations.
(1) Patterns that describe the relationship of low-frequency hearing to high-frequency hearing.
(2) Example of mild gradually sloping to moderate SNHL means that hearing loss in the low frequencies is in the mild range with thresholds become gradually poorer (moderate range) in the higher frequencies.
d. Audiometric patterns that may reflect specific ear conditions (Figure 19-8).
(1) A sensorineural notch at 3,000 or 4,000 Hz is consistent with excessive sound exposure.
(2) Rising conductive loss: reflects stiffness tilt associated with ME effusion (fluid in the ME space).
(3) Sloping conductive loss: reflects mass tilt associated with a variety of conditions such as ossicular discontinuity, ME tumor, and thickened TM.

▶ Hearing Disorders

General Factors Causing Hearing Loss

1. Developmental deficits.
2. Infections.
3. Drugs.
4. Environmental toxins.
5. Trauma.
6. Vascular disorders.
7. Neural disorders.
8. Immune system disorders.
9. Bone disorders.
10. Aging processes.

OE and ME Disorders/ Abnormalities

1. Primary disorders of the OE (the pinna, EAM, or TM) and ME are presented in Tables 19-5 and 19-6, respectively, along with common treatments.
2. Disorders of the pinna and/or EAM typically do not result in hearing loss; cerumen in the EAM will cause hearing loss if it totally blocks the pathway.
3. Disorders of the ME typically cause a CHL; occurs whenever sound is blocked from reaching the IE.
4. Maximum CHL is 60 dB (e.g., case of complete atresia).

IE (Cochlear) Disorders/ Abnormalities

1. Primary disorders and treatments of the IE are presented in Table 19-7.
2. Abnormalities of the IE produce SNHL.
3. Audiometric configurations provide a gross estimation of the regions of the cochlea that are damaged by the pathology (e.g., high-frequency SNHL loss reflects damage to the basal end of the cochlea; a low-frequency SNHL reflects damage more to the apical portion of the cochlea).
4. Mild to moderate SNHL due primarily to damage of the OHC.
5. Severe to profound SNHL due to damage to both the OHC and IHC.

Table 19-5

Outer Ear Disorders	
DISORDER	**BRIEF DESCRIPTION**
Anotia	Absent pinna
Microtia	Small pinna
Atresia	Absent or blocked external auditory meatus or canal
Stenosis	Narrowing of external auditory meatus
Foreign bodies	Miscellaneous objects in canal (e.g., bugs, peas)
Osteoma	Benign bony tumor
Exostosis	Benign bony growth potentially due to swimming in cold water
Cerumen	Wax buildup, which may be impacted due to cotton swab use
Fungal/external otitis	"Swimmer's ear"
Tympanic membrane (TM) TM perforation	Hole in TM (possibly due to trauma or infection)
Tympanosclerosis	Scarring of TM (often due to multiple perforations)

Table 19-6

Middle Ear Disorders	
DISORDER	**BRIEF DESCRIPTION**
Otitis media	Middle ear fluid, which may or may not be infectious (serous—noninfectious; mucoid; purulent); can be chronic or acute
Cholesteatoma	Nonmalignant growth, often following foreign body making its way into the ME space
Ossicular discontinuity	Trauma to any one or more of the ossicles—malleus, incus, stapes
Otosclerosis	"Stiffening" of the ossicles, due to bony growth, especially involving the stapes
Physical trauma/ longitudinal fracture	Partial or total disarticulation of the ossicular chain
Barotrauma	Traumatic injury caused by rapid changes in atmospheric pressure (ascending/ descending in airplane)
Glomus tumor	Neoplasm found in the middle ear that is a mass of cells with a vascular supply accompanied by pulsatile tinnitus
Tympanosclerosis	Formation of white plaques on the tympanic membrane

Table 19-7

Inner (Cochlear) Ear Disorders

DISORDER	BRIEF DESCRIPTION
Autoimmune hearing loss	Associated with autoimmune disorders; loss referring to abnormal immunologic responses where the body produces antibodies against its own tissue
Congenital pathologies	Hereditary or other hearing challenges identified at birth
Congenital infections	Most commonly associated with sensory hearing loss; includes cytomegalovirus (CMV), HIV, rubella, syphilis, and toxoplasmosis
Sound-induced hearing loss **Temporary threshold shift (TTS)** **Permanent threshold shift (PTS)**	 Short-term shift in hearing sensitivity due to acoustic trauma and/or sound Long-term shift in hearing sensitivity due to acoustic trauma and/or sound
Ototoxicity	Hearing loss caused by therapeutic agents (e.g., aminoglycosides; salicylates; loop diuretics; cisplatin) or other chemical substances (e.g., industrial solvents; carbon monoxide)
Ménière's disease	Results from overproduction of an inner ear fluid—endolymph (endolymphatic hydrops); triad of symptoms include unilateral hearing loss; roaring tinnitus; vertigo (balance/nausea challenges) often accompanied by aural fullness
Presbycusis	Hearing loss related to aging process
Physical trauma/transverse fracture	Temporal bone fracture that causes damage to the membranous labyrinth of the cochlea

6. There are several perceptual consequences resulting from cochlear hearing loss.
   a. Loudness recruitment: an abnormally disproportionate increase in the sensation of loudness in response to auditory stimuli of normal volume.
   b. Dysacusis: difficulty understanding speech, which may result from a combination of frequency and harmonic distortion in the cochlea.
   c. Diplacusis: a difference in the perception of sound by the ears, either in time or in pitch, so that one sound is heard as two.
   d. Phonemic regression: significant difficulty in word recognition often associated with presbycusis.
7. Major management strategies for SNHL.
   a. Sudden SNHL is considered a medical emergency and requires medical management.
      (1) Corticosteroids may be delivered systemically or via intratympanic application.
      (2) Hyperbaric oxygen, currently not FDA approved for this indication, may be offered.
      (3) Patients with incomplete hearing recovery should be counseled regarding benefits/limitations of hearing aids (HA/s) and/or other hearing assistive technology.
   b. Ménière's disease: medical and surgical treatment.
      (1) Motion sickness medications (e.g., meclizine [Antivert] or diazepam [Valium]) to reduce vertigo symptoms and antinausea medications (e.g., promethazine) to control nausea and vomiting during episodes of vertigo; long-term use of diuretics to reduce fluid retention.
      (2) Medications injected into the ME and then absorbed into the IE may improve vertigo symptoms (gentamicin, steroids).
      (3) Surgery may be an option and include endolymphatic sac decompression, vestibular nerve section, and labyrinthectomy.
      (4) Noninvasive procedures include vestibular rehabilitation therapy, HA/s, and use of Meniett device (application of positive pressure to the ME to improve fluid exchange).
      (5) Modification of diet, including salt limitation and avoidance of monosodium glutamate (MSG) in prepared food.
   c. Sound-induced hearing loss (SIHL): Table 19-8 displays damage-risk criteria for hearing loss.
      (1) Hearing loss prevention.
         (a) Use of hearing protection. There are different types of hearing protection such as foam earplugs, earmuffs, and custom hearing protection devices; needed when in environment that is 85 dBA for more than 8 hours; if louder, need to reduce time by 50% for every 3 dB increase in intensity above 85 dBA.
         (b) Turn volume down. Reduce volume and time when listening to personal music players or any other device that has a volume control. (Visit https://www.turnittotheleft.org/TTITLfactsheet.pdf).
         (c) Walk away from the noise. Doubling the distance from the sound source decreases the intensity by 50%.
   d. HA/s (see complete section overview of HA/s).
   e. CI/s (see complete section overview of CI/s).

Table 19-8

Damage-Risk Criteria (Based on NIOSH Criteria)		
SOUND PRESSURE LEVEL	LENGTH OF EXPOSURE	EXAMPLES (IN dBA)
<85	>8 hours	Light traffic; dishwasher; blender
85 to 87	8 hours	Train; live show; snowblower
88 to 90	4 hours	Lawn mower; diesel truck; symphony concert
91 to 93	2 hours	Jazz concert; subway
94 to 96	1 hour	Personal stereo
97 to 99	30 minutes	Router; belt sander; drill; MRI machine
100 to 102	15 minutes	Nightclub/discotheque; snowmobile
103 to 105	7.5 minutes	Radial arm saw; chainsaw; rock concert
106 to 108	3.75 minutes	Circular saw; sporting event
109 to 111	1.87 minutes	Air raid siren; firecracker
111 to 113	<1 minute	Revolver; automobile airbag

Table 19-9

Retrocochlear (CN VIII Nerve, Brainstem, Cortex) Disorders	
DISORDER	BRIEF DESCRIPTIONS
Brainstem infarct	Localized areas of ischemia produced by interruption of blood supply
Glioma	Tumor composed of neuroglia, or supporting cells of the brain that can affect auditory pathways
Presbycusis	Hearing loss related to aging process
Vestibular schwannoma	Often referred to as *acoustic tumors* (typically one-sided but can involve bilateral tumors; neurofibromatosis; NF-2)
Multiple sclerosis	Degenerative demyelinating disease, with auditory findings that may be detected during auditory evoked potential testing
Cerebrovascular accident	Stroke caused by interruption of blood supply to the brain due to an aneurysm, embolus, or clot, possibly resulting in language deficits and "cortical deafness"

Retrocochlear (CN VIII, Brainstem, Cortical) Disorders

1. Primary retrocochlear disorders are presented in Table 19-9.
2. There are several audiometric "red flags" associated with CN VIII disorders.
   a. Unilateral high-frequency SNHL.
   b. Unilateral tinnitus.
   c. Poorer word recognition scores that would be predicted based on pure tone audiometry.
   d. Dizziness.
   e. Normal tympanograms, elevated or absent acoustic reflexes, and positive reflex decay.
   f. Abnormal ABR findings with prolongations of wave V.
3. Contrast-enhanced magnetic resonance imaging (MRI) is the gold standard for diagnosing vestibular schwannoma (VS).
   a. VS are slow growing and benign; treatment is recommended because growth may lead to multiple cranial neuropathies, brainstem compression, hydrocephalus, and even death.
   b. A "watch-and-wait" approach may be taken when appropriate (e.g., elderly, medically fragile).
   c. Surgery options include different approaches (retrosigmoid, intralabyrinthine, middle fossa), each having their respective advantages and disadvantages.
   d. Stereotaxic radiosurgery (gamma-knife) is being increasingly used as an alternative to surgical removal of the tumor.
4. Intra-axial disorders (within the brainstem): tests of central auditory function may show contralateral or bilateral effects, oftentimes with normal (or near normal) hearing sensitivity for pure tones.
5. Extra-axial disorders (outside the brainstem): audiometric symptoms are on the same side as the disorder, and patients may show a range (from mild to profound) of hearing sensitivity for pure tones.
6. Vascular accidents: disorders that interfere with blood supply to brainstem pathways and cortex.
   a. Thromboses: clots that form and remain in specific areas of the vessel.
   b. Embolisms: debris that circulates until it reaches a narrow vessel.
   c. Aneurysms: dilation of blood vessels causing the walls of vessels to stretch and dilate.
   d. Cerebrovascular accidents (CVA): obstructions or ruptures of blood vessels within the brain causing a stroke.
   e. Atherosclerosis: hardening of the arteries.
7. (Central) auditory processing disorders (APD): children or adults have difficulty interpreting auditory information (often exacerbated by background noise) even with normal peripheral hearing sensitivity.
   a. Intervention strategies include the enhancement of signal-to-noise ratio (SNR).

(1) Using an FM system to increase teacher's voice over background classroom noise; could be personal or sound field.

(2) Using environment treatments (e.g., curtains on windows, acoustic ceiling tiles, tennis balls on chair legs).

(3) Providing written supplemental instructions/information.

(4) Using preferential seating; this should be the last accommodation implemented.

b. Children with APD may benefit from auditory training therapy and development of compensatory skills.

Auditory Neuropathy Spectrum Disorder (ANSD)

1. Previously known as *auditory neuropathy/auditory dys-synchrony*.

2. ANSD is characterized by evidence of normal cochlear OHC (sensory) function and abnormal auditory nerve function.

3. Cause unknown; children born prematurely and having a stay in a neonatal intensive care unit (NICU) and/or hyperbilirubinemia are at increased risk.

4. Diagnostic criteria.

a. Presence of normal or near-normal OAEs; although OAEs absent in approximately 30% of cases of ANSD.

b. Presence of a cochlear microphonic (CM) assessed using ABR.

c. Absent or markedly abnormal auditory brainstem response (ABR).

5. ABR is required as the screening method for newborns whenever there is a 5-day or longer stay in the NICU.

6. Behavioral audiological assessment.

a. Audiogram: results may suggest any degree of hearing loss.

b. Speech in quiet: results may not be consistent with audiometric findings.

c. Speech in noise: results should show significant decrease in performance compared to testing in quiet.

d. Immittance testing with acoustic reflexes: reflexes should be absent in presence of normal ME function.

e. OAEs: should be present; although if absent does not rule out ANSD.

f. ABR using both a condensation click and a rarefaction click to assess presence of a CM; a no-stimulus run should also be collected to verify that response is biological, not electrical artifact from the headphones.

7. Responses to behavioral testing may not be consistent among tests; need to rely on parental report as well: "some days my child seems to hear—other days my child acts deaf."

8. Management options.

a. HA/s: should be fit using standard pediatric fitting guidelines; however, if OAEs are present, HA/s should be fit to a mild hearing loss.

b. CI/s: considered when progress is limited; CI may bypass the dysfunctional area.

c. Communication methodology: all options are available and presented to parents in an unbiased way to allow them to make an informed decision.

▶ Hearing Sensory Technology

Hearing Aids (HA/s)

1. Components: all HA/s include several basic components (Figure 19-14).

a. Microphone: transducer that converts acoustic sound into electrical signal.

(1) Omnidirectional microphone: equally sensitive to sounds from all directions.

(2) Directional microphone: more sensitive to sounds from specific angles.

(3) Multimicrophones: combines more than one microphone.

b. Amplifier: increases the gain (power) of the incoming signal.

(1) Analog signal processing alters sounds via filters.

(2) Digital signal processing alters sounds via conversion of sound into digital binary code (0, 1) and then by applying mathematical algorithms to the signal.

c. Receiver: converts amplified electrical signal to an acoustic signal delivered to the ear.

d. Battery: power source of HA.

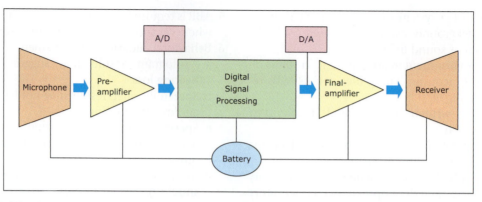

Figure 19-14 Block diagram of the basic components of a digital signal processing hearing aid. A/D, analog-to-digital converter; D/A, digital-to-analog converter.

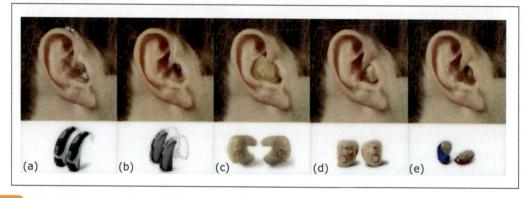

Figure 19-15 Photographs of major hearing aid styles: (A) behind-the-ear (BTE); (B) open-fit micro BTE; (C) full shell in-the-ear (ITE); (D) half-shell ITE; (E) completely-in-the-canal (CIC).

Photographs are courtesy of Phonak.

e. Other HA features:
  (1) Telecoil (t-coil): coil of wire that creates an electromagnetic field when activated that communicates with the electromagnetic field from the telephone.
  (2) Channels: division of the frequency response of the HA into smaller units, permitting greater fitting precision.
  (3) Programs: separate fitting algorithms for specific listening situations (e.g., restaurants); selected either automatically or by push buttons on the devices or remote control.
2. Electroacoustic characteristics.
  a. Gain: amount or magnitude of amplification (in dB); quantified by the difference between the input into the HA and the HA output.
  b. Frequency response: amount of gain across the frequency range of the HA.
  c. Output sound pressure level (OSPL): maximum output level of the HA.
  d. Linear sound processing: equal dB increase for all incoming sounds (i.e., soft, medium, and loud input sounds amplified to the same degree).

  e. Nonlinear sound processing: amount of gain is dependent on the intensity of incoming sound; softer sounds are amplified more than louder sounds; most commonly used processing.
3. HA styles (see Figure 19-15):
  a. Behind the ear (BTE): devices that sit on or behind the ear and are attached to a sound delivery system (e.g., tubing attached to earmold, slim tubing attached to small dome or receiver that sits in the EAM) to the ear canal.
    (1) RITE/RIC BTE: receiver-in-the-ear/receiver-in-canal BTE; used to create an open ear fit.
    (2) Open-fit BTE: EAM is not occluded with earmold; eliminates the occlusion effect (i.e., increased sound pressure level in the ear canal) that causes the HA user's voice to sound louder and hollow; increases physical comfort.
  b. Custom: family of in-the-ear (ITE) devices ranging in size from full shell (FS ITE), half shell (HS ITE), in the canal (ITC), to completely in the canal (CIC); all HA components housed within the shells.

(1) Greater hearing loss requires larger-size device to prevent feedback (high-pitch ringing created by the HA) and provide sufficient gain, in general.

c. Selection of a specific HA depends on a variety of factors, including the patient's ear canal and pinna anatomy, physical fit, degree of hearing loss, listening needs, and patient preference.

d. Contralateral routing of signal (CROS) HA/s: special HA fitting applications when conventional HA configurations may be inappropriate; provide bilateral (i.e., two-sided) hearing; not binaural (two-ear) hearing.

(1) CROS: used to compensate for single-sided deafness (SSD; no aidable hearing in one ear with normal hearing in other ear); microphone worn on weaker ear; signal transmitted wirelessly to receiver worn on stronger ear.

(2) Bilateral CROS (BiCROS): used to compensate for asymmetric bilateral hearing loss; microphones worn on both ears; signal transmitted from weaker ear to stronger ear, which has an HA on/in it.

4. Earmolds (see Figure 19-16).

a. Available in several styles and materials, both of which can alter frequency response of the HA and affect the perceived quality of the patient's voice.

b. Purpose of earmolds.

(1) Attach traditional BTE to ear.
(2) Deliver amplified sound to ear.
(3) Modify the frequency response of the HA.
(4) Prevents feedback.

c. Earmold modifications.

(1) Venting: channel that runs through the earmold; reduces feelings of fullness, prevents moisture in the ear canal, and alters the low-frequency response characteristics.

(2) Damping: acoustic filter/damper in the HA, tone hook, or earmold that reduces the resonant peaks of the response (i.e., smooths the frequency response, providing improved sound quality).

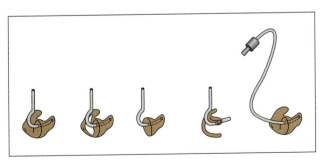

Figure 19-16 Examples of major earmold styles (left to right): full shell, skeleton, canal, free field/CROS, noncustom slim-tube.

(3) Horn effect: use of "horn-shaped tubing" or "belled" bores in the earmold; provides enhancement of the high-frequency response.

5. HA fitting process.

a. Multistep process to determine most appropriate devices to meet the needs of the patient.

(1) Comprehensive audiological evaluation.
(a) Determines degree, type, and configuration of hearing loss.
(b) Determines need for medical treatment.
(c) Assists in selecting specific amplification strategies (monaural versus binaural HA/s).
(d) Assists in setting realistic expectations.

(2) Hearing needs assessment and device selection.
(a) Assessment of communication function and psychosocial consequences of hearing loss: use both objective calibrated speech materials (e.g., Quick Speech in Noise–QuickSIN test) and subjective self-report measures (e.g., Abbreviated Profile of Hearing Aid Benefit–APHAB; Hearing Handicap Inventory for the Elderly/Adult–HHIE/A).
(b) Assessment of biopsychosocial variables such as visual status, manual dexterity, shape and dimension of pinna and ear canal, overall health, cognitive status, motivation, lifestyle, family support, and financial factors.
(c) Special considerations for children include tamper-resistant battery compartment, retention options for securing HA/s, t-coil/direct-audio input options.

(3) HA fitting and orientation.
(a) Verification that HA/earmolds are physically comfortable.
(b) HA/s programmed to meet listening needs, focusing on naturalness of patient's voice, output within comfort level, and without feedback.
(c) Explanation of use and care of devices/earmolds.
(d) Verification of ability to insert/remove HA/s, manipulate controls/switches, and change batteries.
(e) Counseling of realistic expectations and effective communication strategies with the hearing devices.

(4) Verification and validation of devices: processes to determine that the HA/s are performing appropriately and providing the expected benefit.
(a) Verification: assesses adequacy of the HA; variety of strategies include:
• Electroacoustic analysis (verifies frequency response characteristics, input/

Review Questions

1. Which structure is considered part of the outer ear?

   a. Malleus.
   b. Pinna.
   c. Cochlea.
   d. Stapes.

2. Which structure is considered part of the inner ear?

   a. Semicircular canals.
   b. Incus.
   c. Tympanic membrane.
   d. Stapes.

3. Which structure is considered part of the middle ear?

   a. Pinna.
   b. Cochlea.
   c. Stapes.
   d. Reissneir's membrane.

4. What is the function of the cochlea?

   a. To change electrical energy into mechanical energy and finally into neural impulses.
   b. To change mechanical energy into electrical energy and finally into neural impulses.
   c. To change neural energy into mechanical energy and finally into electrical signals.
   d. To change mechanical energy into hydromechanical energy and finally into neural impulses.

5. Which form of audiological evaluation allows a visual inspection of the outer ear and surrounding tissues, external auditory meatus, and tympanic membrane?

   a. Tympanometry.
   b. Otoacoustic emissions.
   c. Otoscopy.
   d. Pure tone audiometry.

6. A 75 dBHL hearing loss would be indicative of what severity of loss?

   a. Slight/minimal.
   b. Mild.
   c. Moderate.
   d. Severe.

7. A 30 dBHL hearing loss would be indicative of what severity of loss?

   a. Slight/minimal.
   b. Mild.
   c. Moderate.
   d. Severe.

8. What is the speech recognition threshold (SRT)?

   a. The highest hearing level at which one can correctly recognize speech stimuli.
   b. The lowest hearing level at which one can correctly recognize speech stimuli.
   c. The highest hearing level at which one can correctly hear auditory stimuli.
   d. The lowest hearing level at which one can correctly hear auditory stimuli.

9. Which form of audiological assessment allows for assessment of middle ear function?

   a. Immittance testing.
   b. Otoscopy.
   c. Otoacoustic emissions.
   d. Auditory-evoked potentials.

10. Which portion of the auditory system is tested using auditory brainstem response?

    a. Outer ear.
    b. Middle ear.
    c. Inner ear.
    d. Semi-circular canals.

11. What is a disorder of the ear that results in a small pinna?

    a. Anotia.
    b. Microtia.
    c. Atresia.
    d. Osteoma.

12. What is a disorder of the ear that results in scarring of the eardrum?

    a. Fungal otitis.
    b. Exostosis.
    c. Tympanosclerosis.
    d. Otitis media.

13. What is a disorder of the ear that is caused by a nonmalignant growth, often following a foreign body making its way into the middle ear space?

    a. Cholesteatoma.
    b. Otosclerosis.
    c. Ossicular discontinuity.
    d. Barotrauma.

14. What is the term for hearing loss associated with the aging process?

    a. Ménière's disease.
    b. Ototoxicity.
    c. Noise-induced hearing loss.
    d. Presbycusis.

15. What is auditory neuropathy spectrum disorder?

    a. A disorder characterized by abnormal cochlear function and normal auditory nerve function.
    b. A disorder characterized by normal cochlear function and abnormal auditory nerve function.
    c. A disorder characterized by abnormal outer ear function with normal auditory nerve function.
    d. A disorder characterized by abnormal outer and middle ear function with normal inner ear and auditory nerve function.

16. What portion of a hearing aid converts acoustic sound into an electrical signal?

    a. Microphone.
    b. Amplifier.
    c. Receiver.
    d. Battery.

17. What portion of a hearing aid converts an amplified electrical signal to an acoustic signal that is delivered to the ear?

    a. Microphone.
    b. Amplifier.
    c. Receiver.
    d. Battery.

18. What is electroacoustic gain?

    a. The amount or magnitude of amplification in dB.
    b. The magnitude of amplification across the frequency range of a hearing aid.
    c. The equal increase in dB for all incoming sounds.
    d. The increase in dB for incoming sounds based on intensity.

19. Which portion of a cochlear implant stimulates cranial nerve VIII (vestibulocochlear nerve)?

    a. External sound processor.
    b. Internal unit.
    c. Electrode array.
    d. Microphone.

20. In the auditory hierarchy of listening, which level describes a person's ability to make a same versus different judgment of auditory stimuli?

    a. Detection.
    b. Discrimination.
    c. Recognition.
    d. Comprehension.

SECTION VI

Examinations

Section Outline

20

Chapter Review Questions and Answers

Anatomy and Physiology of Communication and Swallowing

1. Which plane of section divides the body vertically into anterior and posterior parts?
   a. Frontal.
   b. Sagittal.
   c. Horizontal.
   d. Distal.

2. Which part of the neuron is specialized for receiving signals from other neurons or environmental stimuli?
   a. Axon.
   b. Neurotransmitter.
   c. Dendrite.
   d. Soma.

3. What is cranial nerve VII?
   a. Trochlear.
   b. Trigeminal.
   c. Facial.
   d. Vagus.

4. What is cranial nerve X?
   a. Abducens.
   b. Glossopharyngeal.
   c. Vagus.
   d. Hypoglossal.

5. What are the names of the meninges?
   a. Pia mater, arachnid mater, durable mater.
   b. Pia mater, arachnoid mater, dura mater.
   c. Pterygoid mater, anastomosis mater, durable mater.
   d. Falx mater, subarachnoid mater, epidural mater.

6. How many ventricles are in the brain?
   a. 2.
   b. 3.
   c. 4.
   d. 5.

7. Which portion of the brainstem houses neuronal circuits guiding respiration?
   a. Medulla oblongata.
   b. Midbrain.
   c. Pons.
   d. Cerebellum.

8. In which lobe of the brain will you find the primary motor cortex?
   a. Parietal lobe.
   b. Occipital lobe.
   c. Temporal lobe.
   d. Frontal lobe.

9. Almost all sensory information that reaches the cerebral hemispheres is relayed through which structure of the brain?
   a. Limbic cortex.
   b. Cerebellum.
   c. Thalamus.
   d. Basal ganglia.

10. When a person moves their right leg, which of the following describes the appropriate pathway?
    a. Right upper motor neuron signals carried along the corticospinal pathway.
    b. Right upper motor neuron signals carried along the corticobulbar pathway.
    c. Left upper motor neuron signals carried along the corticospinal pathway.
    d. Left upper motor neuron signals carried along the corticobulbar pathway.

11. From where does the anterior blood supply to the brain originate?
    a. Anterior cerebral artery.
    b. Carotid artery.
    c. Middle cerebral artery.
    d. Posterior communicating artery.

12. What term refers to the volume of air exchanged between a maximum inspiration and a maximum expiration?
    a. Tidal volume.
    b. Vital capacity.
    c. Functional residual capacity.
    d. Total lung capacity.

13. What is the name for the paired cartilages located on the superior, posterior surface of the cricoid cartilage?

   a. Thyroid cartilage.

   b. Epiglottis.

   c. Aryepiglottic cartilage.

   d. Arytenoid cartilage.

14. What is the free-floating bone that serves as an important contributor to laryngeal positioning?

   a. Hyoid bone.

   b. Zygomatic bone.

   c. Maxillary bone.

   d. Styloid bone.

15. Which laryngeal muscle acts as a vocal fold abductor?

   a. Lateral cricoarytenoid muscle.

   b. Transverse interarytenoid muscle.

   c. Oblique interarytenoid muscle.

   d. Posterior cricoarytenoid muscle.

16. Which cranial nerve innervates all laryngeal muscles?

   a. Facial nerve (CN VII).

   b. Glossopharyngeal nerve (CN IX).

   c. Vagus nerve (CN X).

   d. Hypoglossal nerve (CN XI).

17. Which muscle is responsible for mandibular depression?

   a. Masseter muscle.

   b. Temporal muscle.

   c. Lateral pterygoid muscle.

   d. Medial pterygoid muscle.

18. Which muscle forms a majority of the cheek wall?

   a. Mentalis.

   b. Platysma.

   c. Risorius.

   d. Buccinator.

19. Which extrinsic tongue muscle contributes to lingual protrusion?
    a. Hyoglossus.
    b. Genioglossus.
    c. Styloglossus.
    d. Palatoglossus.

20. Which intrinsic tongue muscle contributes to tongue narrowing and elongation?
    a. Superior longitudinal.
    b. Inferior longitudinal.
    c. Transverse.
    d. Vertical.

Acoustics

1. In sound vibration, what term refers to an area of higher density and pressure?
   a. Rarefaction.
   b. Condensation.
   c. Evaporation.
   d. Sublimation.

2. What is frequency?
   a. Physical measurement of the extent of vibrational change from resting position.
   b. The number of repetitions of a cyclic pattern in 1 second.
   c. Intervals between sounds.
   d. The maximum pressure reached by a sound pressure wave.

3. What term refers to the distance traveled by a sound during a single cycle?
   a. Intensity.
   b. Duration.
   c. Wavelength.
   d. Frequency.

4. For what purpose would a narrowband spectrogram be used?
   a. Finding the exact fundamental frequency.
   b. Finding different sounds by manner of articulation.
   c. Checking pitch contour accuracy.
   d. Measuring frequency-related cues.

5. What is a sinusoid?
   a. A sound consisting of multiple frequencies.
   b. A sound consisting of a single frequency.
   c. The peak amplitude observed in a spectrum.
   d. A complex sound produced by vocal fold vibration.

6. In the source-filter theory of speech production, what acts as the filter?
   a. Vocal fold vibration.
   b. Supralaryngeal vocal tract.
   c. Sound radiation from the lips.
   d. Speech.

7. In the source-filter theory of speech production, what acts as the source?
   a. Vocal fold vibration.
   b. Supralaryngeal vocal tract.
   c. Sound radiation from the lips.
   d. Speech.

8. Formant 1 (F1) is most closely associated with which factor?

   a. Pharynx size.
   b. Oral cavity size.
   c. Distinguishing retroflexed vowels.
   d. Listener perception.

9. Formant 3 (F3) is most closely associated with which factor?

   a. Oral cavity size.
   b. Listener perception.
   c. Pharynx size.
   d. Distinguishing retroflexed vowels.

10. Nasal consonants have a complete closure in which location?

    a. Oral cavity.
    b. Nasal cavity.
    c. Glottis.
    d. Subglottis.

11. What is a distinguishing feature of /r/ on spectrographic analysis?

    a. High F1.
    b. High F2.
    c. Low F2.
    d. Low F3.

12. What is characteristic of stop consonants on a spectrogram?

    a. A period of silence followed by a burst.
    b. Continuous high-frequency noise.
    c. A low-frequency formant.
    d. Close resemblance to vowels.

13. What is a distinguishing feature between voiced and voiceless obstruent cognate pairs?

    a. Only voiceless sounds can be obstruents.
    b. Voiced obstruents have a shorter duration.
    c. Voice obstruents have a longer duration.
    d. Voiceless sounds cannot be obstruents.

14. What is a distinguishing feature between sibilant and nonsibilant fricatives?

    a. Sibilant fricatives appear as noise on a spectrogram.
    b. Nonsibilant fricatives appear as noise on a spectrogram.
    c. Sibilant fricatives have higher amplitude noise than nonsibilant fricatives.
    d. Nonsibilant fricatives have higher amplitude noise than sibilant fricatives.

13. How far each score in a data distribution varies from the mean is:
    a. Stability.
    b. Equivalence.
    c. Variance.
    d. Range.

14. Researcher bias is a threat to:
    a. Criterion validity.
    b. Internal validity.
    c. External validity.
    d. Construct validity.

15. What p value is typically accepted as indicating significance?
    a. <0.5.
    b. <0.05.
    c. <0.005.
    d. <0.0005.

16. Subjective aspects of behavioral performance can be explored using what kind of research design?
    a. Randomized.
    b. Qualitative.
    c. Quantitative.
    d. Continuous.

17. An active independent variable is:
    a. Characterized as an outcome.
    b. Manipulated by the researcher.
    c. Constrained as extraneous.
    d. A response of interest.

18. To what does treatment efficacy refer?
    a. The degree to which actual implementation of the treatment in the real-world is consistent with the prototype treatment.
    b. When there is clinical improvement from the treatment when applied in a real-world context.
    c. When research is aimed at demonstrating the benefits of treatment through well-controlled studies.
    d. When research provides best practice guidelines for implementation of treatment methods.

19. What is a positive predictive value?

    a. The number of true positives divided by the combined true and false positives.

    b. The number of true positives divided by the combined true and false negatives.

    c. The number of true negatives divided by the combined true and false positives.

    d. The number of true negatives divided by the combined true and false negatives.

20. Which statistical analysis procedure is most appropriate to use when there are two or more continuous variables?

    a. Correlation.

    b. One-way ANOVA.

    c. MANOVA.

    d. Repeated Measures ANOVA.

The Practice of Speech-Language Pathology

1. What is the professional organization for speech-language pathologists (SLPs) and audiologists that develops standards of practice for both disciplines?
    a. American Speech Correction Association.
    b. American Speech-Language-Hearing Association.
    c. American Speech and Hearing Association.
    d. American Communication and Swallowing Association.

2. Which division of ASHA administers the certificate of clinical competence (CCC)?
    a. Council for Clinical Certification (CFCC).
    b. Council for Academic Accreditation (CAA).
    c. Board of directors (BOD).
    d. Officer-committee board (OCB).

3. How many "big" areas of practice make up the speech-language pathology scope of practice?
    a. 5.
    b. 7.
    c. 9.
    d. 11.

4. In what area of language must SLPs be knowledgeable in?
    a. Respiration.
    b. Morphology.
    c. Orofacial myofunction.
    d. Challenging behaviors.

5. Which of the following is a legal requirement that most SLPs must attain?
    a. The certificate of clinical competence (CCC-SLP).
    b. A passing Praxis score.
    c. State licensure.
    d. Advanced specialty credentialing.

6. What are ASHA special interest groups?
    a. Groups within ASHA that are targeted at raising awareness of SLP practice.
    b. Groups within ASHA that are targeted at raising awareness of benefits of certification.
    c. Groups within ASHA that establish standards for use of evidence-based practice.
    d. Groups within ASHA that engage members in fostering the interchange of information among affiliates who share common professional interests.

Review>Practice>Motivate>Analyze>Apply

7. Which philosophical concept asks what action will do the most good and least harm?
   a. Utilitarian approach.
   b. Rights approach.
   c. Fairness/justice approach.
   d. Virtue approach.

8. Which philosophical concept considers whether people are treated equally or proportionally?
   a. Utilitarian approach.
   b. Rights approach.
   c. Fairness/justice approach.
   d. Virtue approach.

9. Which philosophical concept considers whether an individual acts as the type of person they would like to be?
   a. Utilitarian approach.
   b. Rights approach.
   c. Fairness/justice approach.
   d. Virtue approach.

10. Which philosophical concept considers the action that best respects the rights of all stakeholders?
    a. Utilitarian approach.
    b. Rights approach.
    c. Fairness/justice approach.
    d. Virtue approach.

11. What are the three components of the ASHA Code of Ethics?
    a. Preamble, Rules, Regulations.
    b. Preamble, Principles, Rules.
    c. Rules, Regulations, Principles.
    d. Preamble, Rules, Stipulations.

12. What type of sanction is delivered privately to a person who has made a minor or inadvertent violation?
    a. Censure.
    b. Revocation.
    c. Reprimand.
    d. Suspension.

13. What type of sanction involves repealing membership and certification for some amount of time, in response to a serious violation?

    a. Reprimand.

    b. Revocation.

    c. Warning.

    d. Suspension.

14. What type of sanction involves suspending a clinical fellow's ability to apply for the certificate of clinical competence?

    a. Reprimand.

    b. Suspension.

    c. Withholding.

    d. Cease and desist.

15. What is a multidisciplinary service delivery model?

    a. When a client is seen by multiple professionals who communicate with each other regarding treatment and share information about overall status.

    b. When a client is seen by multiple professionals with some communication between disciplines in regard to referral and follow-up.

    c. When professionals cooperate in the assessment and treatment of a client in a more natural environment.

    d. When a client is seen by a single professional for assessment and treatment of a particular medical condition.

16. What is an interdisciplinary service delivery model?

    a. When a client is seen by multiple professionals who communicate with each other regarding treatment and share information about overall status.

    b. When a client is seen by multiple professionals with some communication between disciplines in regard to referral and follow-up.

    c. When professionals cooperate in the assessment and treatment of a client in a more natural environment.

    d. When a client is seen by a single professional for assessment and treatment of a particular medical condition.

17. What is a transdisciplinary service delivery model?

    a. When a client is seen by multiple professionals who communicate with each other regarding treatment and share information about overall status.

    b. When a client is seen by multiple professionals with some communication between disciplines in regard to referral and follow-up.

    c. When professionals cooperate in the assessment and treatment of a client in a more natural environment.

    d. When a client is seen by a single professional for assessment and treatment of a particular medical condition.

18. What is the role of an SLP in a medical setting?

   a. Assessment and treatment of disorders of swallowing and communication as a result of an underlying medical condition.

   b. Identification, evaluation, and determination of eligible children for receiving speech and language services.

   c. Developmental screening of infants and toddlers.

   d. Billing insurance for services rendered.

19. What is the role of an SLP in a school-based setting?

   a. Assessment and treatment of disorders of swallowing and communication as a result of an underlying medical condition.

   b. Identification, evaluation, and determination of eligible children for receiving speech and language services.

   c. Developmental screening of infants and toddlers.

   d. Billing insurance for services rendered.

20. What is the role of an SLP in an early intervention setting?

   a. Assessment and treatment of disorders of swallowing and communication as a result of an underlying medical condition.

   b. Identification, evaluation, and determination of eligible children for receiving speech and language services.

   c. Developmental screening of infants and toddlers.

   d. Billing insurance for services rendered.

Chapter 7, Appendix 7A, Review Questions

Speech Sound Disorders in Children

1. What is it called when there is vibration of the vocal folds when producing a consonant sound?
   a. Voicing.
   b. Voiceless.
   c. Frication.
   d. Syllabification.

2. Which of the following sounds is considered alveolar?
   a. /k/.
   b. /t/.
   c. /h/.
   d. /g/.

3. What is an allophone?
   a. Different use patterns in terms of pronunciation, vocabulary, and grammar.
   b. One of a pair of sounds that is different by just one phonetic feature.
   c. A nondistinctive phonetic variant for a phoneme.
   d. Obstruents.

4. Which is NOT a component of the Behavioral Theory of speech sound acquisition?
   a. Speech sounds are shaped from the time of babbling.
   b. Reinforcement is necessary for acquisition to progress.
   c. It is related to a broader version of behavioristic theories.
   d. Children are an active participant in their learning.

5. Which theory is attributed to Roman Jakobson?
   a. Generative phonology.
   b. Structuralist theory.
   c. Natural phonology.
   d. Prosodic theory.

6. This therapy approach is best known for its specific therapeutic sequence from least complex to most complex.
   a. Van Riper traditional approach.
   b. Minimal pair approach.
   c. Stimulability approaches.
   d. Cycles approach.

7. Which is NOT a part of the minimal contrast therapy method?
   a. To eliminate the child's production of homonyms.
   b. To pair a set of words that differ by one phoneme.
   c. Only correct sound production is accepted and reinforced.
   d. Error patterns of production are the treatment targets.

8. Which theory attempts to explain children's phonological error patterns?
   a. Distinctive features theory.
   b. Generative phonology.
   c. Natural phonology.
   d. Prosodic theory.

9. Which is NOT one of the three broad categories of phonological processes?
   a. Syllable structure processes change the complexity of how words are structured.
   b. Substitution processes change the complexity of words by substituting relatively earlier to produce sounds for more difficult ones.
   c. Assimilatory processes simplify the production of words by changing sounds in words to become more similar to each other.
   d. Distortion processes change the production to a nonstandard sound.

10. When compared with adults, an infant has all of the following, EXCEPT:
    a. A shorter, flatter vocal tract.
    b. A tongue mass that is placed more forward in the oral cavity.
    c. Lower laryngeal placement.
    d. Different shape for the vocal tract.

11. What is canonical babbling?
    a. Reduplicated babbling of strings of similar CV syllables.
    b. Cooing.
    c. First words.
    d. Squeals, raspberries, trills, direction noises.

12. What is the replacement of a fricative consonant with an affricate consonant?
    a. Affrication.
    b. Alveolarization.
    c. Cluster simplification.
    d. Consonant deletion.

13. How intelligible should a child be by age 3?
    a. 0%–25% intelligible.
    b. 25%–50% intelligible.
    c. 50%–75% intelligible.
    d. 75%–100% intelligible.

14. What is it called when you compare the number of consonants produced correctly to the total number of consonants that should be produced?
    a. Percentage consonants correct.
    b. Contextual testing.
    c. Informal measure of intelligibility.
    d. Phonological mean length of utterance.

15. What is the goal of phonological contrast intervention?
    a. Create meaningful differences in the client's speech using minimal pairs.
    b. Increase stimulability of sounds.
    c. Emphasize multiple input modes.
    d. Maximal cueing.

16. At what age would you expect to hear vocal play, squeals, and fully resonated vowels?
    a. Birth–1 month.
    b. 2–3 months.
    c. 4–6 months.
    d. 6–9 months.

17. Which of the following is an example of canonical babbling?
    a. Ba ba ba ba ba.
    b. Oooooo.
    c. Mommy.
    d. Squeals.

18. Which of the following is an example of alveolarization?
    a. Rabbit → wabbit.
    b. Shoe → Sue.
    c. Funny → money.
    d. Bus → bu.

19. What is phonemic awareness?
    a. Standardized measures of speech sound production.
    b. The ability to identify and manipulate individual phones of spoken words.
    c. Ability to be understood by family and unfamiliar listeners.
    d. Ability to attend to and discriminate or manipulate sounds at the word or sentence level.

20. An approach to therapy for children who have multiple phoneme collapse (use one sound as a substitute for multiple sounds) would be:
    a. Minimal pair therapy.
    b. Multiple oppositions therapy.
    c. Maximal contrast therapy.
    d. Traditional Van Riper therapy.

Language Disorders in Young Children

1. Which approach to language disorders considers society's expectations and the functional impact of the disorder?
   a. Naturalist perspective.
   ▶ **b. Normative perspective.**
   c. Perspective of child's understanding of language.
   d. None of the above.

2. A therapy approach characterized by high naturalness, modeling, and contingent responding by the SLP/adult, low structure, and influenced by social-interactional theory:
   ▶ **a. Child-centered.**
   b. Clinician-directed.
   c. Hybrid.
   d. Behavioral.

3. Which of the following describes milieu communication training?
   a. It is a clinician-directed approach.
   b. It is highly structured.
   ▶ **c. It employs incidental teaching.**
   d. All of the above.

4. Which of the following is true of dynamic assessment?
   a. It uses test-teach-retest procedures.
   b. It helps to determine a child's learning potential.
   ▶ c. It is beneficial for distinguishing difference from disorder.
   d. All of the above.

5. Which of the following statements about early intervention services is MOST accurate?
   a. Early intervention services are more intensive than later services.
   ▶ **b. Early intervention services are family-centered.**
   c. Early intervention services must be prescribed by the child's pediatrician.
   d. Early intervention services should occur in a separate room from the child's parent(s).

6. Which of the following is NOT a potential causal factor for a language disorder?
   a. Environmental.
   b. Genetic.
   ▶ c. Anatomical.
   d. None of the above.

7. Using a screening tool answers which of the following questions?
   a. Should we evaluate further for a language disorder?
   b. What goals should we address in therapy?
   c. What frequency should this child be seen as?
   d. Does this child have a language disorder?

8. For indirect language facilitation techniques, an expansion is:
   a. A comment and questions that serve to extend what the student has said or written.
   b. A contingent verbal response that increases the length or complexity of the child's utterance.
   c. A technique in which the child is provided with concentrated exposures of specific linguistic forms/functions/uses.
   d. When a clinician asks questions to construct a syntactically complete sentence.

9. Which of the following is considered drill work during language therapy?
   a. Sitting on the floor and describing the actions of the child while they play with toys.
   b. Playing with a toy kitchen with a child and describing your own actions.
   c. Having the child repeat the target word multiple times in a row.
   d. Repeating back a phrase the child says during the session verbatim.

10. In what components of language can dialectal differences be found?
    a. Semantics.
    b. Syntax.
    c. Pragmatics.
    d. All of the above.

11. Why is determination of L1 critical during assessment?
    a. A language difference can only be present in L1.
    b. A language disorder cannot be diagnosed in a bilingual child.
    c. A language disorder can be diagnosed only if it is present in L1.
    d. A language disorder can be diagnosed only if it is present in both L1 and L2.

12. Which of the following is NOT a component of Bloom and Lahey's language framework?
    a. Form.
    b. Spelling.
    c. Content.
    d. Use.

13. Which of the following is the BEST example of theory of mind?
    a. Where does Mom think the book is?
    b. Where do you think the book is?
    c. Where did you put the book?
    d. What did you read in the book?

14. What is referred to when a child is able to add a new word to their lexicon after one exposure?
    a. Fast mapping.
    b. Rote learning.
    c. Concept development.
    d. True semantic relationship.

15. Which of the following is an example of a bound morpheme?
    a. Dog.
    b. Eat.
    c. Runs.
    d. Arrive.

16. What is the traditional definition of "late talkers"?
    a. A 24-month-old child with fewer than 50 different words in their expressive vocabulary.
    b. A 30-month-old child with fewer than 100 different words in their expressive vocabulary.
    c. An 18-month-old child with fewer than 10 words in their expressive vocabulary.
    d. A 24-month-old child with fewer than 200 different words in their receptive vocabulary.

17. If a language disorder is identified, how should the SLP prioritize targets for therapy?
    a. Use normative data to determine the aspects of communication that are most significantly deficient.
    b. Teach the child the answers to the standardized assessment that they got wrong.
    c. Talk to colleagues about what areas they think the child needs to work on.
    d. None of the above.

18. Which is the BEST reason that an SLP might choose to do therapy in the home environment?
    a. The SLP may want to focus specifically on words that are only functional at home.
    b. The home environment is where the child is most comfortable.
    c. The SLP may want to see where the child lives to determine whether it is safe.
    d. The home environment is more natural and can help with generalization and carryover.

19. Which of the following is an example of antecedent instructional events?

   a. The SLP models how to say "dog" and the child attempts to say "dog."

   b. The child says, "dog," and the SLP responds, "Yes! Dog!"

   c. The SLP tells the child to say "dog" five times, as fast as they can.

   d. The child says the word *dog* while playing with a toy dog.

20. Which of the following is NOT true of the International Classification of Functioning, Disability and Health: Children and Youth Version (ICF-CY)?

   a. It considers impairment in body functions and structures and the impact on an individual's activity and participation.

   b. It considers the effect of environmental and personal factors on participation.

   c. It adheres to a medical model of disability.

   d. It has been adopted by ASHA as the framework for practice in the field.

Chapter 9, Appendix 9A, Review Questions

Spoken Language Disorders in School-Age Populations

1. What is a criterion referenced–based assessment designed to assess?

   a. The extent to which a child has mastered a specific language skill.

   b. The extent to which a child's performance on a specific language skills differs from other individuals of similar age and background.

   c. The extent to which a child's performance on a specific language skill may be modified.

   d. The extent to which a child's communication disorder impacts daily living.

2. What type of narrative is the following: "The other day I went to the doctor for my annual check-up. I received my flu shot and my arm still hurts 3 days later!"

   a. Retell.

   b. Personal narrative.

   c. Fictional narrative.

   d. Complex episode.

3. At what age is a child expected to be able to relate a narrative with multiple embedded or associated episodes?

   a. 3–4 years.

   b. 4–5 years.

   c. 5–6 years.

   d. 6–7 years.

4. A descriptive sequence is an early form of narrative. Which of the following best illustrates a descriptive sequence?

   a. A story that contains a string of unrelated sentences that depict actions or objects.

   b. A story that contains a series of sentences denoting actions that follow a chronological order.

   c. A story that contains an initiating event (event that motivates the character to take action), actions, and/or consequences.

   d. A story that contains a series of events related coherently and logically using complex language.

5. Which of the following is NOT considered a microstructure in narrative development?

   a. Internal response.

   b. Infinitives.

   c. Mental verbs such as *knew, felt, like*.

   d. Subordination.

6. During preschool, a child is able to determine what another person sees and how it is seen when the other person is in a different location. Which of the following is this an example of?

   a. Linguistic perspective-taking.

   b. Cognitive perspective-taking.

   c. Perceptual perspective-taking.

   d. None of the above.

7. A child is having difficulty with topic maintenance during a conversation. This would be considered a difficulty with which of the following?

   a. Discourse management.

   b. Expressive vocabulary.

   c. Perspective-taking.

   d. Syntax.

8. "I am sad" is an example of which stage of Brown's stages of morphological development?

   a. Stage I.

   b. Stage II.

   c. Stage III.

   d. Stage IV.

9. Which of the following describes the Rehabilitation Act of 1973?

   a. Prohibited discrimination on the basis of disability by programs and agencies receiving federal funding.

   b. Mandated that all children with disabilities be afforded a free and appropriate public education.

   c. Legal document written by health care professionals and caregivers that outlines long-term and short-term education goals.

   d. Stipulated what services are covered in a school-based setting in terms of habilitative services versus rehabilitative services.

10. A child is seen by their SLP in an individual or group session. This would be considered which of the following?

    a. Consultative services.

    b. Collaboration with the classroom teacher.

    c. Indirect services.

    d. Direct services.

11. What are some disadvantages of discrete trial intervention?

    a. Makes target stimuli highly salient.

    b. Maximize opportunities for production.

    c. Skills learned may not readily generalize.

    d. Reduces irrelevant or distracting stimuli.

12. Which laws support the RTI initiative?

    a. FERPA.

    b. IDEA.

    c. Rehabilitation Act of 1973.

    d. Education for All Handicapped Children Act.

13. When is RTI NOT implemented?

    a. Early to prevent academic failure.

    b. When a student is receiving special education services.

    c. As a way to differentiate children with language differences versus language disorders.

    d. As a universal screening.

14. A randomized controlled trial is a(n):

    a. Analysis of a number of studies related to a specific approach.

    b. Experiment in which participants are not assigned randomly to treatment or control groups.

    c. Experiment in which participants are randomly assigned to treatment and control groups.

    d. Opinion of a respected professional.

15. Which of the following is NOT an example of evaluation criteria for external evidence?

    a. Comparison.

    b. Cultural values.

    c. Random assignment.

    d. Participants.

16. Which of the following best describes genetic syndromes?

    a. They may run in families.

    b. They are likely to be associated with language disorders.

    c. They are presumed to be transmitted in genetic makeup.

    d. All of the above.

17. Which is the most prevalent mental health diagnosis made in childhood?

    a. **Attention deficit hyperactivity disorder.**

    b. Bipolar disorder.

    c. Specific reading disability.

    d. Intellectual deficit.

18. Which of the following is TRUE about autism spectrum disorders (ASD)?

    a. Separated into ASD, Asperger's, and PDD-NOS diagnostic criteria.

    b. Can be comorbid with intellectual difficulties.

    c. Must involve language disorder before age 3.

    d. Is exclusively a genetic disorder.

19. In Down syndrome, which of the following statements are FALSE?
    a. Language production is more affected than language comprehension.
    b. Syntax is more affected than semantics.
    c. Vocabulary and syntax growth are asynchronous.
    d. Hearing deficits are unlikely to cause language comprehension issues.

20. A student is observed to say the following: "Josh can help with the chores; Bryan can (help with the chores) too," where the information in the parentheses is not stated out loud. This is an example of which of the following?
    a. Register variation.
    b. Presupposition.
    c. Ellipses.
    d. Indirect request.

Chapter 10, Appendix 10A, Review Questions

Written Language Disorders in School-Age Populations

1. What two processes is written language composed of?
   a. Receptive processes (reading) and expressive processes (writing).
   b. Receptive processes (listening) and expressive processes (speaking).
   c. Phonemic and phonetic processes.
   d. Orthography and morphology.

2. Which of the following is NOT involved in phonic word attack and encoding?
   a. Phonological awareness.
   b. Grapheme-phoneme correspondence.
   c. Cohesive markers.
   d. Syllable recognition.

3. Which of the following is referred to as being able to identify which words start with the same sound?
   a. Rhyme awareness.
   b. Onset-rime awareness.
   c. Mophological awareness.
   d. Word awareness.

4. What is grapheme-phoneme correspondence frequently referred to as?
   a. Sound-symbol correspondence.
   b. Phonetic-phonemic correspondence.
   c. Syntax and morphology.
   d. Onset-rime.

5. What type of reading most involves gestalt recognition?
   a. Phonemic awareness.
   b. Phonetic awareness.
   c. Sight word reading.
   d. Phonics application.

6. Which of the following is an example of the preliterate stage of spelling?
   a. A child makes scribbles on a piece of paper and announces he wrote his name.
   b. The child spells *run* as "rn" and *couch* as "cowch."
   c. The child spells *united* as "younited."
   d. The child spells *bigger, stronger, faster.*

7. In what age range does the emergent writing phase typically occur?
    a. 3–4 years.
    b. 4–6 years.
    c. 7–8 years.
    d. 10–12 years.

8. Which of the following is an example of a phonemic awareness task?
    a. Say "pants" without the /p/.
    b. Use the word *understood* in a sentence.
    c. Repeat back the following numbers: one, nine, eight, five, zero, three.
    d. Name as many words starting with the letter *B* as you can in 60 seconds. Go!

9. According to Chall's stage theory, at what stage is the student "ungluing from print"?
    a. Stage 0.
    b. Stage 1.
    c. Stage 2.
    d. Stage 3.

10. According to the Early Literacy Panel meta-analyses, which is NOT a variable that predicts later literacy performance?
    a. Age of parents.
    b. Alphabet knowledge.
    c. Rapid automatic naming.
    d. Phonological memory.

11. When conducting a literacy assessment and examining underlying spoken language skills, which of the following should be addressed?
    a. Morphology.
    b. Syntax.
    c. Semantics.
    d. All of the above.

12. Which would likely NOT be addressed when assessing automaticity/fluency?
    a. Real words.
    b. Nonwords.
    c. Oral reading of paragraphs.
    d. Reading of tongue twisters.

13. A phonological processing assessment should address which of the following?
    a. Comparison of the student's spelling of regular versus irregular words.
    b. Phonological awareness, phonological short-term and working memory, rapid naming.
    c. Speed of silent reading of a paragraph.
    d. Executive functioning and working memory.

14. When it comes to cultural factors in literacy assessments, it is important to consider which of the following?
    a. Access to reading materials and literacy practices in the home.
    b. Quantity and quality of previous literacy instructions.
    c. Both a and b.
    d. None of the above.

15. Persons with hyperlexia most often show deficits in which of the following areas?
    a. Word recognition.
    b. Spelling.
    c. Underlying language skills.
    d. Automaticity.

16. What are some frequent strengths seen in those with dyslexia?
    a. Word recognition and spelling.
    b. Phonological processing.
    c. Orthographic processing.
    d. Underlying language skills.

17. Top-down processing is also referred to as which of the following?
    a. Whole language processing.
    b. Systematic instruction.
    c. Sensory processing.
    d. Detail-oriented processing.

18. Literacy instruction for at-risk readers should:
    a. Be taught at the students' current grade level.
    b. Be hierarchically structured.
    c. Be supplemental.
    d. Introduce many skills at once.

19. The IDEA:
    a. Does not address the use of an Individual Educational Plan (IEP).
    b. Only pertains to learning disabilities exhibited by children.
    c. Does not have legal implications for the education of handicapped children.
    d. Specifically addresses individuals who struggle with reading and writing difficulties.

20. The National Reading Panel meta-analyses indicated:
    a. Moderate to large effects for systematic, structured word attack and word identification instruction.
    b. Negative effects for vocabulary instruction and summary writing to enhance reading comprehension skills.
    c. Moderate effects for orthographic awareness intervention.
    d. No effect for repeated readings to enhance text-level reading fluency.

Chapter 11, Appendix 11A, Review Questions

Autism Spectrum Disorders

1. What was the original term for autism spectrum disorder?
   - **a. Autistic disturbances of affective contact.**
   - b. Asperger's syndrome.
   - c. Pervasive developmental disorder.
   - d. Autism spectrum disorders.

2. Which of the following is NOT one of the primary symptoms in autism spectrum disorders?
   - a. Impaired development of reciprocal social interaction.
   - b. Abnormal behavioral patterns and interactions with objects.
   - **c. Typical attention span.**
   - d. Deficits in social communication.

3. Autism spectrum disorders are described using different severity levels. Which severity level requires substantial support, such as marked deficits in verbal and nonverbal social interaction?
   - a. Level 1.
   - **b. Level 2.**
   - c. Level 3.
   - d. Level 4.

4. Which of the following is an example of a reciprocal social interaction deficit?
   - **a. Poor conversational turn-taking.**
   - b. Repetition of utterances spoken by others.
   - c. Hand flapping.
   - d. Obsessive preoccupation with cars.

5. Which of the following is the leading theory regarding the etiology of autism?
   - a. Vaccinations.
   - b. Lack of parental/environmental stimulation.
   - **c. Genetic predisposition.**
   - d. Delayed language development.

6. Which of the following are warning signs of autism in a young child?
   - a. Difficulty with pronouncing their name, difficulty following directions.
   - b. Noticeable gross motor delays, not yet potty trained.
   - **c. Lack of response to name, repetitive body movements.**
   - d. Unable to understand *first/then* phrases, poor concept development.

7. Which therapy method focuses on spontaneous, interactive pleasurable activity with the child?

  a. Applied behavior analysis.

  b. Augmentative and alternative communication.

  c. Floor time.

  d. Social stories.

8. Which therapy method focuses on promoting natural interaction and carryover and utilizes peers to provide a model to imitate?

  a. Peer and play mediation.

  b. Floor time.

  c. Social stories.

  d. Theory of mind.

9. Which of the following assessments might a parent and pediatrician fill out if they are concerned a young child has an autism spectrum disorder?

  a. First Year Inventory.

  b. Clinical Valuation of Language Fundamentals.

  c. Hodson Assessment of Phonological Patterns.

  d. Preschool Language Scales.

10. A client who is described as speaking telegraphically is most likely speaking in which way?

  a. Client may use short phrases and omit articles and verb conjugations.

  b. Client may not produce past tense when speaking.

  c. Client has difficulty with conversational turn-taking.

  d. Client may have difficulty with pronouns.

11. Hyper- or hyposensitivities to input would be considered part of which diagnostic criteria for autism spectrum disorder?

  a. Deficits in socioemotional reciprocity.

  b. Restricted, repetitive patterns of behavior, interests, or activities.

  c. Delayed expressive verbal communication.

  d. Clinically significant impairment in social communication.

12. According to the IDEA, autism:

  a. Cannot be diagnosed if there is a delay in cognitive development.

  b. Is a developmental disability that affects verbal and nonverbal communication.

  c. Does not need to be treated using a team-based approach.

  d. Is not a spectrum disorder.

13. Which of the following is true, according to environmental theories regarding autism prevalence?

   a. Toxins present in the environment may cause autism spectrum disorder in some individuals.

   b. Chromosomal abnormalities may cause autism spectrum disorder.

   c. Brain inflammation may be a factor in autism symptoms.

   d. Vaccinations may cause autism spectrum disorders.

14. Which of the following is an example of echolalia?

   a. Clinician says, "cookie," and client says, "kee kee."

   b. Clinician says, "cookie," and client says, "cookie cookie."

   c. Clinician says, "cookie," and client says, "/k/ /k/ /k/ /k/ cookie."

   d. Clinician says, "cookie," and client says, "tootie."

15. Which of the following best describes a child who dislikes being touched?

   a. Auditory sensitivity.

   b. Hyperlexia.

   c. Tactile defensiveness.

   d. Kinesthetic incoordination.

16. Difficulties in what area may lead to a client not being able to modulate their speaking volume in different locations?

   a. Self-regulation in response to tactile stimuli.

   b. Self-regulation in response to sensory stimuli.

   c. Motor deficits.

   d. Hyperacusis.

17. Which of the following defines criterion referencing?

   a. Discrepancy between cognitive ability and motor functioning level.

   b. Discrepancy between cognitive ability and cognitive performance.

   c. Discrepancy between expressive language and receptive language.

   d. Discrepancy between cognitive ability and language functioning level.

18. A pediatrician might indicate further evaluation for autism is needed for a 10-month-old if they see which of the following?

   a. Inability to roll from back to front, limited pointing, low tone.

   b. Lack of turn-taking.

   c. Lack of response to name, limited gestures, poor visual orientation to stimuli.

   d. Limited word production, poor orientation to sound.

19. Which of the following is an example of working on theory of mind?
    a. Teaching a student to play using peer modeling.
    b. Teaching a student to recognize emotions in their classmates.
    c. Teaching a student a specific behavioral response using a story.
    d. Teaching a student to communicate using pictures and photographs.

20. Which of the following is NOT typical of Applied Behavioral Analysis (ABA) treatment design?
    a. Skills taught using a carefully sequenced progression of steps.
    b. Clearly identified antecedent, target behavior, and consequence.
    c. Behavior modification using operant conditioning.
    d. Behavior modification using natural, spontaneous interaction.

Stuttering and Other Fluency Disorders

1. Which is the most common type of fluency disorder?
   a. Psychogenic disorder.
   b. Childhood-onset (developmental) stuttering.
   c. Neurogenic stuttering.
   d. Cluttering.

2. Secondary stuttering behaviors:
   a. Are adjustments in word choice, changes in speech, and changes in motoric behaviors.
   b. Include attitude, feelings, and emotional reactions.
   c. Are atypical speech disfluencies occurring at a higher frequency than typical disfluencies.
   d. Typically are repetitions, prolongations, or blocks.

3. Which of the following situations is a person who stutters more likely to have disfluencies in their speech?
   a. Speaking to a young child.
   b. Speaking to a friend.
   c. Speaking on the telephone.
   d. Singing in a choir.

4. A student with an abnormally rapid and irregular rate of speech and abnormal prosody likely has which of the following diagnoses?
   a. Childhood onset (developmental) stuttering.
   b. Cluttering.
   c. Neurogenic stuttering.
   d. Psychogenic stuttering.

5. Childhood onset (developmental) stuttering is most likely to begin during which age range?
   a. Ages 2–6 years.
   b. Ages 18 months to 3 years.
   c. Ages 5–10 years.
   d. Anytime during the school years.

6. Circumlocutions (talking around a troublesome word) for a person who stutters is considered to be which of the following?
   a. Core behavior.
   b. Secondary behavior.
   c. Emotional reaction.
   d. Attitude.

7. Saying "I want want want to eat a cookie" is an example of which of the following?
   a. Sound repetition.
   b. Word repetition.
   c. Prolongation.
   d. Block.

8. Which type of stuttering occurs around middle school and also sees the child beginning to use methods of avoidance?
   a. Beginning stuttering.
   b. Intermediate stuttering.
   c. Advanced stuttering.
   d. Prestuttering.

9. When determining whether or not a preschool child is likely to persist in stuttering, it is most important to consider all of the following, except:
   a. Whether there is a family history of fluency disorders.
   b. The length of time the fluency disorder has been present.
   c. The child's gender.
   d. Peer attitudes regarding the fluency disorder.

10. When determining appropriate treatment for fluency disorders, which clinical variables should be considered?
    a. Client's educational level.
    b. Motivation for treatment.
    c. Severity of the fluency disorder and preferences or expectations of the client and/or family.
    d. Setting for service delivery.

11. Which guides the primary decision about appropriate treatment for a fluency disorder?
    a. Setting for service delivery.
    b. Age and stuttering stage of the client.
    c. Client/family preferences and expectations.
    d. Motivation for treatment of the fluency disorder.

12. Indirect treatment approaches for young children who stutter are likely to include which of the following?
    a. Parent education.
    b. Client education.
    c. The Lidcombe Program.
    d. Tension reduction at the moment of stuttering.

13. Practicing one's stuttering as a method to decrease fear would be considered what type of treatment approach?

   a. Fluency shaping.

   b. Cancellation of stuttering.

   c. Voluntary stuttering.

   d. Environmental focus.

14. What treatment method would be recommended in order to reduce hard glottal attack at speech onset?

   a. Easy onset of phonation.

   b. Light contact of the articulators.

   c. Rate modifications.

   d. Continuous phonation.

15. When working with a school-age child who has developed a fear of talking after being consistently mocked for stuttering by peers, which of the following would be an important part of therapy?

   a. Helping the child learn to cope with teasing and bullying.

   b. Utilizing both individual and group therapy.

   c. Delivering intensive fluency shaping over a 3-week period.

   d. None of the above.

16. The World Health Organization considers stuttering a disability when:

   a. It is recognized by their employer as a disability.

   b. The client believes it is a disability.

   c. It creates limitations and restrictions on important aspects of a person's life activities.

   d. Diagnostic criteria determines that it is severe.

17. Stuttering often co-occurs in which of the following developmental conditions?

   a. Dysgraphia.

   b. Down syndrome.

   c. Dyslexia.

   d. Attention deficit hyperactivity disorder.

18. When may neurogenic stuttering occur?

   a. When a person has a traumatic brain injury.

   b. When a person is between the ages of 2 and 5 years old.

   c. When a person is in an emotionally charged situation.

   d. None of the above.

19. Psychogenic stuttering:
    a. Is manifested by a rapid rate of speech.
    b. Develops in reaction to stressful or emotional situations.
    c. May be best described as malingering.
    d. Is usually caused by a stroke or tumor.

20. What may a clinician do when implementing the Lidcombe Program with a young child?
    a. Place the primary focus on the child's feelings regarding their disfluencies.
    b. Give the child specific strategies to cope with teasing and bullying.
    c. Use videotaped speech samples to provide a model for prolonged speech.
    d. Train the parent to reinforce fluent speech and respond to stuttering when it occurs.

Acquired Language Disorders: Aphasia, Right-Hemisphere Disorders, and Neurodegenerative Syndromes

1. What is a language disorder caused by brain damage?
   a. Apraxia.
   b. Dysphagia.
   c. Aphasia.
   d. Dysarthria.

2. Which aphasia syndrome is associated with fluent verbal expression, adequate auditory comprehension, and poor repetition?
   a. Wernicke's aphasia.
   b. Conduction aphasia.
   c. Anomic aphasia.
   d. Transcortical motor aphasia.

3. What areas of the left hemisphere make up the language zone?
   a. Frontal, occipital, and insular lobes.
   b. Parietal, temporal, and occipital lobes.
   c. Frontal, parietal, and temporal lobes.
   d. Insular, cerebellar, and frontal lobes.

4. Aphasia is *typically* caused by brain damage in the territory of which artery?
   a. Right anterior communicating artery.
   b. Left middle cerebral artery.
   c. Left internal carotid artery.
   d. Right posterior communicating artery.

5. According to the Boston classification system, what language characteristics are used to determine aphasia syndromes?
   a. Verbal fluency, written expression, auditory comprehension.
   b. Reading fluency, repetition skills, verbal fluency.
   c. Verbal fluency, auditory comprehension, repetition skills.
   d. Verbal fluency, reading fluency, written expression.

6. Who would be a good candidate for the use of voluntary control of involuntary utterances (VCIU)?
   a. A person with fluent aphasia who presents with excessive jargon.
   b. A person with nonfluent aphasia who produces a few single words.
   c. A person with nonfluent aphasia who is totally nonverbal.
   d. A person with fluent aphasia who has few episodes of anomia.

7. A person who shows signs of memory decline but continues to have intact judgment and reasoning skills is most closely associated with which diagnosis?

   a. Traumatic brain injury.

   b. Mild cognitive impairment.

   c. Dementia.

   d. Right-hemisphere aphasia.

8. How are subcortical aphasia syndromes named?

   a. Based on lesion location.

   b. Based on presentation of physical deficits.

   c. Based on presentation of language deficits.

   d. Based on results of EEG.

9. What is the underlying principle for the use of constraint-induced language therapy (CILT)?

   a. Constraining the person with aphasia to use only written expression methods to communicate.

   b. Constraining the person with aphasia to use only their weakest expression method to improve their communicative function in this method.

   c. Constraining the person with aphasia to use only verbal expression methods to communicate.

   d. Constraining the person with aphasia to use only gesturing to communicate.

10. What is the term for aphasia resulting from a right-hemisphere stroke in a right-handed person?

   a. Mixed aphasia.

   b. Crossed aphasia.

   c. Switched aphasia.

   d. Reversed aphasia.

11. What is an appropriate example of a cognitive/communication symptom that may be seen in a person with right-hemisphere brain damage?

   a. Difficulty orienting to time and space.

   b. Poor ability to use correct grammatical constructions.

   c. Difficulty recognizing emotional states in others.

   d. Difficulty naming pictures.

12. What is an example of language change associated with normal aging?

   a. Impaired discourse production.

   b. Moderate decline in auditory comprehension.

   c. Lexical retrieval deficits.

   d. Impaired executive functioning.

13. Which aphasia syndrome is classified by fluent verbal expression, adequate auditory comprehension, and adequate repetition?

   a. Global aphasia.

   b. Wernicke's aphasia.

   c. Transcortical sensory aphasia.

   d. Anomic aphasia.

14. A dementia syndrome that is caused by a significant amount of cerebrovascular disease leading to impairment of multiple cognitive domains is called:

   a. Frontotemporal dementia.

   b. Vascular dementia.

   c. Alzheimer's dementia.

   d. Lewy body dementia.

15. What is an appropriate treatment strategy to utilize in order to reduce agitation and other negative behaviors in a person with dementia?

   a. Simulated presence therapy.

   b. Group reminiscence therapy.

   c. Caregiver-administered active cognitive stimulation.

   d. Computer-assisted cognitive interventions.

16. What is the life participation approach to aphasia (LPAA)?

   a. A treatment approach to aphasia that includes targeting multiple areas of language deficit in order to improve communication of persons with aphasia.

   b. A treatment approach to aphasia targeted at improving participation and quality of life for persons with aphasia, rather than targeting language deficits.

   c. A treatment approach to dementia that allows persons with dementia to better communicate about their favorite activities.

   d. A pragmatic treatment approach to right-hemisphere language disorders that trains persons to better interact within their social environments.

17. When assessing a bilingual person with aphasia, what is the most appropriate means of assessment?

   a. Having a bilingual SLP translate a standardized assessment into both languages.

   b. Having an interpreter translate a standardized assessment into both languages.

   c. Using standardized language assessments for both languages.

   d. Assessing only the person with aphasia's self-selected dominant language.

18. Which aphasia syndrome is classified by nonfluent verbal expression, adequate auditory comprehension, and poor repetition?

   a. Broca's aphasia.

   b. Transcortical motor aphasia.

   c. Wernicke's aphasia.

   d. Global aphasia.

19. What are typical components of a standardized language assessment?

   a. Verbal expression, auditory comprehension, reading comprehension, written expression.

   b. Verbal expression, reading comprehension, writing ability, apraxia assessment.

   c. Auditory comprehension, executive function assessment, verbal expression, speech production.

   d. Oral reading, written expression, apraxia assessment, verbal expression.

20. What is the appropriate label for a temporary loss of neurological function caused by an interruption of blood flow to a brain region?

   a. Cerebrovascular accident (CVA).

   b. Transient ischemic attack (TIA).

   c. Traumatic brain injury (TBI).

   d. Mild cognitive impairment (MCI).

Motor Speech Disorders

1. Which type of dysarthria is associated with hypernasality, imprecise consonants, breathy vocal quality, and damage to lower motor neurons?
   a. Spastic dysarthria.
   b. Ataxia dysarthria.
   c. Hypokinetic dysarthria.
   d. Flaccid dysarthria.

2. What is an appropriate treatment option for a person with dysarthria who presents with a hypoadduction disorder?
   a. Tension reduction.
   b. Loudness training.
   c. Integral stimulation.
   d. Abdominal trussing.

3. What is an appropriate perceptual feature of dysarthria indicating the presence of a resonance disorder?
   a. Monopitch.
   b. Audible inspiration.
   c. Breathiness.
   d. Hypernasality.

4. What is a characteristic that can be used to distinguish apraxia of speech (AOS) from dysarthria?
   a. Persons with apraxia typically present with a co-occurring swallowing disorder (dysphagia), whereas persons with dysarthria do not.
   b. Persons with dysarthria typically present with consistent speech sound errors, whereas persons with apraxia present with inconsistencies.
   c. Persons with apraxia typically perform better with novel speech tasks, whereas persons with dysarthria perform better with rehearsed tasks.
   d. Persons with dysarthria usually only have deficits in articulation and prosody, whereas persons with apraxia have deficits across all speech subsystems.

5. Which type of dysarthria is associated with irregular articulatory breakdowns, excess and equal stress, harsh vocal quality, and damage to the cerebellum?
   a. Hyperkinetic dysarthria.
   b. Unilateral upper motor neuron dysarthria.
   c. Ataxic dysarthria.
   d. Hypokinetic dysarthria.

6. What is true of childhood apraxia of speech (CAS)?
    a. It is usually associated with a lesion in the frontal lobe.
    b. It often co-occurs with childhood dysarthria.
    c. It is often associated with length and disruptive coarticulatory transitions between sounds and syllables.
    d. It usually does not impact literacy development.

7. What is intelligibility?
    a. The overall adequacy or prosody.
    b. The extent of understanding of a speaker.
    c. The rate at which speech units are produced.
    d. The perceptual adequacy of speech sound production.

8. According to principles of motor learning, which practice schedule type leads to best generalization?
    a. Massed practice schedule.
    b. Excessive practice schedule.
    c. Low frequency practice schedule.
    d. Delayed practice schedule.

9. Which type of dysarthria is associated with distorted vowels, monoloudness, voice tremor, and damage to the bilateral cerebral hemispheres?
    a. Spastic dysarthria.
    b. Ataxic dysarthria.
    c. Hyperkinetic dysarthria.
    d. Hypokinetic dysarthria.

10. Which is typically a treatment method used to improve the articulatory subsystem?
    a. Lee Silverman Voice Treatment (LSVT).
    b. Integral stimulation.
    c. Expiratory muscle strength training.
    d. Contrastive stress.

11. What best describes the motor learning principle of "type of feedback"?
    a. Knowledge of results (KR) is feedback regarding the quality of motor behavior.
    b. Knowledge of performance (KP) is feedback regarding the success in achieving a motor behavior.
    c. Knowledge of results (KR) leads to improved acquisition.
    d. Knowledge of performance (KP) leads to improved acquisition.

12. Which is typically a treatment method used to improve the respiratory and phonatory subsystems?

    a. Lee Silverman Voice Treatment (LSVT).

    b. Integral stimulation.

    c. Expiratory muscle strength training.

    d. Contrastive stress.

13. Which clinical characteristic most closely represents a diagnosis of childhood apraxia of speech?

    a. Consonantal distortions with adequate vowel production.

    b. Adequate vowel production with vowel distortions.

    c. Slow rate of speech with initiation difficulties.

    d. Inconsistency of speech sound errors for a given phoneme.

14. Which of the following types of treatment for apraxia of speech involves improving spatial and temporal aspects of articulatory movement?

    a. Articulatory kinematic.

    b. High frequency of practice.

    c. Rate and/or rhythm.

    d. Alternative/augmentative communication (AAC).

15. What is apraxia of speech (AOS)?

    a. A motor speech disorder characterized by phonological deficits.

    b. A motor speech disorder characterized by motor planning deficits.

    c. A motor speech disorder characterized by motor execution deficits.

    d. A motor speech disorder characterized by consistent speech errors.

16. Which can help distinguish between childhood dysarthria (CD) and childhood apraxia of speech (CAS)?

    a. In CD, there are frequent groping behaviors for speech postures, whereas in CAS there are not.

    b. In CAS, there are typically impairments to only articulation and prosody, whereas in CD there are typically impairments to all speech subsystems.

    c. In CAS, there are additional neuromuscular conditions, whereas in CD there are not.

    d. In CD, there are a variety of speech errors, whereas in CAS, distortions are most frequent.

17. As a treatment for childhood apraxia of speech (CAS), which speech subsystem is targeted through use of Dynamic Temporal and Tactile Cueing?

    a. Articulation.

    b. Respiration.

    c. Phonation.

    d. Prosody.

18. Which is typically a treatment method used to improve the respiratory subsystem?

    a. Expiratory muscle strength training.

    b. Effortful closure.

    c. Phonetic placement.

    d. Relaxation strategies.

19. Which type of dysarthria is associated with imprecise consonants, decreased loudness, harsh vocal quality, and one cerebral hemisphere?

    a. Hypokinetic dysarthria.

    b. Spastic dysarthria.

    c. Unilateral upper motor neuron dysarthria.

    d. Flaccid dysarthria.

20. What is considered a type of prosodic impairment in motor speech disorders?

    a. Excess and equal stress.

    b. Palilalia.

    c. Diplophonia.

    d. Audible inspiration.

Cleft Palate and Craniofacial Conditions

1. The philtrum is:
   a. Also called Cupid's bow.
   b. Part of the naris.
   c. The middle meatus.
   d. The indentation from the columella down to the upper lip.

2. Complete clefts of the primary palate:
   a. Involve the lip and part of the alveolus.
   b. Extend through the lip and alveolus to the incisive foramen.
   c. Extend from the uvula to incisive foramen.
   d. Has no lip involvement.

3. A bifid uvula:
   a. Is a type of secondary incomplete cleft.
   b. Indicates a complete cleft palate.
   c. Will develop normally at 7 weeks' gestation.
   d. Hinders closure of the velopharyngeal complex.

4. During speech, which of the following rises in a superior and posterior direction to contact the posterior pharyngeal wall?
   a. Eustachian tube.
   b. Velum.
   c. Uvula.
   d. Incisive foramen.

5. The premaxilla is:
   a. A triangular bone that contains the upper incisors.
   b. Part of the soft palate.
   c. Soft tissue of the faucial pillars.
   d. Connected to the columella.

6. For children with cleft palate, breastfeeding:
   a. Causes no issues.
   b. Usually is not possible.
   c. Is highly recommended.
   d. Is considered dangerous.

7. Another name for the pharyngeal tonsils.
   a. Adenoids.
   b. Pharynx.
   c. Velopharynx.
   d. Middle turbinate.

8. Which of the following is caused by micrognathia?

   a. Fetal alcohol syndrome.

   b. Pierre Robin sequence.

   c. Stickler syndrome.

   d. Velocardiofacial syndrome.

9. Velopharyngeal insufficiency:

   a. Is caused by faulty learned speech patterns.

   b. Is due to abnormal structures.

   c. Is the same thing as velopharyngeal incompetence.

   d. Results in speech with frequent nasal snorts.

10. Which of the following is most perceptible on vowels?

    a. Hypernasality.

    b. Hyponasality.

    c. Cul-de-sac resonance.

    d. Nasal emission.

11. A fistula:

    a. Is a bunching of muscles in the pharynx.

    b. Is a hole in the palate due to surgical repair breakdown.

    c. Typically causes hyponasality.

    d. Is identified by an articulation test.

12. Pneumatic activities involve:

    a. Swallowing.

    b. "Velar dimple."

    c. Air pressure.

    d. Gagging.

13. A pharyngeal flap is:

    a. A technique to lengthen the velum.

    b. A prosthetic device.

    c. A technique to close midline velopharyngeal openings.

    d. Always used in conjunction with speech therapy.

14. The main muscle mass of the velum is the:

    a. Inferior constrictor.

    b. Palatopharyngeus.

    c. Superior constrictor.

    d. Levator veli palatini.

15. Which is NOT a compensatory articulation error due to VPI?
    a. Pharyngeal plosive.
    b. Glottal stop.
    c. Distortion of "sh" sound.
    d. Posterior nasal fricative.

16. Craniosynostosis:
    a. Is premature fusion of the sutures, which causes abnormal growth of the skull and facial bones.
    b. Causes a Class II malocclusion.
    c. Causes minor cardiac and vascular anomalies.
    d. Is a characteristic of orofaciodigital syndrome type 1.

17. Treatment of VPI:
    a. Consists of intensive speech therapy.
    b. Requires physical management.
    c. Rarely involves surgery.
    d. Typically uses nonspeech oral motor exercises to strengthen the pharyngeal structures.

18. Which muscles open the eustachian tubes during swallowing?
    a. Palatopharyngeus.
    b. Tensor veli palatini.
    c. Superior constrictor.
    d. Musculus uvulae.

19. Passavant's ridge:
    a. Is not a permanent structure.
    b. Is a clefted alveolar ridge.
    c. Must be evaluated during the oral mechanism examination.
    d. Is a contributor to normal velopharyngeal function.

20. Why is it important to understand a patient's basic pattern of velopharyngeal closure?
    a. It will indicate the success of speech therapy treatment.
    b. It will help differentiate between hyponasality and hypernasality.
    c. It can affect surgical treatment decisions for VPI management.
    d. It allows a nasalance score to be compared with normative data.

Voice Disorders in Children and Adults

1. Which of the following is an extrinsic laryngeal muscle?
   a. Lateral cricoarytenoids.
   b. Mylohyoid.
   c. Posterior cricoarytenoids.
   d. Interarytenoids.

2. Which of the following is an intrinsic laryngeal muscle?
   a. Thyroarytenoid.
   b. Geniohyoid.
   c. Sternothyroid.
   d. Hyoglossus.

3. What are the three layers of the vocal folds?
   a. Cover, vocal ligament, body.
   b. Sheath, thyroid ligament, corpus.
   c. Coat, vocal ligament, body.
   d. Cover, cricoid ligament, frame.

4. Which portion of the vagus nerve innervates the glottal and supraglottal areas?
   a. Pharyngeal nerve.
   b. Internal laryngeal nerve.
   c. Superior laryngeal nerve.
   d. Inferior laryngeal nerve.

5. Which portion of the vagus nerve innervates the glottal and infraglottal areas?
   a. External laryngeal nerve.
   b. Recurrent laryngeal nerve.
   c. Pharyngeal nerve.
   d. Superior laryngeal nerve.

6. Which phonation type is best described as noise plus an air burst?
   a. Normal voice.
   b. Strained voice.
   c. Breathy voice.
   d. Glottal fry.

7. What is a modal register?
   a. The lowest portion of one's phonational range.
   b. The largest portion of one's phonational range.
   c. The highest portion of one's phonational range.
   d. The smallest portion of one's phonational range.

Review>Practice>Motivate>Analyze>Apply

8. What term refers to the number of times per second the vocal folds open and close during phonation?
   a. Intensity.
   b. Fundamental frequency.
   c. Jitter.
   d. Shimmer.

9. What term refers to the average cycle-to-cycle change in amplitude from one cycle to the next?
   a. Intensity.
   b. Fundamental frequency.
   c. Jitter.
   d. Shimmer.

10. Which form of aerodynamic testing measures pressure below the vocal folds and is related to the degree of medial compression of the closed vocal folds?
    a. Airflow rate.
    b. Subglottic pressure.
    c. Glottal resistance.
    d. Maximum phonation time.

11. What term refers to the aspect of voice perceived by listeners?
    a. Fundamental frequency.
    b. Vocal intensity.
    c. Vocal quality.
    d. Symmetry.

12. What aspect of voice, assessed via stroboscopic means, refers to the regularity of successive cycles of vibration?
    a. Symmetry.
    b. Amplitude.
    c. Periodicity.
    d. Phase.

13. Which form of vocal fold excrescence is usually bilateral in nature and occurs at the junction of the anterior one-third and posterior two-thirds of the vocal folds?
    a. Polyps.
    b. Cysts.
    c. Nodules.
    d. Edema.

14. Which form of vocal fold excrescence is caused by an infection and may result in restriction of breathing and stridor?

    a. Reinke's edema.

    b. Muscle tension dysphonia.

    c. Human papillomavirus.

    d. Puberphonia.

15. Damage to which nerve will lead to difficulty with pitch control and reduced pitch range?

    a. Superior laryngeal nerve.

    b. Inferior laryngeal nerve.

    c. Pharyngeal nerve.

    d. Maxillary nerve.

16. What is the most common acquired voice problem in children?

    a. Vocal fold paralysis.

    b. Vocal fold polyps.

    c. Bilateral nodules.

    d. Sulcus vocalis.

17. The *CAPE-V* is a form of what type of assessment?

    a. Functional assessment.

    b. Perceptual assessment.

    c. Acoustic assessment.

    d. Aerodynamic assessment.

18. What is an effect of radiation therapy?

    a. Tissue fibrosis.

    b. Fatigue.

    c. Nausea.

    d. Hair loss.

19. What is the term for the permanent opening to the respiratory tract that can be found in the front of the neck following a total laryngectomy?

    a. Trachea.

    b. Stoma.

    c. Dissection.

    d. Esophagostoma.

20. What is a tracheoesophageal prosthesis?

   a. An artificial larynx that produces vibrations through the vocal tract, which is then perceived as voice.

   b. A one-way valve that allows air to pass through and vibrate esophageal tissues, which is then perceived as voice.

   c. A one-way valve through which a person who has a tracheostomy tube can redirect airflow, which is then perceived as voice.

   d. A cap that is placed at the end of a tracheostomy tube, which allows a person to have normal function of their respiratory and phonatory systems.

Chapter 17, Appendix 17A, Review Questions

Dysphagia: Swallowing and Swallowing Disorders

1. Which portion of the pharynx contains the epiglottis?
   a. Nasopharynx.
   b. Oropharynx.
   c. Tracheopharynx.
   d. Laryngopharynx.

2. Which cranial nerve controls taste from the posterior one-third of the tongue?
   a. Trigeminal nerve (CN V).
   b. Facial nerve (CN VII).
   c. Glossopharyngeal nerve (CN IX).
   d. Vagus nerve (CN X).

3. What are the four phases traditionally acknowledged as making up the swallow?
   a. Oral prep phase, lingual phase, pharyngeal phase, esophageal phase.
   b. Oral prep phase, oral phase, epiglottal phase, esophageal phase.
   c. Oral prep phase, oral phase, pharyngeal phase, esophageal phase.
   d. Oral prep phase, lingual phase, tracheal phase, epiglottic phase.

4. How many pharyngeal constrictor muscles are there?
   a. Two.
   b. Three.
   c. Four.
   d. Five.

5. During which phase of swallowing does anterior-posterior bolus transit occur?
   a. Oral prep.
   b. Oral.
   c. Pharyngeal.
   d. Esophageal.

6. What is an impact of normal aging on the swallow?
   a. Delayed pharyngeal swallow initiation.
   b. Decreased lingual pressure.
   c. Increased occurrence of aspiration.
   d. Shortened opening of the upper esophageal sphincter.

7. Which muscle has the main action of elevating the posterior tongue to cause contact with the soft palate?
    a. Hyoglossus.
    b. Styloglossus.
    c. Palatoglossus.
    d. Genioglossus.

8. Which muscle flattens and broadens the tongue?
    a. Superior longitudinal.
    b. Inferior longitudinal.
    c. Transverse.
    d. Vertical.

9. In which neurological condition are lingual rocking, pharyngeal dysmotility, and pharyngeal pooling common features?
    a. Amyotrophic lateral sclerosis.
    b. Myasthenia gravis.
    c. Parkinson's disease.
    d. Multiple sclerosis.

10. What would be the most appropriate classification for a tumor occurring on the epiglottis?
    a. Supraglottic tumor.
    b. Infraglottic tumor.
    c. Hemiglottic tumor.
    d. Glottic tumor.

11. What is the term for food or liquid entering the airway, below the true vocal folds?
    a. Penetration.
    b. Pneumonia.
    c. Aspiration.
    d. Invasion.

12. On the 8-point penetration-aspiration scale, which level is labeled "material enters the airway, contacts the vocal folds, and is ejected from the airway"?
    a. Level 2.
    b. Level 4.
    c. Level 6.
    d. Level 8.

13. What is the absence of esophageal peristalsis and failure of the lower esophageal sphincter to relax?
    a. Zenker's diverticulum.
    b. Esophagitis.
    c. **Achalasia.**
    d. Stricture.

14. Which diagnostic instrumentation for swallow evaluation uses radiological means to assess oropharyngeal function?
    a. **Modified barium swallow study (MBSS).**
    b. Fiber-optic endoscopic evaluation of swallowing (FEES).
    c. Pharyngeal manometry.
    d. Ultrasound imaging (US).

15. Which postural technique may be best suited for use when a person exhibits a delay in pharyngeal swallow initiation?
    a. Right head turn.
    b. Head tilt.
    c. **Chin tuck.**
    d. Side lying.

16. What is sarcopenia?
    a. Muscle rigidity.
    b. Muscle flaccidity.
    c. Muscle hypertrophy.
    d. **Muscle wasting.**

17. Which swallowing exercise has been found to improve anterior laryngeal excursion?
    a. Masako maneuver.
    b. Thermal tactile stimulation.
    c. **Shaker exercise.**
    d. Mendelsohn maneuver.

18. Which postural strategy may be most effective if a person experiences insufficient lingual transit?
    a. Chin tuck.
    b. **Head tilt.**
    c. Side lying.
    d. Head turn.

19. When using the Functional Oral Intake Scale (FOIS), which level indicates a total oral diet with no restrictions?

    a. Level 3.

    b. Level 5.

    c. Level 6.

    d. Level 7.

20. Which swallowing exercise has been found to increase oral lingual pressures?

    a. Thermal tactile stimulation.

    b. Oral motor exercises.

    c. Supraglottic swallow.

    d. Effortful swallow.

Augmentative and Alternative Communication

1. The Americans with Disabilities Act (ADA) requires that hospitals provide which of the following?

   a. There must be an effective means of communication for patients, family members, and hospital visitors.

   b. Assistive technology centers must be present in each state.

   c. Every child must have access to free and appropriate public education.

   d. Students in public schools should initially be seen through RTI.

2. Which of the following are considered low-tech tools for augmentative and alternative communication?

   a. iPad with communication applications.

   b. A button pressed to initiate a single, preprogrammed spoken message.

   c. Printed out pictures for making choices or as a visual schedule.

   d. Mac laptop with text-to-speech capabilities.

3. Which one is NOT a common scanning pattern?

   a. Linear.

   b. Eye gaze.

   c. Circular.

   d. Top-bottom.

4. Which of the following is an appropriate standardized assessment to determine an appropriate AAC system?

   a. Clinical Evaluation of Language Fundamentals.

   b. Preschool Language Scales.

   c. Boston Diagnostic Aphasia Evaluation.

   d. There are currently no standardized assessment batteries in AAC.

5. What is feature matching in augmentative and alternative communication?

   a. Matching the skills and needs of the person with communication needs with the features of various AAC systems.

   b. Matching specific vocabulary needs to an individual and making them easily accessible.

   c. Featuring specific people and phrases within a communication system to support individuals with cognitive decline.

   d. Selecting the appropriate communication device based on the SLP's familiarity with devices.

Review>Practice>Motivate>Analyze>Apply

6. Which of the following is an example of a visual scene display?

    a. Two separate pictures presented, one of an orange and one of an apple.

    b. A visual schedule of five different pictures of activities that will occur throughout the day.

    c. A photograph of two kids actively engaged in playing soccer and their puppy is nipping at their feet.

    d. A grid-based communication application using pictures/photographs to help an individual communicate.

7. Which of the following is a knowledge barrier for a family or individual needing AAC?

    a. When the individual does not yet have a device due to funding.

    b. When the individual has a device but does not know how to use it.

    c. When the individual is not allowed to use the device outside of a hospital.

    d. When the individual has a device but thinks the device will stop their child from learning to speak.

8. An SLP would consider trialing eye-gaze technology to establish access to a communication system for a client that:

    a. Has two or three viable sites for switch access.

    b. Can't use any switches or any other means of access.

    c. Is a direct selector using their right index finger.

    d. is legally blind in both eyes but has good audition.

9. Which of the following conditions might require permanent AAC usage?

    a. Intubation following surgery.

    b. Prescription of voice rest.

    c. Total glossectomy.

    d. Severe laryngitis.

10. What are manual signs considered?

    a. Unaided communication.

    b. Aided communication.

    c. Temporary AAC.

    d. Permanent AAC.

11. Using a speech-generating device:

    a. Is no longer stigmatizing.

    b. May delay oral speech and language development.

    c. Is covered by insurance when recommended by a physician.

    d. May promote increased verbal communication.

12. Which of the following occurs in message co-construction?
   a. The client is able to share basic content elements of the message, which the communication partner confirms and expands.
   b. The client is able to, when given additional time, create their messages independently.
   c. The communication partner interrupts and guesses at the client's meaning.
   d. The client pantomimes and uses gestures to communicate their message.

13. Which act mandated assistive technology centers in each state and territory?
   a. Assistive Technology Act Amendments of 2004.
   b. Free Appropriate Public Education.
   c. Rehabilitation Act of 1973.
   d. Individuals with Disabilities Education Act.

14. Which of the following is NOT considered unaided AAC?
   a. Gestures.
   b. Manual signs.
   c. Pantomime.
   d. Pictures.

15. Which of the following describes a communication device that does not have access to Wi-Fi and no other applications?
   a. Low-tech device.
   b. Mid-tech device.
   c. Dedicated device.
   d. Nondedicated device.

16. Which type of symbol does NOT resemble the referent?
   a. Opaque.
   b. Translucent.
   c. Transparent.
   d. Real objects.

17. Which of the following describes a static display?
   a. When a screen changes following input.
   b. When a screen does not change when touched.
   c. When a device does not move location.
   d. When a device is considered high-tech.

18. Which of the following is an example of alternative access?
    a. When a user uses their finger to directly touch their selection.
    b. When a user uses eye gaze and looks at their selection.
    c. **When a user uses linear scanning and the device highlights each item in a row individually when the row is selected.**
    d. When a user uses natural speech to dictate what they wish to type.

19. When is partner-assisted scanning used?
    a. **When the person who uses AAC cannot initiate the scan independently.**
    b. When visual interaction with the device is not possible.
    c. When auditory interaction with the device is not possible.
    d. When the person who uses AAC uses direct selection.

20. Which of the following professionals is unlikely to be involved in an assessment for AAC?
    a. Speech-language pathologist.
    b. Vocational counselor.
    c. Biomedical engineer.
    d. **Computer programmer.**

Audiology and Hearing Impairment

1. Which structure is considered part of the outer ear?
   a. Malleus.
   b. Pinna.
   c. Cochlea.
   d. Stapes.

2. Which structure is considered part of the inner ear?
   a. Semicircular canals.
   b. Incus.
   c. Tympanic membrane.
   d. Stapes.

3. Which structure is considered part of the middle ear?
   a. Pinna.
   b. Cochlea.
   c. Stapes.
   d. Reissneir's membrane.

4. What is the function of the cochlea?
   a. To change electrical energy into mechanical energy and finally into neural impulses.
   b. To change mechanical energy into electrical energy and finally into neural impulses.
   c. To change neural energy into mechanical energy and finally into electrical signals.
   d. To change mechanical energy into hydromechanical energy and finally into neural impulses.

5. Which form of audiological evaluation allows a visual inspection of the outer ear and surrounding tissues, external auditory meatus, and tympanic membrane?
   a. Tympanometry.
   b. Otoacoustic emissions.
   c. Otoscopy.
   d. Pure tone audiometry.

6. A 75 dBHL hearing loss would be indicative of what severity of loss?
   a. Slight/minimal.
   b. Mild.
   c. Moderate.
   d. Severe.

Review>Practice>Motivate>Analyze>Apply

7. A 30 dBHL hearing loss would be indicative of what severity of loss?
   a. Slight/minimal.
   b. Mild.
   c. Moderate.
   d. Severe.

8. What is the speech recognition threshold (SRT)?
   a. The highest hearing level at which one can correctly recognize speech stimuli.
   b. The lowest hearing level at which one can correctly recognize speech stimuli.
   c. The highest hearing level at which one can correctly hear auditory stimuli.
   d. The lowest hearing level at which one can correctly hear auditory stimuli.

9. Which form of audiological assessment allows for assessment of middle ear function?
   a. Immittance testing.
   b. Otoscopy.
   c. Otoacoustic emissions.
   d. Auditory-evoked potentials.

10. Which portion of the auditory system is tested using auditory brainstem response?
    a. Outer ear.
    b. Middle ear.
    c. Inner ear.
    d. Semi-circular canals.

11. What is a disorder of the ear that results in a small pinna?
    a. Anotia.
    b. Microtia.
    c. Atresia.
    d. Osteoma.

12. What is a disorder of the ear that results in scarring of the eardrum?
    a. Fungal otitis.
    b. Exostosis.
    c. Tympanosclerosis.
    d. Otitis media.

13. What is a disorder of the ear that is caused by a nonmalignant growth, often following a foreign body making its way into the middle ear space?

a. Cholesteatoma.

b. Otosclerosis.

c. Ossicular discontinuity.

d. Barotrauma.

14. What is the term for hearing loss associated with the aging process?

a. Ménière's disease.

b. Ototoxicity.

c. Noise-induced hearing loss.

d. Presbycusis.

15. What is auditory neuropathy spectrum disorder?

a. A disorder characterized by abnormal cochlear function and normal auditory nerve function.

b. A disorder characterized by normal cochlear function and abnormal auditory nerve function.

c. A disorder characterized by abnormal outer ear function with normal auditory nerve function.

d. A disorder characterized by abnormal outer and middle ear function with normal inner ear and auditory nerve function.

16. What portion of a hearing aid converts acoustic sound into an electrical signal?

a. Microphone.

b. Amplifier.

c. Receiver.

d. Battery.

17. What portion of a hearing aid converts an amplified electrical signal to an acoustic signal that is delivered to the ear?

a. Microphone.

b. Amplifier.

c. Receiver.

d. Battery.

18. What is electroacoustic gain?

a. The amount or magnitude of amplification in dB.

b. The magnitude of amplification across the frequency range of a hearing aid.

c. The equal increase in dB for all incoming sounds.

d. The increase in dB for incoming sounds based on intensity.

19. Which portion of a cochlear implant stimulates cranial nerve VIII (vestibulocochlear nerve)?

    a. External sound processor.
    b. Internal unit.
    c. Electrode array.
    d. Microphone.

20. In the auditory hierarchy of listening, which level describes a person's ability to make a same versus different judgment of auditory stimuli?

    a. Detection.
    b. Discrimination.
    c. Recognition.
    d. Comprehension.

Online Examinations

Guidelines for Effective Use of the Online Exams

The three online exams included with this text are designed to simulate the Speech-Language Pathology Praxis® exam.

We advise you to take the first simulated exam after you have reviewed the content chapters of this text. Taking a practice exam before you have studied the information that will be tested on the Praxis® exam will only reinforce what you do not know. Learning what you know, not just what you don't, will help you identify your individual content knowledge strengths and weaknesses. This information can then be used to develop a targeted study plan and acquire mastery of the knowledge you need to pass the Praxis® exam.

Each TherapyEd online practice exam, like the actual Praxis® exam, consists of 132 multiple choice items designed to be completed in 2½ hours. This replication of the Praxis® exam format enables you to simulate the exam experience and practice your timing for the actual test.

Upon completing each TherapyEd online exam, you will receive an analysis of your exam performance. This detailed analysis will identify your strengths and weaknesses by Domain of Knowledge and Category, as well as which items you answered incorrectly. Extensive answer rationales are provided for all questions.

If the feedback provided shows a particular area of weakness, TherapyEd's Online Learning Portal includes content-specific mini-exams, drawn from the full exams, to help you focus on individual areas. Using this feature can help you better focus your studying.

We believe engaging in this extensive (and at times challenging) preparation based on your simulated exam performance is far better than being underprepared for the high-stakes SLP Praxis® exam. Students consistently report taking the TherapyEd online exams, reviewing the answer rationales, and focusing their study plans is well worth the effort when they successfully pass the Praxis® exam. To start taking an exam, follow the instructions found on the inside cover of this book to access TherapyEd's Online Learning Portal.

Exam A

Domains of Knowledge

- Anatomy and Physiology of Communication and Swallowing
- Acoustics
- Language Acquisition: Preverbal and Early Language
- Research, Evidence-Based Practice, and Tests and Measurements
- The Practice of Speech-Language Pathology
- Speech Sound Disorders in Children
- Language Disorders in Young Children
- Spoken Language Disorders in School-Age Populations
- Written Language Disorders in School-Age Populations
- Autism Spectrum Disorders
- Stuttering and Other Fluency Disorders
- Acquired Language Disorders
- Motor Speech Disorders
- Cleft Palate and Craniofacial Conditions
- Voice Disorders in Children and Adults
- Dysphagia: Swallowing and Swallowing Disorders
- Augmentative and Alternative Communication
- Audiology and Hearing Impairment

Categories

 Category 1—Foundations and Professional Practice

 Category 2—Screening, Assessment, Evaluation and Diagnosis

 Category 3—Planning, Implementation and Evaluation of Treatment

Examination A

A1

Audiology and Hearing Impairment

A speech-language pathologist (SLP) in a public school is asked to assist with completion of yearly hearing screenings. The SLP completes a screening on a child and observes that the child did not identify any of the higher pitched sounds presented to the left ear. Which of the following options is BEST for the SLP to take?

Choices:
A. Diagnose the patient with a hearing loss in the left ear and work to set up systems in the classroom to aid in the child's learning.
B. Refer the patient for further hearing assessment and management options to be completed by a certified audiologist.
C. Repeat the screening procedure to ensure the child truly did not hear the presented high-pitched sounds.
D. Pass the child on their hearing screening as they responded to most of the presented sounds and are a high-achieving student.

Teaching Points

Correct Answer: B

A hearing screening is a pass/fail procedure that an SLP is qualified to complete. In this procedure, the SLP instructs the client to raise their hand upon hearing tones of various pitch in both ears. As this is a screening process, either the client identifies all tones and "passes" the screening or needs to be referred for further assessment. Audiologists are the health care providers who are most qualified to conduct hearing assessment and intervention.

A2

Acoustics

A speech scientist has recently become interested in aspects of nasal consonant productions, as they have been working on a project regarding hyper- and hyponasality. The speech scientist finds that nasal consonants have a low-frequency nasal formant because the nasal cavity acts as which of the following?

Choices:
A. A side cavity, resulting in a zero between F1 and F2.
B. A side cavity, resulting in a low-frequency F1.
C. The largest resonating cavity, resulting in a zero between F1 and F2.
D. The largest resonating cavity, resulting in a low-frequency F1.

Teaching Points

Correct Answer: C

Children with fragile X syndrome present with language difficulties in syntactic development, organization, auditory memory, fluency, and prosody. For this reason, the most appropriate targets for the SLP to choose in working with this student would be auditory skills (i.e., targeting auditory memory) and pragmatic skills (i.e., fluency and prosody). In contrast to this, semantic skills, receptive language, and visual skills are a relative strength for this population and would not be most appropriate for target selection.

A15

Language Disorders in Young Children

A child has been diagnosed with a cognitive disability with expected and associated language difficulties. Using this information, which intervention approach is MOST EFFECTIVE to implement in therapy sessions?

Choices:

A. Complex sentence structure and increasing relative clauses.
B. Pragmatic communication and increasing vocabulary.
C. Phonological memory and increasing attention span.
D. Simple sentence structure and increasing sight-word recognition.

Teaching Points

Correct Answer: A

Children with cognitive disabilities generally show delayed morphological development, due to their tendency to use less complex sentences and fewer relative clauses. By targeting these language structures through intervention, these children can make improvements in both syntax and morphology. While there are semantic deficits associated with cognitive disability, it tends to be deficits in understanding abstract vocabulary, rather than vocabulary acquisition. Additionally, pragmatic communication is generally commensurate with cognitive age and is not the most appropriate treatment target for this population. Phonological combinations would be appropriate if the child demonstrated an associated speech sound disorder, and attention span would be appropriate with associated attention deficits (i.e., ADHD). Finally, children with cognitive disability often use simple sentence structure, thus more advanced skills should be targeted.

A16

Acoustics

An SLP is using spectrographic analysis to compare voiced and voiceless phonemes. Using this analysis method, the SLP would expect that, compared to voiced stops, word-initial voiceless stops in English are expected to have which features?

Choices:

A. Shorter voice onset time.
B. Longer voice onset time.
C. More compact spectrum.
D. More diffuse spectrum.

Teaching Points

Correct Answer: B

Voice onset time (VOT) duration distinguishes voiced and voiceless stops, with voiceless stops having longer VOTs, especially in word-initial position. A compact versus diffuse spectrum distinguishes stop place of articulation, with bilabial stops having diffuse falling spectra, alveolar stops having diffuse rising spectra, and velar stops having compact spectra.

A17

Acquired Language Disorders

An SLP working at an outpatient clinic would like to start a community group for persons with acquired speech and language deficits. The SLP would like to structure this group around the common good approach to ethical standards. Which scenario would BEST describe use of this standard in the setup of this group?

Choices:
A. Using only verbal means of communication so all group members are working toward treatment goals.
B. Using alternative means of communication so all group members have multiple means.
C. Using alternative means of communication so all group members become more proficient in their use.
D. Using all means of communication in order to allow for all group individuals to participate in the group.

Teaching Points

Correct Answer: D

Given that the SLP would like to structure the group around the common good approach, she should structure the group in a way that best serves the entire community and not just some members. As such, the SLP should encourage group members to utilize whatever means of communication they would prefer in order to participate in the group. While focusing a single use of communication may be best for some members and may help a few others improve in that form of communication, there may be some members of the group who would not be able to participate should the focus be on a sole means of communication.

A18

Cleft Palate and Craniofacial Conditions

After receiving surgical correction of velopharyngeal insufficiency (VPI), a child is referred to speech therapy. Which activity is BEST for correction of compensatory errors following the child's surgical procedure?

Choices:
A. Articulation placement procedures.
B. Velopharyngeal exercises.
C. Blowing exercises.
D. Oral motor exercises.

Teaching Points

Correct Answer: A

Following correction of VPI, speech therapy may be indicated to improve any remaining speech errors. VPI often requires only one instance of surgical management to fix the problem and blowing exercises and velopharyngeal exercises are not effective as treatment methods for this population. Therefore, the best selection would be articulation placement, in order to help the client learn proper placement of the articulators following the surgical change.

A19

Acoustics

An SLP is examining a spectrogram and waveform for the initial sounds in a child's production of the word *spaghetti*. The waveform begins with a silence followed by a transient noise. In the spectrogram, the transient noise is followed by formants, then by high-amplitude, high-frequency continuant noise. When listening to the word, what does the SLP expect to hear?

Choices:
A. A normally produced initial part of the word.
B. A metathesized /s/ and /p/.
C. An /s/ produced as /f/.
D. A /p/ produced as /m/.

Teaching Points

Correct Answer: B

A silence followed by a transient noise indicates a stop manner of articulation; therefore, the word begins with a stop. Formants indicate a resonant sound such as a vowel. Continuant noise is a characteristic of fricatives, and high-amplitude, high-frequency continuant noise is characteristic of /s/. Therefore, the sequence in the child's production is stop-vowel-/s/, while the expected sequence is /s/-stop-vowel. If /s/ were produced as /f/, the frication noise would be low amplitude with no high-frequency peak. If /p/ were produced as /m/, there would be no silence or transient noise.

A20

Stuttering and Other Fluency Disorders

An SLP provides intervention for a young child who stutters. The SLP notes that the parents speak quickly, interrupt frequently, and ask the child questions. The SLP decides to work with the parents on developing a more relaxed communication approach when interacting with their child. What is the primary goal for implementing this approach?

Choices:
A. Improve the quality of their home life.
B. Allow them to serve as a model for communication.
C. Reduce the demands on communication for the child.
D. Improve fluency without providing therapy that might cause anxiety.

Teaching Points

Correct Answer: C

It has been demonstrated that fluency can be enhanced by modifying the speaking environment of young children. Thus, ensuring that the child is exposed to less demanding communication experiences allows for that to occur. Because making these types of communication changes is challenging, it is important to help the family structure these experiences, and usually in short, focused activities.

A21

Acoustics

An SLP is analyzing the speech characteristics of vowels. A pitch contour for a vowel shows a frequency of 150 Hz at the midpoint. Which frequency is expected of the fifth harmonic at the same location?

Choices:
A. 500 Hz.
B. 750 Hz.
C. 1,000 Hz.
D. 1,250 Hz.

Teaching Points

Correct Answer: B

All harmonics are integer multiples of F0. If F0 = 150 Hz, then H5 = 5×150 Hz or 750 Hz.

A22

Language Disorders in Young Children

An SLP is preparing to perform a language assessment with a child whose cultural background is unfamiliar to the SLP. The SLP is concerned about using assessment materials that may assume all cultural populations have the same life experiences. Which type of bias is this SLP identifying with the assessment materials?

Choices:
A. Content.
B. Linguistic.
C. Material.
D. Cultural.

Teaching Points

Correct Answer: A

Content bias refers to test stimuli, methods, or procedures reflecting the assumption that all populations have the same life experiences and have learned similar concepts and vocabulary. If the child from this scenario has not been exposed to the material covered in this test, there may be an inaccurate diagnosis of a language disorder. In contrast to this, linguistic bias is the disparity between the language or dialect used by the examiner, the child, and/or the language or dialect expected in the child's response. Material bias and cultural bias are not forms of bias that are applicable in the evaluation of children from culturally diverse backgrounds.

A23

Anatomy and Physiology of Communication and Swallowing

A patient who has recently been diagnosed with Parkinson's disease has started to experience changes in their mobility and speech production. Which of the following is the BEST description as to the underlying cause of this patient's symptoms?

Choices:
A. There is degradation in areas of the frontal lobe that produce acetylcholine, which causes hyperkinetic movements.
B. There is degradation in areas of the amygdala that produce serotonin, which causes hypokinetic movements.
C. There is degradation in areas of the basal ganglia that produce dopamine, which causes hypokinetic movement.
D. There is degradation in areas of the parietal lobe that produce glutamate, which causes hyperkinetic movement.

Teaching Points

Correct Answer: C

Parkinson's disease is a neurodegenerative disorder caused by the breakdown of neurons in the basal ganglia, leading to a reduction in dopamine. Dopamine is a neurotransmitter that is important in regulating body movements. In the case of Parkinson's disease, the reduction in dopamine leads to hypokinetic, or reduced, movements, such as shuffling gait, masked faces, and hypokinetic dysarthria.

A24

Spoken Language Disorders in School-Age Populations

An SLP is determining whether a 6-year-old client is making progress. How can the SLP determine progress on the target of answering *wh-* questions?

Choices:
A. Discuss with the teacher how the student is doing in her class, in terms of answering questions.
B. Ask questions during a therapy session that have never been asked before.
C. Determine how many correct answers the child gives on questions frequently used during therapy.
D. Ask the student how she is feeling about how she is doing on the skills.

Teaching Points

Correct Answer: B

Administration of untrained probe items will reveal the extent of the child's learning of the targets. This will indicate whether or not generalization is taking place and if the child has truly learned the specific skill being targeted during therapy or has memorized rote answers to the targets during the sessions. Discussing with a teacher whether or not the student is doing these tasks in a classroom can give good insight on generalization as well, but administration of a probe during a therapy session will better reveal progress as the SLP will be able to control prompting and support levels.

A25

Language Acquisition: Preverbal and Early Language

A 2-year-old child demonstrates typical development. Which of the following semantic structures would the child MOST LIKELY demonstrate?

Choices:
A. Declarative sentences and contracted forms.
B. Gestures and phonological process suppression.
C. Relational terms and interrogative terms.
D. Derivational affixes and bound morphemes.

Teaching Points

Correct Answer: C

Relational (e.g., *on, under, next, to*) and interrogative (e.g., *what, who, how, why*) terms are semantic structures that are typically developed by 24 months of age. Additional terms that are developed include temporal relationship terms (e.g., *when, before*), physical relations (e.g., *big, little, wide, narrow*), and kinship terms (e.g., *son, parent, aunt, nephew*). Declarative sentences and contracted forms are syntactic structures, gestures are pragmatic constructs, phonological process suppression deals with phonology, and derivational affixes and bound morphemes are morphological structures.

A26

Dysphagia: Swallowing and Swallowing Disorder

Following a car accident, a patient is being treated by an SLP. The patient exhibits weakness in the orbicularis oris and buccinator muscles. Which problems would the patient MOST LIKELY exhibit as it relates to dysphagia?

Choices:
A. Oral incontinence with anterior loss and lateral residue.
B. Pharyngeal delay with excessive residue.
C. Reduced opening of the upper esophageal sphincter.
D. Piecemeal deglutition with silent aspiration.

Teaching Points

Correct Answer: A

The orbicularis oris and buccinator are the muscles of the lips and cheeks, respectively. If these muscles are weak, the bolus may leak through the lips or be left as residue in the anterior sulcus (i.e., the space between the bottom lip and the teeth) or the lateral sulci (i.e., the space between the cheeks and the teeth).

A27

Speech Sound Disorders in Children

Following a speech evaluation of a child, an SLP has determined that the child demonstrates significant amounts of homonymy in speech. The child produces the word /bo/ for both /bot/ and /bo/. However, the child does produce the /t/ phoneme in other word positions. Which intervention approach would be MOST EFFECTIVE for the SLP to utilize?

Choices:
A. Maximal contrast approach.
B. Integral stimulation.
C. Traditional approach.
D. Minimal pairs approach.

Teaching Points

Correct Answer: D

The goal of the minimal pairs method is to eliminate a child's creation of homonyms, or a singular production for multiple words. In this case, the child is producing /bo/ for both /bot/ and /bo/, which could be directly targeted utilizing this approach. In contrast, the maximal opposition method focuses on contrasting a target word with a maximally distinct sound (i.e., one that varies across a variety of features). However, in this method, reduction of homonymy is indirectly addressed, unlike in the minimal pairs method. Both the traditional method and integral stimulation method are used to treat phonetic errors and are utilized to establish a sound that is not present in a child's repertoire. Because this child is able to produce /t/ in other word positions, these methods would not help alleviate the homonymy being experienced.

A28

Augmentative and Alternative Communication

A 10-year-old child has been identified as a student who would benefit from augmentative and alternative communication (AAC). During the evaluation, the SLP trials use of printed-out photographs and pictures to help the child express wants and needs during the day. Which statement BEST describes the type of AAC utilized during this trial?

Choices:
A. Mid-tech, nondedicated AAC supports.
B. No-tech, dedicated AAC supports.
C. Low-tech, dedicated AAC supports.
D. Low-tech, nondedicated AAC supports.

Teaching Points

Correct Answer: D

Low-tech refers to a picture- and paper-based communication system. As there are no technological parts, these are frequently referred to as low-tech or light-tech options for AAC. *High-tech* refers to how much technology is used in the communication system. An iPad or other communication device would be considered high-tech. *Dedicated* would refer to a device that does not have Wi-Fi access and is exclusively used for communication purposes.

A29

Augmentative and Alternative Communication

An SLP works with a patient in an outpatient augmentative communication center. The SLP has implemented an unaided AAC device for the patient to use in order to facilitate communication with family and friends. Which means of AAC would the SLP MOST LIKELY utilize?

Choices:
A. Line drawings.
B. Speech-generating device.
C. Picture board.
D. Eye gaze.

Teaching Points

Correct Answer: D

Unaided AAC refers to the use of only the body to communicate, with no external aids or equipment. As eye gaze is a form of AAC that does not require equipment or aids to utilize, this would be the best choice for implementation with this patient. In contrast to this, line drawings, speech-generating devices, and picture boards all require external equipment and would be in direct opposition to the needs of the patient from this scenario.

A30

Voice Disorders in Children and Adults

A patient experiences essential tremor of the voice and is approximately 65% intelligible in unfamiliar settings. This patient is highly motivated to participate in speech-language therapy in order to improve their communicative effectiveness. Which treatment options are BEST for the SLP to implement?

Choices:
A. Elevating pitch and shortening phrase length.
B. Lowering pitch and semi-occluded vocal tract tasks.
C. Resonant voice therapy and shortening vowel durations.
D. Elevating pitch and optimizing breath groups.

Teaching Points

Correct Answer: A

Although there is limited evidence at this time, shortening phrase duration, shortening vowel length, and slightly elevating pitch have been found to be effective in alleviating the symptoms of essential tremor. By utilizing these approaches to treatment, the rhythmic oscillations of the tremor are effectively "masked" and do not appear during phonation. No other specific treatment approaches are uniformly efficacious in the treatment of this disorder, including lowering pitch, semi-occluded vocal tract tasks, resonant voice therapy, and optimizing breath groups.

A31

The Practice of Speech-Language Pathology

SLPs are required to gain knowledge of the nature of communication disorders, differences, and swallowing disorders across different age groups, cultures, and practice locations. Which of the following BEST describes a scenario that an SLP should not find themselves?

Choices:

A. Assessment and treatment for a patient experiencing a voice disorder after intubation trauma.

B. Assessment of and training in an alternative mode of communication for a patient with amyotrophic lateral sclerosis.

C. Programming and fitting of a hearing aid for a patient experiencing a sensorineural hearing loss.

D. Assessment and treatment for a patient experiencing a nonfluent aphasia after having a severe cerebrovascular accident.

Teaching Points

Correct Answer: C

The Big 9 areas of speech-language pathology practice include (1) articulation; (2) fluency; (3) voice and resonance (including respiration and phonation); (4) receptive and expressive language (phonology, morphology, syntax, semantics, and pragmatics) in speaking, listening, reading, writing, and manual modalities; (5) hearing (including impact on speech and language); (6) swallowing (including all phases of the swallow, oral function for feeding, and orofacial myofunction); (7) cognitive aspects of communication (attention, memory, sequencing, problem-solving, and executive functioning); (8) social aspects of communication (challenging behavior, ineffective social skills, lack of communication opportunities); and (9) communication modalities (oral, manual, augmentative, and alternative communication techniques and assistive technologies). While SLPs are educated to perform hearing-related services for individuals who are hard of hearing or Deaf/deaf (e.g., speech production, aural [re]habilitation, troubleshooting problems with a hearing aid), an audiologist is the professional trained to program and fit hearing aids for patients.

A32

Written Language Disorders in School-Age Populations

During a speech therapy session, an SLP asks a child the following question: "Which word starts with the same sound as dog? *Tiger*, *drink*, or *hog*?" Which aspect of phonological awareness is the SLP targeting?

Choices:

A. Rhyme awareness.

B. Onset-rime awareness.

C. Phonemic awareness.

D. Word awareness.

Teaching Points

Correct Answer: B

Onset-rime is when a child is able to identify which sounds start with the same sound. Rhyme awareness would require the child to identify which ending sounds were the same—in this case, the word *hog* out of the three choices.

A33

Motor Speech Disorders

A patient incurred a left hemorrhagic infarct with resulting apraxia of speech. Verbal communication consists of a few automatic words and phrases. When speech sound errors occur, they are distorted. Reading and receptive language skills are intact. Adaptive techniques used to suggest writing skills appear to be intact. Which treatment approach is BEST for improving verbal expression?

Choices:
A. A linguistic approach to treatment targeting increased length of utterance.
B. Adoption of melodic intonation therapy.
C. An articulatory kinematic approach.
D. Training communication partners in the use of repair strategies.

Teaching Points

Correct Answer: C

Because this patient demonstrates relatively intact receptive language skills and has a moderate-to-severe apraxia of speech, they are a perfect candidate for an articulatory kinematic approach. Use of this approach focuses on improving spatial/temporal aspects of articulatory movement as a means to improve speech production. This would help improve the patient's distortion of phonemes, thus improving verbal expression.

A34

The Practice of Speech-Language Pathology

A speech-language pathology student is preparing to submit final paperwork to the American Speech-Language-Hearing Association (ASHA) before beginning the clinical fellowship experience. Which requirement must be met by graduate student clinicians?

Choices:
A. Clinical experience during the educational program of at least 400 clock hours.
B. Thirty semester credit hours of study focused on the knowledge pertinent to speech-language pathology.
C. Graduate coursework and clinical practicum completed in an advanced level program.
D. Knowledge of the "Big 10" areas of speech-language pathology practice.

Teaching Points

Correct Answer: A

Graduate student clinicians are required to gather 400 direct hours of clinical experience with persons who have communication and swallowing disorders throughout their education. Additionally, graduate students are required to maintain a minimum of 36 semester credit hours at the graduate level, must complete graduate coursework and clinical practicum in a CAA-accredited program, and gain knowledge in the Big 9 areas of speech-language pathology practice.

A35

Dysphagia: Swallowing and Swallowing Disorder

A patient arrives for a videofluoroscopic swallowing assessment, after experiencing a few weeks of coughing while drinking. During the assessment, the SLP observes that the patient is experiencing difficulty narrowing the laryngeal inlet with incomplete posterior epiglottic movement. In which muscle is the patient MOST LIKELY experiencing an impairment?

Choices:
A. Lateral cricoarytenoid muscle.
B. Posterior cricoarytenoid muscle.
C. Oblique interarytenoid muscle.
D. Superior longitudinal muscle.

Teaching Points

Correct Answer: C

Contraction of the oblique interarytenoid muscle (along with the aryepiglottic fibers) narrows the laryngeal inlet and draws the epiglottis posteriorly to protect the airway during swallowing. While the lateral cricoarytenoid muscles help in vocal fold adduction, which also helps protect the airway during swallowing, this muscle does not play a role in narrowing of the laryngeal inlet. The posterior cricoarytenoid muscle is involved in vocal fold abduction. Finally, the superior longitudinal muscle runs the body of the tongue and is involved in elevation of the tip of the tongue.

A36

Voice Disorders in Children and Adults

A patient visits a local voice clinic for a consultation, with a primary complaint of rough vocal quality. Upon patient interview, the SLP notes that the patient complains of persistent bad breath and a globus sensation over the past month that has progressively worsened. While a medical diagnosis would need to confirm the findings, which is MOST LIKELY the cause of the patient's complaints?

Choices:
A. Vocal fold cyst.
B. Laryngeal papilloma.
C. Vocal fold atrophy.
D. Laryngeal cancer.

Teaching Points

Correct Answer: D

A hallmark characteristic of laryngeal cancer is hoarse or rough vocal quality. Additionally, patients suffering from laryngeal cancer may experience globus, as the tumor may invade other healthy tissue. As cancer is a progressive disorder, if left untreated, these symptoms may continue to worsen. While human papillomavirus (HPV) and cysts could cause hoarse/rough vocal quality, HPV, cysts, and vocal fold atrophy are all not associated with persistent bad breath or globus. Thus, these disorders would not be the problem for this patient and may be effectively ruled out.

A37

Stuttering and Other Fluency Disorders

A 3-year-old child has shown disfluencies in speech since beginning talking in sentences at about 2 years of age. Over time, the disfluencies have increased and now occur on about 12% of words. The child never comments about the stuttering moments and seems to be unaware when they occur. The child has no other speech and language problems, is socially engaged and interactive, and has normal motor skills. The parent reports having stuttered as a child as well but grew out of it. Which statement is MOST accurate?

Choices:

A. The child is showing normal disfluency and an SLP should help the parent see if the child will "grow out of it."

B. The child appears to be at the borderline stage of stuttering and is at risk because there is a family history.

C. When preschoolers stutter, it is best to take a wait-and-see approach.

D. Direct therapy is indicated to address the child's deficits.

Teaching Points

Correct Answer: B

This child is showing signs of beginning stuttering in that his disfluencies exceed 10% and have lasted longer than 6 months. He also shows risk factors (gender, persistence, and genetics) that increase the probability that he will need treatment to resolve his fluency problem.

A38

Autism Spectrum Disorders

An 11-year-old child engages in aberrant behaviors, including pushing and pinching, when unable to access something that is desired. The child does not have a reliable means of expressing needs due to being nonverbal. Which intervention approach is MOST EFFECTIVE to address the deficits?

Choices:

A. Augmentative and alternative communication.

B. Applied behavioral analysis (ABA).

C. Floor time.

D. Theory of mind.

Teaching Points

Correct Answer: A

Augmentative and alternative communication is used when an individual is unable to get their needs met through natural speech. In this case study, the child is a nonspeaking individual and therefore unable to get their needs met through natural speech and will need an alternative way to communicate with those around them. While ABA and/or floor time may be able to address their aggressive behaviors when the child is frustrated, the core of the difficulty in this situation is not being able to be understood or to request what they want.

A39

Motor Speech Disorders

An SLP in a skilled nursing facility is working with a patient diagnosed with dysarthria. The SLP notices that the patient fails to take a breath to replenish their air supply, which leads to the patient talking into reserve volume. The patient exhibits loudness decay when this occurs, and breath group lengths are longer than age and gender-matched controls. Which treatment approach is BEST for this patient?

Choices:
A. A thorough assessment of respiratory shape.
B. Improving coordination of the respiratory and phonatory systems.
C. Reducing maladaptive respiratory behaviors.
D. Adopting the Lee Silverman Voice Treatment (LSVT).

Teaching Points

Correct Answer: C

The type of breathing patterns that this particular speaker is exhibiting are not efficient from a communicative perspective. Focusing on reduction of the maladaptive respiratory behaviors can lead to reduction in loudness decay and age- and gender-appropriate breath groups. The speaker should be instructed in optimal breath groups and to replenish air supply at appropriate conversation junctures.

A40

Speech Sound Disorders in Children

A parent brings a 2-and-a-half-year-old child to a speech and language clinic over concerns with speech sound development. The parent reports that the child is unable to say the last part of their name, substitutes /w/ for /r/, and is unable to produce the /l/ sound. Which statement BEST describes this child?

Choices:
A. The child demonstrates normal phonological development and does not qualify for speech services.
B. The child has gliding and qualifies for speech services.
C. The child has devoicing and qualifies for speech services.
D. The child demonstrates liquid simplification and qualifies for speech services.

Teaching Points

Correct Answer: A

Given the child's young age, it is not yet expected for them to have mastered these speech sounds, so while they do glide and exhibit liquid simplification at this time, they do not yet qualify for speech services based on the given information, as these sounds are not yet expected to be mastered.

A41

Motor Speech Disorders

An SLP has recently changed job settings to work in a clinic specializing in the treatment of motor speech disorders. A new patient arrives for a comprehensive motor speech evaluation, during which the SLP records a speech sample for later review. Upon review of the speech sample, the SLP is questioning whether the patient demonstrates dysarthria or apraxia of speech (AOS). Which would be the BEST characteristic to differentiate these two motor speech disorders?

Choices:
A. Speakers with apraxia often demonstrate co-occurring neuromuscular conditions, while speakers with dysarthria do not.
B. Speakers with apraxia often demonstrate co-occurring dysphagia, while speakers with dysarthria do not.
C. Speakers with dysarthria often have deficits in the respiratory subsystem, while speakers with apraxia do not.
D. Speakers with dysarthria often demonstrate inconsistent speech errors, while speakers with apraxia are more consistent.

Teaching Points

Correct Answer: C
While there are many differences present between dysarthria and apraxia that can help with differential diagnosis of the two conditions, the best characteristic from this scenario is that speakers with dysarthria often demonstrate respiratory subsystem deficits not seen in apraxia. In dysarthria, there is often some level of damage in all five speech subsystems (e.g., articulation, phonation, respiration, phonation, and prosody), while speakers with AOS often only demonstrate deficits in articulation and prosody. Additionally, speakers with dysarthria often have co-occurring neuromuscular deficits and dysphagia, and typically demonstrate consistency in speech errors, whereas speakers with AOS do not typically have co-occurring neuromuscular deficits or dysphagia, and speech errors are characterized by being inconsistent.

A42

Acquired Language Disorders

An SLP working in a skilled nursing facility has received an order to evaluate a new patient presenting with language disturbances and cognitive dysfunction. Upon completing a chart review, the SLP learns that the patient has a history of multiple cerebrovascular accidents, each with new symptoms. The SLP hypothesizes that the patient MOST LIKELY has which underlying condition?

Choices:
A. Vascular dementia.
B. Frontotemporal dementia.
C. Dementia with Lewy bodies.
D. Alzheimer's dementia.

Teaching Points

Correct Answer: A
Vascular dementia is generally considered a dementia syndrome caused by cerebrovascular disease of sufficient severity that multiple cognitive domains (e.g., language, cognition) are impaired. By contrast, Alzheimer's dementia is caused by neurofibrillary tangles and amyloid plaques. Frontotemporal dementia is caused by atrophy in the frontal and temporal lobes. Finally, dementia with Lewy bodies is a disorder of the area of the brain involved in the production of dopamine.

A43

Anatomy and Physiology of Communication and Swallowing

An SLP is completing an oral motor examination with a patient who was recently admitted to an acute care hospital. The patient had an onset of neurological symptoms of unknown etiology. Upon completing the examination, the SLP observes deficits consistent with damage to the facial nerve (CN VII). Which deficit is the patient MOST LIKELY experiencing?

Choices:
A. Reduced facial sensation.
B. Unilateral facial droop.
C. Reduced head rotation.
D. Impaired phonation.

Teaching Points

Correct Answer: B

If the patient experiences damage to her facial nerve, she may experience deficits in any of the following areas: taste sensation for the anterior two-thirds of the tongue, motor innervation to the muscles of facial expression, lacrimation (crying), and salivation (from all glands except the parotid gland). If a patient demonstrates reduced facial sensation, this would be indicative of damage to the trigeminal nerve. Reduced ability to turn the head indicates damage to the spinal accessory nerve. Finally, impaired phonation (from a neurological standpoint) could be indicative of damage to the vagus nerve.

A44

Audiology and Hearing Impairment

An SLP provides consulting services to a local construction company. After making multiple observations of the company's practices, the SLP observes that many of the employees on the construction site are complaining about tinnitus and difficulty hearing at the end of their shifts. Which is the BEST procedure for the SLP to recommend to management?

Choices:
A. Practice reduced shifts in order to minimize noise exposure.
B. Split time between construction work and desk work to minimize noise exposure.
C. Implement use of hearing protection to minimize noise exposure.
D. Hire an audiologist to fit all the employees with hearing aids.

Teaching Points

Correct Answer: C

Given that the company in this scenario is a construction company, it is likely that their workforce is surrounded by multiple means that could lead to a noise-induced hearing loss. This may include working near many different forms of heavy machinery, dropping heavy building materials, and so on. The best way to reduce risk of a noise-induced hearing loss is to implement some form of prevention. While reducing shifts and working differing types of shifts may be a form of prevention, these options may not be available to companies. As such, use of hearing protection is the most appropriate means to prevent a noise-induced hearing loss.

A45

Acoustics

A speech scientist is studying the impact of tongue position on frequency. The speech scientist is particularly interested in tongue position and the F1 frequency during speech. Which finding is the speech scientist MOST LIKELY to conclude?

Choices:
A. When the tongue is low in the mouth, F1 is low.
B. When the tongue is low in the mouth, F1 is high.
C. When the tongue is at the front of the mouth, F1 is low.
D. When the tongue is at the front of the mouth, F1 is high.

Teaching Points

Correct Answer: B

Tongue position determines the size of the pharynx and oral cavity. The pharynx is larger than the oral cavity and is therefore associated with F1. Tongue height is most strongly associated with pharynx size: When the tongue is pulled up toward the roof of the mouth, the air cavity in the pharynx is large and F1 is low; when the tongue is low in the mouth, it occupies most of the space in the pharynx, leaving a small air pocket and resulting in a high F1.

A46

Speech Sound Disorders in Children

An SLP in a private practice has been asked to perform a speech and language evaluation on a child. After completing the evaluation, the SLP notices the following speech sound errors: /sʌpun/ for /spun/, /dzu/ for /zu/, and /tsɪt/ for /sɪt/. Which terms BEST describe the child's speech sound errors?

Choices:
A. Epenthesis and affrication.
B. Tetism and deaffrication.
C. Backing and reduplication.
D. Fronting and stopping.

Teaching Points

Correct Answer: A

Epenthesis is the addition of a vowel sound in a consonant cluster, such as when the child from this scenario produces the word /sʌpun/. Affrication is the replacement of a fricative speech sound with an affricate-like speech sound, such as in the productions of /dzu/ and /tsɪt/. The other phonological processes collectively did not occur in this child's speech sample. Tetism is a phonological process that occurs when sounds are moved to the alveolar position, similar to consonant neutralization. Deaffrication occurs when a child replaces an affricate consonant with a fricative consonant. Backing is a phonological process that occurs when mid and front consonants are replaced with back consonants. Reduplication occurs when there is a repetition of a phoneme or syllable. Fronting occurs when back sounds are replaced by front or mid consonants. Finally, stopping occurs when continuant consonants are replaced by stop consonants.

A47

Motor Speech Disorders

An SLP working in an acute care hospital completes a comprehensive speech and language evaluation on a patient presenting with a left frontal lobe cerebrovascular accident. During the evaluation, the patient presents with a slow rate of speech production with lengthened intersegment durations and articulatory groping behaviors. Which condition BEST coincides with the patient's symptoms?

Choices:
A. Hyperkinetic dysarthria.
B. Ataxic dysarthria.
C. Spastic dysarthria.
D. Apraxia of speech.

Teaching Points

Correct Answer: D

Apraxia of speech is a motor speech disorder often seen occurring following frontal or parietal lobe damage. Hallmark characteristics for this disorder include lengthened speech and intersegment productions, slow rate of speech, articulatory breakdown, and inconsistent error productions. The patient in this practice scenario demonstrated multiple examples of these conditions, which would be indicative of apraxia of speech.

A48

Written Language Disorders in School-Age Populations

A child presents with classic features of dyslexia and another child presents with a broad-based language learning disability (LLD). Which area of cognitive or linguistic ability is MOST LIKELY impaired in both children?

Choices:
A. Orthographic processing.
B. Phonological processing.
C. Receptive oral vocabulary.
D. Oral discourse production.

Teaching Points

Correct Answer: B

Students with LLD and dyslexia demonstrate deficits in phonological processing, which includes their abilities with word recognition and spelling. The difference between these two diagnoses is that students with LLD also demonstrate deficits in underlying language skills (i.e., vocabulary, morphology, syntax, and discourse), whereas students with dyslexia have relative strengths in these areas.

A49

Voice Disorders in Children and Adults

An infant is brought to a speech and language clinic for an evaluation. The parent complains of an "unnatural cry and loud sounds when the child is breathing." This problem has been present since birth and has remained stable since that time. Which disorder is this child MOST LIKELY experiencing?

Choices:
A. Subglottic stenosis.
B. Laryngomalacia.
C. Laryngeal web.
D. Vocal fold nodules.

Teaching Points

Correct Answer: B

This child is most likely experiencing laryngomalacia, or immature development of laryngeal cartilages. This disorder is the most common congenital disorder and results in stridor and respiratory distress. As this child is experiencing "loud sounds when breathing," they are experiencing the typical stridor associated with this condition. Additionally, as the laryngeal cartilages are underdeveloped and collapse inward, there would most likely be co-occurring vocal problems, such as hoarse or raspy cries. Alternatively, if the child was experiencing subglottal stenosis, then laryngeal web may cause respiratory problems but would not cause an unnatural cry. Lastly, vocal fold nodules would cause a change in vocal quality but would not cause respiratory problems.

A50

Written Language Disorders in School-Age Populations

An SLP receives a referral to assess the literacy skills of a child. The SLP utilizes evaluation tasks that look at the child's ability to manipulate and understand sounds, letter awareness and understanding, and automaticity skills. What other area is BEST for the SLP to address in order to perform a comprehensive evaluation?

Choices:
A. Underlying language testing.
B. Articulation assessment.
C. Pragmatic profile.
D. Classroom observation.

Teaching Points

Correct Answer: A

The SLP needs to make sure he assesses the underlying language of his client, including examining morphology, syntax, semantics, and discourse. Examining underlying language abilities will allow the SLP to determine gaps in the child's basic language abilities and understanding. Children typically acquire these skills at an early age, prior to literacy structure. Students with deficits in these oral skills will be at a disadvantage to their peers during literacy instruction.

A51

Acoustics

An SLP is analyzing a spectrogram of an utterance made up of three phonemes. The first phoneme demonstrates a low-frequency nasal formant. The second phoneme is a vowel with high F1 and high F2. The third phoneme consists of a short period of voicing followed by a closure and then frication noise. Which is the MOST LIKELY utterance captured on the spectrogram?

Choices:
A. Madge.
B. Badge.
C. Pour.
D. Four.

Teaching Points

Correct Answer: A

Because the first phoneme has a low-frequency nasal formant, it can be assumed that the final phoneme is a nasal consonant, such as /m/. For the second phoneme, because there is a high F1 and high F2, it can be assumed that the vowel is a low front vowel, such as /æ/. Finally, as the final consonant demonstrates a short period of voicing followed by a closure and then frication noise, it can be assumed that the final phoneme is a voiced affricate, such as /ʤ/. The only option from this scenario that matches these three conditions is /mæʤ/ or "madge."

A52

Audiology and Hearing Impairment

An audiologist working at a local hospital is approached by a surgical team to assist during an upcoming procedure to remove a patient's vestibular schwannoma. The team asks the audiologist to recommend an assessment method to monitor function of the vestibulocochlear nerve (CN VIII) during the procedure. Which assessment method is BEST to recommend to the team?

Choices:
A. Auditory brainstem response.
B. Otoacoustic emissions.
C. Acoustic reflex testing.
D. Tympanometry.

Teaching Points

Correct Answer: A

Auditory brainstem response is a form of auditory evoked potential (e.g., bioelectric responses) that reflects neural activity in the auditory pathway. This assessment method is able to monitor auditory nerve status during surgical procedures. As such, this is the most appropriate assessment method for the audiologist to recommend. Otoacoustic emissions are low-intensity sounds generated by the cochlea. Acoustic reflex testing is measured by assessing the change in acoustic admittance of the ear caused by contraction of the stapedius muscle following presentation of a high-intensity stimulus. Finally, tympanometry is a dynamic measure of energy flow through the tympanic membrane.

A53

Cleft Palate and Craniofacial Conditions

During a comprehensive speech evaluation, an SLP asks a child to prolong the vowel /i/. The SLP asks the child to repeat the same vowel, but while pinching their nose closed. Upon completing this action, the SLP notices a change in the sound of the vowel. Which type of resonance does the child MOST LIKELY demonstrate?

Choices:
A. Hypernasality.
B. Hyponasality.
C. Cul-de-sac resonance.
D. Mixed resonance.

Teaching Points

Correct Answer: A

Hypernasality would occur if excessive amounts of acoustic energy were released into the nasal cavities during speech. By occluding the nares, any energy in the nasal cavity would be forced into the oral cavity, and there would be no perception of hypernasality during these speech tasks. This type of evaluation would not reveal hyponasality, as this is a problem with normal nasal resonance. Additionally, cul-de-sac resonance would not be revealed, as this is a problem with sound already being obstructed in the pharyngeal or nasal cavities. Further obstruction would not make a change in perception.

A54

Spoken Language Disorders in School-Age Populations

A child is referred to an SLP by a teacher, who reports that the child's language sounds more "babyish" than peers. The SLP conducts an observation and hears the child say, "I putted away all of my toys" and "Me goed to school tomorrow." Which areas of language BEST defines this child's language disorder?

Choices:
A. Morphology and syntax.
B. Semantics and pragmatics.
C. Phonology and pragmatics.
D. Morphology and semantics.

Teaching Points

Correct Answer: A

This child has demonstrated difficulty with appropriate verb conjugation and appropriate pronoun usage. Verb conjugation is an aspect of morphology, and pronoun usage would be considered syntax. Semantics would be if the child is having difficulty using the correct word in the appropriate situation.

A55

Spoken Language Disorders in School-Age Populations

A high school student has been referred to an SLP for assessment of language and executive functioning skills. During the initial interview, the student tells the SLP about significant difficulties making friends and has not been able to hold down a job. Following the assessment, the SLP notes that the student presents with significant impairments in recognizing safe and unsafe behaviors. Which impairment does the student MOST LIKELY have?

Choices:
A. Cognitive disability.
B. Autism spectrum disorder.
C. Spina bifida.
D. Cerebral palsy.

Teaching Points

Correct Answer: A

The American Association on Intellectual and Developmental Disabilities defines a cognitive disability as a limitation in at least two of the following areas: communication, self-care, home living, social skills, community use, self-direction, health and safety, functional academics, leisure, and work. As the student in this scenario has stated that she has difficulty making friends (i.e., social skills) and has difficulty holding down a job (i.e., difficulty with work), she most likely presents with a cognitive disability. In contrast to this, there is no strict association of work difficulties or safety deficits in the populations of autism spectrum disorder, spina bifida, or cerebral palsy.

A56

Speech Sound Disorders in Children

A child is brought to a speech and language clinic by a parent, who provides a chief complaint of "being hard to understand." The SLP administers a comprehensive speech evaluation and reveals the following errors: /bu/ for /blu/, /gin/ for /grin/, and /ser/ for /ster/. Which phonological process does this child MOST LIKELY demonstrate?

Choices:
A. Nasal assimilation.
B. Affrication.
C. Metathesis.
D. Cluster simplification.

Teaching Points

Correct Answer: D

The child from this scenario is eliminating one consonant from a consonant cluster (i.e., two or more consonants not separated by a vowel), which is known as the phonological process of cluster simplification. This occurs in this child's speech sample when he removes the /l/ phoneme from the /bl/ cluster or the /r/ phoneme from the /gr/ cluster. In contrast, nasal assimilation occurs when production of a phoneme is more like a nasal phoneme in the target word. Affrication occurs when a fricative consonant is replaced with an affricate consonant. Finally, metathesis occurs when there is transposition of phonemes or syllables in a target word.

A57

Dysphagia: Swallowing and Swallowing Disorder

An SLP is completing a videofluoroscopic swallow study with a patient. During the assessment, the SLP observes that the patient has near absent inflection of the epiglottis, leading to penetration and aspiration across various consistencies. Which strategy would be BEST to attempt in order to improve airway protection?

Choices:
A. Chin tuck.
B. Head tilt.
C. Supraglottic swallow.
D. Head back.

Teaching Points

Correct Answer: C

The epiglottis is a primary source of airway protection during the swallow, with the others being the true and false vocal folds. In cases in which the epiglottis is not adequately inverting, use of the supraglottic swallow maneuver can be indicated, in order to improve closure at the level of the vocal folds. The chin tuck, head tilt, and head back positions are all meant to alter bolus flow, but do not necessarily help with airway closure.

A58

Research, Evidence-Based Practice, and Tests and Measurements

An SLP has finished analyzing the data collected during a research study. The SLP has found that the p-value is 0.04. Considering this level of statistical significance, which is BEST for the SLP to reject?

Choices:
A. Hypothesis.
B. Null hypothesis.
C. Means of analysis.
D. Conclusion.

Teaching Points

Correct Answer: B

The null hypothesis is a statement made that expresses beliefs that no change will occur. Because this SLP has found statistical significance (i.e., $p < 0.05$), they are able to demonstrate that some amount of change has occurred. As this is a direct contrast to "no change will occur," the SLP may confidently reject the null hypothesis for their research. In contrast, if the SLP did not demonstrate statistical significance, they would have to reject their hypothesis, as there truly would be no change made.

A59

Language Acquisition: Preverbal and Early Language

A 13-month-old child is brought to a speech and language clinic for a comprehensive evaluation with a speech-language pathologist. The child is typically developing and meeting language milestones. Which key language milestone(s) would the child MOST LIKELY demonstrate?

Choices:
A. Ability to use present progressive verb endings.
B. Fifty-word vocabulary size, word spurt, and combining words.
C. Naming familiar objects, pointing to items, and demonstrating joint attention.
D. Cooing, gurgling, and beginnings of babbling.

Teaching Points

Correct Answer: C

Cooing and gurgling are early language pieces. Cooing, gurgling, and the beginning of babbling is expected to appear around 6 to 9 months of age. Between 12 and 15 months of age, a child is expected to be naming familiar objects, engaging in joint attention. Being able to put two words together and having a minimum of 50 words is expected by the age of 24 months.

A60

Voice Disorders in Children and Adults

An SLP works at an outpatient voice clinic with a new transgender client. The client is transitioning from male to female and would like to pursue voice therapy to have their voice better match their gender identity. Which approach would be BEST for the SLP to emphasize in treatment?

Choices:
A. Vocal quality.
B. Fundamental frequency.
C. Airflow rate.
D. Loudness patterns.

Teaching Points

Correct Answer: B

Identification and adjustment of a speaker's fundamental frequency often is a focus in the treatment of transgender individuals pursuing voice therapy, as research studies have shown that fundamental frequency provides listeners with information to perceive gender information. By training the client from this scenario to speak with a higher fundamental frequency, their voice will provide information to listeners that is reflective of their gender identity.

A61

Cleft Palate and Craniofacial Conditions

A young child with developmental dysarthria exhibits hypernasality and nasal emissions on pressure conso-nants. Examination of the hard palate failed to note any structural deviations while range of motion for eleva-tion of the soft palate appeared limited. Occlusion of the nose via a nose clip normalized breath group length and improved clarity of speech sound production. Which step is BEST for the SLP to choose next?

Choices:
A. Immediately fit the child with a palatal lift to improve speech sound production.
B. Complete an evaluation of the velopharyngeal system prior to initiating treatment.
C. Initiate treatment targeting the respiratory system in order to improve breath group length.
D. Refer the child for reconstruction of the velopharyngeal system.

Teaching Points

Correct Answer: B
The fact that this pediatric client is experiencing improvements in speech clarity with occlusion of the nose is an indicator that further assessment is warranted. Further assessment would allow the SLP working with this client to determine the extent of weakness that this patient is experiencing and allow the SLP to determine what changes can be made in order to aid in reduction of nasal emission and hypernasality.

A62

Augmentative and Alternative Communication

An SLP works in a rehabilitation hospital with a patient who developed severe spastic dysarthria following a motor vehicle accident. The SLP believes that the patient is a candidate for an AAC device. The SLP wants to prioritize essential messages for recording on the device, such as "hungry," "thirsty," and "bathroom." Which type of vocabulary is being established for this patient?

Choices:
A. Fringe.
B. Developmental.
C. Inventory.
D. Coverage.

Teaching Points

Correct Answer: D
Coverage vocabulary includes words and phrases that the person with complex communication needs (CCN) must have to communicate essential messages that typically relate to basic needs. As the SLP would like to program the patient's AAC device with vocabulary relating to basic needs, the SLP is interested in using coverage vocabulary. In contrast to this, fringe vocabulary includes words and phrases that are specific to a particular topic/activity/individual, which are often content-rich and not used frequently. Developmen-tal vocabulary includes words/phrases that the person with CCN does not yet know but are included on the system to encourage vocabulary growth. Finally, inventory vocabulary includes all the vocabulary in the AAC user's inventory.

A63

Autism Spectrum Disorders

An SLP is working with a young child recently diagnosed with autism spectrum disorder (ASD). The SLP believes that the child would benefit from the use of a floor-time approach to intervention. Which intervention BEST represents this approach?

Choices:
A. Teach the child social skills through a story-time format.
B. Establish a reciprocal communication system for the child.
C. Engage in a play-based activity with the child and an age-matched peer.
D. Engage in a semi-structured play activity that interests the child.

Teaching Points

Correct Answer: D

When utilizing the floor-time approach of intervention for ASD, the SLP would engage the child in a spontaneous, interactive, pleasurable activity, while following the child's leads and interests. This would be completed in a semi-structured play scenario. In contrast to this, teaching children with ASD social skills through stories would be utilized in the social stories intervention approach. Picture exchange communication system (PECS) is a reciprocal communication system in which the child exchanges pictures for desired objects. Finally, matching the child with ASD with an age-matched peer would be utilized in the peer and play mediation intervention approach.

A64

Motor Speech Disorders

A speaker with cerebral palsy can utter only a few words and phrases understood by unfamiliar listeners. Evaluation of the speech production system indicates severe impairment, with a limited ability to compensate. Which approach would be the BEST course of therapy in order to maximize the speaker's comprehensibility?

Choices:
A. Using alternative forms of communication such as an alphabet board.
B. Modifying speaking patterns such as slowing the speaking rate.
C. Reducing impairment through pharmacological therapies.
D. Training communication partners to adopt signal-independent strategies.

Teaching Points

Correct Answer: A

Because the patient has a significant disorder, and minimal ability to compensate on their own, alternative and augmentative communication modalities should be explored in an effort to increase this patient's ability to communicate effectively with conversational partners.

A65

Research, Evidence-Based Practice, and Tests and Measurements

An SLP is designing a research study to determine the effectiveness of a new treatment approach for aphasia, utilizing a time-series treatment design. The SLP wants to ensure that the outcomes are valid and aims to strengthen the treatment design as much as possible. Which design is BEST to include to maximize the strength of this study?

Choices:
A. Meta-analyses and systematic reviews.
B. Control groups and an analysis of variance.
C. Randomization and counterbalancing.
D. Multiple alternating treatments and baseline segments.

Teaching Points

Correct Answer: D

Time-series treatment designs is a type of treatment design used for studying treatment efficacy. This specific type of design includes repeated baseline measures prior to treatment and includes systematic ongoing measurement of participant performance. The research performed using this type of design may be strengthened by including control subjects, a second baseline segment after treatment has begun, or multiple alternating treatment and baseline segments.

A66

Acquired Language Disorders

An SLP working in a skilled nursing facility is designing a treatment plan for a resident. The patient was diagnosed with Alzheimer's disease 5 years earlier and is in the middle stages. The patient has one adult child who is involved in the patient's care but lives across the country. The SLP observes that the patient has been increasingly agitated and difficult for clinical staff to interact with. Which intervention approach is BEST for this patient?

Choices:
A. A course of melodic intonation therapy to increase phrase length and improve fluency of verbal output.
B. Using a simulated presence therapy technique in which taped messages are played to the patient in times of agitation.
C. Using caregiver-administered active cognitive stimulation techniques, assisting the family in administering cognitively stimulating tasks.
D. Training the patient on the use of a computerized augmentative communication system such as Dynavox.

Teaching Points

Correct Answer: B

A person with Alzheimer's dementia who is in the midstage of the disorder and who has been increasingly agitated in the skilled nursing facility is not a candidate for melodic intonation therapy or for treatment to improve functional writing or for using a computerized augmentative communication device. The patient is also not appropriate for caregiver-administered active cognitive stimulation techniques because the daughter lives across the country. Simulated presence therapy has been shown to calm agitation and improve social functioning in people with dementia.

A67

Research, Evidence-Based Practice, and Tests and Measurements

A speech scientist has incorrectly interpreted data collected during a recent study and has claimed that the treatment method led to participant progress when no progress was actually made. Which error BEST describes the scientist's interpretation?

Choices:
A. A type II error.
B. An order effect.
C. A type I error.
D. A treatment effect.

Teaching Points

Correct Answer: C

A type I error occurs when a true null hypothesis is rejected (i.e., a researcher rejects results showing that no improvement was made). Because this scientist has incorrectly claimed participant improvement, they have committed a type I error. On the other hand, if there was actual participant improvement, but the scientist dismissed this as no improvement, a type II error would have occurred.

A68

Language Acquisition: Preverbal and Early Language

An SLP has completed an observation of an interaction between a parent and a child. The parent states to the child: "Look at the doggie! See how pretty? What a pretty doggie! Look! Woof woof!" Which term BEST characterizes this interaction?

Choices:
A. Mutual exclusivity.
B. Baby-ese.
C. Aided language stimulation.
D. Motherese.

Teaching Points

Correct Answer: D

Motherese is characterized by shorter phrases, singsong voice, enthusiasm, contextually redundant phrases, and concrete vocabulary. Motherese is not used in the same way throughout all cultures. *Baby-ese* is not a term that has been used within the field. *Aided language stimulation* is a term typically used in the augmentative and alternative communication (AAC) field to indicate that communication partners are modeling their language output utilizing similar communication strategies to the person who uses AAC.

A69

Speech Sound Disorders in Children

Following a comprehensive speech sound evaluation, an SLP selects specific sound error patterns to target in intervention with a pediatric client aged 4 years. The SLP considers multiple factors when choosing treatment targets. Which option is BEST when selecting treatment targets for this client?

Choices:
A. The child has difficulty producing a speech sound that typically develops at age 6, so this sound should not be targeted, as it is not age appropriate.
B. The child is not stimulable for a specific speech sound that is in error, so this speech sound should be targeted, as it would likely not improve independently.
C. The child demonstrates "later occurring" phonological errors, so this child does not need to participate in speech therapy at this time.
D. The child is stimulable for specific speech sounds in error, so these speech sounds should be targeted, as the child would likely not improve independently.

Teaching Points

Correct Answer: B
Several factors are important in choosing treatment targets for intervention. One such factor is stimulability. Sounds that are stimulable for production most often remediate on their own and do not require intervention. However, those that are nonstimulable may be direct targets for intervention, as these sounds are not likely to remediate independently. In contrast, when discussing the factor of age, there has been work that shows targeting later developing sounds (i.e., those more "age advanced" for children) may allow generalization to errored, age-appropriate sounds. Finally, as the child is demonstrating a speech sound error, they are a candidate for speech therapy, which should begin as soon as possible and not when the child has matured.

A70

Stuttering and Other Fluency Disorders

A child arrives to a private practice speech and language clinic to address his stuttering. The SLP does a comprehensive evaluation and determines that the child is in the beginning stage of stuttering. The parents want to support the child, help with more fluent communication, and are very motivated to work on this fluency disorder. Which information from the evaluation is MOST LIKELY to guide the treatment approach?

Choices:
A. Setting for service delivery.
B. Age and stuttering stage of the client.
C. Client/family preferences and expectations.
D. Motivation for treatment of the fluency disorder.

Teaching Points

Correct Answer: B
Age and stuttering stage are the pieces of information that will most benefit the SLP's decision-making when determining an appropriate treatment plan. While motivation is highly important, and client/family training will occur in most treatment plans, understanding the type of stutter and how old the client is will have the largest impact on the treatment strategies.

A71

Language Acquisition: Preverbal and Early Language

A 20-month-old child is brought to a speech and language clinic for a comprehensive evaluation with a speech-language pathologist. The child displays typical development. Which key language milestones would the child MOST LIKELY demonstrate?

Choices:

A. Embedding sentences, expanding sentence types, conjoining sentences.
B. Showing objects, giving objects, pointing to objects.
C. Fifty-word vocabulary size, word spurt, combining words.
D. Increase in verb vocabulary, mastery of copula and auxiliary morphemes, phonological awareness skills.

Teaching Points

Correct Answer: C

It is well documented that young children at around 18 months of age show a period of rapid growth in vocabulary and making two-word combinations. The other choices in this answer are either seen much earlier (showing objects) or later in development.

A72

Spoken Language Disorders in School-Age Populations

A child in an elementary school is currently producing one-word utterances and has demonstrated difficulty producing more advanced utterances. The SLP has decided to use expatiations during play activities, as a means of increasing utterance length. If the child produces the utterance "kitty," which is the BEST response for the SLP to use?

Choices:

A. What does the kitty like to do?
B. That is a kitty.
C. What's the kitty's name?
D. That is a soft kitty.

Teaching Points

Correct Answer: D

Expatiations are contingent verbal responses that add new but relevant information to a child's utterance and can be used to indirectly target language facilitation. By adding the information that the kitty is "soft," the SLP is offering new information and vocabulary to the child. In contrast to this, an expansion is a contingent verbal response that increases the length or complexity of the child's utterance. The response "That is a kitty" is an example of expansion. The response "What does the kitty like to do?" is an example of a prompt, which is a comment or question that serves to extend what the child has said. Finally, the response of "What's the kitty's name?" utilizes the vertical structure method, where the SLP asks questions in order to construct a syntactically correct sentence.

A73

Autism Spectrum Disorders

A young child and their parents arrive to an outpatient clinic, with a child complaint of "strange behaviors." The parents explain that the child recently received a diagnosis of autism spectrum disorder. After a thorough evaluation, the speech-language pathologist notes significant impairments in syntactic aspects of language. Which deficit is MOST LIKELY exhibited by this child?

Choices:
A. Not being able to establish joint attention.
B. Adding extraneous speech sounds.
C. Omitting past tense markers.
D. Speaking telegraphically.

Teaching Points

Correct Answer: D

Children with autism spectrum disorder may demonstrate specific deficits in syntactic structure of language. Specifically, young children may speak telegraphically and omit articles, verb conjugations, and small connective words. In contrast to this, failure to produce past-tense markers would be considered a deficit in morphology, addition of excessive speech sound would be considered a deficit in phonology, and difficulty establishing joint attention would be considered a deficit in pragmatic language.

A74

Voice Disorders in Children and Adults

The voice team at an outpatient voice clinic has been asked to evaluate an infant client presenting with a parent-reported "weak cry." Following a comprehensive evaluation, which finding would NOT be considered a typical laryngeal characteristic for this infant?

Choices:
A. A relatively small portion of vibrating vocal fold tissue.
B. Prominent arytenoid processes of the vocal folds.
C. Laryngeal positioning around cervical vertebra three.
D. The soft palate contacting the epiglottis at rest.

Teaching Points

Correct Answer: B

Differences between adult and infant larynges include shorter membranous vocal fold tissues, higher positioning of the larynx in the neck, and the soft palate and epiglottis coming into contact with each other. Prominent arytenoid processes are associated with elderly vocal folds, as the vocal fold tissues begin to atrophy and reveal the arytenoid processes in this population. If there are prominent arytenoid processes seen during an infant's evaluation, this should be considered a red flag, and steps to treat this problem should be taken.

A75

Language Disorders in Young Children

A child has been referred to an SLP in a pediatric outpatient facility for comprehensive speech and language evaluation. During the evaluation, the SLP identifies that the child demonstrates significant deficits in non-word repetition. Which is the BEST explanation for this difficulty?

Choices:
A. The child has significant difficulty learning phonological structures.
B. There are unstable underlying phonological representations.
C. There are severe deficits in phonological awareness.
D. The child has difficulty producing words with complex syllable structure.

Teaching Points

Correct Answer: B

Students who demonstrate difficulty repeating nonwords often have unstable phonological representations, which is suggestive of a language disorder. In contrast to this, students with poor phonological awareness often have difficulties with sound categorization, blending, segmentation, elision, and deletion. Students with language disorders in general often have difficulty producing words containing complex syllable structures, but this does not strictly apply to nonword repetition. Finally, while difficulty learning phonological structures may be indicative of a language disorder, this too would not be strictly related to nonword repetition.

A76

Autism Spectrum Disorders

An SLP runs a private practice. A new patient with a language disorder secondary to autism spectrum disorder receives services. The SLP recently received a declination of reimbursement from the patient's insurance company, stating the treatment diagnosis of "speech and language disorder" is not a covered diagnosis. The SLP is preparing to resubmit the paperwork and is considering changing the treatment diagnosis to "autism spectrum disorder." Which is the BEST way for the SLP to proceed?

Choices:
A. Resubmit the original paperwork to reattempt receiving reimbursement.
B. Proceed with changing the treatment diagnosis to autism spectrum disorder.
C. Discharge the patient from services due to lack of insurance coverage.
D. Seek reimbursement from the person designated as responsible for payment.

Teaching Points

Correct Answer: D

In this scenario, the only appropriate response is for the SLP to seek reimbursement from the patient's family. It is unethical for the SLP to resubmit under a treatment diagnosis for which they are not treating (e.g., the SLP is treating the language disorder, not the autism spectrum disorder). While the SLP *could* resubmit the paperwork with the original treatment diagnosis, the insurance company will continue to decline the submission if the treatment diagnosis is not a covered service for the patient. Finally, although the SLP may ultimately not be able to provide services to this patient if they are not able to receive any form of reimbursement, the patient's family should be approached about paying out of pocket prior to any discontinuation of services.

A77

Language Disorders in Young Children

During an intervention session, a child produces the utterance "Mommy go run." The child's SLP uses an expansion approach to increase the complexity of the child's utterance. Which statement is BEST for the SLP to use in response to the child?

Choices:
A. Mommy's going to run.
B. Mommy's going to run to the house.
C. Where is Mommy going?
D. Say "Mommy is going to run."

Teaching Points

Correct Answer: A

An expansion (also known as a *recast*) is a form of experiential instruction in which the SLP provides a corrected version of a child's word or utterance. Because the SLP from this scenario is utilizing an expansion for this child, they would provide only the corrected utterance (i.e., "Mommy's going to run"). In contrast to this, an expatiation is when the SLP provides a corrected version of a child's word or utterance, and goes beyond the child's original meaning (i.e., "Mommy's going to run to the house"). Questioning occurs when the SLP asks follow-up questions to the child's original utterance (i.e., "Where is Mommy running?"). Finally, imitation occurs when the SLP provides a model and expects the child to replicate it (i.e., "Say 'Mommy's going to run.'")

A78

Anatomy and Physiology of Communication and Swallowing

A patient has been admitted to an acute care hospital after presenting with right hemiparesis and aphasia. After being evaluated by an SLP, the patient is diagnosed with Broca's aphasia. This patient is MOST LIKELY to have damaged which lobe of the brain?

Choices:
A. Frontal.
B. Temporal.
C. Parietal.
D. Occipital.

Teaching Points

Correct Answer: A

Broca's area can be found in the frontal lobes of the brain in the inferior frontal gyrus. Refer to Section II "Neuroanatomy and Neurophysiology for Speech, Language, and Swallowing" from the "Anatomy and Physiology of Communication and Swallowing" chapter of this textbook for more information and visualization of this structure.

A79

Research, Evidence-Based Practice, and Tests and Measurements

Two researchers are analyzing data collected from a research study. The researchers have found that their measurements are in good agreement, thus demonstrating adequate interobserver agreement. Which is the BEST description of their finding?

Choices:
A. Accuracy.
B. Agreement.
C. Precision.
D. Consistency.

Teaching Points

Correct Answer: D

Interobserver agreement is a measurement of how consistent two or more researchers are in making a particular measurement. As the two researchers from this scenario demonstrate good interobserver agreement, it is safe to say that they are being consistent in their measurements.

A80

Speech Sound Disorders in Children

After a speech and language evaluation, an SLP has diagnosed a 3-year-old client with an articulation disorder, characterized by difficulty producing the phonemes /l/, /r/, and /ð/. However, due to the child's young age, the SLP decides that this is an age-appropriate finding, as the child hasn't learned many sounds that "come before" the problem sounds. Which theory of development is this SLP MOST likely using in their practice?

Choices:
A. Natural phonology theory.
B. Structuralist theory.
C. Behavioral theory.
D. Cognitive theory.

Teaching Points

Correct Answer: B

According to the distinctive features theory, articulatory aspects of speech sounds are defined as binary feature contrasts (i.e., + or –), which are learned in hierarchical development. Because the SLP in the scenario has determined that earlier developing sounds have not yet been learned, it then follows that the child would not have learned later developing sounds according to this theory. In contrast to this, the natural phonology theory dictates that children learn to repress the use of specific phonological processes. Behavioral theory views verbal development as learned using the processes of contingent reinforcement and stimulus-response, and as there is no mention of lack of reinforcement for this child this would not be an appropriate selection. Finally, according to interactionist-discovery theory, the child is an active learner in phonological development and discovers phonological patterns at any point in development.

A81

Language Acquisition: Preverbal and Early Language

A typically developing 4-year-old preschooler is brought to a speech and language clinic for an evaluation. Which of the following structures would MOST LIKELY be in the child's language repertoire?

Choices:
A. Suggesting intention, emerging mastery of copula "to be," identifying the first sound in a word.
B. Predominantly nouns, calling and requesting action intentions, ritual request gestures.
C. Spurts in word learning, combining two to three words, deletion of possessive -*s*.
D. Combining single words with pointing, 50 words in his expressive vocabulary, word composed of open syllables.

Teaching Points

Correct Answer: A

A typical four-year-old child usually exhibits more sophisticated pragmatic, metalinguistic, and grammatical forms. The other items in this question all occur earlier in development.

A82

Written Language Disorders in School-Age Populations

A child on an SLP's caseload is a typically developing second grader. However, the child shows specific impairments in both word recognition and spelling. In which component abilities would this client be MOST LIKELY to show deficits?

Choices:
A. Phonological processing and phonological memory.
B. Receptive vocabulary and orthographic processing.
C. Pragmatics and receptive vocabulary.
D. Phonological and orthographic processing.

Teaching Points

Correct Answer: D

With regards to word recognition, success is contingent on the ability to break words down into corresponding graphemes while understanding the relationship between these graphemes and their associated phonemes. This corresponds to appropriate phonological processing. Orthographic processing, as it relates to spelling, is the ability of students to associate spoken sounds (i.e., phonemes) with the appropriate graphemes. Therefore, if a student has deficits in both orthographic and phonological processing, they would have difficulty with word recognition and spelling.

A83

Augmentative and Alternative Communication

An SLP is administering an AAC evaluation for a patient with chronic, severe spastic dysarthria. In order to determine the most appropriate means of communication, the SLP engages in an assessment style that compares the skills of the patient with various AAC systems. Following the assessment, the SLP is able to recommend multiple AAC devices that the patient may be able to utilize. Which type of assessment BEST aligns with this process?

Choices:
A. Scanning.
B. Direct selection.
C. Feature matching.
D. System selection.

Teaching Points

Correct Answer: C

Feature matching is the process by which the skills and needs of the person with complex communication problems are matched against the features of various AAC systems. As the SLP from this scenario is engaging in an assessment to determine how the skills of the patient match the AAC devices present, they are utilizing a feature-matching approach. In contrast to this, direct selection is when the AAC user directly makes a choice on the system via touching, pointing, looking, or speaking. Scanning is an indirect method of access in which choices are presented to the AAC user, and the person indicates when the desired target is reached through a predetermined signal. Finally, system selection is the final step of the assessment process in which an AAC user selects the AAC system through which they will communicate.

A84

Speech Sound Disorders in Children

An SLP has been asked to evaluate a child who recently moved to their school from a different part of the country. During the evaluation, the child produces the following utterances: /hæn/ for /hænd/, /dɪs/ for /ðɪs/, and /æks/ for /æsk/. What is the NEXT step in the assessment process?

Choices:
A. Determine if the productions are appropriate for this child's dialect.
B. Diagnose the child with a language disorder.
C. Perform a standardized childhood language assessment.
D. Perform in-depth research regarding the child's cultural background.

Teaching Points

Correct Answer: A

Because this child has recently moved from a different part of the country, there is a chance that they speak a different dialect than the typical one for the area that they live in. Dialectal differences must be distinguished from language disorders, in order to prevent misdiagnosis, inappropriate labeling, and inappropriate referral for therapy. If the child's productions are appropriate for the dialect in which they were raised, this would not constitute a language disorder but rather would be a language difference, and therapy would not be an appropriate recommendation.

A85

Acoustics

A speech scientist is using acoustic analysis to quantify different aspects of vowel production. The pitch contour of a vowel used by the speech scientist shows that the pitch begins at 200 Hz. Assuming the pitch contour is accurate, the speech scientist finds that the period at the beginning of the vowel is MOST LIKELY to occur at what measure?

Choices:
A. 0.005 second.
B. 0.05 second.
C. 0.005 Hz.
D. 0.05 Hz.

Teaching Points

Correct Answer: A

Frequency and period are in an inverse relationship. Period is a time measurement. If F0 = 200 Hz, the period will be 1/200 = 0.005 sec.

A86

Acoustics

An SLP is analyzing a spectrogram of an utterance made up of three phonemes. The first phoneme consists of high-frequency frication noise of a longer duration. The second phoneme is a vowel with high F1 and high F2. The third phoneme demonstrates a low-frequency nasal formant. Which utterance was MOST LIKELY captured on the spectrogram?

Choices:
A. Sam.
B. Tom.
C. Todd.
D. Sid.

Teaching Points

Correct Answer: A

Because the first phoneme demonstrates high-frequency frication noise, it can be assumed that this phoneme is a fricative. As it is of a longer duration, it can be assumed that it is a voiceless fricative, such as /s/. For the second phoneme, because there is a high F1 and high F2, it can be assumed that the vowel is a low front vowel, such as /æ/. Finally, as the final phoneme has a low-frequency nasal formant, it can be assumed that the final phoneme is a nasal consonant. The only option from this scenario that matches these three conditions is /sæm/ or "Sam."

A87

Voice Disorders in Children and Adults

An SLP is working as a member of a comprehensive voice team. A new patient is referred who presents with an onset of voicing deficits. When the patient arrives for the evaluation, the SLP observes that the patient presents with irregular and uncontrolled spasms of voicing during phonation, leading to a strained-strangled vocal quality. Which condition is the patient MOST LIKELY experiencing?

Choices:
A. Abductor spasmodic dysphonia.
B. Mixed abductor/adductor spasmodic dysphonia.
C. Adductor spasmodic dysphonia.
D. Essential tremor.

Teaching Points

Correct Answer: C

In adductor spasmodic dysphonia, a patient experiences irregular, uncontrolled, and random closing spasms of the vocal folds, which leads to the perception of a strained-strangled vocal quality. Abductor spasmodic dysphonia, by contrast, leads to irregular, uncontrolled, and random opening spasms of the vocal folds, leading to a breathy vocal quality. Mixed adductor/abductor spasmodic dysphonia would lead to a combination of both of these qualities. Finally, essential tremor is caused by rhythmic oscillations of the larynx, leading to a "quavering" voice.

A88

Language Acquisition: Preverbal and Early Language

An infant is being evaluated by an SLP during an early intervention home visit. The SLP notes that the infant demonstrates vocal play, raspberries, trills, and marginal babbling during the evaluation. Which stage of linguistic development is the infant MOST LIKELY in?

Choices:
A. Exploration/expansion stage.
B. Coo and goo stage.
C. Canonical babbling stage.
D. Phonation stage.

Teaching Points

Correct Answer: A

Hallmark characteristics of the exploration/expansion stage include vocal play, squeals, raspberries, trills, frication noises, fully resonated vowels, marginal babbling, and great variation in pitch and loudness. As the child from this scenario demonstrates several of these characteristics, it is appropriate to say that he is in the exploration/expansion stage. In contrast, during the phonation stage, a child would demonstrate predominantly reflexive and vegetative sounds. If the child was in the coo and goo stage, he would demonstrate quasi-resonant nuclei, sounds similar to back consonants and vowels, and possible self-imitations. Finally, if the child was in the canonical babbling stage, he would demonstrate reduplicated and nonreduplicated babbling, in addition to producing stops, nasals, glides, and some vowels.

A89

Autism Spectrum Disorders

An SLP works with an 8-year-old child diagnosed with autism spectrum disorder. The SLP has determined that the child would benefit from social skills development. Which strategy is BEST for the SLP to implement with the child?

Choices:

A. Addressing theory of mind.
B. Discrete trial teaching (DTT).
C. Augmentative and alternative communication (AAC).
D. Social stories.

Teaching Points

Correct Answer: D

Social stories can be used to teach social skills through a story format and can be individualized to the client and their specific needs. The story can be introduced regularly and repetitively until it becomes a routine social response. In contrast, discrete trial training focuses on teaching skills through carefully sequenced steps of objectives and theory of mind focuses specifically on the client being able to understand the mental states of their peers or communication partners.

A90

Stuttering and Other Fluency Disorders

A patient arrives to an outpatient clinic with a report of stuttering throughout life. Disfluencies are notable in complicated social situations. The patient reports significant struggles in many communication situations and uses avoidance as the main tool to deal with stuttering. The patient avoids answering the phone when others are present and frequently substitutes words. Which description MOST accurately represents the patient's report?

Choices:

A. Hysterical stuttering.
B. Occasional stuttering with prolongation.
C. Frequent stuttering with interjection.
D. Covert stuttering.

Teaching Points

Correct Answer: D

This pattern of "covert" stuttering is not unusual in individuals who have stuttered throughout life and have used avoidance as a primary method for dealing with stuttering.

A91

Voice Disorders in Children and Adults

A patient recently admitted to an acute rehabilitation hospital is presenting with hoarse vocal quality following spinal surgery. After a consult with an SLP, the patient reports a change in vocal quality since the surgery and that it is beginning to affect their self-perception. Following comprehensive voice assessment, the SLP notes that the patient is presenting with mild vocal fold edema, most likely caused by intubation during surgery. Which intervention approach is BEST for the SLP to implement?

Choices:
A. Vocal function exercise regimen.
B. Vocal hygiene principles.
C. Lee Silverman Voice Treatment (LSVT).
D. Augmentative communication.

Teaching Points

Correct Answer: B

Vocal fold edema arises from phonotrauma, such as being intubated. As this patient has no previous history of voice problems and has recently undergone intubation during surgery, this suggests that the voice problem is still relatively acute. Introducing vocal hygiene information to this patient can help them reduce the trauma to their vocal folds and reduce the amount of swelling that is present. As the edema resolves, the patient's vocal quality should return to baseline. Vocal function exercises and LSVT require excessive vocal fold movements and could cause further damage to the patient's vocal folds. Additionally, as the patient is able to communicate vocally, AAC approaches are not recommended.

A92

Stuttering and Other Fluency Disorders

An SLP provides a community presentation to teachers about stuttering. A participant asks when a child who is showing stuttering should be evaluated. The SLP responds, "The earlier the better." Which statement BEST describes when evaluation should NOT be delayed?

Choices:
A. When the child is unaware of the disfluencies.
B. When a parent reports that someone in the family stuttered.
C. When the child is showing secondary behaviors of stuttering.
D. When a child is ready to begin preschool.

Teaching Points

Correct Answer: C

If the child is beginning to exhibit secondary behaviors that evidence struggle, then it is a good time for referral. The SLP can help the family and referral source determine the appropriate course of treatment, if indicated. While family history is a risk factor, it is less critical for determining need for referral than are secondary behaviors or the child's educational or social situation.

A93

Spoken Language Disorders in School-Age Populations

A young child with a language disorder has recently been struggling with their Tier 1 coursework for language arts. After consulting with the student's teacher, the SLP who works with the child has suggested the student may be a candidate for Tier 2 instruction. Which is the BEST form of instruction for this child?

Choices:
A. The child receives in-class support from the SLP.
B. The teacher alters the coursework for the entire class.
C. The child receives one-on-one instruction from the SLP.
D. The teacher allows multiple resubmissions of all homework.

Teaching Points

Correct Answer: A

At Tier 2 in the response to intervention (RTI) model, a child will receive supportive or different forms of instruction as a means of helping them better grasp the material. If the child in this case was placed in RTI Level 2, they would most likely receive altered teaching from their classroom teacher or in-class supports (e.g., SLP or paraprofessional intervention). In contrast to this, if the child received one-on-one instruction for the material, this would fall under Level 3 of the RTI model, in which there is more intensive instruction, and possible referral for special education services. The teacher altering the coursework for the entire classroom would not be a practical approach, as this may hinder the learning of other students. Finally, multiple resubmissions of homework assignments may not directly assist in the learning of the child from this scenario and would not be considered a part of the RTI model.

A94

Language Disorders in Young Children

An SLP is working with a 3-year-old child. The child is able to use one to two words in order to communicate with others. The SLP wants to increase phrase length by introducing additional information into utterances. Which is the BEST strategy for the SLP to use in this child's treatment?

Choices:
A. Expatiation.
B. Imitation.
C. Expansion approach.
D. Self-talk.

Teaching Points

Correct Answer: C

In this scenario, the SLP is going to use expansion of the child's utterances. Such as when the child might say "Car go" the SLP might expand to "The car is going." The SLP is recasting what the child was saying and providing a grammatically correct version of the child's utterance.

A95

Language Disorders in Young Children

A child is brought to a speech and language clinic by the parents, who have told the speech-language pathologist that their child refers to all round items as "ball." This production includes describing words such as *moon*, *circle*, and *orange*. Which term BEST describes this child's productions?

Choices:
A. Undergeneralization errors.
B. Phonological errors.
C. Overgeneralization errors.
D. Morphological errors.

Teaching Points

Correct Answer: C

Overgeneralization errors are a type of semantic error in which a child thinks a word's meaning may be more broadly applied to other words. In this case, the child believes the meaning of the word *ball* can be applied to other round items. In contrast, undergeneralization errors are a different type of semantic error, in which the child believes a word's meaning is restricted to only a specific exemplar, such as "dog" for only their family dog. Phonological errors are a type of speech sound error and are not a type of language disorder. Finally, a morphological error would include errors in morphemes (i.e., application of the incorrect morpheme to reflect pluralization).

A96

Stuttering and Other Fluency Disorders

A speech-language pathologist's report for a 4-year-old with a history of disfluencies states that the child exhibits simple phrase repetitions and occasional grammatical interjections of one iteration. Occasionally, the child prolongs speech sounds at the beginning of an utterance for up to 3 seconds and occasionally shows tense lip posturing on certain sounds. Which of the following statements is the MOST accurate regarding these findings?

Choices:
A. The child is showing core behaviors of stuttering.
B. The prolongations and tense posturing are insignificant.
C. There is a low risk for the child to have advanced stuttering.
D. The child shows core and secondary stuttering behaviors.

Teaching Points

Correct Answer: D

The child is showing the emergence of secondary stuttering behaviors (borderline stuttering) as evidenced by the presence of secondary behaviors as well as core behaviors. The presence of these secondary behaviors is significant in that they signal attempts to control the core elements of stuttering.

A97

Spoken Language Disorders in School-Age Populations

A young child presents with a diagnosis of a language disorder. The speech-language pathologist has observed difficulties with the child manipulating and blending different sounds as well as difficulty with rhyming words together. This would be MOST indicative of deficits in which area of language?

Choices:
A. Presupposition.
B. Metalinguistic competencies.
C. Pragmatic discourse.
D. Discourse management.

Teaching Points

Correct Answer: B

Metalinguistic competencies are important in learning how to put words together and how to take them apart into sounds and syllables. This would include phonological awareness activities. As the child is having difficulty blending and rhyming, he is struggling in the area of metalinguistic competency. In contrast, presupposition is a skill that involves judging what the listener already knows and making appropriate accommodations to facilitate successful communication.

A98

Dysphagia: Swallowing and Swallowing Disorder

An SLP in a skilled nursing facility is informed of a new patient admission. The patient's paperwork has not fully transferred yet. Only the results from a recent modified barium swallow have been received, which states, "Severe weakness throughout all phases of swallowing, requiring a feeding tube to be placed." When the SLP sees the patient later that day, the reported weakness seems to have improved greatly. Which disorder is MOST consistent with this patient's description?

Choices:
A. Multiple sclerosis.
B. Guillain-Barré.
C. Post-polio syndrome.
D. Parkinson's disease.

Teaching Points

Correct Answer: B

Guillain-Barré syndrome is an autoimmune disorder, which is characterized by demyelination and severe weakness, sometimes to the point of paralysis. However, the weakness is temporary, and there is spontaneous recovery observed in patients with the disorder. For the patient in this question, the spontaneous recovery could have occurred by the time they were transferred to their new facility.

A99

Spoken Language Disorders in School-Age Populations

A school-aged child and parents arrive to the speech and language clinic. The parents report that the child has a cognitive impairment and language-learning difficulties. When the child is seen by the SLP, the SLP notes articulation difficulties and abnormalities with the child's prosody when speaking; however, receptive language skills remain a strength. Which diagnosis does the child MOST LIKELY have?

Choices:
A. Attention deficit/hyperactivity disorder.
B. Down syndrome.
C. Fragile X.
D. Traumatic brain injury.

Teaching Points

Correct Answer: C

Fragile X is a chromosomal disorder mainly impacting males but impacts females as well. Moderate intellectual impairments and language learning difficulties are frequently present in fragile X, with receptive language skills typically being a strength.

A100

Audiology and Hearing Impairment

A patient with a cochlear implant (CI) arrives at an audiology clinic with complaints of CI malfunction. After performing troubleshooting, the audiologist has determined that the malfunctioning component is the part that converts the sounds into a digital signal. Which part of this patient's CI is MOST LIKELY malfunctioning?

Choices:
A. Microphone.
B. External sound processor.
C. Internal unit.
D. Electrode array.

Teaching Points

Correct Answer: B

The external sound processor is the portion of a CI that filters and processes the sound (i.e., converts sound into a digital signal). As this fits the description given by the audiologist in this scenario, it is likely the external sound processor that is experiencing difficulties. In contrast to this, the microphone is the portion of a CI that picks up sound, the internal unit is the portion of a CI that converts the digital signal into electrical signals, and the electrode array is the portion of a CI that stimulates CN VIII for sound perception.

A101

Language Acquisition: Preverbal and Early Language

A child arrives at a speech and language clinic for a language evaluation. After performing the evaluation, the SLP reviews the following utterances: "look doggy," "more cookie," "no bed," and "mommy good." Which term BEST describes this child's speech sample?

Choices:
A. Babbling.
B. Narratives.
C. Simple sentences.
D. Telegraphic speech.

Teaching Points

Correct Answer: D

Telegraphic speech is characterized by content word combinations that often contain a pivot word or phrase. As this child is producing two-word utterances that contain content words, they are demonstrating telegraphic speech. In contrast, babbling is an early form of communication consisting of CV syllables, such as "bababa." Narratives include decontextualized monologues that convey a story, personal recount, or retelling of a book or movie. Finally, simple sentences are a characteristic of Brown's stages II and III and include some form of grammatical structure, such as "I am walking."

A102

Audiology and Hearing Impairment

A person in the community with hearing loss refers to themselves as being culturally deaf and uses American Sign Language (ASL) as their primary means of communication. Which statement BEST describes this person?

Choices:
A. Capital "D" Deaf.
B. Audiometrically deaf.
C. Hard of hearing.
D. Hearing impaired.

Teaching Points

Correct Answer: A

Capital "D" Deaf refers to persons who identify as culturally deaf, who would typically make use of ASL, and are proud to be deaf, such as the person from this scenario. In contrast to this, *audiometrically deaf* refers to the most significant hearing sensitivity challenge based solely on audiological testing (profound hearing loss). *Hard of hearing* and *hearing impairment* are terms currently used in U.S. federal legislation to describe children and adults with any degree of hearing sensitivity deficits/differences.

A103

Dysphagia: Swallowing and Swallowing Disorder

A speech-language pathologist is completing a flexible endoscopic evaluation of swallowing. The evaluation reveals a delay in pharyngeal swallow initiation that leads to aspiration with liquid consistencies. Which postural strategy may be of MOST benefit to trial with the patient during this study?

Choices:
A. Right head turn.
B. Left head tilt.
C. Side lying.
D. Chin tuck.

Teaching Points

Correct Answer: D

When a patient experiences a delay in pharyngeal swallow initiation, use of the chin tuck posture may prevent a bolus from traveling into the pharyngeal cavity before the patient is ready. Use of the right head turn or left head tilt position are indicated when patients present with unilateral pharyngeal weakness. The side-lying position may be helpful in cases where the patient demonstrates slowed pharyngeal contractions or residue along the posterior pharyngeal wall.

A104

Written Language Disorders in School-Age Populations

An SLP is working with a new pediatric client in a private speech and language clinic. The child is noted to spell words semi-phonetically. Which statement BEST illustrates this writing system?

Choices:
A. "I am watching TV" spelled as "I am waching TV."
B. "I am happy" spelled as "I m hap."
C. "I like cats" spelled as "I lik cats."
D. "I went to the game" spelled as "I goed to the game."

Teaching Points

Correct Answer: B

Semi-phonetic spelling, also called *letter-name spelling,* occurs when the child uses letter names to convey the spelling of words. When the child uses "I M HAP" to spell the sentence "I am happy," they are associating the letters as the appropriate spelling of those words. The other choice includes errors in rule-based spelling (watching/waching, like/lik) and past-tense (went/goed).

A105

Dysphagia: Swallowing and Swallowing Disorder

A patient has been admitted to an acute care hospital after a right middle cerebral artery cerebrovascular accident. Initial symptoms include left-sided pharyngeal weakness and reduced vocal fold closure. The SLP is consulted to perform an evaluation. In order to maximize the limited time spent with the patient, which compensatory maneuver is BEST to use during the modified barium swallow?

Choices:
A. Chin tuck maneuver.
B. Head rotation toward the left.
C. Head tilt toward the left.
D. Head back.

Teaching Points

Correct Answer: B

A head rotation toward the weak side closes off the weak side of the pharynx and allows the bolus to be directed down the strong half of the pharynx. Additionally, when the pharynx is turned toward the side of damage, the airway is narrowed, which would help with the patient's reduced vocal fold closure.

A106

Language Disorders in Young Children

A child arrives to an outpatient speech and language clinic for an evaluation. The child demonstrates relatively intact language comprehension skills but has significant impairments in language production and syntax. Which disorder does the child MOST LIKELY demonstrate?

Choices:
A. Attention deficit hyperactivity disorder.
B. Down syndrome.
C. Specific learning disability.
D. Traumatic brain injury.

Teaching Points

Correct Answer: B

A child with Down syndrome will most likely demonstrate intact language comprehension skills, with significant impairments in language production. Children in this population often demonstrate particular difficulty with expressive syntax and vocabulary acquisition. In contrast to this, children with ADHD present with difficulties in concentration, organization, impulse control, planning, and pragmatic language secondary to distractibility. Children with specific learning disability present with deficits in executive functions (i.e., planning, organizing, and problem-solving), dysgraphia, and social skills. Finally, children with traumatic brain injury present with deficits of telegraphic speech, comprehension difficulties, semantic difficulty, word finding, and disorganized language.

A107

Audiology and Hearing Impairment

A patient has received a comprehensive audiological evaluation after complaints of hearing loss. The patient was diagnosed with a vestibular schwannoma. Which type of hearing loss would this patient MOST LIKELY experience?

Choices:
A. Conductive hearing loss.
B. Mixed hearing loss.
C. Sensorineural hearing loss.
D. Mild hearing loss.

Teaching Points

Correct Answer: C

A sensorineural hearing loss is a type of hearing loss that results from disorders of the cochlea or CN VIII. Vestibular schwannomas are a type of acoustic tumor that affects the vestibulocochlear nerve (i.e., CN VIII). Because this is a disorder of a cranial nerve, it would lead to a sensorineural hearing loss. In contrast to this, a conductive hearing loss results from problems associated with the outer or middle ear. Lastly, mixed hearing loss includes problems congruent with both conductive and sensorineural hearing loss.

A108

Language Disorders in Young Children

A child is brought to a speech and language clinic to receive private speech and language services. The SLP has been targeting appropriate use of past-tense verbs. During their sessions together, the SLP looks at pictures with the child of places visited, encouraging the child to share stories. The SLP occasionally prompts with "Tell me more." Which technique BEST represents this approach?

Choices:
A. Focus stimulation.
B. General stimulation.
C. Production stimulation.
D. Treatment generalization.

Teaching Points

Correct Answer: B

In the general stimulation technique, an SLP will focus on modeling several ways of expressing the same idea and leaving prompts open-ended for the client. The intended outcome would be that the child increases the length and complexity of utterances and is able to understand more complex utterances. In contrast, focus stimulation relies heavily on specific targets during a treatment session with the child expected to produce a greater number of correct examples of production of the target.

A109

Voice Disorders in Children and Adults

An SLP working in an outpatient voice clinic has a new patient hoping to pursue voice treatment. Upon reviewing the patient's intake paperwork, the SLP observes that the patient was recently diagnosed with velopharyngeal incompetency. During comprehensive evaluation, the SLP finds that there is no anatomical or physiological deficit present in the patient's laryngeal mechanism. Still, the patient presents with alterations in perceived voicing. Which statement BEST describes this patient's presentation?

Choices:
A. Impaired resonatory function, leading to hypernasal speech.
B. Impaired respiratory function, leading to smaller breath groups.
C. Impaired articulatory function, leading to imprecise articulation.
D. Impaired prosodic function, leading to excessive stress.

Teaching Points

Correct Answer: A

Persons who present with velopharyngeal incompetence may develop phonatory problems by trying to overcompensate for their velopharyngeal incompetence through excessive closing of the laryngeal valve. However, should the patient demonstrate hypernasality without any occurrence of anatomical/physiological impairment of the phonatory subsystem, they are demonstrating a disorder of resonance only.

A110

The Practice of Speech-Language Pathology

An SLP in an acute rehabilitation hospital has several patients on the caseload and is feeling highly overwhelmed by the amount of work. Which step is BEST for the SLP to take in order to better manage the caseload?

Choices:
A. Request an SLP assistant to perform all patient evaluations.
B. Request a fellow SLP become lead clinician for some patients.
C. Discharge high-functioning patients from the caseload.
D. Continue with the current caseload and take brief breaks during the day.

Teaching Points

Correct Answer: B

According to the ASHA Code of Ethics, Principle of Ethics I, Rule of Ethics E, "Individuals who hold the Certificate of Clinical Competence shall not delegate tasks that require the unique skills, knowledge, and judgment that are within the scope of their profession to assistants, technicians, support personnel, or any nonprofessionals over whom they have supervisory responsibility." As this SLP is feeling significantly overwhelmed, they may not be able to appropriately deliver services to all patients on their caseloads. The ASHA Code of Ethics prevents the SLP from delegating evaluations to an SLPA and doing so would prove to be an unethical decision. In contrast to this, another SLP maintains the knowledge and skills to work with any patient, so relinquishing some patients would prove to be an ethical decision that may lead to better outcomes for all involved. Additionally, it is unethical to discharge patients simply for being "high level." A patient may be discharged from services when an SLP appropriately determines the patient has made maximum amounts of progress.

A111

The Practice of Speech-Language Pathology

An SLP works in a pediatric outpatient clinic, specializing in the treatment of pediatric motor speech disorders. During a conversation with a supervisor, the SLP learns that the clinic is expecting a new adult client for dysphagia therapy, as the client has been unsuccessful in finding a practice that accepts their insurance. The supervisor would like the SLP to treat the client, as the SLP had a rotation in an acute care hospital during graduate school 5 years earlier. Which option is BEST for the SLP to choose?

Choices:
A. Treat the patient, as there is foundational knowledge in the treatment of dysphagia.
B. Decline to treat the patient and refer the patient to an SLP with adult dysphagia experience.
C. Decline to treat the patient due to specialization only in pediatric motor speech disorders.
D. Treat the patient since the clinic is the only one that accepts the patient's insurance.

Teaching Points

Correct Answer: B

Although the SLP has some relevant experience in the treatment of dysphagia from their time in graduate school, practice patterns may have changed since the last time they treated a patient with dysphagia. Assessment and treatment methods and procedures that the SLP knew may have become outdated, and since they have been out of practice, it may not be ethical for the SLP to treat this patient. Instead, they should refer the patient to an SLP who is more knowledgeable in current practice patterns for dysphagia management.

A112

Acquired Language Disorders

An SLP working in an acute care hospital has received a new consult for a comprehensive evaluation of a patient who had a left middle cerebral artery cerebrovascular accident (CVA). The CVA affected only the anterior portion of the brain supplied by this artery. Which deficits are MOST LIKELY to be discovered upon evaluation?

Choices:
A. Significant impairment of auditory comprehension and a right hemiparesis.
B. Visual agnosia and dysprosody.
C. Nonfluent verbal expression and a right hemiparesis.
D. Severe dysphagia but no aphasia.

Teaching Points

Correct Answer: C

A CVA in the anterior portion of the middle cerebral artery territory is likely to affect portions of the language zone in the frontal lobe and the precentral gyrus (motor strip). Therefore, the person is likely to have a nonfluent aphasia and a right hemiparesis. Since posterior language regions were not affected, the person will not have a fluent aphasia or a problem with auditory comprehension.

A113

Speech Sound Disorders in Children

An SLP has been working with an 8-year-old child for the last few weeks in an effort to improve intelligibility. The SLP determines that the child is a candidate for an integral stimulation approach to treatment. Which option BEST represents a key component of this treatment methodology?

Choices:
A. Articulation.
B. Rhythm and rate.
C. Tactile/gestural.
D. Augmentative and alternative communication.

Teaching Points

Correct Answer: A

The integral stimulation treatment approach follows when the speaker is asked to watch the clinician produce an utterance and then say the target after the clinician. Using this treatment approach focuses on the speaker's articulation of specific sounds/words and allows the speaker to compare their production with the production of typical speech from the clinician.

A114

Cleft Palate and Craniofacial Conditions

A child is referred to an otolaryngology and speech-language pathology (ENT/SLP) clinic at an acute care hospital after experiencing multiple episodes of nasal regurgitation in addition to significantly hypernasal speech. Upon full evaluation, it is found that the child has difficulty with elevation and retraction of the velum. Which muscle is MOST LIKELY affected?

Choices:
A. Tensor veli palatini.
B. Musculus uvulae.
C. Palatoglossus.
D. Levator veli palatini.

Teaching Points

Correct Answer: D

The levator veli palatini is the muscle that provides the main muscle mass of the velum. Its functions include velar elevation and retraction in a 45-degree angle and formation of the velar dimple. If the child was experiencing deficits within this muscle, they would have problems with velar elevation and retraction. Contrary to this muscle, the tensor veli palatini opens the eustachian tubes, the palatoglossus depresses the velum, and the musculus uvulae contracts during phonation to create a superior velar bulge.

A115

Acquired Language Disorders

An SLP in an acute care hospital has been tasked with completing a comprehensive speech and language evaluation on a patient with a new onset of aphasia following a cerebrovascular accident. Results from the SLP's assessment showed fluent verbal expression with paraphasias and neologisms, as well as significant anomia. The individual also had severe comprehension deficits. The person was able to repeat single words and sentences without error. Which diagnosis would the patient MOST LIKELY receive?

Choices:
A. Wernicke's aphasia.
B. Transcortical motor aphasia.
C. Conduction aphasia.
D. Transcortical sensory aphasia.

Teaching Points

Correct Answer: D

The combination of fluent output, poor auditory comprehension, and preserved verbal repetition is found in the syndrome of transcortical sensory aphasia. In contrast to this, a person with Wernicke's aphasia would demonstrate fluent verbal output, poor auditory comprehension, and poor repetition of words. A person with transcortical motor aphasia would demonstrate nonfluent verbal output, good auditory comprehension, and good repetition of words. Finally, a person with conduction aphasia would demonstrate fluent verbal output, good auditory comprehension, and poor repetition of words.

A116

Anatomy and Physiology of Communication and Swallowing

A client arrives at a speech-language pathology clinic at an acute care hospital with complaints of "a change in voice." After comprehensive endoscopic evaluation, the SLP notes that the change in voice is most likely not due to problems of velopharyngeal closure, as the client exhibits "the most common patten of velopharyngeal closure." Which statement BEST describes this client's closure pattern?

Choices:
A. Circular pattern with equal activity of the velum, lateral pharyngeal walls, and posterior pharyngeal wall.
B. Coronal pattern with the velum contacting the pharyngeal wall.
C. Sagittal pattern with medial lateral pharyngeal wall motion as the primary contributor to closure.
D. Circular pattern with a Passavant's ridge.

Teaching Points

Correct Answer: B

The coronal pattern of velopharyngeal closure is the most common pattern in normal speakers and involves posterior movement of the soft palate against the posterior pharyngeal wall. If the SLP from this scenario noted "the most common closure pattern," this would be the most appropriate choice. Circular and sagittal closure patterns are the second most and third most common velopharyngeal closure pattern, respectively. For this reason, these answers would not be the most appropriate selection for the client from this scenario.

A117

Dysphagia: Swallowing and Swallowing Disorder

An SLP is working with a patient diagnosed with myasthenia gravis (MG) and dysphagia. What is the MOST EFFECTIVE intervention approach?

Choices:
A. A diet consisting of purees and thickened liquids.
B. Smaller meals eaten more frequently throughout the day.
C. Sensory stimulation (e.g., cold and sour bolus).
D. VitalStim therapy.

Teaching Points

Correct Answer: B

MG is a lower motor neuron disorder characterized by exacerbated weakness with use and improvement with rest. Giving patients with MG smaller meals can reduce their fatigue, and increasing the amount of meals throughout the day ensures that these patients will receive the proper amount of nutrition and hydration.

A118

Cleft Palate and Craniofacial Conditions

A 6-year-old child is referred to an SLP by an otolaryngologist in order to receive speech therapy. According to the parent, the child had normal speech until undergoing an adenoidectomy 2 years ago. Following the surgery, the child demonstrated severe hypernasality, which has slightly improved over the past year. The SLP performs a full evaluation, which reveals normal articulation and significant hypernasality. What is the FIRST treatment option that should be implemented?

Choices:
A. Speech and voice therapy for better sound control and airflow.
B. Exercises to strengthen the velopharyngeal musculature.
C. Discuss the inappropriateness of speech therapy with the referring physician.
D. Auditory training to improve awareness of the hypernasality.

Teaching Points

Correct Answer: D

The child in this scenario had a change in speech quality following a surgery. While there has been some noted improvement, the child continues to present with significant hypernasality, possibly due to lack of awareness. By bringing the deficit to the level of awareness, the child will be able to participate more fully in treatment efforts to reduce the perception of hypernasality. Following this step in their treatment, other treatment options and speech therapy techniques may be utilized with this child.

A119

Autism Spectrum Disorders

An SLP is evaluating the communication skills of a child with autism spectrum disorder. Following the evaluation, the SLP notes that during communicative exchanges, the child demonstrates immediate and delayed repetition of utterances spoken by others. Which deficit is this child MOST LIKELY demonstrating?

Choices:
A. Jargon.
B. Verbal perseveration.
C. Childhood apraxia of speech.
D. Echolalia.

Teaching Points

Correct Answer: D

Echolalia is a communication deficit often present in autism spectrum disorder and is defined by repetition of utterances spoken by others. These repetitions may be immediate (i.e., immediately after being spoken) or delayed (i.e., following a long delay after initial production). In contrast to this, childhood apraxia of speech is an inability to voluntarily program neurological sequences for verbal speech production. Verbal perseveration is the continuous repetition of a sound, word, or phrase. Finally, jargon is idiosyncratic speech production that is nonmeaningful to others.

A120

Research, Evidence-Based Practice, and Tests and Measurements

A speech scientist is conducting a research study on a particular treatment program for childhood language disorders and has decided to utilize effect size as a measure of data outcome. Which is the BEST measure for the scientist to use?

Choices:
A. Cohen's d.
B. Chi-square.
C. Cochran Q test.
D. Analysis of variance (ANOVA).

Teaching Points

Correct Answer: A

Cohen's d is one of the most common measurements of effect size and would be the most appropriate selection for this scientist. If the scientist was interested in measuring the level of significance between any relationships among nominal variables, chi-square would be the most appropriate selection. The Cochran Q test is a nonparametric procedure used to assess nominal level data from related samples and would not be appropriate for measuring effect size. Finally, the ANOVA would be the most appropriate selection if the scientist was interested in simultaneous comparison of several means.

A121

Audiology and Hearing Impairment

An audiologist has recently completed full audiometric evaluation on a patient with complaints of hearing loss with the following hearing thresholds: 43 dB hearing loss (HL) in the right ear, 50 dB HL in the left ear. Which of the following statements BEST describes this patient's deficits?

Choices:
A. Moderate right hearing loss and moderately severe left hearing loss.
B. Mild right hearing loss and moderately severe left hearing loss.
C. Moderate right hearing loss and moderate left hearing loss.
D. Mild right hearing loss and moderate left hearing loss.

Teaching Points

Correct Answer: D

When discussing range HL, 26–40 dB HL would be classified as a mild hearing loss, and 41–55 dB HL would be classified as a moderate hearing loss. As this patient fits these diagnostic markers, they would be diagnosed with a mild right hearing loss and a moderate left hearing loss.

A122

Spoken Language Disorders in School-Age Populations

An SLP working in an outpatient speech and language clinic has been asked to evaluate a new client who was referred with a language disorder. However, when the SLP reads the client's intake forms, he notices that the client comes from a culturally diverse background. The SLP has never worked with someone from this cultural background. Which is the BEST method of assessment for the SLP to utilize?

Choices:
A. Processing-dependent assessment.
B. Curriculum-based assessment.
C. Diadochokinetic assessment.
D. Standardized assessment.

Teaching Points

Correct Answer: A

Many standardized assessment measures are inappropriate to administer to children from these populations, as there may be content bias (i.e., the assessment reflects the assumption that all populations have the same life experiences, concepts, and vocabulary), linguistic bias (i.e., disparity between the language used by the examiner and child), or a disproportionate representation in the normative sample. Processing-dependent assessment includes methods such as testing digit span, working memory, or nonword repetition, and is most appropriate because it is minimally dependent on prior knowledge. In contrast to this, curriculum-based assessment may require a level of background knowledge that the child does not have to perform at their true potential. Finally, diadochokinetic assessment is a form of assessment for speech sound intervention and measures the rate of syllable repetition.

A123

Augmentative and Alternative Communication

A school-aged child with cerebral palsy has been brought to an outpatient augmentative communication clinic by the parents in order to participate in a comprehensive AAC evaluation. According to the parents, the child had been working with a GoPro AAC system at school, but now that it is summer vacation, the school has mandated that the device be returned. The parents are hoping to receive a device for use at home, in order to promote their child's communication. Which barrier to communication BEST represents this situation?

Choices:
A. Policy barrier.
B. Skill barrier.
C. Practice barrier.
D. Access barrier.

Teaching Points

Correct Answer: C

A practice barrier is a type of opportunity barrier (i.e., a barrier that is imposed by forces external to the AAC user) that has become commonplace in the environment. As the school district is preventing this pediatric client from utilizing their AAC device during the summer, this child is experiencing a practice barrier to communication. In contrast, a policy barrier is based on legislative decisions that govern specific environments and a skill barrier is caused by facilitator difficulty implementing an AAC technique or strategy. Finally, an access barrier is different from an opportunity barrier, in that it is imposed by the limitations of the AAC user.

A124

Acquired Language Disorders

An SLP has completed a speech and language evaluation for a patient with aphasia and acquired alexia from a recent traumatic brain injury. The patient was assessed for reading abilities and found to display a pattern consistent with letter-by-letter (LBL) reading. Which statement BEST describes the patient's reading pattern?

Choices:
A. Unable to read through the visual modality but can read from kinesthetic input.
B. Able to access only the "whole word" reading route but cannot use the grapheme-phoneme reading route.
C. Unable to read whole words but can benefit from surrounding context.
D. Exhibits a nonfluent form of aphasia.

Teaching Points

Correct Answer: C

The treatment method called multiple oral re-reading works well for LBL readers because the multiple readings of a given passage allow readers to use the context of remembered words to move away from their tendency to read each word in a letter-by-letter fashion. None of the other response choices in the question are true of LBL readers.

A125

Motor Speech Disorders

An SLP is working with a patient on the use of a pacing board to slow rate and improve speech intelligibility. The SLP is concerned about adversely influencing the naturalness of the speaker's speech. Which option BEST exemplifies how pacing boards can reduce naturalness?

Choices:
A. They can reduce vocal flexibility and stability.
B. They are often used in the acquisition of the earliest speech sounds for some speakers.
C. Speakers tend to breathe in too much air prior to speaking.
D. Their use leads to placement of pauses in linguistically inappropriate locations.

Teaching Points

Correct Answer: D

A pacing board is a method to use when patients exhibit deficits that would benefit from a slowed or altered rate/rhythm of speech. A pacing board usually contains specific areas, differentiated by some type of visual (e.g., wooden slots, tape), during which a patient is allowed to speak a predetermined number of words. Because pacing boards are utilized in a way to limit the amount of speech output (e.g., one word per differentiated space on the board), this can lead to longer pauses in between words and pauses in linguistically inappropriate places.

A126

Spoken Language Disorders in School-Age Populations

An SLP in an outpatient speech and language clinic has been contacted by a patient interested in receiving cognitive therapy. The client states they have been evaluated by another SLP and were then referred to this SLP for specific treatment of their attention and memory deficits. Which option should the SLP select FIRST?

Choices:
A. Administer their own assessment of the patient's cognitive abilities.
B. Accept the previous SLP's report and begin providing services.
C. Deny the patient services until contact with the previous SLP is established.
D. Begin intervention for this patient's cognitive deficits.

Teaching Points

Correct Answer: A

According to the ASHA Code of Ethics, Principle of Ethics IV, Rule of Ethics J, "Individuals shall not provide professional services without exercising independent professional judgment, regardless of referral source or prescription." Although the patient from this scenario may have been evaluated by a previous SLP, they did not divulge the date of their last evaluation, and much may have changed since that time. The SLP is fully within their own right as a professional to administer a cognitive-linguistic evaluation to this patient, and if results show that treatment is indicated, begin therapy. The SLP should always perform their own evaluation to see if their services are, indeed, required.

A127

Voice Disorders in Children and Adults

An SLP working at an outpatient voice clinic completes a comprehensive voice evaluation for a patient with a recently diagnosed vocal fold polyp. During the assessment, the SLP documents that the patient presents with an hourglass glottic closure pattern. Which type of assessment MOST LIKELY led to this observation?

Choices:
A. Acoustic.
B. Stroboscopic.
C. Aerodynamic.
D. Perceptual.

Teaching Points

Correct Answer: B

Use of stroboscopic evaluation allows the SLP to evaluate vocal fold vibratory characteristics, such as glottic closure patterns, symmetry of vocal fold movement, periodicity of vocal fold vibration, amplitude of vocal fold movement, and movement of the mucosal wave.

A128

Written Language Disorders in School-Age Populations

A 6-year-old child is recommended for a speech and language evaluation by a teacher at school. While the child has been observed to read significantly above the current grade level, including reading of complex words, the teacher notes that the child continues to struggle with grade-level reading comprehension. These behaviors are BEST associated with which diagnosis?

Choices:
A. Language learning disability.
B. Dyslexia.
C. Hyperlexia.
D. Attention deficit hyperactivity disorder.

Teaching Points

Correct Answer: C

Hyperlexia presents as relative strengths in word recognition that frequently extend to spelling; however, there are deficits in the underlying language skills needed for comprehension of the read material. Dyslexia is characterized by a weakening in word recognition and spelling, while a language learning disorder also shows difficulty with underlying language skills and also usually includes difficulties with word recognition.

A129

The Practice of Speech-Language Pathology

An SLP has worked in the school system for the last 30 years. Recently, a friend's parent had a stroke, resulting in significant dysphagia. The SLP's friend asks if the SLP can provide services for the parent. The SLP has not provided treatment for a patient with dysphagia since graduate school and has not attended any continuing education classes on the topic. What is the SLP's BEST response?

Choices:
A. Refer the friend to a professional with more experience in the treatment of dysphagia.
B. Refer the friend to a colleague at the school who has expertise in dysphagia in children.
C. Provide services for the parent, as dysphagia falls within the SLP's scope of practice.
D. Provide recommendations for at-home exercises targeting improved functional swallowing abilities.

Teaching Points

Correct Answer: A

According to the ASHA Code of Ethics, Principle of Ethics II, Rule of Ethics B, "Individuals shall engage in only those aspects of the professions that are within the scope of their professional practice and competence, considering their level of education, training, and experience." As the SLP has not provided intervention to adult clients with dysphagia in at least 30 years, her understanding of treatment, including at-home exercises, may be outdated. Therefore, she should make a referral to a professional with the most up-to-date knowledge in order to provide the best services to her friend's mother. Additionally, a clinician working with the pediatric dysphagia population may not have a full understanding of how dysphagia affects the adult population, and therefore should not be consulted.

A130

Autism Spectrum Disorders

An SLP works with a group of school-aged children diagnosed with autism spectrum disorder. The SLP wants to implement pragmatic intervention approaches for the children, while utilizing a social communication group approach. Which intervention approach is BEST to implement with the children?

Choices:
A. Sharing interests with other group members.
B. Generating polite requests and responses.
C. Determining appropriate questions for other group members.
D. Understanding other group members' feelings.

Teaching Points

Correct Answer: A

School-age children require pragmatic skills consistent with peer interaction. For this age group, pragmatic goals include considering others' feelings, sharing interests, expressing preferences politely, and shared attention. In contrast to this, generating polite requests would be an appropriate pragmatic goal for younger children, while determining appropriate questions and understanding others' feelings would be an appropriate pragmatic goal for adolescents and adults.

A131

Acquired Language Disorders

A child is receiving speech and language services at an outpatient clinic. The child demonstrates difficulty with comprehension, telegraphic speech, and word-finding challenges. Which disorder does the child MOST LIKELY demonstrate?

Choices:
A. Attention deficit hyperactivity disorder.
B. Down syndrome.
C. Specific learning disability.
D. Traumatic brain injury (TBI).

Teaching Points

Correct Answer: D

TBI can cause a variety of challenges, depending on the location and severity of the injury. However, TBI is frequently characterized by difficulty with comprehension and telegraphic speech. Presentation and severity will vary with the type of TBI.

A132

Voice Disorders in Children and Adults

A patient arrives at a hospital with complaints of sudden onset of voice loss. During the intake interview, the patient utilizes writing to convey to the SLP that they had recently attended a high school football game with frequent cheering throughout the game. Suddenly, the patient was unable to phonate above a whisper. Which diagnosis will the patient MOST LIKELY receive?

Choices:
A. Vocal fold hemorrhage.
B. Laryngitis.
C. Vocal fold ectasia.
D. Vocal fold bowing.

Teaching Points

Correct Answer: A

Vocal fold hemorrhage, or bleeding into the vocal fold tissues, is often associated with a single, phonotraumatic episode. When the person experiencing the hemorrhage participates in excessive vocally abusive behaviors, a blood vessel in the vocal fold tissues may rupture, causing the hemorrhage. Vocal fold varices and ectasias may predispose the patient to experience vocal fold hemorrhage, as these are vascular structures not normally present on the vocal fold tissues. Laryngitis, vocal fold ectasias, and vocal fold bowing would not occur after a single, isolated incident and are not the appropriate diagnosis for this patient.

B1

Augmentative and Alternative Communication

A patient was recently admitted to an acute rehabilitation hospital. The physician has requested a referral for speech-language pathology, for reasons of "communicative difficulties." After the speech-language pathologist (SLP) performs an evaluation, it is determined that while the patient is a candidate for augmentative/alternative communication (AAC), only temporary use of AAC will be required. Which condition is the patient MOST likely experiencing?

Choices:
A. Intubation-induced vocal fold edema.
B. Severe Broca's aphasia.
C. Total glossectomy.
D. Amyotrophic lateral sclerosis.

Teaching Points

Correct Answer: A

Temporary use of AAC may be implemented for patients with conditions that are likely to alleviate or improve drastically. In intubation-induced vocal fold edema, the patient may present as aphonic, which may reduce their communicative effectiveness. However, this condition typically improves within a short time span and may require temporary means of AAC. In contrast, patients with severe Broca's aphasia, total glossectomy, and amyotrophic lateral sclerosis have chronic or degenerative communication problems and would likely benefit from permanent means of AAC to aid their communicative effectiveness.

B2

Anatomy and Physiology of Communication and Swallowing

A patient has experienced facial trauma, which has impacted their ability to produce some labial sounds, including the vowel /u/ in *boot*. Which muscle is MOST likely impacted by the trauma?

Choices:
A. Orbicularis oris.
B. Levator labii superioris.
C. Zygomatic major.
D. Risorius.

Teaching Points

Correct Answer: A

The orbicularis oris muscle is the sphincter-like muscle that surrounds the lips. Contraction of this muscle can lead to the lip-rounding associated with production of the /u/ phoneme in the word *boot*. In contrast, the levator labii superioris muscle contributes to elevation and everting of the upper lip. The zygomatic major muscle contracts the corners of the mouth backward by simultaneously lifting and pulling the corners of the mouth sideways. Finally, the risorius muscle retracts the angle of the mouth upon contraction.

B3

Speech Sound Disorders in Children

An SLP has been working with a child who demonstrates difficulty producing /k/ in the initial and final word positions. However, the child does correctly produce the following words: /ki/, /kæt/, /bæk/, and /bek/. The SLP decides to utilize a treatment method that capitalizes on these correct productions to aid in faulty productions. Which intervention is the MOST LIKELY method chosen by the SLP?

Choices:
A. Integral stimulation.
B. Multiple phonemes approach.
C. Sensory-motor approach.
D. Paired-stimuli approach.

Teaching Points

Correct Answer: D

The paired-stimuli approach utilizes four "key words" as a starting point, and 10 training words are then paired with the key words to aid in production. As the child from this scenario is able to produce the errored speech sound correctly in four separate words, these may act as the key words and aid further production of the /k/ phoneme. In contrast, the integral stimulation approach may be utilized to establish a speech sound that the child is unable to produce and would not be recommended for this client. The sensory-motor approach uses bisyllable productions of nonerrored phonemes that are used as facilitating contexts to produce a target sound. As the child is able to produce the target /k/, this method of intervention is contraindicated. Finally, the multiple phoneme approach is utilized for children with multiple phoneme errors, and as this child only demonstrates errors on the /k/ phoneme, this method is also contraindicated for use in intervention.

B4

Autism Spectrum Disorders

A speech and language scientist has focused research efforts on proving that there are environmental causes for autism spectrum disorders. Which would this scientist MOST LIKELY accept as a cause of autism spectrum disorders?

Choices:
A. Brain inflammation.
B. Chromosomal deficiencies.
C. Toxins.
D. Maternal blood supply.

Teaching Points

Correct Answer: C

Environmental theories of the cause of autism spectrum disorder often focus on environmental toxins (e.g., lead, chemicals) as the cause of autism spectrum disorder. In contrast to this, chromosomal deficiencies as the cause of autism spectrum disorders fall under genetic research, whereas brain inflammation and maternal blood supply as the cause of autism spectrum disorders fall under neurochemical research.

B5

Language Acquisition: Preverbal and Early Language

During a clinical swallow evaluation, a patient who has recently undergone a brain stem tumor resection reports to the SLP that they are unable to taste the different trials being provided. Which cranial nerve is MOST LIKELY damaged?

Choices:
A. Cranial nerve V—trigeminal.
B. Cranial nerve VII—facial.
C. Cranial nerve X—vagus.
D. Cranial nerve XI—spinal accessory.

Teaching Points

Correct Answer: B

The facial nerve (CN VII) controls taste in the anterior two-thirds of the tongue, sensation to the soft palate, salivation from all the salivary glands (except the parotid gland), and motor control for the face. While the trigeminal nerve controls most sensation for the anterior two-thirds of the tongue (e.g., temperature, pain), it does not control the sensation of taste. The vagus nerve controls sensation for pharyngeal and esophageal components only. Finally, the spinal accessory nerve has motor control aspects only and does not control sensory information for any part of the swallow.

B6

Speech Sound Disorders in Children

A 5-year-old child is brought to a speech clinic for a full articulation and phonological evaluation after being referred by a teacher. The SLP notices that the child does not produce several "age-appropriate" phonemes. Which phoneme is the child MOST LIKELY to have difficulty producing?

Choices:
A. /s/.
B. /m/.
C. /r/.
D. /l/.

Teaching Points

Correct Answer: B

Of the phonemes listed, /m/ is a phoneme that is traditionally considered one of the earlier developing speech sounds, typically occurring by 3 years of age. The other phonemes listed are considered later developing sounds, typically occurring between the ages of 6 and 8. Therefore, if a 5-year-old client is demonstrating problems with production of age-appropriate phonemes, /m/ would be a phoneme that could prove difficult.

B7

Voice Disorders in Children and Adults

A patient has undergone phonosurgery to remove lesions associated with polypoid degeneration. After a period of vocal rest, the patient returns to the hospital's voice center to begin treatment with an SLP. Which option is the FIRST step in the patient's treatment?

Choices:
A. Vocal hygiene information, in order to reduce high-fat foods.
B. Use of hard glottal attack, in order to improve vocal fold closure.
C. Vocal hygiene information, in order to reduce smoking.
D. Recommendations for periodic, repeated phonosurgery as necessary.

Teaching Points

Correct Answer: C

Polypoid degeneration, or Reinke's edema, is a condition caused by a combination of vocal abuse and excessive smoking. Following phonosurgery, a patient with polypoid degeneration should be educated regarding the effects of smoking on the vocal folds and chances of reoccurrence with continued smoking. Hard glottal attacks to improve vocal fold closure are not recommended, as this could cause further phonotraumatic lesions to occur. Additionally, repeated surgeries are not recommended unless the lesion continues to reappear.

B8

Spoken Language Disorders in School-Age Populations

Following the response to intervention (RTI) model, a child is given core curriculum instruction in the general education classroom. The child continues to have difficulty within the classroom setting. Which approach is BEST to select next?

Choices:
A. Tier 1 instruction.
B. Tier 2 instruction.
C. Individualized education plan (IEP).
D. Continue and monitor progress.

Teaching Points

Correct Answer: B

Tier 1 instruction is what the child in this scenario is currently receiving. She is receiving high-quality curriculum within the classroom. She is continuing to struggle, so the next plan of action would be to recommend Tier 2 instruction, which is more supportive or different instruction. If she does well in Tier 2, she may go back to the regular classroom for further instruction. An IEP may be recommended after Tier 3 continues to show that a student is struggling and may need specialized education services.

B9

Audiology and Hearing Impairment

An audiologist is evaluating a child who is hard of hearing by obtaining a speech recognition threshold. Which type of speech stimuli is the MOST optimal to be used in elicitation of this assessment?

Choices:
A. Monosyllabic words.
B. Sentences.
C. Spondees.
D. Trochees.

Teaching Points

Correct Answer: C

As part of the comprehensive audiological evaluation, the audiologist will obtain a speech recognition threshold (SRT). The SRT is used to validate pure tone testing and should be within 6 dB of the pure tone average. SRTs are assessed using spondees. These are bisyllabic words with equal stress on each syllable. Examples of spondees are *baseball, ice cream, playground, railroad,* and *sidewalk.* Word recognition testing uses monosyllabic words that are phonetically balanced. Sentences may also be used for word recognition testing. Trochees are two-syllable words, but the stress is unequal, such as *lemon, coffee, finger,* and *trailer.*

B10

Audiology and Hearing Impairment

An audiologist has completed an audiological evaluation of a patient referred for hearing loss. The audiologist has determined that the patient's hearing loss is localized to the middle ear. Which structure is MOST LIKELY damaged?

Choices:
A. Cochlea.
B. Semicircular canals.
C. Ossicular chain.
D. Bony labyrinth.

Teaching Points

Correct Answer: C

The ossicular chain consists of the three bones or ossicles (malleus, incus, and stapes) housed in the middle ear. As this patient is experiencing a middle ear disorder, the ossicular chain could be damaged. In contrast to this, the cochlea, semicircular canals, and bony labyrinth are considered portions of the inner ear.

B11

Dysphagia: Swallowing and Swallowing Disorder

An SLP has completed a clinical swallow evaluation with a patient and reports that the patient exhibits reduced labial seal, reduced tongue grooving, and reduced tongue-to-palate contact. These results are MOST LIKELY reflective of a dysphagia in which phase of the swallow?

Choices:
A. Esophageal phase.
B. Oral phase.
C. Oral preparatory phase.
D. Pharyngeal phase.

Teaching Points

Correct Answer: B

During the oral phase, the bolus is contained in a central groove on the tongue surface and moves posteriorly until the swallow is triggered. The lips close, the tongue tip elevates, and the floor of mouth (FOM) contracts during this phase as well. Deficits with any of these acts would qualify as an oral stage dysphagia.

B12

Language Disorders in Young Children

A child has been brought into a physician's office for a comprehensive evaluation due to difficulties at home. Following the evaluation, the physician notes that the child demonstrates impairments in social interaction and restricted, repetitive behaviors, but demonstrates no delay in language or cognitive development. Which diagnosis will the child MOST LIKELY receive?

Choices:
A. Asperger's disorder.
B. Autism spectrum disorder (ASD).
C. Rhett's syndrome.
D. PDD-NOS.

Teaching Points

Correct Answer: B

Asperger's disorder was previously considered a separate diagnosis from autism spectrum disorder characterized by qualitative impairment in social interaction and restricted/repetitive behaviors, but with no significant delay in language or cognitive skills. Asperger's has been consolidated into the autism spectrum disorder diagnosis and is now no longer a separately defined disorder. PDD-NOS was also considered a separate form of autism but is now not considered in the *DSM-V*. Rhett syndrome is a genetic condition that was also previously considered a part of autism spectrum disorders but is no longer considered to be as such. Rhett syndrome is a separate diagnosis, and if someone were to meet the criteria, would also receive a separate diagnosis of ASD.

B13

Acquired Language Disorders

An SLP in an outpatient aphasia clinic has decided to use constraint-induced language therapy (CILT) in a group session format. Which statement BEST describes why this choice of treatment method would lead to improvements in persons with aphasia's (PWA) language?

Choices:
A. These persons are not allowed to use their "good," unimpaired limb when making a gestural response to describe pictures, thus forcing them to learn gestures with their impaired limb.
B. Use of nonverbal means of communication is not allowed, such as drawing, gesturing, or augmentative/ alternative communication devices when performing language tasks, thus forcing them to use their spoken language.
C. Use of augmentative communication devices is not allowed but use of other nonverbal means of expression is when performing language tasks, thus increasing the likelihood their message will be understood.
D. The PWA is not allowed to respond immediately but is constrained to respond after delays of increasing length, starting with a 5-second delay, thus increasing the likelihood of their ability to respond appropriately in various conversations.

Teaching Points

Correct Answer: B

In constraint-induced language therapy, PWA must respond verbally when performing treatment tasks. Any nonverbal means of expression is not permitted, and a barrier is used to prevent the communication partner from seeing the PWA.

Exam B

B14

Autism Spectrum Disorders

An SLP in a preschool setting has been working with several children with autism spectrum disorder. The SLP believes the children would individually benefit from a Social Stories approach to intervention. The SLP develops individual stories for each child for the intervention sessions. What is the NEXT step that should be taken?

Choices:
A. Read the stories only during the first intervention session, to model an appropriate social response.
B. Read the stories repetitively during intervention sessions, to establish a social response.
C. Read the stories when the child demonstrates pragmatic difficulty, to model an appropriate social response.
D. Send the stories home with the children, to allow their parents to model appropriate social responses.

Teaching Points

Correct Answer: B

In the social stories method of intervention, social skills are taught through a story format. Each story must be specific to the child and their problem situation. Once the stories are developed, it is important that they are read repetitively until it becomes a routine for the child. Following repetitive reading, the story may be sent home with the child for carryover purposes, but this should occur only after the child has been read the story multiple times.

B15

Speech Sound Disorders in Children

After performing a comprehensive speech evaluation on a pediatric client, a speech-language pathologist has determined that the child demonstrates difficulty producing the /l/ phoneme, consistent with a phonetic error. Which method of intervention would be BEST to utilize with this child?

Choices:
A. Minimal contrast method.
B. Distinctive feature approach.
C. Integral stimulation approach.
D. Cycles remediation approach.

Teaching Points

Correct Answer: C

The integral stimulation approach is an intervention method used for phonetic speech errors, in which emphasis on multiple input modes is used to help a child establish a speech sound into their repertoire. In contrast, the minimal contrast approach, distinctive features approach, and cycles remediation approach are all intervention methods used for children with phonemic speech errors and would not be helpful in remediating this particular child's speech sound disorder, as this child needs to learn the motor pattern to produce the /l/ phoneme.

B16

Stuttering and Other Fluency Disorders

An SLP in a school setting receives a referral from a teacher for evaluation of a 10-year-old. The child has a fast rate of speech, history of language and learning problems, and a high rate of disfluency that occurs in connected speech. The teacher indicates that the child doesn't seem too bothered by this problem. The SLP completes the evaluation, which supports the teacher's assessment. Which fluency disorder is the child MOST LIKELY experiencing?

Choices:
A. Neurogenic fluency disorder.
B. Developmental stuttering.
C. Cluttering.
D. Psychogenic fluency disorder.

Teaching Points

Correct Answer: C

Cluttering is a fluency impairment that is seen in children and becomes prominent as they advance in school years. These children also usually show signs of learning difficulties and other motor problems. Excessive rate and lack of awareness are critical features that distinguish cluttering from other fluency disorders.

B17

The Practice of Speech-Language Pathology

An SLP at a skilled nursing facility currently has no patients on their caseload. After evaluating a newly admitted patient, the SLP determines the patient is functioning in the typical range but on the border of a mild cognitive-linguistic disorder. Which decision is BEST to make regarding this patient?

Choices:
A. The SLP should recommend services for the patient, as there is room on the caseload.
B. As the patient is on the border of a mild disorder, the SLP should recommend services.
C. The patient is functioning in the typical range; therefore, the SLP should not recommend services.
D. The SLP should seek out the director of rehabilitation to determine if the patient should receive services.

Teaching Points

Correct Answer: C

According to the ASHA Code of Ethics, Principle of Ethics III, Rule of Ethics C, "Individuals shall refer those served professionally solely on the basis of the interest of those being referred and not on any personal interest, financial or otherwise." As the patient is functioning in the typical range, it may not be in their best interest to refer them for services. Although the SLP needs to meet productivity standards, they may not ethically recommend the patient for services solely on this reason. Finally, if the SLP feels they do not have the skills to work with this patient, they are still ethically bound to refer in the best interest of the patient and recommend that another SLP be the lead clinician.

B18

Language Disorders in Young Children

An SLP has been working with a young child with a language disorder. The SLP has recently initiated clinician-directed approaches during intervention sessions with the child, as a means of reducing the distracting stimuli. Which method of intervention is the SLP MOST LIKELY utilizing in this child's intervention sessions?

Choices:
A. Demonstration.
B. Modeling.
C. Expansion.
D. Questioning.

Teaching Points

Correct Answer: B

Modeling is a form of clinician-directed approach (i.e., a means of intervention that allows the clinician to specify the materials that are used in intervention, how they are used, and the type and frequency of reinforcement) in which numerous examples of a target structure are provided during an interactive activity. The child is not required to produce the target during intervention sessions. In contrast to this, demonstration, expansion, and questioning are all indirect language facilitation techniques. Demonstration occurs when repeated but variable use of a sentence or text pattern is presented to a child. Expansion is a contingent verbal response that increases the length or complexity of the child's utterance. Finally, questioning (i.e., asking questions to a child) serves to extend what the child has said or written.

B19

Stuttering and Other Fluency Disorders

A 10-year-old boy with a developmental stutter, characterized by whole-word repetitions (particularly of words beginning with velar phonemes), is receiving speech and language services. The SLP observes that the child frequently engages in secondary behaviors. Which observation is MOST LIKELY to occur during reading time?

Choices:
A. The child asking, "Can can can I have the book?" while clenching fists and stomping feet.
B. The child asking, "Can can can I have the book?" and then kicks the ground and yells in frustration.
C. The child stating, "I just won't ask for the book. I'll get up and grab it myself."
D. The child asks, "Can can can I have the book?" and continues on, unaware of the repetition.

Teaching Points

Correct Answer: A

Secondary behaviors involved with stuttering may be circumlocution, talking around the troublesome word, or even physical (motor) actions. In this scenario, during the disfluencies, the child clenched his fist and stomped the ground in an effort to overcome the stutter. In contrast, in one of the options he kicks the ground; this is an emotional response to the stutter after it occurred.

B20

Spoken Language Disorders in School-Age Populations

An SLP is working in a school setting. Many students come from a culturally and linguistically diverse background. The SLP wants to ensure that culturally competent services are provided. Which approach BEST reflects this type of service?

Choices:
A. Using English as much as possible when providing intervention services.
B. Helping the students to appreciate and adapt to the culture of the SLP.
C. Using English-language assessments to predict performance in other languages.
D. Respecting the home culture and adapting to the culture in the school.

Teaching Points

Correct Answer: D

An issue that arises for SLPs working with culturally and linguistically diverse populations includes respecting the home culture of any client and assisting with acculturation as needed. In contrast, SLPs should utilize interpreters as needed, which includes providing intervention in a client's language (i.e., one that may be different from English). Finally, English language test instruments should not always be utilized and do not predict performance in any of the client's other languages.

Exam B

B21

Written Language Disorders in School-Age Populations

An elementary school student has been working with an SLP due to difficulties spelling. The SLP has observed the student producing the following spelling errors: spliting/splitting, pated/patted, glanceing/glancing. Which type of words BEST indicate these difficulties in spelling?

Choices:
A. Semi-phonetic.
B. Irregular.
C. Regular.
D. Rule-based.

Teaching Points

Correct Answer: D

Rule-based spelling includes words that rely on systematic instruction of spelling rules, such as the doubling rule (i.e., splitting, patted) and the drop-e rule (i.e., glancing), which this child demonstrated in their spelling errors. The spelling mistakes exhibited by this child do not follow regular word spellings (e.g., *bat* spelled as *bet*), irregular word spellings (e.g., *yacht* spelled as *yat*), or semi-phonetic spelling patterns (e.g., *are* spelled as *R*).

B22

Language Disorders in Young Children

A 20-month-old toddler has not met several early word-learning milestones. The child demonstrates a small vocabulary and does not make two-word combinations. Which statement BEST describes the child's deficit?

Choices:
A. The child demonstrates an early language disorder.
B. The child demonstrates an early language difference.
C. The child demonstrates a speech sound disorder.
D. The child demonstrates an early language delay.

Teaching Points

Correct Answer: D

Toddlers who do not meet early word-learning milestones in a timely manner, such as the child from this scenario, are referred to as *late talkers*. While most outgrow their early language delay, some will demonstrate language deficits that persist into preschool language disorders. *Language differences* refer to differing but appropriate use of language. As this child has not reached several milestones, she is not a typically developing toddler.

B23

Augmentative and Alternative Communication

A 4-year-old student with a history of cerebral palsy and cortical vision impairment (CVI) is nonspeaking. The SLP at the child's school has been consulted to develop a method of augmentative and alternative communication (AAC) for the child to use. Which symbols are BEST for the SLP to choose for the AAC system?

Choices:
A. Black and white written words.
B. High-contrast written words.
C. High-contrast photos and pictures.
D. Grayscale photos and pictures.

Teaching Points

Correct Answer: C

Individuals with CVI benefit from images that are represented using high-contrast coloration to make them easier to discern. As this child is only 4 years old, it is not age appropriate to expect him to be a fluent reader, so using photos and pictures to support his understanding of the vocabulary terms would be the most appropriate option given the scenario.

B24

Augmentative and Alternative Communication

An older adult has recently sustained a right middle cerebral artery (MCA) infarction, resulting in a significant neglect and severe flaccid dysarthria. The SLP has been implementing use of an AAC device to improve the patient's communicative effectiveness. The SLP has determined a list of high-frequency words for the patient to use in conversation and is determining the most appropriate placement of symbols on the device. Which placement is BEST for the symbols on the device?

Choices:
A. Symbols should be placed on the right, so as to be more readily accessible.
B. Symbols should be placed in the middle, so as to encourage scanning.
C. Symbols should be placed on the left, so as to be more readily accessible.
D. Symbols should be placed on the border, so as to cancel effects of the neglect.

Teaching Points

Correct Answer: A

Placement of symbols should be informed by the person with complex communication's physical and visual limitations to access. The most common form of neglect following a right hemisphere stroke is a left neglect, meaning the patient does not attend to (i.e., realize) stimuli on their left side. For this reason, in this scenario, the most appropriate placement of the user's symbols is on the right, to maximize the chances that they will attend to and utilize their symbols for communication.

B25

Language Acquisition: Preverbal and Early Language

An SLP is completing a language evaluation on a young child. During the evaluation, the child produces the utterance, "The boy pushed the cars." How many bound morphemes should the SLP document from this child's utterance?

Choices:
A. 3.
B. 2.
C. 4.
D. 5.

Teaching Points

Correct Answer: B

There are two bound morphemes in the sentence, the plural morpheme after car and the past-tense morpheme *ed* after push.

B26

Research, Evidence-Based Practice, and Tests and Measurements

In evaluating an adult who stutters, an SLP uses a conversational speech sample and an attitudinal survey about communication. The SLP decides not to record the session, so as to not make the client more nervous. Which statement BEST represents this decision?

Choices:
A. It would have been better to use a standardized test to assess this patient's speech.
B. Attitudinal surveys are not helpful communication assessment measures.
C. There is nothing wrong with this approach; recording is not a necessity.
D. Failure to record the sample makes reliability assessment impossible.

Teaching Points

Correct Answer: D

Recording speech samples allows for determination of the types of disfluencies present, and their frequency (e.g., per 100 words), units of repetition and prolongation, and any secondary behaviors or word avoidances. As the SLP from this case did not utilize recording devices during the assessment of the adult from this scenario, they are unable to perform a reliable assessment of the disfluencies present.

B27

Language Disorders in Young Children

An SLP is working with a school-aged child in an attempt to increase their word learning and use. Which of the following aspects of language learning should this SLP utilize in order to maximize the child's likelihood to increase the number of words they know and can use?

Choices:
A. Phonological density, neighborhood sparsity, and morphological representation.
B. Morphotactic probability, neighborhood density, and phonological representation.
C. Syntactic probability, neighborhood density, and lexical representation.
D. Phonotactic probability, neighborhood density, and semantic representation.

Teaching Points

Correct Answer: D

The characteristics described are all factors for word production as opposed to syllable forms or individual sounds or social rules.

B28

Voice Disorders in Children and Adults

A speech-language pathologist working in an outpatient voice clinic is attempting to collect different acoustic measures on a new patient, including jitter and shimmer. In order to check these measures appropriately, which method is the BEST for the SLP to use?

Choices:
A. Recording the patient in a brief, natural conversation.
B. Recording the patient reading a short, phonetically balanced passage.
C. Recording the patient producing a vowel with a sustained pitch.
D. Recording the patient producing a vowel with a rising and falling pitch contour.

Teaching Points

Correct Answer: C

Jitter and shimmer are cycle-to-cycle variations in frequency and amplitude that reflect the degree of regularity of vocal fold vibration. To examine jitter and shimmer, the recording should be a sustained vowel so that voluntary changes in frequency and amplitude are not misinterpreted as jitter and shimmer.

B29

Anatomy and Physiology of Communication and Swallowing

A patient presents to an emergency department after sustaining a fall, after which the patient is unable to move their limbs. Imaging reveals a high spinal cord lesion at the level of the fourth cervical vertebra, impacting motor movements below this point. Which of the following pathways is MOST likely impacted?

Choices:
A. Corticobulbar tract.
B. Reticulospinal tract.
C. Vestibulospinal tract.
D. Corticospinal tract.

Teaching Points

Correct Answer: D

The corticospinal tract (made up of both the lateral and anterior corticospinal tracts) is the motor pathway involved in control of bodily muscles (lateral tract) and trunk muscles (anterior tract). A high spinal cord lesion that impacts the ability to move the limbs would interrupt signals along the corticospinal tract, specifically the lateral branch. The corticobulbar tract controls the muscles of the face, head, and neck. The reticulospinal tract plays a role in autonomic function and regulation of somatic motor control. Finally, the vestibulospinal tract contributes to body and limb adjustments related to balance.

B30

Motor Speech Disorders

A child with developmental dysarthria is receiving treatment in a speech and language clinic. The SLP decides to focus on reduction of the impairment by targeting motor development of the speech production system. Which treatment approach is BEST to improve the child's communication?

Choices:
A. Treatment to reduce episodes of drooling.
B. Appropriate positioning of the child to maximize breathing for speech.
C. Development of repair strategies when communication breakdowns occur.
D. Targeting both receptive and expressive language skills.

Teaching Points

Correct Answer: D
Although dysarthria is a motor speech disorder, children with this type of speech difficulty are still in danger of lagging behind their peers in terms of receptive/expressive language development. Targeting receptive/expressive language within treatment sessions for children with dysarthria will promote age-appropriate development of language for these clients.

B31

Motor Speech Disorders

An SLP at an acute rehabilitation hospital has received orders to evaluate and treat a patient with flaccid dysarthria. After the first session, the SLP decides that the patient may benefit from abdominal trussing. Which rationale is BEST in selecting this intervention?

Choices:
A. To counter inspiratory weakness and assist in creation of inspiratory force for the generation of subglottal pressure during inspiration.
B. To increase vocal fold tension, leading to increased loudness and improved vocal quality.
C. To counter expiratory weakness and assist in creation of expiratory force for the generation of subglottal pressure during expiration.
D. To improve functioning of both the direct and indirect upper motor neuron pathways.

Teaching Points

Correct Answer: C

Use of abdominal trussing would most likely be used with a patient who has impairments in the respiratory subsystem. This method would be used to counter expiratory weakness and assist in the creation of expiratory force for increased subglottal pressures. Depending upon the needs of the specific patient, abdominal trussing can be used on a short-term or long-term basis.

B32

Language Acquisition: Preverbal and Early Language

A young child is recently diagnosed with a language disorder, with particular deficits in the content and use of language. Which area of language BEST defines this child's language disorder?

Choices:
A. Morphology and syntax.
B. Semantics and pragmatics.
C. Phonology and pragmatics.
D. Morphology and syntax.

Teaching Points

Correct Answer: B

According to Bloom and Lahey's 1978 model, language can be divided into form, content, and use in order to make more evident how language components interface during typical language learning. Language form can be divided into the components of syntax, morphology, and phonology. Language content is constructed of semantics and associated vocabulary. Finally, language use consists of pragmatic language components. If this child is demonstrating deficits in language content and use, they would MOST LIKELY have deficits in the areas of semantics and pragmatics.

B33

Cleft Palate and Craniofacial Conditions

A child is brought to an otolaryngology clinic by the parents, with a presenting complaint of "distorted speech." After a full evaluation, in consult with an SLP, the otolaryngologist and SLP agree that the child is demonstrating phoneme-specific nasal emission. Which is the BEST treatment recommendation for this child?

Choices:
A. Articulation therapy.
B. Blowing exercise.
C. Surgical correction.
D. Palatal lift.

Teaching Points

Correct Answer: A

Phoneme-specific nasal emission is a type of error that responds well to speech therapy. Specifically, articulatory placement intervention (most likely for sibilant sounds) is indicated as the treatment method of choice for this problem. Phoneme-specific nasal emission does not require surgical intervention, as it is responsive to speech therapy. Blowing exercises are not an effective treatment tool and should not be attempted for this problem. Palatal lifts are recommended when there is poor velar movement, which is not the case for phoneme-specific nasal emission. As such, the palatal lift device is not recommended for treatment of this problem.

B34

The Practice of Speech-Language Pathology

A paraprofessional works with a young child with autism spectrum disorder. Recently, the paraprofessional has found that the child's language skills have been lagging behind peers. The paraprofessional contacts the school's SLP in order to discuss potential approaches to aid the child's linguistic development in the classroom. What role is the SLP serving in this capacity?

Choices:
A. Instructor.
B. Interventionist.
C. Consultant.
D. Collaborator.

Teaching Points

Correct Answer: C

When a speech-language pathologist acts as a consultant, they are providing indirect services through giving expert advice to teachers, parents, and paraprofessionals regarding the speech or language needs of a child. In contrast to this, when an SLP acts as a collaborator, they are working with teachers, parents, and paraprofessionals to assess and provide intervention to a student with speech or language needs. Although SLPs may act as educators or interventionists, these are not specific roles they would assume in working with paraprofessionals or teachers.

B35

Acquired Language Disorders

An SLP receives an order to perform a comprehensive speech, language, and cognitive-linguistic evaluation on a patient who had a recent cerebrovascular accident. The referral indicates that the patient has trouble with "theory of mind" tasks, indicating difficulty understanding what another person's beliefs or thoughts might be. Which diagnostic group would this patient MOST LIKELY be categorized?

Choices:
A. Alzheimer's disease in the early stages.
B. Wernicke's or conduction aphasia.
C. Parkinson's disease and dementia.
D. Right-hemisphere strokes.

Teaching Points

Correct Answer: D

Deficits in theory of mind are associated with damage to the right hemisphere in adult stroke patients. None of the other diagnostic groups listed are known to display difficulties with theory of mind tasks to the same extent as right-hemisphere stroke patients.

B36

Augmentative and Alternative Communication

A student with a diagnosis of autism spectrum disorder is evaluated for an augmentative and alternative communication device. During the evaluation, the SLP determines that the patient is best supported by translucent symbols within a speech-generating device. Which symbol is BEST for the SLP to use?

Choices:
A. A picture of a cup representing the word *cup*.
B. A picture of a cup representing the word *drink*.
C. A picture of a cup representing the word *snack*.
D. A picture of a cup representing the word *thirst*.

Teaching Points

Correct Answer: B

Translucent symbols are symbols that bear some resemblance to the referent. They are more obviously understood than an opaque symbol; however, additional information may be needed to initially learn the symbol. A picture of a cup representing "cup" would be a transparent symbol and a cup representing both "snack" and "thirst" would be opaque.

B37

Anatomy and Physiology of Communication and Swallowing

An SLP is completing an oral motor examination with a patient who recently incurred a right middle cerebral artery cerebrovascular accident. During the examination, the SLP observes that the patient has weakness on the left side of their face, resulting in a facial droop. Which cranial nerve is MOST LIKELY damaged?

Choices:
A. Trochlear.
B. Trigeminal.
C. Facial.
D. Vagus.

Teaching Points

Correct Answer: C

The facial nerve (CN VII) controls motor innervations to the muscles of facial expression. Damage to the lower motor neurons would cause ipsilateral (same-sided) weakness, which could result in the facial droop that this patient is experiencing.

B38

Audiology and Hearing Impairment

A person with hearing loss complains that listening to conversational partners in noisy restaurants is very difficult. However, they still enjoy going out to eat with family and friends. Which level of the WHO International Classification of Functioning (ICF) BEST describes this person's hearing problem?

Choices:
A. Activity limitation.
B. Impairment.
C. Participation restriction.
D. Behavioral limitation.

Teaching Points

Correct Answer: A

An activity limitation reflects the impact of a hearing loss on the person's ability to communicate and understand environmental and speech signals. As this patient describes deficits with hearing in noisy environments, they are describing an activity limitation. In contrast, if this problem stopped this person from going into the community, this would be described as a participation restriction. An impairment refers to the measurable loss of hearing function (i.e., what is causing the hearing loss). Finally, there is no behavioral limitation as a part of the WHO ICF.

B39

Spoken Language Disorders in School-Age Populations

An SLP working in an elementary school has been asked to perform a comprehensive language evaluation with a new student. The SLP determines the best assessment for the child and begins administration. The SLP uses a dynamic approach to assessment in order to better understand the child's language skills. Which approach will BEST determine how well the child performs?

Choices:
A. On tasks of daily living.
B. On a classroom assignment.
C. With modeling techniques.
D. With no comparison to peers.

Teaching Points

Correct Answer: C

In a dynamic assessment, the assessment is designed to measure the extent to which a child's performance in a specific task may be modified or extended with contextual support. Because this SLP offered modeling techniques in order to see how the child responded, they engaged in a dynamic assessment of the child's learning abilities. In contrast to this, a curriculum-based assessment measures how well the child would perform on a classroom assignment, a functional assessment measures the extent to which a language disorder impacts daily living, and a criterion referenced assessment measures the child's capabilities with no comparison to peers.

B40

Dysphagia: Swallowing and Swallowing Disorder

A patient in a long-term acute care setting complains of gastroesophageal reflux disorder–like symptoms during and after every meal. The physician asks the SLP to perform an evaluation, which comes back negative. Instrumental assessment methods are used next, and it is discovered that the patient's lower esophageal sphincter is not functioning properly. Which is the MOST LIKELY cause for the patient's symptoms?

Choices:
A. Pharyngeal weakness, including muscle atrophy.
B. A change in medication, including addition of steroids.
C. Lingual weakness, including fibrillation.
D. Zenker's diverticulum, including residue.

Teaching Points

Correct Answer: B

When evaluating patients, it is important to keep in mind that medications are able to cause previously undiagnosed dysphagic problems. Lower esophageal sphincter dysfunction has been attributed to medication, including steroids, anti-thyroid drugs, and antacids, to name a few.

B41

Speech Sound Disorders in Children

An SLP is performing an evaluation on a new pediatric client. The SLP wants to perform an analysis to compare the client's correct consonant productions to the entire speech sample. Which means of assessment would be the BEST choice?

Choices:
A. Percent consonants correct.
B. Phonological mean length of utterance.
C. Phonological error patterns analysis.
D. Traditional analysis.

Teaching Points

Correct Answer: A

The percent consonants correct is an analysis procedure that compares the number of consonants produced correctly to the total number of consonants that should have been produced. It gives the clinician a percentage of correct use, which is then corresponded to a severity rating for the child's disorder. In contrast, the phonological error pattern analysis allows the clinician to understand the error patterns that the child produces and provides a means of categorizing the errors into syllable structure, substitution, and assimilation errors. Phonological mean length of utterance attempts to determine the length and complexity of words the child attempts to say, and how well the child matches their target word. Finally, traditional analysis displays the child's errors across word or syllable positions, records the types of errors, and is most useful for those children with few errors.

B42

Stuttering and Other Fluency Disorders

A 4-year-old child who is beginning preschool stutters on about 8% of words and language is mildly delayed. The pediatrician advises against early referral for assessment by the SLP because of concerns that labeling the problem will make it worse. The parent is concerned about the child's stuttering problem and calls the school-based SLP for advice. Which discussion topic is LEAST BENEFICIAL to have with the parent?

Choices:
A. Assessment of the child's speech will not make it worse and should be completed if there is concern.
B. There might be some benefit in providing the parent with some evidence-based materials that clarify the purpose of early assessment.
C. The various goals of early stuttering assessment and treatment.
D. Explaining where the pediatrician is in error.

Teaching Points

Correct Answer: D
These are all points that might be helpful in dealing with this common concern. Many individuals in health care and education have been taught that delaying evaluation is a good idea, so as not to label symptoms as "stuttering." There is no evidence that identification and differential diagnosis of stuttering causes stuttering to worsen or persist.

B43

The Practice of Speech-Language Pathology

An SLP owns a thriving private practice clinic. The SLP learns of a family emergency that requires a move across country, thus necessitating the closing of the clinic. Which decision is BEST for the SLP to make in the management of current clients?

Choices:
A. The SLP should provide ample notice of closure and offer help transitioning clients to other service providers.
B. The SLP should provide notice of closure at each of the clients' next treatment sessions and indicate they will receive only one more session.
C. The SLP should provide ample notice of closure, finish the clients' treatment sessions, and finalize their move.
D. The SLP should hire another SLP to run their private practice and keep the clinic open for services.

Teaching Points

Correct Answer: A

As health care providers, SLPs are not able to abandon their patients, even in the event of a move and need to close a practice center, such as this scenario. The SLP must provide ample notice of closure for their practice and should assist their clients in finding another location to receive services to their full abilities. While hiring another SLP to run the practice may be an attractive option, there is no guarantee that the SLP will find another person to take over in time or find a person who is qualified enough to run a practice.

B44

Autism Spectrum Disorders

An SLP works in an outpatient speech and language clinic. A nonverbal adolescent with autism spectrum disorder (ASD) is referred for services. Upon reviewing the patient's intake paperwork, the SLP learns that the parents have sought services from two other SLPs in the past year to address the patient's verbal expression abilities, as "no other therapists have been successful." Which decision is BEST in this situation?

Choices:
A. Meet with the patient's parents to discuss expectations of speech therapy.
B. Attempt to treat the patient's verbal expression and closely monitor for progress.
C. Refer the patient to an SLP who specializes in complex cases of ASD.
D. Dismiss the patient from speech therapy due to no progress in previous therapy.

Teaching Points

Correct Answer: A

The SLP in this scenario finds themselves in a difficult situation. Given that the reason the patient was referred to them in the first place was for language treatment, it makes sense that the SLP would want to perform these services to the best of their abilities. However, it is also important to understand that the patient is a teenager and remains nonverbal despite, what can be assumed, years of speech therapy. As such, the SLP should have an open and honest discussion with the patient's parents to set realistic expectations for therapy services and suggest possible areas to target in therapy, such as the development of an augmentative or alternative means of communication. This is the best way for the SLP to remain ethical in their practice.

B45

Acoustics

An SLP is studying different acoustic characteristics of vowel sounds. The pitch contour for a vowel shows several abrupt changes that the SLP suspects may be inaccurate. Which is the BEST way to objectively document accuracy or inaccuracy of the pitch contour?

Choices:
A. Listen to the vowel sounds to determine if abrupt changes in pitch can be detected.
B. Observe the waveform to see if it shows abrupt changes in pitch associated with the vowel sounds.
C. Look at an amplitude spectrum to see if the harmonics show abrupt changes in spacing.
D. Look at a narrowband spectrogram to see if the harmonic contours show abrupt changes.

Teaching Points

Correct Answer: D

A pitch contour should follow the same contour as the sound's harmonics. Harmonic contours are visible in a narrowband spectrogram. Listening to a vowel provides useful information but not objective documentation. Pitch changes are more difficult to see in a waveform. Since an amplitude spectrum has no time access, it does not show pitch over time.

B46

Augmentative and Alternative Communication

An older adult with primary progressive aphasia is working with an SLP to implement an appropriate AAC system to facilitate the patient's communication. The patient's spouse does not understand AAC and has not been able to adequately perform partner-assisted scanning, despite ongoing training. Which type of barrier BEST describes this occurrence?

Choices:
A. Access barrier.
B. Skill barrier.
C. Knowledge barrier.
D. Attitude barrier.

Teaching Points

Correct Answer: B

A skill barrier is a form of opportunity barrier (i.e., one caused by forces external to the AAC user) that is caused by facilitator difficulty implementing an AAC technique. As the patient's wife is demonstrating significant difficulty with implementing her husband's AAC strategies, the patient is experiencing a skill barrier to communication. In contrast to this, a knowledge barrier is caused by a lack of information on the part of the person with complex communication needs' (CCN's) facilitator and an attitude barrier is caused by incorrect, outdated, outmoded, or discriminatory attitudes regarding the abilities of people with CCN. Finally, an access barrier is a communicative barrier caused by limitations of the person with CCN.

B47

Voice Disorders in Children and Adults

An SLP is working in an outpatient clinic. A patient arrives for an evaluation, with complaints of a strained voice and difficulty breathing. After completing an endoscopic evaluation, the SLP observes that the patient demonstrates difficulty with vocal fold abduction and the vocal folds are left in a paramedian position. Which muscles are MOST LIKELY impacted?

Choices:
A. Lateral cricoarytenoids.
B. Posterior cricoarytenoids.
C. Transverse interarytenoids.
D. Oblique interarytenoids.

Teaching Points

Correct Answer: B

The posterior cricoarytenoid muscle is the sole muscle of vocal fold abduction. Should there be any damage to this muscle, a person will demonstrate an inability to open their vocal folds, leading to difficulty breathing and potentially to altered phonation. The lateral cricoarytenoids, transverse interarytenoids, and oblique interarytenoids are all muscles involved in vocal fold adduction, which move the vocal folds to midline.

B48

Stuttering and Other Fluency Disorders

A 12-year-old child is referred to an SLP with a fluency disorder. Teachers report that the child rarely speaks at school and the parents report that when attending classmates' parties, the child will spend time with a few close friends. The child is motivated to work on the disfluencies but states willingness to work on them only in one-on-one sessions. Which approach should NOT be part of the intervention plan?

Choices:
A. Building fluency skills.
B. Addressing coping skills to handle teasing and bullying.
C. Providing a family-centered, indirect approach.
D. Helping the child to explore feelings regarding the disfluencies.

Teaching Points

Correct Answer: C

While family training will be important in all stages of stuttering treatment, a family-centered and indirect approach is most typically used with young children in the beginning stuttering stage. This child is in middle school and is aware of his stuttering, putting him at the intermediate stuttering stage. He is a motivated participant, making direct therapy a beneficial option.

B49

Autism Spectrum Disorders

A 24-month-old child has been brought into an outpatient speech and language clinic for a comprehensive evaluation. According to the parents, the child has started demonstrating "strange" behaviors, and the parents believe the child may have autism spectrum disorder (ASD). Which observation is MOST CONSISTENT with signs of ASD?

Choices:
A. Unusual prosody in speech.
B. Lack of pointing to share interest.
C. Repetitive movements with objects.
D. No response to calling the child's name.

Teaching Points

Correct Answer: B

There are several social communication warning signs for autism spectrum disorder, which can be observed at varying points in development. At 24 months, if children demonstrate a lack of pointing to share interest, this could be a warning sign of ASD. In contrast to this, unusual prosody in speech and repetitive movement with objects are warning signs for ASD often seen at 18 months. Finally, lack of response to their own name is a warning sign for ASD seen at 9–12 months.

B50

Language Disorders in Young Children

An SLP is working with a young child who has demonstrated significant difficulty with narrative generation. The SLP selects an initial treatment target to produce recounts. Which goal is MOST BENEFICIAL for this child?

Choices:
A. To produce narratives to relate a routine event or activity.
B. To spontaneously produce narratives about a specific weekend event.
C. To produce narratives about shared experiences when prompted.
D. To produce narratives about ongoing experiences during play activities.

Teaching Points

Correct Answer: C

A recount is a narrative that relates unique, shared experiences using past tense, which a child produces when prompted. In contrast to this, a personal narrative is a spontaneously given narrative, which relates specific experiences or events. An event cast is a type of narrative that is produced as a description of an ongoing activity, often during play. Finally, a script is a type of narrative that relates routine events or activities that occur with some degree of frequency.

B51

Speech Sound Disorders in Children

A child is brought into a local speech and language clinic for treatment of a speech sound disorder. When the SLP interviews the child's parents, they reveal that their child has severe hypernasal speech. With which type of speech sound would this child's hypernasality be MOST audible?

Choices:
A. Nasals.
B. Velars.
C. Plosives.
D. Vowels.

Teaching Points

Correct Answer: D

Hypernasality occurs when too much sound is resonating in the nasal cavity during speech. This type of resonance disorder is most perceptible on vowels, because this type of sound class is always voiced and always produced with a completely occluded nasal cavity. Hypernasality may affect some types of voiced consonants, but voiceless consonants would remain unaffected, as hypernasality is the result of sound vibration, which is not present during production of voiceless consonants.

B52

Autism Spectrum Disorders

An SLP is preparing to administer an assessment to a child suspected of having ASD. The assessment chosen will determine eligibility for intervention. Which consideration is MOST IMPORTANT in completing the assessment?

Choices:
A. The avoidance of criterion-referenced measurements in the assessment of ASD.
B. Informal observation of behaviors as a means of assessment is not accepted by most school systems.
C. Formal assessment measures are the most widely accepted method of determining eligibility.
D. The child must receive a diagnostic label following assessment in order to receive services.

Teaching Points

Correct Answer: A

When determining a child with autism spectrum disorder's eligibility for speech and language services, criterion referencing should be avoided. With this type of evaluation, cognitive and linguistic skills may be revealed as commensurate, which prompts many people to advocate against SLP intervention. In contrast to this, informal observations of behaviors exhibited by these children is critical in determining eligibility, and performance on a formal assessment may not be an accurate reflection of the child's abilities and diagnostic labels may not be appropriate due to the heterogeneity of the ASD population.

B53

Language Disorders in Young Children

A young child arrives to a speech and language center with parents, who suspect that the child may have a language disorder. When the SLP escorts the child into the office, the child plays and interacts with one parent. When the SLP retrieves assessment measures, the child runs into a corner to continue playing. What is the BEST means of assessing this child?

Choices:
A. Waiting until the child is willing to participate in the standardized measures.
B. Talking with the child to see what types of responses will be produced.
C. Administering a standardized case history with the child's parents.
D. Collecting data through observation of the child's interactions with parents.

Teaching Points

Correct Answer: D

When children become noncompliant during assessment, there are several methods that SLPs may implement to gather sufficient data. One such measure is watching the child's interactions as a means of collecting language information. As the child may not become compliant during the session, waiting to administer standardized measures is not an efficient use of time. Additionally, administering a standard case history form may not deliver sufficient information regarding the child's language patterns. Finally, while it may be appropriate to attempt conversation with this child, if she remains noncompliant, this method may not deliver appropriate information.

B54

Motor Speech Disorders

A patient with a diagnosis of flaccid dysarthria exhibits hypernasality. During visualization of the velopharyngeal system, the patient is able to inconsistently achieve closure of the velopharyngeal port. Which intervention approach would be MOST BENEFICIAL for this patient?

Choices:
A. Fit the patient with a palatal lift.
B. Teach the patient to speak with increased effort.
C. Strengthen velopharyngeal muscles through nonspeech exercises.
D. Improve velopharyngeal port closure through pharyngeal flap surgery.

Teaching Points

Correct Answer: B

Because this patient exhibits mild hypernasality, effortful speech production would be the most appropriate treatment route. Palatal lifts and pharyngeal flap approaches are appropriate for those dysarthric speakers who exhibit significant velopharyngeal weakness, whereas velopharyngeal strengthening regimens are more appropriate for those individuals with moderate impairments leading to hypernasality. Speaking with an increased effort may be effective as a compensatory technique for patients with mild deficits.

B55

Anatomy and Physiology of Communication and Swallowing

A person places their hand on a hot surface and experiences the sensation of heat. The feeling of heat is conveyed up to the primary somatosensory cortex in the parietal lobe. This sensory information is relayed to the cortex via which sensory pathway?

Choices:
A. Lateral corticospinal tract.
B. Anterior corticospinal tract.
C. Anterolateral system.
D. Posterior column-medial lemniscal system.

Teaching Points

Correct Answer: C

If a person places their hand on a hot stove, this will cause pain and temperature sensation, which would be conveyed through the anterolateral system (pain, temperature, and crude touch). The posterior column-medial lemniscus system is responsible for transmission of vibration, pressure, and fine touch information. The lateral corticospinal tract and anterior corticospinal tract are both motor tracts, which control limb movement and girdle movement, respectively.

B56

Acoustics

An SLP is analyzing a spectrogram of an utterance made up of three phonemes. The first phoneme consists of lower frequency frication noise of a longer duration. The second phoneme is a vowel with low F1 and high F2. The third phoneme consists of a period of closure followed by a burst. Which utterance is MOST LIKELY captured on the spectrogram?

Choices:
A. Pete.
B. Sheet.
C. Seat.
D. Dan.

Teaching Points

Correct Answer: B

Because the first phoneme demonstrates frication noise of a lower frequency, it can be assumed that it is a fricative sound produced farther back in the oral cavity, such as /ʃ/. For the second phoneme, because there is a low F1 and high F2, it can be assumed that the vowel is a high front vowel, such as /i/. Finally, as the final phoneme is characterized by a closure (e.g., silent period) followed by a burst, it can be assumed that it is a stop consonant. As there is no mention of voicing, it can be assumed that it is a voiceless stop, such as /t/. The only option from this scenario that matches these three conditions is /ʃit/ or "sheet."

B57

Dysphagia: Swallowing and Swallowing Disorder

An SLP working in a skilled nursing facility is asked to complete a clinical swallow evaluation for a resident with dementia. Upon interviewing the primary caregivers, the SLP learns that the resident is consuming less with each meal. During a lunch observation, the resident attempts to use a spoon as a straw, becomes frustrated, and stops eating and drinking. Which recommendation will BEST address the mealtime issues?

Choices:
A. Assign a nursing assistant to feed the resident all of their meals.
B. Encourage the resident to eat alone to reduce distractions.
C. Provide finger foods during meals as available.
D. Referral to occupational therapy, as this is not dysphagia related.

Teaching Points

Correct Answer: C

When a person with dementia exhibits cognitive deficits such as silverware confusion that impacts their ability to participate in meals, use of finger foods is an appropriate means of treatment that allows the person to continue to experience independence with eating and allows them to continue to eat around familiar persons. Removing a person from a communal dining area or assigning them to have feeding assistance can be a dignity issue and can reduce the person's overall independence. Occupational therapy may be able to help with silverware use if the patient is experiencing inability to adequately hold silverware, through use of adaptive tools, such as "built-up" silverware.

B58

Stuttering and Other Fluency Disorders

A parent reports that a 4-year-old child repeats the initial sound of many words when speaking. The parent also states that the child doesn't seem to be bothered by these sound repetitions and doesn't always notice when it is occurring. What type of fluency disorder does the child MOST LIKELY have?

Choices:
A. Neurogenic stuttering.
B. Cluttering.
C. Developmental stuttering.
D. Psychogenic stuttering.

Teaching Points

Correct Answer: C

Developmental stuttering is characterized by disfluencies, typically appearing between the ages of 2 and 5 years. It is the most common type of fluency disorder and more likely to occur in males than females. In contrast, neurogenic stuttering is characterized by disfluencies occurring after a neurological event such as a traumatic brain injury.

Exam B

B59

Language Acquisition: Preverbal and Early Language

A parent brings a typically developing 15-month-old toddler to an outpatient speech and language clinic. The parent is concerned that the child is delayed in speaking words and knows only about 10 words. What is the BEST response to the parent's concerns?

Choices:
A. Recommend a full speech and language evaluation to determine why the child is delayed.
B. Reassure the parent that the child's delays are mild and with time will learn more words.
C. Inform the parent that speaking 10 words is typical for a 15-month-old child.
D. Provide a brief screening to determine if the child would benefit from speech-language services.

Teaching Points

Correct Answer: C

By the time children are 15 months old, their expressive lexicon is around 10 words in size. By the time they are 19 months old, this expressive lexicon has steadily increased to around 100–300 words.

B60

Language Acquisition: Preverbal and Early Language

A 6-month-old is being evaluated through a local early intervention clinic. During the evaluation, the SLP observes the infant exclaiming "mamamama" and "babababa" happily and frequently. Which stage of linguistic development has the infant MOST LIKELY achieved?

Choices:
A. Exploration/expansion stage.
B. Coo and goo stage.
C. Canonical babbling stage.
D. Phonation stage.

Teaching Points

Correct Answer: C

In the canonical babbling stage, a baby is engaging in reduplicated babbling, which is characterized by frequent CVCV sound combinations such as "babababa" and "mamama." Alternatively, if the child was in the phonation stage, the majority of sounds are reflexive, and the exploration/expansion stage would be characterized by the baby engaging in raspberries, squeals, and trills.

B61

Acquired Language Disorders

An SLP in an outpatient clinic is working with a patient with aphasia. The patient demonstrates severe non-fluent verbal expression and is able to intermittently produce single words spontaneously. Additionally, the patient has some preserved reading comprehension. Which treatment method is BEST for the SLP to use?

Choices:
A. Melodic intonation therapy.
B. Treatment of underlying forms.
C. Sentence Production Program for Aphasia.
D. Voluntary control of involuntary utterances.

Teaching Points

Correct Answer: D

The optimal patient profile for use of voluntary control of involuntary utterances includes persons with non-fluent aphasia who have the ability to produce single words intermittently and some level of intact reading. The premise of this treatment method is to use words that the patient has produced spontaneously and work to get these words under conscious, volitional control for production. Melodic intonation therapy utilizes singing to assist in the production of highly functional and selected phrases. Treatment of underlying forms targets grammatical deficiencies in verbal expression. Finally, Sentence Production Program for Aphasia uses a structured hierarchy of sentences to facilitate sentence-level verbal output.

B62

Written Language Disorders in School-Age Populations

An SLP is working on narrative structure with an adolescent. Recently, the adolescent wrote a story about their weekend, which reads, "My family was going to a friend's birthday party. We were late to the birthday party." Using this information, the SLP wants to document the narrative episode level. Which narrative level BEST describes the story?

Choices:
A. Abbreviated episode.
B. Incomplete episode.
C. Complete episode.
D. Action sequence.

Teaching Points

Correct Answer: B

An incomplete episode is a narrative episode level in which the child includes two out of three initiating events, action, and consequence. For this child's story, there is an initiating event (i.e., family members going to a birthday party) and a consequence (i.e., being late for the party), but no action event. If the child had included an action, such as getting a flat tire on the way to the party, this would constitute a complete episode, which includes an initiating event, an action, and a consequence all related to the initiating event. An action sequence consists of a series of actions that follow a chronological order but are not causally linked. Finally, an abbreviated episode is one that contains causally related actions that are not associated with an initiating event, or specific, goal-directed behavior.

B63

Voice Disorders in Children and Adults

A young child arrives at a local voice clinic with their parents for a full voice assessment battery. After completing and reviewing all test measures, the SLP and otolaryngologist have determined that the child is presenting with early stage, bilateral vocal fold nodules, most likely due to phonotraumatic behaviors. The parents explain that the child often yells for siblings and makes funny voices. Which approach to treatment would be MOST IMPORTANT for the child?

Choices:
A. Use of confidential voice.
B. Use of laryngeal massage.
C. Use of pushing/pulling exercises.
D. Surgical intervention.

Teaching Points

Correct Answer: A

Confidential voice therapy is a treatment approach that has the participant engage in low-volume phonation, which effectively reduces contact between the vocal folds. Reducing vocal fold contact reduces the chances of increasing phonotraumatic lesions, such as this pediatric patient is experiencing. Surgical intervention is not recommended in the pediatric nodule population, as their nodules often spontaneously improve as the patient improves. Use of laryngeal massage would not provide benefit to this patient, as it is not excessive laryngeal tension causing their problems. Pushing and pulling exercises would increase the contact between the vocal folds and exacerbate the child's problem.

B64

Language Disorders in Young Children

A child arrives at an early language learning clinic to receive speech and language intervention. The SLP has set goals to increase the child's understanding of vocabulary, utilizing principles of neighborhood density. Which vocabulary word should the child learn FIRST?

Choices:
A. Jump.
B. Cat.
C. Five.
D. Fruit.

Teaching Points

Correct Answer: B

Neighborhood density is a lexical representation variable that influences word learning. When words are in a high neighborhood, there are several "neighbor" words that differ by a single phoneme, which aid in word learning. *Cat* is a high-density neighborhood word, which includes neighbors such as *bat, fat, hat, coat, rat*, and so on. Low-neighborhood words have fewer neighbor words and are more difficult for children to initially learn. *Jump, five,* and *fruit* are all low-density words, and while they would be harder for the child to learn, they would be easier for the child to retrieve after they have learned the words.

B65

Motor Speech Disorders

An SLP at an acute rehabilitation hospital is evaluating a newly admitted patient with flaccid dysarthria. Following a comprehensive speech evaluation, the SLP notes that the patient demonstrates significant hypernasality secondary to poor velum mobility and makes recommendations for a prosthodontist consult. Which prosthetic devices would be BEST for the patient to use?

Choices:
A. Speech bulb.
B. Palatal lift.
C. Palatal obturator.
D. Palatal expander.

Teaching Points

Correct Answer: B

The palatal lift device is recommended for use with patients who have poor velar mobility, such as the patient in this scenario. The palatal obturator (used to close/occlude an open cleft or fistula) and speech bulb (used to occlude the nasopharynx when the velum is short) would not be an appropriate choice for this patient, due to the nature of their disorder.

B66

Motor Speech Disorders

An SLP specializes in the treatment of motor speech disorders. The SLP works with a patient who has apraxia of speech. The SLP acquires percent correct scores for spontaneous (without cueing) productions of one-, two- and three-syllable words targeting a specific transition involving the /s/: 98%, 68%, and 15%. Using integral stimulation, the percentage correct for the same stimuli was 100%, 84%, and 42%. Which option BEST identifies where treatment for this patient should begin?

Choices:
A. With three-syllable words in the absence of any cuing, followed by the addition of tactile, visual, and auditory cuing.
B. With one-syllable words in the absence of any cuing, followed by two-syllable words without cuing.
C. With two-syllable words in the presence of integral stimulation while gradually decreasing cuing.
D. With two-syllable words in the presence of integral stimulation while gradually increasing cuing.

Teaching Points

Correct Answer: C

Because this patient is highly intelligible at the spontaneous one-syllable level, beginning treatment at this level may lead to lower motivation for the participant, as there is not much room for improvement. However, as the patient has significantly reduced intelligibility at the two-syllable level and is stimulable to the use of cues at this level, they are an appropriate candidate to begin treatment by focusing on production of two-syllable words. As this skill builds, and the patient is able to spontaneously produce intelligible utterances at the two-syllable level, treatment focus may transition to the three-syllable level.

B67

Motor Speech Disorders

An SLP working in an acute rehabilitation hospital receives orders for a patient with severe flaccid dysarthria. When the SLP arrives at the patient's room, the patient expresses a change in communication that has significantly affected their self-image and is feeling depressed. The SLP provides supportive statements and reassurance, which does not improve the patient's state of mind. What is the SLP's BEST response?

Choices:
A. Develop a treatment plan to address intelligibility for improvements in psychological outlook.
B. Refer the patient to another SLP who has more experience in working with persons with dysarthria.
C. Refer the patient for a psychological consult to assess the patient's state of mind.
D. Discuss the impact of communication disorders on psychological outlook with the patient.

Teaching Points

Correct Answer: C

According to the ASHA Code of Ethics, Principle of Ethics I, Rule of Ethics B, "Individuals shall use every resource, including referral when appropriate, to ensure that high-quality service is provided." As this patient is showing obvious signs of difficulty coping with their change in communication, referral to a psychological professional is warranted. While improvements in intelligibility may lead to an improved psychological outlook, the need for a referral is warranted and should be capitalized on in this scenario.

B68

Acoustics

An SLP is analyzing a spectrogram of an utterance made up of three phonemes. The first phoneme consists of a short period of voicing followed by a closure and short duration voice onset time. The second phoneme is a vowel with low F1 and low F2. The third phoneme demonstrates a low-frequency nasal formant. Which is MOST LIKELY the utterance captured on the spectrogram?

Choices:
A. Seed.
B. Teeth.
C. Doom.
D. Reem.

Teaching Points

Correct Answer: C

Because the first phoneme demonstrates a short period of voicing followed by a closure (e.g., silent period), it can be assumed that this phoneme is a stop consonant. As it has a short duration voice onset time, it can be assumed that it is a voiced stop consonant, such as /d/. For the second phoneme, because there is a low F1 and low F2, it can be assumed that the vowel is a high back vowel, such as /u/. Finally, as the final phoneme has a low-frequency nasal formant, it can be assumed that the final phoneme is a nasal consonant. The only option from this scenario that matches these three conditions is /dum/ or *doom*.

B69

Dysphagia: Swallowing and Swallowing Disorder

During a patient's bedside swallowing evaluation, the SLP observes copious amounts of residue present throughout the patient's oral cavity following their swallow. Which portion of the oral phase is the patient MOST LIKELY having difficulty?

Choices:
A. Bolus formation.
B. Anterior-posterior movement.
C. Labial seal.
D. Mastication.

Teaching Points

Correct Answer: A

The patient would most likely be experiencing difficulty with bolus formation. If the patient is not able to form a cohesive bolus prior to swallowing, this would most likely lead to residue being left at any location in the oral cavity.

B70

The Practice of Speech-Language Pathology

An SLP has recently expanded into providing telepractice services to clients who are unable to be treated at a private practice center. A friend of the SLP who lives in another state asks the SLP to treat a family member, who has Wernicke's aphasia. The friend would like the family member to receive more treatment than is currently being received. What is the BEST response to this request?

Choices:
A. Recommend against treatment, as telepractice has not been proven effective in treating Wernicke's aphasia.
B. Recommend against treatment, as the family member is already receiving services.
C. Share the family member's case information with a local SLP in the state in which the friend lives.
D. Refer the friend to another SLP who has licensure in the state in which the family member lives.

Teaching Points

Correct Answer: D

Currently, SLPs are required to maintain licensure in any state that they perform telepractice in (i.e., the state in which the client lives). As the SLP does not live in the same state as his friend, he is legally not able to provide services for the friend's mother and should recommend a licensed SLP in that state. While there is currently limited efficacy regarding telepractice, it is regarded as a promising method of intervention and can lead to patient progress for all forms of communication disorders, including Wernicke's aphasia. Individuals who receive telehealth are always eligible for further in-person sessions. Lastly, all rules for privacy and confidentiality apply to all patients, and for this reason, the SLP is unable to share the mother's case information without prior consent.

B71

Speech Sound Disorders in Children

An 11-year-old child is evaluated by an SLP at a private clinic. After completion of the speech evaluation, the SLP observes a pattern with the child's articulation errors: *fishbowl* as /fɪtʃbol/, *parachute* as /pærədʒut/, and *trashcan* as /trætʃkæn/. Which statement BEST describes this child's speech pattern?

Choices:
A. Affrication of medical fricatives.
B. Fronting of initial fricatives.
C. Final consonant deletion of stops.
D. Initial consonant deletion of nasals.

Teaching Points

Correct Answer: A

When examining these errors, it is important to look at placement of the error within the syllable as well as the specific sound error. The error is observed exclusively in the middle of the word, or the medial position. These words all have fricatives, or the ʃ sound specifically. The error this child is making is changing the ʃ to either a dʒ or tʃ, both affricates. While all of these sounds are produced at the palate, the manner in which the sound is being made is being changed by the individual.

B72

Voice Disorders in Children and Adults

An SLP working in a neonatal intensive care unit is assigned to evaluate an infant. The infant demonstrates an abnormal cry and co-occurring respiratory distress, which has been present since birth approximately 3 days prior to SLP consult. Which condition is the infant MOST LIKELY experiencing?

Choices:
A. Vocal fold nodules.
B. Vocal fold polyps.
C. Supraglottic atrophy.
D. Subglottic stenosis.

Teaching Points

Correct Answer: D

Subglottic stenosis is a disorder characterized by narrowing of the space below the glottis (i.e., space between the vocal folds), which can lead to altered voice production and respiratory distress, as this disorder narrows the trachea. While vocal fold nodules and polyps can also cause vocal alterations, these are not expected to occur so early in life. Finally, supraglottic atrophy would imply muscle wasting of the area above the glottis, which would not lead to respiratory distress.

B73

Voice Disorders in Children and Adults

An SLP in an outpatient voice clinic receives orders to complete a comprehensive voice assessment with a patient who presents with a recently diagnosed vocal fold hemorrhage. During the assessment, the SLP documents that the patient has a rough vocal quality with intermittent breaks in phonation. Which type of assessment MOST LIKELY led to these observations?

Choices:
A. Acoustic.
B. Stroboscopic.
C. Aerodynamic.
D. Perceptual.

Teaching Points

Correct Answer: D

Perceptual assessment involves making clinical observations and judgments of a speaker's vocal quality, amplitude, and pitch. These observations include such comments as rough/breathy/strained vocal quality, excessive/reduced loudness, and elevated pitch, among others. These judgments tend to not have the best interrater reliability, necessitating the use of assessment measures such as the GRBAS and CAPE-V.

B74

Spoken Language Disorders in School-Age Populations

A child has been referred to an SLP for a comprehensive language evaluation, with reports of "global language problems." Following evaluation, the SLP determines that the child is demonstrating word-finding difficulties, comprehension deficits, and disorganized language. Which disorder does the child MOST likely demonstrate?

Choices:
A. Traumatic brain injury.
B. Cerebral palsy.
C. Autism spectrum disorder.
D. Down syndrome.

Teaching Points

Correct Answer: A

Language difficulties associated with traumatic brain injury include comprehension difficulties, telegraphic speech, word-finding deficits, disorganized language, and potential pragmatic difficulties. In contrast to this, children with cerebral palsy may demonstrate general difficulties in both receptive and expressive language. Children with autism spectrum disorder demonstrate significant impairments in pragmatic language, as well as restricted interests and behaviors. Finally, children with Down syndrome demonstrate deficits in syntax, rather than semantics, and have a greater difficulty with language production over comprehension.

B75

Stuttering and Other Fluency Disorders

An adult is seeking support from an SLP who specializes in fluency disorders. The person reports stuttering throughout life; however, the disfluencies occur less when relaxed and then they are less bothered by them. The person is hoping to obtain a job as an administrative assistant but is concerned about being able to complete the job requirements. The SLP discusses specific work situations that may occur and ways to practice decreasing the disfluencies. Which intervention approach will BEST address the person's concerns?

Choices:
A. Practicing speaking to a family member with fewer disfluencies.
B. Practicing speaking on the telephone with fewer disfluencies.
C. Seeing a psychologist to overcome negative feelings regarding the disfluencies.
D. Joining a choir to utilize music to decrease the number of disfluencies.

Teaching Points

Correct Answer: B

While working with a therapist may be beneficial to address any self-esteem issues that this patient might have, he is specifically interested in working toward his goal of becoming an administrative assistant. A person who stutters is more likely to have disfluencies while speaking on the telephone, which is a large part of what an administrative assistant would do during the day.

B76

Augmentative and Alternative Communication

An adult with progressive amyotrophic lateral sclerosis (ALS) reports progressive symptoms that significantly affect verbal communication. The patient maintains limited use of fingers on the left hand. The SLP has been updating the patient's AAC device, so it utilizes alternate access to aid in communication. The device now highlights each item in the first row of a selection set, followed by the second row, until the patient makes a selection. Which type of access BEST represents the patient's device?

Choices:
A. Linear scanning.
B. Circular scanning.
C. Row-column scanning.
D. Group item scanning.

Teaching Points

Correct Answer: A

Linear scanning refers to a scanning pattern in which the device highlights each item in the first row of the selection set, followed by each item in the second row, and so on, until the user makes a selection. As this matches the description of the method utilized by the SLP in this scenario, it is likely they are implementing linear scanning. In contrast to this, circular scanning occurs when the device presents the selection set in a circle and scans them item by item until a selection is made. Row-column scanning proceeds by highlighting each row until the user makes a selection, at which time items are then highlighted until the user makes a selection. Finally, group item scanning proceeds by presenting groups (i.e., semantically related items) until the user has made a selection, at which time items are presented until the user has made a selection.

B77

Dysphagia: Swallowing and Swallowing Disorder

A patient presents to a hospital as an outpatient in order to complete a videofluoroscopic swallow study (VFSS) after experiencing dysphagia for a number of months. Results from the VFSS indicate that the patient is experiencing difficulty with hyolaryngeal elevation. Which muscle is MOST LIKELY impacted?

Choices:
A. Omohyoid.
B. Transverse interarytenoid.
C. Sternohyoid.
D. Mylohyoid.

Teaching Points

Correct Answer: D

The muscles most responsible for laryngeal elevation are the suprahyoids, which include the digastric, stylo-hyoid, geniohyoid, and mylohyoid muscles. The sternohyoid, sternothyroid, omohyoid, and thyrohyoid are infrahyoid muscles and contribute to laryngeal depression.

B78

Autism Spectrum Disorders

An SLP is working with a child with autism spectrum disorder. The child demonstrates significant difficulty in understanding perception and beliefs from others' perspectives, which has negatively impacted their social relationships. Which intervention approach is BEST for the SLP to implement with the child?

Choices:
A. Picture Exchange Communication System.
B. Social stories.
C. Theory of mind.
D. Peer and play mediation.

Teaching Points

Correct Answer: C

This child's significant difficulty in understanding perception and beliefs from others' perspectives, which has negatively impacted their social relationships, is a deficit known as *mindblindness*. The theory of mind method of intervention is targeted at improving mindblindness through teaching the individual to understand mental states. In contrast to this intervention, Picture Exchange Communication System, social stories, and peer and play mediation are forms of intervention targeted at deficits in social communication.

B79

Written Language Disorders in School-Age Populations

A student reads seven research articles regarding recycling challenges and methods. The student summarizes and critiques the articles and then, based on their synthesis, proposes a novel strategy to solve urban recycling efforts. This cluster of behaviors is BEST associated with which of Chall's reading stages?

Choices:
A. Stage 2: Confirmation, Fluency, Ungluing from Print.
B. Stage 3: Reading for Learning the New.
C. Stage 4: Multiple Viewpoints.
D. Stage 5: Construction and Reconstruction.

Teaching Points

Correct Answer: D

This student would fall into Chall's Stage 5 as they synthesized multiple viewpoints in order to generate their novel hypothesis. The hallmark characteristics of Chall's Stage 5 include creating new theories based on analysis, synthesis, and evaluation of existing sources of information, which this student has demonstrated. Because the student has generated their own hypothesis regarding the material, they have advanced past Chall's Stage 4.

B80

Acquired Language Disorders

An SLP in a home health setting is working with an individual who has right hemisphere brain damage and is exhibiting significant left neglect. Which treatment approach is BEST for the client?

Choices:
A. Determining reading comprehension by having the client match written words with pictures.
B. Targeting augmentative and alternative communication through computerized programs such as C-Speak Aphasia.
C. Focusing on the client's written expression abilities by training phoneme-grapheme conversion rules.
D. Addressing the client's attention by using a brightly colored border on the edge of pen and paper tasks.

Teaching Points

Correct Answer: D

Left neglect is an attention deficit in which those affected do not attend to stimuli on the left side of their world. By using a treatment method in which brightly colored borders are added to the left edge of paper tasks, the person with left neglect may be "cued" to continue looking until the border is found, thus targeting their attention.

B81

Autism Spectrum Disorders

A child is brought to an outpatient clinic for a neuropsychological evaluation. Following the evaluation, the child is diagnosed with autism spectrum disorder, specifically with Level 2 severity in social communication. Which behaviors are MOST LIKELY to be observed?

Choices:
A. Difficulty initiating social interactions with peers.
B. Abnormal responses to social overtures.
C. Very limited social interaction.
D. Decreased interest in social interactions.

Teaching Points

Correct Answer: B

A Level 2 severity rating for social communication in autism spectrum disorder is characterized by marked deficits in verbal and nonverbal social communication, which are apparent even with supports and reduced or abnormal responses to social overtures. In contrast to this, Level 1 severity ratings are characterized by noticeable deficits in social communication without supports, difficulty initiating and decreased interest in social interactions, and odd/unsuccessful attempts to make friends. Finally, Level 3 severity ratings are characterized by severe deficits in verbal and nonverbal social communication, as well as very limited social interaction and response to social overtures.

B82

Motor Speech Disorders

An SLP is working with a pediatric client with childhood apraxia of speech. The SLP initiates treatment that involves using a set of utterances chosen specifically for the child, structured to use mass and distributed practice schedules. Which treatment approach is the SLP MOST LIKELY utilizing?

Choices:
A. Dynamic temporal/tactile cuing.
B. Nuffield Centre Dyspraxia Programme.
C. Integral stimulation treatment.
D. Articulatory kinematic treatment.

Teaching Points

Correct Answer: A

In the dynamic temporal/tactile cueing method for motor speech treatment, individual utterances are targeted from a set of utterances chosen specifically for the child. Mass and distributed practice are used throughout treatment sessions with different forms of feedback in order to heighten motor learning. The Nuffield Programme, by contrast, uses a hierarchical approach, beginning with isolated sounds and building slowly to the level of conversational speech. Integral stimulation is a traditional approach to articulation treatment, involving the clinician modeling an utterance for the patient prior to the patient attempting to produce it. Finally, articulatory kinematic approaches work to improve spatial and temporal aspects of articulatory movements as a means to improve speech production.

B83

The Practice of Speech-Language Pathology

An SLP discontinues treatment for a child who has achieved the maximum amount of progress possible. What is the MOST IMPORTANT factor to consider when discontinuing treatment?

Choices:
A. The child has met all measurable goals and objectives.
B. The child is refusing to participate in further language treatment sessions.
C. The child's family no longer wishes to receive language services.
D. The child is able to meet all communication demands for daily activities.

Teaching Points

Correct Answer: D

There are multiple factors that are interrelated when considering dismissal from therapy for language disorders. Among these factors is whether the child is able to meet all of the communication demands imposed through their activities of daily living. From a speech-language pathologist perspective, being able to demonstrate adequate language skills for daily life is the ultimate goal of treatment. Once a client has demonstrated this ability, this may be indicative of dismissal from therapy. In contrast, if the child has met all language goals but is unable to meet the communicative needs of the activities of daily living, the child may benefit from further therapy sessions. Finally, if the child and family would not like to receive language intervention, this is also an important factor to consider, as SLPs are ethically bound to provide services that the family would like to receive, but this is not a factor from a speech and language perspective.

B84

Acquired Language Disorders

An SLP works with persons with aphasia (PWA) in a private practice setting. Recently, the SLP has learned about the Life Participation Approach to Aphasia (LPAA) and wants to implement some of the principles into practice to better serve patients. Which scenario BEST demonstrates use of the Performance Assessment of Contributions and Effectiveness (PACE) principles?

Choices:
A. Encouraging a PWA to remain in the home, to work on home-based communication.
B. Hiring a gardener for a PWA with hemiparesis, in order to keep their garden in adequate condition.
C. Providing emotional support services to only the PWA, in order to keep their psychological outlook positive.
D. Providing suggestions for audiobooks at the local library, to aid PWA who have reading deficits.

Teaching Points

Correct Answer: D

The LPAA is an approach to intervention that has five core values and seeks to improve the life participation of people with aphasia by focusing on intervention at all stages and for all people affected by aphasia, and that requires documentation of life participation enhancement as the outcome measure. By providing audiobooks to PWA who have reading deficits, this encourages these individuals to continue a hobby they had prior to their stroke. In contrast to this, the PWA should be encouraged to participate fully in their community and not be restricted to the home. Additionally, gardening could be adapted to allow the PWA to tend to their garden, rather than have another person do this completely. Finally, according to LPAA principles, all people affected by aphasia, including family members and caretakers, are entitled to services.

B85

Voice Disorders in Children and Adults

A patient seeks treatment from an otolaryngologist after experiencing "a lump at the back of the throat." After a full medical workup, the patient is diagnosed as having squamous cell carcinoma of the base of the tongue, with recommendations for a partial glossectomy. Following completion of this procedure, which deficit is MOST LIKELY to be observed during an instrumental evaluation?

Choices:
A. Reduced base of tongue retraction.
B. Reduced hyolaryngeal elevation.
C. Reduced labial seal.
D. Reduced epiglottic inversion.

Teaching Points

Correct Answer: A

The term *glossectomy* is the name of the medical procedure for removal of the tongue. In a partial glossectomy, a portion of the tongue is removed, which in this case would be near the base of tongue (the location of the tumor). If the patient had a portion of the base of their tongue removed, they would experience difficulty with base of tongue retraction. As long as the patient's suprahyoid muscles were left intact, they should not experience any significant reduction in hyolaryngeal elevation, which in turn would lead to no significant change in epiglottic inversion. Finally, as this surgery takes place at the base of the tongue, there should be no impact to the lips, therefore not leading to reduced labial seal.

B86

Motor Speech Disorders

An SLP is working to facilitate performance in the speech of a 4-year-old child with apraxia of speech. During a treatment session, the child articulates a word incorrectly. The SLP provides specific feedback regarding how to produce the movement more successfully and then has the child attempt to produce the word again. Which approach BEST represents the type of feedback provided?

Choices:
A. Blocked practice.
B. Knowledge of performance.
C. Variable practice.
D. Knowledge of results.

Teaching Points

Correct Answer: B

Knowledge of performance consists of specific feedback provided to the patient following practice (i.e., the production of a sound) regarding the quality of the motor behavior. Because this patient was given specific feedback on how to improve the speech sound from the faulty production, this constitutes feedback to the quality of the motor movements. This is in contrast to knowledge of results, in which feedback is given to the degree of success in achieving a motor behavior.

B87

The Practice of Speech-Language Pathology

An SLP is employed in a skilled nursing facility. The SLP reviews practice guidelines in order to provide comprehensive services to patients. Which is NOT a role of this SLP?

Choices:
A. Use of all modes of service delivery, including those that are technology based.
B. Participation in the evaluation, selection, and use of assistive devices.
C. Counseling patients, families, and caregivers regarding assessment and treatment.
D. Evaluation and determination of eligibility for special education and related services.

Teaching Points

Correct Answer: D

SLPs who work in medical settings are required to use all modes of service delivery (including those that are technology based); participate in the evaluation, selection, and use of assistive devices; and counsel patients, families, and caregivers regarding assessment and treatment. In contrast, SLPs in educational settings are required to evaluate and determine eligibility for special education and related services.

B88

Written Language Disorders in School-Age Populations

A typically developing fourth-grade child reads grade-level single words accurately and promptly, and spelling is appropriate for the grade level. When the child reads a passage from an English language arts textbook aloud, the reading, while accurate, is extremely slow and halting. When the SLP asks the child questions that assess understanding of what was read, the child formulates responses clearly and accurately. Which deficit does the child MOSTLY LIKELY have?

Choices:
A. Reading fluency.
B. Orthographic memory for letter patterns.
C. Rules for orthographic-phonological association.
D. Underlying vocabulary skills.

Teaching Points

Correct Answer: A

This student is demonstrating adequate automaticity, as she is able to accurately and quickly read individual words. However, because she has difficulty with the reading of connected text, she is presenting with problems in reading fluency. Fluent reading reflects appropriate rhythm, intonation, and syntactic chunking, all of which would be affected in this student's slow, halting oral reading.

B89

The Practice of Speech-Language Pathology

An SLP is providing a social language group for students with pragmatic language difficulties. The SLP wants to utilize means of intervention that provide the greatest benefit to all the members and is not willing to accept less progress by any member. Which philosophical approach BEST fits the SLP's approach to practice?

Choices:
A. Utilitarian approach.
B. Common good approach.
C. Fairness/justice approach.
D. Rights approach.

Teaching Points

Correct Answer: B

The common good approach seeks to find the action that best serves the whole community and not just some members. As this SLP seeks to find a means of intervention that is best for all the children in the social language group, they are utilizing principles of the common good approach. In contrast, the utilitarian approach seeks to find the action that will do the most good and the least harm to the most amount of people. The rights approach seeks to find the action that best respects the rights of all stakeholders. Finally, the fairness/justice approach seeks to find the option that treats people equally.

B90

Written Language Disorders in School-Age Populations

An SLP at a speech and language clinic is working with a client with dyslexia. During an evaluation, the client writes, "I went to the zu" after being prompted with the cue "write about something you did over the weekend." With which aspect of literacy does the client MOST LIKELY have difficulties?

Choices:
A. Phonological memory span.
B. Syntax.
C. Orthography.
D. Discourse.

Teaching Points

Correct Answer: C

Orthography is a symbolic system that is superimposed over an oral language system, which lends itself to writing. Because the student demonstrates impairments in the spelling of particular words (e.g., *zoo*), they are experiencing orthographic errors. As the sentence is written with correct grammar, the student does not demonstrate syntactic errors. Phonological memory span is measured using oral means (e.g., nonword repetition or digit span), and discourse includes more involved writing processes, both of which do not apply to this particular student.

B91

Dysphagia: Swallowing and Swallowing Disorder

An SLP at a skilled nursing facility is asked by a nurse to perform a swallowing evaluation on an older adult patient. The SLP must consider the multiple, typical changes to the swallow as one ages. Which finding BEST indicates an abnormal result from the examination?

Choices:
A. Increased duration of the swallow.
B. Reduction in smell and taste.
C. Increased presence of aspiration.
D. Lower salivary flow.

Teaching Points

Correct Answer: C

Because of decreased muscle tone with aging, there are typical amounts of associated increased duration of swallowing, delayed hyoid elevation, and longer opening of the upper esophageal sphincter. Additionally, while it does not occur with everyone, there is a typical decrease in smell and taste abilities in the elderly population. However, any presence of aspiration is considered a deficit in the swallow, regardless of the age group.

B92

Spoken Language Disorders in School-Age Populations

An SLP is engaged in reading and writing intervention in a grade school. The SLP wants to determine on a bimonthly basis whether the intervention techniques being implemented are effective or need to be modified. Which approach BEST represents this process?

Choices:
A. Progress monitoring assessment.
B. Diagnostic testing.
C. Outcomes assessment.
D. Screening.

Teaching Points

Correct Answer: A

Progress monitoring assessment includes taking steps throughout an academic year to ensure that adequate progress in reading growth is being achieved. As this SLP is making attempts to produce bimonthly reports about the progress of their client, they are engaging in progress monitoring. The results of these assessments are critical for determining a student's response to intervention as a means of advancing their overall progress in therapy.

B93

Spoken Language Disorders in School-Age Populations

An SLP in an elementary school setting is working with a student on their text-level reading fluency. Which approach would be MOST BENEFICIAL in enhancing the student's reading fluency?

Choices:

A. Diadochokinetic exercises.
B. Practice with repeated reading.
C. Vocabulary instruction.
D. Teaching oral sentence formulation skills.

Teaching Points

Correct Answer: B

The National Reading Panel indicates multiple approaches to intervention for improving children's reading skills. Small to moderate effects have been found for repeated reading, whereas moderate to large effects have been found for phonological awareness intervention and word attack/work identification instruction. Positive effects for systematic vocabulary and summary writing instruction have also been found.

B94

Language Acquisition: Preverbal and Early Language

A 15-month-old toddler is reported to be pointing but does not yet have any discernible words. The child babbles and appears to understand some words when the parents say the names of family members or favorite toys. Which statement BEST describes the child's language development?

Choices:

A. There is an early language disorder.
B. There is an early language difference.
C. The child is typically developing.
D. The child has an early language delay.

Teaching Points

Correct Answer: D

By the age of 15 months, a typical language learner would have on average 12 words. A 15-month-old with no words would draw concern from the speech language pathologist and indicate a language delay.

B95

Anatomy and Physiology of Communication and Swallowing

A patient presents to an emergency room with the complaint of uncoordinated gait and impaired speech production. The patient states that their speech makes it sound as though they are drunk. Which central nervous system structure is MOST LIKELY impaired?

Choices:
A. Midbrain.
B. Pons.
C. Medulla.
D. Cerebellum.

Teaching Points

Correct Answer: D

The cerebellum is the structure below the cerebral hemispheres that is highly responsible for coordination of movements. Damage to the cerebellum would result in ataxia, or uncoordinated movement, on the ipsilateral side of the body.

B96

The Practice of Speech-Language Pathology

An SLP is contacted by a family member. During their conversation, the SLP learns that the family member's child has been diagnosed with childhood apraxia of speech for which they have been receiving speech therapy services. The family member asks the SLP to provide supplemental services to the child to ensure the child's apraxia improves. Which statement BEST describes this scenario?

Choices:
A. The request is a violation of the utilitarian approach.
B. It is a violation of the rights approach.
C. It is a violation of the fairness approach.
D. The request is a violation of the virtue approach.

Teaching Points

Correct Answer: C

This scenario most optimally describes a violation of the fairness or justice approach to ethical considerations. In this scenario, should the SLP provide treatment to their family member "as a favor," this implies that they may be providing services in a manner that their other clients do not receive (e.g., without pay, at a greater frequency). Should this be the case, the SLP is not providing equal or proportionate care.

B97

Audiology and Hearing Impairment

An SLP working in a neonatal intensive care unit is part of the newborn hearing screening team. The SLP assists in the completion of gathering otoacoustic emissions (OAEs) from one of the newborns. During the assessment, the SLP observes that the infant has absent OAEs. Which statement BEST represents this finding?

Choices:
A. The infant demonstrates some degree of hearing loss and should be referred to audiology for further management.
B. The infant demonstrates complete hearing loss and should be referred to audiology for further management.
C. The infant demonstrates normal hearing function and does not require any further hearing intervention.
D. The infant demonstrates near-normal hearing function and should be referred to audiology for further management.

Teaching Points

Correct Answer: A

OAEs are low-intensity sounds generated by the cochlea that travel through the middle ear and are recorded in the external auditory meatus via microphone. Absence of OAEs is suggestive of some degree of hearing loss. SLPs are able to identify individuals who would benefit from further hearing assessment but are not qualified to complete hearing assessment past hearing screening. As the infant from this scenario qualifies as having some degree of hearing loss, they would benefit from an audiology consult for further evaluation and management.

B98

Acoustics

An SLP is using spectrographic analysis of vowels in their clinical practice. In a narrowband spectrogram, the SLP can see that harmonic spacing becomes narrower throughout a vowel. When listening to the vowel, what will the SLP MOST LIKELY hear?

Choices:
A. The vowel is a diphthong that shifts from a low vowel to a high vowel.
B. The vowel is a diphthong that shifts from a front vowel to a back vowel.
C. The vowel begins at a lower pitch and ends at a higher pitch.
D. The vowel begins at a higher pitch and ends at a lower pitch.

Teaching Points

Correct Answer: D

The spacing between harmonics in the human voice is equal to F0. If harmonic spacing shifts from wider to narrower, the harmonics are getting closer together and F0 is getting lower.

B99

Motor Speech Disorders

An SLP in an outpatient clinic works with a patient with a motor speech disorder, characterized by difficulties with speech prosody. The SLP plans to implement a contrastive stress exercise in treatment sessions, in order to improve the prosodic features of their speech. Which statement BEST describes this type of exercise?

Choices:
A. Having the patient produce a targeted feature in a written passage, followed by the SLP indicating the feature heard.
B. Having the patient produce a scripted response multiple times, during which only the stress pattern changes between utterances.
C. Identifying a prosodic feature that the patient is able to modify, which has the greatest impact on speech naturalness.
D. Training the patient to insert short pauses throughout their speech production, in order to maximize naturalness of speech.

Teaching Points

Correct Answer: B

A contrastive stress exercise is one in which the same phrase or sentence is repeated multiple different times while altering one or two words at a time in order to emphasize certain aspects of that phrase/sentence (e.g., in the sentence "Mary is coming to dinner," emphasizing "*Mary* is coming to dinner" compared to "Mary is coming to *dinner*"). Comparatively, production and confirmation of a particular prosodic feature is called a referential task. The final two examples in this scenario are independent modification of certain aspects of prosody, which may or may not improve the naturalness of a person's motor speech production.

B100

Motor Speech Disorders

An SLP works with a patient who is receiving treatment for spastic dysarthria. The patient's intelligibility is primarily impacted by a strained/strangled vocal quality, caused by hyperadduction of the vocal folds. Which treatment method is BEST for the SLP to implement?

Choices:
A. Effortful closure techniques.
B. Relaxation techniques.
C. Postural adjustments.
D. Lee Silverman Voice Treatment (LSVT).

Teaching Points

Correct Answer: B

The appropriate answer to this scenario can be found through means of elimination. Effortful closure techniques, postural adjustments, and LSVT are all treatment methods indicated in cases of vocal hypoadduction. Given that the patient is experiencing vocal hyperadduction, relaxation techniques would be the preferred treatment method of those available. However, it is important to observe that relaxation techniques, while used in clinical practice, do not have a great deal of research evidence behind their use.

B101

Anatomy and Physiology of Communication and Swallowing

An SLP in an inpatient rehabilitation hospital works with a patient who displays the following symptoms: poor ability to explain the meaning of metaphorical language, inability to produce a melody when asked to sing, hemiplegia, tendency to bump into items on their left side when using a wheelchair. Which is MOST LIKELY the cause of this patient's symptoms?

Choices:
A. A brain stem cerebrovascular accident (CVA).
B. A left-hemisphere CVA.
C. Dementia with Lewy bodies.
D. A right-hemisphere CVA.

Teaching Points

Correct Answer: D

The constellation of symptoms described in the patient profile is characteristic of someone with damage to the right hemisphere (i.e., difficulty with metaphorical language, poor ability to produce and comprehend melodies, and visual neglect of items in the left visual field). While hemiplegia may be the result of a right- or left-hemisphere CVA, the other symptoms are more likely only in a right-hemisphere CVA.

B102

Augmentative and Alternative Communication

A patient is admitted to a skilled nursing facility following a left middle cerebrovascular artery infarction. The patient has severe Broca's aphasia and verbal apraxia, with verbal expression characterized by content words, paraphasias, and overly stereotyped utterances. Cognitive skills are preserved, including memory and attention. The SLP believes the patient would benefit from AAC intervention. Which approach would be MOST BENEFICIAL for the patient?

Choices:
A. Supplement verbal expression with an eye gaze system.
B. Provide a speech-generating device.
C. Supplement verbal expression with writing.
D. Supplement verbal expression with a picture board.

Teaching Points

Correct Answer: D

As the patient demonstrates agrammatical speech and paraphasias, their verbal expression is significantly compromised. However, as they demonstrate intact cognitive skills, they may be taught to utilize a picture board to improve their communicative effectiveness by using picture symbols to supplement verbal expression. In contrast, patients with Broca's aphasia demonstrate writing that typically mirrors their verbal expression, making writing an inappropriate selection for use with this patient. For the same reason, selection of a speech-generating device would be inappropriate for this patient, as their written expression is compromised, and they would demonstrate difficulty formulating messages. Finally, as the patient is able to produce some means of verbal expression and is ambulatory, utilizing only eye gaze would not improve the communicative effectiveness for this patient.

B103

Stuttering and Other Fluency Disorders

A client arrives to a speech and language clinic for an evaluation. The client is employed as a teacher who recently transferred to a different school district due to reorganization. The new school has a history of conflict with parents and students, and the client reports feeling stressed by the additional hour of commute time. The client describes stuttering during teaching, and when students laugh, it gets worse. During the evaluation, the client responds to cues provided by the SLP and speech is fluent. Which statement is MOST ACCURATE for this client?

Choices:
A. The client is exhibiting psychogenic stuttering.
B. The client has developmental stuttering.
C. The SLP should recommend returning to the previous school position.
D. The SLP should refer to a psychiatrist for further evaluation.

Teaching Points

Correct Answer: A

The onset of disfluency associated with significant stress is most likely psychogenic. Because the onset is in adulthood, it rules out developmental stuttering. The focus of the SLP should be on helping the client recover her fluent speech. If her psychological difficulties were significant, ideally she might benefit from a referral and some coordination of treatment between the mental health professional and the SLP.

B104

Augmentative and Alternative Communication

An SLP receives orders to evaluate and treat a patient with a neurodegenerative communication disorder with very limited verbal output. The SLP learns that the patient is illiterate and struggles with any literacy-based material. Which approach to intervention is BEST for this patient?

Choices:
A. Intervention that targets cognitive rather than communicative skills.
B. Avoiding use of AAC due to illiteracy.
C. Use of alphabet supplementation and training in phoneme/grapheme association.
D. Use of an AAC device with symbolic representation of words and phrases.

Teaching Points

Correct Answer: D

Persons with complex communication needs do not need to be literate in order to be eligible for AAC use. If a patient is not literate, a speech-language pathologist may utilize symbolic representations that aid in the person's communicative effectiveness, similar to this scenario. As this patient was not interested in literacy-based approaches, direct instruction in phoneme-grapheme association would be contraindicated. Lastly, if a patient is referred for AAC, communication should be directly targeted, and cognitive skills may also be targeted during intervention sessions.

B105

Language Disorders in Young Children

A 3-year-old child is having difficulty communicating with others. At school, the child has a habit of interrupting and appears rude. The parent states the child has clear speech but has trouble getting to the point when talking, making it hard to understand the intent of the message. Which word BEST describes the language difficulty for the child?

Choices:
A. Morphology.
B. Semantics.
C. Gestural.
D. Pragmatics.

Teaching Points

Correct Answer: D

This child's behaviors indicate difficulty using the social rules of communication, rather than trouble with the grammar (syntax) or meaning (semantic) levels of language. There was no description of gesturing in this question.

B106

Cleft Palate and Craniofacial Conditions

An SLP works at a pediatric hospital. The SLP receives a referral to evaluate an infant who was born with a complete cleft of the secondary palate. The SLP is a recent graduate and has not worked with this condition before, necessitating review of the evidence-based information. Upon review of the literature, which structure will the SLP find is MOST LIKELY not affected?

Choices:
A. Hard palate.
B. Velum.
C. Alveolar ridge.
D. Uvula.

Teaching Points

Correct Answer: C

Secondary palate structures include the hard palate, velum, and uvula. If this child was experiencing a complete cleft of the secondary palate, there would be a full cleft extending from the uvula to the incisive foramen. As such, the alveolar ridge would remain intact with this type of cleft.

B107

Research, Evidence-Based Practice, and Tests and Measurements

An SLP in private practice is looking to purchase speech and language evaluations. The SLP is interested in tests that will correctly rule out children who do not have speech and language disorders. Which statistical measure is BEST for the SLP to identify in the evaluation manuals?

Choices:
A. Sample size.
B. Specificity.
C. Evidence.
D. Sensitivity.

Teaching Points

Correct Answer: B

Specificity refers to how well a test detects that a condition is not present when it is actually not present. If the clinician wanted to know information about how well evaluations rule out children who do not actually have speech and language disorders, they should refer to the test manuals' sections on test specificity. Contrary to this, *test sensitivity* refers to how well the test detects a condition that is actually present. Sample size and test evidence would not help this clinician find information about how well the test detects disorders or lack of disorders.

B108

Motor Speech Disorders

A patient presents to an acute care hospital with complaints of a change in their speech production, with initial concern for a cerebrovascular accident. After undergoing head imaging and revealing no acute stroke, it is revealed that the patient has a history of multiple sclerosis (MS). Which of the following is MOST LIKELY the underlying causes for the changes in this patient's speech production?

Choices:
A. The patient's condition leads to decreased dopamine production, impacting the range of motion for the articulators.
B. The patient's condition leads to demyelination of neurons, impacting degree of control over the articulators.
C. The patient's condition leads to death of muscle fiber cells, impacting the ability to move the articulators.
D. The patient's condition leads to excessive muscle fatigue, impacting the duration the articulators may be used.

Teaching Points

Correct Answer: B

MS is a neurological condition caused by the demyelination of neuronal sheaths, which impacts a neuron's ability to adequately transmit neural signals. As such, a person with MS may present with dysarthria characterized by ataxia, spasticity, and so on, which is caused by this demyelination.

B109

The Practice of Speech-Language Pathology

A new SLP is seeking a clinical fellowship position in a medical setting. After months of searching, the SLP receives an invitation for an interview at a skilled nursing facility. During the interview process, the SLP discovers that the staff are encouraged to implement treatment options despite little to no evidence to support them. Which option BEST exemplifies use of the virtue approach for ethical standards in this scenario?

Choices:
A. Accepting the job position in order to secure a medically based position.
B. Declining the job since the management encourages less than ethical practice.
C. Accepting the job in order to change the treatment approaches used at the SNF.
D. Declining the job and waiting for a job offer from a more ethical employer.

Teaching Points

Correct Answer: B

The virtue approach engages ethical considerations by having one ask themselves which option causes them to act in a way that best exemplifies the type of person they want to be. As it can be assumed from this scenario, the SLP would like to practice in a setting that encourages ethical decision-making, so the SLP should decline to take a position with a company that encourages less than that. Although there is an option that suggests attempting to change management's mind-set about treatment approaches, there is no guarantee that this will occur, and the SLP may find themselves in further ethical dilemmas.

B110

Language Acquisition: Preverbal and Early Language

During a speech-language evaluation, a 3-year-old child makes the following utterances: "Me fell down," "Mommy's book!" and "Is she here?" In what stage of Brown's morphological development is the child?

Choices:
A. Stage I.
B. Stage II.
C. Stage III.
D. Stage IV.

Teaching Points

Correct Answer: C

Brown's Stage III of morphological development typically occurs between 36 and 42 months of age and is characterized by a child's ability to indicate possessives, knowledge and use of irregular past tense verbs, and ability to use the full form of the verb *to be* when it is the only verb in the sentence.

B111

Dysphagia: Swallowing and Swallowing Disorder

An SLP in an acute rehabilitation hospital is asked to perform a swallowing evaluation on a newly admitted patient with difficulty eating. After reviewing the patient's medical record, the SLP learns that the patient was diagnosed with Parkinson's disease a few years prior. The SLP foresees that there will be several problems on this patient's modified barium swallow (MBS). Which deficit should the SLP NOT expect to see on the MBS?

Choices:
A. Lingual rocking.
B. Silent aspiration.
C. Oral incontinence.
D. Pharyngeal pooling.

Teaching Points

Correct Answer: C

Oral incontinence, or anterior leakage, occurs when the bolus is not properly contained in the oral cavity and is released through the lips. This is not one of the symptoms of dysphagia associated with Parkinson's disease, although it is associated with other disorders. Dysphagia secondary to Parkinson's disease is defined by lingual rocking, pharyngeal dysmotility, pooling in the pharynx, silent aspiration, and sensory dysfunction of the oropharynx.

B112

Motor Speech Disorders

A patient presents to an outpatient clinic for a motor speech evaluation after a 3-month history of dysarthria of unknown etiology. During the evaluation, the SLP documents that the patient presents with excess and equal stress, telescoping speech production with irregular articulatory breakdown, and excessive loudness variations. Due to the unknown etiology for the dysarthria, the SLP refers the patient to neurology. What is the MOST LIKELY diagnosis for this patient?

Choices:
A. Flaccid dysarthria.
B. Ataxic dysarthria.
C. Spastic dysarthria.
D. Hyperkinetic dysarthria.

Teaching Points

Correct Answer: B

Although the lesion location has not been established in this patient to definitively rule in a particular dysarthria subtype, there are many hallmark characteristics present that would indicate an ataxic dysarthria. Telescoping speech production with irregular articulatory breakdowns are key characteristics seen only in ataxic dysarthria. Additionally, equal and excess stress with excessive loudness variations are also seen in ataxic dysarthria.

B113

Cleft Palate and Craniofacial Conditions

A speech-language pathology student is asked by a clinical supervisor to review speech musculature in preparation for the evaluation of a patient with dysarthria. The student reads about muscles that contract and do not contract during the production of various sounds. The student learns that contraction of the tensor veli palatini and levator veli palatini will NOT occur during the production of which sounds?

Choices:
A. /f/.
B. /s/.
C. /m/.
D. /t/.

Teaching Points

Correct Answer: C

The tensor veli palatini and levator veli palatini muscles contract to raise the soft palate during speech, in order to block off the nasal cavity. /m/ is a nasal phoneme, which means that the nasal cavity remains open during phonation. For this reason, the tensor veli palatini and levator veli palatini do not contract during production of /m/.

B114

Spoken Language Disorders in School-Age Populations

A 12-year-old child is referred by a pediatrician for assessment with an SLP. The physician's referral indicates that the child shows age-delayed communication. Which behavior MOST LIKELY demonstrates a delay in communication?

Choices:
A. Single words or pointing.
B. Combinations of two words.
C. Grammatically complete sentences with minor phonological errors.
D. Vegetative sounds such as coughing, burping, and some vocalizations.

Teaching Points

Correct Answer: A

Children are usually using single words or doing some pointing by about 12 months of age. Grammar emerges later in development. Vegetative sounds are nonlinguistic, and vocalizing comes much earlier in development.

B115

Stuttering and Other Fluency Disorders

A school-aged child has previously been diagnosed with a fluency disorder. The child has recently begun working with an SLP in order to improve their speech fluency. During a treatment session, the SLP observes that the child stomps their feet and snaps their fingers during periods of disfluency. Which of the following statements BEST describes this child's behaviors?

Choices:

A. The child is demonstrating primary stuttering behaviors.
B. The child is demonstrating escape behaviors.
C. The child is demonstrating secondary stuttering behaviors.
D. The child is demonstrating avoidance behaviors.

Teaching Points

Correct Answer: C

Developmentally, when individuals who stutter begin to exhibit secondary behaviors, it serves as an important clinical signal. This indicates that the child has moved in the direction of attempting to control the core behaviors of prolongation and repetition, typically with motoric adjustments and blocks in voicing and airflow. The implications of the appearance of these behaviors may or not indicate any emotional reactions like fear or embarrassment.

B116

Motor Speech Disorders

An SLP in an outpatient clinic is working with a patient with a recently diagnosed bulbar onset of amyotrophic lateral sclerosis. The SLP is considering the best treatment methods to address current symptoms. Which is the BEST treatment approach to implement with this patient?

Choices:

A. Educating the patient in speech intelligibility strategies in order to enhance the patient's ability to be understood.
B. Educating the patient in appropriate breath groups in order to enhance the naturalness of their speech.
C. Training the patient in an augmentative communication system in order to enhance their ability to communicate.
D. Training the patient in Lee Silverman Voice Treatment in order to enhance their vocal production and loudness.

Teaching Points

Correct Answer: C

Given that amyotrophic lateral sclerosis is a neurodegenerative disorder, early implementation of AAC is the most appropriate treatment method to use with this patient. This AAC system should allow the patient to easily communicate throughout the progression of their disease, in order to allow for the most optimal communication. All other treatment methods may be appropriate during some phases of disease progression but will ultimately become ineffective throughout disease progression.

B117

Anatomy and Physiology of Communication and Swallowing

A patient is admitted to an acute care hospital after presenting with stroke symptoms. Imaging reveals a cerebrovascular accident (CVA) in the middle cerebral artery. Which brain region is MOST LIKELY impacted by this CVA?

Choices:
A. The posterior surface of the cerebellum.
B. The lateral surface of the temporal lobe.
C. The inferior surface of the temporal lobe.
D. The lateral surface of the occipital lobe.

Teaching Points

Correct Answer: B

The middle cerebral artery supplies blood to the lateral frontal lobes, lateral temporal lobes, portions of the lateral parietal lobes, and regions deep to the lobes (e.g., the basal ganglia). The posterior surfaces of the cerebellum are supplied by the posterior inferior cerebellar arteries. Finally, the inferior surface of the temporal lobe and all surfaces of the occipital lobe are supplied by the posterior cerebral artery.

B118

Research, Evidence-Based Practice, and Tests and Measurements

A researcher is conducting a study comparing the performance of dyslexic versus nondyslexic participants during oral reading of written words presented rapidly versus slowly. Which statement BEST describes this type of research?

Choices:
A. Experimental research.
B. Descriptive research.
C. Mixed experimental-descriptive research.
D. Qualitative research.

Teaching Points

Correct Answer: C
For this scenario, it is best to separate out the experimental and descriptive portions of the study. The experimental portion comes from the manipulation of the independent variable (i.e., slow versus rapid presentations of written words). The descriptive portion occurs because of the comparison between two groups based on subject attributes (e.g., dyslexic versus nondyslexic readers). Because this study meets both of these conditions, it can be accurately called mixed experimental-descriptive research.

B119

Autism Spectrum Disorders

A research team is investigating genetic theories to establish the cause of autism. The researchers have focused on children with autism spectrum disorder who have a faulty chromosome 11. Which hypothesis is BEST generated by these researchers?

Choices:
A. The children show lack of communication between neurons, causing their autism spectrum disorder.
B. The children show a lack of development of brain circuitry, causing their autism spectrum disorder.
C. The children show intellectual impairments, causing their autism spectrum disorder.
D. The children show faulty cell-to-cell signaling, causing their autism spectrum disorder.

Teaching Points

Correct Answer: A

Chromosome 11 consists of a group of genes involved in communication between neurons during brain development. If this research assumed chromosome 11 was implicated in autism spectrum disorder, they would most likely assume a lack of neuronal communication as the cause of the disorder. In contrast to this, chromosome 5 is responsible for development of brain circuitry, chromosome 15 is associated with intellectual impairment, and chromosome 16 is responsible for cell-to-cell signaling and interaction.

B120

Acoustics

An SLP is analyzing a spectrogram of an utterance made up of three phonemes. The first phoneme consists of a period of closure followed by a burst and a longer voice onset time. The second phoneme is a vowel with high F1 and high F2. The third phoneme demonstrates a low-frequency nasal formant. Which word was MOST LIKELY captured on the spectrogram?

Choices:
A. Pot.
B. Pete.
C. Pan.
D. Pam.

Teaching Points

Correct Answer: D

Because the first phoneme demonstrates a short period of closure (e.g., silent period) followed by a burst, it can be assumed that this phoneme is a stop consonant. As it has a longer duration voice onset time, it can be assumed that it is a voiceless stop consonant, such as /p/. For the second phoneme, because there is a high F1 and high F2, it can be assumed that the vowel is a low front vowel, such as /æ/. Finally, as the final phoneme has a low-frequency nasal formant, it can be assumed that the final phoneme is a nasal consonant. The only option from this scenario that matches these three conditions is /pæm/ or "Pam."

B121

Dysphagia: Swallowing and Swallowing Disorder

While performing a modified barium swallow study, the SLP discovers that the patient is experiencing premature spillage into the pharyngeal cavity, where the bolus sits for many seconds before being swallowed. Which phase of the swallow is this patient MOST LIKELY having difficulty?

Choices:
A. Hyolaryngeal elevation.
B. Initiation of the swallow.
C. Anterior-posterior movement.
D. Bolus formation.

Teaching Points

Correct Answer: B

The swallow is typically initiated when the bolus head reaches the faucial pillars (in younger adults) or the back of the tongue (in older adults). If the bolus is spilling into the patient's pharyngeal cavity prior to hyolaryngeal elevation and excursion, the patient is experiencing difficulty with initiating their swallowing.

B122

Voice Disorders in Children and Adults

An SLP working in an outpatient voice clinic is completing a comprehensive voice evaluation of a newly admitted patient with vocal fold leukoplakia. During the assessment, the SLP documents that the patient demonstrates a reduced phonational pitch range, compared to normal parameters. Which type of assessment MOST LIKELY led to this observation?

Choices:
A. Acoustic.
B. Stroboscopic.
C. Aerodynamic.
D. Perceptual.

Teaching Points

Correct Answer: A

Acoustic assessment measures include phonational range (the pitch range that a patient can achieve, from high to low), perturbation measures (e.g., jitter and shimmer), and programs such as the multidimensional voice profile, which allows for measurement of up to 19 different acoustic parameters.

B123

Autism Spectrum Disorders

A 7-year-old with a diagnosis of autism spectrum disorder level 3 is nonspeaking. The child will typically cry or scream to communicate needs. The child will retrieve a desired item independently if it is within reach. The child will also bring a parent over to items that are out of reach independently and point to them. Which is the BEST goal to address during intervention sessions?

Choices:
A. Cooperative play skills with peers.
B. Establishing a way to get wants and needs met.
C. Conversational discourse.
D. Joint attention.

Teaching Points

Correct Answer: B

Functional communication goals are paramount, particularly in level 3 autism. Establishing a main method of communication in order to decrease frustration is a high priority when working with students who do not have consistent methods to request their wants and needs. While play skills and conversational discourse are also important skills for students to learn, the primary focus should be functional communication.

B124

Dysphagia: Swallowing and Swallowing Disorder

A patient at an acute rehabilitation hospital is working with the SLP on therapy techniques to improve symptoms of dysphagia with decreased laryngeal elevation. Which treatment technique is BEST for this patient?

Choices:
A. Shaker head lifts and the Mendelsohn maneuver.
B. Supraglottic swallow and the super supraglottic swallow.
C. Effortful swallow and the Masako maneuver.
D. VitalStim and thickened liquids.

Teaching Points

Correct Answer: A

The Shaker head lift exercises involve lying down on the floor and lifting only the head until the patient is able to see their toes. This maneuver has been proven to increase upper esophageal sphincter opening through strengthening of the suprahyoid muscles. The Mendelsohn maneuver involves having the patient engage their suprahyoid muscles to hold the larynx at the height of the swallow, thus strengthening that muscle group. Both exercises would be good for a patient who has decreased laryngeal elevation, because increased strength in the suprahyoids would help elevate the larynx.

B125

Autism Spectrum Disorders

An SLP is working with a child who has autism spectrum disorder. The SLP determines that the child would benefit from implementation of picture exchange communication systems to enhance their communicative effectiveness. Which goal is BEST for this child?

Choices:
A. The child will use pictures during play scenarios.
B. The child will perform desired acts in response to pictures.
C. The child will use images to obtain desired items.
D. This child is given pictures in response to desired motor acts.

Teaching Points

Correct Answer: C

The goal of the Picture Exchange Communication System is to establish a functional, reciprocal picture communication system in a social context. In this method of intervention, the child exchanges a picture of a desired item with a communication partner in order to establish communication and receive the desired object. This method of intervention is a form of AAC that focuses on teaching, motivation, and reinforcement.

B126

Acoustics

A speech scientist is analyzing the concept of changes in sound and the impact on the wavelengths of sound. If the frequency of a periodic sound is increased by 100 Hz, the speech scientist would MOST LIKELY observe what effect on the wavelength of the sound?

Choices:
A. There would be no change in wavelength.
B. There would be an increase in wavelength.
C. There would be a decrease in wavelength.
D. There would be a dampening of the sound.

Teaching Points

Correct Answer: C

Wavelength is the distance traveled by a sound during a single period. This measure has an inverse relationship with frequency. This means that higher-frequency sounds would have a shorter wavelength whereas lower-frequency sounds would have a longer wavelength. Therefore, if the frequency of a sound was increased, its wavelength would decrease accordingly.

B127

Speech Sound Disorders in Children

A parent arrives at a local speech and language clinic with a young child, with complaints of "difficulty speaking." A speech-language pathologist provides a comprehensive speech evaluation and determines that the child is exhibiting the phonological processes of affrication, epenthesis, and reduplication. The SLP decides to target only the child's reduplication, as it is determined that the child has not reached an age where affrication and epenthesis should be suppressed. Which theory of phonological development BEST matches this approach to treatment?

Choices:
A. Prosodic theory.
B. Generative phonology.
C. Behavioral theory.
D. Natural phonology.

Teaching Points

Correct Answer: D

The natural phonology theory emphasizes that children are born with a set of natural phonological processes that they need to suppress as they age. These phonological processes are suppressed as the child develops. Because this SLP believes that the child has not developed enough to suppress specific phonological processes, they are utilized principles from the natural phonology theory. In contrast to this, the generative phonology theory is an expansion of the distinctive feature theory and includes concepts such as underlying representations, surface forms, and phonological rules, but does not include suppression of phonological processes. The prosodic theory emphasizes the perception of whole words as early word productions but, again, does not emphasize suppression of phonological patterns. Finally, behavioral theory posits that phonological development is contingent upon reinforcement, not suppression of phonological processes.

B128

Augmentative and Alternative Communication

A speech-language pathologist is working with a patient with severe global aphasia, for whom they are utilizing an AAC device to promote communicative effectiveness. The SLP believes that this patient would benefit from an organization strategy that utilizes individual pictures to capture both environmental and interactional aspects of the communicative context. Which type of organizational strategy is BEST for the SLP to implement with this patient?

Choices:
A. Visual scene display (VSD).
B. Alphabet display.
C. Pragmatic organization dynamic display.
D. Grid display.

Teaching Points

Correct Answer: A

A VSD is an image or picture that captures both environmental and action/interaction aspects of the communicative contexts. As the patient from this scenario would best benefit from a picture-based approach to AAC, the SLP would most likely implement a VSD. In contrast to this, alphabet display is a literacy-based approach in which letters are used for easy access. As this patient has global aphasia, they would demonstrate significant difficulty with reading comprehension and this approach would be ineffective. Pragmatic organization dynamic display is a form of AAC in which pragmatic functions are purposefully added to every page in the AAC user's device. Finally, grid displays are those in which symbols, words, and messages are arranged in a grid pattern.

B129

Cleft Palate and Craniofacial Conditions

An SLP in an outpatient clinic receives a referral by an otolaryngologist for a child. In the referral notes, the physician states that the child demonstrates problems that are not able to be corrected medically or surgically and that speech therapy is indicated. Which deficit is the child MOST LIKELY demonstrating?

Choices:
A. Cul-de-sac resonance.
B. Nasal emission.
C. Pharyngeal fricative.
D. Hypernasality.

Teaching Points

Correct Answer: C

A production of a pharyngeal fricative is a type of compensatory articulation error often seen in individuals with velopharyngeal insufficiency. This type of articulatory error is an appropriate target for intervention through speech therapy. In contrast to this, speech therapy alone cannot improve hypernasality or nasal emission, and these problems require surgical intervention. Cul-de-sac resonance occurs due to a blockage in the pharyngeal or nasal cavity, which traps sound energy. No speech therapy technique can change the quality of resonance for this type of deficit, and surgery is required to remove the blockage (i.e., enlarged tonsils).

B130

Acoustics

A speech scientist is performing analyses on different spectrograms. In examining a spectrogram of the phrase "say sheep" produced by a male speaker, the speech scientist notices that the lower limit of high-amplitude energy noise for both /s/ and /ʃ/ is near 2,500 Hz. Which is MOST LIKELY the cause of this phenomenon?

Choices:
A. /s/ is being produced too far back in the mouth.
B. /s/ is being produced too far forward in the mouth.
C. /ʃ/ is being produced too far back in the mouth.
D. /ʃ/ is being produced too far forward in the mouth.

Teaching Points

Correct Answer: A

The cutoff of high-amplitude energy for sibilant fricatives is related to the size of the oral cavity in front of the obstruction. For /s/, the obstruction should be farther forward than for /ʃ/, resulting in a smaller air pocket and a higher cutoff frequency. /ʃ/ is expected to have a cutoff frequency around 2,500 Hz. If /s/ has a similar cutoff frequency, then /s/ is being produced too far back in the mouth.

B131

Autism Spectrum Disorders

An SLP working in an elementary school has a caseload predominantly of children with autism spectrum disorder. How should the SLP structure intervention sessions to maximize gains made by these children?

Choices:
A. Provide parent training once behaviors have been established.
B. Provide intervention sessions that are lengthy in duration.
C. Provide intervention that utilizes a group format.
D. Provide intervention that promotes active engagement.

Teaching Points

Correct Answer: D

According to the National Research Council's review of intervention evidence for autism spectrum disorder, intervention should be provided intensively and in a way that promotes active engagement through collaboration with family and teachers. Additionally, individualized intervention (as opposed to group treatment), which is brief and focused in nature (as opposed to lengthy treatment), shows greater efficacy. Finally, family members should be trained to implement teaching strategies as a means of reinforcing learning while it is occurring (as opposed to after learning has been established).

B132

Voice Disorders in Children and Adults

After undergoing open-heart surgery, a patient emerges from anesthesia to symptoms of significantly hypophonic, breathy voice. After a few days in recovery, the patient's vocal quality has not improved, and a referral for otolaryngology and speech-language pathology is made. Which condition will MOST LIKELY be discovered upon endoscopy?

Choices:
A. Vocal fold polyps.
B. Presbylaryngis.
C. Vocal fold paralysis.
D. Arytenoid granuloma.

Teaching Points

Correct Answer: C

The left recurrent laryngeal nerve loops under the aortic arch, prior to innervating the muscles of the larynx. Patients who undergo open-heart surgery may experience voice problems resulting from damage to the left recurrent laryngeal nerve. If the recurrent laryngeal nerve is significantly damaged, it could result in complete vocal fold paralysis, as this patient is experiencing. Vocal fold polyps occur due to phonotrauma, such as excessive screaming or cheering, and would not arise due to nerve damage. Similarly, arytenoid granulomas arise from direct vocal fold trauma from intubation or reflux and are not neurological in origin. Finally, presbylaryngis is the term for voice disorders in the elderly and is caused by normal aging.

Examination C

C1

Motor Speech Disorders

A speech-language pathologist (SLP) receives a referral for a pediatric client with a motor speech disorder. The SLP recalls that the organizational framework of the treatment session can both positively and negatively influence success of therapy, especially for pediatric clients. Which statement BEST describes a unique consideration when organizing treatment for children?

Choices:
A. To avoid reinforcements that take too much time to administer.
B. The need for greater amounts of cumulative practice.
C. Clinician preparation.
D. The need for shorter treatment sessions.

Teaching Points

Correct Answer: B

When compared to adults, children exhibit shorter attention spans and reduced short-term memory. Because of these relative reductions when compared to adults, children will require greater amounts of cumulative practice in order to make the same amount of gains. Shorter treatment sessions, clinician preparation, and an appropriate length of time prior to reinforcement are aspects of treatment that apply to both children and adults.

C2

Research, Evidence-Based Practice, and Tests and Measurements

A speech scientist is analyzing data collected from a recently completed study. In order to properly analyze the data, the speech scientist utilizes nonparametric statistical procedures. Which scenario BEST describes the scientist's data?

Choices:
A. The distribution of the data is not normal.
B. The distribution of the data is normal.
C. A small median for the data is present.
D. A small mode for the data is present.

Teaching Points

Correct Answer: A

Nonparametric statistical procedures are those that are not based on a normal curve model or are not normally distributed. Because the data collected from this speech scientist's study was analyzed using nonparametric statistical procedures, it is safe to say that there is not a normal distribution of the data. In contrast, if there was a normal distribution, the speech scientist would be able to implement the more powerful parametric statistical procedures of data analysis.

C3

Language Disorders in Young Children

A 3-year-old child is suspected of having a language disorder and is brought to a speech and language clinic. Upon initial interview, the child's parents reveal that the child first learned to speak English, and they have now begun to teach the child Spanish. Following the evaluation, the speech-language pathologist determines that the child demonstrates age-appropriate linguistic skill with English but presents with significant difficulty with Spanish. Which statement BEST describes this child?

Choices:
A. The child does not present with a language disorder.
B. There is a language disorder for Spanish only.
C. There is a language disorder for both languages.
D. The child presents with a language delay for Spanish only.

Teaching Points

Correct Answer: A

For children who are bilingual, determination of the first language (L_1) is critical because a language disorder can only be diagnosed if the child presents with difficulties in only their L_1. If the child presents with difficulties in L_2, this may be a sign of difficulty learning a new language but is not indicative of a language disorder.

C4

Stuttering and Other Fluency Disorders

An SLP is evaluating a preschool child who stutters. The SLP determines it is beneficial to observe the child interacting with the parent. What is the primary benefit of this observation?

Choices:
A. The most valid sample of communication and speech may be observed in the child's typical interaction with the parent.
B. Comfort with the parent is likely to reduce disfluencies and make the child feel more comfortable.
C. There are a number of legal concerns that should be considered when separating the child from the parent.
D. The use of an informal speech sample reduces the need for any other standardized testing.

Teaching Points

Correct Answer: A

One of the biggest challenges in all speech and language assessment is obtaining a representative sample of an individual's "typical" communication in their own world. This is particularly challenging with very young children. By having the parent participate in a nondirected and noninterrupted conversation with the child, a more realistic and typical sample can usually be obtained.

C5

Augmentative and Alternative Communication

An SLP in private practice receives a referral to evaluate a new patient. After reading the patient's intake file, the SLP learns that the patient has been utilizing an augmentative and alternative communication (AAC) device for communicative purposes for the last few years. The description of the patient's AAC device reads: "a functional computer that utilizes communicative software. The patient is also able to utilize the Internet on their device and has few gaming apps for personal enjoyment." Which statement BEST describes the patient's device?

Choices:
A. A mid-tech, nondedicated AAC device.
B. A no-tech, dedicated AAC device.
C. A high-tech, nondedicated AAC device.
D. A low-tech, dedicated AAC device.

Teaching Points

Correct Answer: C

High-tech AAC refers to more sophisticated electronic devices that support speech and written output. As the patient from this scenario is utilizing a functional computer for communicative purposes, they are most likely utilizing high-tech AAC. Additionally, *nondedicated AAC* refers to devices that support a range of functions in addition to speech output. As this patient utilizes their AAC device for the Internet and for gaming apps, they are utilizing a nondedicated device.

C6

Anatomy and Physiology of Communication and Swallowing

A patient is admitted to an acute care hospital with symptoms of a cerebrovascular accident (CVA). An MRI is completed, which shows a large infarct in the territory of the medial surface of the left cerebral hemisphere. Which artery was MOST likely involved in this patient's CVA?

Choices:
A. Anterior cerebral artery.
B. Middle cerebral artery.
C. Posterior cerebral artery.
D. Anterior spinal artery.

Teaching Points

Correct Answer: A

The telencephalon includes the cerebral hemispheres, which receive blood from the anterior, middle, and posterior cerebral arteries. The anterior cerebral artery branches off from the internal carotid artery and feeds the cerebral hemispheres, starting in the area of the optic chiasm, which can be found in the medial portions of the hemispheres. In contrast to this, the middle cerebral artery supplies blood to a majority of the lateral cerebral hemispheres. The posterior cerebral artery supplies blood to the posterior cerebral hemispheres, including the occipital lobes. Finally, the anterior spinal artery supplies blood to the anterior spinal cord and posterior cerebellum.

C7

Acquired Language Disorders

A patient is admitted to an acute care hospital with symptoms of a cerebrovascular accident. An MRI is completed, which reveals a hemorrhage localized to the left frontal lobe. Which deficit would MOST LIKELY be observed upon evaluation of the patient?

Choices:
A. Broca's aphasia.
B. Tardive dyskinesia.
C. Homonymous hemianopia.
D. Ataxic dysarthria.

Teaching Points

Correct Answer: A

The frontal lobe is the region of the brain that houses Broca's area, which is involved in speech and language production. Broca's aphasia can occur when there is damage to Broca's area, which is characterized by non-fluent verbal expression, relatively preserved auditory comprehension, and impaired repetition.

C8

Voice Disorders in Children and Adults

A patient is admitted to an acute care hospital to have open heart surgery. After the surgery, the patient verbalizes complaints about a change in vocal quality, and an SLP is consulted. The SLP who performs the intake evaluation documents that the patient presents with an excessively high-pitched voice. Which issue MOST LIKELY caused the change in vocal quality?

Choices:
A. Development of vocal fold nodules from screaming at the nurse.
B. A massive hemispheric stroke during the surgery.
C. Damage of the left recurrent laryngeal nerve during the surgery.
D. Persistence of anesthesia effects, resulting in a drug-induced change in vocal quality.

Teaching Points

Correct Answer: C

The recurrent laryngeal nerve innervates the thyroarytenoid muscle, which mediates normal tension in the vocal folds and controls lowering of pitch. This nerve also travels around the aortic arch on its way to innervate the intrinsic laryngeal musculature. If the recurrent laryngeal nerve is damaged (e.g., through open heart surgery complications), it may cause weakness in the thyroarytenoid muscle and reduce the patient's ability to lower pitch. However, the superior laryngeal nerve, which assists in pitch elevation, follows a different course than the recurrent laryngeal nerve and would not be damaged in open heart surgery. As this nerve would remain intact, the patient may experience higher-than-average pitch during oral communication. Although vocal fold nodules may arise from screaming at nurses, it would take prolonged periods of this phonotrauma to cause nodules to form, which would occur long after surgery. A hallmark of upper motor neuron voice disorders, as would be seen in a hemispheric stroke, is a strained-strangled vocal quality, not a heightened pitch. Lastly, prolonged effects of medications may have a drying effect on the vocal folds and would cause a hoarse vocal quality but would not increase pitch.

C9

Spoken Language Disorders in School-Age Populations

A child demonstrates deficits in perspective-taking during conversation. The child is struggling to infer others' feelings and thoughts, which has negatively impacted the ability to converse with others. In which form of perspective-taking is the child demonstrating deficits?

Choices:
A. Linguistic perspective-taking.
B. Perceptual perspective-taking.
C. Cognitive perspective-taking.
D. Phonological perspective-taking.

Teaching Points

Correct Answer: C

Cognitive perspective-taking refers to a child's ability to make inferences about other people's thoughts, feelings, beliefs, and intentions, and involves making judgments about the internal psychological states of another person. In contrast to this, perceptual perspective-taking refers to a child's ability to determine what and how another person sees an object. Finally, linguistic perspective-taking refers to a child's ability to modify the form, content, and use of language in relation to their listener's needs.

C10

Language Acquisition: Preverbal and Early Language

An infant is raised in a home with English-speaking parents, one of whom also speaks German. The parents have decided to expose their child to both languages while the child grows up. Which type of bilingualism BEST describes this scenario?

Choices:
A. Successive bilingualism.
B. Simultaneous biculturalism.
C. Simultaneous bilingualism.
D. Generative biculturalism.

Teaching Points

Correct Answer: C

Simultaneous bilingualism occurs when two or more languages are learned at the same time. Because this child is being exposed to both English and German at the same time, they are experiencing simultaneous bilingualism. This typically begins shortly after birth and continues to be a feature of the caregiving environment. In contrast to this, successive bilingualism occurs when a second language (or more) is learned after the acquisition of a first language. If the child from this scenario learned English first and then his parents taught him German, this would constitute successive bilingualism. Finally, *simultaneous biculturalism* technically refers to being raised in two cultures at the same time. While language is intertwined with a culture, the child's language learning does not have to include learning about the associated culture.

C11

Spoken Language Disorders in School-Age Populations

An SLP works in a public school system. Every year, the SLP completes annual speech and language screenings of all preschool-aged children and provides educational materials to parents in order to prevent speech and language disorders. Which federal law BEST supports the opportunity to complete these tasks?

Choices:
A. Individuals with Disabilities Education Act.
B. Free and appropriate public education.
C. Tier 1 instruction.
D. No Child Left Behind Act.

Teaching Points

Correct Answer: A
IDEA, the Individuals with Disabilities Education Act, allows for SLPs to work in the general classroom offering different levels of support. While there is free and appropriate public education, it is IDEA that specifies the response to intervention initiative. Tier 1 instruction is not a federal law but is an evidence-based high-quality core curriculum instruction for the general population. The No Child Left Behind Act is a law requiring schools to monitor and assess progress within students to hold schools accountable for the materials they are teaching.

C12

Autism Spectrum Disorders

A 24-month-old child is diagnosed with autism spectrum disorder (ASD). The parent has spoken to many doctors about neurochemical studies in order to help the child. Through discussion with the doctor, they have decided to change the child's diet to determine if it positively impacts behaviors. Which dietary modification is MOST LIKELY to show positive benefits?

Choices:
A. No shellfish diet.
B. Gluten-free diet.
C. Vegan diet.
D. Protein-heavy diet.

Teaching Points

Correct Answer: B
Research and observation have supported some autoimmune disorders within ASD, including a report of increased food sensitivities, particularly to gluten, casein, food dyes, and preservatives.

C13

Voice Disorders in Children and Adults

A child is referred to an SLP by an otolaryngologist with a presenting problem of "distorted speech." Following a comprehensive evaluation, the SLP determines that the child is experiencing significant nasal emission during speech. Based on this information, which problem can be eliminated as a cause for this issue?

Choices:
A. Short utterance length.
B. Compensatory errors.
C. Hypernasality.
D. Weak consonants.

Teaching Points

Correct Answer: C

Nasal emissions occur when there is air lost through the nasal cavity during speech production. As this air is required to maintain speech, the quicker loss of air that accompanies nasal emissions causes short utterance length. Additionally, because this air is being released, there is a lack of pressure buildup in the oral cavity, leading to weak consonants, which in turn leads to compensatory productions. Nasal emissions on their own do not cause a change in a client's resonatory capabilities; therefore, the client would not be perceived as hypernasal.

C14

Language Disorders in Young Children

An SLP works in an early childhood education setting. The SLP initiates treatment with a child who has a significant language disorder. The SLP utilizes induction teaching to facilitate the child's learning of language. Which statement BEST describes this approach to intervention?

Choices:
A. Providing an enriched language-learning environment with no specific targets.
B. Targeting of specific forms and functions through repetition and modeling.
C. Increasing the rate at which a targeted form or function is learned.
D. Using a more explicit and systematic set of teaching steps.

Teaching Points

Correct Answer: D

Induction teaching refers to a more explicit and systematic set of teaching steps, beyond modeling. When this form of instruction is utilized, it is not assumed the targeted form would have been learned without intervention or learned to the same degree. Use of induction teaching also leads to concomitant achievements in academic and social contexts. In contrast to this, *facilitation* refers to increasing the rate at which a targeted form or function is learned, *focused stimulation* refers to the targeting of specific forms and functions by the SLP through repetition or modeling, and *general stimulation* refers to a provision of an enriched language-learning environment with no specific target for learning.

C15

Language Disorders in Young Children

An SLP in a preschool setting provides intervention for a child with deficits in morphological developments. The SLP wants to establish that the targeted morphemes in the intervention sessions are being used consistently. Which level of use is BEST for establishing acquisition of morphological structures?

Choices:
A. 85% of use in obligatory contexts.
B. 90% of use in obligatory contexts.
C. 95% of use in obligatory contexts.
D. 100% of use in obligatory contexts.

Teaching Points

Correct Answer: B

The consistency of morpheme use in obligatory contexts is the most appropriate measure for establishing the acquisition of a morpheme. This consistency can be calculated as the number of times the child correctly produced a specific morpheme (in obligatory context) divided by the total number of opportunities for that specific morpheme to have been produced in a spoken or written passage. Traditionally, 90% of use in obligatory contexts has been used as the standard for establishing morpheme acquisition.

C16

Research, Evidence-Based Practice, and Tests and Measurements

An SLP is developing a new assessment for acquired apraxia of speech. The SLP wishes to demonstrate the reliability of the assessment measure, as to better quantify the deficits in apraxia. Which statistical measures are BEST to determine the reliability of the assessment measure?

Choices:
A. Internal consistency, stability, and equivalence of the measurement.
B. Content validity, criterion validity, and construct validity of the measurement.
C. Interobserver agreement, standard deviation of scores, and effect size of the measurement.
D. Sensitivity, specificity, and average participant performance of the measurement.

Teaching Points

Correct Answer: A

In order for an assessment measurement to have good reliability, it needs to demonstrate stability (i.e., the same results upon multiple administrations), equivalence (i.e., comparison of participant results to results from an alternative form of the assessment), and internal consistency (i.e., results from one half of the assessment to the other half from the same assessment). If all three of these conditions are met, the assessment has good reliability.

C17

Stuttering and Other Fluency Disorders

A patient is receiving outpatient speech-language services for disfluencies. The patient is practicing easy onset of phonation in order to decrease symptoms. Which statement BEST demonstrates this skill?

Choices:
A. Softly saying the first sound of the word, then gradually speaking at a regular volume.
B. When saying the /p/ sound, attempting to get lips to touch as lightly and briefly as possible.
C. Singing phrases such as "I can. I can do this. I can do this well."
D. Attempting to avoid trigger sounds by replacing them with alternative words.

Teaching Points

Correct Answer: A

Easy onset of phonation is a common and helpful strategy for individuals with fluency disorders. *Easy onset* refers to the vocal folds coming easily with little force. Light contact of the articulators, such as the lips coming together as gently as possible to create plosives, is another popular technique; however, this is not considered an easy onset.

C18

Voice Disorders in Children and Adults

An SLP at the local speech and language clinic receives orders to evaluate a patient presenting as completely aphonic. After comprehensive evaluation, the SLP finds nothing structurally or physiologically wrong with the patient's laryngeal mechanism. The patient continues to present with difficulties during speech-related activities, and the SLP determines that referral is warranted. Which referral is BEST for this patient?

Choices:
A. Referral to a gastroenterologist in order to establish a potential diagnosis of laryngopharyngeal reflux.
B. Referral to a pulmonologist in order to determine the state of the patient's respiratory mechanism.
C. Referral to a mental health professional in order to establish a potential diagnosis of psychogenic dysphonia.
D. Send the patient home with referral for 2 weeks of complete voice rest until all problems resolve.

Teaching Points

Correct Answer: C

Patients suspected of psychogenic dysphonia present with normal vocal fold tissue and movement during evaluation; however, they continue to present with difficulty during speech-related activities. As psychogenic dysphonia is often associated with emotional distress, a referral to a psychological professional may be warranted to help the patient understand and deal with any psychological underpinnings of their voice disorder. As psychogenic dysphonia is not caused by gastric or pulmonary deficits, referrals to specialists in these areas would not help alleviate the symptoms of the disorder. Lastly, as the patient is unable to produce any voice at all, some form of immediate treatment or recommendation is required, so a period of vocal rest is contraindicated.

C19

Research, Evidence-Based Practice, and Tests and Measurements

A group of speech scientists is attempting to determine the efficacy for an intervention for spastic dysarthria. In order to determine an accurate measure of treatment efficacy, which measure is BEST for the scientists to utilize?

Choices:
A. Test-retest measures and construct validity.
B. Content validity and interobserver agreement.
C. Randomization and effect size.
D. Meta-analysis and systematic review.

Teaching Points

Correct Answer: D

Treatment efficacy is aimed at demonstrating the benefits of treatment through well-controlled studies with internal validity, statistical significance, and practical significance. The strongest evidence of this treatment efficacy comes from meta-analysis (i.e., statistical analysis of accumulated evidence from multiple studies) and systematic reviews (i.e., objective and comprehensive overviews of research focused on a particular clinical issue). The best way for this group of researchers to prove the treatment efficacy for the intervention for spastic dysarthria is to utilize both of these methods.

C20

Audiology and Hearing Impairment

An audiologist has completed an audiological evaluation on a patient and has diagnosed a hearing loss localized to the inner ear. Which disorder does the patient MOST LIKELY have?

Choices:
A. Anotia.
B. Autoimmune hearing loss.
C. Cholesteatoma.
D. Osteoma.

Teaching Points

Correct Answer: B

Autoimmune hearing loss is an inner ear disorder associated with autoimmune disorders. The loss refers to abnormal immunologic responses, where the body produces antibodies against its own tissue, including tissue in the hearing mechanism. In contrast, anotia is an outer ear condition and refers to a lack of the pinna. Cholesteatoma is a middle ear condition, in which a nonmalignant growth occurs in the middle ear, disrupting sound transmission. Finally, an osteoma is a benign bony tumor in the ear canal.

Exam C

C21

Research, Evidence-Based Practice, and Tests and Measurements

A pharmaceutical company has approached an SLP working in the school system regarding their new pills. The company claims that the pills are a cure for childhood apraxia of speech (CAS) and invites the SLP to represent this product in exchange for compensation. Which step should occur FIRST in the potential use of the product?

Choices:
A. Ask to see the research supporting the pill's effectiveness.
B. Try the pills with some of their clients with CAS.
C. Approach their director for permission to be the representative.
D. Accept the position as representative for this product.

Teaching Points

Correct Answer: A

According to the ASHA Code of Ethics, Principle of Ethics III, Rule of Ethics G, "Individuals' statements to the public when advertising, announcing, and marketing their professional services; reporting research results; and promoting products shall adhere to professional standards and shall not contain misrepresentations." As the SLP does not know the research evidence behind the pills, their immediate promotion of the pills may constitute an unethical misrepresentation. If the research shows that the pills are effective, and do in fact cure childhood apraxia of speech, the SLP can then make an appropriate informed decision about whether to promote the product or not. Trying the pills on their clients would also prove to be unethical, as the SLP does not have any information on the product.

C22

Dysphagia: Swallowing and Swallowing Disorder

A patient with dysphagia participates in a flexible endoscopic evaluation of swallowing, which discovers a delay in the initiation of the pharyngeal swallow. Which treatment approach will BEST facilitate a timelier pharyngeal swallow?

Choices:
A. Thermal-tactile stimulation.
B. Diet modification.
C. Sour bolus use.
D. Free water protocol.

Teaching Points

Correct Answer: C

Multiple different treatment approaches have been found to improve the timeliness of pharyngeal swallow initiation, including sour bolus, carbonated bolus, and hot/cold bolus use. While thermal-tactile stimulation is reported to initiate a pharyngeal swallow, studies are inconclusive about the generalizability of this method. Diet modifications may be implemented as a safer option due to the risk of aspiration associated with a delay in pharyngeal swallow initiation, but they do not treat the underlying physiological deficit. Finally, the free water protocol is a method to introduce clean, thin liquids to any person with dysphagia while mitigating the risk for aspiration pneumonia.

C23

Language Disorders in Young Children

A young child is diagnosed with a severe cognitive deficit. The SLP is beginning to formulate a plan for intervention and would like to focus on the most functional treatment targets during intervention. Which approach is BEST to implement during intervention sessions?

Choices:
A. Complex sentence structure.
B. Recreational vocabulary.
C. Phonological memory.
D. Joint attention skills.

Teaching Points

Correct Answer: B

Most children with cognitive deficits will learn some language, although normalization of language skills may not be the most appropriate expectation in these cases. For this population, functional language goals are the most appropriate treatment target, which may include focusing intervention on a limited language repertoire. For this child, as they are still relatively young, the most functional goal may be initially targeting vocabulary surrounding their favorite recreational activities as a means of improving their method of communication. Other functional tasks for this population include understanding different syntactic structures and understanding useful vocabulary for the child's activities of daily living.

C24

Acoustics

An SLP is analyzing a spectrogram of an utterance made up of three phonemes. The first phoneme consists of lower-frequency frication noise of a longer duration. The second phoneme is a vowel with low F1 and high F2. The third phoneme consists of a period of closure followed by a burst. Which is the MOST LIKELY utterance captured on the spectrogram?

Choices:
A. Pete.
B. Sheet.
C. Seat.
D. Dan.

Teaching Points

Correct Answer: C

Because the first phoneme demonstrates frication noise of a higher frequency, it can be assumed that it is a fricative sound produced farther forward in the oral cavity, such as /s/. For the second phoneme, because there is a low F1 and high F2, it can be assumed that the vowel is a high front vowel, such as /i/. Finally, as the final phoneme is characterized by a closure (e.g., silent period) followed by a burst, it can be assumed that it is a stop consonant. As there is no mention of voicing, it can be assumed that it is a voiceless stop, such as /t/. The only option from this scenario that matches these three conditions is /sit/ or "seat."

C25

Augmentative and Alternative Communication

An SLP is providing training with a patient and family in the use of a newly implemented augmentative and alternative communication (AAC) device. The patient doesn't know how to read and has dysarthric speech due to a stroke. Which strategy is BEST to use with the patient and family?

Choices:
A. Alphabet supplementation.
B. Topic supplementation.
C. Augmented input.
D. Message co-construction.

Teaching Points

Correct Answer: B

Topic supplementation is frequently used with individuals with severely dysarthric speech and can work with both literate and illiterate individuals. Topic supplementation involves the AAC user utilizing a list of topics, either written or pictorial, and using the topic/context to cue the communication partner into the correct messages. This strategy is more appropriate than alphabet supplementation, as the patient is described as not being able to read.

C26

Audiology and Hearing Impairment

An SLP is working with a child with hearing loss. Currently, the patient has difficulty making same versus different judgments of presented phonemes. In which level of the auditory hierarchy of listening is this child MOST LIKELY demonstrating deficits?

Choices:
A. Comprehension.
B. Detection.
C. Discrimination.
D. Recognition.

Teaching Points

Correct Answer: C

The discrimination level of the auditory hierarchy of listening requires individuals to make same versus different judgments of sounds. As this child is demonstrating difficulty with making this type of judgment, they are exhibiting deficits in discrimination. In contrast, the detection level requires individuals to identify the presence or absence of sound and is the foundation of the auditory hierarchy of listening. The recognition level requires a listener to point to a picture in response to an auditorily presented sound. Finally, the comprehension level requires that listeners respond to linguistic information and provide a response that proves they have "understood" what was presented.

C27

Motor Speech Disorders

A speech-language pathologist works with a patient with Parkinson's disease in an outpatient clinic. During intervention, the SLP attempts a standard course of pharyngeal strengthening exercises and sensory stimulation, but the patient has made little progress. Which treatment approach would be BEST to implement next?

Choices:
A. Lee Silverman Voice Treatment.
B. McNeil Dysphagia Treatment Program.
C. Semi-occluded vocal tract tasks.
D. Thermal-tactile stimulation.

Teaching Points

Correct Answer: A

While Lee Silverman Voice Treatment (LSVT) was originally developed to treat the vocal deficits often seen in Parkinson's disease, subsequent studies have found that this treatment method can also improve symptoms of dysphagia in the population impacted by Parkinson's disease. The McNeil Dysphagia Treatment Program is a treatment method for dysphagia but is not specifically tailored to use for persons with Parkinson's disease, while LSVT is. Semi-occluded vocal tract tasks are used to treat voice disorders, not dysphagia, and thermal-tactile stimulation is a treatment method that is purported to increase the frequency of pharyngeal swallow initiation, although it has not been found to have good generalization.

C28

Voice Disorders in Children and Adults

A patient is admitted to an acute care hospital after having a cerebrovascular accident. Imaging shows that the stroke affected function of the pharyngeal nerve. Which voice problem would this patient MOST LIKELY experience?

Choices:
A. Strained vocal quality.
B. Aphonia.
C. Breathy vocal quality.
D. Hypernasal vocal quality.

Teaching Points

Correct Answer: D

The pharyngeal nerve is a branch of the vagus nerve that innervates the soft palate. If this nerve is damaged, the soft palate would become weak and would not effectively close off the nasal cavity during phonation. The effect would be air escape through the nasal cavity during phonation, causing hypernasal vocal quality. As the pharyngeal nerve does not innervate the vocal folds (i.e., the vocal folds are innervated by the recurrent and superior laryngeal nerves), breathy vocal quality, strained vocal quality, and aphonia would not result from lesions of this nerve.

C29

Acquired Language Disorders

An SLP in an acute care hospital receives a referral to conduct a speech, language, and cognitive-linguistic evaluation for a patient with a recent traumatic brain injury. Upon review of the patient's medical record, the SLP sees that the neurology team has documented that the patient's occipital lobe is damaged. Which deficit is the patient MOST LIKELY to demonstrate during the evaluation?

Choices:
A. Wernicke's aphasia.
B. Verbal apraxia.
C. Unilateral inattention.
D. Homonymous hemianopia.

Teaching Points

Correct Answer: D

A homonymous hemianopia is a type of visual disturbance in which a person is only able to see one half of the visual field (either right or left) in both eyes. This condition is caused by damage to the occipital lobe, which houses the brain structures involved in vision and visual processing.

C30

Language Acquisition: Preverbal and Early Language

Speech and language researchers are attempting to determine the causes of language disorders in young children. They believe that specific biological feature differences in children are the root cause of language disorders. Which would be the BEST hypothesis for these researchers?

Choices:
A. Language disorders are caused by brain asymmetry in children.
B. Language disorders are caused by a lack of literacy opportunities in children.
C. Language disorders arise due to differences across language-learning environments in children.
D. Children with language disorders demonstrate limited processing capacity.

Teaching Points

Correct Answer: A

Potential causal factors for childhood language disorders may be broken down into biological, environmental, and cognitive differences. Biological features that may account for childhood language disorders include brain asymmetry in children with language disorders and chromosomal differences. In contrast to this, limited processing capacity in children with language disorders are considered a cognitive deficit, and lack of literacy opportunities and limited language-learning environments are considered environmental differences.

Spoken Language Disorders in School-Age Populations

An 8-year-old with a diagnosis of specific learning disability arrives at an outpatient clinic for a speech and language evaluation. When the SLP meets the child, which is MOST LIKELY to be observed?

Choices:
A. Difficulties with articulation.
B. Difficulties in social skills.
C. Strengths in social skills.
D. Strengths in short-term memory.

Teaching Points

Correct Answer: B

Children with specific learning disability frequently have difficulty with social skills and may have emotional/ behavioral challenges. Additionally, children with specific learning disability also frequently have difficulty with short-term memory affecting their spoken language and reading skill development. Articulation is not a hallmark of specific learning disability.

Motor Speech Disorders

An SLP is working with a patient with dysarthria on appropriate pacing methods. The SLP wants to introduce methods to help the patient slow their rate of speech. However, the SLP wants to ensure that these treatment approaches are useful for the patient. The SLP researches criteria for use and discontinuation of these approaches. Which statement BEST indicates a criterion for discontinuing use of slowing rate of speech as a treatment method?

Choices:
A. When the patient exhibits a clinically significant reduction in speech intelligibility with slowing rate of speech.
B. When the patient does not exhibit improvements in speech intelligibility when speaking rate is decreased.
C. When the patient presents with a greater reduction in sentence intelligibility compared to word intelligibility.
D. When the patient exhibits a 25% reduction in vital capacity with a decreased rate of speech.

Teaching Points

Correct Answer: B

Slowing the rate of a person's speech should result in immediate improvement in intelligibility, which can be targeted in further sessions. If patients with severe disorders do not exhibit improvements in intelligibility with a slowed rate of speech, this treatment method should not be targeted. If there is not an immediate effect on intelligibility, other treatment methods should be explored, which can lead to greater overall communicative effectiveness for the patient.

C33

The Practice of Speech-Language Pathology

A patient in a hospital is being seen by multiple professionals, with each professional providing independent assessment and intervention. After each professional has completed an initial assessment, they collaborate about the patient's treatment plan and share information regarding the patient's status for each discipline. Which term BEST describes the service delivery model being utilized in the care of this patient?

Choices:
A. Unidisciplinary.
B. Transdisciplinary.
C. Multidisciplinary.
D. Interdisciplinary.

Teaching Points

Correct Answer: D

The interdisciplinary service delivery model dictates that the client is seen by multiple professionals who communicate regarding treatment and share information about overall status. However, independent assessment is completed by all involved disciplines, such as in this scenario. In contrast, multidisciplinary service delivery models dictate that the client is seen by multiple professionals with some communication between disciplines in regard to referral and follow-up, but with little cooperative service delivery. Transdisciplinary service delivery models dictate that professionals cooperate in service delivery and communicate frequently. Additionally, assessment and treatment are delivered by multiple professionals in a more natural environment. Unidisciplinary is not a service delivery model.

C34

Acquired Language Disorders

An SLP is working with a patient with a diagnosis of primary progressive aphasia who is making progress toward achieving goals. Which is MOST LIKELY true about this patient?

Choices:
A. The patient had a history of progressive impairment of language, with no evidence of global dementia or sign of an acute stroke on neuroimaging.
B. The patient had a dementia syndrome characterized by progressive loss of language functioning and a significant memory impairment, with relative preservation of social graces.
C. The patient experienced acute onset of a language disorder that was getting progressively worse over at least the past 2 years.
D. The patient had a CT scan that showed atrophy in the frontal and temporal lobes and an infarct in the language zone of the left hemisphere.

Teaching Points

Correct Answer: A

A person diagnosed with primary progressive aphasia has a history of at least a 2-year period of decline in language functioning, without displaying a more global dementia syndrome. The onset was not acute, and there is no obvious infarct on neuroimaging. Atrophy may be present in the frontal and temporal lobes. Only the patient with neither global aphasia nor evidence of a stroke meets these criteria.

C35

Acquired Language Disorders

An SLP receives a referral to evaluate a patient with acute onset of aphasia. The patient's primary language is Spanish, with only a few words spoken in English. The SLP is a monolingual, native English speaker. Which step must be taken FIRST in order to ensure an adequate assessment of this patient's linguistic capabilities?

Choices:
A. Proceed as usual with the evaluation and use English-language tests and any Spanish-language tests available in the department.
B. Conduct an informal evaluation with help from the patient's friend or family member who can translate the interaction between SLP and patient.
C. Arrange to have a professional interpreter present during the evaluation to translate the evaluation instructions and items.
D. Delay the evaluation until arrangements can be made to have another SLP who is Spanish speaking conduct the evaluation.

Teaching Points

Correct Answer: C

It is recommended that SLPs use interpreter services whenever they are needed in conducting evaluations of people whose native language is not the same as the SLP's native language. Use of family members or friends as translators should be avoided, and the SLP should not attempt to use a test written in a language with which the patient is not proficient. The SLP should not delay the evaluation just because the native language of the patient is different. Timely and culturally appropriate assessment is important to quality patient care.

C36

Dysphagia: Swallowing and Swallowing Disorder

During a modified barium swallow study, the patient demonstrates penetration to the level of the vocal folds but does not spontaneously clear the material. The SLP selects the Penetration-Aspiration Scale (PAS) to measure the patient's performance so that the score will be widely understood by other speech-language pathologists. Which score BEST represents the patient's performance?

Choices:
A. Level 3.
B. Level 4.
C. Level 5.
D. Level 6.

Teaching Points

Correct Answer: C

Level 5 of the PAS states "Material enters the airway, contacts the vocal folds, and is NOT ejected from the airway." If bolus material reaches the vocal folds and the patient does not clear the material, they would be a PAS Level 5. In contrast, Level 3 of the PAS states, "Material enters the airway, remains above the vocal folds, and is NOT ejected from the airway." Level 4 states, "Material enters the airway, contacts the vocal folds, and is ejected from the airway." Finally, Level 6 states, "Material enters the airway, passes the glottis, and is ejected from the airway."

Exam C

C37

Autism Spectrum Disorders

An SLP in a school setting provides services for a student with a diagnosis of autism spectrum disorder. The SLP has received a report from a local neuropsychologist showing that the student's cognitive abilities are similar to the student's current language abilities. The SLP conducts a full speech-language assessment to determine eligibility. Which factor MUST the SLP consider in the assessment of this student?

Choices:
A. Not to use criterion-referenced measurements.
B. Only utilize standardized assessment results.
C. Do not use informal observations to determine eligibility.
D. The cognitive level of the child is a disqualification for services.

Teaching Points

Correct Answer: A

Criterion-referenced measurements are not considered best practice for treatment and eligibility decisions. Cognitive ability is often negatively influenced by language ability and is not a true indicator of a client's abilities.

C38

Spoken Language Disorders in School-Age Populations

A 6-year-old child receives language therapy through a local private clinic. The child loves to play games with favorite toys in the speech clinic while following the clinician's lead on which games they are going to play. Which type of intervention BEST matches this intervention approach?

Choices:
A. Hybrid approach.
B. Clinician-centered.
C. Experiential.
D. Client-centered.

Teaching Points

Correct Answer: A

A hybrid approach to intervention, including incidental language teaching, focuses on the clinician having a specific set of targets to touch upon in sessions while utilizing preferred materials of the client. In contrast, client-centered approaches would be more free form and involve following the client's lead, while a clinician-centered approach is more structured and adult led.

C39

Acquired Language Disorders

An SLP working in an acute care hospital is asked to complete a comprehensive speech and language evaluation for a patient with a recent large left middle cerebral artery cerebrovascular accident. Upon reviewing the patient's medical record, the SLP notes that the patient speaks only Albanian, necessitating the use of an interpreter. Which approach is BEST in conducting this evaluation?

Choices:
A. Training the interpreter in testing procedures prior to the evaluation so they are able to accurately complete the assessment.
B. Speaking directly to the patient with the interpreter present to translate between the two parties.
C. Speaking directly to the interpreter so the interpreter knows what to say to complete the assessment.
D. Using a family member of the patient who is adept in speaking the patient's native language.

Teaching Points

Correct Answer: B

In any case necessitating the use of an interpreter with a patient, the most optimal way to proceed is through the SLP speaking directly to the patient and having the interpreter translate their message. This shows the patient the respect of speaking to them directly as the provider, rather than using the interpreter as the sole means of communication.

C40

Dysphagia: Swallowing and Swallowing Disorder

An SLP in a skilled nursing facility receives a referral for a patient in the later stages of amyotrophic lateral sclerosis. Nursing staff reports significant dysphagia during all meals, despite implementation of a modified diet. Which treatment approach is BEST?

Choices:
A. Enhancing the sensory capacities of the bolus.
B. Using postural adjustments.
C. Introduction of a percutaneous endoscopic gastrostomy (PEG) tube.
D. Oral range of motion exercises.

Teaching Points

Correct Answer: C

Amyotrophic lateral sclerosis is a neurodegenerative disease that affects both upper and lower motor neurons. Over the course of the disease, patients gradually lose their ability to engage in motor acts, such as walking, speaking, and swallowing. In the later stages of the disease, there may be such a great loss of swallowing ability that patients may not be able to receive their nutrition and hydration orally, indicating the need for a PEG tube to be placed.

C41

Autism Spectrum Disorders

A physician has been consulted by a couple who are hoping to have children. The couple expresses interest in learning about risk factors for having children with autism spectrum disorder (ASD). Which risk factor is BEST associated with having a child with autism spectrum disorder?

Choices:
A. If the father uses antidepressants while trying to conceive.
B. If the mother uses antihistamines during pregnancy.
C. If the mother is over 30 years old.
D. If the father is over 40 years old.

Teaching Points

Correct Answer: D

Two main risk factors associated with having a child with ASD are paternal age and maternal drug use. Specifically, if a father is over 40 years of age, there is a six times greater chance of having a child with autism. Additionally, maternal use of antidepressants during pregnancy has also been linked to a greater chance of having a child with ASD. In contrast to this, there has been no established evidence of maternal age over 30, paternal use of antidepressants, or maternal use of antihistamines associated with having a child with ASD.

C42

Acoustics

An SLP is analyzing a spectrogram of an utterance made up of three phonemes. The first phoneme consists of lower-frequency frication noise of a longer duration. The second phoneme is a vowel with low F1 and low F2. The third phoneme consists of a period of closure followed by a burst. Which is the MOST LIKELY utterance captured on the spectrogram?

Choices:
A. Pot.
B. Shoot.
C. Soup.
D. Pop.

Teaching Points

Correct Answer: B

Because the first phoneme demonstrates frication noise of a lower frequency, it can be assumed that it is a fricative sound produced farther back in the oral cavity, such as /ʃ/. For the second phoneme, because there is a low F1 and low F2, it can be assumed that the vowel is a high back vowel, such as /u/. Finally, as the final phoneme is characterized by a closure (e.g., silent period) followed by a burst, it can be assumed that it is a stop consonant. As there is no mention of voicing, it can be assumed that it is a voiceless stop, such as /t/. The only option from this scenario that matches these three conditions is /ʃut/ or "shoot."

C43

Augmentative and Alternative Communication

An older adult patient is in the middle stages of amyotrophic lateral sclerosis. The patient and life partner have been working with an SLP in order to implement an appropriate AAC system. The patient does not want to appear dependent on others and often refuses to work with the SLP. When asked about future communication needs, the patient states "it is what it is." Which type of barrier BEST represents the patient's statements?

Choices:
A. Access barrier.
B. Attitude barrier.
C. Knowledge barrier.
D. Skill barrier.

Teaching Points

Correct Answer: B

An attitude barrier occurs when an individual has incorrect, outdated, and discriminatory attitudes regarding the abilities of people with complex communication needs. In this situation, the individual believes that using AAC will make her look incompetent, when AAC would actually support her independence at home and in the community.

C44

Written Language Disorders in School-Age Populations

An SLP is tutoring an adolescent who is writing a report for a science class. The student has difficulties setting goals and organizing an approach to writing. These challenges are MOST consistent with deficits in which component area of writing?

Choices:
A. Translating.
B. Planning.
C. Reviewing.
D. Spelling.

Teaching Points

Correct Answer: B

Planning includes the ability to set goals for the writing product, organize a plan, and monitor plans being formulated. As this child demonstrates difficulties with setting goals and organizing plans for her report, she is exhibiting deficits in planning for writing.

C45

Language Disorders in Young Children

A child is receiving treatment by an SLP in an early intervention setting. The child is demonstrating deficits in foundational skills for social use of language. Which skill areas are BEST to address in intervention sessions?

Choices:
A. Gestures and vocalizations.
B. Vegetative sounds such as coughing and burping.
C. Eye contact, joint attention, and taking turns.
D. Talking about objects and events.

Teaching Points

Correct Answer: C

Research has demonstrated that these behaviors are important precursors to the development of social communication in young children. In typical development, children who show these aspects of interaction are believed to be advancing in their communicative development. Gestures and vocalizations and naming behaviors are later-developing occurrences and may or may not signal social awareness.

C46

Cleft Palate and Craniofacial Conditions

A child arrives at an outpatient clinic for a comprehensive speech and language evaluation. While reviewing the child's medical records, the SLP notes a history of vascular malformations. Upon approaching the child for completion of evaluation, the SLP notices that the child presents with micrognathia and hypernasality during speech production. Which diagnosis does this child MOST LIKELY have?

Choices:
A. Stickler syndrome.
B. Velocardiofacial syndrome.
C. Fetal alcohol syndrome.
D. Trisomy 13.

Teaching Points

Correct Answer: B

Velocardiofacial syndrome, or deletion 22q11.2 syndrome, is a disorder characterized by a constellation of features, including velopharyngeal dysfunction (velo-), cardiac issues such as the vascular malformations (-cardio-), and facial structure differences such as micrognathia. As the child from this scenario has all of these features, they are most likely to be diagnosed with velocardiofacial syndrome.

C47

Motor Speech Disorders

An SLP is working with a patient who has flaccid dysarthria. After many weeks of therapy, the SLP has determined that referral for a palatal lift fitting would be beneficial. Fitting of a palatal lift MOST LIKELY results in which outcome?

Choices:
A. Occlusion of the nares during tidal breathing.
B. Improvements in phonation for sustained vowels.
C. Production of perceptually distinct nasal consonants.
D. Increase in nasal emissions during running speech.

Teaching Points

Correct Answer: C

Use of a palatal lift is a compensatory maneuver for weakness in the soft palate, which allows for the reduction of hypernasality and perception of distinct nasal and nonnasal phonemes. Use of a palatal lift does not fully occlude the nares during tidal breathing and allows for appropriate nasal breathing. Nasal emission should be decreased, due to the decrease in size of the velopharyngeal port. As a palatal lift does not directly affect the vocal folds, improvements in phonation would not occur from use of a lift alone.

C48

Augmentative and Alternative Communication

An SLP is working with a severely dysarthric patient in an acute rehabilitation setting, targeting improved functional communication. The patient was nonliterate at the start of treatment and states that literacy is not a priority for communication. The SLP decides to utilize topic supplementation to aid in the comprehension of communicative partners. Which approach BEST matches this choice for intervention?

Choices:
A. Training the patient to utilize their AAC device by modeling and explaining the process.
B. Training the patient's spouse to expand upon their topic of conversation.
C. Providing the patient with a list of letters to utilize in conversation.
D. Providing the patient with a list of pictures to utilize in conversation.

Teaching Points

Correct Answer: D

Topic supplementation may be used for people with complex communication needs (CCN) who have severely dysarthric speech and utilizes a communication board with lists of commonly discussed topics (either pictorial or written). As the user from this scenario is using pictures to supply context clues about their topic of communication, they are engaging in topic supplementation. In contrast to this, alphabet supplementation allows users to select the initial letter of words to provide context clues and improve intelligibility at the word level. Message co-construction occurs when the person with CCN supplies the content words of their message, a facilitator confirms these words, and then expands the person with CCN's message. Finally, augmented input occurs when a facilitator models how a system is used by providing both input and speech.

C49

Augmentative and Alternative Communication

An SLP is working with a nonverbal client to program their AAC device with speech output. The SLP determines that the client would benefit from prerecorded phrases and other stimuli to increase communicative effectiveness, as the client shows poor initiation in generating novel utterances. Which type of speech output is BEST for the SLP to implement for the client's AAC device?

Choices:
A. Computerized speech.
B. Synthesized speech.
C. Digitized speech.
D. Hybrid speech.

Teaching Points

Correct Answer: C

Digitized speech is human speech that has been recorded, stored, and reproduced for use in an AAC system. Additionally, this form of speech cannot be used to generate novel utterances, due to its prerecorded nature. As the patient from this scenario demonstrates poor initiation in developing novel utterances and would benefit from prerecorded speech, the SLP will most likely utilize digitized speech. In contrast to this, synthesized speech and computer-generated speech constitute a form of communication in which words/messages are entered via text. Stored speech data may be used in this form of communication, but it is more likely to be used with individuals who have the ability to formulate novel utterances. Finally, hybrid speech utilizes both synthesized and digitized speech to aid the AAC user in communication.

C50

The Practice of Speech-Language Pathology

An SLP accepts a position in an early intervention (EI) setting. The SLP has no prior experience in this setting and seeks additional information about the role of an EI SLP. Which role BEST represents service in this setting?

Choices:
A. Drafting Individual Education Plans (IEPs).
B. Ensuring free and appropriate public education.
C. Providing an Individualized Family Service Plan.
D. Determining medical means of intervention for newborns.

Teaching Points

Correct Answer: C

SLPs who work in early intervention are responsible for providing and following an Individualized Family Service Plan, which dictates goals and objectives for the child and family, including services to be provided, preservice levels, plan for intervention, and evaluation of services/outcomes. SLPs who work in educational settings are responsible for providing IEPs and free and appropriate public education. No SLP is eligible to provide medical means of intervention for any client seen for services.

C51

Acquired Language Disorders

An SLP receives orders to evaluate a patient with a recent left middle cerebral artery cerebrovascular accident. The SLP wants to obtain a detailed profile of the patient's auditory comprehension abilities. Which method is BEST for the SLP to use to develop a profile of the patient's auditory comprehension skills?

Choices:
A. Asking the person to respond to yes/no questions presented in pairs, such as "Is this shirt blue?" followed by "Is this shirt red?"
B. Asking open-ended autobiographical questions about their name and address, such as "Where do you live?"
C. Asking the patient to follow commands, including naming objects, such as, "Tell me what this is called."
D. Asking the patient to produce automatic spoken sequences, such as, "Count from one to ten."

Teaching Points

Correct Answer: A

When assessing auditory comprehension, the SLP should avoid tasks that are also dependent on other language abilities such as verbal expression that might be impaired as well. Therefore, the scenario most likely to yield reliable information about auditory comprehension is one in which the individual does not have to respond verbally.

C52

Anatomy and Physiology of Communication and Swallowing

During the transmission of an action potential, after a neuron has fired, there is an absolute refractory period. This is a delay during which a neuron is unable to transmit further action potentials. Which of the following describes why this delay must expire before that neuron can fire again?

Choices:
A. Sodium (Na+) ions continue to flow out of the cell after an action potential spike.
B. Potassium (K+) ions continue to flow out of the cell after an action potential spike.
C. Voltage gated sodium (Na+) channels are periodically inactivated after opening.
D. Voltage gate potassium (K+) channels are periodically inactivated after opening.

Teaching Points

Correct Answer: C

During the refractory period, the sodium gated channels are deactivated, so sodium is unable to flow through the neuron's cellular membrane. After a short period, these gates become activated and are able to help with the propagation of an action potential.

C53

Cleft Palate and Craniofacial Conditions

A child arrives at a speech and language clinic for a comprehensive speech and language evaluation. While reviewing the child's records, the SLP notes a history of developmental disabilities and behavioral problems. Upon approaching the child for completion of evaluation, the SLP notices that the child presents with a short nose and a thin upper lip. Which diagnosis does this child MOST LIKELY have?

Choices:
A. Fetal alcohol syndrome.
B. Pierre Robin sequence.
C. Wolf-Hirschhorn syndrome.
D. Van der Woude syndrome.

Teaching Points

Correct Answer: A

Fetal alcohol syndrome is a condition that arises from alcohol exposure during pregnancy. It is characterized by a cluster of symptoms, including possible presence of a cleft (including Pierre Robin sequence), craniofacial features (such as the short nose and thin upper lip the child from this scenario presents with), and functional concerns (such as developmental disabilities and behavioral problems).

C54

Written Language Disorders in School-Age Populations

A fourth-grade child on an SLP's caseload at a school has difficulty with phonological/orthographic associations, automaticity and fluency, and underlying language abilities. Which impairment would the child MOST LIKELY demonstrate?

Choices:
A. Ability to learn spelling rules.
B. Articulation of alveolar fricatives.
C. Spoken language capabilities.
D. Reading comprehension.

Teaching Points

Correct Answer: D

If a student has impaired phonological/orthographic associations and impaired automaticity/fluency, they will present with word recognition deficits and slow, labored reading. When these deficits are coupled with deficits in underlying language abilities, the cognitive load needed to complete reading is greatly increased. This leads to very little cognitive ability for the student to comprehend written material and will present as reading comprehension deficits.

C55

Cleft Palate and Craniofacial Conditions

An SLP is working with a child to improve the hypernasality of their speech. The child has been diagnosed with a cleft palate, but also demonstrates a Pierre Robin sequence, midface hypoplasia, and a mild sensorineural hearing loss. Which disorder does the child MOST LIKELY have?

Choices:
A. Fetal alcohol syndrome.
B. Trisomy 13.
C. Stickler syndrome.
D. Orofaciodigital syndrome, type 1.

Teaching Points

Correct Answer: C

Stickler syndrome includes cleft palate, specific craniofacial features (e.g., Pierre Robin sequence, midface hypoplasia, epicanthal folds), and a function concern for sensorineural hearing loss. Fetal alcohol syndrome, trisomy 13, and orofaciodigital syndrome type 1 include specific craniofacial features but do not include sensorineural hearing loss as a functional concern. Sensorineural hearing loss is a functional concern in individuals with Stickler syndrome, so when this type of hearing loss is present, it is highly indicative of Stickler syndrome.

C56

Stuttering and Other Fluency Disorders

The parents of a 4-year-old are concerned about their child's speech. The child is increasingly hesitant to respond in preschool and has shown disfluencies for the past year, though they never seem to interfere with communication. The child is now holding her breath and closing her eyes when there are episodes of stuttering. Some of these blocks last more than 10 seconds. Which statement BEST represents these findings?

Choices:
A. The child and parents would benefit from a psychologist to help them cope with this problem.
B. The secondary behaviors indicate that the child is trying to control stuttering.
C. A more direct approach to treatment would be beneficial for the child to learn new strategies for stuttering.
D. Due to the child's age, the risk for chronic stuttering is less; therefore, treatment is not needed.

Teaching Points

Correct Answer: B

This child's secondary behaviors indicate that her stuttering is advancing and is a serious concern. Whenever a child has secondary behaviors, it is important to think about the intervention needed. Regardless of the risk factors present, the stuttering behaviors (core and secondary) indicate the need for more careful evaluation and treatment by an SLP.

C57

Spoken Language Disorders in School-Age Populations

A child is having difficulty in school talking with friends. The child frequently goes off topic, changes the topic abruptly, and becomes easily distracted during conversations. During a comprehensive speech and language evaluation, the SLP determines that the child MOST LIKELY has difficulty in which area?

Choices:
A. Expressive vocabulary.
B. Perspective-taking.
C. Discourse management.
D. Syntax.

Teaching Points

Correct Answer: C

Turn-taking, topic initiation, maintenance, and termination are aspects of discourse management. Someone having difficulty in this area may struggle to have cohesive and comprehensive conversations with their communication partners. In contrast, difficulty with perspective-taking would include having difficulty understanding her communication partner's point of view in various situations.

C58

Cleft Palate and Craniofacial Conditions

A child arrives at an outpatient clinic for a comprehensive speech and language evaluation. While reviewing the child's medical records, the SLP notes a history of hearing loss. Upon approaching the child for completion of the evaluation, the SLP notices that the child presents with coloboma of the iris, a prominent nasal bridge, and hypernasality during speech production. Which diagnosis does the child MOST likely have?

Choices:
A. Van der Woude syndrome.
B. Orofaciodigital syndrome, type 1.
C. Saethre-Chotzen syndrome.
D. Wolf-Hirschhorn syndrome.

Teaching Points

Correct Answer: D

Wolf-Hirschhorn syndrome is a genetic disorder that includes a cluster of symptoms, including common presence of a cleft palate (hypernasal speech production), many craniofacial features (including coloboma of the iris and a prominent nasal bridge), and functional concerns (including occasional hearing loss).

C59

Voice Disorders in Children and Adults

A patient presents to the local voice clinic with complaints of difficulty producing voice, which is made worse during prolonged periods of vocal use. After receiving an initial evaluation by both the otolaryngologist and the SLP, the patient is diagnosed with muscle tension dysphonia, specifically with excess tension in the vocal fold adductor muscles. Which treatment approach is MOST BENEFICIAL to utilize to reduce symptoms?

Choices:
A. Lee Silverman Voice Treatment.
B. Head turn maneuvers.
C. Straw phonation.
D. Circumlaryngeal massage.

Teaching Points

Correct Answer: D

Muscle tension dysphonia is a voice disorder characterized by chronic increased tension of the laryngeal musculature. Circumlaryngeal massage is a treatment method that can be utilized to effectively relax the laryngeal muscles and promote phonation in this population. The effects of the massage can last for extensive periods of time, and repeated massages may be utilized as possible. Head turn maneuvers and Lee Silverman Voice Treatment may be utilized in the hypofunctional vocal fold population, such as paralysis and Parkinson's disease. While straw phonation promotes easy onset of phonation, it does not reduce the increased tension in the laryngeal muscles found in muscle tension dysphonia.

C60

Audiology and Hearing Impairment

A patient attends a consultation appointment with an audiologist regarding the potential to receive a cochlear implant (CI). The audiologist educates the patient on candidacy criteria for the placement of a CI. Which statement BEST reflects candidacy criteria for placement of a CI?

Choices:
A. Mild sensorineural hearing loss in both ears.
B. Moderate-to-profound sensorineural hearing loss in a single ear.
C. Preoperative hearing in noise test (HINT) sentence recognition scores of >60% binaurally.
D. Preoperative HINT sentence recognition scores of >50% in the implanted ear and >60% in the opposite ear.

Teaching Points

Correct Answer: B

Candidacy for cochlear implant surgery in adults includes the following criteria: age 18 years or older, moderate-to-profound binaural sensorineural hearing loss, preoperative HINT sentence recognition scores of <50% in the ear to be implanted and <60% in the opposite ear OR <60% binaurally, pre- or postlinguistic onset of severe-to-profound hearing loss, no medical contraindications, and a desire to be a part of the hearing world.

C61

Augmentative and Alternative Communication

An SLP is working with a patient in order to implement an aided AAC device for communicative purposes. Which means of AAC would be of GREATEST benefit for use with this patient?

Choices:
A. Head movements.
B. Pantomiming.
C. Labeled symbols.
D. Manual signs.

Teaching Points

Correct Answer: C

Aided AAC refers to any means of AAC that utilizes external aids or equipment to improve the communicative effectiveness of the user. As a labeled system requires external equipment in order to use, this would be the most appropriate selection for use with this patient. In contrast to this, head movements, pantomiming, and manual signs do not require the use of external aids and would be considered non-aided AAC. These methods would be inappropriate for use with the patient from this scenario.

C62

Speech Sound Disorders in Children

An SLP performs a comprehensive speech evaluation with a child. The SLP determines that although the /s/ phoneme is produced, the child demonstrates the phonological process of final consonant deletion for this phoneme, consistent with a phonemic error. Which method of intervention would be BEST to implement?

Choices:
A. Van Riper traditional approach.
B. Multiple-phoneme approach.
C. Paired-stimuli approach.
D. Minimal-contrast approach.

Teaching Points

Correct Answer: D

The minimal-contrast approach is an intervention method used for phonemic speech errors and is utilized to eliminate excessive homonymy in children's speech. In contrast, the Van Riper traditional approach, multiple-phoneme approach, and paired-stimuli approach are all intervention methods used for children with phonetic speech errors and would not be helpful in remediating this particular child's speech sound disorder, as this child already knows the motor pattern for the /s/ phoneme and requires help to generalize production to new word positions.

Exam C

C63

Research, Evidence-Based Practice, and Tests and Measurements

An SLP is interested in starting a research study to determine the effect of a treatment approach in alleviating symptoms of voice disorders. While the SLP believes that this treatment will be beneficial to individuals with voice disorders of varying etiology, the SLP only has access to persons with voice disorders caused by muscle tension dysphonia. Which type of threat MUST be addressed in this research process?

Choices:
A. Internal validity.
B. External validity.
C. Reliability.
D. Content validity.

Teaching Points

Correct Answer: B

External validity is the amount of generalizability of results to real-life situations. This SLP needs to be aware of the external validity to those with other etiologies of the voice disorder, as he only has participants with muscle tension dysphonia in his study. His external validity would be strengthened further if he had participants with other etiologies.

C64

Autism Spectrum Disorders

A child arrives at a physician's office for a comprehensive evaluation, with parental suspicions of autism spectrum disorder (ASD). Following the evaluation, the child is diagnosed with ASD, with Level 1 severity in repetitive behaviors. Which statement BEST describes the behaviors likely exhibited by the child?

Choices:
A. Difficulty switching between tasks.
B. Becoming distressed when changing focus or activity.
C. Behaviors that markedly interfere with functioning.
D. Inflexible behavior that is obvious to observers.

Teaching Points

Correct Answer: A

Level 1 severity of restricted, repetitive behaviors reflect inflexible behaviors that cause interference with functioning, difficulty switching between tasks, and problems with organization and planning. In contrast to this, Level 2 severity reflects inflexible behaviors that are obvious to the casual observer, and distressed behavior noted when changing focus. Finally, Level 3 severity reflects difficulty in coping with change, repetitive behaviors markedly interfering with functioning, and significant distress upon changing focus.

C65

Language Disorders in Young Children

A child has recently begun to show growth in their language skills, particularly demonstrating increased variety of word classes used and multiple different sentence types. At what age range is this child MOST likely in their development?

Choices:
A. Infancy.
B. Toddlerhood.
C. Preschool.
D. School-age.

Teaching Points

Correct Answer: C

It is during the preschool years that more complex language is noted. Prior to this time, children express language through babbling, which gives way to first words. Children then build their expressive lexicon and begin expressing language through simple sentences before reaching complex language structures.

C66

Audiology and Hearing Impairment

An audiologist completes an audiological evaluation on a patient. During the evaluation, the audiologist utilizes instrumentation that allows determination of the severity of the patient's hearing loss as well as the type of hearing loss the patient is experiencing. Which evaluation method BEST represents the type of evaluation completed?

Choices:
A. Pure tone audiometry.
B. Tympanometry.
C. Acoustic reflex testing.
D. Speech audiometry.

Teaching Points

Correct Answer: A

Pure tone audiometry refers to a form of evaluation that determines the severity of a hearing loss and provides information to help diagnose the type of hearing loss (i.e., conductive, sensorineural, or mixed). In contrast to this, tympanometry evaluates middle ear integrity, tympanic membrane mobility, and middle ear pressure. Acoustic reflex testing assesses the neural pathways. Finally, speech audiometry cross-checks the validity of pure tone threshold results and quantifies suprathreshold speech recognition abilities.

C67

Spoken Language Disorders in School-Age Populations

An SLP working in a public school is asked to evaluate a child to better understand the current level of linguistic functioning. The SLP decides to use a curriculum-based assessment to evaluate the child's linguistic competency. Which statement BEST describes the design of this type of assessment?

Choices:
A. Measures linguistic skill with modifications or support put in place.
B. Measures linguistic skill in order to select targets to improve daily living.
C. Measures the impact of a linguistic disorder on daily living.
D. Measures linguistic skill with no comparison to other students.

Teaching Points

Correct Answer: B

A curriculum-based assessment is designed to measure the extent to which a child's communication disorder impacts academic functioning, in order to select linguistic targets that improve daily functioning. Progress on these targets should be monitored over the course of instruction. In contrast to this, dynamic assessment is designed to assess a child's linguistic skills with modifications or supports put in place. Ecological assessment is designed to measure the extent to which a child's communication disorder impacts daily living. Finally, criterion-referenced assessment is designed to measure a specific linguistic skill with no comparison to other students.

C68

Stuttering and Other Fluency Disorders

An adult who stutters has received speech-language services on and off over the past 10 years. The SLP uses a fluency-shaping approach to improve speech. The patient is able to make progress toward goals but has trouble generalizing fluent speech to work and social settings. The patient and SLP collaborate to try an approach that uses more focus on stuttering modification. Which technique is BEST to emphasize in treatment sessions?

Choices:
A. Use of easy onset of speech.
B. Use of breathing modifications.
C. Use of loose speech contacts.
D. Use of cancellation strategies.

Teaching Points

Correct Answer: D

Cancellation techniques are considered a form of stuttering modification (working directly with the stutter) in which the person who stutters identifies a moment of disfluency, stops their speech production, and begins again. The other options listed are considered fluency-shaping techniques, which are focused on improving fluent speech.

C69

Autism Spectrum Disorders

An adolescent with a diagnosis of ASD Level 1 has been referred for a speech and language evaluation at a local clinic. Which behavior does the client MOST LIKELY demonstrate?

Choices:
A. Difficulty understanding sarcasm used by peers.
B. Difficulty using natural oral speech to get wants and needs met.
C. Distress when changing focus or action during routine tasks.
D. Difficulty with the ability to self-regulate when stressed.

Teaching Points

Correct Answer: A

Level 1 autism is characterized by deficits in social communication and difficulty initiating social interactions. By age 15, sarcasm, metaphors, and idioms are frequently used in everyday speech in nonliteral ways. Difficulty in understanding these aspects may cause challenges in social interactions with peers and would require support. In contrast, in Level 3 autism, the client may have significant communication impairments requiring them to use AAC in order to get their basic wants and needs met.

C70

Dysphagia: Swallowing and Swallowing Disorder

An SLP is completing an oral motor examination for a patient recently admitted to an acute care hospital with a cerebrovascular accident. Upon completing the oral motor examination, the SLP observes symptoms consistent with damage to the glossopharyngeal nerve (CN IX). Which deficit does the patient MOST LIKELY have?

Choices:
A. Unable to produce a smile.
B. Unable to elevate the velum.
C. Unable to elicit a gag reflex.
D. Unable to open their mouth.

Teaching Points

Correct Answer: C

If the patient experiences damage to their glossopharyngeal nerve, they may experience deficits in any of the following areas: taste sensation from the posterior third of the tongue, sensation from the middle ear/upper pharynx/carotid body, salivation from the parotid gland, and contraction of the stylopharyngeus. If a patient is unable to produce a smile, that would be indicative of damage to the facial nerve. Inability to elevate the velum would indicate damage to the vagus nerve. Finally, inability to open the mouth would be indicative of the trigeminal nerve.

C71

Audiology and Hearing Impairment

An SLP working in a school receives a referral to evaluate a child with a newly diagnosed hearing loss. After completing the evaluation, the SLP implements aural rehabilitation principles into intervention sessions. The SLP speaks to a teacher about approaches that can be implemented during class activities to support the child's progress. Which approach is BEST to recommend to the teacher?

Choices:
A. Provide lessons in a large group format to allow the student to fully integrate into the classroom setting.
B. Provide instruction in a one-on-one format in order to optimize the ability to learn.
C. Use a megaphone during lessons in order to optimize the student's ability to hear and learn material.
D. Implement written class content in order to allow the student to fully benefit from instruction.

Teaching Points

Correct Answer: D

There are multiple ways in which an SLP can implement auditory rehabilitation approaches in a classroom, including use of FM or infrared systems, acoustic treatment of the classroom (e.g., recommending lessons occur in a room with a low ceiling or acoustic tiles, carpeting on the floor, and shades/curtains on windows), a small class size, and provision on increased visual cues.

C72

Language Disorders in Young Children

A 5-year-old child has been receiving language therapy at his school. Recently, the child has greatly enjoyed going to see his SLP because he is able to bring in all his favorite toys and the SLP will play along with him while asking questions. What type of language intervention is the child MOST likely receiving?

Choices:
A. Hybrid approach intervention.
B. Clinician-centered intervention.
C. Experiential intervention.
D. Client-centered intervention.

Teaching Points

Correct Answer: D

Client-centered intervention occurs when the client interacts with the clinician and the clinician uses the interests of the child to direct the order and substance of the language intervention session. Because this child's SLP is following the child's lead and utilizing the child's interests, this is most likely a client-centered approach to intervention. In contrast to this, a clinician-centered approach occurs when the clinician chooses the targets and sets the agenda for the therapy session. Hybrid approaches draw aspects from both clinician- and client-centered therapy approaches. Finally, experiential intervention occurs in a conversational context and highlights appropriate conversational practices.

C73

Autism Spectrum Disorders

An SLP is providing language intervention for an adolescent student with autism spectrum disorder (ASD). The SLP establishes a goal to improve semantic language use. Which treatment approach is BEST for the SLP to develop for this student?

Choices:
A. Reading conversation partners' intentions.
B. Understanding sarcastic comments made by conversation partners.
C. Understanding idiomatic expressions mentioned by conversation partners.
D. Determining when to make appropriate decisions.

Teaching Points

Correct Answer: B

Semantic goals for adolescents with ASD could entail comprehending semantic nuances, such as inferred meaning, humor, discourse/conversational rules, and sarcasm. In contrast to this, reading others' intentions and making appropriate decisions are pragmatic language goals for adolescents, while understanding of idiomatic expressions is a semantic language goal for school-aged children.

C74

Motor Speech Disorders

An SLP works with a patient in a skilled nursing facility who is exhibiting signs of an emerging neurological condition. The SLP observes the patient fatigue quickly during completion of a swallowing exercise regimen, but performance improves with use of energy-conservation techniques. The SLP refers the patient for a neurology consult. Which neurological condition does the patient MOST LIKELY have?

Choices:
A. Guillain-Barré.
B. Myasthenia gravis.
C. Parkinson's disease.
D. Progressive supranuclear palsy.

Teaching Points

Correct Answer: B

A hallmark symptom of myasthenia gravis is weakness that is exacerbated with repeated effort, such as that seen in the completion of a swallowing exercise regimen. The weakness seen in myasthenia gravis is best managed through energy-conservation techniques, such as use of smaller, more frequent meals throughout the day, rather than three, larger meals. While persons with Guillain-Barré experience weakness, their weakness is not managed with energy-conservation techniques and often requires prolonged treatment approaches to improve their overall strength. Parkinson's disease and progressive supranuclear palsy are movement disorders in which force of motor movements is reduced, both of which respond to direct treatment of any swallowing impairment.

C75

Spoken Language Disorders in School-Age Populations

A child arrives at a speech and language clinic for a comprehensive speech and language evaluation. While reviewing the child's medical records, the SLP notes a history of developmental disabilities. Upon initiating the evaluation, the SLP notices that the child presents with midface hypoplasia, ptosis of the eyelids, and hypernasality during speech production. Which diagnosis does the child MOST LIKELY have?

Choices:
A. Crouzon syndrome.
B. Apert syndrome.
C. Saethre-Chotzen syndrome.
D. Pfeiffer syndrome.

Teaching Points

Correct Answer: C

Saethre-Chotzen syndrome is considered a type of craniosynostosis syndrome and involves a cluster of symptoms, including cleft palate (hypernasality during speech production), craniofacial features (including midface hypoplasia and ptosis of the eyelids), and functional concerns (including developmental disabilities).

C76

Language Disorders in Young Children

A preschooler overhears a person saying, "The mouse murped the cheese." The child is able to figure out that "murp" is an action based on what was overheard. This demonstrates support for which word-learning principle?

Choices:
A. Syntactic bootstrapping.
B. Early word-learning bias.
C. Semantic bootstrapping.
D. Morphological bootstrapping.

Teaching Points

Correct Answer: A

Syntactic bootstrapping is when a person is able to use/understand morphosyntactic structures based on the word class of a novel word. In this particular example, the child is able to determine the meaning of the new word because he is able to understand syntactic categories such as actions versus things.

C77

Voice Disorders in Children and Adults

An SLP working in an outpatient voice clinic provides intervention for a patient with an unstable phonatory system. The SLP would like to utilize a treatment approach that works on restabilizing the voicing system while also promoting optimal flexibility. Which approach is BEST for the SLP to utilize in intervention sessions?

Choices:
A. Resonant voice therapy.
B. Vocal function exercises.
C. Vocal hygiene training.
D. Lee Silverman Voice Treatment.

Teaching Points

Correct Answer: B

Vocal function exercises are a group of exercises that research has shown to improve vocal range, stability, flexibility, and resonance. As such, this would be the optimal treatment method for the SLP in this scenario to use. Resonant voice therapy would be the best bet for optimizing vocal quality through focusing on maximizing oral-pharyngeal resonance. Semi-occluded vocal tract tasks maximize interaction between vocal fold vibration (sound production) and the vocal tract (the sound filter) and produce resonant voice. Finally, vocal hygiene training works by training individuals to reduce or eliminate vocally abusive behaviors to reduce phonotrauma.

C78

Speech Sound Disorders in Children

A child with speech sound problems is recently diagnosed with a speech sound disorder, characterized by difficulty producing interdental and alveolar fricatives. Which speech sounds would the child MOST LIKELY demonstrate difficulty producing?

Choices:
A. /f/ and /h/.
B. /θ/ and /s/.
C. /z/ and /dʒ/.
D. /ð/ and /b/.

Teaching Points

Correct Answer: B

This child demonstrates speech sound errors on the /θ/ and /s/. The interdental fricatives include /θ/ and /ð/, and the alveolar fricatives include /s/ and /z/. In contrast, /f/ and /h/ are labiodental and glottal fricatives. While /z/ is an alveolar fricative, /dʒ/ is a palatal affricate. Similarly, while /ð/ is an interdental fricative, /b/ is a bilabial stop. There is no mention of the child's ability to produce affricates or stops, so these answers are not the most appropriate.

C79

Voice Disorders in Children and Adults

An SLP working in an outpatient voice clinic is attempting to utilize acoustic measurements to more accurately qualify aspects of the patient's voice. The spectrum of the patient's voice shows that H1 is 15 dB higher than H2 in amplitude. Which is MOST LIKELY indicated through this type of spectrum?

Choices:
A. Breathy voice.
B. Modal voice.
C. Creaky voice.
D. High harmonic-to-noise ratio.

Teaching Points

Correct Answer: A

The relative amplitude of H1 and H2 provides an indicator of spectral tilt, which can differentiate voice quality changes between breathy, modal, and creaky. Breathy voice is distinguished by an H1 that is higher in amplitude than H2. In modal voice, H1 and H2 are approximately equal in amplitude. In creaky voice, H1 is lower in amplitude than H2. Harmonic-to-noise ratio is a measure of overall harmonic to noise ratio rather than a comparison of H1–H2 amplitude.

C80

Language Acquisition: Preverbal and Early Language

The parents of an English-speaking preschooler have decided to send their child to a Spanish-speaking childcare to aid in learning both languages. Which term BEST describes this decision?

Choices:
A. Successive bilingualism.
B. Simultaneous bilingualism.
C. Generative language.
D. Nonstandard dialect.

Teaching Points

Correct Answer: A

Successive bilingualism is when a second language is learned after the acquisition of a first language. In this scenario, the child is already exposed to and able to speak English, so she would be learning Spanish as a second language.

C81

Written Language Disorders in School-Age Populations

An SLP in a high school is working with an adolescent who is struggling with generating detailed essay-length material. The SLP reviews current research to select an optimal method for enhancing quantity and quality of text produced by struggling writers. Which approach is BEST for the SLP to select for this student?

Choices:
A. Sentence combining practice.
B. Repeated copying of sentences.
C. Decontextualized vocabulary instruction.
D. Incidental exposure to authentic textures.

Teaching Points

Correct Answer: A

Sentence combining practice is an efficacious approach to writing intervention that enhances the quantity and quality of text produced. With this type of practice, students gain experience combining different types of sentence structure in order to build their writing skills. The other types of interventions posed in this question are general bottom-up and top-down approaches to reading and writing instruction.

C82

Motor Speech Disorders

An SLP working in an acute care hospital is asked to complete a comprehensive speech and language assessment for a patient who has had a cerebrovascular accident. During the assessment, the SLP is unsure whether the patient demonstrates apraxia of speech (AOS) or aphasia. Which description provides the BEST information for a differential diagnosis, assuming the patient demonstrates only one of these conditions?

Choices:
A. While verbal expression may be impaired in both conditions, other linguistic tasks are often preserved in speakers with AOS.
B. While verbal expression may be impaired in both conditions, speakers with aphasia often have greater difficulty initiating speech.
C. While verbal expression may be impaired in both conditions, speakers with apraxia often have co-occurring auditory comprehension deficits.
D. While verbal expression may be impaired in both conditions, speakers with aphasia often demonstrate groping behaviors.

Teaching Points

Correct Answer: A

As a singularly occurring disorder, AOS is a condition that impacts the speaker's motor speech abilities. This often leads to errors in speech prosody, speech sound distortions, difficulty initiating speech production, and groping behaviors to find articulatory configurations. As this disorder on its own does not typically impact the linguistic system, persons with AOS are often able to complete other linguistic tasks, such as following verbal directions and writing accurately. Use of these types of tasks can help with differentiation between AOS and aphasia.

C83

Language Disorders in Young Children

A young child receives speech-language therapy to remediate a language disorder. After 3 months of services, the SLP would like to assess the progress this child has made during intervention. Which is the MOST EFFECTIVE method for assessing the child's progress?

Choices:
A. Review data collected during intervention sessions.
B. Elicit untrained exemplars during conversation.
C. Administer a standardized assessment and compare scores.
D. Implement dynamic assessment procedures.

Teaching Points

Correct Answer: B

Periodic measurement of client performance is a critical component of advancing clients through therapy. One way to assess progress is to utilize untrained exemplars when eliciting language. For example, if the client has been working on the third-person singular form of *come*, the clinician can probe for generalization to "walk." Administration of standardized assessment is discouraged, as there may be a recall bias for assessment material. Dynamic assessment would reveal how the child is functioning currently but may not probe generalization. Finally, reviewing data collected during intervention—while essential for steering the direction of treatment—will reveal when goals need to be updated but does not probe for current level of progress.

C84

Voice Disorders in Children and Adults

An SLP is working in an outpatient voice clinic. A referral is received to evaluate a patient with a recent diagnosis of vocal fold nodules. The SLP completes a comprehensive evaluation that reveals reduced airflow rate. Which area of assessment BEST captures this assessment finding?

Choices:
A. Acoustic.
B. Stroboscopic.
C. Aerodynamic.
D. Perceptual.

Teaching Points

Correct Answer: C

Aerodynamic assessment measures include maximum phonation time (maximum time an individual can prolong a vowel on one single breath), airflow rate (an estimate of glottic valving efficiency), estimates of subglottic pressure, and laryngeal airway resistance (ratio of air pressure to the flow of air through the glottis).

C85

Acquired Language Disorders

An SLP in an acute care hospital is asked to complete a speech, language, and cognitive-linguistic evaluation for a patient with a recent cerebrovascular accident. Upon reviewing the patient's admitting paperwork, the SLP reviews the chart and learns that the patient has been unable to answer basic questions or follow directions since admission. The SLP determines that the patient MOST LIKELY has a lesion in which brain region?

Choices:
A. Temporal lobe.
B. Parietal lobe.
C. Basal ganglia.
D. Thalamus.

Teaching Points

Correct Answer: A

A deficit in auditory comprehension (e.g., inability to respond to questions or follow verbal directions) could be indicative of a lesion in the primary auditory context, which is housed in the temporal lobe of the brain.

C86

Acoustics

A speech scientist is utilizing spectrum to study different aspects of sibilant phonemes. Pertaining to sibilant fricatives, the speech scientist is MOST LIKELY to find which feature in the center of gravity?

Choices:
A. It is higher than its skewness.
B. It is lower than its skewness.
C. It is at the center of the spectrum.
D. It is off-center in the spectrum.

Teaching Points

Correct Answer: D

Center of gravity for sibilant fricatives is expected to be off-center, whereas for nonsibilant fricatives it should be at or near the center of the spectrum.

C87

Dysphagia: Swallowing and Swallowing Disorder

An SLP is performing both bedside evaluation and instrumental assessment with a patient. The SLP determines the primary feature of the patient's dysphagia is a weak swallow. In order to improve the swallow, the SLP develops swallowing-based exercises using boluses, with a minimum of three different swallowing exercises in each session. Which principle of neuroplasticity is NOT explicitly targeted in the SLP's approach?

Choices:
A. Use it or lose it.
B. Repetition matters.
C. Use it and improve it.
D. Age matters.

Teaching Points

Correct Answer: D

This SLP is using the approaches "use it or lose it" and "use it and improve it" simultaneously, because they are having the patient swallow boluses of real food in order to improve their swallowing. Additionally, because the SLP has chosen to have the patient engage in three swallows per bolus, they are engaging the principle of "repetition matters." While age would more than likely be a factor in deciding treatment approaches, the plan does not specifically address this in the approach.

C88

Audiology and Hearing Impairment

An older adult arrives at an audiology clinic with complaints of hearing loss. After completing an evaluation, the audiologist diagnoses the patient with a symmetric mild-to-moderate sensorineural hearing loss. Which condition does the patient MOST LIKELY have?

Choices:
A. Otosclerosis.
B. Presbycusis.
C. Ototoxicity.
D. Otitis media.

Teaching Points

Correct Answer: B

Presbycusis refers to hearing loss associated with aging. As this patient is an elderly man complaining of hearing loss, and the audiologist did not discover another organic cause of this patient's loss, they are likely experiencing presbycusis. In contrast to this, *otosclerosis* refers to stiffening of the ossicles in the middle ear, *ototoxicity* refers to environmental toxins or pharmaceutical agents causing hearing impairment, and *otitis media* refers to a middle ear effusion.

C89

Acoustics

An SLP is analyzing a spectrogram of an utterance made up of three phonemes. The first phoneme consists of a short period of voicing followed by a closure and short duration voice onset time. The second phoneme is a vowel with high F1 and high F2. The third phoneme consists of a short period of voicing followed by a closure and then frication noise. Which utterance was MOST LIKELY captured on the spectrogram?

Choices:
A. Rad.
B. Sheep.
C. Bat.
D. Badge.

Teaching Points

Correct Answer: D

Because the first phoneme demonstrates a short period of voicing followed by a closure (e.g., silent period), it can be assumed that this phoneme is a stop consonant. As it has a short duration voice onset time, it can be assumed that it is a voiced stop consonant, such as /b/. For the second phoneme, because there is a high F1 and high F2, it can be assumed that the vowel is a low front vowel, such as /æ/. Finally, as the final consonant demonstrates a short period of voicing followed by a closure and then frication noise, it can be assumed that the final phoneme is a voiced affricate, such as /dʒ/. The only option from this scenario that matches these three conditions is /bædʒ/ or "badge."

C90

Speech Sound Disorders in Children

During a speech evaluation, the SLP observes that the patient is able to produce all of the "early" and "mid" eight speech sounds but has difficulty with multiple "late" eight sounds, including /s/, /r/, and /l/. The SLP determines that the maximal contrast approach is best to target the patient's speech sound errors. Which example BEST follows this approach?

Choices:
A. Bat and pat.
B. Ran and bug.
C. Rock and dock.
D. Bird and duck.

Teaching Points

Correct Answer: C

In the maximal oppositional approach, an SLP is going to select a target sound that the client has difficulty with, contrasted with a sound the client can produce that is maximally different in place, manner, and voicing. *Bat* and *pat* both begin with sounds the client is not reported to have difficulty with. While *ran* and *bug* are extremely different words in multiple ways, the words are not pairs and therefore are not specifically addressing the target sound. The /r/ in *rock* is a voiced, rhotic, palatal sound, contrasted with the /d/ in *dock* as a voiced alveolar stop.

C91

Research, Evidence-Based Practice, and Tests and Measurements

A speech and language researcher has demonstrated the benefits of a newly developed treatment method through well-controlled studies that show internal validity, statistical significance, and practical significance. This researcher's method BEST demonstrates which principle?

Choices:
A. Treatment efficacy.
B. Treatment effectiveness.
C. Treatment fidelity.
D. Treatment validity.

Teaching Points

Correct Answer: A

Research that demonstrates treatment efficacy shows the benefits of treatment through well-controlled studies with interval validity, statistical significance, and practical significance. When a research study demonstrates all three of these principles, the study demonstrates good treatment efficacy. On the other hand, if research demonstrates clinical improvement when applied in real-life contexts, it demonstrates treatment effectiveness. When an application of a treatment in real-world context matches the controlled conditions of the original study, this demonstrates good treatment fidelity.

C92

Written Language Disorders in School-Age Populations

An adolescent demonstrates fluent reading at the text level and shows average spelling for regular and irregular words; nevertheless, reading comprehension is quite poor. This pattern of literacy behaviors is BEST associated with deficits in which areas?

Choices:
A. Phonological awareness and grapheme-phoneme correspondence.
B. Word recognition and rapid automatic naming.
C. Oral vocabulary and sentence processing.
D. Sight word reading skills and structural analysis.

Teaching Points

Correct Answer: C

Although this student demonstrates adequate reading of sentence-level material, deficits in oral vocabulary and sentence processing would lead to deficits in reading comprehension. Because this student has difficulty with vocabulary, they would most likely not understand the meaning behind multiple words they encounter. Sentence-level processing deficits would lead to further difficulty with reading comprehension, as the student would not be able to hold the elements of the story in their working memory or comprehend word-order patterns within the sentence.

C93

Autism Spectrum Disorders

A young child demonstrates behaviors consistent with the triad of deficits seen in autism spectrum disorder. Specifically, the child demonstrates severe restricted, repetitive behaviors. Which behavior is MOST LIKELY demonstrated by this child?

Choices:
A. Exaggerated gestures that accompany speech, to the point of interrupting communicative attempts from parents.
B. Aversion of eye contact with parents and siblings to a degree that prohibits communication.
C. Prolonged sustained attention on a stuffed toy and blocking out all communicative attempts from parents.
D. Verbal perseveration of a favorite phrase, with very little other spontaneous verbal output.

Teaching Points

Correct Answer: C

Restricted, repetitive behaviors exhibited by children with autism spectrum disorder may come in the form of stereotyped or repetitive motor movement, insistence on sameness, inflexible adherence to routines, highly restricted interests, and hypo-/hyperreactivity to sensory input. The child's prolonged sustained attention toward her stuffed toy would be classified as a restricted, repetitive behavior, as it is a highly restricted, fixated interest on a single item. This could be considered abnormal in intensity or focus. In contrast to this, exaggerated gestures accompanying speech and aversion of eye contact are considered deficits in social communication, whereas verbal perseveration is considered a language deficit.

C94

Motor Speech Disorders

A patient is transported to the emergency department following a motorcycle accident. After a computerized tomography scan, diffuse bilateral hemispheric damage is revealed. Later results from a speech and language evaluation show that the patient has a strained-strangled vocal quality, hypernasality during speech activities, and a slow, effortful rate of speech. Based on this information, the patient would MOST LIKELY be diagnosed with which motor speech disorder?

Choices:
A. Hypokinetic dysarthria.
B. Flaccid dysarthria.
C. Ataxic dysarthria.
D. Spastic dysarthria.

Teaching Points

Correct Answer: D

Spastic dysarthria arises from bilateral hemispheric damage, which leads to excessive spasticity during speech activities. Associated perceptual correlates include a strained-strangled vocal quality, hypernasality, and effortful speech. Flaccid dysarthria arises from lower motor neuron damage (either unilateral or bilateral), ataxic dysarthria arises from cerebellar damage, and hypokinetic dysarthria arises from basal ganglia damage.

C95

Acquired Language Disorders

An SLP evaluates a patient with a left cerebrovascular accident and determines that the patient exhibits both aphasia and apraxia of speech. Which is the MOST IMPORTANT consideration when planning treatment for this patient?

Choices:
A. Adopting a linguistic approach to treatment.
B. The contribution of both disorders to the communication deficit.
C. Adopting a motor approach to treatment.
D. Identifying alternative forms of communication to compensate for both deficits.

Teaching Points

Correct Answer: B

Considerations from both disorders should be taken into consideration when planning treatment for this particular patient. As aphasia is a language disorder, and apraxia of speech is a motor planning/programming deficit, the focus of treatment will be different for each disorder. Planning for these differences can lead to the greatest amount of improvement for this type of patient. Adopting approaches that target only one of the disorders leads to a lack of gains made in the untargeted disorder. Additionally, AAC could be utilized during treatment to supplement treatment. It should only be used as a complete compensation for both linguistic and motoric deficits if the patient persists with significant deficits in both areas after treatment.

C96

Acquired Language Disorders

An SLP is completing a comprehensive speech and language assessment for a person with aphasia and is assessing their reading and reading comprehension. Following completion of the assessment, the SLP determines that the patient presents with an overreliance on phonetic reading rules but retains adequate grammar. Which condition is the patient MOST LIKELY experiencing?

Choices:
A. Surface dysgraphia.
B. Deep dyslexia.
C. Surface dyslexia.
D. Deep dysgraphia.

Teaching Points

Correct Answer: C

Surface dyslexia is a form of acquired reading disorder in which the person demonstrates an overreliance on phonetic reading rules, meaning that only the grapheme-phoneme reading route is used. Deep dyslexia is the opposite of this profile, in that the person does not have access to the grapheme-phoneme reading route and relies on "whole-word" or lexical reading. Finally, surface and deep dysgraphia are disorders of written expression, rather than reading and reading comprehension.

C97

The Practice of Speech-Language Pathology

An SLP in private practice was recently reported for violating the American Speech-Language-Hearing Association (ASHA) Code of Ethics. ASHA has provided a sanction in which the SLP was officially rebuked, which was published to the membership of ASHA. Which type of sanction was brought against this SLP?

Choices:
A. Reprimand.
B. Revocation.
C. Censure.
D. Withholding.

Teaching Points

Correct Answer: C

When an SLP has been censured, they have been sanctioned with a public reprimand, which is published to the membership of ASHA, such as the SLP in this scenario. If the SLP had received a private rebuke, this is known as a *reprimand*. Revocation occurs for serious violations, and membership/certification can be revoked for a year, years, or life. Finally, withholding may be sanctioned to clinical fellows in violation and their ability to apply for the CCC may be withheld for a period of years, up to life.

C98

Language Disorders in Young Children

An SLP is working on conversational-level goals with a young child. However, the child continues to have significant difficulties with this form of communication. The SLP determines that the child may have deficits in the underlying skills needed for conversation. Which deficit is MOST LIKELY present?

Choices:
A. Phonological memory span, turn-taking abilities, and simple sentence structure.
B. Gestures, complex sentence structures, and joint attention.
C. Intellectual functioning, morphosyntactic development, and fluency.
D. Joint attention, following line of regard, and joint action routines.

Teaching Points

Correct Answer: D

Successful development of conversational abilities, or any discourse type, depends on a child's skill in three areas. Joint attention (i.e., focusing on what the caregiver is focused on) skills set the stage for establishing a topic of conversation. Following line of regard (i.e., recognizing that the caregiver is attending to someone or something) is a prerequisite for seeking out a point of attention. Finally, joint action routines (i.e., repetitive, predictable patterns of interaction) aid in the learning of predictable roles and responsibilities for conversational partners.

C99

Cleft Palate and Craniofacial Conditions

A child arrives at a speech and language clinic for a comprehensive speech and language evaluation. Upon approaching the child for completion of evaluation, the SLP notices that the child presents with a cleft lip, facial asymmetry, and reduced mandibular range of motion. Which diagnosis does this child MOST likely have?

Choices:
A. CHARGE syndrome.
B. Oculoauriculovertebral dysplasia.
C. Treacher Collins syndrome.
D. Beckwith-Wiedemann syndrome.

Teaching Points

Correct Answer: B

Oculoauriculovertebral dysplasia (or hemifacial microsomia) is a genetic condition that is characterized by a cluster of symptoms, including presence of a cleft lip or palate, craniofacial features (including facial asymmetry due to unilateral hypoplasia of the face and dysplasia of the temporomandibular joint), and functional concerns (such as hearing loss and velopharyngeal insufficiency).

C100

Cleft Palate and Craniofacial Conditions

An SLP in an outpatient clinic performs an evaluation for a child presenting with complaints of intermittent hypernasal speech. The SLP selects a dynamic assessment to achieve multiple views of the velopharyngeal valve to observe closure during connected speech. Which assessment is BEST to utilize in the evaluation of this child?

Choices:
A. Aerodynamic instrumentation.
B. Nasometer.
C. Nasopharyngoscopy.
D. Videofluoroscopy.

Teaching Points

Correct Answer: D

Videofluoroscopy is a multiview radiographic procedure that allows evaluation of the velopharyngeal valve. By utilizing videofluoroscopy, an SLP is able to gather multiple views (e.g., lateral, front, and base) to assess velopharyngeal closure during speech. In contrast, a nasometer involves use of a headset to capture acoustic energy from the nasal and oral cavities during speech, aerodynamic assessment uses catheters to measure air pressure and flow during speech production, and nasopharyngoscopy involves placing an endoscope through the nasal cavity to visualize the nasal surface of the velum during speech.

C101

Augmentative and Alternative Communication

An SLP is working with an adolescent with Down syndrome. The adolescent is effectively able to use a communication device. When communicating with parents, they frequently fill in the gaps while the adolescent selects responses, due to slow communication. This frequently leads to frustration when the adolescent is interrupted, as the parents frequently guess incorrectly. Which type of training would BEST support the adolescent and parents?

Choices:
A. Expectant delay.
B. Message co-construction.
C. Topic supplementation.
D. Alphabet supplementation.

Teaching Points

Correct Answer: A

Utilizing an expectant delay would train facilitators to allow extra time when waiting for a response from the AAC user. Training can include counting from one to five or waiting for the client to indicate they have completed their message instead of attempting to complete the statement before they are ready.

C102

Acquired Language Disorders

An SLP is working in an outpatient speech and language clinic. A referral from a neurologist is received for a new patient. Upon reviewing the paperwork, the SLP notes that the patient is referred for language treatment due to a nonfluent aphasia. The SLP hypothesizes that the patient MOST LIKELY has a brain lesion in which brain region?

Choices:
A. Frontal lobe.
B. Parietal lobe.
C. Limbic system.
D. Cerebellum.

Teaching Points

Correct Answer: A

A difficulty with language production characterized by a nonfluent aphasia is most likely indicating a lesion in Broca's area of the brain, which can be found in the inferior frontal gyrus of the frontal lobe.

C103

Written Language Disorders in School-Age Populations

An adolescent in high school has been assigned to read different articles about life in the early 1900s. The student reads three articles discussing different perspectives about this time period and is able to draw conclusions regarding life in the early 1900s. This cluster of behaviors is MOST closely associated with which stage of Chall's reading stages?

Choices:
A. Stage 2: Confirmation, Fluency, Ungluing from Print.
B. Stage 3: Reading for Learning the New.
C. Stage 4: Multiple Viewpoints.
D. Stage 5: Construction and Reconstruction.

Teaching Points

Correct Answer: C

This student would be in Chall's fourth stage of reading development. She was able to analyze and synthesize information from multiple perspectives. She is not yet being tasked to create a new theory around the articles, so she has not yet advanced to Stage 5.

C104

Acquired Language Disorders

An SLP in an inpatient rehabilitation hospital completes a comprehensive speech and language evaluation for a patient with aphasia following a cerebrovascular accident. Results from the assessment show fluent verbal output with frequent episodes of jargon and neologisms, as well as poor recognition of these episodes. The patient also has difficulty with auditory comprehension and repetition. Which type of aphasia does the patient MOST LIKELY have?

Choices:
A. Global.
B. Wernicke's.
C. Conduction.
D. Broca's.

Teaching Points

Correct Answer: B

Wernicke's aphasia is a profile of aphasia characterized by fluent verbal expression, impaired auditory comprehension, and impaired repetition. Global and Broca's aphasias are forms of aphasia that include nonfluent verbal expression. Finally, while conduction aphasia includes fluent verbal expression with impaired repetition, persons with this profile of aphasia have intact auditory comprehension.

C105

Acquired Language Disorders

An SLP in an acute care hospital completes a comprehensive speech and language evaluation for a patient with aphasia following a cerebrovascular accident. Results from the SLP's assessment show nonfluent verbal output with significant agrammatism, with a co-occurring apraxia of speech. The patient has preserved auditory comprehension but difficulty with repetition of single words. Based on these findings, which diagnosis does the patient MOST LIKELY have?

Choices:
A. Global aphasia.
B. Transcortical motor aphasia.
C. Broca's aphasia.
D. Wernicke's aphasia.

Teaching Points

Correct answer: C

A person with Broca's aphasia would present with nonfluent aphasia, significant agrammatism, intact auditory comprehension, deficits with repetition, and possibly a co-occurring apraxia of speech. This is differentiated from global aphasia because of the spared auditory comprehension; from transcortical motor aphasia because of the impaired repetition; and from Wernicke's aphasia because of the nonfluent verbal expression.

C106

Spoken Language Disorders in School-Age Populations

A child demonstrates pragmatic difficulties, including presupposition skills. The SLP designs an intervention program in order to improve the child's conversational abilities. Which is the BEST goal for intervention?

Choices:
A. The child will utilize gestures in conversation to reinforce engaging topics of conversation.
B. The child will understand that communication partners have perspectives and feelings different from oneself.
C. The child will modify communicative attempts based on the needs of a communication partner.
D. The child will understand that communicative partners engage in conversation with certain expectations for communication.

Teaching Points

Correct Answer: C

Presupposition is a skill that involves judging what the listener already knows and making appropriate accommodations to facilitate successful communication. By targeting this ability, the child may have a better understanding of what their conversation partner requires for successful intervention. In contrast to this, theory of mind deals with understanding that conversation partners have differing perspectives and feelings. Joint action routine is a skill that aids in establishing predictable roles and expectations for conversation. Finally, using gestures to reinforce topics of conversation may engage speakers more in conversation but does not necessarily equate to a change in conversation based on the needs of the communicative partner.

C107

Language Disorders in Young Children

A 5-year-old child is in a kindergarten class for 3 months after moving to the United States from a European country. Teachers are concerned that the child is having difficulty in school and is not talking during the day. The teachers believe there is a language disorder and have referred the child to the SLP. During an initial interview, the parents reveal that the child has been exposed to both English and native language since birth but is having difficulty at home and school with both languages. Which statement BEST describes these findings?

Choices:
A. The child does not present with a language disorder.
B. The child presents with a language disorder for the native language only.
C. The child presents with a language disorder for both spoken languages.
D. The child presents with a language delay for the native language only.

Teaching Points

Correct Answer: C

The parents reported that the child in this scenario has been exposed to both languages since birth (simultaneous bilingualism) and that he has had difficulty with both languages. Language disorders will appear in both languages of bilingual speakers. This child most likely qualifies for speech-language services, as the language disorder is in both French and English.

C108

Stuttering and Other Fluency Disorders

An SLP is employed in a school setting. The SLP's caseload includes children who stutter. The SLP reviews a variety of indirect treatments that have been recently developed to determine best practices. Which statement BEST describes indirect treatment?

Choices:
A. It employs counseling on attitudes and fears to improve stuttering and ignores speech production.
B. It reduces social and linguistic demands and helps parents reduce speech pressure.
C. It uses extensive practice in teaching others to provide treatment and eliminates the clinical role.
D. It delays the initiation of treatment until the parent indicates readiness and encourages annual reevaluations.

Teaching Points

Correct Answer: B

Indirect treatments are frequently used with young children as a less intrusive approach to treatment. With these methods, children are engaged in social interactions with the clinician and the clinician models speech that is less complex and slower with no direct response expected from the child. It has been observed that as the speech and language environment of the child is simplified, fluency is often facilitated.

C109

Language Acquisition: Preverbal and Early Language

A child is able to understand the use of dishes and bowls when it is time to eat. The SLP places an unfamiliar item in front of the child and says, "Dish, bowl, and spoon." The child is able to determine that the new item is called a *spoon*. This finding BEST demonstrates which word-learning principle?

Choices:
A. Semantic bootstrapping.
B. Novel name principle.
C. Mutual exclusivity.
D. Shape bias.

Teaching Points

Correct Answer: B

Novel name/nameless principle refers to the belief that a novel word will be taken as the name for a previously unnamed object. Semantic bootstrapping would be when the individual is able to learn syntactic structures of language by first being able to recognize the individual syntactic elements and then building upon them. *Mutual exclusivity* refers to a theory that proposes that when learning new words, a single label is assigned to the item rather than assigning two labels for a single item.

C110

Cleft Palate and Craniofacial Conditions

A child receives surgical correction of velopharyngeal insufficiency. After the surgery, the child is referred to an SLP to improve speech performance, including compensating for errors in speech production. Which approach is BEST for correction of compensatory errors?

Choices:
A. Articulation placement procedures.
B. Velopharyngeal exercises.
C. Blowing exercises.
D. Further surgical management.

Teaching Points

Correct Answer: A

Following correction of velopharyngeal insufficiency, speech therapy may be indicated to improve any remaining speech errors. Velopharyngeal insufficiency often requires only one instance of surgical management to fix the problem, and blowing exercises and velopharyngeal exercises are not effective as treatment methods for this population. Therefore, the best selection would be articulation placement in order to help the client learn proper placement of the articulators following the surgical change.

C111

Language Acquisition: Preverbal and Early Language

An SLP observes a 13-month-old child to make eye contact and to point to interesting items around the room. The SLP documents these findings as consistent with which type of communication?

Choices:
A. Nonverbal behaviors.
B. Discourse-related skills.
C. Theory of mind.
D. Verbal behaviors.

Teaching Points

Correct Answer: A

Nonverbal behaviors are behaviors or actions that a person may engage in without using natural speech to communicate with those around them. Alternatively, discourse-related skills are skills that focus on narratives and being able to integrate various units of language. Verbal behavior is a methodology for teaching natural oral speech, focusing on word meaning and function.

C112

Cleft Palate and Craniofacial Conditions

An SLP receives orders to evaluate a neonate in an intensive care unit. The SLP notes that the neonate has a cleft palate, micrognathia, and airway obstruction. Which disorder does this infant MOST LIKELY have?

Choices:
A. Pierre Robin sequence.
B. Velocardiofacial syndrome.
C. Down syndrome.
D. Pfeiffer syndrome.

Teaching Points

Correct Answer: A

Pierre Robin sequence includes the characteristics of micrognathia (small lower jaw), glossoptosis (downward displacement of the tongue), and airway obstruction. While these characteristics may be individually present in velocardiofacial syndrome, Down syndrome, and Pfeiffer syndrome, when they are collectively present, this indicates a diagnosis of Pierre Robin sequence.

C113

Motor Speech Disorders

An SLP working in an outpatient clinic receives orders to evaluate a child with childhood apraxia of speech (CAS). The SLP has not worked with a child with this diagnosis before and is researching evidence-based intervention approaches. Which considerations are MOST IMPORTANT when treating a child with CAS?

Choices:
A. Number of sessions per week and the number of productions per session.
B. Adoption of nonspeech tasks and number of sessions per week.
C. Syllable shape and the number of cues provided to achieve a correct production.
D. Number of suprasegmental facilitators and the number of sessions per week.

Teaching Points

Correct Answer: A

Session characteristics for clients with CAS include intensive and individualized treatment, maximization of production practice during each session, more frequent occurrence of treatment sessions, and length of the session matched to the attention/learning abilities of the child. Focusing on the number of treatment sessions and maximizing the amount of productions for the client can promote improvements in the client's speech output capabilities.

C114

Audiology and Hearing Impairment

An SLP is working in a rural outpatient setting with no audiologist present. A patient arrives with complaints that their behind-the-ear hearing aid has stopped functioning. The SLP helps the patient troubleshoot the potential issue. Which step should the SLP do FIRST in attempting to resolve the hearing aid malfunction?

Choices:
A. Check the tonehook for blockages.
B. Check the earmold for blockages.
C. Check the status of the battery.
D. Check the status of the microphone.

Teaching Points

Correct Answer: C

In troubleshooting hearing aid problems, there are several steps that an SLP can take. Battery problems (e.g., dead batteries, batteries being placed into the unit incorrectly) are the largest group of problems experienced by hearing aid users. By checking the status of the battery first, the SLP may quickly fix the problem and help the hearing aid user. If this does not work, the SLP can follow a chain and check for debris in the earmold, tonehook, and microphone. If problems persist, the SLP may need to refer the patient to his/her audiologist for further troubleshooting of the device.

C115

Spoken Language Disorders in School-Age Populations

A young child is referred for a comprehensive speech and language evaluation at an elementary school. During the initial assessment in the SLP's office, the child states "No" and "I don't want to" multiple times and refuses to participate. Which is the BEST manner to gather data to determine service eligibility?

Choices:
A. Offer candy at the end of each question prompt.
B. When the child gets a correct answer, state "Great job!"
C. Observe the child in a natural setting and interview the parent(s).
D. Interview the teacher and reattempt the standardized assessments.

Teaching Points

Correct Answer: C

Young children may be noncompliant during testing for a variety of reasons. There are many parent interview forms that can be used to gather information on a child's present level of performance to determine areas of need. Additionally, an observation may give valuable information on how the child interacts in a natural setting. While a teacher may be able to give great insight into development, a parent/caregiver is likely to have more consistent information about a young child.

C116

Voice Disorders in Children and Adults

An SLP in an acute care facility prepares a patient for a total laryngectomy following malignant laryngeal cancer. After education regarding the various forms of alaryngeal communication, the patient chooses a form of communication that allows the most natural vocal quality that also restores spoken communication as quickly as possible. Which treatment option is BEST to introduce for this patient?

Choices:
A. Electrolarynx with neck placement.
B. Tracheoesophageal speech.
C. Esophageal speech.
D. Electrolarynx with intraoral adapter.

Teaching Points

Correct Answer: B

Tracheoesophageal speech involves inserting a prosthesis through the tissue wall separating the trachea from the esophagus in a laryngectomee. This prosthesis diverts air from the trachea in order to vibrate the pharyngoesophageal segment, producing voice. Tracheoesophageal speech produces the most natural-sounding voice for alaryngeal speakers, and following insertion of the prosthesis, there may be immediate restoration of oral communication. Thus, this method of communication may prove the best match for this patient's wishes. Both forms of electrolarynx (i.e., neck placement and with intraoral adapter) produce a very unnatural, robotic-sounding voice. This is in direct contrast with the patient's wishes for a natural vocal quality. Lastly, while esophageal speech offers a more natural vocal quality than the electrolarynx, it takes lengthy periods of time for patients to learn and has a high fail rate. As such, this goes against the patient's wishes for immediate restoration of voice.

C117

Research, Evidence-Based Practice, and Tests and Measurements

A speech and language researcher has completed final analysis on a data set and has discovered a highly homogenous distribution of participant scores. Which result is the researcher MOST LIKELY to find?

Choices:
A. A small mean.
B. A small median.
C. A small standard deviation.
D. A small confidence interval.

Teaching Points

Correct Answer: C

The standard deviation is the average amount that all the scores in a particular distribution will deviate from the mean. When there is more homogeneity of data points in the set, there will be a smaller standard deviation, as there will be less deviation from the median.

C118

Acoustics

An SLP is analyzing a spectrogram of an utterance made up of three phonemes. The first phoneme consists of high-frequency frication noise of a longer duration. The second phoneme is a vowel with low F1 and high F2. The third phoneme demonstrates a low-frequency nasal formant. Which word is MOST LIKELY the utterance captured on the spectrogram?

Choices:
A. Seam.
B. Seat.
C. Sear.
D. Seed.

Teaching Points

Correct Answer: A

Because the first phoneme demonstrates high-frequency frication noise, it can be assumed that this phoneme is a fricative. As it is of a longer duration, it can be assumed that it is a voiceless fricative, such as /s/. For the second phoneme, because there is a low F1 and high F2, it can be assumed that the vowel is a high front vowel, such as /i/. Finally, as the final phoneme has a low-frequency nasal formant, it can be assumed that the final phoneme is a nasal consonant. The only option from this scenario that matches these three conditions is /sim/ or "seam."

C119

Language Acquisition: Preverbal and Early Language

An SLP evaluates a child in an outpatient setting. The SLP observes the parent speaking to the child with exaggerated speech, short utterances, and heightened inflections. Which term BEST describes the parent's speech style?

Choices:
A. Parentese.
B. Bootstrapping.
C. Word-learning biases.
D. Frequent exposure to television.

Teaching Points

Correct Answer: A

Parentese refers to the universally observed style of adjusting speech patterns in interacting with very young children. In contrast to this, *bootstrapping* refers to use of language to infer the meaning of unknown vocabulary words. Finally, word-learning biases help children determine what referent is being labeled during early word learning.

C120

Spoken Language Disorders in School-Age Populations

A child demonstrates mastery of simple sentence structure but continues to present with difficulties in complex syntax. The SLP determines that the child is a candidate for speech-language pathology services. Which intervention approach is BEST for this child?

Choices:
A. *Wh-* questions.
B. Full prepositional complements.
C. Conjoined sentences.
D. Embedded sentences.

Teaching Points

Correct Answer: D

Working on complex syntax is an appropriate intervention for children over the age of 4 who have mastered simple syntactic structures. Appropriate targets include multiple embedding, embedding and conjoining, infinitive clauses with different subjects, relative clauses, gerunds, *wh-* infinitives, and unmarked infinitives. In contrast to this, full prepositional complements, *wh-* questions, and conjoined sentences are simple syntactic structures and would not be an appropriate treatment target for this particular child.

C121

Speech Sound Disorders in Children

A 5-year-old client arrives at a speech-language pathology clinic for a full speech and language evaluation. After completion of the evaluation, the SLP reviews the results and notes that the child produces the words /bo/ (boat), /fɪʃ/ (fish), /kʌ/ (cup), /sʌn/ (sun), and /dɑ/ (dog). Which statement BEST describes this child's speech pattern?

Choices:
A. Affrication of medial fricatives.
B. Fronting of initial fricatives.
C. Final consonant deletion of stops.
D. Initial consonant deletion of nasals.

Teaching Points

Correct Answer: C

When evaluating the child's errors, it is important to note that the child omits some, but not all, of the final consonants of the words produced. Of those omitted, all consonants are stop consonants (e.g., /g/, /t/, /p/). Therefore, the most appropriate phonological pattern that this child demonstrates is final consonant deletion of stop consonants. If the child deleted the first phoneme of each word (e.g., /ot/ for /bot/), then the child demonstrates initial consonant deletion. As the child appropriately produces all of the initial consonants in the sample, they are also not demonstrating fronting. Finally, as the child is producing CVC words, there is no opportunity for them to affricate medical consonants, making this selection incorrect.

C122

Speech Sound Disorders in Children

A child is referred to a speech clinic for a full articulation and phonological evaluation. The SLP notices a pattern in the child's word production, including *dog* as /dɑ/, *cat* as /kæ/, and *rat* as /ræ/. Which term BEST describes the child's speech pattern?

Choices:
A. Final consonant deletion.
B. Metathesis.
C. Initial consonant deletion.
D. Palatalization.

Teaching Points

Correct Answer: A

Final consonant deletion is a pattern of leaving off the final consonant sound at the end of a word. *Metathesis* refers to transposing the sounds within the word. Palatalization is the addition of a palatal component to a nonpalatal target phoneme.

C123

Stuttering and Other Fluency Disorders

A child receives a diagnosis of a developmental stutter. The child has difficulty with words starting with the letter *B* and refuses to use words beginning with the letter *B*. The child instead replaces these words with other words. Which strategy BEST describes the strategy the child is using to control the disfluencies?

Choices:
A. Acceptance.
B. Avoidance.
C. Escape.
D. Perspective-taking.

Teaching Points

Correct Answer: B

When individuals who stutter engage in avoidance behaviors, they are attempting to avoid/not engage in what they consider to be trigger sounds or trigger situations in order to avoid disfluencies. They may substitute a different sound or an entirely different word. In contrast, escape behaviors would include motor adjustments such as eye blinds or head nods to "get out" of the moment of stuttering.

C124

Acoustics

An SLP performs a comprehensive speech and language evaluation with a child. The SLP uses acoustic measurements of /r/ to document the child's progress in producing the sound. Which is the BEST measurement to make to document the child's progress?

Choices:
A. F0.
B. F1.
C. F2.
D. F3.

Teaching Points

Correct Answer: D
Correct articulation of English /r/ results in a clear drop in F3 frequency.

C125

Motor Speech Disorders

For the past month, an SLP has been working with a child with a diagnosis of moderate childhood apraxia of speech. The SLP is using a motor-based approach to treatment. The SLP determines that the child is not making satisfactory progress in treatment sessions. Which is the BEST course of action for the SLP to take?

Choices:
A. Evaluate if motor learning principles have been applied appropriately and adjust as needed.
B. Switch treatment to a phonologically based approach from the previously used motor-based approach.
C. Begin treatment at the isolated phoneme level to ensure all phonemes can be produced accurately before increasing length and complexity.
D. Continue the treatment sessions but include maximal cueing techniques.

Teaching Points

Correct Answer: A

Children with childhood apraxia of speech (CAS) exhibit a motor speech disorder that would not respond appropriately to a phonologically based approach to treatment. Additionally, children with CAS are often able to produce individual phonemes with ease and experience difficulty making the transitions between speech sounds during connected speech. The best approach in this type of situation would be to evaluate the treatment protocol to see if properties of motor-learning approaches (e.g., practice schedule, type of feedback, amount of feedback, learning, specificity of training, intensive practice) are effectively being utilized.

C126

Research, Evidence-Based Practice, and Tests and Measurements

A speech and language researcher is designing a research study to determine the effects of time spent in intervention, dosage of intervention, and type of feedback on the amount of progress made in patients with phonological disorders. Which research method is BEST to use in the study?

Choices:
A. Nonparametric experiment.
B. Parametric experiment.
C. Within-subjects experiment.
D. Between-subjects experiment.

Teaching Points

Correct Answer: B

A parametric experiment is one that is designed to study the simultaneous effects of more than one independent variable on the dependent variable. In this scenario, the researcher is studying the effect of the independent variables of time in intervention, dosage of intervention, and type of feedback on the dependent variable of progress made in intervention. As there are three separate independent variables, a parametric experiment would be the best selection for this researcher.

C127

Acquired Language Disorders

An SLP is working in a skilled nursing facility. A patient on the caseload has severe global aphasia with a co-occurring limb apraxia. The SLP has previously trialed some standard approaches to treatment, including producing automated spoken sequences and modeling simple, functional words. The patient has shown limited progress, and the SLP is considering new treatment options. Which is the BEST approach to implement next in the treatment of this patient?

Choices:
A. Melodic intonation therapy.
B. Visual action therapy.
C. Response elaboration therapy.
D. Anagram Copy and Recall Treatment (ACRT).

Teaching Points

Correct Answer: B

Visual action therapy is a treatment method that can be used with persons with severe aphasia and works to treat limb apraxia in order to allow the person with aphasia to use manual gestures to represent objects (e.g., "pounding" a nail in order to represent a hammer). This allows the person with aphasia to communicate through the use of gestures. Melodic intonation therapy and response elaboration therapy are methods that work to increase verbal expression in persons with aphasia, which may be contraindicated in this case, as the person with aphasia has shown limited improvement through use of methods targeting verbal expression. Finally, ACRT is an approach used to specifically improve written expression.

C128

Research, Evidence-Based Practice, and Tests and Measurements

A speech scientist is employed in a research hospital. The scientist initiates a research study utilizing a between-subjects treatment design. In order to reduce the effect of an extraneous variable, which procedure is BEST to implement?

Choices:
A. Randomly assign participants to a particular treatment condition.
B. Establish a reliable baseline performance for each participant.
C. Match research participants across treatment groups.
D. Randomize the order of treatment conditions for participants.

Teaching Points

Correct Answer: C

Between-subjects research designs involve comparing two or more groups of subjects. For this type of research design, it is critical that extraneous variables are controlled as much as possible, to minimize their effect on the dependent variable. One way that the researcher from this scenario could control extraneous variables is to match participants across groups, either by averages (e.g., average age) or through pairwise matching based on the extraneous variable (e.g., gender, education level).

C129

Acoustics

A speech scientist is studying different aspects of the supralaryngeal vocal tract (SLVT). The speech scientist observes that the SLVT is a broadly tuned filter. Which statement BEST describes this type of filter?

Choices:
A. The SLVT has an infinite number of resonant frequencies.
B. As the shape of the SLVT changes, the resonant frequencies also change.
C. Sinusoids will resonate if they are near a resonant frequency.
D. Sound output dies away immediately when the sound source stops.

Teaching Points

Correct Answer: C

A broadly tuned filter is one in which a sinusoid's frequency does not have to exactly equal the frequency of a filter peak in order to resonate. Frequencies that are near the filter peak will also resonate. When the resonant frequencies of a filter are changeable, it is called a *variable filter*. When sound output dies away immediately, it is called a *heavily damped filter*.

C130

Augmentative and Alternative Communication

A child with a diagnosis of cerebral palsy is evaluated for an AAC device by an SLP due to significant unintelligibility. During the evaluation, the SLP compares the child's abilities and challenges with various AAC systems and access methods. After gathering information from the child and family, the SLP is able to discuss multiple AAC devices to trial to determine the best fit. Which type of assessment is BEST to trial?

Choices:
A. Scanning.
B. Direct selection.
C. Feature matching.
D. System selection.

Teaching Points

Correct Answer: C

Feature matching is the process by which the skills and needs of the person with complex communication problems are matched against the features of various AAC systems. As the SLP from this scenario is engaging in an assessment to determine how the skills of the patient match the AAC devices present, they are utilizing a feature-matching approach. In contrast to this, direct selection is when the AAC user directly makes a choice on the system via touching, pointing, looking, or speaking. Scanning is an indirect method of access in which choices are presented to the AAC user, and the person indicates when the desired target is reached through a predetermined signal. Finally, system selection is the final step of the assessment process in which an AAC user selects the AAC system through which they will communicate.

C131

Cleft Palate and Craniofacial Conditions

A child arrives at a speech and language clinic for a comprehensive speech and language evaluation. While reviewing the child's medical records, the SLP notes a history of vascular malformations and delayed onset of puberty. Upon initiating the evaluation, the SLP notes that the child has a repaired cleft lip and anomalies of the outer ear. Which diagnosis does the child MOST LIKELY have?

Choices:
A. Apert syndrome.
B. Crouzon syndrome.
C. Beckwith-Wiedemann syndrome.
D. CHARGE syndrome.

Teaching Points

Correct Answer: D

CHARGE syndrome is a genetic condition with multiple symptoms, including presence of cleft lip/palate, coloboma, heart disease, atresia of the choanae, retarded growth and development, genital anomalies (including delayed puberty), and ear anomalies. Given that the student from this scenario demonstrates many of these symptoms, they would most likely carry a diagnosis of CHARGE syndrome.

C132

Speech Sound Disorders in Children

A child arrives at a speech and language clinic with parents who state the child is difficult to understand and "doesn't say the whole word." The SLP administers a comprehensive speech evaluation and determines the following errors: "keen" for *queen*, "bu" for *blue*, and "tee" for *tree*. Which phonological process does this child demonstrate?

Choices:
A. Nasal assimilation.
B. Affrication.
C. Metathesis.
D. Cluster simplification.

Teaching Points

Correct Answer: D

Clusters involve multiple consonants being next to each other in a word. In cluster simplification, the cluster is reduced and occasionally replaced by the schwa sound. In contrast, nasal assimilation would involve the words becoming nasalized, as in changing to /m/ or /n/ sounds.

Index

Note: Page numbers with *f* and *t* indicate figures and tables, respectively.